Practical Teaching

A Guide to Assessment and Quality Assurance

Linda Wilson

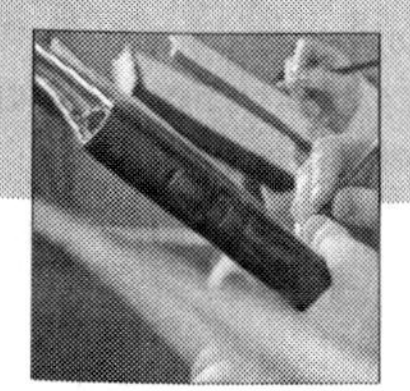 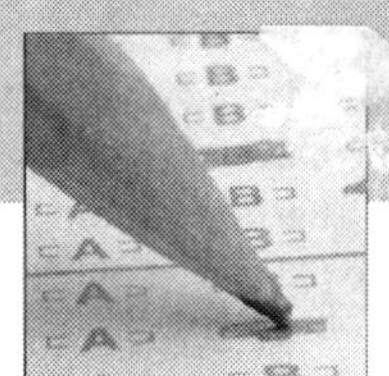   

CENGAGE Learning

Australia • Brazil • Japan • Korea • · United States

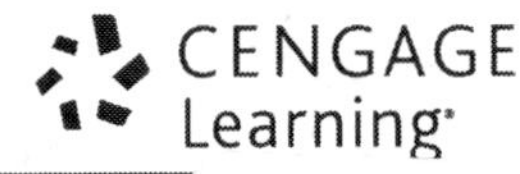

Practical Teaching: A Guide to Assessment and Quality Assurance, 1st Edition

Author: Linda Wilson

For product information and technology assistance, contact **emea.info@cengage.com**.

For permission to use material from this text or product, and for permission queries, email **emea.permissions@cengage.com.**

British Library Cataloguing-in-Publication Data
A catalogue record for this book is available from the British Library.

ISBN: 9781473717336

Cengage Learning EMEA
Cheriton House, North Way, Andover,
Hampshire, SP10 5BE
United Kingdom

Cengage Learning products are represented in Canada by Nelson Education Ltd.

For your lifelong learning solutions, visit **www.cengage.co.uk**

Purchase your next print book, e-book or e-chapter at **www.cengagebrain.com**

Brief contents

Contents

Introduction

I have been involved in assessment and verification since the late 1980s. I have seen many mutations of training programmes, terminology and qualifications, and this is my opportunity to put onto paper helpful hints and identify potential pitfalls for new or inexperienced assessors and quality assurance staff. I hope that the teachers and trainers of assessors and quality assurance staff will also find the activities useful in developing skills and delivering their courses. To date there are very few texts that focus entirely on assessment and quality assurance and fewer that link so clearly to the National Occupational Standards and the new qualifications.

The book is aimed at those wishing to achieve their assessor or internal quality assurance award – the candidate assessors or candidate quality assurers. Some aspects of the book also support the trainers of the qualifications. Chapter 1 The principles of assessment: functions and concepts and Chapter 2 Planning and delivering assessments are concerned with assessment; Chapter 3 Quality assurance of assessment and Chapter 4 Internally assuring the quality of assessment are related to quality assurance and Chapter 5 Managing the quality assurance process is directed at those managing the processes. Chapter 6 Collecting evidence and compiling a portfolio aims to put all the learning together and summarise how candidates might evidence their competence.

The structure of the chapters

Each chapter commences with a clear set of learning outcomes, which are reviewed at the end of the chapter together with a summary of how they were achieved. The content of each chapter is linked to the assessment criteria of the assessment and quality assurance qualifications.

The chapters, which are written in a user friendly manner, include a range of theoretical concepts and practical applications. Throughout the chapters activities, watch points and case studies guide the reader to develop their understanding of the subject. Each concludes with a list of specialist terminology and key words with references to further reading on the topics.

The terminology used in the sector is varied. To clarify, in this edition, candidates are those working towards qualifications (apprentices, trainees, learners, students, etc.).

You will see many references to quality assurance and quality assurer throughout the book. For ease of referencing quality assurance has been given the acronym QA and quality assurer has been written out in full. However quality assurance and quality assurer are interchangeable and if required can be used as such.

The subject matter

Practical Teaching: A Guide to Assessment and Quality Assurance is my third book in a series of teachers' texts relating to the current National Occupational Standards for the sector. This particular book maps directly to the City and Guilds Assessment and Quality Assurance (6317) qualifications. The former relate to teacher training qualifications – PTLLS, CTLLS and DTLLS and are proving to be a valuable help to trainee teachers.

The assessor and quality assurance qualifications are the new generation of assessor and internal verifier (IV) qualifications, the former versions being informally known as the D units (expired in 2002) and more recently the A & V units (expired December 2010). The first noticeable change, therefore, is the change of expression from internal verifier to quality assurance staff. This reflects the broader role of the verifier, which in the new awards includes moderation and other quality assurance processes. At this point it should be noted that holders of those former qualifications do not need to re-qualify, although they may use the new assessor and quality assurance awards to update the currency of their skills. The new units would make ideal continuous professional development opportunities.

> *Ofqual stated in 2010 that there is no mandatory requirement to re-qualify, re-train or upskill to the Assessment and Quality Assurance units. However, all centres must ensure that all their assessors and internal quality assurance staff (IQAs previously*

known as IVs) – irrespective of sector – are working in line with the March 2010 National Occupational Standards (NOS) for Learning and Development.

www.cityandguilds.com

What are they?

They are a series of units of assessment which when clustered together form awards and certificates within the qualifications credit framework. The tables below relate to the qualifications accredited by City and Guilds. Other awarding organisations take the National Occupational Standards and units of assessment (from Lifelong Learning UK) and then make their own qualifications. Each has to go through the same rigorous accreditation so are comparable with each other. They are valid in England, Wales and Northern Ireland. A different set of qualifications is applicable to Scottish assessors and verifiers. At launch, the qualifications were known as the Training, Assessment and Quality Assurance qualifications with an expectation that further qualifications around training will follow.

Qualification clusters – assessment

The table below lists the titles and reference numbers for each qualification, the units of assessment that make up each qualification, the credit value of each unit of assessment on the Qualification Credit Framework (QCF) and the required Guided Learning Hours (GLH) for each qualification.

Title	C&G Code	Units	QCF value	GLH
Level 3 Award Understanding the Principles and Practices of assessment	6317-30	• Understanding the principles and practices of assessment	3 credits	24
Level 3 Award Assessing Competence in the Work Environment	6317-31	• Understanding the principles and practices of assessment	3 credits	54
		• Assess occupational competence in the work environment	6 credits	

Title	C&G Code	Units	QCF value	GLH
Level 3 Award Assessing Vocationally Related Achievement	6317-32	• Understanding the principles and practices of assessment • Assessing vocational skills, knowledge and understanding	3 credits 6 credits	54
Level 3 Certificate Assessing Vocational Achievement	6317-33	• Understanding the principles and practices of assessment • Assess occupational competence in the work environment • Assessing vocational skills, knowledge and understanding	3 credits 6 credits 6 credits	84

Qualification clusters – quality assurance

Title	C&G Code	Units	QCF value	GLH
Level 4 Award Understanding the Internal Quality Assurance of Assessment Processes and Practice	6317-40	• Understanding the principles and practices of internally assuring the quality of assessment	6 credits	45
Level 4 Award Internal Quality Assurance of Assessment Processes and Practice	6317-41	• Understanding the principles and practices of internally assuring the quality of assessment • Internally assure the quality of assessment	6 credits 6 credits	90

Title	C&G Code	Units	QCF value	GLH
Level 4 Certificate Leading the Internal Quality Assurance of Assessment Processes and Practice	6317-42	• Understanding the principles and practices of internally assuring the quality of assessment • Internally assure the quality of assessment • Plan, allocate and monitor work in own area of responsibility	6 credits 6 credits 5 credits	115

So what's changed?

Well the qualification framework has for one. The old qualifications were written against the National Qualifications Framework (NQF) and needed to be rewritten aligning the qualifications to the Qualifications Credit Framework (QCF). This was quite timely given the age of the former qualifications.

Change	Old	New
Written against QCF with credit values and different sizes of qualifications	No	Yes
Knowledge and understanding inclusive in qualifications	Inherent	Mandatory, stand-alone units
Practical assessments	Yes	Yes
Work based assessor routes (pathways)	Generic in (A2)	Bespoke in-service practical units
Vocational assessor routes (pathways)	Yes in (A1)	Bespoke in-service practical units
Suitability for all assessors/quality assurance staff	NVQ only	All assessors and quality assurers

Change	Old	New
Suitable for those working with accredited or non-accredited learning programmes or work based training	No	Yes
Units for aspiring assessors or QA staff or non-practitioners	No	Stand-alone knowledge units
Links to other qualifications, e.g. teaching qualifications	No	Potential RPL
Suitable for those managing or co-ordinating QA process	No	Yes
Assessor Awards and Certificates at Level 3	Yes	Yes
Quality Assurance (Internal Verifier) Awards and Certificates at Level 4	Yes	Yes
Unit Accreditation	Yes	Yes
Holistic assessment available	No	Yes

Who can do them?

The qualifications are suitable for those who work, or want to work, as:

- Assessors/teachers/trainers/tutors in the Lifelong Learning Sector or Adult/Community Education.
- Assessors/trainers of personnel in commerce, industry, public and voluntary sectors or HM Forces.
- Quality assurance/internal verifiers and support staff in Further and Adult Education.
- Quality assurance managers and internal verifiers in workplace training and further and adult education.

The qualifications are suitable provided that assessors are qualified in the subject they intend to assess by virtue of holding an appropriate professional qualification or employed in a training/teaching role. The decision as to what constitutes an appropriate qualification is at the discretion of the training provider or employer (City & Guilds: http://www.cityandguilds.com website, accessed June 2011).

This book seeks to summarise effective strategies in assessment and quality assurance. I hope that new assessors and quality assurers will find it helpful as they gain their skills and develop their competence.

Acknowledgements

I would like to take this opportunity to thank my reviewers, City and Guilds and the staff at Cengage. In particular, John, who once again offered his experience, opinions and support during its preparation.

The author's previous books, published by Cengage Learning are:

Practical Teaching: A Guide to PTLLS and CTLLS (2008)

Practical Teaching: A Guide to PTLLS and DTLLS (2009)

Walk-through tour

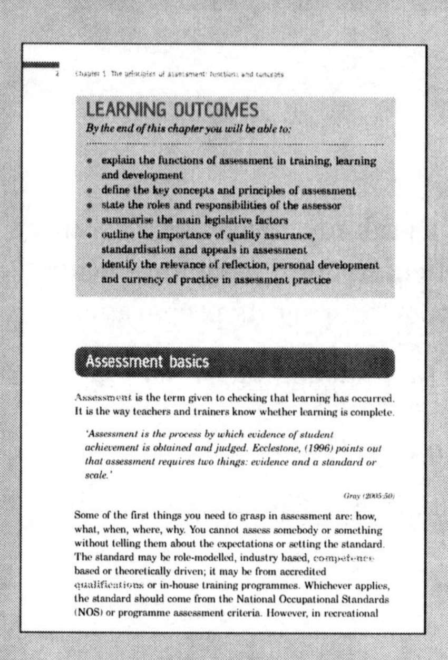

2 Chapter 1 The principles of assessment: functions and concepts

LEARNING OUTCOMES

By the end of this chapter you will be able to:

- explain the functions of assessment in training, learning and development
- define the key concepts and principles of assessment
- state the roles and responsibilities of the assessor
- summarise the main legislative factors
- outline the importance of quality assurance, standardisation and appeals in assessment
- identify the relevance of reflection, personal development and currency of practice in assessment practice

Assessment basics

Assessment is the term given to checking that learning has occurred. It is the way teachers and trainers know whether learning is complete.

> *'Assessment is the process by which evidence of student achievement is obtained and judged. Ecclestone, (1996) points out that assessment requires two things: evidence and a standard or scale.'*
>
> Gray (2005:50)

Some of the first things you need to grasp in assessment are: how, what, when, where, why. You cannot assess somebody or something without telling them about the expectations or setting the standard. The standard may be role-modelled, industry based, competence based or theoretically driven; it may be from accredited qualifications or in-house training programmes. Whichever applies, the standard should come from the National Occupational Standards (NOS) or programme assessment criteria. However, in recreational

Learning outcomes Featured at the beginning of each chapter, you can check at a glance what you are about to learn

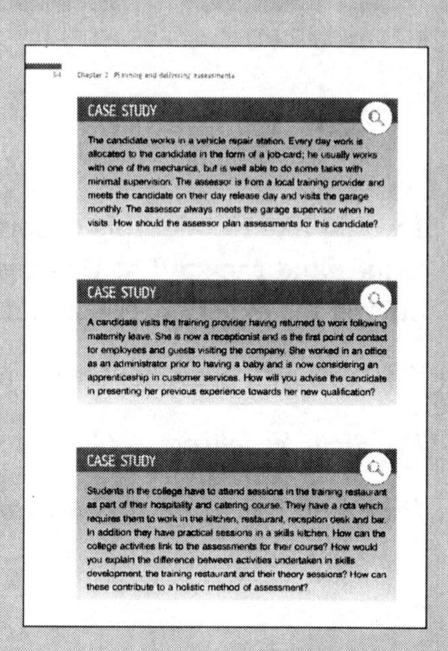

54 Chapter 2 Planning and delivering assessments

CASE STUDY

The candidate works in a vehicle repair station. Every day work is allocated to the candidate in the form of a job-card; he usually works with one of the mechanics, but is well able to do some tasks with minimal supervision. The assessor is from a local training provider and meets the candidate on their day release day and visits the garage monthly. The assessor always meets the garage supervisor when he visits. How should the assessor plan assessments for this candidate?

CASE STUDY

A candidate visits the training provider having returned to work following maternity leave. She is now a receptionist and is the first point of contact for employees and guests visiting the company. She worked in an office as an administrator prior to having a baby and is now considering an apprenticeship in customer services. How will you advise the candidate in presenting her previous experience towards her new qualification?

CASE STUDY

Students in the college have to attend sessions in the training restaurant as part of their hospitality and catering course. They have a rota which requires them to work in the kitchen, restaurant, reception desk and bar. In addition they have practical sessions in a skills kitchen. How can the college activities link to the assessments for their course? How would you explain the difference between activities undertaken in skills development, the training restaurant and their theory sessions? How can these contribute to a holistic method of assessment?

Case study Practical, real-world examples illustrate key points and learning objectives in the text

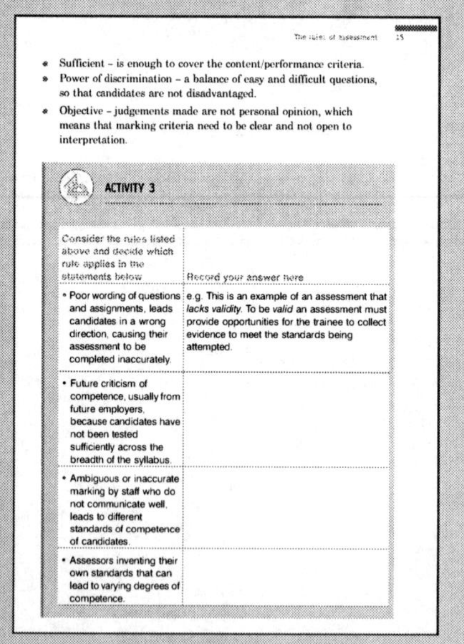

The rules of assessment 15

- Sufficient – is enough to cover the content/performance criteria.
- Power of discrimination – a balance of easy and difficult questions, so that candidates are not disadvantaged.
- Objective – judgements made are not personal opinion, which means that marking criteria need to be clear and not open to interpretation.

ACTIVITY 3

Consider the rules listed above and decide which rule applies in the statements below	Record your answer here
• Poor wording of questions and assignments, leads candidates in a wrong direction, causing their assessment to be completed inaccurately.	e.g. This is an example of an assessment that *lacks validity*. To be *valid* an assessment must provide opportunities for the trainee to collect evidence to meet the standards being attempted.
• Future criticism of competence, usually from future employers, because candidates have not been tested sufficiently across the breadth of the syllabus.	
• Ambiguous or inaccurate marking by staff who do not communicate well, leads to different standards of competence of candidates.	
• Assessors inventing their own standards that can lead to varying degrees of competence.	

Activity Put your knowledge into action with these practical activities

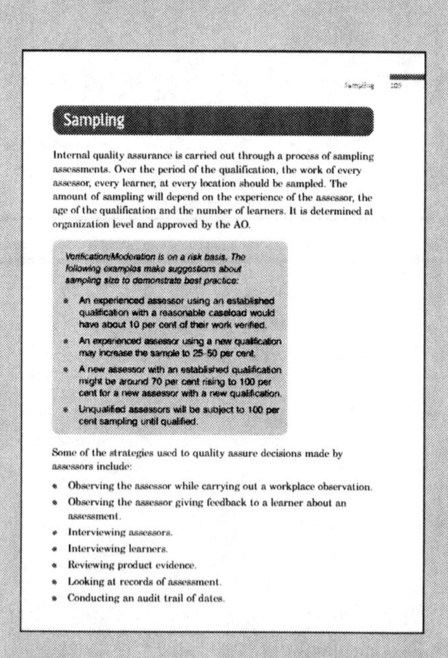

Sampling 105

Sampling

Internal quality assurance is carried out through a process of sampling assessments. Over the period of the qualification, the work of every assessor, every learner, at every location should be sampled. The amount of sampling will depend on the experience of the assessor, the age of the qualification and the number of learners. It is determined at organization level and approved by the AO.

> *Verification/Moderation is on a risk basis. The following examples make suggestions about sampling size to demonstrate best practice:*
>
> - An experienced assessor using an established qualification with a reasonable caseload would have about 10 per cent of their work verified.
> - An experienced assessor using a new qualification may increase the sample to 25-50 per cent.
> - A new assessor with an established qualification might be around 70 per cent rising to 100 per cent for a new assessor with a new qualification.
> - Unqualified assessors will be subject to 100 per cent sampling until qualified.

Some of the strategies used to quality assure decisions made by assessors include:

- Observing the assessor while carrying out a workplace observation.
- Observing the assessor giving feedback to a learner about an assessment.
- Interviewing assessors.
- Interviewing learners.
- Reviewing product evidence.
- Looking at records of assessment.
- Conducting an audit trail of dates.

Note box Key information is drawn out in eye-catching boxes

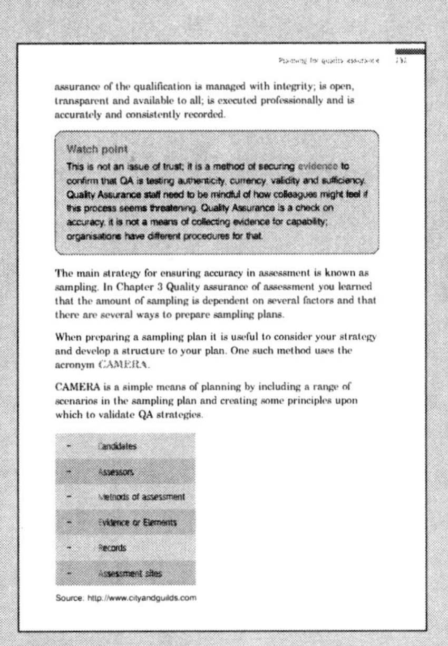

Planning for quality assurance 152

assurance of the qualification is managed with integrity; is open, transparent and available to all; is executed professionally and is accurately and consistently recorded.

Watch point

This is not an issue of trust; it is a method of securing evidence to confirm that QA is testing authenticity, currency, validity and sufficiency. Quality Assurance staff need to be mindful of how colleagues might feel if this process seems threatening. Quality Assurance is a check on accuracy, it is not a means of collecting evidence for capability; organisations have different procedures for that.

The main strategy for ensuring accuracy in assessment is known as sampling. In Chapter 3 Quality assurance of assessment you learned that the amount of sampling is dependent on several factors and that there are several ways to prepare sampling plans.

When preparing a sampling plan it is useful to consider your strategy and develop a structure to your plan. One such method uses the acronym CAMERA.

CAMERA is a simple means of planning by including a range of scenarios in the sampling plan and creating some principles upon which to validate QA strategies.

- Candidates
- Assessors
- Methods of assessment
- Evidence or Elements
- Records
- Assessment sites

Source: http://www.cityandguilds.com

Watch point Useful hints and tips to alert assessors or IQA staff of potential challenges

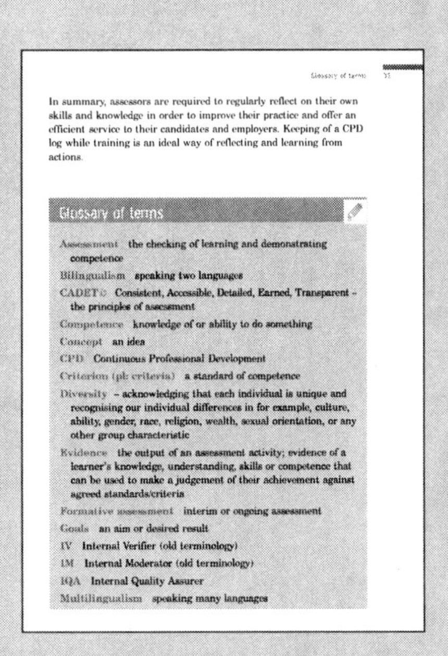

Glossary of terms 35

In summary, assessors are required to regularly reflect on their own skills and knowledge in order to improve their practice and offer an efficient service to their candidates and employers. Keeping of a CPD log while training is an ideal way of reflecting and learning from actions.

Glossary of terms

Assessment the checking of learning and demonstrating competence
Bilingualism speaking two languages
CADET© Consistent, Accessible, Detailed, Earned, Transparent – the principles of assessment
Competence knowledge of or ability to do something
Concept an idea
CPD Continuous Professional Development
Criterion (pl: criteria) a standard of competence
Diversity – acknowledging that each individual is unique and recognising our individual differences in for example, culture, ability, gender, race, religion, wealth, sexual orientation, or any other group characteristic
Evidence the output of an assessment activity; evidence of a learner's knowledge, understanding, skills or competence that can be used to make a judgement of their achievement against agreed standards/criteria
Formative assessment interim or ongoing assessment
Goals an aim or desired result
IV Internal Verifier (old terminology)
IM Internal Moderator (old terminology)
IQA Internal Quality Assurer
Multilingualism speaking many languages

Glossary of terms Glossary of terms highlighted in the text are listed at the end of each chapter with definitions

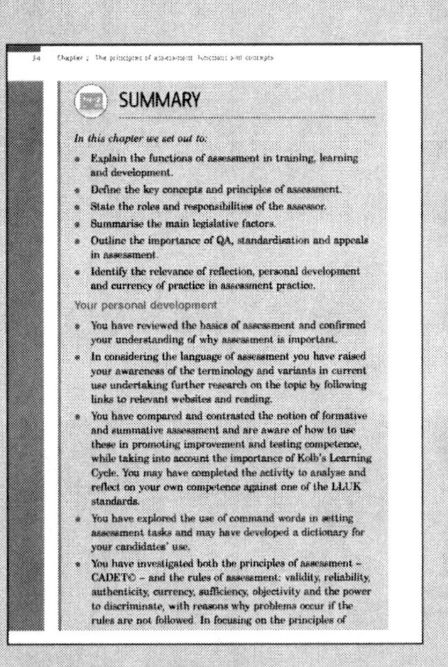

34 Chapter 1 The principles of assessment: functions and concepts

SUMMARY

In this chapter we set out to:

- Explain the functions of assessment in training, learning and development.
- Define the key concepts and principles of assessment.
- State the roles and responsibilities of the assessor.
- Summarise the main legislative factors.
- Outline the importance of QA, standardisation and appeals in assessment.
- Identify the relevance of reflection, personal development and currency of practice in assessment practice.

Your personal development

- You have reviewed the basics of assessment and confirmed your understanding of why assessment is important.
- In considering the language of assessment you have raised your awareness of the terminology and variants in current use undertaking further research on the topic by following links to relevant websites and reading.
- You have compared and contrasted the notion of formative and summative assessment and are aware of how to use these in promoting improvement and testing competence, while taking into account the importance of Kolb's Learning Cycle. You may have completed the activity to analyse and reflect on your own competence against one of the LLUK standards.
- You have explored the use of command words in setting assessment tasks and may have developed a dictionary for your candidates' use.
- You have investigated both the principles of assessment – CADET© – and the rules of assessment: validity, reliability, authenticity, currency, sufficiency, objectivity and the power to discriminate, with reasons why problems occur if the rules are not followed. In focusing on the principles of

Summary Featured at the end of each chapter, summary boxes help you to consolidate what you have learned

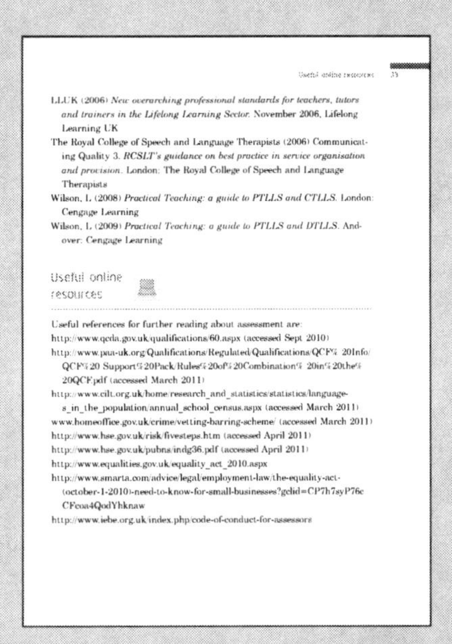

Useful online resources 33

LLUK (2006) *New overarching professional standards for teachers, tutors and trainers in the Lifelong Learning Sector.* November 2006, Lifelong Learning UK

The Royal College of Speech and Language Therapists (2006) Communicating Quality 3. *RCSLT's guidance on best practice in service organisation and provision.* London: The Royal College of Speech and Language Therapists

Wilson, L (2008) *Practical Teaching: a guide to PTLLS and CTLLS.* London: Cengage Learning

Wilson, L (2009) *Practical Teaching: a guide to PTLLS and DTLLS.* Andover: Cengage Learning

Useful online resources

Useful references for further reading about assessment are:

http://www.qcda.gov.uk/qualifications/60.aspx (accessed Sept 2010)

http://www.pua-uk.org/Qualifications/Regulated/Qualifications/QCF% 20Info/QCF%20 Support%20Pack/Rules%20of%20Combination% 20in%20the%20QCF.pdf (accessed March 2011)

http://www.cilt.org.uk/home/research_and_statistics/statistics/languages_in_the_population/annual_school_census.aspx (accessed March 2011)

www.homeoffice.gov.uk/crime/vetting-barring-scheme/ (accessed March 2011)

http://www.hse.gov.uk/risk/fivesteps.htm (accessed April 2011)

http://www.hse.gov.uk/pubns/indg36.pdf (accessed April 2011)

http://www.equalities.gov.uk/equality_act_2010.aspx

http://www.smarta.com/advice/legal/employment-law/the-equality-act-(october-1-2010)-need-to-know-for-small-businesses?gclid=CP7h7syP76cCFcoa4QodYhknaw

http://www.iebe.org.uk/index.php/code-of-conduct-for-assessors

Useful resources Further reading feature offers suggestions for print and online reading material

CHAPTER 1

The principles of assessment: functions and concepts

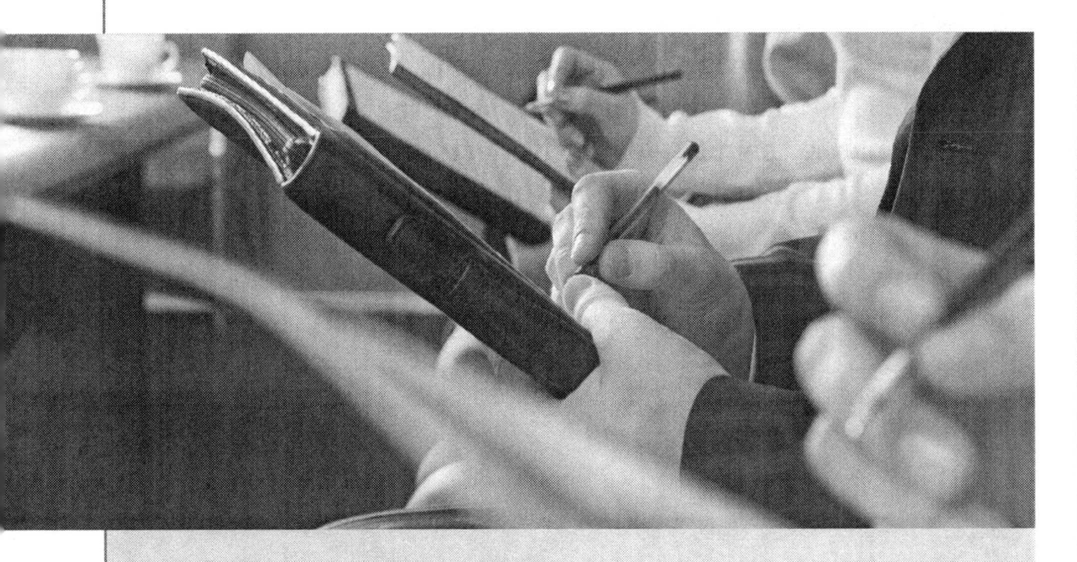

Unit of Assessment	Assessment Criteria
Understanding the principles and practices of assessment	1.1; 1.2; 1.3; 1.4; 6.1; 6.2; 6.3; 8.1; 8.3; 8.4
Assess occupational competence in the work environment	2.3; 3.3; 4.1; 4.2; 4.3; 4.4
Assess vocational skills, knowledge and understanding	2.5; 3.3; 4.1; 4.2; 4.3; 4.4
Understanding the principles and practices of internally assuring the quality of assessment	No direct references
Internally assure the quality of assessment	No direct references
Plan, allocate and monitor work in own area of responsibility	No direct references

LEARNING OUTCOMES

By the end of this chapter you will be able to:

- explain the functions of assessment in training, learning and development
- define the key concepts and principles of assessment
- state the roles and responsibilities of the assessor
- summarise the main legislative factors
- outline the importance of quality assurance, standardisation and appeals in assessment
- identify the relevance of reflection, personal development and currency of practice in assessment practice

Assessment basics

Assessment is the term given to checking that learning has occurred. It is the way teachers and trainers know whether learning is complete.

> *'Assessment is the process by which evidence of student achievement is obtained and judged. Ecclestone, (1996) points out that assessment requires two things: evidence and a standard or scale.'*

Gray (2005:50)

Some of the first things you need to grasp in assessment are: how, what, when, where, why. You cannot assess somebody or something without telling them about the expectations or setting the standard. The standard may be role-modelled, industry based, **competence** based or theoretically driven; it may be from accredited **qualifications** or in-house training programmes. Whichever applies, the standard should come from the National Occupational Standards (NOS) or programme assessment criteria. However, in recreational provision there are unlikely to be such formal **standards**, so the standard becomes the teacher's, employer's and/or the candidate's **goals**. Therefore, standards and goals are the keys to successful assessment.

Watch point

If you know where you are going, you'll be able to tell when you've got there.

The output of assessment is 'evidence'; **evidence** is the confirmation that assessment has occurred and the way it is proven. To summarise, assessment is a 'method of confirming learning'.

Why assess?

Businesses and training institutions are driven by the need to have a qualified workforce. In both the private and public sectors this need is met through a range of opportunities delivered either on their premises or in conjunction with a college or private training provider. Education and training is delivered as part of a professional development programme, apprenticeship, day-release or full-time education programme. Whichever way the education or training is delivered there is a need to ensure that the standards are consistent and recognisable. To this end each occupational sector (see Appendix A Occupational sectors – Sector subject areas (SSA)) has a series of qualifications. Where qualifications do not exist, perhaps because the employer has their own specific training needs, there is still a need to produce standards by which to measure learning.

The need for assessment is, therefore, linked to national or organisational standards. Assessment is required to ensure the integrity of those standards.

The language of assessment

The terminology or language of assessment leads to the introduction of words which demand further explanation. This section introduces the reader to the technical language of assessment.

Assessment can be carried out before recruitment (at interview), at commencement (diagnostic and initial assessment), during and at the end of the learning or training activity and at the end of the module, unit or programme. It may be pertinent at this point to look at how qualifications are structured, as this will lead us to the points at which assessment should occur.

Programme of study

A collection of qualifications which create an apprenticeship framework, a college course or training programme. Also described as a curriculum.

In September 2010 a new qualifications framework was launched. As with the previous National Qualifications Framework (NQF), the Qualifications Credit Framework (QCF) lists a hierarchy of levels of qualifications. In the new system, a tariff was issued with eight levels of qualification of increasing difficulty. These levels meant that qualifications could be matched against each other – for example at Level 3 you will be able to undertake an A level, an Advanced Apprenticeship or a BTEC Extended Diploma. While they will be different sizes within the Level 3, they all have parity in terms of difficulty. Figure 1.1 shows the QCF.

In the vocational sector, NOS are written by the Sector Skills Councils (SSCs). These standards form the basis of the **units of assessment** and the resultant qualifications created by awarding organisations.

Qualification

A certificated qualification, endorsed by an awarding organisation and approved through the Qualifications and Credit Framework (QCF, see www.ofqual.gov.uk for more information).

For example, some qualifications you may come across include:

Entry	Functional Skills Mathematics
Level 1	NVQ Diploma in Hairdressing and Beauty Therapy (QCF)
Level 2	Certificate in Health and Social Care (QCF)

Figure 1.1 The Qualifications Credit Framework

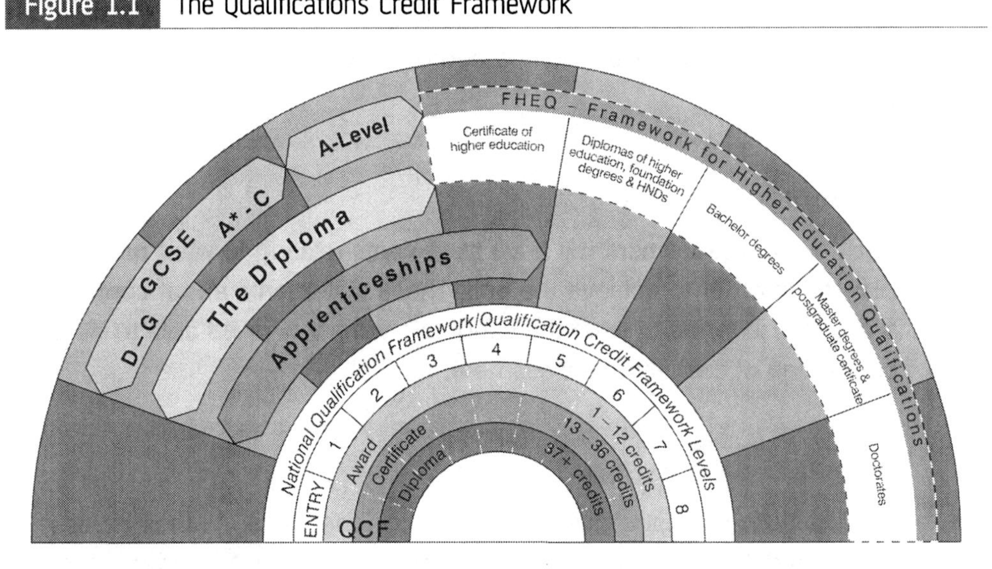

Source: Ofqual, August 2011.

Level 3 Extended Diploma in Public Services (Uniformed) (QCF)
Level 4 Certificate in Teaching in the Lifelong Learning Sector
Level 5 HND Diploma in Business (QCF)

A qualification consists of a number of units of assessment, clustered to create a certificated qualification.

Units of assessment

The smaller subsections of the qualification which focus on a particular aspect of the subject. There will usually be several units in a qualification.

Each unit will have its own specified learning outcomes and assessment criteria. Each will have a specified level and credit value. Additional information may be provided to guide the assessment process. The documentation will also state the name of the sector skills area which owns the unit. In some qualifications, units of assessment from different sector areas will be combined to create meaningful qualifications.

Content

Each unit of assessment will have statements relating to what has to be covered in order to achieve the unit. These statements about content are written in terms of what the candidate will know or be able to do on completion of the unit of assessment.

Rules of combination

Qualifications consist of mandatory and optional units. As their names infer, mandatory units are those which must be achieved and optional ones are usually from a list of units arranged singularly or in groups from which the candidate must select a specified number. The purpose of grouping units is to ensure that qualifications contain the range of competence expected in the industry.

Version 4 http://www.paa-uk.org/Qualifications/Regulated/Qualifications/QCF%20Info/QCF%20Support%20Pack/Rules%20of%20Combination%20in%20the%20QCF.pdf (accessed July 2011)

Accumulation and transfer of credits

In order to provide benchmarks for qualifications, the regulatory body Ofqual requires that each unit in a set of NOS is set at a *level* of learning. This determines the level of difficulty of the unit. It varies from entry (entry 1, entry 2 and entry 3), through level 1 to level 8. Level 2 is roughly equivalent to GCSE level and level 3 equivalent to A level standard, whereas, level 8 is PhD standard (see Figure 1.1 above). Another benchmark is that of *size*. This refers to the volume of learning and is stated as a 'credit'; an award comprises 1 to 12 credits; a certificate comprises 13 to 36 credits; a diploma comprises of 37 credits or more.

Watch point

This change is different to the earlier framework in which a diploma was at a higher level than a certificate. Now there are awards, certificates and diplomas at all levels; they are now determined by their size, not their difficulty.

The final benchmark relates to *subject*; qualifications are categorised into the subject sector classification scheme. For example, Assessor and Quality Assurance units are in subject area 13 – Education and Training, sector area 13.2 – Direct Learning Support.

Programmes of learning and apprenticeships are arranged around these frameworks; you may be employed to deliver a particular unit or module or you may work within a team of people who train towards a whole or part qualification. Whichever strategy is used, the teacher or trainer will have to assess that learning has occurred. In some qualifications this learning is referred to as 'demonstrating competence'.

Term	Alternative expressions
Qualification	Standards, specifications, course, syllabus, programme, apprenticeship written by an awarding organisation following a set of NOS
Learning outcome	Objective, range statements, content, statements of competence
Evidence requirements	Assessment guidance, evidence, portfolio, assignment, assessment criteria
Grading	Grading criteria are the level at which the outcomes are met – e.g. pass merit/credit or distinction
Quality assurance (QA)	Verification, moderation, standardisation
Assessment	Test, exam, evidence (proof)

Unfortunately, assessment is such a wide topic and the qualification frameworks are so varied that there are many different terms used (assessment jargon) and it sometimes takes a while to learn the terminology; usually when you do discover their meaning it is broadly the same as another similar term used in a different qualification team. Let us look at some of those terms.

Command words

Within every set of units of assessment, there are a series of statements to define exactly what a candidate has to do in order to demonstrate their competence against a specific set of standards.

For example: 'explain ...' is frequently seen. Explain can be defined as 'to make something clear by giving a detailed account of relevant facts or circumstances'. How a candidate does this will be 'explained' in Chapter 2, but suffice to say, at this point, it could be written, verbal, demonstrated, or a combination of those strategies. It is the skill of the assessor that will guide the candidate towards an effective method.

ACTIVITY 1

Make a list of command words you use in your training or learning environment when 'explaining' the subject or how it will be assessed.

Consider:

Wording in assignments or instructions to complete question sheets.

e.g.: explain *

* *

* *

* *

Extension activity:

Create a dictionary of terms that your candidates may find helpful.

Clue: look at the learning outcomes in a qualification. Sentences usually start with a word that indicates what needs to be done in order to meet the requirements of the outcome. Awarding organisations also have resources to explain their command words.

Concepts of assessment

A **concept** is an idea, in this instance, about assessment. The concepts that you will commonly see are: **criterion** referencing; **formative assessment** and **summative assessment**.

Criterion referencing When a candidate (trainee, learner, student) achieves a standard, they either can (or can't) do the task, answer the question or demonstrate competence. They can continue in their attempts until the criterion is achieved (plural is criteria). Therefore in this style of assessment the assessor is measuring what a candidate can do. While it is generally associated with a 'can do–can't do' (pass–fail) assessment, it may be linked to a grading scale which determines how well a candidate can do something. In this strategy a candidate can pass, pass with merit or pass with distinction.

ACTIVITY 2

Assess your own performance against the statements of competence:

If you were to measure your performance as a teacher or trainer against the 'New overarching professional standards for teachers, tutors and trainers in the lifelong learning sector' (LLUK, 2006), you would be undertaking an assessment using criteria. For example, this is an extract from Domain E – Assessment for Learning, using criteria related to professional practice (LLUK, 2006: p11–12). By comparing your status against the standard you can complete the self-assessment.

	Standard	How do you measure up to the standard? Do you do this? How? What evidence do you have to prove this?
EP1.1	Use appropriate forms of assessment and evaluate their effectiveness in producing information useful to the teacher and the learner	
EP1.2	Devise, select, use and appraise assessment tools, including where appropriate, those which exploit new and emerging technologies	
EP2.1	Apply appropriate methods of assessment fairly and effectively	
EP2.3	Design appropriate assessment activities for own specialist area	
EP3.2	Ensure that access to assessment is appropriate to learner need	
EP4.2	Use feedback to evaluate and improve own skills in assessment	
EP5.3	Communicate relevant assessment information to those with a legitimate interest in learner achievement, as necessary/appropriate	

In the boxes on the right you will have written statements, made lists, justified your choices and opinions, described strategies and given examples of instances when the competence is demonstrated. As this is a self-assessment, and therefore only an individual's opinion of their ability, the judgements will usually be supported by other assessments.

The units in the assessment and quality assurance qualification also base assessment decisions on criteria (see Appendix B Units of assessment (City & Guilds)). They are different to the LLUK (2006) criteria. It is important, therefore, not to muddle criteria contained within different awards or sets of standards.

Formative assessment An interim judgement, also known as 'continuous assessment'. It has the advantage of being an ideal opportunity to tell a candidate how they are progressing and giving them the chance to improve. This type of assessment is highly motivational because it is seen as a review rather than an assessment. It helps candidates to progress and maximise their potential. There is life after formative assessment! One of the disadvantages of formative assessment (although significantly outweighed by the advantages) is that continuous assessment may feel like *continual* assessment. Kolb's learning cycle (see Figure 1.2) advocates the concepts of formative assessment and feedback clearly within the cycle, indicating their value in personal development and progression. Formative assessment aids learning.

Figure 1.2 Kolb's learning cycle (1984)

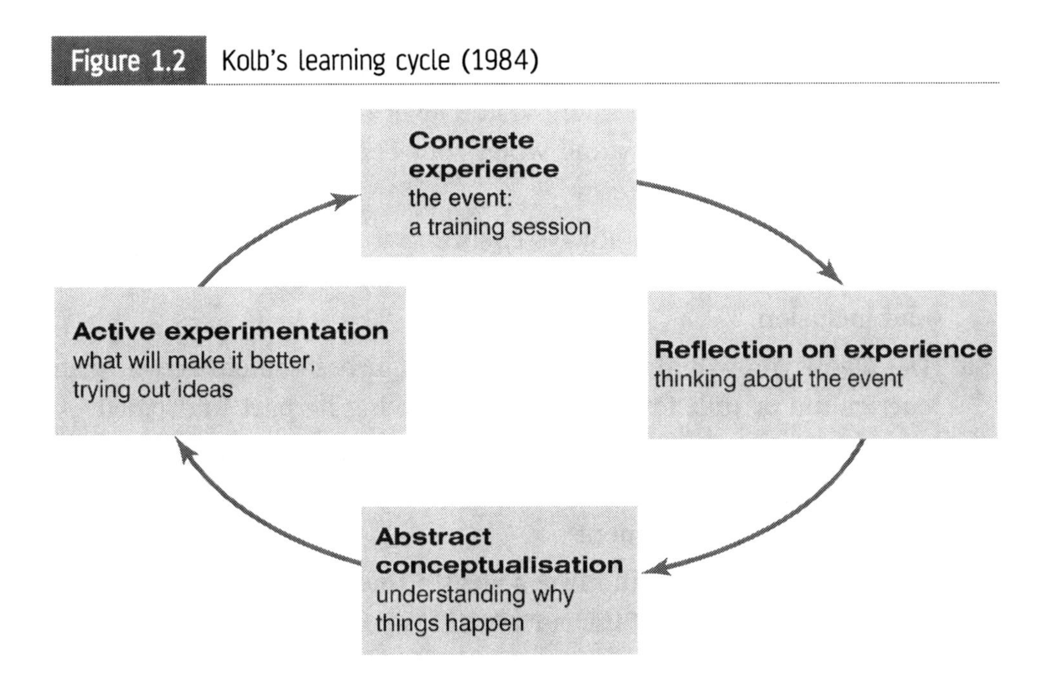

Summative assessment The form of assessment usually associated with tests and exams. It aids the assessment of learning and is a formal process to close a stage of learning or training; thus enabling the whole programme to move forward. In summative assessment styles, a candidate progresses through their qualification or unit of study until the time comes that learning is complete and they are tested on their knowledge or skills. A judgement is made, which is then expressed on a certificate. If a candidate wishes to improve they usually have to 'sit' the examination again. This does put enormous pressure on candidates as the outcomes may determine their future. However, with teaching that prepares a candidate well for their test, such apprehension and anxiety can be lessened. In a less formal situation the summative assessment is usually completed in smaller chunks to build up to the whole qualification. This is where formative and summative concepts overlap and the meaning of the terminology becomes less black and white.

Principles of assessment

A **principle** is a rule that you will follow; it is an underlying standard that you will not compromise. Some of the principles that you should advocate are:

- Consistency – you will always ensure that the methods and timeliness of your assessment is at a level standard, making certain that irrespective of how and when your candidates are assessed, the outcomes are constant.
- Accessibility – you will always ensure that all of your candidates are able to access your assessments and follow systems of equality and inclusion.
- Detailed – you will always ensure that your assessments cover your curriculum or unit fairly and evenly, leaving no part undecided.
- Earned – you will always ensure that your candidates have achieved their qualifications with rigour and others will respect the integrity of the assessment.
- Transparency – you will always ensure that everyone involved in the assessment is crystal clear about its purpose and meaning.

These principles form the acronym **CADET©**:

C	Consistent
A	Accessible
D	Detailed
E	Earned
T	Transparent

So, these are the values and principles that you follow when preparing, implementing and evaluating assessment. It will be these values that will help to determine the effectiveness of your assessment.

It should be remembered that assessment is not merely something which occurs in the workplace or end of year test. In every training session that you do you will set learning outcomes, deliver your topic and then close the session. You must remember that to truly know if you have achieved the learning outcomes you must set an assessment activity. If the close of your session is: 'Is everybody OK with that?' you may be able to claim that you have 'taught' your topic, but you cannot claim that your candidates have learned anything! You must, therefore, include into the structure of your training session, small assessment activities which help you to confirm learning. The easiest to prepare are verbal or written questions – but make sure everyone contributes and remember that you can use similar activities in the follow up session as a recap activity, before moving forward to the next topic. In the next chapter we will review the different ways that this can be achieved.

The rules of assessment

Once you have sorted out the basics of assessment, you can get down to the actual assessment. There are a number of different ways of assessing, but all rely on the fact that you need something to measure against. These are usually written by awarding organisations but there are some courses where you may have to devise your own standards, for example non-qualification courses, industry training schemes or recreational programmes.

Watch point

NEVER substitute your own standards onto qualifications which are approved within the QCF, however well intentioned.

Qualifications are written against NOS and approved as such by organisations charged with the remit to create a standard across the country, e.g. City & Guilds. If you change the specifications contained in the qualifications you will disadvantage your candidates, because you are creating your own qualification, which will not be recognised within your professional area. A similar rule should apply to the delivery of industry training courses; these courses are agreed at head office level and provide a standard across the company.

The first task when planning assessment is to gain sight of the awarding organisation's specifications for your unit/module or qualification. In it you will find a series of paragraphs telling you what a candidate will:

- know
- be able to do
- demonstrate,

at the end of the unit or module.

Some qualifications/units will tell you that you need to collect two of this, a report on that, or an observation for the other. But more often it will be up to you to decide on the appropriate assessment task and the method, usually under the supervision of the Internal Quality Assurer (**IQA**). There are some **rules** that will help you make informed choices. You should ensure that your assessments are:

- Valid/relevant – assesses what it is supposed to, according to the curriculum, in an appropriate manner.
- Reliable/fair – assesses in a consistent manner to the expected standards, regardless of who makes the judgement or when the judgement is made without any bias or preference.
- Authentic – is able to be attributed to the candidate.
- Current/recent – is up to date and recently written.

- Sufficient – is enough to cover the content/performance criteria.
- Power of discrimination – a balance of easy and difficult questions, so that candidates are not disadvantaged.
- Objective – judgements made are not personal opinion, which means that marking criteria need to be clear and not open to interpretation.

ACTIVITY 3

Consider the rules listed above and decide which rule applies in the statements below	Record your answer here
• Poor wording of questions and assignments, leads candidates in a wrong direction, causing their assessment to be completed inaccurately.	e.g. This is an example of an assessment that *lacks validity*. To be *valid* an assessment must provide opportunities for the trainee to collect evidence to meet the standards being attempted.
• Future criticism of competence, usually from future employers, because candidates have not been tested sufficiently across the breadth of the syllabus.	
• Ambiguous or inaccurate marking by staff who do not communicate well, leads to different standards of competence of candidates.	
• Assessors inventing their own standards that can lead to varying degrees of competence.	

Consider the rules listed above and decide which rule applies in the statements below	Record your answer here
• Poor research skills leading to inaccurate citation and/or plagiarism.	
• Work presented in a portfolio is not signed or dated.	

To overcome these issues, you should follow the rules of assessment, by:

- Always ensuring that your candidates are prepared for their assessments.
- Devising tasks that test what you have taught.
- Telling candidates how, when and where assessments will happen.
- Offering study skills to support presentation of research in work.
- Asking colleagues (or IQA) to review the task before submitting to candidates (when devising assessments).
- Creating varied assessment tasks to give good coverage of material and opportunities for differentiation.

The role and responsibilities of the assessor

To develop an understanding of the role of the assessor, it is helpful first to consider who else is involved in an assessment. The key roles of people involved in the assessment process starts with the candidate who is assessed by the assessor who then submits work to the quality assurer (QA). This simplistic process is further explained as:

Title	Role	May also be known as:
Candidate	To attend regularly To achieve award in a timely manner To respect the rules of the organisation	Trainee, learner, student
Trainer	To demonstrate skills To teach underpinning knowledge (UPK) To raise confidence To monitor progress towards assessment	Tutor, teacher, coach, facilitator
Skills assessor	To make judgements about skills, usually in the work environment To ask oral questions to test knowledge related to the task To check validity, currency, authenticity and sufficiency of evidence To feedback the outcome of assessment To make records To process assessments to the QA stage	Assessor, first line assessor, trainer, observer
UPK assessor	To make judgements about knowledge and understanding To check validity, currency, authenticity and sufficiency of evidence To feedback the outcome of assessment To make records To process assessments to the QA stage	Assessor, second line assessor, teacher

Title	Role	May also be known as:
IQA	To confirm that assessments are valid, current, authentic and sufficient to meet the assessment criteria To support and guide assessors To make records To lead on standardisation activities To plan external QA visits To liaise with awarding organisations	Internal verifier (IV) Internal moderator (IM)
External quality assurer	Appointed by the awarding organisation To confirm assessment and QA procedures comply with awarding organisation assessment guidance	External verifier External moderator External examiner

The assessor will work with the candidate in the following ways:

- Providing initial advice and guidance prior to enrolment.
- Preparing and delivering an induction to the programme, qualification and organisation.
- Undertaking initial assessment to ascertain the best **pathway**.
- Undertaking diagnostic assessment to check or confirm previous learning.
- Identifying additional learning requirements.
- Introducing the candidate to the framework or qualification.
- Preparing the programme of study and long- and short-term targets.
- Providing a platform for learning – a trainer may do this.
- Planning assessments.
- Reviewing targets and progress.
- Undertaking a range of assessment activities according to need.

- Supporting and advising the candidate on methods of collecting evidence to support competence.
- Giving feedback to the candidate.
- Confirming validity, sufficiency, authenticity and currency of evidence.
- Keeping records of assessment.

In addition, the assessor is required to participate in QA processes, many of which are described briefly later in this chapter or in detail in Chapter 3 Quality assurance of assessment and Chapter 4 Internally assuring the quality of assessment:

- Be the first point of contact between the candidate and the QA.
- Contribute to QA procedures.
- Attend standardisation activities.
- Fully understand the qualification.
- Maintain and update own expertise and professional development.
- Maintain own licence to practice.

The qualities the assessor will possess include:

- Organisational skills.
- Time management skills.
- Patience.
- Communication skills.
- The ability to evaluate/assess objectively and accurately against units of assessment and NOS.
- An approachable manner within boundaries of role.
- Perception.
- The ability to judge without appearing to interrogate or sanction.
- An ability to create relationships built on trust and integrity.
- Knowledge of systems and procedures and the ability to be the 'guardian of the rules'.
- Advocacy of high standards.

Legislation

This section covers the main items of legislation covering the assessment and QA roles. It should be read within those parameters. Every assessor will also be occupationally competent in their field of expertise and, therefore, will need to be aware of the legislation pertinent to their subject.

Health and Safety at Work Act 1974

Everyone has a responsibility for the safety of themselves and others, therefore, rules must be followed and safe practices adhered to. You should demonstrate a model of best practice, lead by example. There are additional rules relating to taking candidates on educational visits following a series of tragic accidents. Do not consider taking candidates on visits without seeking advice. Health and Safety legislation requires the assessor to comply with the rules of the organisation in which their trainee is working. Assessors should wear appropriate personal protective equipment (PPE) and ensure that their trainees are compliant.

The Management of Health and Safety at Work Regulations 1999

The Regulations seek to prevent unsafe practices and minimise risk. For example: fire and emergency procedures, first aid at work, safe handling practices, visual display unit guidance and risk assessment.

Risk assessment All activities have an element of risk, some more so than others. It is the trainer/assessor's responsibility to assess the level of the risk, to establish practices to minimise risk and record such activities. The five steps to risk assessment recommended by the Health and Safety Executive (HSE) are:

1 identify the hazards

2 decide who might be harmed and how
3 evaluate the risks and decide on the precaution
4 record the findings and implement them
5 review your assessment and update if necessary.

http://www.hse.gov.uk/risk/fivesteps.htm (accessed April 2011)

Visual display units/display screen equipment The HSE give advice to individuals and employers about working in these environments. Employees report eye strain, headaches, tiredness and discomfort, aches and repetitive strain injuries when using such equipment. The HSE advises employees to take regular short breaks to relieve eye strain, and customise chairs, desks and wrist supports to minimise discomfort and injury. The Health and Safety (Display Screen Equipment) Regulations 1992 implement an EC Directive and came into effect from January 1993 (some small changes were made in 2002). The Regulations require employers to minimise the risks in VDU work by ensuring that workplaces and jobs are well designed.
http://www.hse.gov.uk/pubns/indg36.pdf (accessed April 2011)

Child protection and safeguarding Recent high profile cases have brought about the necessity to introduce legislation and guidance on protecting children and vulnerable adults against inappropriate behaviour. Each organisation should exercise their functions with a view to safeguarding and promoting the welfare of children, (Protection of Children Act 1999, The Children Act 2004, Mental Capacity Act 2005). Mandatory Criminal Records Bureau (CRB) checks are required of anyone working closely with children and vulnerable adults. The Government holds lists of those deemed unsuitable to work with these groups and organisations should check these before appointing staff. You may also find that groups of candidates, for example child care trainees, are checked before embarking on their course of study. This is 'due diligence' on behalf of the organisation who may send these candidates into work placements in nurseries and the like.

Safeguarding is an expression which defines the broader implications of child protection as it also includes prevention. Safeguarding has been defined as:

- All agencies working with children, young people and their families taking all reasonable measures to ensure that the risks of harm to children's welfare are minimised.
- Where there are concerns about children and young people's welfare, all agencies taking appropriate actions to address those concerns, working to agreed local policies and procedures in full partnership with other local agencies.

Safeguarding Children (2005)

In February 2011 the Coalition Government published the findings of its Review into the Vetting and Barring Scheme (VBS). One of the key recommendations from the VBS review was the merging of the CRB and Independent Safeguarding Authority (ISA) to form a streamlined new body providing a proportionate barring and criminal records checking service. The guidelines require organisations to liaise with other departments in multi-agency working. This will ensure that isolated incidents collate to create a bigger picture and thus work to prevent abuse and neglect.

www.homeoffice.gov.uk/crime/vetting-barring-scheme/ (accessed March 2011)

Equality of opportunity legislation A series of laws have been passed to ensure that no-one is discriminated against, irrespective of gender, marital status, sexual orientation, disability, race, nationality, ethnic origin, religion or belief, domestic circumstances, trade union membership, social or employment status.

For the assessor this means ensuring language, handouts and other training and learning materials are free from bias, and that inappropriate comments are challenged and excluded from the training environment. When advertising courses and delivering learning, an assessor should not stereotype or in any way disadvantage groups of candidates. The environment and all support structures should enable access and include facilities to meet all candidates' needs.

The Equality Act 2010 brings together separate pieces of legislation into one single Act simplifying the law and strengthening it in important ways to help tackle discrimination and inequality. The single equality scheme aims to meet the requirements of current legislation, which includes the following Acts, Statutory Instruments and other legislation:

- Disability Discrimination Act 1995
- Disability Equality Duty 2006
- Employment Equality (Age) Regulations 2006
- Employment Equality (Religion or Belief) Regulations 2003
- Employment Equality (Sex Discrimination) Regulations 2005
- Employment Equality (Sexual Orientation) Regulations 2003
- Equal Pay Act 1970
- Equality Act 2006
- Equality Act (Sexual Orientation) Regulations 2007
- EU Framework for Equal Treatment in Employment Directive 2000
- EU Race Discrimination Directive 2003
- Gender Equality Duty 2007
- Gender Equality Duty Code of Practice England and Wales 2006
- Gender Recognition Act 2004
- Human Rights Act 1998
- Race Relations Act 1976
- Race Relations (Amendment) Act 2000
- Sex Discrimination Act 1975
- Sex Discrimination (Gender Reassignment) Regulations 1999
- Special Educational Needs and Disability Act 2001
- Statutory Code of Practice on the Duty to Promote Race Equality 2002
- Work and Families Act 2006

Of the Acts, the following impose a duty on all public bodies to positively promote disability, race and gender equality:

- Equality Act 2006

- Disability Discrimination Act 2005
- Race Relations (Amendment) Act 2000

Government Equalities Office http://www.equalities.gov.uk/

Data protection The Data Protection Act 1998 requires any organisation that holds any data on individuals, electronic or otherwise, for more than two months, to register as data users. It restricts the sharing of data. Caution should be taken when holding records associated with candidates, staff or partner companies. It is common sense that you should never reveal personal information about anyone to another person, however convincing the request!

Duty of care Common, civil, statute and criminal law all apply to trainers and assessors. If you are proven to be negligent in an act, then you may have to compensate the injured party. This applies to individuals as well as to corporate responsibility. Trainers and assessors are, in principle, *in loco parentis* to their younger candidates. This means they need to offer a safe environment, while balancing the need to experiment and develop independence. If you and the organisation have taken all reasonable steps to ensure safety, yet a candidate is injured as a result of not following the rules, it is unlikely to be proven that you are in breach of the duty of care. So, if you are using equipment in a workshop, or scissors in a salon, or taking a group on a visit, you should assess the risk, warn of the safety implications and use protective equipment. All organisations including placements providing opportunities for candidates to learn skills and knowledge must hold relevant insurances and have a risk assessment for all activities. Failure to do so is negligence.

Diversity and assessment Equality is ensuring that candidates have fair and equal access to assessment. Although this does not mean treating all people the same, it does require assessors to design training and assessment around the individual needs of all candidates. **Diversity**, however, requires trainers and assessors to respect the difference between individuals.

The current diversity within the population of the United Kingdom is extremely broad. Embedding equality and diversity into all aspects of the programme is now seen as standard practice in helping to raise cultural awareness and prepare candidates for their future experiences in the world of work.

In addition, assessors need to be mindful of specialist needs of those for whom English is not the first language. **Bilingualism** and **multilingualism** is now common, with 16 per cent of primary and 12 per cent of secondary children speaking a first language other than English. This represents a 1 per cent increase on the previous year. Over 300 language categories are reported as spoken in the UK; this does not include dialects.

Annual School Census 2010. Department for Children, Schools and Families. http://www.cilt.org.uk/home/research_and_statistics/statistics/languages_in_the_population/annual_school_census.aspx (accessed March 2011)

Further, there is a promotion of the notion that:

> *'... bilingualism in a child or adult is an advantage and does not cause communication disorders'.*
>
> *The Royal College of Speech and Language Therapists (2006)*

Assessors are, therefore, required to ensure that the language of the qualification or framework is accessible and comprehended by all.

Ethics in assessment

Confidentiality is required in all aspects of the role:

- In planning to ensure timely preparations.
- In appeals and disputes to ensure impartial outcomes.
- In feedback to ensure appropriateness of location and outcome.
- In evidence to ensure the security of information contained in personal journals, portfolios, or corporate information.
- In records to protect candidates' personal information, progress and assessment records.

The Freedom of Information Act 2000 gives candidates the right to access information that is being kept about them both on paper and electronically. The Data Protection Act 1998 requires organisations to store information securely and lawfully.

Finally, the assessor's attitudes, values and beliefs should never influence assessment practice or the way a candidate is treated (see also the various aspects of equality in Diversity in Assessment above). As a professional occupation a code of conduct is required of trainers and assessors.

The Institute for Education Business Excellence sets a code of practice for assessors. It requires assessors to:

- Evaluate objectively, be impartial, with no bias, declaring any conflicts of interests which may undermine their objectivity.
- Report honestly, ensuring that judgements are fair and reliable.
- Carry out their work with integrity, treating all those they meet with courtesy and sensitivity.
- Do all they can to minimise the stress on those involved in the assessment visit, taking account of their best interests and well-being.
- Maintain purposeful and productive dialogue with those being assessed, and communicate judgements clearly and frankly.
- Respect the confidentiality of information, particularly about individuals and their work.
- Attend assessment visits well prepared, having read pre-visit documentation.
- Dress in a professional manner and be punctual.

http://www.iebe.org.uk/index.php/code-of-conduct-for-assessors

Quality assurance and standardisation in assessment

While later chapters will cover these aspects in more detail, at this point you need to have a basic understanding of these terms.

Quality assurance is a process which ensures that assessment decisions are accurate and transparent. In order to provide clarity of this process you will find policies within the organisation to outline expectations and what to do if things go wrong. To meet an awarding organisation's guidance the following policies are expected:

- Assessment policy and/or procedure – outlines assessment procedure, guidance on special assessment requirements, strategy for QA, process for dealing with fails and referrals, and general guidance for teams.
- Assessment malpractice policy and/or procedure – guidance on how an organisation ensures consistency and integrity of assessment, including how the organisation will deal with cheating, plagiarism, collusion and falsifying records either by staff or candidates.
- Appeals policy and/or procedure – guidance on how the organisation will deal with complaints, disputes and appeals against assessment decisions.

Within every training and assessment provider, there will be people appointed to check the work of assessors. Again, terminology will vary here, but most commonly you will see the role of IQA. These people are tasked with the remit of quality assuring the assessment process. Each stage of assessment is subject to QA tactics. Those stages include planning, delivering, making judgements, providing feedback and record keeping.

For example:

- IQAs will call meetings to ensure that all assessors are working to the same set of principles. This is called 'standardisation'. Assessors may be tasked to review a piece of work and collectively agree the judgement; alternatively, they may be required to each bring in some examples and share these with colleagues – again to ensure consistency.
- IQAs will cross check a number of pieces of evidence to confirm that an accurate judgement had been made. The amount of evidence checked will depend upon the experience of the assessor.
- IQAs will co-observe assessments in the workplace to verify the observation process.

- IQAs will check records of assessment to check accuracy of completeness and check that signatures are bona fide. They will look at dates to ensure that candidates are registered in a timely manner, that evidence matches dates on recording documents and that assessment activities are carried out regularly.

These examples constitute the main aspects of the QA process in relation to validating assessment practice. Later chapters will explore this in more detail.

Disputes and appeals

There may be occasions when a candidate disputes the judgement made about the evidence presented by them. In Chapter 3 Quality assurance of assessment, you will find more detail about the process in the context of the role of the IQA. At this point assessors need to recognise that a candidate has the right of appeal against judgements. Appeals are likely to be either against the process – i.e. a candidate believes that part of the planning, delivery or feedback was unfair, or against the outcome – i.e. the candidate believes that the judgement should have been different to that recorded.

In either instance, the candidate should be allowed to discuss the disputed decision without fear of recrimination. During the candidate's induction, they will have been made aware of the process to follow in the case of a dispute or appeal. It would usually commence with an informal, verbal alert to a candidate's dissatisfaction. The assessor and the candidate would discuss the issue and, hopefully, either the candidate will understand more fully the rationale behind the outcome, or the assessor will review the evidence again and over-ride the original decision. Even though informal and resolved there should still be a record of the appeal.

An example of a record for informal appeals is shown opposite.

Irrespective of the potential outcome of the appeal, the IQA must be aware that an appeal is in progress. However, they should not request detail during the early stages in order to remain impartial should a

Candidate name		
Qualification		
Date of appeal		
Record of informal appeal		
Was the appeal/dispute logged verbally or in writing?		
Did a meeting occur to discuss the appeal/dispute?		
Date of meeting: .... Persons present: Assessor: Candidate: Others (state)		
Outline the nature of the appeal or dispute?		
Was the appeal/dispute resolved?		
YES	What actions result from the meeting:	
	Appeal lost: Candidate agreed with original decision following explanation, judgement stands.	
	Appeal upheld: assessment decision amended in the light of review of evidence or policy.	
	Implications for assessment practice: Complete and return this form to IQA.	
NO	The assessor and the candidate failed to agree and wish to enter a formal appeal process. Candidate signature: Assessor signature:	
	Complete and return this form to IQA.	
	Date appeal/dispute forwarded to IQA.	

formal stage be entered. An appeal or dispute conversation is a confidential discussion. If this is discussed with others before an outcome is agreed, then the candidate may have a justified complaint that the appeal was not held in a manner to minimise bias.

ACTIVITY 4

Collect a copy of your organisation's appeals and disputes policy and procedure and ensure you are familiar with its content. Prepare a briefing session about the process to use with candidates during induction.

Reflection, personal development and currency of practice

The role of the assessor is broad and the responsibilities great. Candidates rely on assessors' experience and expertise in their subject. To this end, assessors are required to continuously review their practice, refresh their skills and knowledge and offer their candidates a professional service.

Many awarding organisations and professional bodies specify the extent of that personal and professional development. Thirty hours per year of continuous professional development (**CPD**) is regularly advocated as a requirement to maintain licence to assess. While not regulated in the same way as teachers, trainers and tutors, assessors should aspire to this best practice model. The CPD is made up of:

- Professional updating: for example – by attending assessment updates, standardisation meetings, awarding organisations' training events or sessions to raise awareness of specialist skills in meeting candidates' needs.
- Subject updating: for example – keeping vocational skills current by working in the sector to update assessors on current industry or commercial practices.
- Personal updating: for example – improving own functional skills abilities, time management skills or personal development.

In summary, assessors are required to regularly reflect on their own skills and knowledge in order to improve their practice and offer an efficient service to their candidates and employers. Keeping of a CPD log while training is an ideal way of reflecting and learning from actions.

Glossary of terms

Assessment the checking of learning and demonstrating competence

Bilingualism speaking two languages

CADET© Consistent, Accessible, Detailed, Earned, Transparent – the principles of assessment

Competence knowledge of or ability to do something

Concept an idea

CPD Continuous Professional Development

Criterion (pl: criteria) a standard of competence

Diversity – acknowledging that each individual is unique and recognising our individual differences in for example, culture, ability, gender, race, religion, wealth, sexual orientation, or any other group characteristic

Evidence the output of an assessment activity; evidence of a learner's knowledge, understanding, skills or competence that can be used to make a judgement of their achievement against agreed standards/criteria

Formative assessment interim or ongoing assessment

Goals an aim or desired result

IV Internal Verifier (old terminology)

IM Internal Moderator (old terminology)

IQA Internal Quality Assurer

Multilingualism speaking many languages

National Occupational Standards (NOS) nationally set guidelines defining the level, size and subjects used in designing units of assessment

Ofqual Regulatory body, Office of the qualifications and examiners regulator

Pathway a route. Usually describing the combination of units to achieve the learner's goal

Principle a set of values or beliefs; a rule or moral code

Qualification a set of specifications (units of assessment) leading to an award, certificate or diploma of achievement

Quality assurance a system of review to confirm that processes are in place and applied to guarantee the quality of the service or product; systematic checks to provide confidence

Rules validity/relevance; reliability; authenticity; currency/recency; sufficiency; power of discrimination; objectivity (rules of assessment)

Standards an agreed level of competence

Summative assessment final or summary assessment

Units of assessment statements of knowledge and/or competence, clustered to make a qualification

Recommended reading

Ecclestone, K (1996) *How to assess the Vocational Curriculum.* London: Kogan Page quoted in Gray, D, Griffin, C and Nasta, T (2005) *Training to Teach in Further and Adult Education.* (2nd edn) Cheltenham: Stanley Thornes

Institute of Assessors and Verifiers – an organisation funded by member's subscriptions – to support assessors and QA staff and promote the sharing of best practice (http://www.ivalimited.co.uk)

Kolb, D (1984) *Experiential Learning: experience as a source of learning and development*. Englewood Cliffs, NJ: Prentice-Hall

LLUK (2006) *New overarching professional standards for teachers, tutors and trainers in the Lifelong Learning Sector*. November 2006, Lifelong Learning UK

The Royal College of Speech and Language Therapists (2006) Communicating Quality 3. *RCSLT's guidance on best practice in service organisation and provision*. London: The Royal College of Speech and Language Therapists

Wilson, L (2008) *Practical Teaching: a guide to PTLLS and CTLLS*. London: Cengage Learning

Wilson, L (2009) *Practical Teaching: a guide to PTLLS and DTLLS*. Andover: Cengage Learning

Useful online resources

Useful references for further reading about assessment are:

http://www.qcda.gov.uk/qualifications/60.aspx (accessed Sept 2010)

http://www.paa-uk.org/Qualifications/Regulated/Qualifications/QCF% 20Info/QCF%20 Support%20Pack/Rules%20of%20Combination% 20in%20the%20QCF.pdf (accessed March 2011)

http://www.cilt.org.uk/home/research_and_statistics/statistics/languages_in_the_population/annual_school_census.aspx (accessed March 2011)

www.homeoffice.gov.uk/crime/vetting-barring-scheme/ (accessed March 2011)

http://www.hse.gov.uk/risk/fivesteps.htm (accessed April 2011)

http://www.hse.gov.uk/pubns/indg36.pdf (accessed April 2011)

http://www.equalities.gov.uk/equality_act_2010.aspx

http://www.smarta.com/advice/legal/employment-law/the-equality-act-(october-1-2010)-need-to-know-for-small-businesses?gclid=CP7h7syP76cCFcoa4QodYhknaw

http://www.iebe.org.uk/index.php/code-of-conduct-for-assessors

SUMMARY

In this chapter we set out to:

- Explain the functions of assessment in training, learning and development.
- Define the key concepts and principles of assessment.
- State the roles and responsibilities of the assessor.
- Summarise the main legislative factors.
- Outline the importance of QA, standardisation and appeals in assessment.
- Identify the relevance of reflection, personal development and currency of practice in assessment practice.

Your personal development

- You have reviewed the basics of assessment and confirmed your understanding of why assessment is important.
- In considering the language of assessment you have raised your awareness of the terminology and variants in current use undertaking further research on the topic by following links to relevant websites and reading.
- You have compared and contrasted the notion of formative and summative assessment and are aware of how to use these in promoting improvement and testing competence, while taking into account the importance of Kolb's Learning Cycle. You may have completed the activity to analyse and reflect on your own competence against one of the LLUK standards.
- You have explored the use of command words in setting assessment tasks and may have developed a dictionary for your candidates' use.
- You have investigated both the principles of assessment – CADET© – and the rules of assessment: validity, reliability, authenticity, currency, sufficiency, objectivity and the power to discriminate, with reasons why problems occur if the rules are not followed. In focusing on the principles of

assessment you have decided on the values you will advocate when carrying out assessments.

- You have examined the roles and responsibilities of the assessor and the link between that role and those of the candidate and QA.
- You have perused a list of legislation factors and ethics which should be considered when assessing candidates.
- You are able to briefly describe the function of QA and the ways that IQAs will review the assessor's work in order to guarantee accuracy and completeness.
- You are able to summarise the responsibilities of the assessor in dealing with disputes and appeals and are confident in knowing when to refer an appeal to the internal verifier.
- Finally, you have considered the importance of reflection and CPD in ensuring the currency of your own practice and compliance to professional requirements.

CHAPTER 2
Planning and delivering assessments

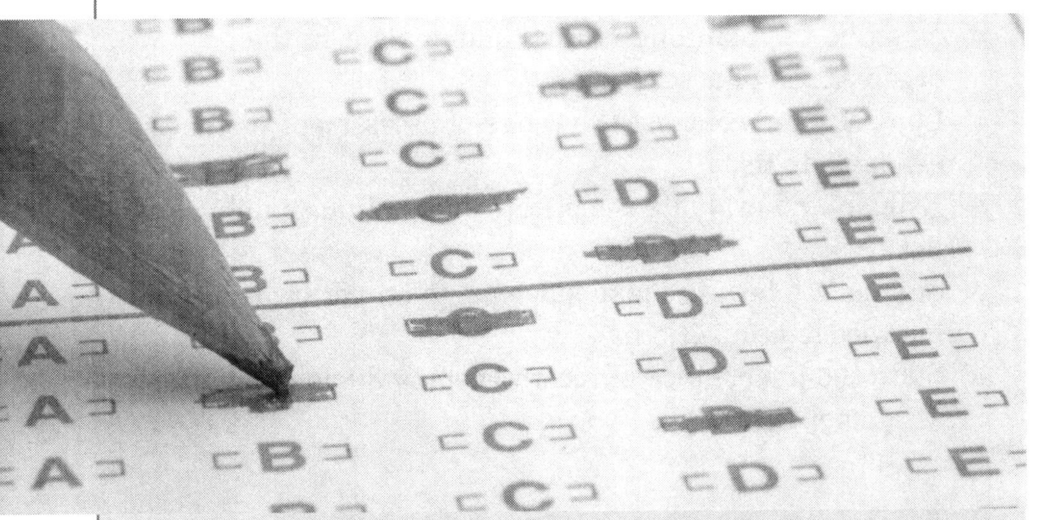

Unit of Assessment	Assessment Criteria
Understanding the principles and practices of assessment	2.1; 3.1; 3.2; 3.3; 3.4; 3.5; 4.1; 4.2; 4.3; 4.4; 5.1; 5.2; 7.1; 7.2; 8.2;
Assess occupational competence in the work environment	1.1; 1.2; 1.3; 1.4; 2.1; 2.2; 2.3; 2.4; 2.6; 3.1; 3.2;
Assess vocational skills, knowledge and understanding	1.1; 1.2; 1.3; 2.1; 2.2; 2.3; 2.4; 2.6; 3.1; 3.2
Understanding the principles and practices of internally assuring the quality of assessment	No direct references
Internally assure the quality of assessment	No direct references
Plan, allocate and monitor work in own area of responsibility	No direct references

LEARNING OUTCOMES

By the end of this chapter you will be able to:

- Describe the planning process and apply it in the organisation of assessments
- Compare and contrast the range of assessment methods available to use
- Explain and evaluate the effectiveness of questioning and feedback
- Summarise how to make judgements on performance and knowledge acquisition
- State the importance of record keeping during and after assessment.

Planning assessment

What is a plan? In short, it is a detailed breakdown (or formal contract) about how the candidate is going to achieve their desired assessment outcomes. It is one of the first stages in the assessment process, namely: plan – collect evidence – make a judgement – give **feedback** and review, and then you are back to the beginning and ready to repeat the process.

There are some protocols to observe when planning assessments:

- Ensure the assessment is fair (equality and diversity).
- Explain the process to the candidate – how, why, where, when, with whom, what?
- Link the plan to the assessment criteria – be transparent.
- Negotiate with the candidate and the employer and get agreement from all parties.

Figure 2.1 The assessment cycle

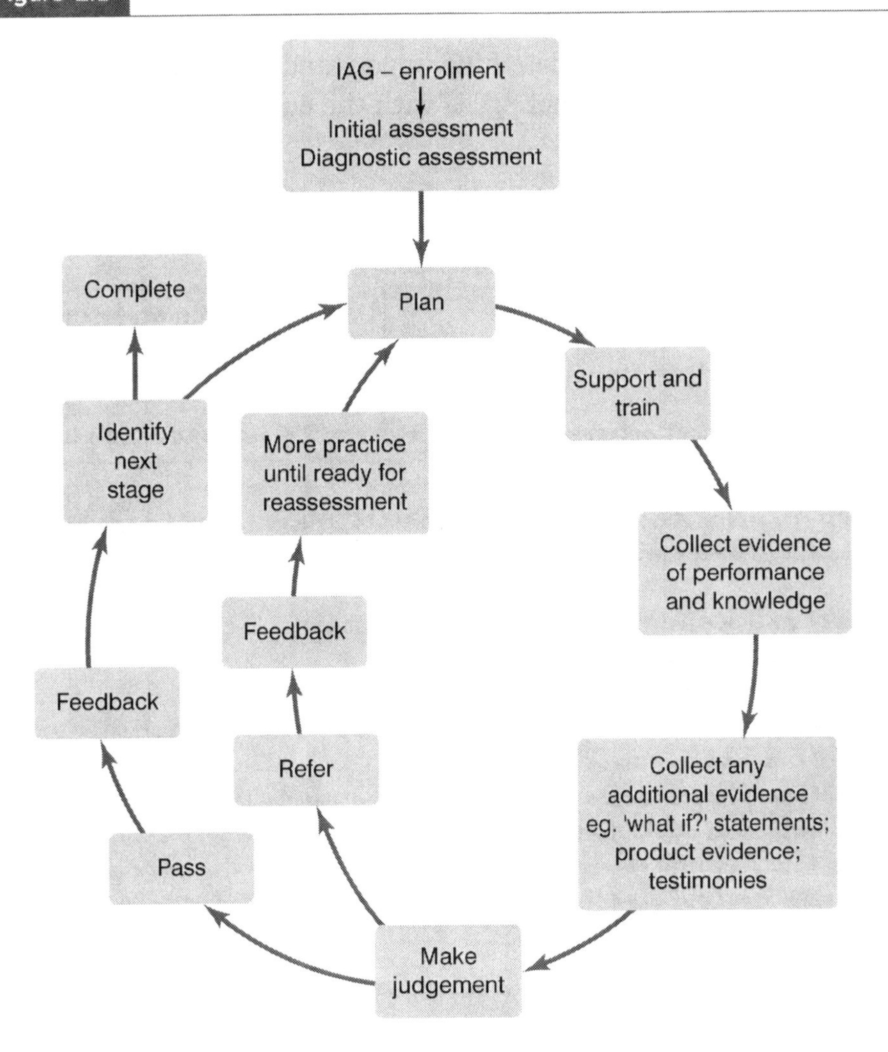

- Ensure that the planned assessment causes minimal disruption to the routine work of the employer's business.
- Confirm shift patterns and resources are available and suitable.
- Factor in any special assessment needs – to suit disability or difficulty.
- Plan to achieve success, not to fail – is the candidate ready for the assessment?
- Always prioritise naturally occurring performance over simulated or contrived performances.

- Maximise assessment opportunities – look for **holistic** assessments rather than unit driven.
- Ensure that the candidate fully understands the whole process and what to do if they do not agree with the outcome – i.e. the appeals process.

An assessment plan might look like this:

<table>
<tr><td colspan="2">Summative assessment plan</td></tr>
<tr><td>Name: A Candidate</td><td>Date of proposed assessment:
14th July 2011</td></tr>
<tr><td colspan="2">Planned activity:
To prepare short crust pastry and fruit for 24 portions of apple pie</td></tr>
<tr><td colspan="2">Expected outcomes/criteria/evidence
(Units: Prepare and cook pastry products, Prepare and cook fruit dishes, Working safely and hygienically)

Select and measure ingredients accurately
Wear appropriate work wear and ppe
Select equipment to prepare pie
Demonstrate health and safety practices throughout activity
Follow the recipe accurately
Assemble prepared commodities for the apple pie, continue to assemble and cook dish for lunchtime customers
Take photographs of product at various stages of the process
Evaluate how successful you were in achieving the outcomes</td></tr>
<tr><td colspan="2">Evidence methods:
Observation by assessor in the workplace
Oral questions
Photographs</td></tr>
<tr><td>Plan signed/dated by assessor:
A.N. Assessor 7th July 2011</td><td>Plan agreed,
signed/dated by candidate:
A Candidate 7th July 2011</td></tr>
<tr><td colspan="2">Special considerations:
Confirm with employer that menu is as agreed and products are available
Prepare recipe card in large font
Feedback after lunch to minimise disruption</td></tr>
<tr><td>Feedback following assessment:</td><td>Actions for development:</td></tr>
<tr><td>Outcome:
Pass ☐
Needs further training ☐</td><td>Assessor signature:
Candidate signature:
Date:</td></tr>
</table>

Planning assessments are key to a problem-free process. By observing the protocols in the bullet points above, you can ensure that planning is effective, comprehensive and meets the standards expected in assessment.

The what, why, when, how, where, who considerations

Most often used in questioning, the 'w' words are equally important in planning assessment.

I keep six honest serving men
(They taught me all I knew);
Their names are What and Why and When
And How and Where and Who.

Rudyard Kipling, Just So Stories 1902, The Elephant's Child

In your planning session, you will not go far wrong if you answer the questions:

- What: what will be assessed – you may need to write this both formally (using the units of competence) and in a way the candidate will understand (task related). The **goals** or short-term **targets** need to be **SMARTER**:

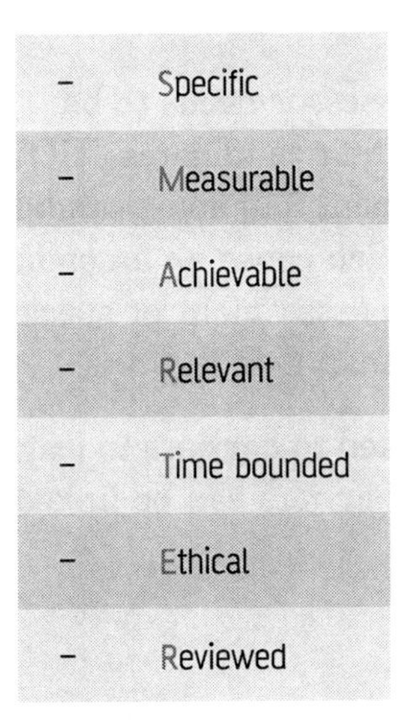

- Why: to achieve success in the chosen qualification, this maybe the long-term target.
- When: specify the date and time of the assessment.
- How: how will the assessment be carried out, by what method/s? The methods will be determined by the type of assessment: is it a practical assessment or is underpinning knowledge to be tested? Any **contingency plan** should be mentioned in case for any reason the assessment is interrupted.
- Where: specify the location of the assessment, e.g. in the workplace.
- Who (with whom): who will be involved, for example an assessor, a witness in the training environment? Is the assessor someone who works in the environment or a peripatetic assessor visiting from a training provider? Are there others in the workplace who may be affected by the assessment?

This detail is required to both create the contract and alleviate any misunderstandings. By being clear about the expectations (from all parties involved), the candidate will be more comfortable in the assessment situation. Irrespective of how much practice a candidate has, and how confident they are in their surroundings, very often the mere mention of the assessment word causes a shiver of trepidation.

In order to meet the 'HOW' statement, an assessor needs to be sensitive and aware of the characteristics of their candidates. 'HOW' is mainly concerned with the method of assessment, but some candidates require special assessment arrangements, which cause an amendment to a selected assessment strategy. Barriers to assessment or special assessment considerations come in many forms:

Using the acronym **DELTA©** (previously linked to barriers to learning in Wilson, 2009:51) the issues of access and barriers can be linked to assessment:

- Disability
- Emotional
- Language
- Technology
- Ability

DISABILITY	EMOTIONAL	LANGUAGE	TECHNOLOGY	ABILITY
Chronic pain Dexterity Dyscalculia Dyslexia Hearing Long illness Mental health Mobility Visual	Behaviour Child care Commitments Concentration Confidence Dependants Discipline Employer pressure Fear of unknown Finance Hormones New surroundings Parental pressure Peer pressure Personal problems Poverty Previous experience Returning to education Stress/worry	Accent Basic skill needs Communication Cultural differences Foreign language Pace Rapport Terminology	Car breakdown Computer skills Fear of technology Heating Lighting Temperature Transport	Absence Inaccurate advice Large classes Motivation Personal skills Punctuality Resources Short illness Study support Support Teaching styles

Types of assessment

Assessment is the term given to checking that learning has occurred and that the candidate is competent in the skills and knowledge of the occupational area. Assessment is not just something that will occur summatively, it will happen throughout the programme as a means of monitoring progress and is essential at the commencement of the programme to identify appropriate training and assessment strategies to meet your candidate's needs. Assessment also refers to the process of collecting proof of competence; this is frequently referred to as 'evidence'. This evidence is generated by undertaking an observation, questioning session, review of products, completion of assignments or another assessment method.

Assessment methods

There are several different ways of assessing or collecting evidence to demonstrate competence. The table on pages 45–50 describes the main ones that you will come across.

Quality versus quantity

Trying to collect sufficient evidence to meet the scope of the assessment criteria has long been a challenge for assessors. There is a tendency, particularly with inexperienced assessors, to collect too much, 'just in case' or, at the opposite end, not enough. This balance is something assessors must confront and test frequently. It is better to collect one piece of really useful evidence rather than a collection of things which only relate to parts of a candidate's qualification.

Here are some suggestions which may be useful:

- Read and comprehend the assessment criteria for the whole qualification, not just part of it. By doing this you will see where there is repetition and be able to attribute evidence to more than

Method	Description
Observation (Direct assessment)	Used in practical situations when a candidate demonstrates their competence (natural performance) while being observed by their assessor. This is considered one of the best forms of assessment – primary assessment – because there can be no doubts in the mind of the assessor that the candidate knows how to do something. The observation should be recorded either on film, electronically or on paper. A phone with a camera is quite useful, but ensure that you have relevant permissions before photographing or filming a candidate, especially if they or those around them are minors. Equally, employers might be quite sensitive to filming in their offices or on their shop floors. There may be occasions when the verifier needs to observe observational evidence to verify standards. Observation is very versatile in assessment as candidates are usually repeating their everyday activities and so will always perform at a level appropriate to their need and ability. Verbal questioning complements observation well.
Simulation	This is similar to observation, but uses a simulated activity rather than natural performance. The rules associated with observation (above) apply. While many qualifications do not generally support this type of evidence, there may be occasions when it is deemed appropriate, for example when using high cost materials or in dangerous situations. You would not expect an airline pilot to be assessed on his or her ability to crash land in a 'natural performance' scenario – this is best done under simulated conditions, which should mirror reality. Fire drills and first aid are other commonly simulated assessments. Assessors should always confirm the validity of using simulation as an assessment method by reading the **Awarding Organisation's** (AO) guidance on assessment.

Method	Description
Project and assignment	These are usually a series of activities which collect together to make a project or assignment. For example, task one may be a written description of something, task two may be a presentation of some findings and task three may be a booklet or poster. Generally, a project is designed by the candidate and an assignment is designed by the assessor; both include a 'brief' which is related to the learning outcomes. AOs may preset assignments in order to standardise practice. There may be different assessment methods within an assignment or project depending on the tasks. The assessor will be assessing learning outcomes which relate to the proposed content of the assignment or project and are used during marking. Some qualifications also include levels of understanding, which are reflected in grading criteria. Assessors can differentiate outcomes of assignments and projects to suit candidate's needs.
Case study	Case studies are scenarios prepared by the assessor to test aspects of the qualification which are not able to be assessed directly. Alternatively case studies can be used to confirm that knowledge achieved in one situation can be applied in other situations. A case study will describe a specific scenario and have questions about the given situation.
Written questions	Essays: A discussion type of question which can be structured or unstructured. The assessor will need detailed assessment marking plans to ensure fairness, especially if the essay is around opinion and therefore has no right or wrong answer. The assessor should also consider what proportion of marks will be attributed to spelling and grammar, content, structure and argument, etc. To be considered fair, the assessment

Method	Description
	marking strategy should be shared with your candidates. Marking is quite complex. Marking could be **subjective**.
	Reports: A descriptive account generally used to explain a particular topic. Reports provide the opportunity to link theory and practice and offer chances for the candidate to cover 'what if' scenarios. There is rarely a right or wrong answer, so marking the report is best linked to the standards of competence or units of assessment to provide validity to the assessment. As they are written by the candidates the level is reflective of ability. Structured reports offer guidance on how much detail to include in the answer and can be helpful to candidates.
	Short answer questions: A series of questions where the answer is usually about a few sentences long. In some cases, e.g. the 'state four reasons for ...' type of questions, only a few words are required. Ideally questions start with how, why, what, etc. The marking plan should include all possible answers that could be offered by candidates to increase the **objectivity**. Short answer questions are quite easy to mark and are suitable for checking knowledge and understanding. They offer many opportunities to differentiate to meet candidate needs in that the complexity of the questioning is easily varied to suit ability. If completed independently, the assessor needs to check that it is the candidate's own work, maybe by asking a few oral questions or comparing the writing style with the candidate's usual style.
	Multiple choice questions (MCQs): A question with (usually) four possible answers. The candidate has to identify which of the offered answers is correct. As a candidate selects an

Method	Description
	answer there is little opportunity to expand or probe understanding. They are very simple to mark; the AO may use computers to scan answer sheets and calculate the number of correct answers. They are quite difficult to write in the first instance but for the candidate they are relatively easy to undertake. This method does not support any differentiation of individual need, but is a very objective way of marking.
Verbal/oral questions (Direct assessment)	These are questions which try to establish depth of knowledge and are a useful assessment tool to complement observation in order to check understanding. For example – 'what would happen if …' type of questions. Verbal questioning is usually informal and sometimes unprepared in that the assessor sees something during an observation and wishes clarification or further information on a particular issue. Verbal questioning should be recorded on tape, electronically or on paper and the candidate should sign to confirm accuracy of answers recorded. Verbal questioning is a very versatile method of assessment and is so easily adjusted to meet individual's needs that it is considered a primary method of assessment.
Professional discussion	This is a semi-structured interview where the assessor and the candidate discuss an issue and the assessor prompts the candidate into answering questions related to subject outcomes. It is very often used to link workplace practice to standards of competence or units of assessment. The method is particularly suited to qualifications which require deeper understanding of a topic or candidates who prefer the autonomy of free expression in their own assessments. It is an effective tool because an experienced assessor will lead the conversation to ensure all aspects are covered. However, authenticity could be questioned – did

Method	Description
	the assessor lead in a way that would elicit only correct answers? Is it really the candidate's own words/actions?
Peer and self-assessment	As an informal strategy it is very common. Reading through a piece of work to ensure everything is covered before handing it in is a form of self-assessment. As a formal assessment strategy it can be used in the format of personal statements, journals, diaries or profiling. All of these assessments require the candidate to write down what they did or would do in a given situation; this is then linked to a set of standards or criteria. There may be a witness testimony to authenticate the validity of the statements. This assessment method requires a good level of self-criticism and personal awareness and may need to be 'taught' before embarking on as a reliable method of assessment. Peer assessment follows the same principles although the review is undertaken by a fellow candidate. Authenticity is the main risk associated with this method of assessment in that candidates may not be familiar with the units of competence or be as confident in deciding sufficiency.
Recognition of Prior Learning (RPL) (indirect assessment)	Also known as 'accreditation of prior learning, achievement or experience' APL or APA. A system of recognising the skills a candidate already has when they come into training. The process of claiming RPL requires a candidate to work either independently or with an assessor to match their previous skills or knowledge with the criteria contained in the qualification they wish to achieve. The assessment of RPL requires the assessor to validate the claim and ensure the authenticity of the evidence and confirm that the skills and knowledge are current. Testimonies, product evidence and skills test may form part of the claim. The complexity of gathering evidence

Method	Description
	may be perceived as a barrier to using RPL as an assessment method.
Reviewing products or artefacts portfolios	Many assessments generate products which will form part of the assessment. Things such as printouts, letters, booklets, photographs and video clips are frequently submitted to prove a candidate has developed skills to the required standard. The use of mobile technology and e-portfolios provides a mechanism to produce a sustainable (i.e. paperless) portfolio.
Testimonials (indirect assessment)	The use of testimonials is important when the assessor needs to rely on others who have a closer contact with the candidate. Workplace supervisors are a valuable source of evidence to prove that a candidate consistently works to a prescribed standard. Testimonials should be written against the units of assessment. However, frequently workplace staff are less familiar with the criteria and therefore the assessor would be required to annotate the testimonial during the assessment process.
e-assessment or online tests	All or parts of qualifications can be achieved using learning technologies. Paper based examinations can be replaced by on-line tests which give instant results. Paper based portfolios are being replaced by e-portfolios which require all evidence to be stored in a more environmentally friendly manner. The evidence is stored electronically on either personal media storage devices or using a training organisation's servers. See Electronic and mobile learning and assessment technologies, page 55.

one aspect of the qualification – this is generally referred to as **cross referencing**.

- Consider linking the job to the qualification rather than the other way around. Many jobs completed by the candidate cover a range of UoA and therefore will be easier for the candidate to understand.

This is referred to as holistic assessment – where the assessor considers the bigger picture. An example of this would be a health and safety unit. It is possible to collect a range of evidence to confer competence in health and safety. However, every job a candidate does in their work environment will then enable them to demonstrate their application of health and safety, supported by some 'what if' questions to check understanding or contingency plans. This would reduce the amount of evidence required and embed it fully into every task completed.

Assessment conditions and environments

The environment in which assessment occurs is as important as the type of technique used. In some instances the technique used will directly impact on the environment and conditions.

- Observations need to occur where the task regularly takes place; after all it is frequently referred to as naturally occurring evidence. An assessor must neither help nor hinder the candidate who is being observed, nor must other colleagues.
- Simulations may occur under replicated or virtual conditions – but these should be as realistic as possible to ensure that the scenario mirrors the event.
- Verbal questions will often be executed in the same environment as the observation or simulation. However, an assessor needs to be mindful that workshops are often noisy or candidates might be distracted, so consideration of the appropriateness of the environment needs to be factored into the assessment plan.
- Written questions, especially those undertaken under examination conditions, need careful planning. An assessor must consider privacy, quiet, desk space, timing and allowable resources, then plan to accommodate the needs of the candidate, especially for those who might need additional support (extra time, signers, scribes, specialist resources, etc.). An assessor needs to establish how much help is allowed, before it would be considered inappropriate. Guidance on this should be taken from the AO, as permission is needed to change formal assessment arrangements.

- Projects and assignments are frequently completed in a more traditional learning environment. An assessor needs to establish to what extent research is a requirement and ensure that the candidate has access to journals, books or the internet.

ACTIVITY 1

Holistic assessment

Consider one of the following jobs frequently carried out in the workplace and, using the National Occupational Standards, create a grid (also know as a plan or matrix) which shows which parts of the qualification can be assessed while observing the task.

1. Hairdressing salon: shampooing a client's hair in preparation for a cut.
2. Construction site: laying a foundation course of bricks for a garden feature.
3. Garage: changing a tyre on a vehicle.
4. Office: typing a set of minutes from your supervisor's notes.
5. Veterinary surgery: preparing a rabbit for a non-surgical procedure.
6. Café: preparing a steak and kidney pie for a lunchtime meal.
7. Care home: helping an elderly patient to dress.
8. Nursery: supervising a play session with a group of three-year-olds.
9. Office: retrieving a document from a computer for your supervisor.
10. Reception desk: dealing with a delivery of office stationery.
11. Leisure centre: preparing an exercise plan for a guest.
12. Beauty salon: preparing a client for a neck and back massage.
13. Newspaper office: receiving an advert for this week's edition.
14. Farm: assisting the farmer with preparations for lambing.
15. Restaurant: serving wine at the table.

To start this activity you will need to break down your chosen task into its component parts. You should also consider additional skills such as customer service, health and safety, equality and diversity. You may wish to expand the case study to set the context.

For example, Restaurant: taking a customer's order.

Observable items: approaches to hygiene and safety, appearance, communication with customers and staff, knowledge of menu (food and drinks), how item is served, organised approach – table laid, crockery, accompaniments, dealing with problems or unexpected situations.

Each of these topics is contained in the Level 2 Diploma in Professional Food and Beverage Service, City and Guilds 7103-02, Qualification handbook, 500/7478/7.

Watch point

Always apply the rules of assessment to the chosen assessment method. Is the method a reliable way of providing valid evidence, authentic to the candidate, demonstrating current practice and will it provide enough (sufficient) evidence to meet the standards? (See also Chapter 1 The principles of assessment: functions and concepts.)

In helping you to compare, contrast and decide upon appropriate assessment methods for a given assessment, consider the following case study scenarios.

CASE STUDY

The candidate works in a hairdressing salon and the assessor is the senior stylist. They work together daily. Clients book into the salon for various services, usually regular clients but sometimes they are spontaneous. In addition, the candidate needs to demonstrate their understanding of how to respond to spontaneous bookings as opposed to regular clients? How does the assessor need to plan this assessment?

CASE STUDY

The candidate works in a vehicle repair station. Every day work is allocated to the candidate in the form of a job-card; he usually works with one of the mechanics, but is well able to do some tasks with minimal supervision. The assessor is from a local training provider and meets the candidate on their day release day and visits the garage monthly. The assessor always meets the garage supervisor when he visits. How should the assessor plan assessments for this candidate?

CASE STUDY

A candidate visits the training provider having returned to work following maternity leave. She is now a receptionist and is the first point of contact for employees and guests visiting the company. She worked in an office as an administrator prior to having a baby and is now considering an apprenticeship in customer services. How will you advise the candidate in presenting her previous experience towards her new qualification?

CASE STUDY

Students in the college have to attend sessions in the training restaurant as part of their hospitality and catering course. They have a rota which requires them to work in the kitchen, restaurant, reception desk and bar. In addition they have practical sessions in a skills kitchen. How can the college activities link to the assessments for their course? How would you explain the difference between activities undertaken in skills development, the training restaurant and their theory sessions? How can these contribute to a holistic method of assessment?

In summary, choosing assessment methods should always be linked to the candidate's needs and appropriateness of the environment.

Electronic and mobile learning and assessment technologies

Supporting assessment through electronic (e-technologies) and mobile (m-technologies) is becoming increasingly popular as the technology, equipment and access is improving. In an era of environmental sustainability the days of lever-arch files full of evidence is diminishing in favour of alternative storage strategies.

Online assessment has been a feature of many qualifications for a number of years. When assessment is undertaken through multiple-choice questioning many AOs host this through easy to access online testing software such as Global On-line Assessment (GOLA) or e-volve. Marking through the use of scanning software has been used for many years where multiple-choice questions or Likert scales are used to analyse answers.

http://psychology.about.com/od/lindex/g/likert-scale.htm

Many organisations now have Virtual Learning Environments (VLEs), for example Moodle or Blackboard. These are hosted through the internet or through an organisation's servers and intranets. They include access to resources, links to websites and documents, provide email facilities and support wikis, blogs and chat rooms. They complement, or offer an alternative to, managed learning environments and have the added benefit of being available 24/7. The VLEs can host forums on which candidates can have conversations, meetings or share ideas. These can be synchronous or asynchronous.

E-assessment is supported by recent developments in software and hardware resources. Digital cameras can easily provide still or video evidence of competence or products. Flip cams record activities and are easily uploaded (transferred) to computer storage systems. Similarly, the internet provides valuable links to downloadable material to support assessment activities. Voting systems provide interesting

mechanisms to vary traditional questioning sessions. The increased access to WiFi and the development of smart phones and associated ppps is really broadening the scope of assessment and learning.
http://www.jiscinfonet.ac.uk/InfoKits/effective-use-of-VLEs/e-assessment

Assessors can accept electronic copy of assignments and other written pieces via e-mail and using 'review' in Word applications are able to provide a timely and trackable marking system. These and other electronic files used to collect evidence can be uploaded to e-portfolios using software systems such as Smart Assessor, Learning Assistant, Pass-Port, Pebble-Pad or iWebFolio.

Questioning techniques

Questioning refers to a process designed to find out what someone understands (or knows) about a topic.

Open, closed and leading questions Good questioning should be of an 'open' type, which means that the candidate has to think of the answer. A good question will test knowledge or understanding and contain opportunities to provide a full answer. **Closed questions**, have limited responses, for example, yes/no or true/false solutions – so a candidate could guess the answer. In **leading questions** the assessor includes a key word which might indicate a preferred response from the candidate – or even suggest the answer.

Nominated or directed questions In group situations, a nominated or directed style of questioning ensures that everyone contributes and that questions offered to candidates are pitched at the candidate's known ability. They are an effective means of differentiating or meeting candidates' needs. In a nominated style the assessor poses the question to the group, then pauses so that candidates can all create their own answer: the assessor then nominates (or directs) a candidate to give the answer. It can be made fun by offering play or pass options to minimise embarrassment if candidates do not know the answer. You may also try the 'ask a friend' strategy, in which a candidate can elicit

ACTIVITY 2

Following on from the descriptions of closed or leading questions, how would you re-write them to become open in style?

Closed question	*Open question*
Are there seven days in a week?	How many days are there in a week?
Is it correct that you inform your manager if you encounter an unexpected situation?	
Are you OK with that?	
Are you happy with the evidence in your portfolio?	
Do you know where your supervisor is?	
Leading question	*Open question*
I can see that you understand about PPE because you are wearing your boots. Do you understand about PPE?	What does PPE mean?
Is it true that blue and red mixed together make purple?	
How well do you get on with the people in the office?	
Have you improved your punctuality on site?	

the help of someone else in the group. In the worst questioning scenarios, the assessor leaves insufficient time for the candidate to answer and completes the question themselves.

Scaffolding questions Scaffolding questions are those that build on a candidate's existing knowledge or understanding. They enable the assessor to take forward the candidate and explore the extent of their knowledge and if they are able to apply it in other contexts or in problem solving.

Probing (or funnel) questions A technique which will take a broad topic and go into it in more detail thus digging for information. The assessor can use an **open question** to launch the discussion and then use probing questions to delve deeper into the subject. How or why did that happen? What would happen if ...? Can you give me more information about ...?

Effective feedback

Feedback is the conversation between the assessor and candidate. It aims to celebrate strengths, give constructive advice on weaknesses and identify areas for further development. It is essential in the assessment process; the main purpose being to let candidates know how well (or not) they are doing.

Feedback is the key to successful development of potential, increasing motivation and assessment. It is part of the learning process, because it tells the candidate how well they are doing. The quality of the feedback is as important as the quality of the teaching or training. Feedback should be frequent and meaningful. There are two types. The praise and criticism model is that which is based on personal judgements and is therefore subjective. In this model you list the strengths and the weaknesses. The constructive feedback model is preferred and more objective, because it is based on specifics and related to the assessment against standards or criteria. Constructive feedback can be positive, when good practice is praised. The assessor will appreciate and value what has been done and comment on how well it has been achieved. Constructive feedback can be negative, when improvement needs are discussed. Giving negative feedback does not mean giving the feedback in a negative (i.e. unsupportive) way. The assessor should not use sarcasm or anger. Be helpful – start with a positive statement and then comment on the improvements that are needed.

Watch point

Don't get over enthusiastic with the praise; it is far more effective when offered as a result of something achieved, rather than responding to everything as 'brill!'

You may also hear the expression feed-forward. Whereas feedback is based on a response to what has occurred, feed-forward is based on the notion of motivating a candidate to develop. It aims to address the difference between 'assessment OF learning' (feedback) and 'assessment FOR learning' (feed-forward). This might merely be an up-to-the-minute response to research in the field as effective feedback in its existing format has always been a method of aiding improvement, but it does reflect the fact that feedback tells someone how they have done and does not necessarily move them forward.

Feedback skills

Giving feedback is not easy; it is particularly difficult at the opposite ends of the feedback spectrum. If observed practice or an assessed piece is particularly good, it is difficult to identify development suggestions, or, conversely, it is difficult to feedback to candidates without destroying confidence when the required standards are not met. Giving effective feedback will test your own skills in listening, objectivity and explaining. It will improve the confidence of your candidates and develop their potential, but it takes time to get it right. Although you will be encouraged to give immediate feedback, in the early days you may wish to consider what you want to say before diving in – so give yourself a few minutes to think and plan what you are going to say.

Feedback should:

- Be planned and carefully thought about.
- Be delivered promptly after the assessment, preferably immediately, especially after observation or verbal questioning sessions.
- Be a two-way process – you can always ask the candidate to say how they think it went and get an idea of their understanding, checking their ideas for development.
- Be motivational – feedback increases confidence and self-esteem and therefore potential attainment.

- Be specific – feedback should only be about the assessment; it should be unbiased, without opinion, unnecessary digression or imposing your own standards.
- Offer choices and solutions – this develops potential.
- Only comment on things that can be changed – e.g. behaviours or values, not appearance or inner character.
- Be positive – use strategies that will encourage a candidate to develop.
- Be constructive – a balance of positive and negative comments should be offered on a one-to-one basis and as privately as possible.
- If circumstances mean that feedback cannot be immediate, then tell the candidate when it will be possible. For example: after the shift, when it quietens down a bit, when you get your next break, etc.

Constructive feedback is the title given to a form of feedback which is helpful and supportive. (It may also be known as feed-forward.) It is motivational in that it neither gives false descriptions of a candidate's ability nor does it destroy their self-esteem, but aims to develop and fine-tune skills. Whether produced verbally or in writing, this effective style of feedback follows a distinct pattern of:

- a positive opener
- a developmental statement
- a motivational close.

This is called the *feedback sandwich*.

By starting with a positive statement, you will reassure and relax the recipient of the feedback. Always identify something good, even if it is only the fact that they turned up on time! The comments you make should always link to the standards being assessed. The feedback should always be about the individual and you should never compare their performance with anyone else or anything other than the standards expected.

Developmental statements are the point at which you should make comments about things which need to be improved. It is good to get contributions from the recipient of the feedback. Using open questions will aid this process and together you will formulate your future plans.

Some questions you might wish to consider are:

- How do you think that the customer felt when you ...?
- What would you do if ...?
- What alternatives are there to ...?
- Why did that happen?
- At what point in the process would you think about ...?

If there is going to be a 'but' the person giving the feedback should build up confidence (i.e. discuss the positive aspects of the work) before delivering the shock. The use of the word 'but' should also be used cautiously. 'But' muddles what you are trying to say and confuses the message. 'It was OK, but ...' *(Is it OK or not?)*

A contextual example of this is:

'It was alright but it wasn't very welcoming' is not particularly helpful. It seems to suggest a negative outcome. An alternative suggestion might be: 'I liked the way that you welcomed the customer and believe it would be improved if you'd stood to greet them.' This is of the same flavour but not as hard as a 'but' statement. In the second statement the 'but' is delivered as an 'and'. Therefore, is not as critical and more developmental.

Ending the feedback in a motivational way will incite the candidate to take on board recommendations and leave them feeling positive about their performance, even if not ecstatic about the outcome. Ideally in a feedback session, you should try to get the recipient to identify their own way forward. This ownership of the actions needed to improve will result in a high level of motivation. It is at this point you can develop reflective skills in your candidates.

The typical feedback conversation example is:

- State what the standard is or what the assessment was about. Describe what has been observed or reviewed, without side tracking.
- Make a comment about what has been achieved.
- Offer alternatives like: have you considered ..., you could try ...
- Avoid 'BUT'.
- Summarise the key achievements.
- Make and state your judgement – you meet/don't meet the standards, you've passed or you need more practice.

In discussing feedback, it is worth noting the research of Prof. John Hattie of Auckland University (1999 and 2003). He investigated the effects of feedback on achievement and the ability of teachers to influence learning.

Having dissected the factors associated with teaching and learning and categorising them into responsibilities, he discovered, not surprisingly, that the teacher has a significant influence on learning. This furthered his earlier research which identified the extent to which feedback impacts on achievement. This all supports the current beliefs in assessment for learning rather than the assessment of learning. In summary, effective feedback is more effective in developing candidate progress than merely providing grades. This is generally because if a candidate is told 'that's a pass' or 'it's a grade B' they are more likely to accept that outcome without seeking development or improvement. When given feedback, 'most' candidates will attempt to develop future work. In combination they are able to meet both candidates' values and aspirations.

Additional reading on this research is widely available on the internet using Hattie, feedback and assessment as key words in a search engine.

Assessment decisions

Following an assessment and the resultant feedback, you will have to make a judgement. The decision will be a summary of what you saw that was good, the standard achieved, how much further development is needed. There will usually be parts of the assessment that are satisfactory, but there may be parts that were not so good – this may be reflected in the grade or pass mark. All criteria contained in the units of assessment must be met, which is why an assessment may consist of more than one method of assessment to cope with the things that don't naturally occur.

When making an assessment decision or judgement it is important that the assessor remains objective. The best way of doing that, to guarantee the reliability and fairness of your decision, is inherent in the make-up of the qualification and the rules of assessment.

- Always use the UoA specified in the assessment plan (validity).
- Always check that documentation is signed and can be attributed to the candidate (authenticity).
- Always check that documentation is dated and that the evidence reflects current industry standards (currency).
- Always check that there is enough evidence to cover all aspects of the targeted assessment criteria (sufficiency).
- Always apply the rules of assessment consistently without bias in all decision-making (reliability/fairness).

It is worth commenting here about authenticity and **plagiarism**. All evidence presented to confirm competence must do that. It must not be someone else's work. For example, in an office a candidate presents to you a number of letters that the candidate alleges to have composed and sent to customers. How do you know? You cannot assume that just because these letters were presented by the candidate that they were created by them.

Plagiarism is similar but refers to the passing off as someone else's published material as their own. It is more usually seen in written statements or assignments where articles, particularly from the internet, are included in a candidate's work without any citation or reference. Plagiarism breaches the Copyright, Designs and Patents Act 1988 in which it is against the law to reproduce material without acknowledging the owner. The acknowledgement is usually in the form of a reference citing the name of the author, the title of the product and the publisher. If using larger pieces of work then permissions from the owner need to be sought.

Unfortunately, one of the downsides of the internet is the apparent ease in which people can download information and cut and paste it into their work, or even acquire whole assignments.

How to spot plagiarism:

- different writing style or writing level to that seen in usual work
- variants in fonts and font size within text
- American spellings
- different referencing to that which has been taught
- typed work when handwritten is usual
- obscure references or sources of information
- different opinions/context to those made in class or recommended textbooks.

If you suspect something, you don't need fancy software tools to detect it, just type a whole sentence or just the key words, especially those that seem obscure, into a search engine and if it appears verbatim in the list of search findings then it has probably been plagiarised.

In terms of authenticity, it doesn't hurt to get candidates into the habit of signing and dating their work.

> I confirm that this [assignment/essay etc.], is all my own work.
>
> Signed: A candidate.
> Today's date

This does not stop plagiarism, but it enters the candidates into a contract concerning ethics.

Triangulation

There are various ways to achieve confidence in your assessment and thus promote effectiveness. One of the easiest is to triangulate judgements. This means, to use more than one assessment method to confirm competence. For example, a candidate presents product evidence; you check out understanding with some oral questions and seek testimony from a workplace supervisor. If the results of all of these assessment methods say the same thing then you can confirm competence. Each method is, therefore, contributing effectively to produce an assessment that is reliable and authentic and provides sufficient evidence on which to confirm competence.

Triangulation also provides variety. By testing learners in different ways, not only does it triangulate, providing confirmation that decisions are accurate and consistent, but it adds interest and meets different learning styles.

Depending upon the type of qualification, purpose of assessment and level of formality in the assessment, the decision will either be:

- Pass or fail – the assessment either meets or does not meet the standard required.
- A graded result – pass, merit [credit], distinction, which describes how well a candidate has achieved, but your feedback needs to explain the development between levels.
- Marks – out of 10, 20, 100 etc. usually expressed as a percentage.

The assessor should be quite clear in stating the outcome of the assessment. Saying the words 'you've passed' is very often the thing that is forgotten at the expense of creating good feedback. Also, sometimes the feedback is so positive that a candidate can misunderstand the outcome, maybe thinking that they have passed or achieved a higher grade than they actually have.

The 'F' word

The word *fail* is rarely used. This is because it is highly de-motivational. Rarely is everything so bad in an assessment that the assessor cannot comment positively on some aspect. If an assessment is not at the required standard, i.e. *fails*, you should consider alternative expressions such as 'needs further training' or 'not yet competent' or simply 'refer'.

Portfolios

Records are kept by candidates in the form of portfolios. Their portfolios will include records and evidence derived in their workplace and documents created by their assessor to record observations, testimonies and questioning.

What is a portfolio?

A portfolio is a collection of evidence – this is more likely to be the best or final copy rather than everything created during the training process. The portfolio tells the story of the candidate's journey from trainee to competence.

A portfolio of evidence, therefore, is a term used to describe the way in which the evidence required to demonstrate competence relating to a particular qualification is kept. A portfolio can be paper based, electronic (either through an e-portfolio or portable storage device) or a combination of both. Brown (1992) defines the term 'personal portfolio' as follows:

> *'... a private collection of evidence which demonstrates the continuing acquisition of skills, knowledge, attitudes, understanding and achievement. It is both retrospective and prospective, as well as reflecting the current stage of the development of the individual ...'*

While the portfolio belongs to the candidate, it is important that the assessor and quality assurer (verifier) also has access to it. The qualification assessor will need to see the evidence in order to make judgements about the validity, authenticity, currency and sufficiency of the contents. The qualification **internal quality assurer** (IQA) will need to see it to sample the decisions made by the assessor for accuracy and transparency. The AO will also require access, via an external quality assurer, to the information for sampling purposes.

A portfolio, despite the fact that it is an individual's record, does not need to include personal or learning materials as that part of the journey to competence is not assessed. It should be evidence relating to how competence is demonstrated against whichever qualification the candidate is registered. Collecting evidence in a logical manner will also enable the person collecting the evidence to reflect on their progress. So by keeping a list of contents, referenced to what the candidate is trying to achieve, both the assessor and the candidate will always know how much more needs to be done in order to complete the qualification. The principles will apply to any qualification for which a portfolio is used to store evidence. In the assessor or quality assurer qualification, you are additionally required to demonstrate your own occupational competence to be an assessor/quality assurer as this is a requirement of the role. Mindful of this, there is a suggestion in the format (below) that the candidate assessor or candidate quality assurer adds their CV and copies of relevant occupational certificates to their portfolio.

On the occasions when a portfolio is paper based, it is generally stored in a file or folder. However, it is not essential to copy absolutely everything. Whenever possible, a qualification assessor will view evidence in its normal location and 'testify' to its existence. This will ensure that folders do not become excessively large with lots of photocopies of documents. It also supports the notion that confidential material or records can be retained within the organisation. Similarly, products, for example, brick walls, cooked food items or clients' hairstyles cannot be 'put' into a folder. Admittedly, photographic evidence can be made, but qualification assessors observing or viewing the real thing are sufficient. This evidence may need to be seen as part of QA sampling, by both the qualification internal and external QA teams. This may mean site visits to view the evidence judged as competent by the qualification assessor.

ACTIVITY 3

Make a list of five typical pieces of evidence that could be retained in the workplace.

1.

2.

3.

4.

5.

(Answers might include: fire evacuation procedures, office procedures, cooked products from a catering outlet, staff appraisals, environmental/ layout of space, safe working practices, clients' treatments, confidential files, etc.)

City and Guilds, in these instances, recommend that when evidence is assessed in situ, the record of that assessment must state:

- Who and what was assessed and by whom.
- The date and location of the assessment.
- The assessment methods used to collect the evidence.
- The assessment decision.
- The units, learning outcomes and assessment criteria achieved.
- The location of the supporting evidence.

Qualification Handbook for Centres (February 2011, p11)

What constitutes evidence?

Evidence is defined as the output of an assessment activity; evidence of a learner's knowledge and understanding, skills or competence that can be used to make a judgement of their achievement against agreed standards/criteria. As such, evidence collected by assessors can be:

- Observation of performance
- Oral questions
- Written questions
- Products, documents, artefacts, photographs, video clips, records
- Professional discussion
- Personal statements or logs, reflective accounts
- Witness testimony
- Supplementary evidence – i.e. that which contextualises or explains the context of other pieces of evidence.

Each of these is discussed as an assessment method earlier in this chapter, pages 45–50.

Unfortunately, it is not possible for an assessor or candidate to just say 'I do that'. They need to be able to prove it.

An artist or model has used a portfolio for many years; it being a collection of pictures or images to prove their ability and versatility. A qualification portfolio is exactly the same; it is a collection of proof. Evidence may be stored in a file or folder (a portfolio) or electronically (e-portfolio or portable storage device).

Observation of performance Candidates may be observed by their assessors while working within their workplace. Observations will be planned in advance in order to ensure that candidates are prepared and their employer can expect additional people to be attending their establishment. Observation records would record the context and describe what has been seen.

Oral questions These will probably be asked following an observation. They will be asked to clarify something seen during the observation or to confirm something related to it. They will probably start 'what would you do if …' or 'can you explain why …'. Oral questions are not exclusively part of an observation; alternatively, candidates and assessors may select this method of testing knowledge evidence.

Written questions These are likely to be pre-set by the assessor and used to confirm your knowledge and understanding. Typically questions may be short answer type, written in such a way so that candidates can demonstrate understanding of aspects of the qualifications – especially those not observed or evidenced by producing products. They are unlikely to be tests or exams with time constraints – many will allow the use of texts to complete the questions (i.e. open book questions).

Products, documents, artefacts, photographs, video clips, records Work products are items, for example, business/service documents (minutes, print-outs, forms, procedures, diagrams), finished goods, commodities or commissions, or anything similar produced during normal work activities. Candidates should obtain authorisation to use any document or procedure. If using mobile technology to video an assessment or take photographs of others, candidates and assessors must ensure that appropriate permissions are sought and received before using them in evidence. This would demonstrate awareness of Safeguarding procedures and Data Protection requirements.

Professional discussion This is when a candidate and their assessor engage in conversation about a topic. In some parts of your qualification, it is not possible to cover all of the evidence requirements by observation. In these circumstances candidates and assessors will agree topics of conversation. This is likely to be a structured conversation and the assessor may ask specific questions or direct the discussion in a particular direction.

Personal statements or logs, reflective accounts These can be used as an alternative to professional discussion. Whereas a discussion involves a candidate and assessor, in statements a candidate writes how they do (or would do) something. A statement should be referenced to a particular topic rather than a rambling piece of text about general issues.

Witness testimony A witness is someone who is able to testify (validate) what they have seen. A witness might be an employer, customer or team member.

You will find these are the most commonly used methods of assessment. Candidates will produce evidence relating to performance – i.e. evidence of doing the job. This forms half of the evidence, the rest being derived from knowledge evidence – i.e. what is understood about the job.

Portfolio extras

You will need to check with your quality assurer whether or not there is a requirement to include the unit specifications in a candidate portfolio. Some assessors find it useful if their candidates' portfolios contain these to save them time when assessing. Other assessors provide grids which link the specifications to the evidence – called tracking sheets (see below).

Assessors need to mark according to professional standards, particularly relating to presentation of work, accuracy of spelling, grammar and the use of English. Assessors should always correct inaccuracies.

Confidentiality in assessment is part of the ethical responsibilities of an assessor and an IQA. An assessor/IQA is required to keep records securely, and respect the confidentiality of candidates and their employers. For example, an assessor will more than likely come into contact with systems and procedures in many different organisations. They must be mindful of 'commercial in confidence' which requires them to look at documents only for the purpose of assessment and not divulge information to others. If you use photographs in your portfolio, you must seek permission to use them. If people are in the photograph, especially minors or vulnerable adults, this should be in writing (from parents/guardians/carers of minors or vulnerable adults).

Copyright legislation exists to protect intellectual ownership and misuse of published materials. Plagiarism is when there is a lack of accurate referencing of published information. To overcome this, candidates should not 'cut and paste' or cite published works without referencing the source. For example, to cite a part of this paragraph the writer should write it as follows: Wilson (2012) states: 'Plagiarism … is a lack of accurate referencing of published information'. Then, in a bibliography or reference list at the end of the essay or statement, you would include the reference: Wilson, L (2012) *Practical Teaching: a teaching guide to assessment and assurance*. Andover: Cengage.

Supporting candidates to complete their portfolio is common. An assessor needs to decide at what point the support is complete and assessment starts. The evidence contained in a portfolio must be authentic – i.e. the candidate's own work, so it cannot include work which has been created by the assessor. There are ways of showing development within a portfolio, for example to include draft versions of evidence and final copy. This way, internal and external QA staff can see the candidate's journey to competence. In discussing authenticity, it should be noted that everything contained in a portfolio should be signed and dated. When assessing e-portfolios, signatures are not possible (in that e-signatures could be attached by anyone), so the assessor must make other investigations to ensure that the work is authentic and owned by the candidate.

Portfolios do have a shelf-life. Evidence contained in a portfolio is required to be current practice. This means that evidence contained in a portfolio which is more than 12–24 months old (depending on the sector) is likely to be considered too old to be valid. Awarding Organisations will provide advice on currency of evidence and it will change according to the sector. For example: the technology sector is advancing very quickly, so the evidence needs to reflect current versions of hardware and software. The Arts sector is likely to allow evidence built up over a longer period of time.

Exemplar portfolios are commonly requested by candidates. These are not advised because they remove the spontaneity of the evidence methodology. Candidates (and assessors) tend to replicate the style of the example and this restricts the efficiency of assessment.

Tracking evidence

Once all the evidence has been collected, it will need to be indexed and linked back to the assessment criteria of the award the candidate is hoping to achieve.

Depending upon the type of qualification being undertaken, one of the following would be an appropriate method to track evidence.

In these grids each piece of evidence is given a reference (or a page number) to indicate where it is located. Remember this could be at the workplace or saved to a file or folder on a portable storage device. Then the evidence is linked to the standards. In the first example you will notice that there is no piece of evidence that is recorded against 2.3. This means that any reviewer of this tracker would alert the

	REF	1.1	1.2	1.3	1.4	1.5	2.1	2.2	2.3	3.1	3.2	etc
Xyz document	p 5			✔	✔		✔	✔		✔	✔	
Observation 30/11/11	p 8	✔	✔	✔	✔	✔		✔				
Oral Question record 1	p12					✔	✔					
etc												

	REF	P1	P2	P3	P4	P5	P6	M1	M2	D1
Assignment 1	Doc 1	✔	✔	✔				✔		✔
Assignment 2	Doc 2				✔	✔	✔		✔	

candidate to gain some evidence to evidence it – alternatively it might be an error in the tracking.

Watch point

Assessors should always check the tracking sheets as they will need to sign to say that the evidence they have assessed does in fact cover the criteria claimed.

Tracking is a difficult task if a candidate is not very organised or the qualification has some complex cross referencing – so as an assessor you should be prepared to support them in this task.

Record keeping

Records are an essential part of the assessment process; they provide evidence of achievement and competence. They also have a wider purpose in respect of supporting organisational processes.

The part of the job associated with record keeping often seems bureaucratic and repetitive. It sometimes takes longer to prove you did the job than it took to do the job in the first place. These feelings are quite common and you should not feel guilty about having them, although to move on you need to see the value in the process so here goes …

Paperwork: The necessary evil or the answer to your prayers?

The need to record assessments or in fact any other aspect of the role is essential to you, your candidates, your colleagues and your managers. Completing the necessary paperwork on time and distributing it to those who need it, is essential to support efficient and effective working practices.

Record keeping is best done in smaller chunks and not all left to the end of a programme; this ensures a distribution of the workload and timely completion of records which ultimately saves time. Records help you to remember what has occurred and act as a guide to others in case you are not available. A filing system suits methodical workers but not spontaneous types and so it is something that may need personal development time to fine tune. Records need to be kept in a logical sequence; chronological, alphabetical, by name, by programme or any combination of those. They may be stored as a paper record or saved electronically.

The stakeholder table: who needs records and why?

Who	Why
Candidates	• To provide records to evidence achievement, progress and support needs. Candidates will need advice on how to store their information.
Assessors	• To replicate progress records of candidates (in case of loss); to inform reports to others. • To inform reflective personal and professional practice. • To know who has done what and when. • To provide a record of the variety of assessment methods used. • To raise awareness of the overall assessment strategy of a candidate.
Colleagues	• To support team members during absence. • To share in team meetings and self-assess the effectiveness of their programmes.

Who	Why
	Colleagues will need your records to be accessible and stored logically.
Managers	• To monitor performance. • To plan for responsive provision. • To make strategic and financial decisions.
Quality unit	• To generate comparative analysis across the organisation. • To compare performance with national averages and organisational trends.
Parents	• To inform about the progress of their child on the programme. Candidates may not communicate well with their parents and so this is the only definite link. Don't rely on candidates to give reports to their parents, especially if they are anticipating less complimentary reports.
Schools	• To create a link between vocational and academic studies. • To develop a standardised approach to a candidate's development.
Employers	• To inform about the progress of their employee on the programme. • To inform their business processes. As the financial sponsor, they require accurate and reliable progress information.
AO	• To register and certificate achievement. • To action and record external quality monitoring processes. • To inform responsive development.

Who	Why
Auditors	● To check funding claims are legitimate and business processes are legal and above question. ● To scrutinise accountability and responsibility.
Inspectorate	● To quality assure performance at organisation level against national standards. ● To justify appropriate use of public funds.

What are the consequences of failure to keep records?

- Candidate's progress is haphazard and unstructured.
- Mistakes and trends are not noticed so they continue to impact on practice, possibly in a downward spiral.
- There is a lack of accountability with no-one taking the lead on responsibility to candidates and other stakeholders.
- Candidates don't gain their qualifications, or if they learn the required elements they will not be accredited through a recognised organisation.
- Public confidence is reduced, which results in lower enrolments, which leads to fewer classes, fewer jobs, and eventually the demise of the organisation.

Hints and tips for record keeping:

- Keep copies for third parties.
- Write in an appropriate style for the reader – the candidate, parent, AO, etc.
- Keep notes about informal processes – development needs and actions, late work, resubmission dates, problems, etc.
- Documentation should give an overview rather than record every 'if, but and maybe'.

- Documents should be fit for purpose.
- Keep records relating to the process and product of assessment.
- Records may be self-devised or devised by the organisation – ask what is in use before going your own way.

Assessment documentation

Watch point

- Methods of recording assessments will differ according to the qualification type.
- Always use the forms agreed within the organisation.
- Suggestions for improvements should be made through the IQA.
- All forms should, at the very least, include the qualification title, names of the assessor and the candidate and the date.

The forms below are examples of format in order to recognise style. They should not be considered as 'approved' documents. The forms described, which are examples and not an exhaustive list, are:

- observation records
- records of questioning
- assignment front sheets
- tracking sheets.

Observation records

These forms are most commonly associated with the recording of observed evidence. The purpose of keeping documents relating to observation is to ensure that *what is seen is accurately matched to the assessment criteria*. Whether this is completed by the assessor or the candidate will depend on how confident the candidate is and how familiar with the criteria they are. In my experience it is usually the assessor's job! The observation record would be a piece of evidence to demonstrate what was seen, when and should be confirmed or 'witnessed' by the parties involved – usually in the form of signatures. The most common use of observation documents is to record workplace activities. They are usually descriptive and are written as a chronological record. For example:

> *2nd March 2011 – Reception area of Smith's Engineering, Sometown. At 09.15, Sheila greeted the customer in a polite manner, asking the purpose of their visit and who they wished to see. She then used the telephone to inform the Director's secretary that the visitor had arrived. Sheila gave the visitor's name and the company they represented. While waiting for the visitor to be collected, she issued a visitor's badge and asked the visitor to 'sign-in'. Two incoming calls were taken using the standard greeting and directed to the extension required. At 09.20, as the secretary still hadn't arrived to collect the visitor she invited them to take a seat in the waiting area. A package arrived and was signed for; rang to inform addressee of its arrival. She smiled when the visitor left reception with the secretary at 09.25.*

When writing up observations, it is useful to have a copy of the assessment criteria to hand and to be mindful of everything that is occurring; this will enhance the holistic approach to assessment.

An observation record might look like the following.

<table>
<tr><td colspan="2">Name of candidate: Date:
Qualification: Level:
Location of assessment:</td></tr>
<tr><td>A description of the event or activity</td><td>Links to performance criteria</td></tr>
<tr><td></td><td></td></tr>
<tr><td colspan="2">Assessor's signature: Date:
Candidate's signature: Date:</td></tr>
</table>

Records of questioning

These documents are more associated with verbal questioning rather than written questioning. Written questions automatically create a record, but verbal questions could just happen. The purpose of the document is to provide evidence of what question was asked and the answer given (whether right or wrong). This should then be linked to relevant criteria. Valid questions are those which are related to theory and underpin a practical activity.

For example, following the observation above, typical questions might be:

What would you do if the telephone extension had been busy?

What would you do if the addressee on the parcel had not been a member of staff?

Why is it important to use a standard greeting when answering a telephone?

If a visitor is very early for their appointment, what do you do?

At the end of the record of questioning, it is important that both the assessor and the candidate sign to say that the document is 'a true record of questions and their responses'.

A record of questioning might look like the first form opposite.

Assignment front sheets

The purpose of an assignment front sheet is to provide a standardised method of briefing candidates on components of the assignment. For example, it will list the tasks to be completed and target dates; it will identify any key/basic or functional skills that are derived from the assessment; it will state the criteria for gaining pass, merit or distinction grades; and usually provide a space for assessors to give feedback on the work. It is customary that the person who designs the tasks should submit the brief to the IQA for approval before launching it with their group. This ensures consistency within the organisation and a double check before issuing the assignment to candidates.

Record of Questioning

<table>
<tr><td>Name of candidate:</td><td>Date:</td></tr>
<tr><td>Qualification:</td><td>Level:</td></tr>
<tr><td colspan="2">Unit/Assessment:</td></tr>
<tr><td>Question</td><td>Response given by candidate/learner</td></tr>
<tr><td></td><td></td></tr>
<tr><td></td><td></td></tr>
<tr><td></td><td></td></tr>
<tr><td>Assessor's signature:</td><td>Date:</td></tr>
<tr><td>Candidate's signature:</td><td>Date:</td></tr>
</table>

An assignment front sheet might look like the following:

Assignment Front Sheet

<table>
<tr><td colspan="2">Qualification title:</td></tr>
<tr><td colspan="2">Unit title and number:</td></tr>
<tr><td>Launch date:</td><td>Submission date:</td></tr>
<tr><td>Task</td><td>Criteria reference
Including links to Functional Skills</td></tr>
<tr><td></td><td></td></tr>
<tr><td colspan="2">Feedback</td></tr>
<tr><td colspan="2">Grade achieved:</td></tr>
<tr><td>Assessor signature:</td><td>Date:</td></tr>
</table>

Tracking sheets

These are the forms that record progress during a qualification. They may be used in a way that the assessor can plot achievement of tasks within an assignment, units or modules within a qualification or framework or completion of homework/class-work activities. It is usual to record the date the unit/task/activity is completed. Best practice models include the date commenced and who assessed the work, with a space to date and initial if the work is internally quality assured. A similar document can be used to plan internal quality assurance strategies – i.e. identify which part of the qualification and which candidates' work are to be sampled.

A tracking sheet might look like the following:

Qualification title:									
Name	Unit, task or activity								
	1	2	3	4	5	6	7	8	Etc.
Candidate A									
Candidate B									
Etc.									

To be effective and meaningful, you should devise a simple marking code to visualise the progress. For example:

- / means a candidate has started on the unit/module.
- X means they have completed the unit/module.
- Always add a date when completed, together with the assessor's initials.
- If verified the verifier could date and initial maybe in a different colour pen.

Reporting progress

Reporting progress (or tracking as it is commonly known) is part of the record keeping process. The keeping of records is about organisation, transparency and accountability, but recording progress is the part of the process concerned with sharing those records with others in order to initiate a development. This is the move discussed earlier: record keeping is associated with 'assessment OF learning', progress reporting is concerned with 'assessment FOR learning'. As we have already seen, the benefits to the candidate when the focus of assessment is changed from measurement to development impacts significantly on the candidate's achievement.

Why does progress need to be reported?

Progress needs to be reported, quite simply, because common sense (and current research) says it is the best way to develop potential. If the assessor tells the candidate how they are doing, they can engage in a discussion to move forward, rectify mistakes and build on their strengths. It is highly motivational for the candidate to be told how well they are progressing. Equally, with constructive feedback, it is valuable to know what isn't going so well, and, maybe through motivational interviewing, you will come up with strategies to overcome this.

The assessor will have to report progress to **stakeholders** (see The stakeholder table: who needs records and why? above). There are three stakeholders directly involved in the assessment process: the candidate; their parents or guardians if under 18; their employer if employed.

Parents are also interested to know how their child is performing in the classroom. It is increasingly important that the learning ethos is shared between home and the learning organisation. If additional work is being set to complete at home, it is good to know that parents are helping to ensure it is done.

Employers are interested because they have identified training needs in their employees and have contracted with learning organisations to realise those goals. They need to know that their employees are getting value for money and that they are attending and contributing to learning.

How and when is progress reported?

- One-to-one reviews – informally and formally at regular intervals throughout the programme.
- Feedback – after assessments and with all marked work.
- Reports – once or twice a year as a summary to parents or employers.
- Employer forums – to develop partnerships and collaborative activities.
- Parent's evening – to formalise candidate development – this is more common in the post-16 sector.

The timing of reporting is only a suggestion; it will be determined by cost and availability of resources and staff. It is hoped that informal chats will ensure that progress is summarised and reported frequently with more formal monitoring and stakeholder reporting targeted at specific periods throughout the training period.

Glossary of terms

Awarding organisation a body approved by Ofqual to create and certificate qualifications (AO)

Closed questioning limited response type of questions

Contingency plan planning for the unexpected occurrence

Cross reference linking evidence to more than one aspect of the qualification

DELTA © Disability, Emotional, Language, Technology, Ability.

Feedback verbal or written comments about the assessment intended to bring about improvement

Goal an aim or desired result

Holistic the big picture; the whole qualification or curriculum

Internal Quality Assurance validating the integrity of the assessment

Leading questioning a question (with an indicated answer contained within the question)

Objectivity without bias

Open questioning question designed to elicit a detailed response

Plagiarism the passing off of someone else's work as your own without reference

SMARTER Specific, Measurable, Achievable, Relevant, Time-bounded, Ethical and Reviewed

Stakeholder a person, either directly or indirectly, associated or interested in the candidate or organisation

Subjectivity decisions influenced by other factors

Targets an objective or focused path towards an outcome

Recommended reading

City and Guilds (2009) *Level 2 Diploma in Professional Food and Beverage Service, 7103-02*, Qualification handbook, 500/7478/7. November 2009.

Fautley, M and Savage, J (2008) *Assessment for Learning and Teaching in Secondary Schools.* Exeter: Learning Matters

Gardener, J (ed) (2006) *Assessment and Learning*. London: Sage

Gravells, A (2009) *Principles and Practice of Assessment in the Lifelong Learning Sector.* Exeter: Learning Matters

Wilson, L (2008) *Practical Teaching: a guide to PTLLS and CTLLS*. London: Cengage Learning

Wilson, L (2009) *Practical Teaching: a guide to PTLLS and DTLLS.* Andover: Cengage Learning

Useful online resources

Balancing Assessment of and for learning. Enhancement Themes – various researchers summarised on: http://www.enhancementthemes.ac.uk/themes/IntegrativeAssessment/IABalancingFeedforwardAss.asp (accessed May 2011)

Likert Scales: http://psychology.about.com/od/lindex/g/likert-scale.htm (accessed May 2011)

E-assessment: http://www.jiscinfonet.ac.uk/InfoKits/effective-use-of-VLEs/e-assessment

SUMMARY

In this chapter we set out to:

- Describe the planning process and apply in the organisation of assessments.
- Compare and contrast the range of assessment methods available to use.
- Explain and evaluate the effectiveness of questioning and feedback.
- Summarise how to make judgements on performance and knowledge acquisition.
- State the importance of record keeping during and after assessment.

Your personal development

- You have looked at the planning process and studied its position within the assessment cycle. You are able to explain the protocols and design features of effective planning and have reviewed the factors which may provide barriers to successful assessment.

- You can describe and compare the various methods of assessment and have considered how they are appropriate within different assessment situations. By completing the case studies you have shown how you devise assessments to ensure that they meet the rules of assessment, i.e. validity, reliability, authenticity, currency and sufficiency. Further you have developed this concept by exploring how using holistic assessment minimises the quantity of evidence required to demonstrate competence.
- You have reviewed the importance of an appropriate environment in which to carry out your assessment.
- You have analysed how you can modify your questioning techniques to ensure that you are able to assess the knowledge and understanding of your candidates. You can differentiate questions by using different techniques for individual and group situations. You have practiced re-writing questions to make them more efficient in gathering accurate information.
- You explain the importance of effective feedback in both assessment of learning and assessment for learning. In each you can use feedback to express achievement and development of candidates' competence, following a constructive feedback model. You have scrutinised the protocols required in delivering an effective feedback session.
- You have evaluated the importance of making accurate judgements following an assessment. You are able to explain how to judge evidence against the rules of assessment.
- Finally, you have noted the importance of record keeping both in recording judgements and their part in reporting progress to stakeholders. You have looked at some examples of recording documents and are able to critically evaluate how they are fit for purpose.

CHAPTER 3
Quality assurance of assessment

Unit of Assessment	Assessment Criteria
Understanding the principles and practices of assessment	8.1; 8.3
Assess occupational competence in the work environment	4.1; 4.2
Assess vocational skills, knowledge and understanding	4.1; 4.2
Understanding the principles and practices of internally assuring the quality of assessment	1.1; 1.2; 1.3; 1.4; 4.2; 4.3; 5.1 6.1 Legislation: see Chapter 1 6.4 Equality and Diversity: see Chapter 1
Internally assure the quality of assessment	2.2; 2.3; 2.6; 3.1; 3.2; 4.1; 4.2; 5.1 Legislation: see Chapter 1 5.2 Equality and Diversity: see Chapter 1
Plan, allocate and monitor work in own area of responsibility	No direct links although underpins management of quality assurance

LEARNING OUTCOMES

By the end of this chapter you will be able to:

- Review the regulations and requirements of QA
- Explain the main functions and principles of QA models
- Define the key terms relating to QA
- State the roles and responsibilities of the QA practitioner
- Explain the disputes and appeals process
- Identify the key external organisations involved in the QA processes.

The regulations and requirements of quality assurance

In England, the Office of the Qualifications and Examinations Regulation (**Ofqual**) is bound under **statute** to ensure that **awarding organisations** and their approved centres comply with a set of **regulations** relating to **quality assurance**. They are also responsible for vocational qualifications in Northern Ireland. University degrees are regulated by the Quality Assurance Agency (QAA).

In respect of Ofqual, the regulations are:

- The Statutory Regulation of External Qualifications in England, Wales and Northern Ireland 2004
- NVQ Code of Practice 2006 (revised)
- Regulatory Principles for e-Assessment 2007
- Regulatory Arrangements for the Qualifications and Credit Framework 2008
- Operating rules for using the term 'NVQ' in a QCF qualification title 2008
- The Apprenticeship, Skills, Children and Learning Act 2009

You do not need to be able to recite these, but you should know that they underpin the values of delivering and assessing **accredited** qualifications. The various regulations aim to meet the needs of learners, maintain standards and comparability, promote public confidence, support equality and diversity and ensure value for money. To this end they specify that AOs and approved centres must:

- Maintain standards by confirming compliance to approval criteria.
- Offer a robust, consistent approach to QA and internal **verification**.
- **Sample** assessment decisions to confirm validity and authenticity.
- Provide valid and reliable outcomes against NOS.
- Keep accurate records relating to assessment decisions.
- Have policies and **procedures** in place for assessment and QA.
- Provide administrative systems to support **registration** and **certification**.
- Ensure that QA systems are consistently applied.
- Recruit appropriate staff to ensure integrity in all aspects of provision.
- State clear roles and responsibilities of staff to maintain high standards.
- Ensure staff have relevant qualifications and experience to undertake their roles.
- Review and evaluate to promote improvements.
- Have effective systems to recruit candidates and ensure their needs are met.
- Provide human and physical resources to support the delivery and assessment of accredited qualifications.
- Ensure fairness in assessment with appropriate references to appeals processes.

Ofqual also regulates vocational qualifications in Northern Ireland, with the Council for the Curriculum, Examinations and Assessment (CCEA) which regulates other qualifications in Northern Ireland.

In Scotland, qualifications are regulated by the Scottish Qualifications Authority (SQA).

In Wales, the regulatory body is the Department for Children, Education, Lifelong Learning and Skills (DCELLS).

In Eire, the National Qualifications Authority of Ireland (NQAI) has responsibility.

Useful online resources

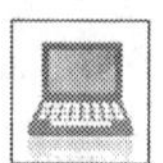

For additional detailed information use the following links to the websites:
Ofqual: http://www.ofqual.gov.uk/
CCEA: http://www.rewardinglearning.org.uk/
SQA: http://www.sqa.org.uk/
DCELLS: http://wales.gov.uk/
NQAI: http://www.nqai.ie/

This chapter sets out to explore how this can be achieved.

Quality assurance models

Quality assurance is a business model which manages **quality control** systems to reassure senior managers and other stakeholders that systems are in place to guarantee the output of the organisation – in training terms the timely success of its candidates. Quality assurance systems will check that processes are fit for purpose, value for money, of a high standard and that they meet legal and regulatory requirements. Following the QA **process**, **quality improvement** is a mechanism to record the required and/or necessary developments and then monitor progress toward achievement of any identified goals. Quality improvement is informed by the outcomes of QA strategies. Quality assurance systems, therefore, are a continuous cycle of audit, review and development aimed to:

> *'Delight the customer by fully meeting their needs and expectations.'*
>
> *http://www.businessballs.com*

In all aspects of quality, the customer experience should be at the core, but it also has sound business principles. Quality assurance increases the levels of confidence in the value of assessment and the decisions made during assessment. It is a series of mechanisms or policies for ensuring reliable, effective assessment, i.e. guarantees of quality. Quality assurance also provides the mechanism to identify error and implement improvements. A wider purpose of QA is to assure the integrity of product nationally, to set entry and exit standards that are equal so that all stakeholders know that, regardless of where the qualification was achieved, the outcomes are equal. This is one of the main differences between accredited qualifications and un-accredited company training. Accredited qualifications have to be seen to be of a specific standard, whereas company training is designed to meet the unique requirements of a particular organisation – these un-accredited qualifications are not regulated by Ofqual. Both assure quality of provision, but company training certificates are less transferable between other sectors due to the training being designed around individual company practices.

In any QA model, the principle driver will be to strive for excellence. In a Total Quality Management (TQM) strategy, there is zero tolerance towards poor quality and a notion that quality is at the heart of an organisation rather than a process of the organisation. The TQM motto is 'right first time'. Total quality management focuses on the customer and advocates an 'everyone is committed to quality' strategy.

Standards model An organisation positions itself against a set of standards. The International Organization for Standardization (ISO) and business excellence models are examples of typical QA models which use standards to determine the quality of the product or organisation.

Benchmarking model An organisation pitches itself against others or sets of perceived good practice. This can be internal – one department against another, or with competitors, or looking at functions or general performance. This model is used by Ofsted.

Team ethos model The organisation measures itself according to values and contributions, particularly relating to staff. They look at these values and how they promote its services, through training and development and a collective strategy to strive for best practice. Investors in People is an example of this model.

Motivational leadership model In this model there is a notion of 'evolution not revelation'. This means that organisations look for small steps towards excellence and aim to be more reflective. Originating in Japan, *Kaizan* is Japanese for 'improvement' and forms the basis of many motivational theorists' works. These advocate that organisations that create ownership of the quality encourage a culture of continuous development.

In the context of assessment, quality systems provide a means for **intervention**. Quality is driven by effective leadership and works best in the absence of a blame culture. Staff at all levels need to commit to the same high standards and generally, if one aspect of the process goes wrong, very often the others will in something of chain reaction.

Quality = a better way of working.
Prevention is better than cure.

This statement means that effective quality systems, as well as checking compliance, need to be able to locate the cause of the problem, preferably before it occurs. Errors are minimised when procedures are followed.

The aspects of an organisation which will be subject to QA include:

- the learner experience
- training, assessment, verification and **moderation**
- support for candidates
- complaints, **appeals** and **disputes**
- self-assessment
- procedures and documentation.

ACTIVITY 1

Take one aspect of your job role and investigate how it is quality assured. Consider how it is done and when it is done. Who is involved and how is it reported. Give an example of something that has improved as a result of a QA intervention.

One of the main methods of assuring quality is to have good policies and procedures which will guide staff on the expectations and protocols used within the organisation. You would expect to see the following:

- Assessment policy and/or procedure – outlines assessment procedure, guidance on special assessment requirements, strategy for QA, process for dealing with fails and referrals, and general guidance for teams.
- Assessment malpractice policy and/or procedure – guidance on how an organisation ensures consistency and integrity of assessment, including how the organisation will deal with cheating, plagiarism, collusion, or falsifying records either by staff or candidates.
- Appeals policy and/or procedure – guidance on how the organisation will deal with disputes and appeals against assessment decisions.
- Internal quality assurance (IQA) policy and/or procedure – outlines the procedures for ensuring accurate and consistent assessment decisions and processes to ensure that actions identified are carried out.
- IQA implementation strategy – a course or programme specific document to state how the IQA policy will be put into practice.
- External Quality Assurance policy and/or procedure – advises staff on processes to be followed in preparing for and after a visit from an AO.
- CPD Policy – outlines the commitment to training and development and how it is prioritised.

These policies would be supported by corporate policies covering the legislative requirements, for example: health and safety policy, single equality scheme and safeguarding. Additional policies relating to the recruitment, admissions and other aspects of the staff and learner journey will also apply to the QA processes.

ACTIVITY 2

Find the location and acquire copies of policies and procedures relating to your job role. To be sustainable you should ideally save these electronically to your personal storage folder on your computer.

Functions and principles of quality assurance

Centre approval

Approval is the process of seeking permission to run particular programmes, under the auspices of an AO. Thus, a training provider or college (or similar organisation) becomes an approved centre. Awarding organisations, who certificate the programmes, are required to meet stringent criteria (set by Ofqual) to ensure their QA practices are sound. Similarly an approved centre has to meet a number of criteria to ensure its suitability to offer qualifications on behalf of the AO.

Approved centres will receive QA reviews to ensure that they comply with the regulatory aspects of delivering qualifications. This is known as external quality assurance (verification). Whilst likely to be an annual event, the frequency is based on risk. An analysis of an organisation will determine not only frequency but the model. It could be a visit to the centre or a remote/desk based sampling.

Registration and certification

Every approved centre is required to maintain relevant administrative and management information systems to support the enrolment of candidates and claiming certificates. While organisations will vary, either the assessor or the IQA will be required to liaise with designated administrative or examinations staff to process registrations and certifications.

Watch point

Check the specific timeframes for registering and applying for certificates specified for your course or programme. The AO will specify timeframes for this in their assessment guidance.

Record keeping

An essential part of the process is that of keeping records to demonstrate that quality procedures have been carried out. In the next

ACTIVITY 3

Does your organisation or AO provide guidance on:

- The time between centre enrolment and AO registrations. For example: scheme registration to be completed within 12 weeks of commencement of the programme. Does the AO you use make any rule about this?
- The amount of learning that must take place before certification is allowed. For example: under QCF guidelines each qualification has a tariff referring to the amount of notional and guided learning – each credit in a QCF qualification attracts 10 hours of notional learning – of which some is direct contact (guided learning) and some will be self-directed study. Historically NVQs were subject to a 10-week rule in that certification should be greater than 10 weeks following the scheme registration. What is the notional learning for your course?

chapter you will find some suggestions for these. As an IQA you will need to keep forms relating to:

- How IQA is being planned to cover every aspect of the programme.
- Confirming that assessors are making accurate judgements. This may be by observing them making those decisions and/or sampling the evidence collected to inform the decision.
- The suitability of the staff on the programme. This will be achieved by keeping CVs or profiles demonstrating occupational competence and competence in assessment or QA. Specimen signatures will be stored on file to compare with signatures seen on the evidence.
- How the assessors are allocated to candidates. There may be certain assessors who can only assess specific units due to their expertise – a tracking sheet would show how that works.
- Confirmation that assignment or project briefs are approved as valid prior to their use by candidates.
- The amount of hours CPD and professional updating the staff delivering, assessing and Quality Assuring have completed.

All records will need to be kept for three years after the certificate has been issued. As this might mean an accumulation of paperwork, your organisation may require you to store records electronically or scan completed paper-based documents to store electronically. All records whether stored in filing cabinets or in computerised systems are subject to the specifications of the Data Protection Act 1998 and may be applicable to the openness of the Freedom of Information Act 2000.

The Data Protection Act 1998 states that personal data needs to be stored fairly and lawfully and only for the intended purpose (e.g. enrolment, registration, assessment or certification procedures). It must be accurate and kept up-to-date and not kept for any longer than is necessary. All data must be kept securely and systems must be in place to ensure that it remains confidential to the organisation. Individuals have the right to see information you store about them and question any decisions made about them.

The Freedom of Information Act 2000 gives individuals the right to request information, on a particular subject, from public sector organisations. It also allows individuals access to information stored about them.

One key document is the assessment record. This document summarises the assessment activity and provides a system to 'sign off' units as they are achieved. An example would look as follows:

<table>
<tr><td colspan="4">Qualification title:</td></tr>
<tr><td colspan="2">Name of candidate</td><td colspan="2"></td></tr>
<tr><td colspan="2">Name of assessor</td><td colspan="2"></td></tr>
<tr><td colspan="2">Name of quality assurer</td><td colspan="2"></td></tr>
<tr><td>Unit/module name</td><td>Date achieved</td><td>Assessor signature</td><td>Quality assurer signature and date (if sampled)</td></tr>
<tr><td></td><td></td><td></td><td></td></tr>
</table>

This could easily be modified to 'sign off' the component parts of a module or unit if required.

Standardisation

Standardisation relates to ensuring consistency and making agreements concerning the expected standards or content of an award. In a competency based framework this is checking the consistency and accuracy of decisions. In the context of technical certificates or assignment based qualifications, then standardisation will be used to create a consistency in marking.

Standardisation, therefore, is usually a series of meetings aimed at ensuring and monitoring the quality of assessment, the outcome of which is to provide a level of confidence in the assessment outcomes: credible assessment.

The Standardisation process can occur before assessment to set unified expectations and agree on how a particular part of the award is interpreted or to be evidenced. This is particularly useful when working with inexperienced assessors or new qualifications.

Standardisation after assessment is to agree the standard of assessment (or marking) and to check that there is a consistent approach to the validity and sufficiency of evidence. One of the pitfalls in leaving standardisation until the end of a unit is that if something untoward is discovered, the assessor may need to go back to candidates and ask for additional evidence. One way of resolving this is for assessors to be cautious in their feedback and use expressions like, 'subject to moderation'.

Ideally, therefore, standardisation needs to cover the span of the entire assessment period. The standardisation process is aimed at ensuring all assessment decisions are equal. It ensures that assessors are fully conversant with assessment requirements and consistently make the correct decisions. It is also effective in ensuring compliance to the assessment and QA procedures. Where non-compliance is detected the team can together resolve issues and develop practice.

A standardisation meeting would be convened by the IQA coordinator and everyone involved in the programme would discuss the assessment process, identify good practice and support new or weak assessors. The team would be able to devise a CPD plan to support their development.

Some examples of typical standardisation activities would be:

- Every assessor brings candidate work. For example, a 'competent' judgement and a 'not yet competent' judgement OR one 'refer' and one 'pass' standard piece of work (or merit and distinction if applicable). They justify to the group why they have assessed to that level.
- The assessors agree on what constitutes good practice in a particular activity which they then use during their observations of workplace practice.
- Assessors submit an unmarked/unassessed piece of work prior to the event, which is assessed by the IQA or moderator. Then at the meeting everyone assesses the same piece of work, the outcome being that everyone should reach the same assessment decision, mark or judgement. This is also known as 'blind marking'.
- Every assessor involved in a particular unit or module brings ideas or samples of product evidence or assignments, etc. to the meeting to establish the expected standard for that unit or module, which is then implemented by all assessors.
- A particular aspect is evaluated, for example, the use of **witness** testimony. This would provide the benchmark for future activity.

The IQA would run these meetings, which should be recorded. External quality assurers will need to see evidence of how the centre ensures consistency and accuracy in assessment.

Second (and third) marking refers to a process similar to standardisation, when one piece of work is independently marked by another person to (hopefully) get the same result. It is frequently applied to written work.

Another important role of standardisation is concerned with ensuring that the assessment decisions made within consortia organisations are consistent. Here, there is a great risk of inequality borne from the different cultures and methods of working within an organisation. Therefore, when working collectively, effective standardisation is of paramount importance.

ACTIVITY 4

Select a unit or part of a qualification and make a list of how it should be evidenced. Use this to check against a piece of work assessed by a colleague and one of your own. Do they match?

Internal quality assurance – verification and moderation

An internal quality assurance team aims to ensure that assessments are valid (relevant to what is being assessed), reliable (consistent standard) and sufficient (covers everything) to meet the requirements. The IQA checks, through standardisation and sampling processes, that assessment decisions are reliable and that judgements made by the assessment team are accurate.

In the organisation there will be a strategy for quality assuring its training, learning and assessment. While QA is the responsibility of everyone in the organisation, an IQA will take on the responsibility of checking and auditing to confirm the quality and consistency of assessment (and other related processes).

Internal quality assurance comprises two facets.

Moderation The confirmation that marks or grades are accurate. It is a procedure which involves sampling of completed or assessed work to arbitrate on the declared outcomes. This may be done by comparing a result with agreed models or standards to ensure equality of outcomes against others in the sample. Moderation 'evens out' the assessment outcomes and limits variance in interpretation of standards which may occur. Standardisation activities used in the moderation process can be before assessment (to set the standard) or after assessment to compare to the standard and correct marking if necessary. External moderation will take place through visits to approved centres or by posting samples to a nominated representative from the AO. Moderation is most common in assignment based or examined qualifications.

Verification The confirmation that the processes leading to assessment decision-making are compliant, accurate and complete. It is more common in vocational or competency based qualifications. Verification may also include aspects of moderation, but is mainly concerned with process. For example, is the range and type of assessment appropriate to the assessment opportunity, is the documentation complete, are the rules of assessment applied when making assessment decisions? Evidence is rarely re-assessed during the verification process. Verification should take place throughout the assessment cycle (Chapter 2 Planning and delivering assessments, Figure 2.12.1). In order to create transparency in verification, assessors should encourage candidates to reference (index) their evidence against the units of assessment.

Supporting assessors

Another of the roles of the IQA is that of advising and supporting assessors, in particular, new assessors. The types of support that would be implemented would commence with an **induction** programme for new staff. During an induction a new assessor would be issued with guidance on the organisation's systems and procedures, any corporate documentation and introduced to key personnel. If it hasn't already been completed, a **training needs analysis** (TNA) would be started to establish the extent and experience of the assessor, their expertise being matched to units or modules within the qualification. Sample signatures would be collected and stored for future authentication of evidence. New unqualified assessors would require additional support until they had completed their assessor's qualification. Until qualified all of their assessment judgements should be **countersigned** by an experience, qualified assessor. This countersigning process also applies to unqualified quality assurance staff.

Experienced assessors would require less support but should still be introduced to organisation-specific information – a CPD plan or mentoring is probably more appropriate for them.

Continuous professional development for assessors might include:

- How to complete centre documentation.
- The use of the organisation's software programs.
- Assessment or QA updates.
- Attendance at standardisation events.
- Familiarisation with new units or qualifications.
- Subject specific updating or professional/industrial secondments.

In addition to a CPD programme covering current requirements, an organisation may choose to offer development to prepare staff for the future, including succession planning, curriculum development, quality processes or supervisory roles.

Once established in the organisation, the assessor will make assessment decisions. At this point the support needs will be around interpreting criteria, advice of appropriate evidence sources and methods – especially if working with a team collecting evidence holistically. New assessors will need all of their assessment decisions to be countersigned until qualified – this includes observations, scrutiny of product evidence, questioning sessions and feedback meetings. This is quite an expensive quality assurance strategy, but is necessary to ensure the integrity of the qualification. Assessors should, therefore, gain their assessor (or IQA qualifications) promptly, even though many AOs will give them up to 18 months to achieve.

Following quality assurance sampling or standardisation any actions required must be clearly imparted to the assessor. In many cases the IQA and the assessor will sign the IQA sampling record to agree the actions and how/when they will be resolved. It is important that those records are re-visited when the actions are completed in order to 'close-the-loop'. Any corrective actions taken should be signed off to demonstrate successful completion of the actions. The corrective actions will either be:

Essential: i.e. must be completed to enable the candidate to progress.

Advisory: i.e. should be completed in future assessments to raise standards.

Desirable: i.e. could be completed to develop professional and occupation standards.

Watch point

Experienced assessors and QA staff who already hold an Assessor or QA qualification (D32, D33 or D34; A1, A2 or V2) do not need to re-qualify. However, they are required to maintain their professional practice and ensure that their practice complies with current NOS.

ACTIVITY 5

Look at the following scenarios and decide what the recommended corrective actions should be and whether those actions should be considered essential, advisory or desirable.

Scenario	Recommended actions: Corrective action status:
The questioning record states the questions asked and the assessor has noted 'correctly answered' in the answer box.	
The assessment record has not been signed and dated by the candidate.	
The witness testimony from the candidate's employer is written very descriptively and does not comment on how well the candidate has completed the activity.	
It has been five years since the assessor worked in the occupational sector.	
One criterion about 'what to do in case of fire' has been evidenced with a copy of the evacuation procedure.	

Sampling

Internal quality assurance is carried out through a process of sampling assessments. Over the period of the qualification, the work of every assessor, every learner, at every location should be sampled. The amount of sampling will depend on the experience of the assessor, the age of the qualification and the number of learners. It is determined at organisation level and approved by the AO.

Verification/Moderation is on a risk basis. The following examples make suggestions about sampling size to demonstrate best practice:

- An experienced assessor using an established qualification with a reasonable caseload would have about 10 per cent of their work verified.
- An experienced assessor using a new qualification may increase the sample to 25–50 per cent.
- A new assessor with an established qualification might be around 70 per cent rising to 100 per cent for a new assessor with a new qualification.
- Unqualified assessors will be subject to 100 per cent sampling until qualified.

Some of the strategies used to quality assure decisions made by assessors include:

- Observing the assessor while carrying out a workplace observation.
- Observing the assessor giving feedback to a learner about an assessment.
- Interviewing assessors.
- Interviewing learners.
- Reviewing product evidence.
- Looking at records of assessment.
- Conducting an audit trail of dates.

Every organisation will have their own IQA policy, which will depend on resources. Quality Assurance should be part of the process of assessment rather than a product of assessment. This means quality assuring judgements as they occur; during the programme. Further information about how to plan and undertake sampling is detailed in Chapter 4.

Watch point

Beware the IQA who pays lip-service to the QA process. Look for detailed developmental feedback to assessors.

CASE STUDY

Assessor A has a cohort of 15 candidates working at one organisation in the outskirts of town. They are experienced, but this is the first time the assessor has worked with this new qualification since it moved over to the new QCF. One of the candidates submitted a week ahead of the rest and the IQA identified that the assessor had misinterpreted one of the criteria and the evidence provided by the candidate was insufficient to meet the evidence requirements. The IQA rejected the portfolio and told the assessor that more evidence was needed.

1. What strategies should the IQA adopt to resolve this situation?
2. What actions should the IQA recommend to ensure the error is not repeated in the remaining portfolios?
3. What preventative measures would have been needed to ensure this did not occur?
4. What are the implications had the IQA not seen the error?

Roles and responsibilities of IQA staff and other related roles

The duties of an IQA may include:

- Inducting new assessors.
- Confirming the suitability and competence of assessors.

- Supporting and advising assessors.
- Organising team meetings.
- Dealing with enquiries and queries about assessment, programmes and QA processes.
- Checking assessment processes both during and at the end of the programme.
- Monitoring records made by candidates and assessors.
- Tracking and monitoring the progress of candidates.
- Liaising with managers and other support departments to ensure compliance with procedures.
- Organising standardisation events.
- Dealing with appeals and disputes.
- Organise external verification visits.
- Communicating with internal and external parties to deliver an effective service.

In addition, they may need to:

- Recruit candidates.
- Organise inductions for candidates.
- Create administrative processes to ensure appropriate documentation is available and completed.
- Process registrations and applications for certificates.
- Train new assessors.

The basic duties of assessors and IQAs have been described here but you may find references to other roles and responsibilities.

ACTIVITY 6

Research the information provided by the AO and/or SSC in relation to the expectations of the roles and responsibilities of assessors and quality assurers. Does your organisation have a job description for either role?

Expressions used to describe roles

Term	Also known as	Abbreviations
Awarding organisation – appoints the EQA	Awarding body	AO
External quality assurer – represents the awarding organisation to quality assure the QA processes	External verifier External moderator External examiner	EQA (EV, EM, EE)
Approved centre – appoints the IQA and assessment teams	Training provider College Work place	
Internal quality assurer – ensures the integrity of the assessment process	Internal verifier Internal moderator	IQA (IV, IM)
Independent assessor (second tier of assessment)		IA
Lead internal verifier or Lead quality assurer Co-ordinates a number of IQAs		LIV LQA
Assessor	See Chapter 1 The principles of assessment: functions and concepts for further guidance on role	
Trainer/tutor/teacher	Needs to be qualified with learning and development or teacher training qualifications	
Witness	Expert (familiar with the target qualification) Non-expert (unfamiliar with the target qualification)	

Lead internal verifier/lead quality assurer

In larger organisations/centres, there are likely to be programmes where there are a number of internal quality assurers. It would, therefore, be necessary to have an Internal Quality Assurer Co-ordinator (IQAC, IVC) or LIV. Although there may be a difference in their job title, their role is to co-ordinate the duties of a number of IQAs and be a first point of contact between the AO, EQA and centre staff. See Chapter 5 Managing the quality assurance process for more detail about this role.

Edexcel have recently created a role of LIV as part of a revised QA strategy. This role, for which applicants have to sit an assessment test called OSCA2 (online support for centre assessors), is where LIVs are assigned to an area of learning, for example Business, and all Edexcel qualifications within that sector are co-ordinated by this person. They liaise with Edexcel and are a key member of the QA team. Edexcel's external quality assurance staff are known as standards verifiers, who

sample work during the lead IVs three-year accreditation. In this model, the LIV is taking on the duties of an EQA in terms of checking and auditing verification processes.

Independent assessor

There is an increasing requirement to use IAs. This is to support the accuracy and **reliability** of assessment decisions. As many assessors are also involved in the delivery of training, it is difficult to assure objectivity when an assessor and learner have built up a successful learning and training rapport. By building another tier into the assessment, the quality of the assessment decisions are made more robust. Independent assessment usually means that a particular component must be assessed by someone not previously involved in the training, learning or assessment process. It is not validation of an assessment decision as this remains the role of the quality assurer or moderator.

Advantages:

- Assessors are protected from accusations of unreliability by using a third party to make certain assessment decisions.
- Learners are guaranteed unbiased judgements.

Disadvantages:

- Another tier of assessment means additional costs.

Witnesses

The testimony of others is invaluable to the assessment process. There are many events that occur randomly during the candidate's daily routine. If the assessor is not working in close proximity to the candidate, then these assessment opportunities would be missed. The solution to this is to use witness testimony.

As you would expect, keeping records about who is contributing to a candidate's achievement is paramount. There are two documents suggested.

The first collects sample signatures and the designations of those contributors:

Name	Position/role	Contact	Status	Sample signature
	For example: head of department, assessor, internal verifier, supervisor, colleague, witness	Please give a telephone or email contact – to be used to verify testimony	Qualified Assessor Qualified IQA Expert Witness – Unqualified assessor, but familiar with qualification requirements Unqualified assessor and unfamiliar with qualification	This should be the mark used when signing documents for a candidate/ learner. It might be a signature and/or initials
A TRAINEE	CANDIDATE	atrainee@ trgprovider.com	N/A	A Trainee
A Foreman	SUPERVISOR	aforeman@ trgprovider.com	Expert Witness	A Foreman

The second records the event being witnessed:

Witness testimony (also include detail about the candidate, dates, signatures, etc.)	
Detail:	Link to criteria
A Trainee uses the telephone more than 10 times per day to talk to our customers. They are always polite and answer the telephone with our standard greeting. A Trainee makes notes during the conversation and seeks to summarise key points regularly during the conversation. They close the call thanking them for their order or comment. A summary of the conversation is recorded neatly on the message pad and put in the supervisor's tray. If the conversation related to an order A Trainee completes the order on the computerised order system and sends it to the despatch office. This complies with our company policy.	1.3; 1.4. 3.6; 3.7; 7.6; 8.1

With regard to QA, a degree of caution will be necessary when using witness testimony as part of the assessment. The assessor must review the evidence to ensure that it complies with the rules of assessment:

Valid:	Who linked it to the criteria – was it the expert witness, the assessor, the candidate or a non-expert witness?
Authentic:	Was it signed. Can you be sure that the witness wrote it? Have you contacted the witness to check the authenticity?
Sufficiency:	Does the text cover the criteria, meeting the evidence requirements fully? Are additional pieces of evidence required?
Current:	Possibly the easiest, but does the text reflect current industry standards?

It would be unusual for a single piece of testimony to cover the requirements of a whole module or unit, but not impossible. The IQA should consider how much of the unit or module is suited to witness testimony – this would make a good standardisation topic. Expert witnesses are a valuable resource and it might be worth encouraging them to become workplace assessors.

External quality assurance and the tariff of sanctions

One of the quality assurance roles of the awarding organisation is to comment on the effectiveness of the IQA and to measure its confidence in the organisation accordingly. Organisations will strive for 'direct claims', which means that awarding organisations are confident that they are able to quality assure with integrity, and they are authorised to apply for registrations and certificates without constantly seeking approval from EQAs.

Every assessment team strives to get to a 'direct claim' status. This means that their systems and procedures are sound and that the AO has high levels of confidence in the assessment and QA strategies in existence. It is kudos for the team and ensures continuance of the organisation's good reputation.

During the EQA's visits to the centre, the EQA will ask to see policies and check that the associated procedures are being complied with. They will sample candidate work including those that have been sampled as part of the approved centre's QA process and those that were not sampled. They will make a judgement about the extent to which the centre and the team comply with the regulations. If it is discovered that there are breaches in compliance, i.e. there is a risk to the integrity of the qualification, then the EQA will apply a **sanction**.

The NVQ Code of Practice 2006 lists a tariff of sanctions which are applied when approved centres transgress from the regulations specified by Ofqual. While originally only applicable to NVQs, many AOs have adopted a similar series of tariffs to classify the reliability of the approved centre.

At the highest level of sanction the centre may be closed and risks losing reputation and the ability to deliver qualifications.

- Level 0 tariff: The qualification has **direct claims status** (DCS) without any identified action points.
- Level 1 tariff: The qualification has DCS with minor action points which must be addressed before the next visit.
- Level 2 tariff: The qualification has DCS withheld or removed. This is either as a result of a serious assessment or verification concern or a previously identified action not being met. The EQA has to sign off qualifications before a certification claim can be made.
- Level 3a tariff: Registration of new candidates is suspended. The EQA considers that the centre is at risk of not upholding quality standards if more registrations were to be allowed.
- Level 3b tariff: Registration and certification is suspended. There are significant serious concerns about the integrity of the assessment and internal QA within the programme.
- Level 4 tariff: Suspension of specified qualification. The AO considers that there is an irretrievable breakdown in the management and QA processes which compromise the integrity of

the qualification. The centre must note this on any future applications for course approval.

- Level 5 tariff: Suspension of all qualifications. The AO considers that there is an irretrievable breakdown in the management and QA processes which compromise the integrity of all qualifications run at the centre. The centre must note this on any future applications for course approval.

Appeals and disputes

REVISION

In Chapter 1 The principles of assessment: functions and concepts, you considered aspects of the appeals and disputes procedure as part of the assessment process and in the context of the assessor's role and responsibilities. You learned how to deal with an appeal in the initial stages. This part extends that process exploring the role of the IQA.

'Appeal' and 'dispute' broadly mean the same thing, however, they can be defined as:

- Appeal: A request to reconsider a judgement made.
- Dispute: A difference in opinion in an outcome.

There are two very important words associated with the process – fairness and consistency.

It is important to clearly express the process by which candidates can appeal against assessment decisions. This transparency is equally important to the candidate, assessor and organisation. The process should state the organisation's commitment to high standards of equality and be applied consistently throughout the organisation.

A policy will define what the organisation's viewpoint is. It ensures that its stakeholders are aware of its commitment to those who wish to appeal or dispute some aspect if its work.

> *'... aims to ensure that all of its assessments and assessment results are fair, consistent and based on valid judgements. However, it recognises that there may be occasions when a centre or a candidate may wish to question a decision made.'*
>
> *City & Guilds – Enquiries and Appeals policy (August 2008)*

A procedure will define the process a complainant will need to follow in order to make an appeal or log a dispute. It will define the circumstances within which an appeal or dispute is allowed, the time parameters (deadlines) and make assurances regarding confidentiality, impartiality and transparency.

While every organisation will have a variant on their policy and procedure, it should always default to the AO's guidance on appeals and disputes. In essence the process will follow a system similar to the following.

Stage one Candidate refers to the assessor to log an appeal or dispute. They will discuss, clarify and review the assessment and hopefully agree an outcome. Whether the appeal is upheld or lost, then the assessment team should review its assessment processes to identify training needs, support for staff, or confirm and rectify any resultant errors to ensure rigour is maintained. Where there is a failure to agree, then the next stage of the process is entered.

Stage two The candidate will formally state their grounds for appeal or dispute, usually within a specified timeframe to the IQA or designated person. The quality assurer will consider the appeal which may include a re-assessment of the evidence, another observation or interviews with all relevant parties. A decision will be made and notified to the complainant – again within a specified timeframe. If the appeal or dispute is still not resolved, then the next stage is entered.

Stage three This stage is broadly similar to the previous stage although the complainant is referred to the AO, who will allocate a representative to investigate the complaint; this is usually the centre's EQA. Their decision is final, although a candidate would have the right to appeal directly to the AO.

All stages of the process should be documented and stored securely in line with the organisation's policy. The AO will want to see records relating to appeals whether upheld or lost.

External audits and charter marks

As discussed earlier, there are many models of QA. In this section the role and purpose of the organisations involved in QA are summarised. Quality assurance will be undertaken by teams from within the organisation, but at times will also be subject to external audit.

For example:

- AOs
- Inspectorial organisations: Ofsted, QAA
- Charter Mark organisations: Investors in People, Matrix, Training Quality Standard, ISO.

Each of these organisations or charter marks (and there is a summary of each later in the chapter) will inspect or assess to a set of published standards and make judgements in the same way that the assessor would make a judgement about a candidate's competence. Colleges and training providers frequently undertake assessment against the various charter marks in order to market their provision and provide a level of credibility to the public.

Awarding organisations

These are the organisations responsible for devising and accrediting qualifications. They entrust that responsibility to centres who agree to uphold standards. The AO remains accountable for the integrity of the qualifications. They do this by reviewing centre performance to confirm the effectiveness of IQA, by sampling assessments, confirming staff competence and providing advice and support to centres.

Ofsted

The Office for Standards in Education is the government department tasked with the role of inspecting quality and standards in education and training organisations. It publishes its findings on its website and thus it creates the opportunity for stakeholders to review quality of provision prior to deciding which educational establishment to attend. It uses a 'common inspection aramework' (CIF) to set the performance standards. It makes a judgement about the 'overall effectiveness' and 'capacity to improve' through seeking answers to questions relating to outcomes for learners, quality of provision, and leadership and management. The questions in the CIF are answered in the organisation's self-assessment report (SAR), which demonstrates how high quality is achieved, sustained and improvements are ensured. (www.ofsted.gov.uk). The current process is applicable to inspections in a four-year period from September 2009.

Equivalent organisations:

Wales	Estyn (www.estyn.gov.uk)
Scotland	HM Inspectorate of Education (www.hmie.gov.uk) – inspection of schools
Northern Ireland	Department for Education (www.deni.gov.uk)

Quality Assurance Agency

Established in 1997, the organisation seeks to safeguard and help to improve the academic standards and quality of higher education (HE) in the United Kingdom. It is funded through subscriptions from universities and project work undertaken for funding bodies.

(source: www.qaa.ac.uk)

The review process is the integrated quality enhancement review – IQER – and is a two-stage process. The developmental engagement precedes the summative review over a, usually, 12-month period. Each stage commences with a self-evaluation and students can supply a student written submission to offer their views. The review team conducts an assessment relating to the management of the HE provision with the second stage resulting in a published report. It considers the extent to which a HE provider maintains academic standards, the quality of learning and its public information. The IQER process is currently under consultation to revise the methodology (2011).

Investors in People (IiP)

A set of standards designed to recognise and value the importance of people and their contributions to business improvement. It mirrors the teaching/training cycle in that the standards reflect the planning, implementation and evaluative stages of development. The standards seek to address the answers to the following questions and assessors gather evidence from both managers and employees.

Developing strategies to improve the performance of the organisation

1. A strategy for improving performance of the organisations is clearly defined and understood.
2. Learning and development is planned to achieve the organisation's objectives.
3. Strategies for managing people are designed to promote equality of opportunity in the development of the organisation's people.
4. The capabilities managers need to lead, manage and develop people effectively are clearly defined and understood.

Taking action to improve the performance of the organisation

5. Managers are effective in leading, managing and developing people.
6. People's contribution to the organisation is recognised and valued.
7. People are encouraged to take ownership and responsibility by being involved in decision-making.
8. People learn and develop effectively.

Evaluating the impact on the performance of the organisation

9. Investment in people improves the performance of the organisation.
10. Improvements are continually made to the way people are managed and developed.

(source: http://www.investorsinpeople.co.uk)

International Organisation for Standardisation

The ISO is recognised throughout the world, and due to language differences has adopted ISO as its acronym. Based on the training cycle, it enables organisations to work more efficiently and effectively by checking that the systems and procedures are implemented consistently throughout the organisation. There are over 17 000 different standards covering a wide variety of sectors, disciplines and initiatives. The two most commonly seen in the lifelong learning sector are those associated with quality management and environmental management. The current series for quality is the ISO 9001 standard and the ISO14001 is the standard for environmental management. These international standards certify the process rather than the product.

(source: http://www.iso.org)

Matrix assessment

Matrix standards are service standards relating to information, advice and guidance. They look at the work of those involved in giving assistance to learners as they embark on their post-compulsory learning. There are eight standards:

Delivering the service:	Awareness Defining the service Access to information Support in exploring options

Managing the service:	Planning and maintaining the service Staff competence and support Feedback from customers Quality improvement through evaluation

(Source: http://www.matrixstandard.com)

Training Quality Standard (TQS)

NOTE: 19 April 2011. The Department for Business, Innovation and Skills took the decision to withdraw funding for TQS and is winding down accreditation. This will have the effect of making existing accreditations valueless as a charter mark; however it would still act as a measure of an organisation's responsiveness to their employers, pending alternative solutions.

This charter mark helped to measure how effective a training provider is at delivering their employers' needs. When engaging in a training programme the employer would have specific business needs and expected impacts of that training – for example: increased productivity, fewer accidents, faster response times, etc. For the employer, TQS is useful in measuring the effect of training; providing a benchmark for training standards; and how it impacts on procurement decisions. For the training provider, TQS is useful in measuring systems and the effectiveness of the employer/provider communications. It provides a statement about efficiency and therefore is a marketing tool.

Assessment is in two parts: Part A is about responsiveness to employer needs, Part B is about specific sector expertise, i.e. high standards of delivery in a particular occupation.

While inspections by Ofsted and the QAA are done to an organisation, IiP, ISO, Matrix and TQS are voluntary assessments selected by the organisation as part of its assumed role and character.

(source: http://www.trainingqualitystandard.co.uk)

A potential alternative to TQS is investors in excellence (IiE). It aims to deliver sustainable improvements within an organisation. The Standard is based on the European Foundation for Quality Management model (EFQM), which is widely adopted in Europe.

In summary, QA in assessment is a model that can be applied internally and externally, with the sole purpose of making guarantees about the accuracy of assessment. In the next chapter we consider the practical approaches to QA.

Glossary of terms

Accredited a qualification written under Ofqual regulations

Appeal a request to reconsider a judgement made

Awarding organisation a body approved by Ofqual to create and certificate qualifications (AO)

Certification a process of claiming a certificate following successful completion of a qualification

Continuous professional development on-the-job training for staff (CPD)

Countersign a guarantee of reliability in assessment decisions, made by unqualified assessors

Direct claims status a high level of confidence from an AO, resulting in the ability to claim certification without a visit from an EQA (DCS)

Dispute a difference in opinion of an outcome

Induction an introduction to a programme or duty

Intervention to interrupt for the purpose of resolving issues

Moderation the confirmation that marks or grades are accurate

Ofqual regulatory body, office of the qualifications and examinations regulation

Policy a statement of proposed actions

Procedure a way of working

Process a series of actions to meet a specific outcome

Quality assurance a system of review to confirm that processes are in place and applied to guarantee the quality of the service or product; systematic checks to provide confidence

Quality control checks on the integrity of the process

Quality improvement process to improve reliability of quality assurance systems

Registration an official list of entrants to a qualification

Regulation a rule or directive made by an official organisation

Reliability strategy to ensure that assessment decisions are consistent

Sample a representative of the whole to show trends

Sanction a penalty for disobeying the rules

Standardisation process to confirm decisions and create norms

Statute a written law passed by a legislative body

Training needs analysis identification of required training (TNA)

Verification the confirmation that the processes leading to assessment decision-making are compliant, accurate and complete

Witness a person, other than assessor, who provides evidence of competence.

Recommended reading

Wilson, L (2008) *Practical Teaching: a guide to PTLLS and CTLLS*. London: Cengage Learning

Wilson, L (2009) *Practical Teaching: a guide to PTLLS and DTLLS*. Andover: Cengage Learning

Useful online resources

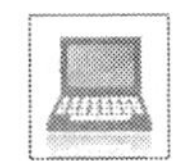

Useful references for further reading about assessment are:

http://www.businessballs.com/dtiresources/total_quality_management_TQM.pdf
http://www.ofqual.gov.uk/files/Regulatory_arrangements_QCF_August08.pdf
http://www.ofqual.gov.uk/files/qca-06-2888_nvq_code_of_practice_r06.pdf
http://www.matrixstandard.com
http://www.trainingqualitystandard.co.uk
http://www.iso.org
http://www.investorsinpeople.co.uk
www.qaa.ac.uk
www.deni.gov.uk
www.hmie.gov.uk
www.estyn.gov.uk
www.ofsted.gov.uk

SUMMARY

In this chapter we set out to:

- Review the regulations and requirements of QA.
- Explain the main functions and principles of QA models.
- Define the key terms relating to QA.
- State the roles and responsibilities of the QA practitioner.
- Explain the disputes and appeals process.
- Identify the key external organisations involved in the QA processes.

Your personal development

- You have reviewed the main regulations which apply to QA, considering both the requirements for AOs and those for approved centres. You are able to describe the role of Ofqual in regulating processes.

- You have looked at quality as a business model and are able to define the benefits of systems and procedures in maintaining and raising standards. You have considered a zero tolerance model and are able to broadly describe TQM.
- You have explored in detail the various functions and principles of a QA system. You have thought about the purpose of centre approvals and the link between the centre and the AO in processing registrations and certifications. In completing this review you have considered the records that you will be required to keep in order to demonstrate compliance to the regulations and comply with the Data Protection Act 1998 and the Freedom of Information Act 2000.
- You have focused on the functions relating to standardisation of evidence and can describe several different types of activity that would be deemed appropriate as standardisation mechanisms.
- You have scrutinised internal quality assurance and the role of supporting assessors and the checking of the accuracy of assessments. You have completed an activity which confirms your ability to compare the difference between the levels of corrective actions and how to make recommendations for improvement. Further, you have looked at the types of sampling systems available and how they confirm accuracy of assessment. In the completion of a case study you have demonstrated how you use information gained during sampling in order to improve performance.
- Finally, in this section, you have reviewed the levels of sanction that would be imposed should a centre be in default of the regulations.
- Then, you looked at the role of the IQA and their relationship to others in the QA stage and considered the importance of the role in bringing about high levels of confidence in assessment. When reviewing the role of witnesses, you have studied two exemplar documents on which to record testimony.

- You have examined the various stages of the appeals and disputes process and can define who is involved and at what stage. You are aware of the role of the awarding organisation as the final arbiter.
- Finally, in this chapter you have reflected on the roles of the various inspectorial and charter mark organisations and how they help organisations to develop and measure themselves against standards and position themselves in the public eye.

In the next chapter we will consider the practicalities of the role.

CHAPTER 4

Internally assuring the quality of assessment

Unit of Assessment	Assessment Criteria
Understanding the principles and practices of assessment	No direct references
Assess occupational competence in the work environment	No direct references
Assess vocational skills, knowledge and understanding	No direct references
Understanding the principles and practices of internally assuring the quality of assessment	2.1; 2.2; 2.3; 3.1; 3.2; 4.1; 6.2; 6.3 6.1 Legislation: see Chapter 16.4 Equality and Diversity: see Chapter 1
Internally assure the quality of assessment	1.1; 1.2; 2.1; 2.2; 2.3; 2.4; 2.5; 2.6; 5.3; 5.4
Plan, allocate and monitor work in own area of responsibility	No direct references although content underpins management aspects of the award

LEARNING OUTCOMES

By the end of this chapter you will be able to:

- Describe the importance and key attributes of planning processes in assuring quality
- Summarise the main sampling strategies
- Identify activities which contribute to quality assurance procedures
- Outline the role feedback has in developing assessment practice
- Reflect on current practice and plan to develop skills and knowledge

Internal quality assurance

REVISION

In Chapter 1 The principles of assessment: functions and concepts and Chapter 2 Planning and delivering assessments you have learned about the main principles of assessment and the importance of the rules of assessment, i.e. the assessed work is **valid**, **authentic**, has **currency** and is **sufficient**. You have reviewed a number of assessment methods and discovered the importance of planning, delivering, making judgements and providing feedback to candidates. In Chapter 3 Quality assurance of assessment you looked at the regulatory **requirements** of QA and explored the purpose of sampling and standardisation. In this chapter we put all of that together in a practical look at QA in action by reconsidering these components in the context of planning and delivering QA.

Any training organisation approved to deliver qualifications on behalf of an AO must have effective QA systems in place to ensure that the delivery and assessment of qualifications is of a high standard. These

Figure 4.1 The quality cycle

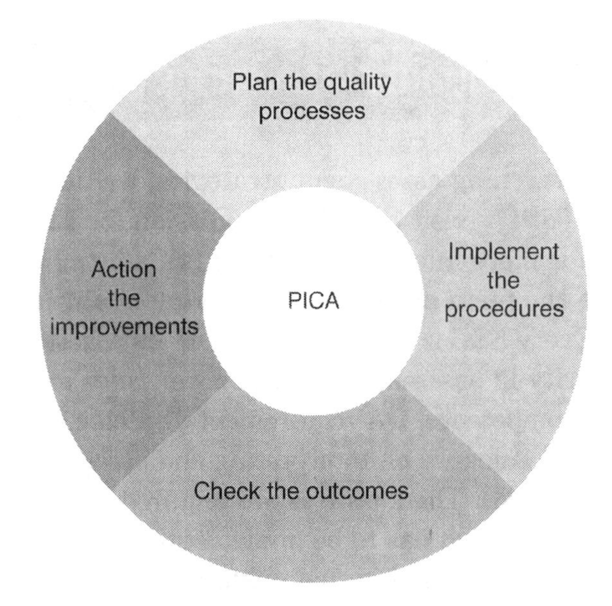

approved centres are responsible for internal quality assurance while the AO will undertake external quality assurance. The AO, during either site visits or remote activity, will check the policies and procedures of approved centres and confirm that staff comply with procedure and are able to manage the assessment and QA processes.

The quality process follows a cyclical strategy of planning, implementing, checking and actioning improvement. This is shown in Figure 4.1.

P	Plan for quality processes
I	Implement the quality procedures
C	Check the outcomes
A	Act on the improvements required

PICA is an acronym designed to help you remember the various stages of the quality cycle. Each relates to a particular aspect of QA procedures and on completion of the cycle there will be an inevitable requirement to recommence the cycle, thus ensuring continuous improvement.

Planning for quality assurance

The various overarching assessment strategies, written by the Sector Skills Councils (SSC) (visit the UK Commission for Employment and Skills website for more information on the SSCs http://www.ukces.org.uk), will define the main protocols for assuring quality for the qualification. Every SSC is required to define its assessment strategy to ensure integrity in assessment. It will cover rules such as assessor experience and competence, QA requirements, specific sector idiosyncrasies and guidance on interpreting and assessing the occupational standards. Then, centres are required to develop a working strategy and a plan which has to be implemented by all those undertaking assessment and internal quality assurance roles. This plan must also meet the requirements of the approved centre and the AO.

Those requirements can be broadly categorised as assessment strategy, legislation and organisation specific methods of working:

- Assessment strategy will define who can assess and the IQA decides what to assess, e.g. the frequency and issues such as the policy on simulated assessment.
- Legislation will cover the requirements of, for example, the Health and Safety at Work etc Act 1974, the Equality Act 2010 and the Data Protection Act 1998.
- Working methods will consider security aspects, shift working, acceptable dress codes, contractual or staffing issues.

In summary, the requirements of the AO and the centre cover aspects which will ensure that the assessment and the internal quality

ACTIVITY 1

Locate your organisation's assessment and QA policy and procedure and develop a strategy to monitor the QA of two assessors in your team. Be careful to include a sampling plan relevant to their experience and contingencies to address difficulty in interpreting assessment criteria.

assurance of the qualification is managed with integrity; is open, transparent and available to all; is executed professionally and is accurately and consistently recorded.

Watch point

This is not an issue of trust; it is a method of securing **evidence** to confirm that QA is testing authenticity, currency, validity and sufficiency. Quality Assurance staff need to be mindful of how colleagues might feel if this process seems threatening. Quality Assurance is a check on accuracy, it is not a means of collecting evidence for capability; organisations have different procedures for that.

The main strategy for ensuring accuracy in assessment is known as sampling. In Chapter 3 Quality assurance of assessment you learned that the amount of sampling is dependent on several factors and that there are several ways to prepare sampling plans.

When preparing a sampling plan it is useful to consider your strategy and develop a structure to your plan. One such method uses the acronym **CAMERA**.

CAMERA is a simple means of planning by including a range of scenarios in the sampling plan and creating some principles upon which to validate QA strategies.

–	Candidates
–	Assessors
–	Methods of assessment
–	Evidence or Elements
–	Records
–	Assessment sites

Source: http://www.cityandguilds.com

In this model, the following considerations would be made:

Candidates	Evidence (complete units) from every candidate should be seen at least once during the qualification. This ensures that there is **equality** and fairness between the different candidate characteristics, needs and special requirements. Every candidate should have at least one aspect of their work quality assured.
Assessors	Something from every assessor should be seen at least once during the qualification. The plan would take into consideration the experience of the assessor and the newness or complexity of the qualification. For examples see below. Every assessor should have at least one aspect of their work quality assured. This may occur indirectly through the sampling of **learner** work, but experience may affect the percentage of sampling.
Methods	From the whole of the qualification the plan should include something assessed by each of the different methods of assessment used in the qualification. Particular attention should be given to the use of witnesses or third party assessors when collecting evidence. Every method used to collect candidate evidence should be quality assured during the programme.
Evidence	Evidence types might include electronic or paper versions of evidence collection. You may also see this written as 'elements', although as qualifications are being re-validated the use of elements to break down units or modules is less visible. The expression 'evidence requirements', however, is being seen frequently and IQA should verify against the guidance given. Evidence and assessment relating to 'problem' units would also be offered more scrutiny.
Records	Auditing of records is important to confirm that assessments occur within the registration and that IQA is timely. Dates, signatures, accuracy and compliance are frequent IQA checks when looking at record keeping.

Assessment sites	Where assessment takes place at different locations, it is important to check consistency of practice across those sites, even if the assessor is the same. On occasions working practices of organisations might impact on a candidate's access to assessment and so this check is required to ensure **fair** access. Every assessment site should be included in the QA sampling plan.

While CAMERA suggests a methodology, there are other aspects of QA to take into consideration when preparing sampling plans.

Assessor experience An experienced assessor would be one who has assessor qualifications (D32/33, A1/A2 or 6317 Assessment and Quality Assurance), who is occupationally competent (qualified at least to the level above the qualification to be assessed plus trade, industry or professional experience) and is familiar with the occupational standards. While the size of the sample depends upon risk, this might be as little as a 10 per cent sample of their assessment decisions. However, newly qualified assessors working with new qualifications would have a considerably larger sample taken. As the risks associated with accuracy of decisions might be greater, unqualified assessors (working towards assessor and QA qualifications) should have all of their work checked through a countersigning process. Unqualified people, unfamiliar with the occupational standards should be treated as witnesses rather than assessors.

Countersigning This is when an unqualified assessor, who is working towards an Assessment and Quality Assurance qualification, works with an experienced assessor. Every assessment decision they make is checked and countersigned for accuracy. Their candidate's work will then become part of the evidence they require to complete their own qualifications.

Watch point

Ensure that it is clear who has made the assessment decision and who is countersigning that decision.

Communication It is important that the assessment and IQA teams communicate, share ideas and work together to achieve goals. This is more important when assessment is offered away from the main site of the organisation. Sound administrative practice will be required to set up a communication and meeting schedule which is open to all in the assessment and IQA team. Meetings should be minuted and shared among the team. Organisations might need to consider issues around sustainability when arranging meetings and assessments to minimise travel and time demands. Can video conferencing or Skype be used to minimise the impact of excessive travel on the environment?

When to QA? Quality assurance should never be left until the end of the award, although this remains a common practice! QA at this point is '**summative QA**'. By undertaking internal quality assessment during the assessment process, any issues relating to inaccurate interpretation of standards, poor practice or non-compliance can be intercepted and resolved before the actions impact on candidate achievement. One way to do this is to assess the assessor assessing. By observing assessment practice IQAs can get a feel of what support assessors need and plan accordingly. Inexperienced assessors might require more internal quality assessment during the process – interim internal quality assessment – thus requiring less summatively.

Watch point

Identify the problems before they become issues. Don't be frightened to ask for advice. If assessment is going wrong, it is better tackled during the programme than after the candidates have completed it.

Standardisation This process ensures a consistent approach to assessment and agreed standards of working. The concept of standardisation was discussed in Chapter 3 Quality assurance of assessment. Insofar as it relates to internal quality assessment, it is a successful method of preparing assessors prior to undertaking assessments or, alternatively, ensuring that judgements made are consistently applied. Where discrepancies occur, the IQA can arrange additional help, training and guidance to support the assessment team.

One of the benefits of standardisation activities is that of preventing error in assessment practice; consider it risk management. It is a pro-active approach to ensure that assessments are valid and consistent. Another benefit is that of pre-empting problem units. To discuss a unit that is difficult or can be interpreted in different ways is a typical standardisation activity and very helpful to the assessment team. A final benefit is that of agreeing standards of practice – for example: what to ask witnesses to write on their statements? What does a personal statement look like? How much of a programme could be evidenced through recognition of prior learning?

Basic QA planning document

This simple strategy shown below will ensure that something from every candidate is seen at least once during the period of study. It is called **horizontal sampling**. It is the most commonly adopted sampling strategy. By ensuring that every unit or module is subject to QA review, by default, it means that if different units are assessed by different assessors all will be reviewed during the QA period. There are, of course, things that make this process more complex – for example, ensuring that if assessors work on different sites then every site is compared. Similarly, planning must include a strategy to ensure that every assessment method is covered.

	Qualification Units/Modules							
	Start date	1	2	3	4	5	etc	Date complete
Name	Sep 11	QA Nov11						
Name	Sep 11		QA Dec 11					Feb 12
Name	Jan 12			QA Mar 12				
Name	Jan 12				QA Mar 12			
Name	Jan 12					QA May 12		
etc								

Another method of sampling, known as **vertical sampling** would involve all assessors bringing in a unit to compare practice. For example, each assessor submits unit one, the sampling might investigate how each assessor has assessed the unit, whether problem criteria have been interpreted in the same way, has evidence generated as proof been evaluated in the same way? Are the assessment decisions the same (**reliable**) across the unit and assessors? This would go a long way to prove that your assessment practice offers a fair and equitable service regardless of assessor, location, work experience, etc.

A final sampling strategy, called **themed sampling**, is concerned with themes. In this situation, assessors would produce work assessed by a specific method. Witness testimony is frequently a chosen theme. In this sample the quality assurerwill investigate how each assessor accepts the chosen method, makes reliable judgements on it and confirms the rules of assessment – validity, accuracy, currency and sufficiency. Another frequent theme is one of auditing the date trail. This is a method of ensuring that candidates enrol with the training provider, then with an AO. Then, checking that their assessments are within the period of the programme, allowing time for learning before assessment. Finally, checking that QA dates follow assessment and that there is time for assessors to rectify errors before certification is claimed. This type of activity is also useful in checking that candidates complete in a timely manner, which on Government funded programmes is an essential criteria to secure outcome related funding.

Just a final note in terms of planning. It should also be borne in mind that a plan means exactly that. It is not a 'tablet of stone' and things will impact on the plan.

For example:

- Seasonal influences in horticulture awards will impact on the order the units can be delivered.
- Menus will impact on the completion of catering awards.
- Candidates achieve quicker or slower than expected.
- Sickness of candidates, assessment staff or employers may delay the process.

- Employer's response to business needs create different assessment opportunities.

It is, therefore, important to manage the QA process, prepare for unexpected situations and always record the actual QA date against the planned date.

ACTIVITY 2

Examine the tracker below and decide on your sampling strategy. Explain how you made your decision.

	Qualification Units/Modules							
	Start date	1	2	3	4	5	6	Date complete
Eliza Workplace: JB & Co	Sep 11	Ach'd Nov 11 Assr: Sarah	Ach'd Nov 11 Assr: Sarah	Ach'd Nov 11 Assr: Sarah				
Bill Workplace: ABC Ltd	Sep 11	Ach'd Nov11 Assr: Derek	Ach'd Nov11 Assr: Derek	Ach'd Nov11 Assr: Derek	Ach'd Dec11 Assr: Derek	Ach'd Jan12 Assr: Derek	Ach'd Feb12 Assr: Derek	Feb12
Sahid Workplace: ABC Ltd	Jan 12	Ach'd Feb12 Assr: Derek	Ach'd Feb12 Assr: Derek				Ach'd Feb12 Assr: Derek	
SammyJo Workplace JB & Co	Jan 12	Ach'd Mar12 Assr: Sarah					Ach'd May12 Assr: Sarah	
JJ Workplace Ditty & son	Jan 12	Ach'd Apr12 Assr: Goran		Ach'd Mar12 Assr: Sarah	Ach'd Mar12 Assr: Sarah			
Winston JB & Co	Feb12	Ach'd Mar12 Assr: Sarah						

Implementing the quality assurance

Adherence to the organisation's assessment and QA policies is the only way to implement effective QA. The policies are agreed and approved by AOs and are tested in their visits. It is, therefore, essential that whatever arrangements have been planned, they are carried out fully. Failure to do this is the main reason for sanctions from the AOs.

Without repeating too much, the main policy and processes are concerned with:

- Sampling to verify and/or moderate decisions.
- Standardisation to confirm consistency and moderate between assessors.
- Record keeping to create an audit and reference trail.
- Communication to ensure everyone knows what is going on.

This will ensure that inaccuracies are identified quickly and are rectified before they impact on candidate achievement.

Quality Assurance occurring during the assessment process is known as **interim QA**. It is likely to involve looking at assessor practice and talking to candidates. Rarely will it look at evidence, as it is likely to be incomplete, although formative assessment will accurately identify the missing components. As a result, **formative feedback** sessions will either be observed or documentation reviewed.

Simple documents can be used to record any observation of assessment activity or formative feedback sessions.

Assessor:		IQA:
Candidate:		Date:
Standard:	Y/N	Comment:
PLANNING		
Was the assessment planned?		
Did the plan include information about what was to be assessed, how, when, where and who was involved?		

Were appropriate risk assessments in place relevant to the assessment task?		
Was the assessment planned to ensure fair, equitable and reliable assessment?		
Were any special arrangements made to meet candidate needs – e.g. timing, resources and/or support?		
Did the assessment use a standalone or holistic approach?		
Did the candidate understand the proposed assessment process? Was it agreed before being undertaken?		
If others were affected by the assessment or involved in the assessment, did the assessor make relevant arrangements before the commencement of the assessment?		
DELIVERY		
Did the assessor remain unobtrusive, neither helping nor hindering the process?		
Were the standards interpreted correctly?		
Was questioning used? If so, were the questions designed to test knowledge without leading the candidate?		
Did the methods chosen seem the most appropriate for the assessment?		
GIVING FEEDBACK		
Was the feedback provided in a timely manner?		
Was the feedback given in a setting appropriate to candidate confidentiality?		
Did the feedback include a clear statement about the outcome of the assessment?		
Was the feedback constructive?		

RECORD KEEPING		
Were the appropriate documents completed to record the assessment?		

An observation of the assessor can be supplemented by asking candidate's some questions. This will either provide an alternative sampling strategy or complement and/or confirm an existing one. An example of a candidate interview form might look like this:

Candidate	IQA:
	Date:
Question	Comment:
How are you involved in the planning of assessments? In what way?	
Do you require any special arrangements when you are assessed? Are these provided?	
Are you given the opportunity to present evidence in different ways, for example, electronically?	
Are you aware of the procedure if you wish to appeal against an assessment decision?	
Is the feedback you are given after an assessment helpful and supportive? Does it provide you with ideas for improving your practice?	
Are you on target to achieve? How do you know?	

A verification strategy, common in written assignment types of assessment is that of verifying the assignment brief before launching to candidates. In this process, the assessors will write the assignment (probably consisting of a number of tasks which collectively evidence the assessment criteria) and submit it to the QA team. In Edexcel programmes this may be the lead internal verifier (LIV). Their role is to check the content of the brief to ensure that it is fit for purpose.

Assessor:	IQA:	
Proposed launch date: Proposed hand-in date:	IQA date:	
Qualification:	Unit/Module:	
QA Check	Yes/No/In part	Comments
Validity		
Do the tasks relate to the assessment criteria of the unit/module?		
Are the tasks at the appropriate level?		
Is the language of the brief relevant to the target group?		
Does the brief offer a fair and equitable opportunity for all candidates to complete the tasks?		
Does any aspect of the task risk contravention of any legislative requirement or moral value?		
Does any aspect of the tasks require additional risk assessments to be undertaken?		
Authenticity		
Does the brief require the candidate to declare that it is their own work?		
Does any part of the assignment require the candidate to reference their citations?		
Currency		
Do the tasks mirror current industry or commercial practice?		
Does the brief require candidates to date their work?		

Sufficiency		
Do the specified tasks cover the content of all assessment criteria in the unit/module?		
Do the specified tasks cover any range requirements? e.g. four types of ...		
Does the brief include reference to functional skills?		
Other		
Is the brief fit for purpose?		
Has the brief been verified prior to issue to candidates?		
Feedback to the assessor		
Areas of good practice: Areas for future improvement: Are any actions required PRIOR to issuing to candidates? Signed: Date:		
I confirm that this brief meets the rules of assessment and organisational policy and that it can be issued to candidates. Signed: Date:		

E-assessment

In Chapter 2 Planning and delivering assessments you looked at the benefits and types of e-assessment tools. This method of storing and collecting evidence provides different challenges in verification and moderation. Quality Assurance systems will need to reflect the method of retrieving and collecting evidence. As well as subject expertise, IQA staff will need to have IT skills and security permissions to access the information, even though the ethos of QA remains the same – checking the validity, authenticity, currency and sufficiency of evidence. Many software programs have systems in-built which record verification activity. In e-assessment, confirming authenticity poses the biggest test, as both the assessor and the QA team need to be confident that the evidence presented is a true demonstration of a candidate's ability. The use of e-signatures needs care to ensure evidence is signed off by the correct person. Authenticity checks can be strengthened through the use of security levels and passwords to limit access to only those with permission to use the software. Additional conversations with assessors, witnesses and candidates as part of the QA process should be carried out to confirm competence and actions recorded in the e-portfolio.

For example:

- Ask candidates questions about the observations and knowledge recorded as achieved to verify competence.
- Ask assessors to confirm visits to candidates and check against assessment dates.
- Ask witnesses what types of statements they have made recently about their candidate's achievements in the workplace.

Watch point

Are you absolutely sure that the evidence is attributed to the candidate? How do you know?

Checking the quality assurance

Lets us now consider what QA staff need to judge when verifying or moderating evidence.

Validity	Is the evidence referenced and linked to the units of assessment? Is the evidence collected appropriate to the qualification? Who has made the assessment decisions – qualified, experienced assessors or others, e.g. expert or non-expert witnesses?
Authenticity	Is there evidence to confirm that it is the candidates own work? Is the evidence signed?

	Do the signatures match the signatures in the 'sample signature' file? Is the assessor competent to make the decision? Is the evidence plagiarised? Have any quotations been accurately referenced using a system like Harvard referencing?
Currency	Has the evidence been collected after the date of registration with the awarding organisation? Has the evidence been collected during the period of enrolment with the training provider? Is the evidence dated? Does the evidence reflect current industry or commercial standards? If RPL is used as an assessment method, then is it recent practice, i.e. derived within the past 12 months (or in line with the assessment strategy)?
Sufficiency	Is there enough evidence to cover the content of the UoA? Is there enough evidence to cover the range of evidence requirements specified in the assessment guidance? Does the evidence provide proof of competence over a period of time?
Reliability	Is the practice consistent across all assessors and locations? Are assessment records accurate and complete? Is evidence stored securely?
Fairness and equity	Do the chosen assessment methods enable access by all candidates regardless of gender, age, ethnic background, disability, marital status, sexual orientation, etc.? Do assessors consider shift patterns and seasonal factors, etc., when assessing evidence?

Acting on and identifying improvements

A vital part of the QA process is concerned with creating opportunities for improvement. There are various stages within the QA process which seem to provide such situations.

Induction is the first opportunity to establish how experienced or confident an assessor is in their duties. It is at this point that certificates will be confirmed. When a new assessor (or IQA) is appointed, their original certificates will be required to be seen by the AO. Generally, this occurs at the first visit where the EQA will view originals and sign copies of the certificates for the centre to keep in its management files. Sample signatures will be taken and stored and appropriate passwords issued to retrieve electronically stored information.

When collecting signatures, it might be pertinent to collect not only the full signature used to sign off assessment, but if the assessor uses initials to sign evidence, then that symbol should also be taken.

At commencement of assessment activity, the assessor should also be given access to information, documentation and records relating to assessment, organisational policy, candidates and employers or training and assessment venues. Ideally this is either stored electronically with an explanation of how it can be accessed or as part of a pack of materials. This information should clearly describe who will be assessed, against what standards, when and where they will be

INDUCTION CHECKLIST			
	Y/N		Y/N
CV		Username and password issued	
Signature – full and initials		Specifications issued	
Original certificates (to be presented at visit on .. /.. /....)		Assessment documentation issued	
Photocopied certificates		QA documentation discussed	
Schedule of standardisation events and meetings issued		Candidates allocated	
Candidate records issued		Assessment sites identified	
Training record established		Mentor/IQA allocated	

assessed, guidance on how those assessments are conducted and all relevant processes. The IQA appointed should take the opportunity to conduct an initial assessment and training needs analysis to establish a solid foundation for the new assessor.

At standardisation and moderation meetings there will be opportunities to review what decisions the assessment team is making. Where there is inconsistency or a lack of compliance, then the IQA will be able to target training and development to those individuals and teams requiring such support.

Ongoing throughout the working life as an assessor, the assessor should update their own personal, professional and vocational practices. This is widely known as CPD. Assessors, who belong to the Institute for Learning (IfL), are required to complete up to 30 hours of CPD per year.

The Institute for Verifiers and Assessors (IVA) is another professional body that uses member subscriptions to organise CPD opportunities.

What constitutes CPD?

Awarding Organisation require assessors and QA staff to engage in CPD activities. Some will specify how many hours per year are required to demonstrate up-to-date practice. CPD activities include:

- development of functional skills – e.g. literacy, mathematics, ICT
- development of personal skills – e.g. time management, problem solving
- development of professional skills – e.g. assessment specific updating
- development of vocational skills – e.g. industry or commercial updating
- development of study skills – e.g. note taking, researching
- development of training skills – e.g. differentiating, planning, e-learning
- development of legislative changes – e.g. copyright, health/safety, equality
- development of support skills – e.g. special educational needs, learner support
- development of skills to embed functional skills into sessions
- awareness of imminent changes in policy or practice
- awareness of new management information systems
- awareness of organisational processes and procedures.

Feedback following quality assurance

One of the most valuable tools to inform improvements is feedback. We read in Chapters 1 The principles of assessment: functions and concepts and Chapter 2 Planning and delivering assessments about the importance of feedback in terms of moving a candidate forward. Assessors are no different. They require feedback to develop and hone their skills. They also need to know when they are doing a good job and can share their good practice.

Feedback to assessors should use the constructive feedback model. These are the aspects of the job that you do well, the areas to improve upon and the suggestions offered to make those improvements. As with many processes, the quality assurer needs to re-visit the feedback and actions to 'close' the action once it has been achieved, i.e. close the loop.

Below are two examples of forms to record QA activity and provide feedback to the assessor. These are important as they both confirm accuracy in assessment and indentify development needs.

Basic QA feedback sheet – Individual feedback

Assessor			
Candidate			
Describe the QA sample:			
Unit/module			
Assessment methods used:			
Location/site of assessment			
Records reviewed			
Did the sample meet the rules of evidence, was it:			
Valid?	Authentic?	Current?	Sufficient?
Feedback to assessor Was the assessment decision agreed?			
Further actions identified To be completed by (date and by whom)			
Actions completed. Checked by:		Date completed:	

In this simple form, the IQA is required to check that the assessment decisions are accurate. It also leads the IQA to ensure that there is enough evidence across the range and scope of provision to make a judgement about the confidence in this assessor's decisions. The feedback here is aimed at assessors not candidates so it should be written to reflect the actions an assessor must undertake, either to improve this particular assessment, or their future practice. It should be clear, factual and honest, with constructive and helpful comments. It should identify the strengths and weaknesses of the assessment practice, stating what needs to change and if relevant, identify strategic improvements, i.e. those required over the longer term.

Basic QA feedback sheet – Multiple feedback

In assignment based work there is a tendency to undertake internal quality assurance on a unit and to gather a number of candidate's work to make the QA decisions. An example is shown overleaf.

In this basic form, the IQA would look at a number of samples from submitted work. While each would be checked against the rules of assessment, the **summative feedback** to the assessor would address the whole of the sample. At the planning stage you would ensure that different candidates' work is looked at over the total number of units or modules in the qualification, thus ensuring every candidate, every unit and every assessor is reviewed.

Reflection

Assessors and QA staff are encouraged to be reflective practitioners. At regular points in the assessment and quality cycles it is useful to sit back and review what has transpired.

The cycle of QA is now complete. At this point the process would start again with improved practices in assessment. A revised sampling strategy would be planned to check that the issues identified had been implemented and that there was a discernible impact, namely more rigorous assessment. This would again be checked and further improvements identified and implemented.

<table>
<tr><td>Assessor</td><td colspan="5"></td></tr>
<tr><td>Candidate</td><td colspan="5"></td></tr>
<tr><td colspan="6">Describe the QA sample:
candidate work on final submission of assignment</td></tr>
<tr><td>Unit/
module</td><td colspan="5"></td></tr>
<tr><td colspan="6">Did the sample meet the rules of evidence, was it:</td></tr>
<tr><td></td><td>Valid?</td><td>Authentic?</td><td>Current?</td><td>Sufficient?</td><td>Decision agreed</td></tr>
<tr><td>A</td><td></td><td></td><td></td><td></td><td></td></tr>
<tr><td>B</td><td></td><td></td><td></td><td></td><td></td></tr>
<tr><td>C</td><td></td><td></td><td></td><td></td><td></td></tr>
<tr><td>D</td><td></td><td></td><td></td><td></td><td></td></tr>
<tr><td>E</td><td></td><td></td><td></td><td></td><td></td></tr>
<tr><td colspan="6">Feedback to assessor</td></tr>
<tr><td colspan="6">Further actions identified

To be completed by (date and by whom)</td></tr>
<tr><td colspan="6">Actions completed.

Checked by: Date completed:</td></tr>
</table>

ACTIVITY 3

Make a list of three things that have gone particularly well, and three things that have given rise to most concern.

1. ☺
2. ☺
3. ☺

1. ☹
2. ☹
3. ☹

Why do you think the good things went well and what are the circumstances surrounding the not so good bits?

Glossary of terms

Authentic being the learner's own work

CAMERA acronym for a suggested sampling strategy

Currency reflects current or recent work practices

Equality a state of fair treatment that is the right of all the people regardless of the differences in, for example, culture, ability, gender, race, religion, wealth, sexual orientation, or any other group characteristic

Evidence the output of an assessment activity; evidence of a learner's knowledge understanding, skills or competence that can be used to make a judgement of their achievement against agreed standards/criteria

Fair ensuring that everyone has an equal chance of getting an objective and accurate assessment

Formative feedback on-going feedback to support development

Horizontal sampling sampling across all units in the programme

Interim QA quality assurance within the programme designed to support and develop practice

Learner the person being assessed by the candidate assessor

PICA acronym for components of the quality cycle; plan, implement, check, action

Reliable consistently achieves the same results with different assessors and the same (or similar) group of learners

Requirements these could be the requirements of the practitioners own organisation or those of an external organisation such as awarding organisation

SSC Sector Skills Council (part of UK Commission for Employment and Skills)

Sufficient enough evidence as specified in evidence requirements or assessment strategy

Summative feedback feedback at the end of the unit or programme in which the final judgement is made

Summative QA quality assurance at the end of the unit or programme

Themed sampling sampling focused on a specific aspect of assessment

Valid relevant to the standards/criteria against which the candidate is being assessed

Vertical sampling sampling of a single units across all assessors

Recommended reading

City and Guilds (2011) *Level 3 and 4 Awards & Certificates in Assessment and Quality Assurance: qualification handbook for centres*. February 2011

Collins, D (2006) *A survival guide for college managers and leaders*. London: Continuum

Hill, C (2003) *Teaching using Information and Learning Technology in Further Education*. Exeter: Learning Matters

Hoyle, D (2007) *Quality Management Essentials*. Oxford: Heinemann (Elsevier)

Sector Skills Councils: UK Commission for Employments and Skills –

Whalley, J, Welch, T and Williamson, L (2006) *E-Learning in FE*. London: Continuum

Wilson, L (2008) *Practical Teaching: a guide to PTLLS and CTLLS*. London: Cengage Learning

Wilson, L (2009) *Practical Teaching: a guide to PTLLS and DTLLS*. Andover: Cengage Learning

Wolf, A (2011) *Review of Vocational Education – The Wolf Report*. March 2011

Wood, J and Dickinson, J (2011) *Quality Assurance and Evaluation*. Exeter: Learning Matters

Useful online resources

Useful references for further reading about assessment are:

http://www.ukces.org.uk/

https://www.education.gov.uk/publications/standard/publicationDetail/Page1/DFE-00031-2011 (accessed May 2011)

SUMMARY

In this chapter we set out to:

- Describe the importance and key attributes of planning processes in assuring quality.
- Summarise the main sampling strategies.
- Identify activities which contribute to QA procedures.
- Outline the role feedback has in developing assessment practice.
- Reflect on current practice and plan to develop skills and knowledge.

Your personal development

- You have commenced learning in this chapter by revising assessment practices, originally discussed in Chapter 1 The principles of assessment: functions and concepts and Chapter 2 Planning and delivering assessments. The new information was introduced through 'The Quality Cycle' using the acronym PICA, which stands for plan, implement, check and act.
- In the first section, you studied the importance of the UK Commission for Employment and Skills' role in licensing Sector Skills Councils who set the benchmarks and requirements of QA – both internal to the training organisation and external to it. You may also need to review the importance of legislation and the role of Ofqual to further your understanding.
- You explored the use of CAMERA as a means of establishing a sampling strategy and reviewed each aspect of the expression to consider how each could be sampled.
- You thought about the processes which impact on planning effective internal quality assurance, namely assessor experience, countersigning assessments, communication, and standardisation and then you scrutinised some suggested planning documents. Please note that you should

always default to your organisation's agreed documentation, the ones displayed here are only ideas.

- When devising plans, you compared and contrasted the merits of horizontal, vertical and themed strategies of sampling. Hopefully, you have concluded that each has a number of values and that over a period of time all methods should be included to establish a broad range of sampling.
- You then moved on to looking at implementing an internal quality assurance strategy. This section generally reinforced the activities in the planning section earlier, but extended your knowledge by considering the impact of observing the assessors assessing and questioning candidates about the assessment process. Also in this section, you explored the importance of quality assuring assignments briefs before they were issued to candidates to ensure that they were decreed fit for purpose.
- You then had an opportunity to reflect on the specific challenges facing the internal quality assurance team when verifying or moderating e-assessment activity – especially in relation to confirming authenticity.
- The chapter progressed and caused you to focus on the rules of assessment and what actions the internal quality assurance team need to carry out to check that they have been applied consistently and in line with organisational policy and procedures.
- In the final component of this chapter, you evaluated what all of this meant and what the next stage was. You looked at how internal quality assurance is a means to improvement, but equally so are an effective induction, regular standardisation events, constructive feedback mechanisms and the emergent CPD.
- All of the processes together form the quality cycle – a continuous strategy to promote improvement.

In the next chapter we will look at the management of quality assurance in an organisation.

CHAPTER 5

Managing the quality assurance process

Unit of Assessment	Assessment Criteria
Understanding the principles and practices of assessment	No direct links although theory underpins the management of the assessment process
Assess occupational competence in the work environment	No direct links although theory underpins the management of the assessment process
Assess vocational skills, knowledge and understanding	No direct links although theory underpins the management of the assessment process
Understanding the principles and practices of internally assuring the quality of assessment	No direct links although theory underpins the management of the quality assurance process
Internally assure the quality of assessment	No direct links although theory underpins the management of the quality assurance process
Plan, allocate and monitor work in own area of responsibility	1.1; 1.2; 1.3; 1.4; 2.1; 2.2 3.1; 3.2; 4.1; 4.2

LEARNING OUTCOMES

By the end of this chapter you will be able to:

- Describe the processes involved in managing the quality assurance of assessment
- Plan for quality assurance management
- Identify the resources required in quality assurance
- Implement and monitor quality assurance in own area
- Organise an external quality assurance activity
- Manage and implement improvements

The management of quality assurance

This chapter is concerned with managing the assessment and QA processes. The chapter will cover aspects in relation to planning, monitoring, improving and providing an impact on actions. The concepts and principles referred to are those previously described in earlier chapters.

O'Connell (2005: 182) describes the management of quality assurance as:

> *'Putting systems in place to ensure that high standards are achieved: as little as possible is left to chance in ensuring "right first time".'*

He states that by being proactive in the approach to QA there will be a more productive outcome than relying on a reactive approach, i.e. discovering problems and putting actions into place to resolve them.

Cole and Kelly (2011: 332) maintain that quality management is both proactive and reactive. They agree that:

> *'Written procedures, instructions, forms or records help to ensure that everyone is not just "doing his or her own thing" and that the organisation goes about its business in a structured way.'*

Effective QA, therefore, starts with procedures and systems to describe the correct way. The manager of the QA process will, therefore, be responsible for ensuring compliance.

Typical procedures seen in the assessment and QA process are:

- assessment policy and procedure
- assessment malpractice procedure
- assessment appeals procedure
- internal QA policy and procedure
- internal QA strategy
- enrolment and registration procedures
- information, advice and guidance policy
- support for learners policy and procedures
- management Information procedures
- equality policy and procedures
- health and safety policy and procedures
- safeguarding policy and procedures.

The management of quality assurance practices

In the context of assessment and QA, this is the tier of the QA process that monitors or manages a particular area of provision or a particular qualification. Those responsible for the management of assessment and QA may be called programme managers or coordinators, IVCs or LIVs. The role may or may not be part of the organisation's (centre's) management structure. In this instance 'management' is perceived as a function as well as a role. For the purpose of clarity, in this chapter people managing the assessment and QA processes will be referred to as lead quality assurers (LQAs). Figure 5.1 attempts to represent a typical organisational structure for an assessment and QA team.

Figure 5.1 Organisational chart for quality assurance process

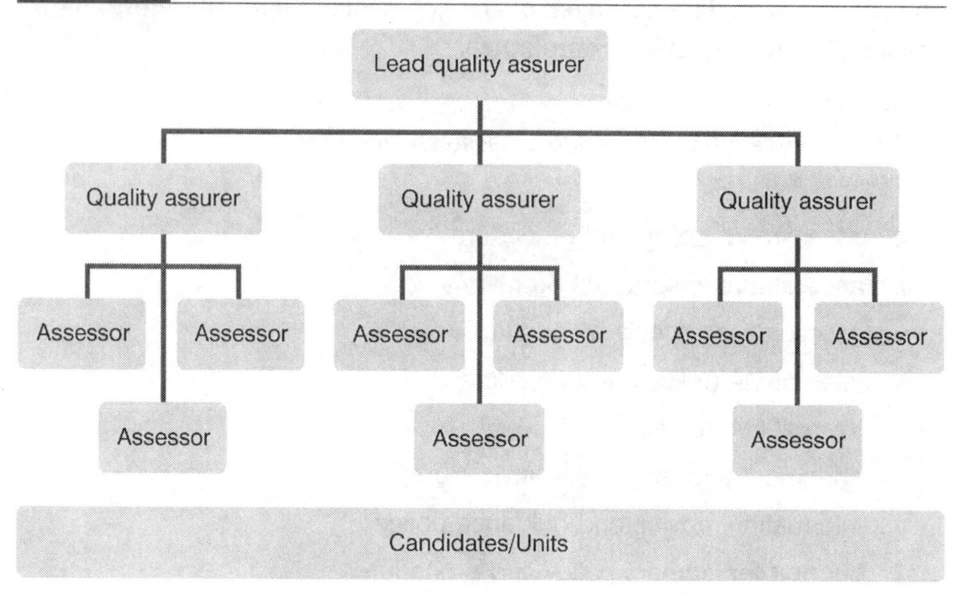

In essence, the LQA is likely to coordinate a number of internal quality assurers (IQAs) each of whom will be working with a number of assessors. Their role is to standardise, communicate, disseminate and monitor QA practice within their area of coordination. The holder of the role may not necessarily be a subject expert, but will have supervisory or management experience, probably within the broad subject sector area. The structure may be arranged so that assessors are responsible for a number of candidates, each completing a full qualification, or, alternatively, assessors may be responsible for specific units which collectively form a qualification. Quality assurance staff will be appointed to oversee the work of a number of assessors, or specific levels or qualifications. As there is no 'right way', each centre should arrange the structure of its QAs to suit its needs and methods of delivery. The important aspect is that it is clearly described and justified and then agreed with the AOs.

Some AOs are modifying their QA processes to devolve more of the responsibility of compliance and summary sampling to their approved centres. Edexcel introduced the role of LIV in September 2010 to coincide with the launch of the new QCF qualifications. Edexcel, the AO, then samples activity within the centre at a management level and a few qualifications rather than in every subject/qualification area.

As this role is quite obviously a managerial or supervisory role the occupational standards and learning outcomes for this part of the assessor and quality assurance qualifications are taken from the leadership and management standards. These are:

Plan, allocate and monitor work in own area of responsibility:	
1. Be able to produce a work plan for own area of responsibility.	1.1 Explain the context in which work is to be undertaken. 1.2 Identify the skills base and the resources available. 1.3 Examine priorities and success criteria needed for the team. 1.4 Produce a work plan for own area of responsibility.
2. Be able to allocate and agree responsibilities with team members.	2.1 Identify team members' responsibilities for identified work activities. 2.2 Agree responsibilities and SMART (specific, measurable, achievable, realistic and time-bound) objectives with team members.
3. Be able to monitor the progress and quality of work in own area of responsibility and provide feedback.	3.1 Identify ways to monitor progress and quality of work. 3.2 Monitor and evaluate progress against agreed standards and provide feedback to team members.
4. Be able to review and amend plans of work for own area of responsibility and communicate changes.	4.1 Review and amend work plan where changes are needed. 4.2 Communicate changes to team members.

The LQA has a responsibility to manage and oversee the QA and assessment processes by:

- Defining the roles and responsibilities of the team.
- Preparing and implementing the assessment strategy in line with their organisation's assessment policy and procedure.
- Preparing and implementing the QA strategy in line with their organisation's QA policy and procedure.
- Ensuring assessment and QA practice is fit for purpose.
- Creating opportunities to quality assure all aspects of the learner journey.
- Planning QA throughout the assessment process.
- Observing assessment and QA practice.
- Providing support to assessors and QA teams and monitoring CPD activity.
- Implementing standardisation activities to ensure consistency in assessment.
- Ensuring learning and assessment practices meet trainee's needs and aspirations.
- Ensuring learning, assessment and QA practices meet the requirements of the NOS.
- Ensuring learning, assessment and QA practices comply with the SSC's and AO's assessment strategy.
- Communicating effectively with all relevant people.
- Monitoring that all of the above happens in a timely manner and is recorded and reported in line with their organisation's policy.

In order to achieve this, the LQA must have a good grasp of the principles of assessment and QA as well as the skill of management. Aspects of assessment can be found in Chapter 1 and Chapter 2; aspects of QA can be found in Chapter 3 and Chapter 4.

Assessment	Quality assurance	Management
Roles/responsibility Criterion based assessment Formative assessment Summative assessment Principles of assessment (consistent, accessible, detailed, earned and transparent) Rules of assessment (valid, authentic, current, sufficient, reliable) Assessment language Qualification structure Assessment cycle Legislative requirements Equality and diversity Ethics Disputes and appeals Recording keeping E-technology Assessment methods Questioning skills Feedback skills	Roles/responsibility Regulatory requirements Legislative requirements Models of QA Centre approval Candidate registration and certification Record keeping Sampling strategies Standardisation Inducting and supporting assessors CPD Sanctions Disputes and appeals Charter marks Quality cycle	Communication Decision-making Delegation Data management Financial management Leadership Problem solving Target setting Conflict management Planning Motivation and feedback

Resourcing quality assurance

When an organisation commits to delivering a qualification – i.e. becoming an approved centre – it does so by assuring the AO that it has both the physical and human resources required to deliver the qualification with integrity. The role of the LQA is to ensure that this is upheld.

Physical resources covers:

- Traditional resources – teaching and learning materials, access to placements/work, accommodation, paper based resources.
- E-technologies – computer hardware, internet, log-ins, specialist software.

ACTIVITY 1

Using the NOS for your area of work, review the standards to list the resources that are needed to implement training, assessment and QA procedures.

Divide your list into learning/assessment, technological and specialist equipment.

Carry out an audit of your work area – including placements – and prepare a report to confirm suitability of resources including a rationale for any additional requirements.

- Additional support – computerised adaptations, e.g. voice recognition software.
- Specialist equipment – technical machinery, software, equipment to support the learning and assessment of all units of assessment within the qualification.

Human resources covers:

- Qualifications – sufficient qualified assessors and QA staff to meet the learners' needs and availability.
- Experience and skills – assessors and QA staff who meet the role specifications. (See Chapter 1 The principles of assessment: functions and concepts and Chapter 3 Quality assurance of assessment.)

The LQA is responsible for maintaining assessor and QA practitioner profiles and keeping accurate records of the team's CPD.

Each member of staff in the team should complete a profile document to keep in the management file (see Documenting and recording quality assurance management below). This provides an overview of the team and should be updated annually. Staff who are 'working towards' qualifications should be included as the LQA will need to make additional arrangements to support countersigning requirements. For best practice, a similar document should be included in the candidate's portfolio to include people who are signing evidence in their portfolios.

Name	Role	Technical qualification	Professional qualification	Sample signature
	This might be trainer, assessor or QA or combination of all.	List the highest level qualification held relating to the qualification delivered. Inc. Awarding Organisation and year of achievement.	Include training, teaching and assessment or QA qualifications. These should be commensurate with role.	Include a full signature and the mark or initials used on evidence.
For example:				
Joe Bloggs	Trainer & assessor	HND in xxyy (BTEC, 2002) GCSE English (AQA, 1996)	L4 CTLLS (C&G, 2010) A1 (C&G, 2008)	Joe Bloggs JB

Each member of the assessment or QA team should submit an up-to-date CV, their CPD plan, a list of CPD attended during the last 12 months and copies of certificates held. At an External Quality Assurance (EQA) visit, the AO's representative will want to see original certificates; they will then sign the centre's file to confirm 'original seen'. Once validated, the QA will only wish to see updated and recently acquired certificates.

Watch point

A note about certificates:

- Certificates issued by an AO represent nationally recognised qualifications. Assessors are usually required to be qualified to level three in their subject, but experience is also valid – if proven.
- Certificates issued by employers represent in-house qualifications relating to specific methods of working. They may not be transferable.
- Quality assurers will need to make a judgement about the importance of any certification in relation to age, validity and relevance to the target qualification or NOS.

- Attendance certificates mean just that; the owner attended the event – it does not mean they listened, learned or were even awake!

The CPD plan should be linked to the comments and actions reported during QA sampling as well as other generic personal, professional and technical updates identified. An example would be:

CONTINUOUS PROFESSIONAL DEVELOPMENT PLAN COVERING THE PERIOD FROM: 2012–2013 Extract from entries:				
Planned CPD activity and date identified	Aims and desired outcomes of activity	Suggested methods to achieve the planned outcomes	Target date for completion	Actions
Performance Development Review: September 2012 Diversity Awareness	To identify key legislation and implications. To raise awareness of impact in lessons. To modify handouts to ensure all are inclusive.	Online diversity package on the Intranet	August 2013	Enrol for programme. To find out how to enrol check with Personnel. Check date of next inset day.
Peer observation Any identified actions	To improve the quality of assessment practice.	Mentor support LQA Advice Standardisation meetings	July 2013	Check with manager before embarking on activities requiring funding.
TARGET CPD HOURS: 30	IfL Membership No: AA123456 Organisation: A N Other Training			
Name: Joe Bloggs I agree to support the Continuous Professional Development plans identified above. Manager's signature: Ima Boss Date: September 2012				

CONTINUOUS PROFESSIONAL DEVELOPMENT RECORD

COVERING THE PERIOD FROM: 2012–2013

Extract from entries:

Date of event/hours	Nature of event	Why?	What did I learn from this?	How the organisation, teams and I have benefited
27/10/12 7 hours CPD	Diversity Awareness Training Internal online programme of study	Identified in my PDR. This is becoming high profile and all staff are required to attend.	What diversity means, what constitutes discrimination and how it impacts on teachers.	I have been more conscious when devising assessment plans to check for discriminating practices. I will now challenge unacceptable behaviours more confidently; my planning seeks to include a wider variety of experiences. In team meetings we discuss how to create more diversity in the curriculum.
08/02/13 3 hours CPD	Standardisation meeting Research activity	My LQA suggested that my assessment practice could be developed.	Using the internet I found a lot of information about assessment mostly to do with setting clear feedback and future goals.	I ensure that I give each candidate the opportunity to check/identify what evidence they wish or need to present to meet the criteria. At the end of the assessment I set SMART targets for improvement and future actions, which means I can measure their achievement against standards.
TOTAL No CPD HOURS 10 hours	IfL Membership No: AA123456 Organisation: A N Other Training			

Name: Joe Bloggs

This document is agreed to be a true record of Continuous Professional Development undertaken.

Manager's signature: Ima Boss Date: February 2013

CPD records can be stored in a portfolio type of system, either paper based or electronically. A CPD record should be reviewed annually by a manager or colleague to offer peer support and guidance.

The Institute for Learning (IfL), although the professional body for teachers, is also open to membership from assessors. Members of the IfL have access to RE*f*LECT©, which is an electronic recording system, to plan, record and reflect on CPD opportunities (www.ifl.ac.uk).

Documenting and recording quality assurance management

As established at the start of this chapter, managing the assessment and QA processes is largely a matter of ensuring everyone complies with the procedures laid down by the organisation and when those procedures are compromised, errors will inevitably occur. In this section we look at the documentation that is required to:

- record the outcomes of assessment
- record QA activity

- record compliance to procedure
- record LQA activity.

In the earlier chapters, you will find a number of documents relating to assessment and QA, including:

Assessment

- initial assessment records
- candidate induction record
- assessment plan
- record of observation
- records of oral questions
- written question sheets
- assignment cover sheets
- declaration of authenticity
- feedback to candidates
- candidate achievement tracking sheets
- witness signature sheet
- records of witness testimony

Internal quality assurance

- assessor induction record
- sampling plans
- observation of assessment records
- candidate interview records
- validation of assignment brief
- feedback to assessors
- outcome of sampling records
- standardisation meeting minutes
- appeals and disputes record

Lead quality assurance

- staff profiles

- qualification management information:
  - specifications
  - candidate listings – registrations
  - team structure
  - records of certifications
  - EQA details
  - EQA report and action plan
  - quality improvement plan
  - minutes of meetings
  - copies of QA records
- QA summary.

Records of assessment and QA are auditable documents. An approved centre is required to keep them for at least three years following accreditation. The documents relating to registration, progress monitoring (tracking) and certification should be kept for three years; documents relating to candidate assessment (e.g. candidate work) and QA processes should be retained until the next EQA activity.

Even if a centre is classified as 'direct claims status' it still has to retain portfolios and records for the next EQA monitoring. This offers a challenge for centres:

- Do you return portfolios to candidates and recall them if required for sampling?
- Do you retain everything until the EQA process is complete?

By returning work to candidates, and after all it is their work (!), you alleviate storage problems. Candidates can use their portfolio evidence to secure future learning or employment opportunities. However, if they leave the area or fail to return them, how will your EQA be able to sample evidence?

If you retain the portfolios, even after certification but until the EQA monitoring, where will you keep them?

Possible solutions to resolve this would be:

- Wherever possible scan documentation and store in electronic portfolios. However, many candidates still use paper-based storage for their evidence, in which case ...

- When returning paper portfolios, state that they should be kept intact for at least 12 months in case requested for sampling. However, candidates may move or just not realise the importance of the request, so, try the reverse. Retain the work but provide a testimonial for candidates to use offering a reference pending return of their work – and buy a large, secure cupboard!

An ideal solution would be to keep in regular contact with your EQA. External quality assurers are usually practitioners so will understand the dilemma. As each candidate cohort completes, let the EQA have the sampling information:

- name
- date of birth
- registration number
- start date
- assessment site
- assessor name
- IQA name, if sampled
- completion date.

Ask them to indicate which units or portfolios should be retained and which can be returned. This eliminates the recall issue and minimises the storage requirements. High volume centres may be entitled to more frequent 'desk-based' sampling to keep things moving along. The key to this is communication and building up a relationship with your EQA to ensure business efficiency is suited to centre requirements.

What you need to keep

Forms to summarise verification activity across the qualification/period. This is best kept as a spreadsheet which will enable better searching and filtering of information, but the headings should be as shown on the next page.

This chart collects information, which an EQA or LQA can used to prepare sampling at a management level.

A. N. Other Training Co

Qualification title:

Cohort/group: Start date: End date:

Candidate name	Date of birth	Centre enrolment date	Awarding organisation registration number	Awarding organisation registration date	Assessor name	Assessment site/workplace	Assessment methods used	IQA name	Date of last sampling (if applicable)	Unit accreditation or complete qualification	Completion date	Date certificate claimed (if DCS)

By including in this chart whether or not a unit has been internally quality assured, the EQA or LQA can plan to look at both sampled and unsampled materials – this will be in addition to the usual criteria in a CAMERA style of sampling.

- Candidates
- Assessors
- Methods of assessment
- Evidence or elements
- Records
- Assessment sites

Source: http://www.cityandguilds.com

Lead quality assurers should keep a centre, management or QA file. They all mean the same thing, but you may hear any of these expressions. The file keeps information about the programme, the candidates, the staff and process documentation in one place. This may be electronic or paper-based, but needs to be accessible to the team and AO staff. Contents might include:

- list of candidates
- candidate/assessor allocations
- details of work placements and/or employers (location, insurances, contacts)
- risk assessments
- copies of specifications – or links to where they are stored
- centre organisation chart and reporting lines
- list the team and their role within the team
- staff CVs, qualifications, CPD records and sample signatures
- minutes of meetings
- standardisation records
- QA strategy and plans (including justification of sampling ratios)
- verification and moderation records
- EQA contact details and copies of communications
- recent EQA reports and action plans.

Making improvements

An effective QA process which is systematically and consistently applied should result in few errors. Where errors do occur, the LQA needs to decide whether it is a system or procedure fault or a compliance error.

Systems and procedures should be reviewed annually to confirm that they remain fit for purpose. Documents should be checked to ensure that they record the correct issues. Feedback from EQA staff and internal audits will provide an opinion on how effective the process is.

The alternative error of compliance is more about the fault of individuals in following the procedure; you will have to decide if this is due to lack of training or shoddy practices. Each will have a different action to resolve the issue.

How you deal with errors will depend upon the complexity of those errors and the potential negative impact that may result from the error. All errors should result in a clear target to identify the improvement required. SMART target setting is widely considered the appropriate strategy. There are several different words associated with the acronym, but the meaning is clear and the table below explains the concept:

SMART

Specific	Goals that clearly refer to what is expected
Measurable	Goals using verbs and phrases that can be judged
Achievable/ Agreed	Goals that can be succeeded A more powerful expression because it appears contractual
Realistic/ Relevant	Goals that are reasonable, practical and logical Goals that are appropriate and important (Avoid using achievable and realistic because they mean broadly the same thing.)
Time-bound	Goals that express when things must be done by

Many of the improvements within a programme will come from standardising practice and the team striving to make the candidate's experience an efficient and successful process.

Improvements come from assessors and QA staff looking at their current practices and deciding if and how it can be made better.

Problem units/modules Certain criteria in some qualifications cause problems for assessors. This might be in how they are interpreted or in how they might be evidenced. In a standardisation event the team comes together and talks things through. This will lead to a consensus of opinion on how it will be assessed in the future.

Assessment opportunities Assessment methods or procedures are discussed in order to ensure that they are efficient in collecting the correct amount of evidence to cover the evidence requirements specified. This leads to a development and because it is jointly agreed is owned and understood by the team.

However, not all improvement arises from natural development of ideas to promote improved practice. Sometimes through either capability or failure to comply with processes, remedial actions are required to correct errors and bring about improvement.

What might the errors be and how would you action them?

Many of the actions will be around minor issues, for example missing signatures and dates here and there, or documents completed too quickly maybe with some parts incorrectly filled in. These are easily checked and resolved, because they are not fundamental errors. An action plan to the assessor would suffice with a request for a future sample to confirm that the actions have been met. These types of action do not compromise the integrity of the qualification. However, systematic failure to sign and date anything in the candidate's portfolio is a different matter!

In this scenario, SMART Targets might include:

- Check and complete future assessment records to include a signature and date on all pieces of work.
- Identify a set time each week to complete assessment paperwork. Ensure paperwork is completed fully. Submit paperwork for review by the IQA by the end of the month.

At the other end of the scale are assessments which fail to meet the rules of assessment. Look at the following case study examples.

CASE STUDY 1

You identify that old specifications are being used in current assessments. The rules being broken here are VALIDITY and CURRENCY. This compromises the assessment in that the candidate is assessed against standards that are out-of-date and therefore any certificate claimed would be invalid. The annoying part of this scenario is that candidates rely on their assessors to provide them with assessment material and probably do not realise the error. They would do the work asked of them and not realise that there is a problem.

ACTIVITY:

How would you ensure, through QA processes, that the scenario in this example did not occur?

Answer:

When qualifications change, teams should be brought together in briefing and standardisation activities to discuss the changes and develop new assessment materials. Regular standardisation meetings at which all assessors bring examples of assessed work would identify any problems in interpreting standards. Sampling to cover all assessors during the assessment process would also indicate any problems. Sampling should be carried out within the assessment process rather than at the end of it, when an error has more serious consequences. Audit procedures – for example, each assessor to supply pieces of assessed work for review either by peers or an audit team – would further establish the validity of the assessment content.

IQAs should ensure that new assessors or those working remotely have sufficient materials to carry out their roles. This places an importance on induction and the benefit of electronic resources stored on shared servers. If staff are not able to attend standardisation meetings, the IQA should provide additional support.

SMART targets might include:

- Attend the standardisation meeting on 21/09/2012.
- Bring three examples of assessed work to the IQA by next weekend.

CASE STUDY 2

You identify that a significant part of a candidate's work, is 'cut and pasted' from the internet. There is no referencing or statement to say that it is not the candidate's work. The rule being broken here is AUTHENTICITY. This compromises the assessment in that by presenting work that is not their own, an assessor cannot guarantee that the candidate understands the concept or activity that they require an explanation of. If unchallenged both the assessor and the candidate are guilty of cheating or assessment malpractice. The integrity of the qualification and the reputation of the organisation are compromised.

ACTIVITY:

How do you advise your assessors and candidates to reference or cite published information in their work? Is this included in your induction material or candidate information pack?

Answer:

Organise a themed standardisation meeting to look at referencing and assessment malpractice. At the meeting assessors and IQAs should agree the system of referencing to be used – for example Harvard referencing. Develop and distribute a cover sheet (A Declaration of Authenticity) in which the candidate has to declare that 'all the work contained in the assessment/ assignment is my own work and I have acknowledged any sources from published materials'. This should be signed and dated.

A standardisation activity might include an activity in which an unreferenced paragraph is provided and IQAs provide guidance on how to identify whether it is plagiarised or not. There is software available to check work, but the simplest solution is to type the text into an internet search engine. More often than not the plagiarised paragraph appears as the first hit or can be found on an open source website, such as Wikipedia.

Candidate induction should include how to reference published work.

Include in the IQA system a process which requires all bona fide assessors, IQAs, candidates and witnesses to provide a sample signature.

SMART targets might include:

- Complete an induction activity with every new candidate about referencing and the consequences of plagiarism.
- All assessors to countersign the declaration coversheet to confirm that they have checked the authenticity of the candidate's work.

CASE STUDY 3

A candidate has been assessed by observation in their workplace. There is a record of the observation and a record of a few oral questions. All of the documentation is fully completed and the assessor has signed off the unit as complete. However, there is a criterion which is not readily evidenced through natural workplace practice. The rule being potentially broken here is SUFFICIENCY. Rarely do qualifications only require observational evidence. There are usually criteria relating to knowledge and understanding which underpins the practical aspects of the qualification. Unless fully assessed to meet all of the criteria, the assessor is making inaccurate decisions.

ACTIVITY:

How would you use QA practices to ensure that all criteria are assessed correctly? What feedback would you give to the assessor responsible, and what feedback would you give to an IQA if this had gone through a QA process without being identified?

Answer:

Any method of sampling should identify insufficiency of evidence, although in this case vertical sampling would identify it most easily. This is because you will have a number of the same units assessed by different assessors, and will notice different types of evidence being presented. That would alert you to investigating more deeply into why assessors are accepting different types of evidence. Hopefully you would have agreed in a standardisation activity what evidence is typical for particular units, and allowing for minor differences due to different work environments, the evidence base is usually broadly similar. This means that if something is surplus or missing it is quickly noticed. Similarly, units may have a particular criterion that is known to be either problematic in interpretation or in evidencing; consequently you will look at these in detail.

When an assessor reviews evidence, they are checking that the candidate's evidence is sufficient to meet all of the performance and knowledge evidence. In the case above, you would be suspicious in that only performance evidence seems to have been presented and knowing there is a criterion that is not evidenced by observation you would check to see how it has been assessed.

SMART targets might include:

- Arrange to meet the candidate to discuss the issue.
- Resubmit additional evidence in relation to criterion (a) by next week.
- Re-assess the unit and present for QA.

Where issues of weak or poor assessment practice emerge from QA activities, they should always result in an action plan for the assessor. However, some of the issues might be more generic or be concerned with a particular assessor and, therefore, show a lack of consistency. In this case the QA team might want to prepare a Quality Improvement Plan (QIP) for the team. The following example takes the issues in the three case studies above and demonstrates what the QIP might look like.

By preparing a QIP, it provides a mechanism to record issues, note what needs to be done and review frequently to check how well you are progressing. In many organisations this is done quite formally with an independent committee challenging teams on their performance. This has the effect of increasing confidence, promoting responsibility and making people accountable for improvements.

Source	Area for improvement	Success indicator	Actions (SMART)	By whom	By when	Progress
How did you identify it?	Write an evaluative statement about the weakness.	What impact do you expect from the actions?	List what needs to be done to achieve the required impact	Who is responsible for ensuring actions completed?	When must the actions be completed by?	How well are you progressing towards the desired impact
QA activity or EQA activity	Invalid assessment decisions due to wrong specifications being used.	All assessment decisions valid.	Prepare induction pack for assessors to include documents. Arrange six weekly standardisation meetings. Audit all candidate log books for currency. Complete sampling plan to increase % verified.	State who, e.g. LQA.	State dates – do not say 'ongoing.'	Schedule issued to all assessors for present year. Plans updated to increase sampling from 10% to 20%.
QA activity or EQA activity	Poor referencing practice leads to potential assessment malpractice.	All candidate work attributed as authentic.	Update candidate induction material to include guidance on referencing. Arrange themed standardisation activity. Arrange staff dev. in Harvard referencing. Prepare a declaration of authenticity sheet.	State who, e.g. LQA.	State dates – do not say 'ongoing.'	Scheduled into plan. Speaker contacted. Sheet devised – awaiting approval.

Source	Area for improvement	Success indicator	Actions (SMART)	By whom	By when	Progress
QA activity or EQA activity	Inaccurate assessment decisions.	All assessment decisions valid and sufficient to meet specifications.	Modify QA Plan to include vertical sampling. Arrange a standardisation meeting to discuss unit. Allocate additional sampling of named assessor.	State who, e.g. LQA.	State dates – do not say 'ongoing.'	Plan amended. Activity scheduled for next month. Additional QA planned for assessor.

There are many ways of identifying improvement:

- internal quality assurance
- external quality assurance
- audit
- reflection
- self-assessment
- peer review.

Internal and external quality assurance activities are mainly those around standardisation and sampling. An effective IQA process will eliminate potential for poor practice or provide the platform for identifying issues. If issues are discovered by the external QA, it leads the EQA to have less confidence in the approved organisation's ability to lead improvement. This may lead to sanctions on the approved centre.

Audit is a specific activity which looks at aspects of the core business. These may be real or simulated inspections carried out, either by organisations like Ofsted, or consultants or internal teams.

Another method of improvement is to undertake reflective activities, such as self-assessment or peer review. These offer teams the opportunity to be self-critical and identify what needs to happen to improve. The chances are that the same actions would result as those stated on the exemplar QIP above.

However, issues are identified, many of the resultant actions required to make improvements are going to centre on CPD activities. Every assessor and IQA is required – through the SSC's assessment strategy or the approved centre's policies to keep up-to-date and possibly engage in a specified number of hours of training and development. An LQA is, therefore, required to keep records relating to this, as described earlier in the chapter.

Creating an impact

How do you know if what you have done has made any difference? This is a key question. Unless you are able to show an impact on your actions you can't really say if they have improved to the benefit of the candidates or organisation.

In order to ascertain the impact you will need to either:

- use data to show the improvement, or
- seek the views of candidates and assessment teams.

Impact is only relevant if it demonstrates an improvement on the learner experience, financial efficiencies, staff morale. For example: you have worked hard to get all of your documentation into a corporate format; it looks really good and professional. So what? How does this affect candidate achievement? Does it mean you have a healthier recruitment? Unfortunately, this is one valuable improvement that has little impact other than aesthetic. It does not mean that it didn't need to be done; just that it doesn't easily show an impact.

Using and interpreting data and information to demonstrate impact

Organisations, particularly those using public funds, are measured on their success. The data does help in other aspects though, for example it can lead you to required improvements or demonstrate that improvements have had an impact on outcomes.

And now for some numeracy ...

CASE STUDY 4

	Unit Number										
	1	2	3	4	5	6	7	8	9	10	completed
	Assessor: Joe QA: Mary				Assessor: Simon QA: Joe		Assessor: Mary QA: Simon				
Ann	✔	✔	✔	✔	✔	✔	✔	✔	✔	✔	y
Briar	✔	✔				✔	✔				withdrawn
Carrie	✔		✔					✔	✔		
Dena	✔			✔						✔	
Edward	✔	✔	✔	✔	✔	✔	✔	✔	✔	✔	y
Fiona	✔	✔	✔	✔	✔	✔	✔	✔	✔	✔	y
George				✔	✔	✔	✔	✔			
Henry	✔	✔	✔	✔	✔	✔	✔	✔	✔	✔	y
Ingrid	✔	✔	✔	✔	✔	✔	✔	✔	✔	✔	y
Jumar	✔	✔	✔	✔	✔	✔	✔	✔	✔	✔	y
Khalid	✔		✔					✔			
Lucy	✔		✔								withdrawn
Mohamed	✔	✔	✔	✔	✔	✔	✔	✔	✔	✔	y
Norman	✔	✔	✔	✔	✔	✔	✔	✔	✔	✔	y
Oscar	✔	✔	✔	✔	✔	✔	✔	✔	✔	✔	y

✔ = completed units (shaded squares indicate sampled units)

This table can tell us several things:

- how far the candidates have progressed
- the retention percentage
- an achievement rate
- overall success
- the percentage of samplings.

Candidate information

There are 15 candidates in this cohort of the qualification. The qualification consists of 10 units. Nine candidates have completed all 10 units. Two have unfortunately withdrawn from the programme leaving four who have yet to complete.

To calculate the unit progress to date:

To calculate the units achieved as a percentage of the whole the formula is:

$$\text{Number completed} \div \text{total units} \times 100$$

For example: when Briar withdrew she had completed 4 of the 10 units

$$4 \div 10 \times 100 = 40\%$$

How near to completion is George?

Answer:

Half way through. George has achieved 5 of his 10 units = 50 per cent

To calculate the retention rate:

Number of candidates at the start − number of candidates leaving = number remaining

Number remaining ÷ number of starters ×100 = retention rate/percentage

For example: 15 candidates started this programme, 2 have now left therefore there are 13 remaining.

$$13 \div 15 \times 100 = 86.6666\% \text{ (87\% to nearest whole number)}$$

Recalculate the retention rate if you find out that Dena no longer wishes to continue

Answer: 80%
(15 - 3 = 12) remaining
(12 ÷ 15) x 100 = 80% retention rate

To calculate the achievement rate:

Achievement is the number of candidates who have achieved the qualification as a percentage of those that remain on the programme.

$$\text{Number completed} \div \text{Number retained} \times 100$$

For example: 9 candidates from the remaining 13 on programme have achieved the qualification.

$$9 \div 13 \times 100 = 69.23\% \text{ (69\% to nearest whole number)}$$

Re-calculate the achievement rate now that Dena has left. What impact does this have on the achievement figure? What conclusions might you draw from this?

Answer: 75%
9 learners have completed, but now only 12 remain on-programme.
9 ÷ 12 = 75%
This has the effect of raising the achievement rate, which initially looks like an improvement.

To calculate success:

Success is the number of candidates who have achieved as a percentage of those that started on the programme.

$$\text{Number completed} \div \text{Number of starters} \times 100$$

For example: 9 candidates from the original 15 starters have now succeeded in achieving their qualification.

$$9 \div 15 \times 100 = 60\%$$

Re-calculate the success rate now that Dena has left. What impact does this have on the success rate? What conclusions might you draw from this?

Answer: No change

However, by Dena withdrawing from the programme there is no chance that she will achieve and therefore the success rate will be lower.

In the original scenario (with 2 leavers) if everyone else achieved the success would be 13 out of 15 = 87%, but Dena leaving means that the maximum success will now be 12 out of 15 = 75%. As many providers and colleges are measured on success, this one learner leaving means a reduction of 12% in the overall success. This is a worrying scenario. By interpreting and predicting this, QA staff can intervene and maybe offer Dena alternative assessment opportunities to ensure her success.

What else does this table tell you?

It tells you what the current percentage of units sampled are against the total required. There are 15 candidates, each with the potential of completing 10 units. This means that there are 150 sampling opportunities. To achieve a 10 per cent sample you should verify 15 units. In this example, 111 units have been completed by the candidates and of those 15 have been sampled.

$$15 \div 111 \times 100 = 13.5\%$$

This tells the LQA that a sufficient QA sample has been applied to this cohort.

What kind a sampling strategy has been used in this example? If each of the candidates had a different assessor, what is the percentage sample size per assessor?

Answer: Horizontal sampling (see Chapter 4 Internally assuring the quality of assessment page 135).

There has been a 10 per cent sample size from every assessor.

ACTIVITY 2

Using the case study above answer the following.

What are the implications if:

Units 1–4 are assessed by Joe, 5 and 6 by Simon and 7–10 assessed by Mary.

Recalculate the sampling percentages per assessor and decide if additional sampling is required.

Answer:

Joe: 15 candidates × 4 units = 60 sampling opportunities. 8 units sampled = 13%

Simon: 15 candidates × 2 units = 30 sampling opportunities. 3 units sampled = 10%

Mary: 15 candidates × 4 units = 60 sampling opportunities. 4 units sampled = 7%

This would indicate that additional sampling is required on Mary's assessments.

Preparing for external quality assurance

The EQA (also known as external verifier) is appointed by the AO to check that approved centres are meeting the requirements of the awarding organisation and is tasked to ensure that Ofqual's standards are being upheld.

The role of the EQA is a valuable part of the quality assurance processes. They have a multiple role; they are both the 'guardian of the rules' and will check that the centre is coping with the managerial,

ACTIVITY 3

Using the case study above answer the following.

The table shows us that Unit 1 has been sampled three times, Units three, four and five sampled twice and the remaining units once each. No unit has been omitted from the sampling strategy. What information can be gleaned from this information?

Answer:

This is very typical in a horizontal sampling strategy, in that there may be variance between the sampling patterns in different units. Overall every candidate has been sampled and every unit is sampled. Either by the strategy that every candidate has a different assessor, or by the scenario above where Joe, Mary and Simon assess different units, this means that the work from all assessors has also been sampled.

The LQA might extend this by undertaking a standardisation activity with Unit 1, to see if the assessment practice is consistent; this would be particularly valuable if there were many different assessors assessing Unit 1, but less so if the same assessor made the decisions alone for this unit.

administrative and practical requirements of assessment and quality assurance. They are also a means of cascading and sharing best practice. They are likely to be working with a number of centres and, as such, will be able to talk about good ideas they have seen on their travels. While maintaining confidentiality about their centres' practices they will pick up tried and tested examples of good assessment and QA practices and are happy to convey them as part of other centres' development. The conversations occurring during EQA activity are therefore invaluable in suggesting actions to improve practice. These informal conversations are the most satisfying part of the role of the EQA. The EQA therefore is the best CPD a centre can access.

In order to raise standards, *'City & Guilds is working to support and guide centres to be better able to assess their own performance and to focus on quality management. The External Verifier role is evolving into a Qualification Consultant role. Because for the future the focus will be to advise, support and guide centres to excellence rather than to "police" standards. City and Guilds believes that "Quality" and "quality" assurance should be built into all activities from the start – it is much easier to build good quality in than to audit poor quality out ...'*

Charmain Campbell, City and Guilds 2011

External quality assurance will take place in one of two ways; either by a visit to the centre or remotely through postal or electronic sampling. Increasingly the AO's external quality assurance strategy is based on a risk assessment of the approved centre, this will determine the frequency of EQA activities, but it is usually an annual process. The risk is based on the level of confidence that an AO can place on an approved centre's ability to plan, assess, quality assure and certificate its qualifications.

Whether by a visit or a postal verification, EQA activity should be managed. Once candidates are registered with an AO it will trigger EQA activity.

If this is done by a visit, the activities are likely to be centred on meeting staff and candidates and looking at completed work. The following listing, much of which is contained in a centre management or QA file, can be used as a checklist to prepare for a visit:

Item required at visit	Checked and confirmed
Copy of previous EQA report	
Copy of action plan to show progress of previous actions	
Relevant staff/departments notified of EQA visit	
Copy of pre-visit planner (from EQA) completed and sent to EV	
Confirm dates with EQA	
Base room booked for visit	

Car parking space reserved if appropriate	
Reception notified of EQA arrival date and time	
Check all portfolios and/or logbooks requested for sampling are available for inspection	
Cross check portfolios and/or logbooks for: • date compliance • evidence of assessments • evidence of IQA • all signatures and dates complete • cross referenced to standards, learning outcomes, assessment criteria • evidence of constructive feedback to candidates	
All candidates requested for interview with EQA are available (a telephone appointment is acceptable)	
All assessors requested for interview with EQA are available (a telephone appointment is acceptable)	
Assessor's records/documents available and audited	
All quality assurance staff requested for interview with EQA are available (a telephone appointment is acceptable)	
QA records/documents available and audited	
IQA actions set previously have been closed and signed off	
Minutes of standardisation events, team meetings and attendance at CPD is documented	
If EV requests: has observation of assessment been arranged?	
If necessary, inform candidate's employer that EQA will require a site visit	
Details of team – candidate /unit allocations with sample signatures available	
New team members – CV + original certificates	

Notes regarding preparing for a visit or postal verification:

- Only candidates registered with an AO can be externally verified. Candidates enrolled at a centre but not registered with an AO cannot submit work for verification.
- Any assessments recorded in portfolios or log books which pre-date the AO registration date are not valid.
- An EQA is checking that the IQA process is being applied. This is to ensure that the IQA policy, procedure and guidance are being followed.
- The rules of evidence are: valid, sufficient, authentic and current; ensure that evidence presented by candidates satisfies these rules and assessors can state how they ensure these rules are applied.
- The principles relating to the IQA sample size are that the sample should cover a range of assessments for every candidate, every module/unit, every assessor, the assessor's experience, at every assessment location, over a range of assessment methods. An IQA strategy should be presented to show how the IQA has created the sample and an IQA should be prepared to answer questions on their justification/strategy.
- Documents stored electronically must be available for EQA scrutiny.
- New assessors need to be introduced to the EQA, they should bring with them a CV and original certificates appropriate to the qualification – for example: evidence of occupational experience/ qualifications, assessment and/or verifier certification. An EQA will require copies which will be signed 'original seen' for their files.
- If the activity is a visit then prepare an agenda, remembering to include all meetings requested by the EQA and time and space for the EQA to review paper based or electronic evidence. You will not be required to sit with the EQA for the duration of the visit but should remain close and at the end of a telephone.
- Meetings with candidates, assessors and IQAs ideally are face-to-face interviews. In exceptional circumstances a telephone appointment can be made. In which case the EQA will need access

to the phone number and a telephone to make appropriate contacts.

- If preparing a postal verification, then remember that an EQA can only make judgements on what is seen. If you do not send key explanatory documents then you may cause additional work to validate the sample.

The outcome of a successful EQA activity is the confirmation that the approved centre is confident and competent in delivering, assessing and quality assuring its qualifications on behalf of the AO. The role of the LQA in making that happen is paramount, and the sense of satisfaction as the EQA says 'no actions identified' is second to none and worth the effort required to achieve it.

Glossary of terms

EQA external quality assurer (appointed by an AO)

Learner journey the learner's experience of an organisation from first to final contact

LQA lead quality assurer (appointed by an approved centre)

Malpractice improper or negligent actions

Policy a statement of proposed actions

Procedure a way of working

Process a sequence of activities

Recommended reading

Bush, T and Middlewood, D (1997) *Managing People in Education*. London: Paul Chapman Publishing

City and Guilds (2011) *Level 3 & 4 Awards & Certificates in Assessment and Quality Assurance.* www.cityandguilds.com (version 1.3 February 2011, p. 16 accessed April 2011)

Cole, G A and Kelly, P (2011) *Management Theory and Practice*. Andover: Cengage

Collins, D (2006) *Survival Guide for Managers and Leaders*. London: Continuum

Ellis, C W (2004) *Management Skills for new Managers*. New York: AMACOM

O'Connell, Sir B (2005) *Creating an Outstanding College*. Cheltenham: Nelson Thornes

Wilson, L (2009) *Practical Teaching: a guide to PTLLS and DTLLS*. Andover: Cengage Learning

In this chapter we set out to:

- Describe the processes involved in managing the quality assurance of assessment.
- Plan for quality assurance management.
- Identify the resources required in quality assurance.
- Implement and monitor quality assurance in own area.
- Organise an external quality assurance activity.
- Manage and implement improvements.

Your personal development

- You commenced learning in this chapter by considering how the management of the QA process differs from the role of a quality assurer. This caused you to think about how to manage the implementation of QA to ensure that it is procedurally compliant.
- You have explored the role of the LQA and the possible roles and responsibilities the role attracts. You have reviewed how the management of physical and human resources are key to ensuring that QA is effective and carried out with integrity and how this is demonstrated to AOs. In this section you checked that the physical resources were

appropriate to the qualification. You evaluated staff experience and qualifications against the requirements of the qualification and AO, touching briefly on CPD and how this is identified, recorded and demonstrated.

- In the next section you looked at documentation and what is required of managers of the QA process. You were reminded of the assessment and QA records originally described in earlier chapters and how you summarise QA activity. You examined a document used by EQA staff which offers an overview of assessment and QA and is used to identify sampling.
- In considering managing the QA process, the next section caused you to reflect on how improvements can occur, and how you can measure the impact of your development actions. This explored SMART target setting and provided several case studies which enabled you to theorise on how you would use QA processes to take development and remedial actions. This led to a review of how QIPs are used to develop and record improvement.
- In the penultimate section, you scrutinised a case study and used numerical statistics to demonstrate how to improve sampling strategies. This same case study was used to calculate retention, achievement and success information and then enable you to conclude that data is deceptive and needs to be carefully analysed to be an effective development tool.
- Finally, you considered how to prepare for an external quality assurance visit and by ensuring that this process is as methodical as others in the QA processes, it will realise a successful outcome, that is: no action points.

In the next chapter you will find help and advice on how to achieve this and other units of your QA award.

CHAPTER 6

Collecting evidence and compiling a portfolio

Unit of Assessment	Assessment Criteria
Understanding the principles and practices of assessment	1.1; 1.2; 1.3; 1.4; 2.1; 3.1; 3.2; 3.3; 3.4; 3.5; 4.1; 4.2; 4.3; 4.4; 5.1; 5.2; 6.1; 6.2; 6.3; 7.1; 7.2; 8.1; 8.2; 8.3; 8.4
Assess occupational competence in the work environment	1.1; 1.2; 1.3; 1.4; 2.1; 2.2; 2.3; 2.4; 3.1; 3.2; 3.3; 4.1; 4.2; 4.3; 4.4
Assess vocational skills, knowledge and understanding	1.1; 1.2; 1.3; 2.1; 2.2; 2.3; 2.4; 2.5; 2.6; 3.1; 3.2; 3.3; 4.1; 4.2; 4.3; 4.4
Understanding the principles and practices of internally assuring the quality of assessment	1.1; 1.2; 1.3; 1.4; 2.1; 2.2; 2.3; 3.1; 3.2; 4.1; 4.2; 4.3; 5.1; 6.1; 6.2; 6.3; 6.4
Internally assure the quality of assessment	1.1; 1.2; 2.1; 2.2; 2.3; 2.4; 2.5; 2.6; 3.1; 3.2; 4.1; 4.2; 5.1; 5.2; 5.3; 5.4
Plan, allocate and monitor work in own area of responsibility	1.1; 1.2; 1.3; 1.4; 2.1; 2.2; 3.1; 3.2; 4.1; 4.2

LEARNING OUTCOMES

By the end of this chapter you will be able to:

- Describe the main features of your portfolio of evidence relating to the assessor and QA qualifications
- Prepare a programme suitable for the delivery of knowledge and understanding
- Develop and accumulate knowledge and understanding evidence
- Aid and support the compilation of your performance evidence to meet the evidence requirements

The assessment and quality assurance qualifications

This chapter of the book refers to the reader as the candidate of the **assessor** and QA **qualifications**. It should be remembered that the **evidence** produced will also be assessed by an assessor and verified by a **qualification quality assurer**. To this end, the person compiling the evidence is referred to as the **candidate assessor** or **candidate quality assurer**. The **principles** of assessment previously described in the rest of this book refer to both the candidate assessor/quality assurer and the **qualification assessor**/quality assurer.

It is this two tier, yet same subject focus, which, in the early stages causes much confusion. In essence, everything you are being asked to complete as part of your assessor or QA qualification, will also be completed by your assessor in their role as a judge of your competence.

Figure 6.1 demonstrates the people involved in the process of achieving assessor and quality assurer qualification/awards. The darker shaded boxes relate to the person registered to complete either the assessor units or the quality assurance units. They are referred to

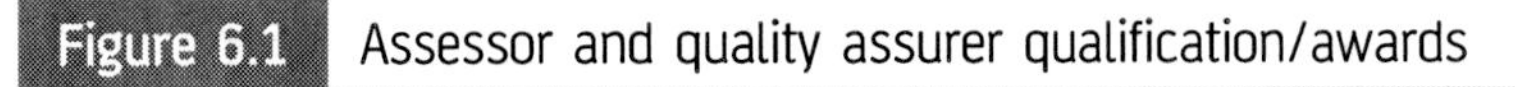
Figure 6.1 Assessor and quality assurer qualification/awards

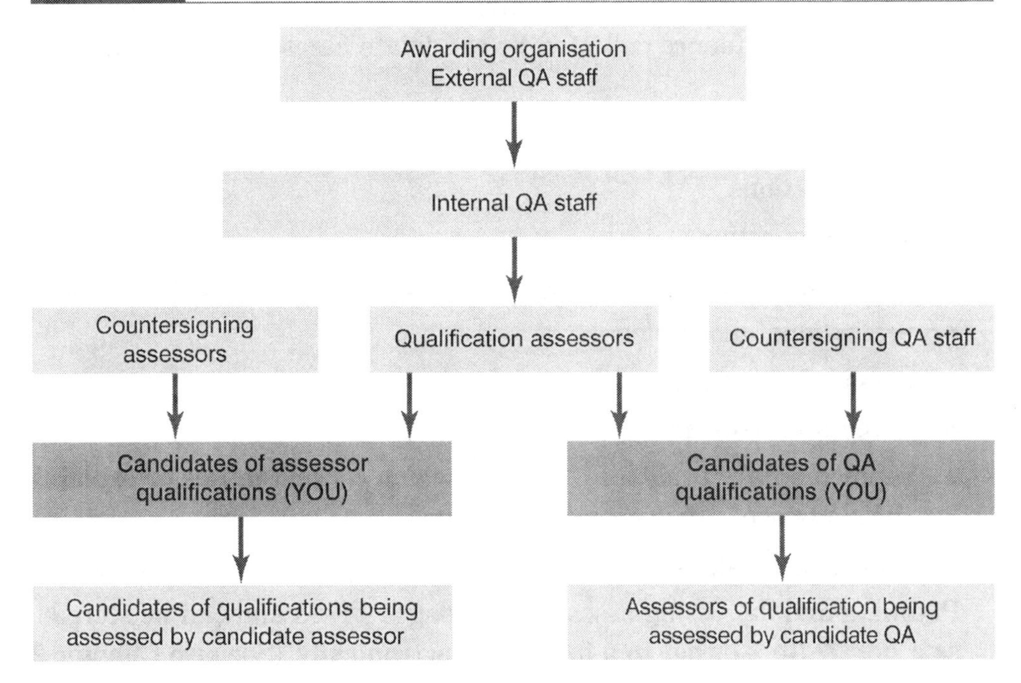

as the candidate assessor or candidate quality assurer. The person assessing you is referred to as the qualification assessor or qualification internal quality assurer – i.e. someone accredited to assess the assessor and quality assurance qualifications.

The candidate assessor will work with **trainees/learners** completing either an accredited qualification or in-house/industry devised training competences. The candidate quality assurer will work with assessors of either accredited qualifications or industry devised training competences. In this context the word 'qualification' is used but applies to both categories.

What constitutes evidence?

Evidence is defined as the output of an assessment activity; evidence of a learner's knowledge and understanding, skills or **competence** that can be used to make a judgement of their achievement against agreed standards/criteria. In this section we take a look at the evidence that would be required of someone completing an assessor or internal QA qualification. Evidence collected by candidate assessors and quality assurers can be:

- observation of performance
- oral questions
- written questions
- products, documents, artefacts, photographs, video clips, records
- professional discussion
- personal statements or logs, reflective accounts
- witness **testimony**
- supplementary evidence – i.e. that which contextualises or explains the context of other pieces of evidence.

Each of these is discussed as an assessment method in Chapter 2 Planning and delivering assessments, pages 44–53 and can be stored as a **portfolio** – either in a folder or electronically. (See also Chapter 2 Planning and delivering assessments, pages 66–67 – Portfolios).

Unfortunately, it is not possible for an assessor or candidate to just say 'I do that'. They need to be able to prove it.

An artist or model has used a portfolio for many years; it being a collection of pictures or images to prove their ability and versatility. A qualification portfolio is exactly the same; it is a collection of proof.

Observation of performance Candidate assessors will be observed by their qualification assessor while working with their trainees/candidates; candidate quality assurers will be observed by their qualification assessors while undertaking activities relating to internal monitoring of quality requirements. Your qualification assessor will observe (listen) while you give feedback to your trainees/learners or assessors – dependent upon the qualification you are working towards. This would be planned in advance in order to ensure that you can alert your trainees/learners/assessors and their employer to the fact that additional people will be watching the process.

Oral questions These will probably be asked following an observation. They will be asked to clarify something seen during the observation or to confirm something related to it. They will probably start 'what would you do if …' or 'can you explain why …'. Oral questions are not exclusively part of an observation; you and your assessor may select this method of testing knowledge evidence. Your assessor will need to record the question and your answer. The assessor may record on a document, voice recorder or by video. You may use Skype if it is not convenient to meet with your assessor. You must include the evidence that questioning has occurred in your portfolio.

Written questions These are likely to be pre-set by your qualification assessor and used to confirm your knowledge and understanding. Typically questions may be short answer type, written in such a way so that you can demonstrate your understanding of aspects of the qualifications – especially those not observed or evidenced by producing products. They are unlikely to be tests or exams with time constraints – many will allow the use of texts to complete the questions (i.e. open book questions). There are two sets of suggested pre-set written questions below which may help in your gathering of evidence for either the assessor or internal QA qualifications.

Products, documents, artefacts, photographs, video clips, records
Work products are items, for example, business/service documents (minutes, print-outs, forms, procedures, diagrams); finished goods, commodities or commissions; or anything similar produced during normal work activities. For a candidate assessor these are likely to be things like assessment plans or records of progress/achievement related to your assessments. For a candidate quality assurer they are likely to be minutes of meetings, verification documents, procedures or other products relating to your QA actions. You should obtain authorisation to use any document or procedure. If using mobile technology to video an assessment or take photographs of learners, you must ensure that appropriate permissions are sought and received before using them in your evidence. This would demonstrate awareness of safeguarding procedures and data protection requirements.

Watch point

Policies – what do they prove? Do not encourage policies as evidence – it is more appropriate for the candidate to make a statement or engage in discussion about how they apply the policy. Including policy documents says more about the candidate knowing where to find them rather than how to use them!

ACTIVITY 1

Locate the Policy for Assessment or Internal Quality Assurance at your place of work. Write a statement about how you use or apply either of those policies in your area of work.

Professional discussion This is when you and your qualification assessor engage in conversation about a topic. In some parts of your qualification, it is not possible to cover all of the evidence requirements by observation. In these circumstances you talk to your qualification assessor about how you would, for example, use RPL or case studies as assessment methods. This is likely to be a structured conversation and the qualification assessor may ask specific questions or direct the discussion in a particular direction. You should prepare for a professional discussion. Plan with your assessor the types of topics you will cover and practise what you want to say. You may need to provide documentary evidence to support your statements. You professional discussion will be noted or recorded to provide a record of the conversation.

Personal statements or logs, reflective accounts These can be used as an alternative to professional discussion. Whereas a discussion involves you and your qualification assessor, in statements you write how you do (or would do) something. For example, you might use personal statements to demonstrate your knowledge of legislation or equal opportunities in situations – especially those that were not observed. You might use them to describe how you prepare **contingency plans** or meet specialist requirements of some learners. A statement should be referenced to a particular topic rather than a rambling piece of text about general issues.

Witness testimony A witness is someone who is able to **testify** (validate) that they have seen you do something. A witness might be one of your learners or their employer, or for a candidate quality assurer, one of your assessors. They will testify to things such as effective communication in the planning of assessment or QA. As a candidate assessor/quality assurer your assessments need to be confirmed by a qualified assessor who is a subject expert. This is known as **countersigning**. Because you are in training (to be an assessor or quality assurer) you will find this support invaluable in deciding if evidence is to the required standard, i.e. meets the rules of evidence (valid, authentic, current and sufficient). The countersigning of decisions made by candidate assessors or candidate quality assurers is part of many SSCs' assessment strategies.

You will find these the most commonly used methods of assessment when completing your qualification. You will produce evidence relating to the performance evidence – i.e. evidence of you doing the job. This forms half of the evidence, the rest being derived from knowledge evidence – i.e. what you understand about the job. Acquiring knowledge of the subject is most likely to be by attending some training sessions. Personally, I find that learning about assessment and quality assurance (the theory) is best when it precedes the application. Therefore, I would do a training session before embarking on a task. Others may find the theoretical aspects easier to comprehend after they have done the tasks, allowing them to 'hang'

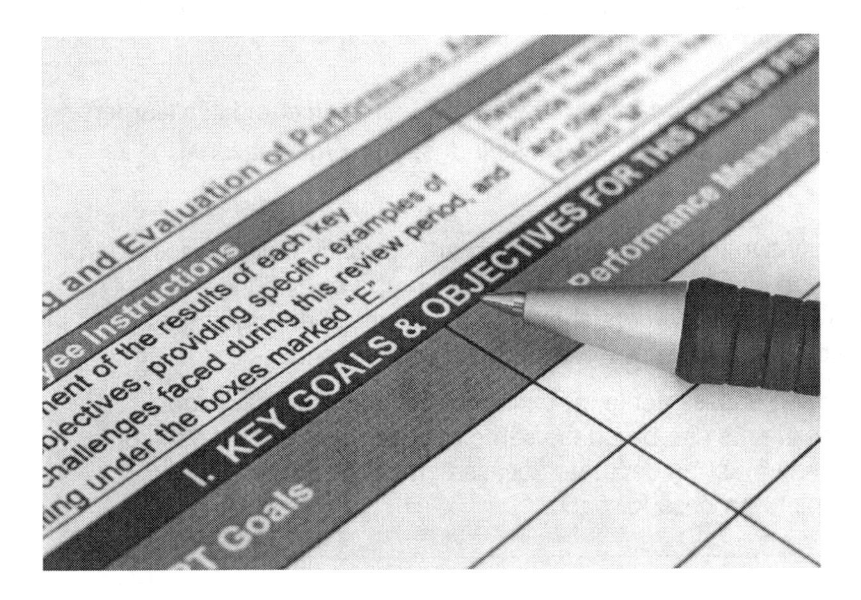

their knowledge onto actions. The order is less important than the fact that both aspects need to be completed to create a deep understanding and proficient application of the roles. Your preference should be discussed as part of your personal development plan when embarking on the chosen qualification.

Evidence requirements

In order to achieve the units you need to collect the following evidence.

Unit 301: Understanding the principles and practices of assessment

This unit is assessed by assignments, written questions or professional discussion. There is no requirement to be assessing trainees in their workplaces as the content of this unit is concerned with the theory that underpins assessment practice. It is a unit suitable for practising assessors or those seeking to become assessors.

Unit 302: Assess occupational competence in the work environment

To achieve this unit you can be assessing trainees/candidates/learners attempting qualifications or in-house/industry or organisational standards. In the first instance:

- Identify two trainees/learners who are currently being assessed in the workplace. To provide a broader range of evidence, one of these trainees/learners should require special arrangements to enable them to work towards their qualifications.
- Plan two assessments for each trainee/learner. These four assessments can be on the same day with one following the other, but they must be separate assessments with a planned and complete process for each.

- Arrange for your qualification assessor to observe at least one of the briefings for each trainee/learner with the others evidenced by witness testimony.
- Undertake the assessments – all four must be observed by your qualification assessor. During the four assessments you should use observation, examination of work products and questioning – you do not need to use them all in each observation, but overall they should all be observed by your assessor. A statement is required to show how you would plan and execute other methods – discussion, use of testimony, personal statements, RPL. At least one assessment must include an observation of you giving feedback to your trainee/learner.

Collect all documentation used during the four assessments: plans, observation and assessment records, feedback to trainees/learners, and assessment outcome. See Figure 2.1. To confirm the accuracy of the judgements, the evidence should be countersigned by an accredited assessor who is a subject expert, and ideally quality assured. Your qualification assessor will supply documentation relating to their observation of you, i.e. plans, observation, records of questioning, feedback, and assessment outcome.

Submit additional personal statements, written questions and/or transcript of professional discussion to complete the evidence requirements.

Unit 303: Assess vocational skills, knowledge and understanding

To achieve this unit you can be assessing trainees/candidates/learners attempting qualifications or in-house/industry or organisational standards. In the first instance:

- Identify two trainees/learners who are currently being assessed in contexts other than the workplace (e.g. workshop, classroom, simulated environment, distance/virtual learning environment, area at work away from main work space). To provide a broader range of evidence, one of these trainees/learners should require special arrangements to enable them to work towards their qualifications.

- Plan two assessments for each trainee/learner. These four assessments can be on the same day with one following the other, but they must be separate assessments.
- Arrange for your qualification assessor to observe at least one of the briefings for each trainee/learner with the others evidenced by witness testimony.
- Undertake the assessments – all four must be observed by your qualification assessor. During the four assessments you should use a minimum of three methods of assessment from: simulation, skills test, oral/written questioning, assignment, project, case study, RPL – you do not need to use them all in each observation, but overall your chosen methods should be observed by your assessor. For some methods your assessor will observe you 'managing an assessment'. A statement is required to show how you would plan and execute the remaining methods. At least one assessment must include an observation of you giving feedback to your trainee/learner.

Collect all documentation used during the four assessments: plans, assessment records, feedback to trainees/learners, and assessment outcome. See Figure 2.1. To confirm the accuracy of the judgements, the evidence should be countersigned by an accredited assessor who is a subject expert, and ideally quality assured. Your qualification assessor will supply documentation relating to their observation of you, i.e. plans, observation, record of questioning, feedback, and assessment outcome.

Submit additional personal statements, written questions and/or transcript of professional discussion to complete the evidence requirements.

Unit 401: Understanding the principles and practices of internally assuring the quality of assessment

This unit is assessed by assignments, written questions or professional discussion. There is no requirement to be quality assuring the assessor or their trainees in their workplaces, as the content of this unit is concerned with the theory that underpins QA and assessment practice. It is a unit suitable for practising quality assurance staff or those seeking to become QA staff.

Unit 402: Internally assure the quality of assessment

To achieve this unit you can be assessing assessors delivering qualifications or in-house/industry or organisational standards. In the first instance:

- Identify two assessors who are currently assessing at least two candidates each through part of a qualification or in-house/industry or organisational standards. To provide a broader range of evidence, one of these assessors should be less experienced than the other and therefore require more support as they work through their qualifications.
- Plan moderation activities relating to the two assessors, including, managing assessment risk, standardisation and sampling activities (interim and summatively). Collect planning documentation. An example of a sampling plan is seen in Chapter 4 Internally assuring the quality of assessment page 135.
- Collect records relating to the two assessors, including, CV, occupational certificates, CPD logs and feedback resulting from internal QA.
- Arrange to be observed while your assessors are engaged in QA activities.

Collect all documentation used during the QA (moderation, verification) activity. See Figure 4.1. This should include interim QA – for example observing the assessment process, and summative QA – for example reviewing and evaluating assessment products. To confirm the accuracy of the judgements, the evidence should be countersigned by an accredited quality assurer who is a subject expert, and ideally externally quality assured. Your qualification assessor will supply documentation relating to their observation of you, i.e. plans, observation, feedback and assessment outcome. Examples of QA/ verification documents are seen in Chapter 4 Internally assuring the quality of assessment pages 139–142.

Undertake a standardisation activity and submit minutes of the meeting, records relating to decisions made and feedback, advice and support given. Arrange for your qualification assessor to observe at least one feedback session to one of your assessors with the other evidenced by witness testimony.

Submit additional personal statements, written questions and/or transcripts of professional discussion to complete the evidence requirements.

Unit 403: Plan, allocate and monitor work in own area of responsibility

Identify the area of work that you are responsible for. The 'work' is the QA practices that are supervised. A personal statement will describe this. This will be in the context of your LIV/quality assurer role. The success criteria are those that will demonstrate effective QA, for example, no or few actions identified in EQA visits, success data and acceptable standards of practice.

The work plan will be the sampling plan the lead verifier creates to ensure effective and efficient QA and assessment practice.

Describe the team in this area and their responsibilities. This might be an organisation chart with role and job descriptors, showing other QA, assessor and trainee allocations. In this context the resources are the assessors and their competence as well as the physical resources required to assess the target qualifications. Additional evidence will come in the style of individual plans and records relating to the IQA and assessor team, job descriptions or work schedules. These will contain targets and deadlines which need to be written in a SMART way.

Collect documentation relating to: the setting of SMART work targets for the team; minutes of meetings; monitoring progress and performance; giving feedback; arranging/delivering CPD; and other improvement mechanisms. You may need to describe how annual performance reviews or developments plans aid the monitoring of performance and lead to improvements.

Provide testimony to demonstrate effective contacts. An observation of a team event would provide evidence of effective communication, advice and support to the team.

Knowledge and understanding

In the following section you will find some questions which will help you to demonstrate your knowledge and understanding of the assessor and IQA qualifications. They also address the additional requirements of the 'best practice' statements. Written questions can be completed as an activity in their own right or used as part of a professional discussion, or a combination of both.

Questions for the assessor qualifications, comprising:

Unit 301: Understanding the principles and practices of assessment

Unit 302: Assess occupational competence in the work environment

Unit 303: Assess vocational skills, knowledge and understanding

QUESTIONS FOR UNITS 302, 302 AND 303

C&G Ref.	Question	Answers to include:
301.1.1 301.1.2	Describe the main functions and principles of assessment?	Initial assessment, formative and summative assessment Making judgements against the rules of assessment – valid-authentic – current – sufficient. Fairness and objectivity.
301.1.3	What are the key roles and responsibilities of an assessor?	Interpreting standards, planning and carrying out assessments, communicating, making judgements about assessments, recording and giving feedback about assessments, attending standardisation and CPD events.
301.1.4	What role do the AO and SSCs have in regulating assessment practice?	The role of Ofqual in setting the regulations The role of the SSCs in writing NOS, UoA and Assessment Strategy. The role of the AO in writing and upholding standards in assessment.
301.2.1 302.1.1 302.2.1 303.1.1 303.1.2 303.2.1 301.4.3 302.4.3 303.4.3	Choose four assessment methods and compare the strengths and limitations of each. Explain how self- and peer assessment promotes learner involvement. Evaluate the assessment methods used in your assessments.	Choose from: observation, reviewing products, **professional discussions**, **personal statements**, **recognising prior learning**, simulations, tests, oral and written questions, assignments and projects, case studies, **witness testimony.** Aids preparation and timing of assessment and empowers the learner. (Choosing the emboldened four will also meet parts of 302, others if used should be evaluated to confirm they were most appropriate and comply with assessment strategy.)

C&G Ref.	Question	Answers to include:
301.3.1 302.1.3 303.2.2 301.4.1 301.4.2	List the main factors to consider when preparing assessment plans. Why do you need to involve the learner and others in planning?	What, when, where, how of assessment. Arrangements for dealing with special requirements (e.g. support needs, shifts, not reassessing, normal work opportunities). Communicating with others about the plans. Raised awareness leads to transparency and efficiency in assessment.
301.3.2 301.3.3 302.1.4	What are the benefits of creating holistic assessments and how would these be planned?	Efficiency of assessment covering more than one unit Linking work practice to assessment rather than the other way around.
301.3.4 301.3.5	What are the main risks that an assessor needs to consider when planning and delivering assessment, and how might they be minimised?	Health and safety, stress, malpractice, over-assessment, unfairness, not adhering to assessment strategy. Ensuring planning considers all of these issues and complies with the rules of assessment.
301.5.1 301.5.2 302.2.2 303.2.3 303.2.4 303.2.5	How do you make judgements about competence?	Rules of assessment. Using criteria. Liaise with others. Consider equality of opportunity. Comply with assessment strategy. (Testimony from a subject specialist should corroborate this statement.)
301.6.1 301.6.2 302.2.3	Briefly outline the main QA processes and how your assessments conform to standardised practice.	Sampling, standardisation, fairness, reliability to ensure consistency and credibility.
301.6.3	Describe the process a learner would follow if they wanted to appeal against an assessment judgement.	Informal and formal stages. When to involve the IQA and EQA. How standardisation activities can limit the risk of unfair assessment.

C&G Ref.	Question	Answers to include:
301.7.1	What is the purpose of assessment records? How are assessment records stored? How frequently would they be completed?	To provide points of reference which are accurate and accessible. To support feedback to trainee/ learner. To aid quality processes. Records should be made in a timely manner and available to the trainee, assessor, IQA and EQA.
301.7.2	How does feedback and questioning support trainees/learners?	Aids progression. Provides opportunity to clarify issues. Feedback needs to be constructive. Questions should not lead or hinder attainment.
301.8.1 301.8.3 302.3.3 302.4.1 302.4.2 303.3.3 303.4.1 303.4.2	What are the main pieces of legislation and procedure that need to be considered in your subject area? How do you comply with them?	Legislation: Health and Safety, Equality Act (E&D), Data Protection, Children Act, specialist legislation. Procedure: confidentiality, record keeping, compliance to assessment strategy. Security of information.
301.8.2	How do/might you use e-assessment or technology in your subject area?	E-portfolios, mobile technology, internet, blogs, VLEs, video/audio evidence – flip cams, recordings, etc. On-line testing.
301.8.4 302.4.4 303.4.4	What reflections have you made during this process? What CPD activities have you engaged in?	Personal development plan, feedback from others, standardisation meetings. Personal and professional development – inc. occupational updates.

Questions for the IQA Qualifications, comprising:

Unit 401: Understanding the principles and practices of internally assuring the quality of assessment

Unit 402: Internally assure the quality of assessment

QUESTIONS FOR UNITS 401 AND 402

C&G Ref.	Question	Answers to include:
401.1.1 401.1.2	Describe the main functions and principles of internal quality assurance.	Credibility, respect, ensuring and monitoring quality, compliance, accuracy and consistency, managing risk, identifying cpd, supporting assessors, promoting improvement. Planning, sampling, standardisation.
401.1.3	What are the key roles and responsibilities of an internal quality team?	Roles of IQA (and also – trainer, expert/non-expert witnesses, independent assessors). Involvement in ensuring and monitoring quality of planning, delivery and assessment outcomes.
401.1.4	What role do the AO and SSCs have in regulating assessment and quality practices?	The role of Ofqual in setting the regulations. The role of the SSCs in writing NOS, UoA and assessment strategy. The role of the AOs in writing and upholding standards in assessment and QA.
401.2.1	Explain the benefits of planning IQA activities.	How QA reduces risks relating to accuracy, validity, fairness and consistency.
401.2.2 401.2.3	Describe what an IQA plan should include and what arrangements need to be made to prepare for QA.	Includes: timeframes relating to sampling – interim and summatively, monitoring assessment, standardisation, supporting assessors and minimising risk. Sampling to meet **CAMERA** Arrangements: collating info, communicating.

C&G Ref.	Question	Answers to include:
401.3.1	Compare and contrast a range of sampling strategies and explain what considerations you make regarding deciding upon sample sizes.	Vertical, horizontal and themed sampling. Observing assessors, candidate interviews, discussions with witnesses, sampling products and records. CAMERA, experience, difficult units, size of provision, current assessment activity.
401.3.2	How do you make judgements about the quality of assessment?	Rules of evidence. Using criteria. Liaise with others. Consider equality of opportunity. Comply with assessment strategy. (Testimony from a subject specialist should corroborate this statement.)
401.4.1 402.2.2 402.2.4 402.2.5 402.3.1	Describe how you support assessors. Explain how you evaluate assessor competence. What types of things might you need to feedback to assessors?	Feedback to assessors (not learners). Constructive feedback. Detailed inductions and ongoing support. Development plans. Protocols or strategies to determine experience of assessors. Observing assessors giving feedback. Checking reliability of assessments. Confirming appropriateness of assessments.
401.4.2 402.2.6	How do you maintain consistency in assessment decisions?	Standardisation activities. Recording outcomes of standardisation. Making improvements and agreeing actions following standardisation. Comparing assessments across units, assessors and themes.
402.2.3	What do you look for in your assessors planning and how do you decide if that planning is appropriate?	Special assessment needs. Documentation. All key components of an assessment plan completed. Validity in assessment against the criteria. Planning will lead to sufficient evidence to meet criteria and range.

C&G Ref.	Question	Answers to include:
401.4.3	Describe the process a learner would follow if they wanted to appeal against an assessment judgement.	The role of the IQA in informal and formal stages. Liaising with assessors and when to involve the EQA. How standardisation activities can limit the risk of unfair assessment.
401.5.1 401.6.1 401.6.4 402.5.1 402.5.2	What are the main pieces of legislation and procedure that needs to be considered in your subject area? How do you comply with them?	Legislation: Health and Safety, Equality Act (E&D), Data Protection, Children Act, specialist legislation. Procedure: confidentiality, record keeping, compliance to assessment strategy. Security of information.
401.6.2	How do/might you quality assure assessments collected using e-assessment or technology in your subject area? How do/might you support assessors using e-assessment?	E-portfolios, mobile technology, internet, blogs, VLEs, video/audio evidence – flip cams, recordings, etc. On-line testing. Virtual standardisation. Electronic communication.
401.6.3 402.5.3 402.5.4	What reflections have you made during this process? What CPD activities have you engaged in?	Personal development plan, feedback from/to others, standardisation meetings. Personal and professional development – inc. occupational updates and current assessment/ QA practice.

Additional questions for those undertaking Unit 403: Plan, allocate and monitor work in own area of responsibility are listed overleaf.

QUESTIONS FOR UNIT 403

C&G Ref.	Question	Answers to include:
403.1.1 403.1.2 403.1.3	What do you consider when preparing to work with IQAs and assessors?	Skills of team, workloads of team. Recency/age of qualifications. Experience of assessors and IQA team. Previous EQA reports. Audit outcomes.
403.3.1	What strategies do you employ to monitor progress of the assessment and IQA team?	Standardisation meeting and records. Sampling of work. 1:1 discussions – appraisals, etc. Observing and questioning practice. External and internal audit. CPD events – Personal development plans. Written and verbal communication. IQA/Assessment feedback. Testimony from others.

Putting it together

This section explains what you need to do with all of this evidence in order to achieve the qualifications. When compiling your portfolio you need to consider how the evidence relates to the assessor or QA qualifications, including the additional 'best practice' requirements.

- *Collect* – either chronologically, by subject or by unit (but keep an index to avoid repetition).
- *Reflect* – review what you have collected and choose want to keep; identify missing parts and plan for how you will collect them.
- *Connect* – link to the standards (your assessor will help with this).

Whether your portfolio of evidence is stored in a substantial file or folder, an e-portfolio or portable storage device, it should be clear and tracked to the criteria of the qualification being attempted. You should also check with your tutor about the use of plastic wallets in paper based portfolios – some providers like them, some hate them. If used, you should balance the one piece of paper per wallet with the overstuffed wallets that burst out their contents!

The portfolio needs to be clearly accessible by the owner, the assessor, the IQA and the EQA. Try to avoid the strategy of putting everything in, in case it might be useful.

Watch point

Good quality evidence rather than high volumes of evidence makes for happy assessors!

Incomplete or poorly referenced portfolios will be rejected at assessment or quality assurance on the grounds that the evidence is not easily located and therefore makes it difficult to prove competence.

Suggested portfolio content:

- Title page, including the owner's name and qualification title.
- Index of contents.
- A tracking sheet – linking evidence pages to the standards (referencing), this should also indicate when one piece of evidence is linked to more than one assessment criteria (cross-referencing).
- List of witnesses and sample signatures of those involved.
- Personal information – CV, copies of certificates.
- A contextual statement is useful in understanding who the owner is and the context in which the evidence has been collected.
- The evidence – records of observations, records of questioning, products, personal statements.

Tracking your evidence

An example of a tracking sheet is shown on the next page.

In this example, the candidate assessor has produced evidence of assessment and has been observed relating to one of the four assessments required to sufficiently cover this unit. This grid gives a flavour of how one piece of evidence meets more than one criterion and

Name: A Candidate Date: 20th November 2012

Unit: Assess occupational competence in the work environment

Ref	Evidence	LO 1				LO 2				LO 3			LO 4			
	Learning Outcomes	1.1	1.2	1.3	1.4	2.1	2.2	2.3	2.4	3.1	3.2	3.3	4.1	4.2	4.3	4.4
1	Assessment Plan 1	✓		✓	✓								✓			
2	Observation 1					✓			✓				✓	✓		
3	Feedback and Assessment Records 1								✓	✓	✓		✓	✓		
4	Witness Testimony re communication with learner prior to assessment		✓													
5	Work Products - email		✓													
6	Personal Statement re assessment methods not used	✓				✓										
7	Personal statement evaluating methods used														✓	
8	Written Questions/ Professional Discussion			✓	✓	✓	✓	✓				✓	✓	✓		✓

that each criterion is evidenced at least once. A tracking sheet similar to this should be presented towards the start of the portfolio. The centre will provide this document. If evidence is stored electronically, then the 'Ref' column should indicate the file name where the evidence is located. These grids need to be signed and dated by your assessor when they agree that the evidence you have presented does in fact meet the claimed criteria. You would sign and date them also, as would the IQA if they have sampled this unit.

Preparing for the delivery of knowledge and understanding

This section is particularly useful to those delivering assessor and quality assurer awards to candidates. You will find a scheme of work (programme or agenda) relating to the two knowledge units – one to underpin the assessor qualifications and one for the QA qualifications.

Assessor qualification

Scheme of work for knowledge unit – understanding the principles and practices of assessment

The following scheme of work is a suggestion for how the content of this unit might be broken down and delivered to candidate assessors. It requires a minimum of 24 hours of **guided learning hours (GLH)**. It assumes 12 sessions of 2 hours duration, but this may vary according to organisational need. There is also an assumption that this unit is delivered to a group rather than an individual. It would need to be modified if that were not the case. The detailed content would be planned according to the specific preferences and needs of the learning cohort, with teaching and learning methods arranged accordingly.

Prior to the commencement of the programme, the potential candidate assessors should receive appropriate advice and guidance. This may include assessments relating to acquisition of English skills and other diagnostic assessments in order to identify levels of support required.

UNIT 301 SCHEME OF WORK

Session	Content	Extension/assessment activity	Links to Unit 301
1	Introduction to unit and course; ice breaker and introductions. Issue course handbook (assessor qualification). The language of assessment: understanding the terminology. The roles and responsibilities of the assessor and the assessment team (suggested activity: thought shower the duties and summarise into: roles, responsibilities and characteristics).	Prepare a dictionary of terms with their meanings. Locate and save/print (probably from the internet) a copy of the NOS, units of assessment or in-house standards for your subject area. Collect or review a copy of the qualification/ course or student handbook for the qualification/training programme you are to assess.	1.1 1.3 1.4
2	Key concepts and rules of assessment. Legislation and regulation (suggested activity: each group researches a piece of legislation and offers key findings to other groups). Policy and procedure, why do we need them?	Locate and print/save a copy of your organisation's assessment policy and procedure. OR Review an example of an assessment policy and procedure.	1.1 1.2 1.4 8.1
3	Assessment methods – traditional and e-assessment techniques. Questioning techniques. Risks and barriers to assessment. Special assessment requirements (suggested activity: thought shower key barriers to assessment and identify a strategy to support each).	Create a list of the main assessment methods used to collect knowledge and performance evidence for your subject area assessments. Review *four* methods in detail and identify the main strengths and weaknesses of the chosen methods.	2.1 3.4 3.5 4.4 8.2

Session	Content	Extension/assessment activity	Links to Unit 301
4	Planning assessments – key components of an assessment plan. Holistic v unitised assessment. Preparing for assessment – how to prepare the candidate; liaising with others in the assessment process; peer and self-assessment as an indicator of readiness and development needs.	Collect a copy of your organisation's document for planning assessment. OR Review a planning document. Download the assessment strategy for your subject area (from the AO). Describe a holistic assessment to cover a number of units from a chosen set of occupational standards.	3.1 3.2 3.3 4.1 4.2 4.3
5	Practice workshop Using a set of occupational standards, prepare plans using appropriate assessment methods. Recap – rules of assessment.	Compare and contrast methods and offer suggestions to modify practice to suit: learner with communication barriers; learner who lacks confidence; learner with limited access to assessment opportunities.	5.1 5.2
6	Making assessment judgements and giving feedback (suggested activity: role play feedback models and examples). Record keeping.	Collect copies of your organisation's documents for recording assessment and feedback. OR Review examples of recording documents.	7.1 7.2

Session	Content	Extension/assessment activity	Links to Unit 301
7	Disputes and appeals. Assessment etiquette: confidentiality. E-technology – demonstration of e-portfolio. E&D: meeting the needs of individuals.	Locate your organisation's appeal procedure. OR Review an appeals procedure (for example from an AO).	6.3 8.1 8.2 8.3
8	Brief outline of QA process – what is QA, key practices: moderation and verification: sampling, standardisation, grading.	Collect or review samples of assessed work and annotate to show how it meets the rules of assessment. Attend and collect minutes from a standardisation meeting or simulate a standardisation meeting in class.	5.1 5.2 6.1 6.2
9	Preparing for professional discussion. Create appointment schedule for next week/s.	Prepare personal statements. OR Recap main theoretical aspects of the qualification. Review Chapter 1 The principles of assessment: functions and concepts and Chapter 2 Planning and delivering assessments of *Practical Teaching: A Guide to Assessment and Quality Assurance.*	
10	Professional discussions.	Prepare own discussion topics.	All

Session	Content	Extension/assessment activity	Links to Unit 301
11	Either professional discussions continued or extension activities.	Review evidence requirements for your qualification and prepare evidence for your qualification.	All
12	Reflection. Key learning. Making improvements to practice. Next steps.	Create a personal development plan. Identify key areas for improvement.	8.4

Internal quality assurance qualification

Scheme of work for knowledge unit – Understanding the principles and practices of internally assuring the quality of assessment

This scheme of work is a suggestion about how the content of this unit might be broken down and delivered to candidate quality assurers. It requires a minimum of 45 hours of guided learning. It assumes 15 sessions of 3 hours duration, but this may vary according to organisational need. There is also an assumption that this unit is delivered to a group rather than an individual. It would need to be modified if that were not the case. The detailed content would be planned according to the specific preferences and needs of the learning cohort, with teaching and learning methods arranged accordingly.

Prior to the commencement of the programme, the potential candidate quality assurers should receive appropriate advice and guidance. This may include assessments relating to acquisition of English skills and other diagnostic assessments in order to identify levels of support required.

Session	Content	Extension/assessment activity	Links to Unit 401
1	Introduction to unit, course: ice breaker and introductions. Issue course handbook (internal quality assurance qualification). The language of QA: understanding the terminology. The roles and responsibilities of the IQA and the assessment team (suggested activity: thought shower the duties and summarise into role – responsibilities – characteristics).	Create a mini job description for the role of IQA and link to others in the team (link to Unit 403).	1.1 1.3
2	Recap assessment principles and rules of assessment.	Review Chapter 1 The principles of assessment: functions and concepts and Chapter 2 Planning and delivering assessments of *Practical Teaching: A Guide to Assessment and Quality Assurance.*	1.1 1.2 3.2
3	The functions of IQA. Suggested activity: thought shower purpose of QA. Key concepts, principles and rules of QA. Legislation and regulation including confidentiality. (suggested activity: each group researches a piece of legislation and offers key findings to other groups). Policy and procedure, why do we need them?	Create an information leaflet for a new assessor about the role of IQA. Locate and print/save a copy of your organisation's QA/verification/ moderation policy and procedure. OR Review an example of a QA policy and procedure.	1.1 1.2 1.4 5.1 6.1 6.2

Session	Content	Extension/assessment activity	Links to Unit 401
4	Overview of internal quality assurance strategies: sampling, standardisation, moderation, verification. QA in e-assessment.	Collect examples of IV documentation or review samples of IV documentation.	1.2 2.1 6.2
5	Planning for internal quality assurance (what, why, how, when). Identify the key risk points. The rules of assessment and their relationship to QA.		2.1 2.2 2.3 3.2
6	Sampling models. (suggested activity: prepare exemplar IQA plans and justify the chosen strategy against CAMERA).	Justify how QA models of sampling can lead to effective and efficient assessment.	3.1
7	Preparing for a standardisation meeting. Note taking. Communication and chairing meetings.	Simulate or undertake a Standardisation meeting.	2.2 2.3 4.2
8	Feedback from formative and summative assessment. (Suggested activity: role play or case study examples of weak assessment requiring feedback.) Supporting and inducting assessors.	Prepare an induction plan for a new assessor.	4.1 6.3
9	Dealing with appeals and disputes. Referral to EQA if necessary. Equality and diversity: dealing with and developing assessment to meet the needs of individuals. IQA strategies to standardise and moderate difference.	Locate your organisation's appeal procedure. OR Review an appeals procedure (for example from an AO).	4.3 6.4

Session	Content	Extension/assessment activity	Links to Unit 401
10	Keeping records. Using or developing documentation to lead to accurate and complete IQA practices. Review legislation to ensure transparency in record keeping.		5.1 6.1
11	Preparing for an EQA visit. Internal and external audit. Communication between centres and AOs. Keeping AOs informed.		
12	Preparing for professional discussion.	Review Chapter 3 Quality assurance of assessment and Chapter 4 Internally assuring the quality of assessment of *Practical Teaching: A Guide to Assessment and Quality Assurance.*	
13	Professional discussions.		All
14	Either professional discussions continued or extension activities.		
15	Reflection. Key learning. Making improvements to practice. Next steps.	Create a personal development plan. Identify key areas for improvement.	6.3

Deliverers of programmes, maybe using the suggested programmes above, should ensure that content and activities address the evidence guidelines stated in the AO's published material.

Glossary of terms

Assessor a person in the workplace or other learning environment who is quality assured by a candidate quality assurer

CAMERA acronym for a suggested sampling strategy (candidate, assessor, method, evidence, records, assessment site)

Candidate assessor a person seeking to achieve an assessor qualification

Candidate quality assurer a person seeking to achieve the QA qualification

Competence knowledge of or ability to do something

Contingency plan planning for the unexpected occurrence

Countersign a guarantee of reliability in assessment decisions, made by unqualified assessors

Evidence the output of an assessment activity; evidence of a learner's knowledge understanding, skills or competence that can be used to make a judgement of their achievement against agreed standards/criteria

Guided learning hours (GLH) the number of hours of direct contact required to deliver a qualification

Portfolio a storage tool, used either paper based or electronically to collect evidence

Principle a set of values or beliefs; a rule or moral code

Qualification a set of specifications (units of assessment) leading to an award, certificate or diploma of achievement; an accredited QCF, NQF or NVQ qualification or in-house/industry or organisationally devised set of standards used to assess the competence of trainees/learners

Qualification assessor a person accredited to assess assessor and quality assurance qualifications

Qualification quality assurer a person accredited to quality assure assessor and quality assurance and QA qualifications

Testify/testimony to bear witness to; to concur; to give evidence of

Trainee/learner a person in the work place or other learning environment who is assessed by the candidate assessor

Recommended reading

City and Guilds (2011) Level 3 and 4 Awards and Certificates in Assessment and Quality Assurance – Qualification handbook for centres. Qualification: 6317. February 2011

Useful online resources

Developing a portfolio of evidence: www.eoedeanery.nhs.uk

SUMMARY

In this chapter we set out to:

- Describe the main features of your portfolio of evidence relating to the assessor and quality assurance qualifications.
- Prepare a programme suitable for the delivery of knowledge and understanding.
- Develop and accumulate knowledge and understanding evidence.
- Aid and support the compilation of your performance evidence to meet the evidence requirements.

Your personal development

- Having established the tiers of assessment and comprehended who is who and who does what in terms of

QA, assessors, candidate assessors/quality assurers and trainees, you started this stage of learning by exploring the meaning of the word portfolio and are now able to describe what it is, what it consists of and how it is compiled. You have looked at evidence of competence and understand the difference between performance and knowledge evidence and how these are demonstrated in your portfolio. You completed this section by confirming your understanding of some key assessment methods for this qualification – observation, oral and written questioning, work products, professional discussion, personal statements and witness testimony.

- Then you considered a suggested programme or scheme of work to gain sufficient knowledge to meet the standards. The topics included in the scheme are explored in detail in the previous chapters (Chapters 1 to 5). If you are reading this as an assessor of the asessor and QA awards you have considered how these could be translated into learning sessions.
- In the next part, you discovered what you need to do in order to achieve the qualification. The main findings here are that to gain the assessor qualification you need to work with two trainees, each doing two assessments. You need to follow a complete cycle of assessment for each of the four assessments – see Figure 2.1, page 39. For the QA qualification, you need to work with two assessors, each of whom has two trainees. Each assessor should complete a full cycle of the 'quality cycle' – see Figure 4.1, page 129. Both units require additional evidence to supplement the performance evidence (best practice evidence) as well as evidence to confirm knowledge and understanding.
- This part of the chapter followed on by making some suggestions regarding what the supplementary and knowledge evidence should consist of. These are written as questions but can be evidence by simply answering them, by using them to reference some personal statements or as a

focus for a professional discussion with your qualification assessor.

- Finally, you looked at how all of this is put together and tracked (referenced to the assessment and learning outcomes). The final stage of your development is concerned with doing the job. Your qualification assessor at your chosen centre will support you in achieving your goal.

Good luck!

Appendices

A Occupational sectors – Sector subject areas (SSAs)

B Units of assessment (City & Guilds)

C Abbreviations and acronyms

Appendix A: Occupational sectors – Sector subject areas (SSAs)

	Area – First Tier		Area – Second Tier
1	Health, Public Services and Care	1.1	Medicine and Dentistry
		1.2	Nursing and Subjects and Vocations Allied to Medicine
		1.3	Health and Social Care
		1.4	Public Services
2	Science and Mathematics	2.1	Science
		2.2	Mathematics and Statistics
3	Agriculture, Horticulture and Animal Care	3.1	Agriculture
		3.2	Horticulture and Forestry
		3.3	Animal Care and Veterinary Science
		3.4	Environmental Conservation
4	Engineering and Manufacturing Technologies	4.1	Engineering
		4.2	Manufacturing Technologies
		4.3	Transportation Operations and Maintenance
5	Construction, Planning and the Built Environment	5.1	Architecture
		5.2	Building and Construction
		5.3	Urban, Rural and Regional Planning
6	Information and Communication Technology	6.1	ICT Practitioners
		6.2	ICT for Users
7	Retail and Commercial Enterprise	7.1	Retailing and Wholesaling
		7.2	Warehousing and Distribution
		7.3	Service Enterprises
		7.4	Hospitality and Catering
8	Leisure, Travel and Tourism	8.1	Sport, Leisure and Recreation
		8.2	Travel and Tourism

9	Arts, Media and Publishing	9.1	Performing Arts
		9.2	Crafts, Creative Arts and Design
		9.3	Media and Communication
		9.4	Publishing and Information Services
10	History, Philosophy and Theology	10.1	History
		10.2	Archaeology and Archaeological Sciences
		10.3	Philosophy
		10.4	Theology and Religious Studies
11	Social Sciences	11.1	Geography
		11.2	Sociology and Social Policy
		11.3	Politics
		11.4	Economics
		11.5	Anthropology
12	Languages, Literature and Culture	12.1	Languages, Literature and Culture of the British Isles
		12.2	Other Languages, Literature and Culture
		12.3	Linguistics
13	Education and Training	13.1	Teaching and Lecturing
		13.2	Direct Learning Support
14	Preparation for Life and Work	14.1	Foundations for Learning and Life
		14.2	Preparation for Work
15	Business, Administration and Law	15.1	Accounting and Finance
		15.2	Administration
		15.3	Business Management
		15.4	Marketing and Sales
		15.5	Law and Legal Services

Source: Ofqual http://www.ofqual.gov.uk/files/sector_subject_areas_with_indicative_content.pdf, for a complete version, including the detailed topics within each area and sub-area tiers.

Appendix B: Units of assessment (City & Guilds)

Understanding the principles and practices of assessment

1. Understand the principles and requirements of assessment	1.1 Explain the functions of assessment in learning and development. 1.2 Define the key concepts and principles of assessment. 1.3 Explain the responsibilities of the assessor. 1.4 Identify the regulations and requirements relevant to assessment in own area of practice.
2. Understand different types of assessment method	2.1 Compare the strengths and limitations of a range of assessment methods with reference to the needs of individual learners.
3. Understand how to plan assessment	3.1 Summarise key factors to consider when planning assessment. 3.2 Evaluate the benefits of using a holistic approach to assessment. 3.3 Explain how to plan a holistic approach to assessment. 3.4 Summarise the types of risks that may be involved in assessment in own area of responsibility. 3.5 Explain how to minimise risks through the planning process.
4. Understand how to involve learners and others in assessment	4.1 Explain the importance of involving the learner and others in the assessment process. 4.2 Summarise types of information that should be made available to learners and others involved in the assessment process. 4.3 Explain how peer and self-assessment can be used effectively to promote learner involvement and personal responsibility in the assessment of learning. 4.4 Explain how assessment arrangements can be adapted to meet the needs of individual learners.

5. Understand how to make assessment decisions	5.1 Explain how to judge whether evidence is: ● sufficient ● authentic ● current. 5.2 Explain how to ensure that assessment decisions are: ● made against specified criteria ● valid ● reliable ● fair.
6. Understand quality assurance of the assessment process	6.1 Evaluate the importance of quality assurance in the assessment process. 6.2 Summarise quality assurance and standardisation procedures in own area of practice. 6.3 Summarise the procedures to follow when there are disputes concerning assessment in own area of practice.
7. Understand how to manage information relating to assessment	7.1 Explain the importance of following procedures for the management of information relating to assessment. 7.2 Explain how feedback and questioning contribute to the assessment process.
8. Understand the legal and good practice requirements in relation to assessment	8.1 Explain legal issues, policies and procedures relevant to assessment, including those for confidentiality, health, safety and welfare. 8.2 Explain the contribution that technology can make to the assessment process. 8.3 Evaluate requirement for equality and diversity and, where appropriate, bilingualism in relation to assessment. 8.4 Explain the value of reflective practice and continuing professional development in the assessment process.

Assess occupational competence in the work environment

1. Be able to plan the assessment of occupational competence	1.1 Plan assessment of occupational competence based on the following methods: • observation of performance in the work environment • examining products of work • questioning the learner • discussing with the learner • use of others (witness testimony) • looking at candidate statements • recognising prior learning. 1.2 Communicate the purpose, requirements and the processes of assessing occupational competence to the learner. 1.3 Plan the assessment of occupational competence to address learner needs and current achievements. 1.4 Identify opportunities for holistic assessment.
2. Be able to make assessment decisions about occupational competence	2.1 Use valid, fair and reliable assessment methods including: • observation of performance • examining products of work • questioning the learner • discussing with the learner • use of others (witness testimony) • looking at candidate statements • recognising prior learning. 2.2 Make assessment decisions of occupational competence against specified criteria. 2.3 Follow standardisation procedures. 2.4 Provide feedback to learners that affirms achievement and identifies any further implications for learning, assessment and progression.
3. Be able to provide required information following the assessment of occupational competence	3.1 Maintain records of the assessment of occupational competence, its outcomes and learner progress. 3.2 Make assessment information available to authorised colleagues.

	3.3 Follow procedures to maintain the confidentiality of assessment information.
4. Be able to maintain legal and good practice requirements when assessing occupational competence	4.1 Follow relevant policies, procedures and legislation for the assessment of occupational competence, including those for health, safety and welfare. 4.2 Apply requirements for equality and diversity and, where appropriate, bilingualism, when assessing occupational competence. 4.3 Evaluate own work in carrying out assessments of occupational competence. 4.4 Maintain the currency of own expertise and competence as relevant to own role in assessing occupational competence.

Assess vocational skills, knowledge and understanding

1. Be able to prepare assessments of vocational skills, knowledge and understanding	1.1 Select methods to assess vocational skills, knowledge and understanding which address learner needs and meet assessment requirements, including: • assessments in simulated environments • skills tests • oral and written questions • assignments • projects • case studies • recognising prior learning. 1.2 Prepare resources and conditions for the assessment of vocational skills, knowledge and understanding. 1.3 Communicate the purpose, requirements and processes of assessment of vocational skills, knowledge and understanding to learners.

2. Be able to carry out assessments of vocational skills, knowledge and understanding	2.1 Manage assessments of vocational skills, knowledge and understanding to meet assessment requirements. 2.2 Provide support to learners within agreed limitations. 2.3 Analyse evidence of learner achievement. 2.4 Make assessment decisions relating to vocational skills, knowledge and understanding against specified criteria. 2.5 Follow standardisation procedures. 2.6 Provide feedback to the learner that affirms achievement and identifies any further implications for learning, assessment and progression.
3. Be able to provide required information following the assessment of vocational skills, knowledge and understanding	3.1 Maintain records of the assessment of vocational skills, knowledge and understanding, its outcomes and learner progress. 3.2 Make assessment information available to authorised colleagues as required. 3.3 Follow procedures to maintain the confidentiality of assessment information.
4. Be able to maintain legal and good practice requirements when assessing vocational skills, knowledge and understanding	4.1 Follow relevant policies, procedures and legislation relating to the assessment of vocational skills, knowledge and understanding, including those for health, safety and welfare. 4.2 Apply requirements for equality and diversity and, where appropriate, bilingualism. 4.3 Evaluate own work in carrying out assessments of vocational skills, knowledge and understanding. 4.4 Take part in continuing professional development to ensure current expertise and competence in assessing vocational skills, knowledge and understanding.

Understanding the principles and practices of internally assuring the quality of assessment

1. Understand the context and principles of internal quality assurance	1.1 Explain the functions of internal quality assurance in learning and development. 1.2 Explain the key concepts and principles of the internal quality assurance of assessment. 1.3 Explain the roles of practitioners involved in the internal and external quality assurance process. 1.4 Explain the regulations and requirements for internal quality assurance in own area of practice.
2. Understand how to plan the internal quality assurance of assessment	2.1 Evaluate the importance of planning and preparing internal quality assurance activities. 2.2 Explain what an internal quality assurance plan should contain. 2.3 Summarise the preparations that need to be made for internal quality assurance, including: • information collecting • communications • administrative arrangements • resources.
3. Understanding techniques and criteria for monitoring the quality of assessment internally	3.1 Evaluate different techniques for sampling evidence of assessment, including use of technology. 3.2 Explain the appropriate criteria to use for judging the quality of the assessment process.
4. Understand how to internally maintain and improve the quality of assessment	4.1 Summarise the types of feedback, support and advice that assessors may need to maintain and improve the quality of assessment. 4.2 Explain standardisation requirements in relation to assessment. 4.3 Explain relevant procedures regarding disputes about the quality of assessment.
5. Understand how to manage information relevant to the internal quality assurance of assessment	5.1 Evaluate requirements for information management, data protection and confidentiality in relation to the internal quality assurance of assessment.

6. Understand the legal and good practice requirements for the internal quality assurance of assessment	6.1 Evaluate legal issues, policies and procedures relevant to the internal quality assurance of assessment, including those for health, safety and welfare. 6.2 Evaluate different ways in which technology can contribute to the internal quality assurance of assessment. 6.3 Explain the value of reflective practice and continuing professional development in relation to internal quality assurance. 6.4 Evaluate requirements for equality and diversity and, where appropriate, bilingualism, in relation to the internal quality assurance of assessment.

Internally assure the quality of assessment

1. Be able to plan the internal quality assurance of assessment	1.1 Plan monitoring activities according to the requirements of own role. 1.2 Make arrangements for internal monitoring activities to assure quality.
2. Be able to internally evaluate the quality of assessment	2.1 Carry out internal monitoring activities to quality requirements. 2.2 Evaluate assessor expertise and competence in relation to the requirements of their role. 2.3 Evaluate the planning and preparation of assessment processes. 2.4 Determine whether assessment methods are safe, fair, valid and reliable. 2.5 Determine whether assessment decisions are made using the specified criteria. 2.6 Compare assessor decisions to ensure they are consistent.
3. Be able to internally maintain and improve the quality of assessment	3.1 Provide assessors with feedback, advice and support, including professional development opportunities, which help them to maintain and improve the quality of assessment. 3.2 Apply procedures to standardise assessment practices and outcomes.

4. Be able to manage information relevant to the internal quality assurance of assessment	4.1 Apply procedures for recording, storing and reporting information relating to internal quality assurance. 4.2 Follow procedures to maintain confidentiality of internal quality assurance information.
5. Be able to maintain legal and good practice requirements when internally monitoring and maintaining the quality of assessment	5.1 Apply relevant policies, procedures and legislation in relation to internal quality assurance, including those for health, safety and welfare. 5.2 Apply requirements for equality and diversity and, where appropriate, bilingualism, in relation to internal quality assurance. 5.3 Critically reflect on own practice in internally assuring the quality of assessment. 5.4 Maintain the currency of own expertise and competence in internally assuring the quality of assessment.

Plan, allocate and monitor work in own area of responsibility

1. Be able to produce a work plan for own area of responsibility	1.1 Explain the context in which work is to be undertaken. 1.2 Identify the skills base and the resources available. 1.3 Examine priorities and success criteria needed for the team. 1.4 Produce a work plan for own area of responsibility.
2. Be able to allocate and agree responsibilities with team members	2.1 Identify team members' responsibilities for identified work activities. 2.2 Agree responsibilities and SMART (specific, measurable, achievable, realistic and time-bound) objectives with team members.

3. Be able to monitor the progress and quality of work in own area of responsibility and provide feedback	3.1 Identify ways to monitor progress and quality of work. 3.2 Monitor and evaluate progress against agreed standards and provide feedback to team members.
4. Be able to review and amend plans of work for own area of responsibility and communicate changes	4.1 Review and amend work plan where changes are needed. 4.2 Communicate changes to team members.

Source: City & Guilds, 2010

Appendix C: Abbreviations and acronyms

AO	Awarding organisation
APA	Accreditation of prior achievement
APL	Accreditation of prior learning
BTEC	Trade mark for Edexcel qualifications
CADET©	Consistent, accessible, detailed, earned, transparent (acronym for principles of assessment)
CAMERA	Candidate, assessor, method, evidence, records, assessment site (acronym for a suggested sampling strategy)
CCEA	Council for the Curriculum, Examinations and Assessment
CIF	Common inspection framework
CPD	Continuous professional development
CRB	Criminal Records Bureau
CV	Curriculum vitae
DCELLS	Department for Children, Education, Lifelong Learning and Skills
DCS	Direct claims status
DELTA	Disability, Emotional, Language, Technology, Ability (acronym to remember barriers to learning and assessment)
EE	External examiner
EFQM	European Foundation for Quality Management
EM	External moderator
EQA	External quality assurance/assurer (appointed by an awarding organisation)
EV	External verifier
GLH	Guided learning hours

GOLA	Global online assessment
HE	Higher education
HSE	Health and Safety Executive
IA	Independent assessor
IAG	Information, advice and guidance
IfL	Institute for Learning
IiE	Investors in Excellence
IiP	Investors in People
IM	Internal moderator
IQA	Internal quality assurer/assurance
IQAC	Internal quality assurance co-ordinator
IQER	Integrated quality enhancement review
ISA	Independent safeguarding authority
ISO	International Organization for Standardization
IV	Internal verifier
IVA	Institute for Verifiers and Assessors
IVC	Internal verification co-ordinator
LIV	Lead internal verifier
LLUK	Lifelong Learning UK – SSC – disbanded March 2011
LQA	Lead quality assurer (appointed by an approved centre)
MCQs	Multiple choice questions
NOS	National Occupational Standards
NQAI	National Qualifications Authority of Ireland
NQF	National Qualifications Framework
NVQ	National Vocational Qualification
Ofqual	Office of the Qualifications and Examinations Regulator
Ofsted	Office for Standards in Education
OSCA	Online support for centre assessors
PPE	Personal protective equipment
PICA©	Plan, implement, check, action (acronym to remember the stages of the quality cycle)
QA	Quality assurance

QAA	Quality assurance agency
QCF	Qualifications and Credit Framework
QIP	Quality improvement plan
RPL	Recognition of prior learning (formerly APL/E/A – accreditation of prior learning or experience or achievement)
SAR	Self assessment report
SMART	Specific, Measurable, Achievable, Relevant, Time bounded (acronym for target setting)
SMARTER	Specific, Measurable, Achievable, Relevant, Time-bounded, Ethical, Reviewed (extended acronym for target setting)
SQA	Scottish Qualifications Authority
SSC	Sector Skills Council
TNA	Training needs analysis
TQM	Total quality management
TQS	Training quality standard
UoA	Units of assessment
UPK	Underpinning knowledge (theory of a subject)
VBS	Vetting and barring scheme
VDU	Visual display units (in relation to display screen equipment regulations)
VLE	Virtual learning environment

Glossary

A

Accredited a qualification written under Ofqual regulations

Appeal a request to reconsider a judgement made

Assessment the checking of learning and demonstrating competence

Assessor a person in the workplace or other learning environment who is quality assured by a candidate quality assurer

Authentic being the learner's own work

Awarding organisation (AO) a body approved by Ofqual to create and certificate qualifications

B

Bilingualism speaking two languages

C

CADET© consistent, accessible, detailed, earned, transparent principles of assessment

CAMERA candidate, assessor, method, evidence, records, assessment site (acronym for a suggested sampling strategy)

Candidate assessor a person seeking to achieve an assessor qualification

Candidate quality assurer a person seeking to achieve the quality assurance qualification

Certification a process of claiming a certificate following successful completion of a qualification

Closed questioning limited response type of questions

Competence knowledge of or ability to do something

Concept an idea

Contingency plan planning for the unexpected occurrence

Continuous professional development (CPD) on-the-job training for staff

Countersign a guarantee of reliability in assessment decisions, made by unqualified assessors

Criterion (pl: criteria) a standard of competence

Cross reference linking evidence to more than one aspect of the qualification

Currency reflects current or recent work practices

D

DELTA disability, emotional, language, technology, ability (acronym to remember barriers to learning and assessment)

Direct claims status a high level of confidence from an AO, resulting in the ability to claim certification without a visit from an EQA (DCS)

Dispute a difference in opinion of an outcome

Diversity acknowledging that each individual is unique and recognising our individual differences in for example, culture, ability, gender, race, religion, wealth, sexual orientation, or any other group characteristic

E

EQA external quality assurer (appointed by an AO)

Equality a state of fair treatment that is the right of all the people regardless of the differences in, for example, culture, ability, gender, race, religion, wealth, sexual orientation, or any other group characteristic

Evidence the output of an assessment activity; evidence of a learner's knowledge understanding, skills or competence that can be used to make a judgement of their achievement against agreed standards/ criteria

F

Fair ensuring that everyone has an equal chance of getting an objective and accurate assessment

Feedback verbal or written comments about the assessment intended to bring about improvement

Formative assessment interim or ongoing assessment

Formative feedback on-going feedback to support development

G

Goal an aim or desired result

Guided learning hours (GHL) the number of hours of direct contact required to deliver a qualification

H

Holistic the big picture; the whole qualification or curriculum

Horizontal sampling sampling across all units in the programme

I

Induction an introduction to a programme or duty

Interim QA quality assurance within the programme designed to support and develop practice

Internal quality assurance validating the integrity of the assessment

Intervention to interrupt for the purpose of resolving issues

IV Internal verifier (old terminology)

IM Internal moderator (old terminology)

IQA Internal quality assurer

L

Leading questioning posing a question (with an indicated answer contained within the question)

Learner the person being assessed by the candidate assessor

Learner journey the learner's experience of an organisation from first to final contact

LQA lead quality assurer (appointed by an approved centre)

M

Malpractice improper or negligent actions

Moderation the confirmation that marks or grades are accurate

Multilingualism speaking many languages

N

National Occupational Standards (NOS) nationally set guidelines defining the level, size and subjects used in designing units of assessment

O

Objectivity without bias

Ofqual regulatory body, Office of the Qualifications and Examinations Regulation

Open questioning posing a question designed to elicit a detailed response

P

Pathway a route; usually describing the combination of units to achieve the learner's goal

PICA acronym for components of the quality cycle; plan, implement, check, action

Plagiarism the passing off of someone else's work as your own without reference

Policy a statement of proposed actions

Portfolio a storage tool, used either paper based or electronically to collect evidence

Principle a set of values or beliefs; a rule or moral code

Procedure a way of working

Process a series of actions to meet a specific outcome

Q

Qualification a set of specifications (units of assessment) leading to an award, certificate or diploma of achievement; an accredited QCF, NQF or NVQ qualification or in-house/industry or organisationally devised set of standards used to assess the competence of trainees/learners

Qualification assessor a person accredited to assess assessor and quality assurance qualifications

Qualification quality assurer a person accredited to quality assure assessor and quality assurance qualifications

Quality assurance a system of review to confirm that processes are in place and applied to guarantee the quality of the service or product; systematic checks to provide confidence

Quality control checks on the integrity of the process

Quality improvement process to improve reliability of quality assurance systems

R

Registration an official list of entrants to a qualification

Regulation a rule or directive made by an official organisation

Reliability strategy to ensure that assessment decisions are consistent

Reliable consistently achieves the same results with different assessors and the same (or similar) group of learners

Requirements these could be the requirements of the practitioner's own organisation or those of an external organisation such as awarding organisation

Rules validity/relevance; reliability; authenticity; currency/recency; sufficiency; power of discrimination; objectivity (rules of assessment)

S

Sample a representative of the whole to show trends

Sanction a penalty for disobeying the rules

SMARTER specific, measurable, achievable, relevant, time-bounded, ethical and reviewed

SSC Sector Skills Council (part of UK Commission for Employment and Skills)

Stakeholder a person, either directly or indirectly, associated or interested in the candidate or organisation

Standards an agreed level of competence

Standardisation process to confirm decisions and create norms

Statute a written law passed by a legislative body

Subjectivity decisions influenced by other factors

Sufficient enough evidence as specified in evidence requirements or assessment strategy

Summative assessment final or summary assessment

Summative feedback feedback at the end of the unit or programme in which the final judgement is made

Summative QA quality assurance at the end of the unit or programme

T

Targets an objective or focused path towards an outcome

Testify/testimony to bear witness to; to concur; to give evidence of

Themed sampling sampling focused on a specific aspect of assessment

Trainee/Learner a person in the work place or other learning environment who is assessed by the candidate assessor

Training needs analysis (TNA) identification of required training

U

Units of assessment statements of knowledge and/or competence, clustered to make a qualification

V

Valid relevant to the standards/criteria against which the candidate is being assessed

Verification the confirmation that the processes leading to assessment decision-making are compliant, accurate and complete

Vertical sampling sampling of a single units across all assessors

W

Witness a person, other than assessor, who provides evidence of competence

References and bibliography

Printed references

Brown, R A (1992) *Portfolio development and profiling for nurses*. Lancaster: Quay Publishing Ltd

Bush, T and Middlewood, D (1997) *Managing People in Education*. London: Paul Chapman Publishing

City and Guilds (2011) *Level 3 and 4 Awards & Certificates in Assessment and Quality Assurance: qualification handbook for centres*. February 2011

City and Guilds (2009) *Level 2 Diploma in Professional Food and Beverage Service, 7103-02*, Qualification handbook, 500/7478/7. November 2009

Cole, G A and Kelly, P (2011) *Management Theory and Practice*. Andover: Cengage

Collins, D (2006) *A survival guide for college managers and leaders*. London: Continuum

Ecclestone, K (1996) *How to assess the Vocational Curriculum*. London: Kogan Page quoted in Gray, D Griffin, C and Nasta, T (2005) *Training to Teach in Further and Adult Education*. (2nd Edition) Cheltenham: Stanley Thornes

Ellis, C W (2004) *Management Skills for new Managers*. New York: AMACOM

Fautley, M and Savage, J (2008) *Assessment for Learning and Teaching in Secondary Schools*. Exeter: Learning Matters

Gardener, J (ed) (2006) *Assessment and Learning*. London: Sage

Gravells, A (2009) *Principles and practice of Assessment in the Lifelong Learning Sector*. Exeter: Learning Matters

Gray, D Griffin, C and Nasta, T (2005) *Training to Teach in Further and Adult Education*. (2nd Edition) Cheltenham: Stanley Thornes

Hill, C (2003) *Teaching using Information and Learning Technology in Further Education*. Exeter: Learning Matters

Hoyle, D (2007) *Quality Management Essentials*. Oxford: Heinemann (Elsevier)

Kolb, D (1984) *Experiential Learning: experience as a source of learning and development*. Englewood Cliffs, NJ: Prentice-Hall

LLUK (2006) *New overarching professional standards for teachers, tutors and trainers in the Lifelong Learning Sector*. November 2006. Lifelong Learning UK

O'Connell, Sir B (2005) *Creating an Outstanding College*. Cheltenham: Nelson Thornes

The Royal College of Speech and Language Therapists (2006) Communicating Quality 3, *RCSLT's guidance on best practice in service organization and provision*. London: The Royal College of Speech and Language Therapists

Walklin, L (1991) *The Assessment of Performance and Competence: a handbook for teachers and trainers*. Cheltenham: Stanley Thornes

Walklin, L (1996) *Training and Development NVQs: a handbook for FAETC candidates and NVQ trainers*. (reprinted 2001) Cheltenham: Nelson Thornes

Whalley, J, Welch, T and Williamson, L (2006). *E-Learning in FE*. London: Continuum

Wilson, L (2008) *Practical Teaching: a guide to PTLLS and CTLLS*. London: Cengage Learning

Wilson, L (2009) *Practical Teaching: a guide to PTLLS and DTLLS*. Andover: Cengage Learning

Wood, J, and Dickinson, J (2011) *Quality Assurance and Evaluation*. Exeter: Learning Matters

Web sourced references

Balancing Assessment of and for learning. Enhancement Themes – various researchers summarised on: http://www.enhancementthemes.ac.uk/themes/IntegrativeAssessment/IABalancingFeedforwardAss.asp

Award Handbook – City and Guilds: City and Guilds (2011) *Level 3 & 4 Awards & Certificates in Assessment and Quality Assurance*. www.cityandguilds.com (version 1.3 February 2011, p. 16, accessed April 2011)

City & Guilds – Enquiries and Appeals policy (August 2008): http://www.cityandguilds.com/documents/Centre%20(Generic)/Enquiries_and_Appeals_-_policy_and_procedures_V1_Dec_08 (1).pdf

Code of Conduct: http://www.iebe.org.uk/index.php/code-of-conduct-for-assessors

Developing a portfolio of evidence: www.eoedeanery.nhs.uk

Equality Act: http://www.equalities.gov.uk/equality_act_2010.aspx

Equality Act: http://www.smarta.com/advice/legal/employment-law/the-equality-act-(october-1-2010)-need-to-know-for-small-businesses?gclid=CP7h7syP76cCFcoa4QodYhknaw

Investor in People: http://www.investorsinpeople.co.uk

ISO: http://www.iso.org

Matrix Assessment: http://www.matrixstandard.com

Ofqual: http://www.ofqual.gov.uk/files/Regulatory_arrangements_QCF_August08.pdf and http://www.ofqual.gov.uk/files/qca-06-2888_nvq_code_of_practice_r06.pdf

Ofsted and regional equivalents: www.ofsted.gov.uk; www.deni.gov.uk; www.hmie.gov.uk; www.estyn.gov.uk

QAA and IQER: www.qaa.ac.uk

Qualifications and Credit Framework: http://www.qcda.gov.uk/qualifications/60.aspx

Risk Assessment: http://www.hse.gov.uk/risk/fivesteps.htm

Rules of Combination: Version 4 http://www.paa-uk.org/Qualifications/Regulated/Qualifications/QCF%20Info/QCF%20 Support%20Pack/Rules%20of%20Combination%20in%20the%20QCF.pdf

Sector Skills Councils: UK Commission for Employments and Skills – http://www.ukces.org.uk/

Sector/Subject Areas: http://www.ofqual.gov.uk/files/sector_subject_areas_with_indicative_content.pdf

Total Quality Management: http://www.trainingqualitystandard.co.uk http://www.businessballs.com/dtiresources/total_quality_management_TQM.pdf

TQS Mark: withdrawn April 2011: http://www.trainingqualitystandard.co.uk

VDU Guidelines: http://www.hse.gov.uk/pubns/indg36.pdf

Vetting and Barring Scheme: www.homeoffice.gov.uk/crime/vetting-barring-scheme/

Wolf, A (2011) *Review of Vocational Education – The Wolf Report*. March 2011 https://www.education.gov.uk/publications/standard/publicationDetail/Page1/DFE-00031-2011 (accessed May 2011)

Index

Lightning Source UK Ltd.
Milton Keynes UK
UKOW03f1339170215

246404UK00001B/25/P

Contents

Illustrations

Preface

Research for this book was supported by grants from the Social Sciences and Humanities Research Council of Canada, from Concordia University, Montreal, and from York University, Toronto. I would like to thank a number of research assistants over the past few years who have played some role in the making of this book: Angela Brkich, Sacha Mathew, Julia Campbell-Such, Mayjee Philip, Daniel Bernard (Concordia University), Agnes Choi (University of Toronto), and William den Hollander, who prepared the indices (York University).

I am grateful to many colleagues who in some way contributed to the completion of this work. I would especially like to thank John S. Kloppenborg, Steve Mason, Richard Ascough, and Giovanni Bazzana, who read and commented on some or all of the manuscript. I am grateful to the members of the Context Group, who discussed chapters 1–2 at the meeting in Stella, New York (March 2009). Among those who provided feedback on earlier incarnations of the chapters presented here are Michel Desjardins (Wilfrid Laurier University), Harold Remus (Wilfrid Laurier University), Jinyu Liu (DePauw University), Jonathan Scott Perry (University of Central Florida), and Zeba Crook (Carleton University). Several chapters were also previously presented at conferences, and I would like to thank participants in the Greco-Roman Religions, Hellenistic Judaism, and Greco-Roman Meals sections of the Society of Biblical Literature and members of the Religious Rivalries seminar of the Canadian Society of Biblical Studies.

Most of all, I would like to thank my wife, Cheryl Williams, who read all of the manuscript in some form or another, making valuable suggestions for improvement. As always, friends and family, who know who they are, have been a support throughout the project. This book is dedicated to my wife, Cheryl, and my sons, Nathaniel and Justin.

All photos that appear in this volume were taken by me (© 2009 Philip A. Harland). I would like to thank the organizations and staffs responsible for maintaining the archeological sites and museums for permission to view and photograph these ancient archeological materials. The map base is used with permission from the Ancient World Mapping Center, University of North Carolina at Chapel Hill (www.unc.edu/awmc).

Chapters 1 and 5 are, on the whole, new and appear here for the first time. The following articles or portions of them form the basis of certain chapters in this book, and I would like to thank the following publishers or organizations for permission to incorporate material, in significantly revised form, from these articles: *Part 1:* "Christ-Bearers and Fellow-Initiates: Local Cultural Life and Christian Identity in Ignatius's Letters," *Journal of Early Christian Studies* 11 (2003): 481–99, with permission from the journal. *Part 2:* "Familial Dimensions of Group Identity: "'Brothers' (ἀδελφοί) in Associations of the Greek East," *Journal of Biblical Literature* 124 (2005): 491–513, with permission from the journal and the Society of Biblical Literature. "Familial Dimensions of Group Identity (II): 'Mothers' and 'Fathers' in Associations and Synagogues of the Greek World," *Journal for the Study of Judaism* 38 (2007): 57–79, with permission from the journal. *Part 3:* "Acculturation and Identity in the Diaspora: A Jewish Family and 'Pagan' Guilds at Hierapolis," *Journal of Jewish Studies* 57 (2006): 222–44, with permission from the journal and the Oxford Centre of Jewish and Hebrew Studies. *Part 4:* "Spheres of Contention, Claims of Pre-Eminence: Rivalries among Associations in Sardis and Smyrna." In *Religious Rivalries and the Struggle for Success in Sardis and Smyrna,* vol. 14, edited by Richard S. Ascough; Studies in Christianity and Judaism, 53–63, 259–62 (Waterloo, ON: Wilfrid Laurier University Press, 2005), with permission from the publisher and the Canadian Corporation for the Studies in Religion. "'These People Are . . . Men Eaters': Banquets of the Anti-Associations and Perceptions of Minority Cultural Groups." In *Identity and Interaction in the Ancient Mediterranean: Jews, Christians and Others. Essays in Honour of Stephen G. Wilson,* edited by Zeba A. Crook and Philip A. Harland, 56–75 (Sheffield: Sheffield Phoenix Press, 2007), with permission from Sheffield Phoenix Press.

Dynamics of Identity in the World of the Early Christians

Italy and the Eastern Roman Empire

Map base copyright 2009, Ancient World Mapping Center, University of North Carolina at Chapel Hill <www.unc.edu/awmc>. Used by permission. Map prepared by Philip Harland.

Introduction

Drawing on insights from the social sciences, this study suggests that we can better understand certain dynamics of identity among groups of Judeans (Jews) and Christians by looking at archeological evidence for other contemporary associations and cultural minority groups. Ancient Judean and Christian answers to the question *Who are we?* come into sharper focus through close attention to the cultural environments and real-life settings of associations in the cities of the Roman Empire. Despite the peculiarities of both Judean gatherings and Christian congregations, there were significant overlaps in how associations of various kinds communicated their identities and in how members of such groups expressed notions of belonging internally.

Recent studies are shedding light on aspects of identity in the world of the early Christians.[1] And yet there is a tendency to neglect archeological evidence regarding real-life groups at the local level, groups that might provide a new vantage point to early Christianity. For instance, Judith Lieu's important contributions to the study of early Christian identity are particularly notable.[2] In her latest work, *Christian Identity in the Jewish and Graeco-Roman World* (2004), Lieu investigates the emergence of Christian identity in literature of the first two centuries, drawing on concepts from the social sciences along the way. The strength of this work lies in its comparative approach, investigating various identity issues among Judeans, Christians, and both Greeks and Romans. Thus, for instance, Lieu shows how similar ethnographic discourses were at work in Roman perspectives on "foreign" peoples (e.g., Tacitus on the Germans and on the Judeans), in Judean definitions of the "gentiles," and in some early Christian processes of self-definition in relation to the "other."[3] Like Denise Kimber Buell (2005), Lieu also helpfully notes the importance of discourses of ethnicity in the construction of Christian identity, to which I return below.[4]

However, Lieu's attempt to cover so much ground and her concentration on literary sources to the exclusion of archeology did not permit a focus on identity within small *groups and associations* in Greco-Roman settings. This lack of attention to group

1. See, for instance, Lieu 2004; Buell 2005.
2. See Lieu 1996 and 2002.
3. Lieu 2004, 269–97.
4. Lieu 2004, 239–68. Cf. Lieu 2002, 49–68.

identity and local groups as a comparative framework is, in part, a result of Lieu's stress on what she sees as a more "universal," "translocal identity" shared by Christians that, she implies, is a unique trait of the Christians.[5] So despite her aim of comparison, she tends to focus on what is distinctive or unique about Christian identity, often to the exclusion of areas of overlap in identity formation and negotiation within groups in the Greco-Roman world.[6] In the introduction, she explicitly sets aside "voluntary associations" (*collegia*, θίασοι) as somehow too "local" to be of any use in assessing dynamics of identity among early Christian groups, which are presumed to be primarily "translocal."[7] An abundance of archeological and inscriptional evidence for group identity in the Greco-Roman world thereby gets left aside as somehow irrelevant.

Other scholars do see the value in comparisons that look to local archeological and epigraphic materials, including evidence for associations in the world of early Christian groups and Judean gatherings. Yet the topic of identity formation and negotiation with regard to associations is only beginning to be addressed. Associations in the Greco-Roman world first drew the attention of numerous scholars in the late nineteenth century, such as Jean-Pierre Waltzing (1895–1900), Erich Ziebarth (1896), and Franz Poland (1909), who focussed primarily on things such as the types of groups, group terminology, internal organization, and legal issues. As I discuss at length elsewhere, there were some initial attempts—by scholars such as Edwin Hatch (1909 [1880]) and Georg Heinrici (1876, 1881)—to compare such groups with Christian congregations.[8] Yet many were hesitant to engage in such comparisons due, in large part, to ideological or theological assumptions concerning the supposed uniqueness and incomparability of early Christianity.[9]

As interests turned to social history since the 1970s, there has been renewed attention to studying such associations within the disciplines of Greek and Roman studies. There are many recent works, including those by Frank M. Ausbüttel (1982), Ulrich Fellmeth (1987), Halsey L. Royden (1988), Onno M. van Nijf (1997), Imogen Dittmann-Schöne (2000), Brigitte Le Guen (2001), Holger Schwarzer (2002), Carola Zimmermann (2002), Ulrike Egelhaaf-Gaiser and Alfred Schäfer, eds. (2002), Sophia Aneziri (2003), Jinyu Liu (2004), Jonathan Scott Perry (2006), and Stefan Sommer (2006), to name a few.

This resurgence in interest was also reflected in the study of diaspora Judean gatherings and Christian congregations. There are now a significant number of works that compare associations with either Judean or Christian groups in the Roman period,

5. Lieu 2004, 4.

6. Lieu 2004, 11. At times, this focus on distinctiveness seems to reflect an idealizing approach to early Christians, as when Lieu speaks of "mutual support" or "love" (*agapē*) as "an inalienable element in the shared symbols that shaped early Christian identity" (Lieu 2004, 169).

7. Lieu 2004, 4. On problems with such local vs. translocal contrasts, see Ascough 1997a.

8. See Kloppenborg 1993; Harland 2003a. For other subsequent attempts at comparison before the resurgence since 1980, see, for instance, Besnier 1932; Gilmour 1938; Reicke 1951; Guterman 1951 (on synagogues and the *collegia*); Judge 1960.

9. See J. Z. Smith 1990; Kloppenborg 1993.

including those by Robert Wilken (1972, 1984), S. C. Barton and G. H. R. Horsley (1981), Hans-Josef Klauck (1981, 1982), Moshe Weinfeld (1986), John S. Kloppenborg (1993), John S. Kloppenborg and Stephen Wilson, eds. (1996), Thomas Schmeller (1995), Peter Richardson (1996), Albert Baumgarten (1998), Paul R. Trebilco (1999), Anders Runesson (2001), Richard S. Ascough (1997b, 2003), Eva Ebel (2004), and my own previous works listed in the bibliography, especially *Associations, Synagogues, and Congregations* (2003a).

Such comparative studies are setting the stage for focussed explorations of specific aspects of association life, including issues relating to identity and belonging in the context of small groups. Explorations of this sort will provide new perspectives on both Judean gatherings and Christian congregations. The present study of identity in the world of the early Christians contributes towards this scholarly enterprise. I focus attention on the question of how associations and ethnic groups in the ancient Mediterranean provide a new angle of vision on questions of identity formation and negotiation among Judean gatherings and Christian congregations in the first three centuries. Archeological evidence and inscriptions provide a window into dynamics of identity within group settings in antiquity. Insights from the social sciences offer a constructive framework for making some sense of these materials.

Social-Historical Study of Group Life in the Greco-Roman World

This study is social-historical in at least two senses of the word. On the one hand, I am interested in the everyday life settings of average people in antiquity, in down-to-earth social interactions and cultural practices at the local level. Social history in this sense originally emerged as "history from below" in the discipline of history beginning primarily in the post–World War II period, especially since the 1960s.[10] "History from below" or social history is history from the perspective of those who are often left out of traditional approaches to political and intellectual history. It gives attention to those who did not necessarily hold positions of influence or power, or who were not necessarily educated enough to write things down themselves (e.g., the lower social strata of societies, and women).

In time, this interest in social history began to play a role in other disciplines including classical studies and New Testament studies. Works by Ramsay MacMullen (1974), G. E. M. de Ste. Croix (1981), and Géza Alföldy (1985) illustrate the budding interest in social history of the Greek and Roman periods, for instance. Among the earlier cases of social-historical approaches to the early Christians are influential contributions by

10. See Burke 1992 [1980], 13–16. Among the earlier and more influential social historians were those of the French Annales school, including Fernand Braudel (1949) and, later, Marxist historians such as Eric Hobsbawm (1959, 1969), E. P. Thompson (1964), and Christopher Hill (1971, 1972).

scholars such as Gerd Theissen (1982 [1973], 1978), John G. Gager (1975), Abraham Malherbe (1983 [1977]), John H. Elliott (1990 [1981]), Wayne A. Meeks (1983), and Richard Horsley (1985).

In the case of small group life in the ancient world, archeological and inscriptional evidence is particularly important in approaching social history. This is because this evidence frequently offers glimpses into everyday social and cultural interactions that are not as visible in literary sources. Literary sources were produced by a small segment of the population, the educated elites (although there was a range of statuses among this segment). Usually literacy levels are estimated to be approximately 10 percent of the population for antiquity and for the period before the invention of the printing press in 1453.[11] Nonetheless, one can approach literary evidence in careful ways to shed light on social and cultural practices among the population generally, keeping in mind the specific perspectives of the ancient authors in question.

On the other hand, this study is social-historical in the sense that it employs the social sciences. The social sciences in question are sociology (the study of social groups and structures), anthropology (the study of humans and human culture), and social psychology (the study of individual human behaviour in social group contexts). The social sciences came to play a role in social-historical studies in history quite early, as Peter Burke's survey of 1980 (repr. 1992) on *History and Social Theory* illustrates. Eventually such approaches began to be employed in the study of early Christianity and the New Testament, initially by scholars such as those I mentioned above in connection with social-historical studies and those belonging to the Context Group (formed in 1986).

Before outlining the social-scientific concepts that inform this volume, it is important to say a few words about how one goes about using social sciences in historical study. There is now a broad consensus among scholars of early Christianity, for instance, that the social sciences can and should be employed to shed new light on early Christianity. However, as Dale Martin (1993) also notes, this consensus is marked by a spectrum of opinion on how to approach the enterprise, as recent debates between Philip Esler and David Horrell also illustrate.[12] While some tend to emphasize the scientific nature of the enterprise and focus their attention on developing, applying, and testing models, others are less focussed on models and take what they would call a more interpretive approach to their use of the social sciences.

On the one hand, the Context Group has been particularly instrumental in developing social-scientific approaches to early Christianity. Scholars such as Philip Esler, Bruce Malina, John H. Elliott, and others associated with that group take what they would consider a scientific, model-based approach to their research.[13] They correctly emphasize the value of employing explicit models or theories from the social sciences, since this approach helps the scholar to avoid the negative effect of implicit assumptions when our models of social interactions remain unrecognized or unstated.[14]

11. On the Roman era, see Harris 1989 and Beard 1991, for instance.

12. See, for example, Horrell 1996, 2000, 2002; Esler 1998a, 1998b. Cf. Martin 1993.

13. See esp. Elliott 1993 for a summary of this approach.

14. See Elliott 1993.

Elliott defines a model as an "abstract representation of the relationships among social phenomena used to conceptualize, analyze, and interpret patterns of social relations, and to compare and contrast one system of social relations with another."[15] Such models are considered to serve as heuristic devices in raising questions that help to explain the significance of social and cultural data reflected in the New Testament. It is particularly common for scholars such as Malina and Jerome Neyrey, for instance, to draw on models from recent studies of modern Mediterranean cultures, such as those associated with honour-shame societies, and to adapt them in ways that shed light on the ancient Mediterranean.[16]

Beyond participants in the Context Group, other scholars such as Gerd Theissen (1982, 1999), Wayne Meeks (1983), Margaret McDonald (1988), John M. G. Barclay (1996), and David Horrell (Horrell 1996, 2000, 2002) have engaged in historical studies of Christian origins or ancient Judean culture that employ the social sciences in various ways. Some of these scholars take a more interpretive approach to the use of the social sciences and tend to speak of themselves as social historians rather than social scientists. Some tend towards a piecemeal approach to the use of sociological theory, including Meeks. Others, such as Horrell, speak in terms of using social theory to develop a theoretical framework for the analysis of ancient materials, and such scholars focus less on models specifically.[17]

Building on contributions from both of these scholarly areas, I approach the social sciences as heuristic devices, as things that help the social historian develop questions and *find* or notice things that might otherwise remain obscure. I tend to draw on social-scientific insights to develop a research framework for analysis, and I am less focused than some other scholars on testing models specifically. In this respect, I consider myself more a social historian than a social scientist. Throughout this interdisciplinary study, I explain and adapt social-scientific concepts and theories in order to further our understanding of specific historical cases in the ancient context.

Key Concepts and Insights from the Social Sciences

This study is informed by insights from two overlapping areas of social-scientific investigation: identity theory, on the one hand, and studies of ethnic groups and migration theory, on the other. For both of these areas of research, there is a high degree of interdisciplinarity involving sociology, anthropology, and social psychology. Let me begin by briefly introducing these two areas and by defining key theoretical concepts for this study along the way. It is important to stress that the concepts that I define here in the introduction are scholarly outsider (etic) terms that help us to make sense of social relations and cultural interactions in the ancient world. Most of the time these

15. Elliott 1993, 132.

16. See Malina 1981, or subsequent editions of that work.

17. Horrell 1996, 9–32, esp. p. 18.

concepts would not be used by the ancient subjects we are studying. Often, however, scholars take into consideration insider, or emic, perspectives or conceptions as part of their definition of an etic category, as we will see with both "identity" and "ethnic group."

Identity Theory

Broadly speaking, there are two main ways in which the concept of "identity" is used in this study, corresponding to variant, though related and overlapping, uses in the social sciences, each with different purposes.[18] There is the collective use of the term identity and the more individual-focused use of the term. In both uses, however, identity is seen as socially constructed by the subjects under investigation and as malleable, not as primordial, engrained, or static.

First, there is the *collective view* of identity that is most common in ethnic and migration studies. Roughly speaking, this view of identity best corresponds to our subjects answering the question Who are *we*? as well as What distinguishes us from other groups in this society? and Where do we draw the lines (or boundaries) between our group and others? This tradition within sociology and anthropology, which underlies much of my discussion in the following chapters, employs the concept of identity and especially ethnic identity in a collective way to refer to group-members' common sense of belonging together in a particular ethnic or cultural minority group.

In the wake of the work of anthropologist Fredrik Barth (1969), "ethnic identity" is often used to refer to a particular group's shared sense of belonging together because of certain experiences and notions of connection deriving from group-members' *perceptions* of common cultural heritage and common geographical and/or ancestral origins (emic perspectives are incorporated into an etic category).[19] As Jonathan M. Hall emphasizes in his discussion of ethnicity in the archaic and classical Greek periods, fictive kinship is often central to the definition of ethnicity, alongside the historical subjects' notions of a common history and a shared homeland.[20]

The imagined connections and the categories used by participants to classify themselves or others in ethnic terms may, and often do, change over time (despite the common perceptions of some actors that such things are in-born, primordial, or static). Nonetheless, if a given ethnic group is to continue, what is maintained is the "continued interest on the part of its members in maintaining the boundaries" which are considered to separate members of the ethnic group ("us") from others ("them").[21] It is important to emphasize that ethnicity or ethnic identity, in this view, is ascriptive and subjective rather than primordial and objective. What matters is how the partici-

---

18. Cf. Howard 2000; Stets and Burke 2003.

19. On ethnic identity see, for instance, Barth 1969; Romanucci-Ross and de Vos 1995, 13; de Vos 1995; Verkuyten 2004.

20. Hall 2002, 9–19.

21. Goudriaan 1992, 76; de Vos 1995.

pants categorize themselves and how they adopt a perspective that sees their belonging together as engrained.

There is a sense in which this collective concept of identity will be most appropriate in the present study. There are at least a couple of reasons why this is so. The fragmentary nature of ancient evidence means that we lack sufficient data on individual roles or individual self-conceptions, but we do catch glimpses of group life and interactions. Furthermore, recent studies by scholars such as Malina and others draw attention to the primarily collective character of ancient Greco-Roman societies and the dyadic or group-oriented nature of ancient personalities.[22] This contrasts somewhat to the more individualistic tendencies of modern, Western societies and personality development in those societies. So a collective concept of identity is particularly fitting in studying the world of the early Christians.

Recent works have usefully employed such concepts of ethnicity in studying groups in the ancient context, including Hall's (1997, 2002) important studies of the emergence of *Hellenicity*; Philip F. Esler's (2003) discussion of tensions between ethnic groups within the Christian congregations at Rome; and Barclay's (2007) study of Josephus's expression of Judean identity in terms of common descent, history, territory, language, sacred texts, and temple. In the following section, I return to defining related concepts including "ethnic group" and "cultural minority group," but for now we need to consider some other social-scientific theories of identity.

The second main way in which the concept of identity can be employed relates to sociological and, especially, social psychological theories of identity. Here the term relates primarily to the *individual's self-concept* as it pertains to positions or roles within social groupings. This nonetheless has implications for group identity as a whole. Roughly speaking, this view of identity best corresponds to our subjects answering questions such as Who am I in this particular situation and how does this relate to who I am in other social groups? and How is my own self-conception based on, or affected by, my belonging in this particular group? The focus here, one could say, is on the interaction of individuals and the group in the construction and negotiation of identities and in affecting social behaviours.

There are at least two schools of research that employ identity in this second way. The most important for this study is what is known as "*social* identity theory."[23] The "social" descriptor in social identity refers to the part of one's self-conception that is based on, and influenced by, membership in a group, be that an ethnic group or some other cultural or social group.[24] Social identity theorists who follow the lead of the social psychologist Henri Tajfel (1981) tend to use the term "social identity" to refer to an "individual's knowledge that he/she belongs to certain social groups together with some emotional and value significance to him/her of the group membership."[25]

22. Malina 1981.

23. For social identity theory see, for instance, Tajfel 1981; Tajfel, ed. 1982; Tajfel and Turner 1986; Abrams and Hogg 1990; Verkuyten 2004, 39–73.

24. See Tajfel 1981, 13–56.

25. Tajfel as cited by Abrams and Hogg 1990, 2.

Social identity theorists in line with Tajfel also pay attention to interactions between different groups as they affect social identity. So issues concerning outsiders' categorizations of a particular group or its members, including stereotypes, are important here. Esler (1998a, 2003) is among the scholars that have fruitfully employed social identity theory to shed light on dynamics of group conflict reflected in Paul's letters to the Galatians and to the Romans.

Another variant of the second main approach to identity is represented by sociologists such as Sheldon Stryker and Peter J. Burke, who speak of their own approach as "identity theory" (to be distinguished from Tajfelian "*social* identity theory").[26] This symbolic interactionist tradition in sociological social psychology stresses the interplay of self and social structure, paying special attention to "individual role relationships and identity variability, motivation, and differentiation."[27] In this view, the "core of an identity is the categorization of the self as an occupant of a role and incorporating into the self the meanings and expectations associated with the role and its performance."[28] "Identities are the meanings that individuals hold for themselves—what it means to be who they are," as Burke states.[29] This approach is focussed on the individual self, on identities housed in the individual, and on how these manifest themselves in social relations or social structures. Stryker and Burke's approach is most suited to conditions where the individual behaviours of subjects can be carefully analyzed, which is not the case in studying people in antiquity. I will nonetheless occasionally draw on insights from their theories and findings.

Both this interactionist approach to identity and other studies of ethnic identity specifically give attention to the multiple nature of identities among individuals, something that will be important to keep in mind when we turn to multiple affiliations among associations in chapters 6 and 7. Burke is interested in "questions of how multiple identities relate to each other, how they are switched on or off, and, when they are on, how the person manages to maintain congruence between perceptions and standards for each identity."[30] For Burke here, identities are "housed" in the individual and activated within certain situations. He notes three different conditions, the second of which is relevant to the discussion in chapters 6 and 7: (1) persons may have multiple role identities within a single group, (2) persons may have similar role identities in more than one group, (3) persons may have different role identities within intersecting groups.[31]

It is important to note that studies of ethnicities and migration make similar observations concerning the "situational" character of social and ethnic identities.[32] How one identifies oneself in terms of social, ethnic, and other identities may shift

26. See Stryker and Burke 2000; Stets and Burke 2003.

27. Stets and Burke 2003, 133.

28. Stets and Burke 2003, 134.

29. Burke 2003, 196.

30. Burke 2003, 196–97.

31. Burke 2003, 200–201.

32. See Kaufert 1977; Howard 2000, 381–82; Waters 2000; Verkuyten 2004, 149–181.

from one situation to another, and there is potential for a blending of identities, or hybridity. Rina Benmayor, a historian of migration, stresses that the personal testimony of immigrants speaks "to how im/migrant subjects constantly build, reinvent, synthesize, or even collage identities from multiple sources and resources, often lacing them with deep ambivalence."[33] Membership in, or affiliation with, multiple groups plays a role in these options for identification. Joseph M. Kaufert notes that studies of "multiple ethnic loyalties have stressed that individuals and groups have an array of alternate identities from which to choose. They will adopt—or be perceived by others as maintaining—different ethnic identities in different situations."[34] Kaufert also notes the potential for "dissonance" between conflicting identities in different situations.[35]

The collective and individual perspectives on identity outlined above do share in common certain features, including a recognition of the dynamism, malleability, and multiplicity of identities, as well as the situational nature and development of identities as understood and expressed in particular places and times. In other words, the answers to the questions Who are we? or Who am I in relation to this group or situation? varied and changed over time despite elements of stability.[36] Identities of groups or individuals are negotiated and renegotiated, expressed and reexpressed; they are not static.

Several recent social-scientific studies usefully combine insights from the perspectives outlined above to help explain dynamics of identity in terms of two main, interdependent factors: "internal definitions" within the group and "external definitions" (or "external categorizations") by contemporary outsiders. This corresponds to ascribed (internal) and attributed (external) identifications. These two factors frame the discussion of identity throughout the chapters in this book, with some chapters concentrating more on the former or on the latter, and others dealing with both of these formative identity factors simultaneously.

Let me briefly explain internal and external definitions here, and then I will expand this explanation in subsequent chapters with case studies of Judeans, Christians, and others in the Greco-Roman world. Richard Jenkins (1994), for instance, who builds on the work of both Barth (1969) and Tajfel (1981), explains how social and ethnic identities are constructed and reconfigured in relation to both internal definitions and external categorizations.[37] Internally, members of a group express their identities and formulate what they consider to be the basis of their belonging together as a group, engaging in self-definitions and in the construction of boundaries between insiders and outsiders.

Externally, outsiders categorize and label a particular group or members of a group. This external process of categorization can range from a high level of consensus

33. Benmayor 1994, 15.

34. Kaufert 1977, 126.

35. Kaufert 1977, 127.

36. On the primordial vs. circumstantial debate about ethnicity, which cannot be fully addressed here, see Scott 1990; Verkuyten 2004, 81–90.

37. Cf. Tajfel 1981.

with internal modes of definition (as when an outsider's categories overlap significantly with internal modes of self-definition) to conflictual categorizations (as when outsiders categorize or label members of another group in terms of negative stereotypes). The relational nature of identity formulations and the shifting boundaries between a group and others means that even these negative categorizations or stereotypes of outsiders come to play a role in identity constructions through the process of internalization. Internalization involves the categorized person or group reacting in some way to external categorizations, as I explain in chapters 5 and 8. These interdependent internal definitions and external categorizations occupy the chapters in this volume.

Ethnic Studies and Migration Theory

Closely related to studies of identity, particularly ethnic identity, are social-scientific studies of ethnic groups, minority groups, and migration, including processes of assimilation or acculturation. Ethnic and migration studies have developed into somewhat of a subdiscipline within the social sciences, as reflected in journals such as *The Journal of Ethnic and Migration Studies*, *Ethnic and Racial Studies*, and *Diaspora: A Journal of Transnational Studies*.[38] I have already touched on the ascriptive (rather than primordial) nature of ethnicity as it is understood in the wake of Barth's (1969) anthropological study of ethnic boundaries. Although precise definitions vary within the social-scientific literature, there is a commonly shared use of the term "ethnic group" to describe a group that is perceived by members and, secondarily, by outsiders in particular ways. As Jimy M. Sanders's survey of the literature points out, there are two common denominators in the social constructions of members and of outsiders that form the basis of many scholarly definitions of ethnic group—the cultural and the geographical:

> The first of these elements is usually viewed as a social construction involving insiders and outsiders mutually acknowledging group differences in cultural beliefs and practices. Insiders and outsiders do not necessarily agree over the details of the acknowledged cultural division. . . . The second basic element used to define an ethnic group pertains to geographical origins, and therefore social origins, that are foreign to the host society. While this element usually has an objective basis, it is also partly subjective. The native-born generations of an ethnic group sometimes continue to be identified by outsiders, and in-group members may self-identify, in terms of their foreign origin. The ways in which insiders and outsiders go about characterizing a group, and thereby positioning it and its members in the larger society, are responsive

38. For an overview of this subdiscipline, see Brettell and Hollifield 2000, Banton 2001, and Vertovec 2007.

to the social and historical context within which intergroup interactions take place.[39]

So an ethnic group is a group that sees itself as sharing certain distinctive cultural characteristics that are associated with a particular geographical origin or homeland. As mentioned earlier, this distinctiveness is usually described by participants in terms of a shared history and ancestry (regardless of whether or not this is objectively the case). The ethnic group is characterized by fictive kinship and participants often interpret these notions of kinship as primordial or inborn.[40] The existence of an ethnic group is maintained through what Barth and others call "ethnic boundaries" between the group and other groups within society. Ethnic identities are dependent on the everyday interactions among members of the group and between members and other groups. These interactions result in the formulation of notions of "us" and "them."

The quotation from Sanders also indicates the primary importance of the category ethnic group in studying migration and in studying what I also call "immigrant groups" or "immigrant associations." The majority of ethnic group studies in the social sciences are focussed on immigrants in a host society or a "diaspora," as well as the relation of such groups to the homeland.[41]

Although related to the concept of ethnic group, it is important to clarify another concept that I employ in a particular way in this study: "cultural minority group" or "cultural minorities."[42] This concept is more generic than the specific category ethnic group. I use the term cultural minority group to describe a group that is, numerically, in the minority in a particular context and which has certain cultural customs that are often highlighted as distinctive by both its members and by those outside the group, especially by the "cultural majority" in a particular locale or region. So it is possible to have a cultural minority group that is not an immigrant or ethnic group that shares notions of ancestral kinship (e.g., certain Christian groups in the first two centuries, as I explain below). Still most migrant ethnic groups that settle elsewhere and represent a minority position in terms of certain key cultural practices (e.g., Judeans in the Greek cities of Asia Minor) would also be cultural minority groups.

My use of "minority" in this terminology is in line with that of the British sociologist Michael Banton, for whom a minority is "a category consisting of less than half the number of some named population."[43] Philip Gleason's (1991) history of the concept "minority" shows how Banton is here avoiding popular, political, and certain sociological definitions (e.g., avoiding Louis Wirth's definition). These other definitions tend to problematically emphasize experiences of discrimination or prejudice as the main criterion in defining "minority" (even to the point of calling a group that

---

39. Sanders 2002, 327–328.

40. Cf. Verkuyten 2004, 81–90.

41. On the concept of "diaspora" as it has been developed in this area, see Brubaker 2005.

42. On problems with definitions of "minority," see Meyers 1984 and, more importantly, Gleason 1991. Cf. Layton-Henry 2001.

43. Banton as cited by Gleason 412. See Banton 1977; Banton 1983, 130–31.

is statistically in the majority a minority based on social discrimination).[44] Although groups to whom I apply the term did, at certain times and places, experience discrimination, I do not consider victimization integral to my use of the descriptor "minority" in cultural minority group.

This is also a good place to briefly state what I mean by "culture," which is a concept that is closely bound up in discussions of ethnicity and identity. William H. Sewell's (1999) helpful survey of debates concerning the use of the concept of culture within anthropology argues that, despite certain anthropologists' observations concerning its problems and ambiguities, we should carefully refine definitions of the concept. The concept of culture continues to be useful not only in anthropology but also in social history, Sewell's own area. Sewell shows how two different approaches to defining culture can be seen as complementary in certain respects: culture-as-system-of-symbols, on the one hand, and culture-as-practice, on the other.

Clifford Geertz's influential explanation of culture sees it as a coherent "system of inherited conceptions expressed in symbolic forms by means of which men [*sic*] communicate, perpetuate, and develop their knowledge about and attitudes towards life."[45] Both cultural anthropologists and cultural sociologists tend to use the term culture to refer to processes of human *meaning-making* embodied in symbols, values, and practices that are shared and passed on by a particular group.[46] Yet Sewell appropriately notes that such definitions of culture as a coherent system tend towards synchronic analysis (at a particular time), rather than diachronic analysis (through time): "Historians are generally uncomfortable with synchronic concepts. As they took up the study of culture, they subtly—but usually without comment—altered the concept by stressing the contradictoriness and malleability of cultural meanings and by seeking out the mechanisms by which meanings were transformed."[47] This, Sewell points out, is more in line with some trends among certain anthropologists who emphasize the performative and changeable character of culture (much like my observations about the changeability of ethnicity and identity). These anthropologists see culture less in terms of symbols and more in terms of tools that are called upon in particular situations and with particular aims in mind.

Sewell suggests that both the "system" and "practice" approaches may be understood as complementary in certain respects, and I adopt this view:

> The employment of a symbol can be expected to accomplish a particular goal only because the symbols have more or less determinate meanings. . . . Hence practice implies system. But it is equally true that the system has no existence apart from the succession of practices that instantiate, reproduce, or—most interestingly—transform it. Hence system implies practice.[48]

---

44. Gleason 1991, 399–400; cf. Meyers 1984, 8, 11.
45. Geertz 1973, 89.
46. Cf. Geertz 1973; Sewell 1999; Spillman 2007.
47. Sewell 1999, 45.
48. Sewell 1999, 47.

Certain theories and conceptual tools that have been developed in the study of culture, migration, and ethnicity are useful in understanding interactions between a given ethnic group or cultural minority group and other groups in surrounding society. Issues of identity are once again central in such interactions. Benmayor characterizes migration as "a long-term if not life-long process of negotiating identity, difference, and the right to fully exist and flourish in the new context. . . . [T]he experience and effects of migration are long-term and critical in shaping and reshaping both collective and individual identities."[49]

Anthropologists, sociologists, and social psychologists often explain such processes of negotiation in the place of settlement using theories of acculturation and assimilation. At the outset I should acknowledge that my own exploration into these social-scientific methods was inspired, in part, by two scholars who usefully apply similar insights in studying ancient Christians and Judeans respectively: David Balch (1986) shows the value in understanding the household codes in 1 Peter in terms of acculturation, and Barclay (1996) engages in an excellent study of assimilation among diaspora Judeans, particularly though not solely in connection with literary sources.

Theories of assimilation and acculturation deal with processes that take place when two groups come into contact with each other, with resulting changes in the boundaries and cultural ways of either or both groups. In chapters 6 and 7, I expound a particular framework for assessing such processes among Syrian and Judean immigrant or ethnic groups based on the works of Milton Yinger, Martin N. Marger, John W. Berry, and others. There I explain three main clusters of concepts relating to (1) cultural assimilation, or acculturation; (2) structural assimilation, which has both formal and informal dimensions; (3) and dissimilation (differentiation) or cultural maintenance.[50] Processes of assimilation and dissimilation take place at both the individual and group levels, resulting in the renegotiation of boundaries between a given cultural minority group or its members and other groups within their contexts. So issues of group identities and boundaries are bound up in this area of analysis.

Concepts relating to dissimilation or cultural maintenance are particularly important to emphasize since these reflect a turn away from older models of assimilation in sociology. Certain older models, which are not the basis of the present study, tend to assume the ultimate disintegration of ethnic or cultural minority group boundaries and, with them, the vanishing of distinctive cultural practices in relation to the majority culture. Closely related is the tendency to view acculturation as a one-way process rather than a cultural exchange.

Similar methodological problems are also noted in recent studies of the concept of "Romanization" (a specific approach to acculturation in the Roman era) specifically. As Jane Webster (2001) stresses in her survey of the literature on the concept of Romanization, we need a more sophisticated approach to cultural exchanges in antiquity that does not assume adoption of Roman practices as the principal mode of

---

49. Benmayor and Skotnes 1994, 8.

50. Berry 1980; Yinger 1981; Marger 1991, 117–20; Berry 1997.

acculturation in the provinces. Instead, acculturation was a process of blending, and Webster suggests that the concept of "Creolization"—developed in connection with Early Modern processes of cultural exchanges in the interaction of European peoples and Native American, African, and African Caribbean societies—better captures this blending element. Although I agree with the problems that Webster identifies, I nonetheless consider the concepts of assimilation and acculturation appropriate so long as we recognize the complexities of cultural exchanges which do indeed often involve blending and two-way interchanges. Such an approach that recognizes the multidimensional processes involved in cultural exchanges and the resulting "blending" factor fits well with the multiple and situational character of identities and ethnicities as I explained those concepts earlier.

Judeans and Christians as Ethnic Groups or Cultural Minority Groups

The applicability of the modern scholarly (etic) category ethnic group to gatherings of Judeans and to other immigrant groups in the ancient context may be somewhat uncontroversial. As peoples with *shared notions* regarding common ways of life and geographical and genealogical origins, migrant groups of Judeans, Phoenicians, and others naturally fit under this rubric. Both ancient observers and Judeans conceived of Judeans specifically in terms of what a modern social scientist would consider an ethnic group.

In this connection, it is important to note where I stand in current scholarly debate regarding the most appropriate way to translate the term Ἰουδαῖοι (*Ioudaioi*). The term is traditionally rendered "Jews" but rendered "Judeans" throughout my study when referring to subjects in the Hellenistic and Roman eras, up to at least the third century CE. I agree with recent scholarly contributions by Esler (2003), Mason (2007), and Barclay (2007), who argue that "Judeans" is the most accurate and most appropriate way to translate this term in the first centuries.[51] The ancient use of the term "Judeans" involves geographic, ethnic, and cultural associations with the region of Judea (tribal Judah) proper or with a broader conception of Judea (e.g., Strabo *Geogr.* 16.2.21; Pliny *Nat. Hist.* 5.15; Josephus *War* 2.232), encompassing Galilee and other areas historically associated with the Israelites or with the temple-state of Jerusalem in the wake of Hasmonean expansion in the late second century BCE.[52]

---

51. Mason (2007, 493–510) convincingly challenges the views of Schwartz (1992) and Shaye J. D. Cohen (1999, 69–106), who argued for a supposed shift from "ethnic" meanings to "religious" meanings of *Ioudaioi* in the Babylonian (Schwartz) and Hasmonean (Cohen) periods respectively. Now also see Elliott 2007.

52. This general use of the term Judeans does not preclude instances when ancient persons or authors use more specific geographic or ethnic identifications, such as identifications based on a particular district (e.g., Galilean) or city/village (e.g., Jerusalemite [*IJO* II 21.9]; Nazarene). When detailing peoples gathered in Jerusalem for a festival, for instance, Josephus himself distinguishes

Adopting this geographic, ethnic, and cultural understanding of the term helps to avoid misunderstandings among modern lay readers and some modern scholars who may tend to separate "religion" from its ethnic or cultural matrix. Along with this, what has traditionally been called "Judaism," with implications of a religious category, is better described using terms such as Judean cultural ways, or Judean customs, or Judean approaches to honouring their God. Rather than repeating the convincing arguments of Mason and others, I instead clarify aspects of this debate at key points in subsequent chapters. There is a sense in which this study, as a whole, is an argument for approaching Judeans in the diaspora primarily as one among many immigrant and ethnic groups in the Greco-Roman world (rather than as a "religious" group more specifically).

Judean groups were immigrant groups settled in a diaspora where certain aspects of their way of life put them in a minority position in particular cultural and social respects. Most important among these cultural practices and worldviews was the Judean tendency to honour only the God of their homeland. Unlike some other immigrant ethnic groups in the Greek cities, this entailed Judean nonrecognition of the gods of others, and nonparticipation in honouring, or sacrificing to, those gods in social contexts (what is traditionally called their "monotheism"). At times, this became a source of tensions with other groups and led certain people to label Judeans "atheists," "haters of human kind," and other more extreme charges which I explain in chapter 8. Certain ancient observers also noticed other customs of the Judeans which these observers considered peculiar, including the Judeans' abstinence from pork, their Sabbath day of rest, their practice of circumcision, and their avoidance of images.[53] Although secondary to the outstanding practice of honouring only the Judean God, these peculiarities, too, suggest ancient perceptions of Judeans that fit with a scholarly use of the category cultural minority group. In this sense, diaspora Judean gatherings are both ethnic groups and cultural minority groups as I employ these etic concepts in this study.

Despite the applicability of ethnic group and cultural minority group to Judeans, it is important to make some clarifications here, which will be spelled out more fully in subsequent chapters. The cultural landscape of the Roman Empire was significantly diverse, and this diversity involved local or regional customs and peculiarities, including those of other ethnic, immigrant, or minority groups. As well, there were local cultural variations and differences not only from one region or people to another, but even from one Greek city to the next in the same region (see Strabo's descriptions of local customs and practices in his *Geography*, for instance). Within this context, those who honoured the Judean God were not the only group of people to engage in activities that could, at times, be viewed as distinctive, peculiar, strange, or superstitious by an elite author, as Plutarch's and Seneca's treatises on "superstition" illustrate.[54]

Galileans and Idumeans from Judeans; here he is thinking of the more specific meaning of inhabitants of Judea proper (*Ant.* 17.254).

53. See the discussion in Schäfer 1997.

54. Plutarch *On Superstition*. Seneca's treatise is preserved only in Augustine's *City of God*: *Civ.* 6.10–11 (cf. Tertullian *Apol.* 12). Both Plutarch and Seneca include discussion of the "superstitious"

Seneca critiques castration practices among devotees of the Syrian goddess and Sabbath observance among devotees of the Judean God. Interestingly enough, Seneca's complaint about the latter is not that "the customs of this accursed race" (as he calls them) are universally rejected or viewed as strange superstitions by the majority, but that these practices among a minority "are now received throughout all the world" (a claim that needs to be taken with a grain of salt).[55] Notwithstanding certain Roman upper-class authors' perspectives, the existence of such a range of local customs among various peoples would also mean that *such variety was in some sense normal and expected among contemporaries,* only some of whom would happen to be more or less familiar with the customs of the Judeans specifically.[56]

Furthermore, the list of Judean customs mentioned above that some pinpointed as distinctively Judean or as strange should not lead us to ignore the many other ways in which Judeans were indistinguishable from their neighbours in the diaspora. Shaye J. D. Cohen (1993) makes this point clearly: in respect to significant factors for identity, including "looks, clothing, speech, names, or occupations," Judeans were indistinguishable from many Greeks, Romans, and others.

The applicability of the categories ethnic group and cultural minority group to early Christians deserves further attention here. I would argue that, in some cases, "ethnic group" is applicable to Christian groups, or groups of Jesus-followers. Yet, in general, the scholarly, etic concept of "cultural minority group" is more appropriate in describing a significant number of ancient Christian groups in the first two centuries in many locales.

"Ethnic group" would most obviously be appropriate in reference to groups of Jesus-followers that consisted primarily of Judeans, such as some groups that were labelled "Ebionites" by certain Christian authors.[57] It is important to remember that the earliest Jesus movements began within the Judean cultural sphere, and certain groups continued to reflect that origin more than others. In the primordial understanding of ethnicity as inborn (based on shared blood) and unchanging, which is a popular usage *not* adopted in this study, most other Christian groups whose membership consisted mainly of gentiles (non-Judeans) from various ethnic groups could not be described as an ethnic group at all.

However, from the perspective of modern social-scientific definitions, which see ethnicity in more flexible and ascriptive terms, some other Christian groups may well be understood within the context of ethnic identities. As I show in chapter 8, ancient

customs of those who follow the Syrian goddess, for instance (Seneca in *Civ.* 6.10; Plutarch *Superst.* 170D). Plutarch, like Seneca, pinpoints the peculiarity of the Judeans' Sabbath observance (Plutarch *Superst.* 169C).

55. Trans. W. M. Green (LCL) as cited by Stern 1974–76, 1.431.

56. A general lack of knowledge about Judean ways is shown, for instance, in Josephus's assumption that some among his educated audience of Greeks and Romans in Flavian Rome will be ignorant of Judean abstention from work on the seventh day (*War* 1.146), the very issue about which Seneca happens to know and complain (cf. Mason 2008, 61).

57. On such Judean followers of Jesus, see the studies in Skarsaune and Hvalvik 2007.

Greek and Roman observers sometimes categorized early Christian groups drawing on stereotypes that were associated with "foreign" peoples and ethnic groups. The perspectives of insiders are particularly important here since the modern concept of ethnic identity is defined in terms of the participants' perceptions of belonging together as a people with a shared origin, fictive kinship, and a particular way of life. Certain early Christian authors (who were not themselves originally from Judea) describe Christian groups in terms of ethnicity, depicting the early Christians as a people or nation comparable to other ethnic groups, as recent studies by Buell (2005) and Aaron P. Johnson (2006) show so well.

An early example of such discourses of ethnicity is 1 Peter, which is appropriately described as a diaspora letter. Although some scholars suggest that 1 Peter's language of "foreigners," "exiles," and "dispersion" may refer to the actual immigrant status of these Christians, many other scholars suggest it is likely that such concepts are used metaphorically to express early Christian identities in a particular way.[58] Here my working hypothesis is the latter. In this case, 1 Peter describes the identities of his addressees in the provinces of Asia Minor in terms of them being "foreigners" (πάροικοι) and "exiles in the diaspora" (παρεπιδήμος διασπορᾶς). The author of 1 Peter draws heavily on Judean ethnic identities to express the self-understanding of these non-Judean (gentile) followers of Jesus: "But you are a chosen race (γένος), a royal priesthood, a holy nation (ἔθνος), a people (λαός) for God's possession. . . . Once you were no people but now you are God's people" (1 Pet 2:9–10).[59] The author also expresses group identity in terms of kinship, calling them a "brotherhood" (1 Pet 2:17; cf. 5:9). Here, then, a Christian defines groups of non-Judean Jesus-followers (cf. 1 Pet 4:3–5) in terms of ethnicity, particularly drawing on discourses of Judean ethnicity. They are described as though they are immigrant or ethnic groups, and he hopes his hearers will adopt a similar way of thinking about their memberships in these groups (cf. *Diogn.* 5.1–5).

Johnson cites many similar examples of early Christian authors defining Christians in terms of ethnicity. Among the more important ones is a passage in one of the earliest Christian apologies (defensive writings) by Aristides of Athens (early second century). There Aristides speaks of Christians as kin (γένος) and a nation or people (ἔθνος) comparable to other peoples:

> For it is clear to us that there are three races (*genē*) of humans in this world. These are the worshippers of those whom you call gods, the Jews [Judeans] and the Christians. And again, those who worship many gods are divided into three races: the Chaldaeans, the Greeks and the Egyptians. For these have become the founders and teachers of the veneration and worship of the many-named gods to the other nations (*ethnesin*; Aristides, *Apol.* 2.2).[60]

---

58. See, for instance, Feldmeier 1992. John H. Elliott (1990 [1981], 59–100, esp. pp. 70–72) is among those that hold to a literal understanding of the terms.

59. Trans. RSV, with adaptations.

60. Trans. Johnson 2006, 6.

Elsewhere Aristides claims common ancestry for Christians and traces their "genealogy" from Christ (*Apol.* 15; cf. Justin *Dial.* 123.9). It is also noteworthy that an early Christian author such as Aristides would group together and closely ally Judeans and Christians as peoples who do not "worship many gods" (monolatrists or monotheists) in contradistinction from those peoples that did (polytheists). A minority cultural position is contrasted to the majority position. Johnson, who also fully explores such ethnic argumentation in a writing by Eusebius, concludes that

> [e]thnic (or national) identity played a fundamental role in the ways in which Christians argued and articulated their faith. When Christian apologists went about the task of defending themselves within this conceptual framework, the "others" with whom they engaged were all seen as the representatives of distinct peoples, nations, or ethnicities. These apologists, therefore, defined Christianity as the way of life of a particular people whose strong roots in the distant past were superior to the other peoples from whom they marked themselves off.[61]

So there are good reasons to consider certain early Christians within the context of ethnic identities and rivalries in antiquity, at least in the case of those that did adopt such discourses of identity construction.

"Cultural minority group" is another closely related, though broader, concept which may be even more applicable to many Christian congregations in the first two centuries. My use of the term is less technical than it is descriptive, and I employ it in a way that is meant to draw attention to the fact that Christian congregations were not the only minority groups in the Greco-Roman world, something that I underline in subsequent chapters. In the case of groups of Jesus-followers in most locales in the first two centuries, these groups were in the minority with respect to their rejection of sacrificing to the Greek or Roman gods. Quite often this cultural choice was noticed and highlighted by outsiders and insiders, who sometimes recognized that these practices derived in some way from Judean customs (with some exceptions, such as certain "gnostic" Christian groups or Marcionite groups). As Michele Murray (2004) documents so well, there is also considerable evidence of the continuing involvement of certain gentile Jesus-followers in the activities of diaspora synagogues, including attending synagogue and celebrating Judean festivals.[62] The adoption of honouring the Judean God (and his messiah) and the rejection of recognizing and sacrificing to the gods of surrounding peoples in the majority culture was a highlighted feature of the cultural practices of many Christian congregations, both in terms of internal self-definition (e.g., 1 Thess 1:9–10; 1 Pet 4:1–5) and in terms of external categorizations (e.g.,

61. Johnson 2006, 6.

62. Cf. Dunn 2008, 2: "Writers such as Justin, Origen, Aphrahat, and Chrysostom had to warn Christians forthrightly on the subject. The Councils of Antioch (341) and Laodicea (363) explicitly prohibited Christians from practicing their religion with Jews, in particular from celebrating their festivals with them."

"atheists," as in *Mart. Poly.* 3.2; 9.2). This highlighted feature sometimes played a role in social harassment or persecution of members of these minority groups, as I discuss in chapter 8.[63]

In using this more general descriptive term in reference to Christian groups, I am quite self-consciously avoiding a more specific and common etic categorization of Christian groups using the sociological concept of the "sect." In *Associations, Synagogues, and Congregations* (2003a), I have explained what I see as some key problems in the wholesale application of sect typologies to early Christian groups, and I do return to some of these issues in subsequent chapters. The purpose in my calling many Christian congregations "cultural minority groups" is not to make the same mistake in lumping all Christian groups together as though they were the same in contradistinction to other groups in that societal context. Rather, this terminology helps us to recognize that certain Christian congregations, like some other ethnic or cultural minorities in specific locales, were in the minority with respect to certain highlighted cultural practices. It is also important to stress that, despite this shared minority position based on rejection of the gods of others, there were nonetheless considerable differences from one Christian congregation to the next with respect to various other cultural and other factors. This internal diversity among Christian congregations despite a shared minority position in other respects will become clear as we proceed. Furthermore, circumstances would change over time and differ from one locale to another, and as Christianity became more prominent in particular locales into the third and fourth centuries, the descriptor "cultural minority" would no longer be appropriate.

So in certain ways both Judean gatherings and Christian congregations can be studied as instances of cultural minority groups in cities of the Roman Empire whose perceived distinctiveness arose—to varying degrees—from Judean cultural connections (e.g., honouring the Judean God and drawing on similar Judean scriptural traditions associated with that God).[64] The degree to which these distinctive cultural practices were highlighted, or overlooked in favour of shared cultural ways, would depend on the situation and on the particular people involved, both insiders and outsiders.

This cultural minority position makes it particularly appropriate to employ modern social-scientific tools for assessing acculturation and assimilation in studying both Judean gatherings and Christian congregations, even though many of the latter were not ethnic or immigrant groups. In other words, as with Judeans who were also minority groups, we can address Christian congregations in terms of members' *en*culturation into the minority group, on the one hand, and acculturation or dissimilation in relation to aspects of majority cultures, on the other. Members of Christian congregations would be enculturated to varying degrees into the ways of the minority group. These members, or the group as a whole, would assimilate or dissimilate in relation to certain aspects of life in the cities of the Roman Empire. The more precise balance of each of these two factors would differ from one Christian group or individual to the next.

---

63. See Harland 2003a, 239–264.

64. Cf. Stowers 1995.

Overview of This Study

Now that we have some sense of my social-historical approach and my theoretical framework, let me briefly outline the progression of this study. In important respects, both diaspora Judeans and followers of Jesus shared much in common with other associations when it comes to dynamics of identity and belonging. Part 1 introduces associations and explains how both Judean gatherings and Christian congregations were often viewed as associations, both by insiders (e.g., Philo and Josephus) and by outsiders (e.g., Roman authorities, Lucian, and Celsus; ch. 1). Followers of Jesus, such as Ignatius of Antioch, further illustrate how Christians themselves could express their identities in terms drawn from local cultural life, including the world of associations (ch. 2). Here external categorizations by outsiders and internal self-definitions by insiders overlap in processes of identity formation and negotiation.

In part 2, I explore internal definitions of identity with a focus on familial language of belonging among members in certain groups. Quite well known is the early Christian use of sibling language ("brothers") to express and strengthen bonds within congregations. Contrary to assumptions within scholarship, however, this practice was not uniquely Christian, and epigraphic and papyrological evidence shows that "brother" language was also used within some other groups and associations (ch. 3). Furthermore, parental language, such as "mother of the synagogue" or "father of the association," was another important way in which members within Judean gatherings and other associations expressed social hierarchies and identified with other members of the group (ch. 4). The Judean use of such parental terminology mirrors similar practices within Greek cities in the Roman Empire, pointing to one instance of acculturation to the practices of civic communities generally and associations specifically.

In part 3, I turn to evidence for ethnically based associations of immigrants, including Judeans. Placing Judean gatherings within the framework of other, less-studied, immigrant associations and cultural minority groups provides new perspectives on dynamics of identity maintenance and acculturation. The case of associations formed by Phoenicians or Syrians abroad illustrates the value of comparing immigrant populations and ethnic groups within this milieu (ch. 5). A regionally focussed study of Judeans at Hierapolis in Asia Minor then offers further insights into the complexity of interactions between cultural minorities and other groups within cities in the Roman Empire, including processes of assimilation and cultural maintenance (ch. 6).

Finally, in part 4 I turn to evidence for tensions and competition in intergroup relations. I show how rivalries and external categorizations play a role in the formation, negotiation, and expression of identities. Cohabitation and cooperation among various groups in the ancient city did not preclude rivalries among associations, such as those in cities addressed by John's Apocalypse (ch. 7). In Sardis and Smyrna, for instance, associations of various kinds could express their identities in ways that countered other groups. Such groups were, in some respects, competitors for the allegiances of members. Evidence for certain individuals' memberships in multiple associations draws further attention to the plural nature of identities in the ancient context, as well as the potential for links among groups through certain individuals' social networks.

In the case of Greek and Roman perspectives on foreigners or cultural minority groups, such as Judeans and followers of Jesus, ethnic rivalries and processes of identity formation could take place, in part, through stereotypes of the "alien" other and the portrait of the "anti-association" (ch. 8). Charges of human sacrifice, cannibalism, and incest which were laid against certain Christian groups and other cultural minorities are better understood within this ethnographic framework. Sometimes cultural minorities themselves engaged in analogous characterizations of the majority culture (or of associations in the majority culture). Furthermore, similar techniques were also used in rivalries between different cultural minority groups, such as the rivalries that took place among various Christian groups (orthodox groups vs. heretical groups). These ethnographic discourses were, in themselves, part of ongoing processes of internal self-definition and external categorization in relation to the "other" on the part of a given cultural group, whether in the majority or in the minority.

Moreover, depending on the perceiver and the moment of perception, Judean gatherings and Christian congregations could be viewed as either typical associations or "foreign" anti-associations. Giving attention to both sides of this dynamic, this study places Judeans and their close relatives, the followers of Jesus, within the framework of identity formation, negotiation, and communication in the Greco-Roman world.

Part 1

Judean and Christian Identities in the Context of Associations

1

Associations and Group Identity among Judeans and Christians

Introduction

In this chapter, I argue that certain social dimensions of group life among Judean (Jewish) gatherings and Christian congregations, including issues of identity, are better understood when we place these groups within the framework of unofficial associations in the Greco-Roman world. Despite their position as cultural minority groups, synagogues and congregations should not be studied in isolation from analogous social structures of that world. This is something that certain scholars are increasingly recognizing, especially since the 1980s.[1] Still, in categorizing many Judean gatherings and Christian congregations as associations, I am going against the grain of a more common scholarly categorization in social-historical studies of Christian origins.

It has become standard—one might even say orthodox—within scholarship on early Christianity to categorize virtually all congregations of Jesus-followers, and sometimes Judean gatherings as well, as "sects" in terms drawn from modern sociological studies, particularly studies by Bryan R. Wilson.[2] In some cases, scholars who categorize these groups as sects are hesitant about the value of comparing synagogues and congregations with contemporary associations, stressing supposed differences between the groups precisely concerning the relationship between the group and society.[3] The emphasis in such sectarian categorizations is often placed on the negative or ambivalent social relations that existed between the sect and surrounding society. Discourses of separation and distinction predominate.[4]

There may be benefits to viewing *some* minority groups or associations through the lenses of sociological typologies of sects in order to provide insights into certain types of social and intergroup relations. However, we should not assume that all Judean gatherings

1. On the history of scholarship, see the introduction and, more extensively, Harland 2003a, 177–212.

2. Wilson 1967, 1970, 1973, 1990. See Harland (2003a, 177–195) for further discussion of problems in the application of Wilson's typology to early Christianity.

3. E.g., Meeks 1983, 78–80. Cf. Schmeller 1995; McCready 1996.

4. E.g., Elliott 1990 [1981], 79; Meeks 1983, 35, 77–78.

or Christian congregations are best categorized and understood within a typology of "sects." As I began to show in *Associations, Synagogues, and Congregations*, such wholesale categorizations tend to obscure a range of evidence, and this includes the sort of evidence for integration and common modes of identity construction, negotiation, and communication that I explore throughout the present study.

Alongside this overall statement regarding where Judeans and Christians fit on a social map of the ancient Mediterranean, I draw attention to important implications for identities in this chapter. In particular, I begin to outline the importance of both external categorizations and internal definitions of identity. In this case, there are many instances when both outsiders and insiders identified Judean gatherings and Christian congregations in terms drawn from association life. So my scholarly choice to categorize these groups as associations is based, to a significant degree, on how many people in the ancient context, including some Judeans and Christians, viewed such groups. I begin by defining associations and outlining some common social sources of association membership before turning to ancient external and internal definitions of Judean gatherings and Christian congregations as associations.

What Are Associations?

Basic Definition

Let me begin by clarifying what I mean by "associations" and how this relates to the concept of "voluntary associations" as it is used in the social sciences. Then I will move on to social networks that contributed to their memberships. I use the term "associations" to describe social groupings in antiquity that shared certain characteristics in common and that were often recognized as analogous groups by people and by governmental institutions. Associations were small, unofficial ("private") groups, usually consisting of about ten to fifty members (but sometimes with larger memberships into the hundreds), that met together on a regular basis to socialize with one another and to honour both earthly and divine benefactors, which entailed a variety of internal and external activities.

With regard to external relations, these groups engaged in ongoing connections with those outside the group, particularly with wealthier members of society who could assume the role of benefactors (donors) or leaders of the group in question. In return these benefactors received honours from the association, a system of benefaction that I explain more fully in chapter 7. Sometimes associations could also return the favour by supporting particular members of the elite in their political goals or honour-pursuing competition with others.[5] Associations could on occasion interact with civic and imperial institutions or functionaries as well. The level and frequency of involvement in such contacts varied from one group to the next.[6]

5. See, for example, Philo's discussion of Isodoros and associations in Alexandria (*Flacc.* 135–45). Cf. Cicero, *In Piso.* 8–9; *Pro Sestio* 33–34; *Dom.* 74; Quintus Cicero, *Pet.* 8.29–30. On *collegia* and elections at Pompeii, see Tanzer 1939 and Franklin 1980.

6. On external relations of associations, see Harland 2003a, 115–76.

Internally, associations participated in a range of activities, including honouring the gods through rituals, including sacrifice and the accompanying meal. The importance of the meal in connection with the gatherings and festivals of such groups draws attention to the fact that what we as moderns might distinguish as "religious" (sacrificing to the gods) and "social" (meals) were intimately tied together in antiquity, as Stanley Stowers's study of sacrifice also stresses.[7] All associations were in some sense religious, and it is problematic to speak of particular groups as religious associations simply because their patron deities happen to be mentioned in their title. Associations served other functions for their membership internally, including burial-related activities, which I discuss in chapter 6.[8]

A variety of corporate terms for a "gathering" or "grouping," some of which were shared within broader civic or imperial institutional contexts, were used to identify such informal groups. In the Greek-speaking areas that are the focus of this study, some common general group designations include κοινόν (pronounced *koinon* and translated "association" in this study), σύνοδος (*synodos*, "synod"), θίασος (*thiasos*, "society"), συνέδριον (*synedrion*, "sanhedrin"), ἔρανος (*eranos*, "festal-gathering"), συνεργασία (*synergasia*, "guild"), συμβιωταί (*symbiotai*, "companions"), ἑταῖροι (*hetairoi*, "associates"), μύσται (*mystai*, "initiates"), συναγωγή (*synagōgē*, "synagogue"), and σπεῖρα (*speira*, "company"). There were also group titles characteristic of certain cultural regions, such as δοῦμος (*doumos*), which was characteristic of Phrygia and Lydia (in central Asia Minor); κλῖνη (*klinē*), "dining-couch," which was used of both a "banquet" and of an "association" in Egypt; and συνθείς (*syntheis*), which was used for "those placed together" in Macedonia.[9] In Latin-speaking areas (especially in Italy and the West), one of the most well-attested terms for an association was *collegium*, which is why many scholars have adopted the practice of using the plural of that term, *collegia*, as a designation for associations generally.

Other associations developed a more specific title that incorporated the patron deity of the group, including names such as the Dionysiasts (in honour of the god Dionysos), the Isiasts (in honour of Isis), and the Aphrodisiasts (in honour of Aphrodite). Still, an array of other group designations, some of which we will soon encounter, shows that there was no standard approach to group titles, and the same thing can be said about variations in internal leadership titles.

My definition of associations here seeks to distinguish these rather informal (or "private") groups from official "institutions" of the cities and provinces, from official "boards" in charge of administering temples or other similar institutions, and from age-based "organizations" connected with the gymnasia (e.g., ephebes, elders), for instance. I should mention, however, that the evidence is sometimes ambiguous, and it is not always easy to clearly identify whether a particular group is a board of cultic functionaries within a god's temple rather than a less formal group of devotees of a god. A further complication is that associations frequently designated themselves using corporate terminology shared within broader

7. Cf. Stowers 1995.

8. On internal activities, see Harland 2003a, 55–88.

9. For the first term, see *TAM* V 179, 449, 470a, 536. For the second, see *POxy* 110, 1484, 1755, 3693, 4339; Youtie 1948; *NewDocs* I 1; Philo *Flacc.* 136–37. For the third, see *SEG* 27 (1977), no. 267; IG X.2 288, 289, 291, all from Thessalonica.

civic and imperial contexts (e.g., *koinon, synedrion, speira*), which sometimes makes a group sound more official or public than it actual was.

Voluntary Associations in the Social Sciences

There are certain affinities between my definition here and the quite broad concept of "voluntary associations" as it is used in sociology and anthropology, and yet some distinctions are important to note.[10] In the social sciences, the concept of voluntary associations often encompasses a large spectrum of groups, referring to "secondary organisations that exist between the primary links of kinship and the equally non-voluntary arrangements of tertiary institutions like the state."[11] As Jose C. Moya goes on to note, defined in this broad way, the term has been used in reference to a spectrum of groups that have proliferated in the modern period, from local choirs or bowling leagues to neighbourhood associations, immigrant groups, and more international organizations, such as Amnesty International.

According to Maria Krysan and William d'Antonio, modern voluntary associations are "independent of control from sources outside themselves, people were free to join or leave, and members established their own objectives and goals and the means to achieve them."[12] This intersects with ancient groups under evaluation here in the sense that they were generally not controlled by outside organizations and they did indeed establish and pursue their own goals. Yet quite often these goals (e.g., honouring earthly and divine benefactors) were relatively limited in comparison with those of some modern voluntary associations, such as politically focussed groups such as Amnesty International. When the same sociologists go on to explain the commonly perceived functions of modern voluntary associations, they are describing something quite different from the groups we are looking at in antiquity: associations "serve an important governing role at the local level and perform tasks as varied as community decision-making, emergency relief, fund-raising, public information campaigns, and professional licensing."[13]

Furthermore, it is important to heavily qualify the "voluntary" nature of the groups under examination in this study. Although there is some truth in the statement that, for many associations in antiquity, people might join or leave of their own volition, there were certain factors at work in limiting the voluntary nature of membership in associations of particular types, as I soon discuss in connection with social networks and the composition of associations. So our definition of associations here in this volume is more limited and specific, though at times it overlaps with or is encompassed within such social-scientific definitions dealing with associations in modern societies.

One further observation about modern studies of voluntary associations is in order before surveying social sources of ancient associations. Much of the literature on voluntary associations in modern, developed and developing countries (e.g., North America, Africa,

---

10. Social-scientific studies of voluntary associations include Mishnun 1950; Little 1957; Geertz 1962; Anderson 1971; Kerri 1976; Thomson and Armer 1981; Krysan and d'Antonio 1992; Moya 2005.

11. Moya 2005, 834.

12. Krysan and d'Antonio 1992, 2231.

13. Krysan and d'Antonio 1992, 2231.

Indonesia) is devoted to the question of the primary functions of such groups in relation to surrounding society. In particular, as Randall J. Thomson and Michael Armer (1981) clarify, scholarly debates have centred on whether voluntary associations primarily serve integration or mobilization functions in relation to society.

On the one hand are studies that emphasize the role of voluntary associations in the integration or adjustment of individuals and communities within broader society, serving as "adaptive mechanisms."[14] In part, this integrative focus was a result of another assumption within the social sciences in earlier generations: namely, the notion that urban settings are alienating environments characterized by relative deprivation and social dislocation, especially for immigrants.[15] As I discuss in chapter 5, such assumptions still impact studies of social life in the ancient world, including the study of immigrants. Thomson and Armer critique this view, which involves problematic assumptions and oversimplifications regarding city life that are not consistent with a range of findings in other more recent social-scientific studies. This view also tends to assume that the formation of associations was primarily a means to compensate for a lack of meaningful ties, or for feelings of rootlessness in the urban milieu.[16] On the other hand are social-scientific studies that show that "instead of integration, voluntary associations reinforce the cultural distinctiveness of various ethnic and minority groups" and serve to mobilize individuals to effect change in the host society.[17]

Despite clear differences between the ancient and modern contexts, Thomson and Armer's argument here is particularly noteworthy in connection with my own findings in subsequent chapters regarding associations in the ancient context, particularly ethnic groups or cultural minority groups. Thomson and Armer point to the "multifunctional and dynamic capabilities of voluntary associations" and the various types of groups and types of societal contexts. They argue that "voluntary associations can serve both adjustment and mobilization functions; which is most important depends in part on the interaction between the type of organization and the dominant urban culture."[18] I continue to address the role of associations in cultural adaptation and identity maintenance in subsequent chapters.

Social Networks and the Membership of Associations

Now that we have some sense of what is meant by the term association, I turn to our ancient sources for these groups and to the question of what types of associations existed, which will also flesh out my earlier definition. Sometimes there are literary sources that shed light on such groups. Still, evidence for most groups is primarily archeological, including

14. E.g., Mishnun 1950; Little 1957; Geertz 1962; Anderson 1971; Kerri 1976.

15. See, for instance, Wirth 1938, for the traditional view of urban life. On problems with theories of relative deprivation, see Gurney and Tierney 1982; Wallis 1975; Beckford 1975, 1530–59; Berquist 1995.

16. See Thomson and Armer 1981.

17. Thomson and Armer 1981, 288.

18. Thomson and Armer 1981, 288.

Figure 1. Banqueting hall of the cowherds at Pergamon (second cent. CE*)*

epigraphy (inscriptions). To some extent, this is why associations have only recently begun to draw the attention of disciplines such as New Testament studies and classical studies that, traditionally at least, privilege literary evidence.

Some of the meeting places of associations have been discovered and excavated, offering a window into aspects of the internal life of such groups, including their ritual lives. Thus, for instance, the meeting places of associations devoted to the god Dionysos have been excavated at Athens and at Pergamon, and numerous buildings have been found on the Greek island of Delos and at Ostia near Rome.[19] Figure 1 shows a photo of a second-century banqueting hall of a group that honoured the god Dionysos at Pergamon, calling themselves the "cowherds" (βουκόλοι) in reference to some of the mythology of this god.[20]

By far the most extensive source of materials on association life comes from monuments and inscriptions.[21] These inscriptions include honorary plaques or monuments for benefactors, dedications to gods, internal regulations or statutes, membership lists, and grave stones that were commissioned by associations or their members. Pictured in figure 2 is a photograph of a monument dedicated to "Zeus Most High (Hypsistos) and the village." Below the inscription, it depicts the gods (Zeus, Artemis, and Apollo) along with the asso-

19. See Hermansen 1981; Schwarzer 2002; Trümper 2002 and 2004; Harland 2003a, 63–69, 78–83; Ascough 2007, 82–90.

20. On these cowherds, see the following inscriptions: *SEG* 29 (1979), no. 1264 (found in the meeting place); *IPergamon* 485–88; Conze and Schuchhardt 1899, 179, no. 31. On the building, see Radt 1989 and Radt 1988, 222–28.

21. On the value of inscriptions for history, see Millar 1983; Oliver 2000; Bodel 2001.

Figure 2. Monument depicting three gods (Zeus, Artemis, and Apollo), an association, and entertainment, from Panormos near Kyzikos, now in the British Museum (GIBM IV. 1007)

ciation gathered for a meal as several other figures provide entertainment (*GIBM* IV. 1007). Although limited in what they tell us, such material remains nonetheless provide important information regarding social and cultural life among many segments of the population, rather than only the literary elites.

The inscriptional evidence attests to an array of associations, and it is important to explain the groups that are found, building on my previous work in this area. Previous typologies of associations, such as the influential, multivolume work of Jean-Pierre Waltzing (1895–1900), tended to approach categorization with issues of primary purpose in mind, resulting in a threefold typology of (1) occupational, (2) cultic, and (3) burial associations. Besides the now generally recognized embeddedness of religion within social life in antiquity, such that all associations were cultic associations, this typology is also problematic in that it implies that occupational associations were not interested in honouring the gods or in the burial of members, for example. Instead, groups of various kinds served a variety of purposes for their members, not just one. So, building on a suggestion by John S. Kloppenborg (1996a), I have proposed a typology of associations that entails attention to the composition of membership and the role of social network connections in the formation and growth of groups.[22]

---

22. See Harland 2003a, 25–54.

Social scientists have long recognised the significance of social networks—intricate webs of connection that exist within a social structure—for understanding and explaining the workings of society, including the formation of social movements and groups. The term "social network" refers to the webs of ties and interactions among actors (individuals, groups, communities) within a social structure.

Since the mid–1950s social scientists have come to use the concept of social networks as an analytical tool for studying specific phenomena within society in relational terms.[23] Several sociologists have employed this tool in the study of modern social and religious groups, and have stressed the importance of preexisting social ties within networks for the dissemination or expansion of groups of various kinds (e.g., new religious movements, sects, and churches). For instance, in studies of the Korean-based Unification Church of the Reverend Sun Myung Moon and of recruitment to Pentecostal churches it was found that, more often than not, prior social contacts or interpersonal connections between members of a religious group and a nonmember preceded entrance of new members into a group.[24] Subsequent sociological studies, including those by Rodney Stark and William S. Bainbridge, confirm the vital importance of linkages through social networks not only as a precondition of joining, but also as a continuing factor in explaining the social workings of a given group.[25] In light of the importance of social networks for group membership, it is worth considering what webs of social linkages were at work in the ancient context.[26]

Several social networks, at times overlapping, framed social relations in the Greco-Roman world and played a role in the formation and growth in membership of particular associations.[27] Although such networks were overlapping, there are cases when certain groups drew membership primarily from one or another of these five important areas. There were associations that drew membership primarily from social connections associated with (1) the household; (2) the neighbourhood; (3) the workplace; (4) the sanctuary or temple; and (5) common geographical origins or a shared sense of ethnic identity. Groups could, of course, draw membership from several of these overlapping networks, but often a certain set of connections seems more prevalent.

First, the ties of the family and household could play a fundamental role in affiliations and in the membership of associations. Family networks encompassed a far greater set of relations in the ancient context than in modern Western societies. Household relationships seem to account entirely for the membership and existence of groups like the "initiates" of Dionysos headed by Pompeia Agrippinilla in Torre Nova, Italy (*IGUR* 160; ca. 160 CE).[28] The whole range of social strata found in the ancient household or *familia* belonged to this group, including free, freed, and servile dependents alongside members of the imperial

23. See, for instance, Mitchell 1969, 1974; Boissevain 1974; Wellman 1983; Wasserman and Faust 1994.

24. Lofland and Stark 1965; Gerlach and Hine 1970.

25. Cf. Stark and Bainbridge 1985, 307–324; Welch 1981; Cavendish, Welch and Leege 1998.

26. For other studies that analyze social networks in the ancient context, see White, ed., 1992, Chow 1992, and Remus 1996.

27. The following discussion builds on Harland 2003a, 25–53. For a recent discussion of growth in association memberships, see Ascough 2007.

28. Cf. *LSAM* 20, with discussion in Barton and Horsley 1981 (household-based group in Philadelphia in Asia).

elites such as Agrippinilla herself, who was married to the influential M. Gavius Squilla Gallicanus (a senator and consul who became proconsul of Roman Asia in 165 CE).[29]

A second important web of connections was found in the neighbourhood where one lived and worked. There are several examples of ongoing associations in Asia Minor and elsewhere who drew primarily on these local links and whose identity was expressed in terms of the neighbourhood or district in question.[30] Persons living or working in a particular area were more likely to reflect similar social brackets of society, yet such neighborhood associations could include a mixture in terms of occupation (e.g., *IPergamon* 393) or gender.

Third, social networks related to occupation could in many ways be a determining factor in group affiliations. Daily social contacts in the workshops and marketplaces could often develop into an occupational association or guild of a more permanent type. We know of a wide range of such associations that identified themselves primarily in terms of their shared occupation, including groups of producers and dealers of foods (e.g., bakers, fishers), clothing manufacturers (e.g., leather cutters, linen workers, purple-dyers), builders (e.g., carpenters, masons), other artisans (e.g., potters, copper-, silver-, or goldsmiths), merchants, shippers, bankers, physicians, philosophers, athletes, theatrical performers, and soldiers (e.g., associations devoted to Mithras). I would suggest that membership in such occupationally based associations was less than voluntary in the sense that there would be considerable social pressure to join with fellow-workers. Failure to join might result in some degree of alienation, with economic repercussions. At the same time, Russell Meiggs does note evidence for multiple memberships in guilds at Ostia, which also shows that engagement in a particular occupation was not necessarily a requirement for membership in a guild based on that occupation.[31]

Although there are clear exceptions, membership in occupational associations was predominantly male and in many cases the social makeup of a guild was rather homogeneous in social-economic terms. Nevertheless, there are guilds that reflect a wider spectrum of social-economic levels, such as the fishers and fishmongers at Ephesos (*IEph* 20 = *NewDocs* V; 50s CE). This group, together with their families, contributed towards the building and dedication of the fishery toll-office, and they set up a monument that is pictured in figure 3. The one hundred (or so) contributors included Roman citizens (about forty-three to forty-four members) and a mixture of persons of free or freed (about thirty-six to forty-one) and servile status (about two to ten). The donors are listed in order of the size of donation ranging from the Roman citizen who could afford to provide four marble columns to those who could afford to give five denaria or less.

Fourth, social contacts arising from regular attendance at a particular temple or sanctuary could become the basis for an ongoing association. Harold Remus's (1996) study of social networks at Asklepios's healing sanctuary at Pergamon, as reflected in the works of Aelius Aristides, demonstrates well the complicated webs of connection that formed in such a setting. These connections could also be translated into associations such as the

---

29. See Vogliano 1933; Scheid 1986.

30. See, for instance, *IEph* 454, 3080; *IGR* IV 788–91 (Apameia, Phrygia); *IPergamon* 393, 424, 434; *ISmyrna* 714.

31. Meiggs 1960, 321–22.

Figure 3. Monument set up by fishermen and fishmongers at Ephesos, now in the Selçuk Archaeological Museum (IEph *20; 50s* CE*)*

"therapeutists" (θεραπευταί) attested at this sanctuary at Pergamon. Some, though not all, groups of initiates in the mysteries, including some discussed in the next chapter, may have formed from sanctuary-related networks.

A fifth important set of social links were those established among immigrants or in connection with common geographical origins, ethnicity, or cultural minority positions. This type of ancient association may also be understood in relation to social-scientific concepts of ethnic groups and cultural minorities, which I defined in the introduction.[32] There were various associations of immigrants from Rome and Alexandrians who had resettled in cities in other provinces, for instance (e.g., *IPerinthos* 27–28; *IGR* I 446). In chapter 5, I devote significant attention to Syrians or Phoenicians who migrated elsewhere and formed associations. Gatherings of Judeans, which occupy us considerably in this study, need to be placed alongside these other ethnically based associations. While this type of association may be formed in connection with shared ethnic identity or minority cultural practices,

32. For social network studies of ethnic groups in the modern context, see Sanders 2002, 329–31.

these associations could also come to include participants or members from other ethnic groups.

Some Judean associations happen to illustrate the interplay of the five overlapping webs of networks that I have outlined above. Secondary to links associated with ethnic identification, several other subsets of social connections could be operative in the formation and membership of particular immigrant or minority groups. At Rome, three Judean associations derive their names from the neighbourhood where they lived (Calcaresians, Campesians, and Siburesians) and two appear to be founded by Judeans who shared in common previous settlement in Greek cities elsewhere ("Tripolitans" and the "synagogue of Elaia").[33] Both neighbourhood and occupational networks played a role in the organization of the Judean population at Alexandria as well, and Shaye J. D. Cohen discusses several other locales where we know of neighbourhoods being specifically identified as Judean.[34]

The interplay of various social networks also means that it was possible for those who did not initially share the minority cultural position or ethnic identity of a particular group to become involved in some way within such minority groups, potentially becoming ongoing participants or members. Non-Judeans (gentiles) joining Judean associations is a case in point. Yet further on I discuss similar interactions between Syrian groups and outsiders who could attend meetings and join in honouring the deities of the ethnic group. This also has implications for Christian associations as cultural minority groups of a Judean variety, associations that nonetheless came to incorporate members with varying ethnic identities. So multiple networks, corresponding to a plurality of identities, could be at work in the formation of certain associations.

These same social networks seem to have played a role in the formation and growth of Christian associations. A pattern of recruitment and communal gathering in Paul's letters and in Acts suggests the importance of family-based networks: again and again an entire family of dependents was baptized along with the head of the household and the home was used as a meeting place.[35] Though Acts may exaggerate the point, social connections related to ethnicity served as an avenue for the spread of Christianity, as Judean networks in the diaspora coincided with the movement of figures such as Paul. Occupational networks, too, were important for early Christianity.[36] Richard S. Ascough (2000) shows that the Christian group at Thessalonica in the mid-first century may be considered a professional guild of hand-workers, for instance (cf. 1 Thess 2:9; 4:9–12). Although we should not take at face value Celsus's characterization of the Christian movement as a whole as predominantly lower class, there is truth in his observation, about a century after Paul, that attachments through workshops of "wool-workers," "shoemakers," and "clothing-cleaners" continued as a source of newcomers to some Christian groups (Origen *C. Cels.* 3.55).

---

33. For the former, see *IEurJud* 69, 98, 165, 558, 584 (Calcaresians = "Lime-burners" district); 288, 560, 577 (Campesians); 338, 428, 451, 452, 527, 557 (Siburesians). For the latter, *IEurJud* 406, 576 (Elaia); 166 (Tripolitans). Also see Leon 1995 [1960], 135–66; Richardson 1998.

34. Cf. Philo *Flacc.* 55; *CPJ* III 454, 468; Kasher 1985, 352–53; Cohen 1999, 56–58.

35. Acts 11:14; 16:15; 18:8; cf. 1 Cor 16:19; Phlm 2; Rom 6:10–16; Col 4:15.

36. Cf. Hock 1980; Humphries 1998, on the importance of trade networks in the dissemination of Christian and other groups in Italy.

Group Designations and Identity: Judean and Christian Groups as Associations

What we as social historians look for and notice in studying such groups is not necessarily what an ancient Greek, Roman, Egyptian, Syrian, or Judean would notice. For instance, even the typology of associations based on social network connections outlined above in some respects represents the outsider (etic) perspective of a scholar, not necessarily the insider (emic) perspective of the subjects we are studying. And when we call an early Christian congregation a "cultural minority group" or a Judean gathering an "ethnic group," we are once again using etic categories, not concepts that were used by our historical subjects. Such scholarly constructs assist us in understanding and explaining social phenomena in our terms.

Nonetheless, there is considerable evidence that people in the ancient world—both outsiders and members of the groups in question—did indeed notice the analogous nature of associations of various kinds, even if they would not develop a typology based on social networks such as the one outlined above. This adds a further dimension to our own categories and comparisons. Such evidence of comparisons in the ancient world is particularly valuable for approaching issues of group identity since it involves cases where the two main sources of identity construction and negotiation are at work, where ancient external categorizations and internal definitions of the group intersect or overlap considerably. Ancient observers, on the one hand, and both Judeans and followers of Jesus, on the other, sometimes used common social and cultural categories drawn from association life to describe group identities. This was done alongside other more specific or distinctive terms of identification that are not our focus in this chapter, and which varied from one association to the next.

Let me illustrate these common categories and group designations here before going on to detail one specific case of internal self-definition from the letters of Ignatius of Antioch in the following chapter. Here the focus is on outlining common group designations. I am by no means making any Herculean attempt to discuss the myriad self-identifications or external categorizations (some of them strongly negative, as we will see in chapter 8) that were used in reference to Judeans or Christians. I begin with designations of Judean groups generally. Then I move on to groups of Jesus-followers, groups that shared in common some degree of connection with certain Judean cultural ways and the Judean God. In each case I begin with external categorizations by contemporaries before considering internal self-designations that overlap with common association terminology.

On the Judean side, both Philo of Alexandria (early first century) and Josephus of Jerusalem (late first century, born in 37 CE) supply us with information regarding both external and internal definitions and corporate designations for groups of Judeans in the diaspora. As Judean authors writing to Greek-speaking audiences in the Roman period, Josephus's and Philo's own characterizations of Judean groups are already informed by Greek or Roman categorizations, I would suggest.[37] So, in certain ways, they may reflect

37. Note, for instance, Josephus's characterization of educated Judean groups in the homeland as "philosophies," using Greek philosophical debates about the soul and about Fate as his focal points (*Ant.* 18.12ff.; *War* 2.119).

what some social scientists call the internalization of external categorizations. Internalization, as I mentioned in the introduction and discuss further in chapter 8, involves members of a particular group adopting, adapting, or reacting to outsiders' labels or definitions of them.

Josephus presents numerous official statements by civic and imperial institutions that reflect the perspectives of outsiders to some degree, including Roman imperial authorities (*Ant.* 14.185–267 and 16.160–78). Although these official documents may already be affected by, or revised in accordance with, Josephus's own apologetic (defensive) purposes, they nonetheless provide some insights into common external categorizations by Greek civic authorities or Roman imperial institutions.

Josephus shows that a Judean group might be considered a "society" (*thiasos*). This term has a long history dating back to subgroups within the phratries in the Athenian sphere as early as the fifth century BCE; by the first century CE, it was among the more common self-designations adopted by associations and it was used almost exclusively for associations.[38] It was often used as a general catch-all category for associations generally, as a comment by Philo (cited below) also shows.[39] Josephus preserves a letter ostensibly from Julius Caesar to the civic institutions of the Greek city (*polis*) of Parion in Asia Minor, located just west of Kyzikos on the map (*Ant.* 14.213–16). In it, Julius Caesar refers to Judean emissaries from the Greek island of Delos who claimed that others in the cities had been preventing them from practicing their "ancestral customs and sacred practices." The letter then mentions and applies to the Parion situation previous actions by Caesar which specified that, although societies were forbidden "to assemble in the city" of Rome, societies formed by Judeans specifically were provided an exception in response to specific diplomatic contacts with imperial authorities.

It is important to at least note here that associations of various kinds, including the Dionysiac initiates at Smyrna whom I discuss in chapter 7, engaged in such diplomacy with civic or imperial authorities, which resulted in similar recognitions or privileges.[40] So we should not always assume that the Judeans were a special case among associations in regard to such diplomatic relations, despite the participants' claims that they were special. As Tessa Rajak has clearly established, there was no "Roman charter for the Jews," and the problematic scholarly idea that Judeans were a specially recognized "legal religion" (*religio licita*) with such a charter is unfounded in ancient evidence.[41]

Another document presented by Josephus has a Roman official, Lucius Antonius (about 49 BCE), responding positively to the request of Judean ambassadors from Sardis in Asia Minor regarding their "synod" (*synodos*). The term "synod," which has the basic meaning of a "coming together," was used in a variety of contexts for an assembly of people and had a significant range of meanings, so the passage from Josephus involving the use of "society" (*thiasos*), discussed above, is stronger evidence of an association context than this

38. For discussion of the early use of the term, see Costello 1938, 178–79; Ferguson and Nock 1944, 133–34.

39. See *Flacc.* 136.

40. See Rajak 1984; Harland 2003a, 157, 220–24.

41. Rajak 1984; cf. Millar 1973, 145.

instance of "synod."[42] Nonetheless, synod is among the most used Greek self-designations for associations specifically in the Roman period, and it is likely that its use in the passage in Josephus reflects the milieu of associations.

These Judeans at Sardis had apparently argued that "from the earliest times they have had a synod of their own in accordance with their ancestral laws and a place of their own" (Josephus *Ant.* 14.235).[43] The Roman official responded by reaffirming this claim and, in this case, it seems that civic institutions of Sardis likewise acknowledged the claim (*Ant.* 14.259–61). Here it is difficult to sort out whether this language of "synod" was the term used by ambassadors of the Judean group themselves (internal definition) or by Roman officials (external definition), or by both. Whatever the case may be, it seems that the group is being described using common group-designations that were used by associations in the same context.

It is worth noting some evidence that may provide insight into similar uses of this designation, "synod," in self-definitions among Judean groups. One inscription from Nysa, located east of Ephesos, apparently confirms the internal use of this corporate term by Judeans themselves (cf. *CPJ* I 138). In it, a man named Menandros had established a place "for the people and the synod (τῶι λαῶι καὶ τῇ συνόδωι) which are gathered around Dositheos son of Theogenes."[44] Here the somewhat culturally distinctive Judean usage of "people" (λάος), as also attested at Smyrna and Hierapolis—likely reflecting notions of the "people of God" as in the Septuagint—is coupled with the standard use of "synod" for the group.[45] If Margaret H. Williams's recent interpretation of a fragmentary papyrus from late Ptolemaic Egypt (first cent. BCE) is correct, then we have another case involving a guild of Judean "embalmers" (ἐνταφιασταί / συνταφιασταί) that designated itself a "synod" and met in a "prayer house" (προσευχῆι) for its meetings (the term συναγωγῆ is used for its "meeting").[46] Other Judean groups who did not necessarily adopt "synod" as a main group designation nonetheless could use the term in reference to a regular meeting of the group, as with the corporate body of Judeans in Berenice in Cyrenaica, to which I return below.[47]

Further evidence of both external and internal definitions comes from Philo. In these cases, too, "synod" is a common designation which is linked closely with the more distinctive "society" (*thiasos*) and with imperial actions in relation to such associations. Philo was himself among the five Judean ambassadors to Emperor Gaius (in 38 or 39 CE) in connection with ethnic conflicts in Alexandria.[48] Philo records the essence of his speech in

---

42. Josephus himself uses the term "synod" twenty-five times but it does not have any stable, technical sense in his writings (I am grateful to Steve Mason for his suggestions in this area).

43. Trans. Marcus 1933–63 (LCL).

44. *IJO* II 26 = *DFSJ* 31 = Robert 1960c, 261 (first cent. BCE, according to Ameling 2004, in IJO).

45. *IJO* II 44 (Smyrna), 206 (Hierapolis). Also see the discussion in Noy, Panayatov, and Bloedhorn 2004, 109–10, regarding the phrase "farewell to the people" at Larissa in Thessaly (*IJO* I Ach 1–4, 8–14, 25; probably third or fourth cent. CE). On the connection with the "people of God," see Robert 1960c, 260–61.

46. Williams 1994b, 174. For the repeated reference to "the synod," see lines 4, 8, and 16. For the fragmentary mentions of the embalming occupation, see lines 10 and 13. On various names for burial related occupations in Egypt, see Youtie 1940, 650–57.

47. Reynolds 1977, 244–47, no. 17 (line 24) and no. 18 (line 16). Cf. Rajak 2002 [1996], 382.

48. On these conflicts see Barclay 1996, 48–59; Schäfer 1997, 163–69.

a writing titled the *Embassy to Gaius*. There he appeals to the positive actions of Gaius's great-grandfather, Augustus himself, as a precedent for Gaius to follow in siding with the Judeans of Alexandria over against the Greeks. In support of his position, Philo cites two documents reflecting positive diplomatic relations between Romans and Judeans which once again reveal external categorizations.

The second document involves a letter by Gaius Norbanus Flaccus, the proconsul of Asia, to the civic magistrates of Ephesos (dating ca. either 24 BCE or 12 BCE).[49] Philo suggests that this reflects the perspective of Augustus as well (cf. Josephus *Ant.* 16.166, 171). In this case, Philo first quotes portions of the letter before paraphrasing its essence in this way: Augustus "did not think that the form generally adopted about synods should be applied to do away with the gatherings of the Judeans to which they resort for collection of the first-fruits and their other pious activities" (*Leg. Gai.* 316).[50] As Torrey Seland (1996) points out, elsewhere Philo employs the term "synod" as one among several synonyms for a general concept of associations, a general concept which he identifies using the term "societies": "In the city there are societies (θίασοι) with a large membership . . . "Synods" and "dining couches" (σύνοδοι καὶ κλῖναι) are the particular names given to them by the people of the country" (*Flacc.* 136).

The first document cited by Philo is Augustus's letter to the governors of the provinces of Asia (likely the provinces of Asia Minor are in mind). Here Philo paraphrases the letter and suggests that Augustus proclaimed that "Judeans alone be permitted by them [the governors] to assemble in synagogues (τὰ συναγώγια συνέρχεσθαι). These synods, he said, were not based on drunkenness and carousing to promote conspiracy . . . but were schools of temperance and justice" (*Leg. Gai.* 311–13).

Here the point is that Judean gatherings are called not only "synagogues" but, once again, "synods," and Philo himself compares the groups to the advantage of Judean associations. This suggests the importance of "synods" and the associations generally for internal Judean self-definition, despite the occasions on which authors like Philo engaged in moral critique of the associations of others, to which I return in chapter 8. Diaspora Judeans like Philo sometimes considered associations as the framework within which to define themselves, it seems, at least in addressing Greek or Roman audiences. Not surprisingly, in light of the rivalries that existed among associations, there were claims of superior status for the Judean associations nonetheless, both in Josephus and in Philo.

This picture of Judean gatherings viewed as associations is confirmed by internal designations in the inscriptions, which may also reflect nonelite Judean perspectives on group identity. I have already noted Judean use of the self-designation "synod" in inscriptions. Other instances suggest further that Judean groups could view and present themselves as associations. The evidence that has survived does not suggest consistent, empire-wide practices regarding self-designations among Judeans abroad in the first centuries of the common era, and various terms were employed. "Synagogue," one of the many Greek terms for a "gathering together," was among the more commonly used terms for a Judean gathering, especially in the city of Rome, for instance.[51] As early as the first century CE,

---

49. See Millar 1966, 161 (who prefers 12 BCE) and Rajak 1984, 113–14.
50. Trans. Colson 1929–62 (LCL).
51. E.g., *IRomJud* 96, 165, 189, 194, 288, 406, 542, 549, 560, 562, 576, 584.

the term "synagogue" could also be used as a designation for the *building* in which such a Judean gathering took place.[52] Ultimately "synagogue" came to be the Judean standard in subsequent centuries, and we now regularly use it when speaking of ancient diaspora Judeans or of both ancient and modern Jewish meeting places (buildings) today. Yet it was not the only term used and it was not specific to Judean cultural contexts in the Hellenistic and Roman periods.[53]

The term "synagogue" and its cognates were used by other associations in various locales, pointing to shared means of group identification. Thus, for instance, a group of male and female "society members" devoted to the god Zeus in Apamea (east of Kyzikos) in Bithynia set up an honorary monument for a priestess of Mother Cybele and Apollo in the "synagogue of Zeus" (*IApamBith* 35; likely 85 CE). Across the Marmara Sea (Propontis) from Apamea, at Perinthos (Herakleia) in Thracia, there were at least two occupational groups in the first or second centuries that adopted this designation: one a "synagogue of barbers" that included a "synagogue leader" (ἀρχισυνάγωγος) at its head and the other a "synagogue of oar-dealers."[54] Numerous associations called synods or societies at Tanais, Panticipaion, and elsewhere in the Bosporan region (north of the Black Sea), had a similar functionary (called simply a συναγωγός), who was likely in charge of arranging the sacrificial feasts. This functionary is attested as early as the second century BCE, and there is no evidence to support a Judean connection with these groups, as I discuss more fully in chapter 3.[55]

There is considerable evidence for non-Judean synagogues or synagogue leaders from the province of Macedonia as well. Synagogue leaders are found within a *collegium* at Acanthus, within an association (συνθείς) devoted to Poseidon at Beroia, within a group of worshippers (θρησκευταί) devoted to Zeus Most High at Pydna, and within an association (συνθείς) at Thessalonica devoted to the god Herakles.[56] From Egypt there is evidence of a "synagogue of fellow-farmers" in the Ptolemaic era, as well as a military group of horsemen headed by a synagogue leader.[57] So, clearly, designating one's group a "synagogue" was a relatively common practice in some areas, a practice that also happened to be adopted by some Judean gatherings, ultimately becoming the prominent term.

Many other group titles were used by Judeans themselves and some likewise overlap with those adopted by other associations. When we compare Judean self-designations to

52. See John S. Kloppenborg's (2000) discussion of the Theodotus inscription (*CIJ* 1404) from Jerusalem, which most likely dates before 70 CE (*contra* Howard Clark Kee 1995).

53. The most common term for meeting places of Judeans in Hellenistic Egypt, on the other hand, was "prayer house" (προσευχή) (e.g., *IEgJud* 9, 13, 22, 24, 25, 27, 28, 117, 125, 126). It seems that this usage was particular to Judeans (see the notes by Horbury and Noy in *IEgJud* 9 and 126).

54. *IGR* I 782; *IPerinthos* 59, on which see Robert 1937, 261 (first or second cent. CE). Cf. *IGLSkythia* I 58.

55. See Ustinova (1999, 190–91, 196, 203–39), who convincingly challenges Levinskaya's (1996) conjecture of Judean influence. Cf. Ascough 2003, 71–81.

56. *CIG* 2007f (second century); *SEG* 27 (1977), no. 267; *NewDocs* I 5 (250 CE); *IG* X.2 288–89 (154 CE). Cf. *SEG* 42 (1992), no. 625 (90/91 CE) also from Thessalonica. For associations in Macedonia, see Ascough 2003.

57. *SB* 7457; *IFayum* I 9 (80–67 BCE). Cf. *IAlexandriaK* 91–92 (ca. 4–5 CE); *SB* 4981, 7307; Brashear 1993, 12–18.

those of other ethnic groups specifically, there are at least two crossovers beyond those noted for associations generally. We lack evidence for a standard terminology adopted by associations based on common geographic origin, but the term for "settlement" or "those settled" (οἱ κατοικοῦντες) is among the better attested ones. This was a favourite identification used by associations of settlers from the city of Rome, especially those settled in Asia Minor, and it is attested in connection with Tyrians who migrated to Puteoli in Italy.[58] So it is not surprising to find at least one second-century Judean group, which I discuss in chapter 6, adopting local cultural practice by identifying itself as the "settlement of the Judeans who are settled in Hierapolis" (*IJO* II 205).

Another term used by associations of immigrants, as well as Judean groups, was borrowed from civic and military contexts. *Politeuma* (πολίτευμα) or "corporate body" was sometimes used as a term for a civic body of those in charge, either the ruling class or the citizenry, at least at Cyrene in Cyrenaica and on the Aegean island of Chios.[59] It was also used for settlements of immigrants or, especially in the Hellenistic period, for military colonies based on ethnic identity. The papyri recently published by James M. Cowey and Klaus Maresch (2001) provide a Judean example of the sort of ethnic-based military settlements established under Ptolemaic rule in Egypt, in this case at Herakleopolis (ca. 144–132 BCE).[60] There were also groups of soldiers from Kaunos, Termessos, and Pinaria at Sidon who designated themselves a "corporate body," for instance.[61] Furthermore, as Constantine Zuckerman (1985/88) and Gert Lüderitz (1994) show, the term was used of regular associations including "corporate bodies" of Phrygians at Alexandria and of devotees of the goddess Sachypsis in the Fayum in Egypt.[62] I would suggest that this is the associational framework in which to understand the group of Judeans at Berenice in Cyrenaica in the first century CE who employed somewhat interchangeably the designations "the corporate body of Judeans in Berenice" and "the synagogue of Judeans in Berenice."[63] This is not the place to rehearse studies by Zuckerman (1985/88) and Lüderitz (1994) except to say that they have clearly disassembled an unfounded scholarly theory espoused by Mary Smallwood and others. This problematic view (as espoused by Smallwood) asserts that "*politeuma* was a recognized, formally constituted corporation of aliens enjoying the right of domicile in a foreign city and forming a separate, semiautonomous civic body, a city within

58. *IGR* IV 785–86, 788–91, 793–94; *MAMA* VI 177 (ca. 65–69 CE), 183; *OGIS* 595 = *CIG* 5853 (Tyrian merchants at Puteoli). Cf. *CIG* 2287.

59. See Lüderitz 1994, 185–88; cf. Ascough 2003, 77–78, regarding Paul's use of the term in Philippians 3:20.

60. I am indebted to Giovanni Bazzana, who pointed me to the recently published Herakleopolis materials.

61. For other "corporate bodies" of foreign soldiers in Egypt, see *SB* V 8757 (120 CE); *IFayum* II 121 (from Philadelphia; 93 CE); *PTebtunis* 32 (145 BCE); *IFayum* 15 (third to first cent. BCE); *SB* III 6664 (165–145 BCE; from Xois, near Alexandria). Cf. *OGIS* 145 (146–116 BCE), involving Ionians on Cyprus.

62. Macridy 1904 = Mendel 1912–14, vol. 1, nos. 102–8 (*politeumata* at Sidon); *IAlexandriaK* 74 (Phrygians).

63. Reynolds 1977, 242–47, nos. 16, 17, 18. For a translation and discussion of no. 17, see Harland 2003a, 224–25. I do not agree with Lüderitz's (1994, 210–22) conjecture, based on the voting procedures in the inscriptions, that the usage at Berenice is an anomaly in relation to the usual usage of "corporate body" for an association.

the city. . . . It had to be officially authorized by the local ruler or civic body, presumably by a written charter."[64] Instead, in many cases (particularly in the Roman imperial era) the term *politeuma* is a synonym for "synod" and related terms for an association, not a "public" institution as held in the scholarly tradition.[65]

So smaller gatherings of Judean groups in the diaspora could be viewed as synods, societies, and synagogues, and their members could communicate their own internal identifications drawing on the model of the association. It is not surprising, therefore, to find a similar situation in the case of Jesus-followers, who, at least in some cases, could be viewed by outsiders as obscure groups with Judean cultural connections (e.g., Tacitus *Ann.* 15.44). Several Greek and Roman literary sources show that the world of associations often came to mind when outsiders encountered the little-known groups of Jesus-followers. Robert Wilken (1972, 1984) and, more recently, Richard S. Ascough (1998) have surveyed at some length the models that were at work in how Greek and Roman outsiders viewed groups of Jesus-followers, including the synagogue, the philosophical school, the mysteries, and the association. Here we want to focus on cases when the association informed external or internal definitions of Christian identity.

One of the earliest Roman descriptions of Jesus-followers is Pliny the Younger's correspondence with the emperor Trajan. In about 110 CE, Pliny was appointed governor (legate) of the province of Bithynia and Pontus in northern Asia Minor. Pliny's appointment was special, as there were numerous perceived administrative and other problems in the cities of the province, and Pliny was sent to clean things up. As part of his ongoing activities, this Roman governor sometimes wrote letters both to report on his successes and to request advice from the emperor or from other elite friends.

One of these letters involves followers of Jesus and reveals how a member of the Roman elite might view such people. It is important to note that Pliny was familiar with the associational tendencies of populations in Asia Minor, as he refers to associations in two other letters involving groups at Nikomedia and at Amisos (Pliny *Ep.* 10.33–34, 93–94). Because of Pliny's special appointment to correct problems specific to this province at this time, most of these references involve Pliny's hesitancy about such groups, and it seems that he had passed at least one edict limiting associational activities in some way, perhaps forbidding night-time meetings.

When Pliny writes to the emperor concerning those labeled "Christians" (*Christiani*) that had been brought before him, perhaps at Amisos or Amastris, he speaks disparagingly about them.[66] He dismisses them as an upper-class Roman author would dismiss many other forms of cultural activity among the lower classes, namely, as a "superstition"—"a debased and excessive superstition (*superstitionem pravam et immodicam*)."[67] However, at

---

64. Smallwood 1976, 225, also cited by Lüderitz 1994, 201.

65. Cf. Rajak 2002 [1999], 469–70; Barclay 1996, 25 n. 18, 64–65.

66. On Pliny, the Christians, and trials see, for example, de Ste. Croix 1963 and 1964; Sherwin-White 1966, 691–712; Wilken 1984, 1–30. On the label "Christian" and its eventual adoption by the followers of Jesus, see Horrell 2007. However, I do not agree with elements of his interpretation of 1 Peter with regard to the nature of persecution, and I am not as convinced that the label emerged in "legal" contexts.

67. See Tacitus *Annals* 15.38–44, who also speaks of following Christ as a "superstition," and

the same time he describes their gatherings in terms familiar from the activities of associations among the population:

> they also declared that the sum total of their guilt or error amounted to no more than this: they had met regularly before dawn on a fixed day to chant verses alternately amongst themselves in honour of Christ as if to a god, and also to bind themselves by oath, not for any criminal purpose, but to abstain from theft, robbery, and adultery, to commit no breach of trust and not to deny a deposit when called upon to restore it. After this ceremony it had been their custom to disperse and reassemble later to take food of an ordinary, harmless kind. (*Ep.* 10.96.6–7)[68]

Also important is Pliny's reference to an edict that he had passed regarding restrictions on meetings of associations (*hetaeriae*, sometimes a synonym for *collegia*), where he specifically notes that the devotees of Christ had obeyed his edict.[69] Some of Christ-devotees still met together regularly, it seems, but now certain meetings (likely those held at night) were avoided. This suggests that both this Roman official and the Christians themselves understood these groups to fall under the rubric of associations (*Ep.* 10.96.7–8). So here there are indications not only of external categorizations but also of internal self-definitions (or internalization of external categories) among these followers of Jesus in northern Asia Minor.

Subsequent external categorizations of Christian groups that likewise see such groups as associations are found in the writings of Lucian of Samosata and of Celsus (both in the second century CE). In the midst of his ridiculing satire on the (once) Christian Peregrinus, Lucian refers to Peregrinus's time in Palestine among Christian "priests and scribes." Lucian ridicules the Christians' ready acceptance of this man and characterizes Peregrinus's authority among them by calling him: "prophet, leader of the society, and leader of the synagogue" (προφήτης καὶ θιασάρχης καὶ ξυναγωγεὺς [*sic*]) (*Peregrinus* 11). Although writing considerably later (in the early fourth century), the Christian historian Eusebius reveals that the term "society" could be used by insiders, as when he speaks of Christian congregations as "our society" (*HE* 10.1.8). Lucian's description of the Christians also draws on the analogy of associations devoted to the mysteries: he labels the movement an "initiation rite" (τελετή) in referring back to "the man who was crucified in Palestine because he introduced this new initiation rite into the world" (*Peregrinus* 11).[70] In the next chapter, we will see that analogies drawn from associations that engaged in "mysteries" were also important for internal Christian self-definition in some cases, at least for Ignatius and the congregations he addressed in Asia Minor.

In a manner similar to Lucian, the critic Celsus characterizes followers of Jesus as

---

see the discussion of Caecilius (in Minucius Felix) in chapter 8 of this volume. Cf. Beard, North, and Price 1998, 215–27.

68. Trans. Radice 1969 (LCL). For comparable "moral" expectations of association members, compare the association devoted to Zeus and Agdistis in Philadelphia in Asia Minor (see Barton and Horsley 1981).

69. On the question of legal actions (or lack thereof) in relation to associations, see Arnaoutoglou 2002 and Harland 2003a, 161–73.

70. Trans. Harmon 1913–67 (LCL).

"members of a society" (θιασῶται; Celsus as cited in Origen *C. Cels.* 3.23). Sometimes Celsus's critique of the Christians reflects the same sort of general upper-class disdain for the activities of the lower strata that we saw in Pliny. This is the case when Celsus characterizes members of such groups as a bunch of "wool-workers, cobblers, laundry workers, and the most illiterate and bucolic yokels" (*C. Cels.* 3.55).[71] Yet he also specifically complains about something that has to do with (Judean) cultural practices of these groups, rather than their social level: the Christians' strange avoidance of "setting up altars, images and temples." Celsus interprets these strange avoidances as a "sure token of an obscure and secret fellowship" (ἀφανοῦς καὶ ἀπορρήτου κοινωνίας) (8.17; cf. 1.1). So, as with Judean groups, Greek and Roman spectators readily categorized Christian groups—however strange they may have otherwise seemed because of certain minority cultural practices—using concepts that reflect association life in that milieu.

Unlike the internal epigraphic evidence for Judean groups generally, archeological evidence for early Jesus-followers that is distinguishable from other materials only becomes recognizable in the late second century CE.[72] So our ability to compare the self-designations of associations with those of Christian groups is somewhat limited by a lack of corresponding types of material evidence. Among the archeological evidence that has been found, it is worth mentioning one building inscription from Barata, near Lystra in Lycaonia (north of Lamos, at the top of the label "Cilicia" on the map in this volume), with the Christian *chi-rho* symbol that does refer to "the *collegium*" (in transliterated Greek) with no further clarification (third century or earlier).[73]

For the first two centuries, we have to rely on specific Christian literary sources that reflect identification practices in only some groups of Jesus-followers (from the perspective of those who claimed authority over them). Among the self-designations in the literature, the most common term within Pauline circles was "assembly," or "congregation" (ἐκκλησία, often anachronistically translated "church"). This term is drawn from civic life in the Greek East, where a particular gathering or assembly of the civic institution of "the people" (δῆμος), namely, the citizen body, was frequently called an "assembly" (ἐκκλησία). Paul's (or other Jesus-followers') adaptation of this term from its origins in reference to an occasional assembly or meeting to an ongoing title for a group reflects a common process that can be seen with many other associations and their titles, including the groups that came to use a general designation for a specific "gathering together" (*synag-* root words) of people as an ongoing title for the group.

The use of "assembly" (ἐκκλησία) specifically is not widely attested as a title or self-designation among other associations in the inscriptions that have survived and been found. Two inscriptions from Aspendos in Pamphylia (just inland from the Gulf of Antalya about half way between Tlos and Lamos on the map) may involve an association that was called an "assembly" (*IGLAM* 1381–82).[74] Although the term does not seem to have become a widespread group self-designation, there is clear evidence that certain associa-

71. Trans. Chadwick 1953, 165 (Greek text from TLG).

72. See Snyder 2003 [1985].

73. Laminger-Pascher 1992, no. 69.

74. See Poland 1909, 332; *IGLAM* 1381–82, which were first noted by Heinrici 1876, 1877. I am indebted to Kloppenborg (1993, 215–16, 231), who also briefly discusses these inscriptions.

tions did use it in reference to a specific "assembly" or "meeting," as in the case of the synod of Tyrian merchants on Delos, which I discuss in chapter 5.[75] In subsequent chapters, I return to some other cases where Christian groups and other associations share common terminology in processes of internal self-definition, particularly sibling terminology and other fictive familial language used to express belonging among members.

It is not entirely clear what key self-designations or titles were used by the followers of Jesus reflected in the epistles of John, which likely involve groups in western Asia Minor.[76] Only the author of 3 John happens to employ Paul's favourite, "the assembly" (3 John 1:6, 9, 10), but there is some other suggestive language used within these letters that happens to intersect with internal association terminology in Asia Minor. In particular, "the elder" who authored this same letter to Gaius closes the letter with the following: "The friends (οἱ φίλοι) send you their greetings. Greet the friends there, each by name" (3 John 15). The collective reference to "*the* friends" using the article rather than a possessive (e.g., "my friends" or "your friends") here in both cases suggests the possibility that the members of each group, the group to which the elder belonged and the group to which Gaius belonged, might term themselves, corporately, "the friends" (οἱ φίλοι). "The friends" (οἱ φίλοι) was not merely a common means of expressing positive connections with others within associations in Asia Minor and elsewhere. It was sometimes used as the main title for the group itself.[77] We will return to some examples of association members addressing one another as "friends" in chapter 3.

Conclusion

In this chapter we have defined and outlined a variety of unofficial groups that can be discussed together as "associations." We have found that ancient observers would group together many of the gatherings considered under the rubric of associations by a modern scholar (cf. Philo *Flacc.* 136). I have suggested that we can make better sense of these groups not by categorizing them based on supposed primary purposes, which were varied, but by thinking in terms of overlapping social networks that formed the bases of these groups, sometimes with one set of connections predominating for a particular group.

In looking at both external categorizations and internal definitions, which are at the centre of social-scientific explanations of identity, we have found common ground among ancient observers and group members alike. Both could define Judean gatherings and Christian congregations in terms drawn from association life generally. This is despite the

75. *IDelos* 1519, lines 1–2 = *CIG* 2271 = Foucart 1873, 223–25, no. 43. Similarly, a gymnastic organization (the ἀλειφομένοι) on Samos refers to its meeting as an ἐκκλησία. See McCabe 1986, no. 119 (accessible via http://epigraphy.packhum.org/); Poland 1909, 332.

76. See Raymond E. Brown 1979 and 1982.

77. "The friends": *IGLAM* 798 (Kotiaion, Aezanatis valley); *IIasos* 116; *IMagnMai* 321; *IDidyma* 502 (a Dionysiac group); *IMylasa* 571–75; *TAM* V 93 (Saittai; 225 CE); *ISmyrna* 720; *MAMA* III 580, 780, 788 (Korykos); *SEG* 35 (1985), no. 1337 (Amastris, Pontus); *IPrusaOlymp* 24 (first cent. CE); *IAsMinLyk* I 69 (Xanthos, Lycia). Cf. *IG* II.2 1369 (Athens; second cent. CE); *IG* III 1081, 1089, 1102 (Athens; ca. 120s CE; ephebes); *IGUR* 1169 (Rome).

fact that, in other respects, these groups could be viewed as peculiar because of certain cultural practices arising from Judean ways, such as a devotion to the Judean God to the exclusion of the gods of other peoples. This also suggests that these Christian associations can be viewed by a scholar as cultural minority groups alongside Judean gatherings, as I explained in the introduction.

The shared language of identity and the comparison of associations with both Judean gatherings and Christian congregations are not surprising. After all, these groups were, like the local devotees of Zeus or Dionysos or the guild of purple-dyers, groups that assembled regularly to socialize, share communal meals, and honour both their earthly and their divine benefactors. From an outsider's perspective, this general similarity might help to make sense of what was in other respects quite strange: minority groups whose cultural ways of life included an insistence that only their god and no one else's was deserving of their recognition or honour. From the perspective of these cultural minorities, describing oneself in terms drawn from the world of associations might simultaneously establish a sense of place within local society while also forming a basis from which to assert distinctiveness or preeminence for the group or its God. This twofold process of cultural adaptation and identity maintenance occupies us in subsequent chapters.

2

Local Cultural Life and Christian Identity

"Fellow-Initiates" and "Christ-Bearers"

Introduction

An individual member's place within a group and that group's identity in relation to surrounding society is an ongoing, shifting process of negotiation as we are beginning to see. In the case of minority groups, such as associations of Jesus-followers, processes of negotiation entail both differentiating and assimilating forces. On the one hand, the self-understanding of a member or the group as a whole can be expressed in terms of distinction from common cultural categories in the majority culture. We are the precious few "holy ones," and outsiders are the vast sea of "the wicked" who engage in morally abhorrent or perverted activities, for instance (e.g., 1 Pet 4:3–4; Philo *Vit. Cont.* 40–41; *Leg. Gai.* 311–13).

On the other hand, that majority culture can supply a primary means by which identity is expressed. Specific concepts and categories from the majority culture or local manifestations of that culture can be central to the expression of identities in a minority group. Both of these forces are often at work at the same time. The processes of internal self-definition and external social categorization can, at times, overlap significantly, as I demonstrated in chapter 1.

There are clear instances when followers of Jesus in the Roman era express their identities in terms that draw on widely shared cultural categories, including categories drawn from association life. Simultaneously, these Christians could reinterpret such categories in a way that made claims regarding distinctive identity or the superiority of the group. The letters of Ignatius of Antioch, which reflect group life in two central hubs of early Christianity—western Asia Minor and Syrian Antioch—provide a case in point.

Ignatius draws quite heavily on categories from the culture of the Greco-Roman cities in order to build up the identity of the Christian groups, expressing their identities in terms drawn from local social and cultural life in Asia Minor. He uses several analogies and metaphors in his letters to speak of the identity of congregations in Roman Asia. Followers of Jesus at Ephesos, for instance, are likened to a choral group in a temple, "attuned to the bishop as strings to a lyre" (*Eph.* 4; cf. *Phld.* 1.2). They are "fellow-initiates" (συμμύσται) of

Paul that share in the "mysteries" (*Eph.* 12.2; 19.1; cf. *Magn.* 9.1; *Trall.* 2.3). Together they take part in a procession in honour of their patron deity, bearing images and sacred objects as groups (σύνοδοι) of "God-bearers" (θεοφόροι) and "Christ-bearers" (χριστοφόροι; *Eph.* 9.2; cf. *Smyrn.* inscript.). The Ephesians were by no means the only ones to hear these characterizations, however, as the letters of Ignatius soon circulated more widely to other groups in Asia and elsewhere (cf. Polycarp, *Phil.* 13.2).

Over a century ago, J. B. Lightfoot devoted attention to Ignatius's "vivid appeal to the local experiences of an Ephesian audience," particularly regarding the Christ-bearer metaphor and local evidence for processions.[1] In doing so, Lightfoot was drawing on then recent archeological discoveries by John Turtle Wood published in 1887 (repr. 1975). Yet there is far more archeological evidence now available, evidence that provides further insight into such expressions of identity.

Other scholars have since given some attention to these metaphors, but often in a cursory way and rarely, if ever, with reference to local cultural life as attested in archeological evidence from Roman Asia. William R. Schoedel's commentary rightly understands the Christ-bearers in terms of a Greek religious procession, noting that "bearers" of sacred things can be found within this milieu (citing Plutarch, *Moralia* 352B, where the image is also used metaphorically). Schoedel also notes the importance of the background of the mysteries for understanding Ignatius's use of "fellow-initiates."[2] Yet Schoedel and other scholars do not give attention to artefactual remains that can illuminate what, concretely, these passages would spark in the imaginations of Ignatius and the addressees of his letters.

Here I explore the cultural images Ignatius evokes, particularly with reference to associations of initiates and processions. This illuminates how authors such as Ignatius could express Christian identity in terms familiar from local social and cultural life, particularly association life. Specifically, I examine epigraphic evidence from Ephesos, Smyrna, Magnesia (southeast of Ephesos), Tralles (east of Magnesia), and other cities that sheds light on what Ignatius may have had in mind. Perhaps more importantly, I explore what the listeners or readers of Ignatius in these cities of Roman Asia in the early second century would likely think of when Ignatius used these analogies to speak of their identities.

Fellow-Initiates and Their Mysteries

Ignatius designates the Christian assembly at Ephesos as "fellow-initiates of Paul" engaging in their own "mysteries" (μυστήρια). The specific designation "*fellow*-initiates" (συμμύσται) is common for unofficial associations engaging in mysteries throughout Asia Minor, including those cities addressed by Ignatius, and "initiates" (μύσται) is even more widespread.[3] Ignatius sustains this analogy in several of his letters, including those to the Magnesians and Trallians, and continues to speak of the revelation of "mysteries of Jesus Christ," which

1. Lightfoot 1889–1890, 2:17–18, 54–57.

2. Schoedel 1985, 67–68, 72–73, 89–90. H. Paulsen's (1985, 35–36) reworking of Bauer's commentary adds little on this.

3. For "fellow-initiates" see *ISmyrna* 330; *IStratonikeia* 845–46; *IApamBith* 103; *IPrusiasHyp* 845; *CCCA* I 60 (Pessinos, Galatia).

suggests this is a fairly consistent way of expressing identity. The mysteries he identifies center on the (virgin) birth, death and resurrection of Jesus, as well as the celebration of these in the Lord's Supper, which was administered by the "deacons of the mysteries" (*Eph.* 19.1–3; *Magn.* 9.1–2; *Trall.* 2.3).

Alongside the staple ritual of sacrifice, mysteries (μυστήρια, ὄργια, τελετή) were among the most respected ways of honouring the gods in the Roman era.[4] The term could encompass a variety of practices, including sacrifice, communal meals, reenactment of the myths of the gods, sacred processions, singing of hymns, and, of course, the revelation of holy things. There was an expectation that aspects of these practices were secretive, to be fully experienced only by the initiated. In some cases, those who followed the prescribed steps towards initiation, witnessing the mysteries of a given deity, joined together in an ongoing association of initiates. In Asia Minor, it is most common to hear of mysteries in connection with Dionysos, Demeter, the Great Mother (Cybele), and Isis, but there were mysteries for other deities as well. In fact, the notion of separate "mystery religions" (hence the old scholarly term) is problematic in that one could encounter mysteries as rituals in honour of deities within various contexts, from official civic and imperial cults to unofficial guilds and associations. It is the latter, more unofficial associations that best illuminate Ignatius's descriptions of Christians as initiates with their own mysteries.

Despite secretive dimensions of their rituals, associations of initiates were by no means shy in making their presence known within their hometowns. Ignatius and the followers of Jesus he addressed would have encountered public statements (inscriptions and visual representations on monuments) by such groups or by individual initiates. On a monument from Magnesia on the Maeander River (a locale addressed by Ignatius), an initiate of Dionysos publicizes the importance of Dionysiac associations in that community (*IMagnMai* 215; mid-second cent. CE). The initiate's republication of an "ancient oracle" claims that a divine manifestation of Dionysos, followed by consultation of the oracle of Apollo at Delphi, resulted in the foundation of Dionysiac "societies" (θίασοι) before there were any temples there. Implied is that the very foundation and continued well-being of the Magnesian community depended on such initiates and their deity. Secretive though the mysteries were, the presence of associations of initiates was, to say the least, public knowledge in Roman Asia Minor.

There were many such associations of initiates in the cities addressed by Ignatius, including Magnesia, Philadelphia, Tralles, Smyrna, and Ephesos.[5] There were several such associations in Smyrna, for instance, where Ignatius spent some time and from which he wrote his letters to congregations at Ephesos (*Eph.* 21.1), Magnesia (*Magn.* 15.1), and, probably, Tralles (*Trall.* 13.1). Particularly well attested in monuments from Smyrna are the initiates of Dionysos Breseus, a synod that was active at least from first to the third century.[6] A decade or so after Ignatius, these "initiates of the great Dionysos Breseus, preeminent

---

4. On the mysteries, see Burkert 1987 and the works cited by him. On comparison and the mysteries see Jonathan Z. Smith 1990; Gasparro 1985; and Harland 2003a, 90–97.

5. Cf. *IMagnMai* 117, 215 (Dionysos; early–mid second cent. CE); *ILydiaKP* I 42 (Philadelphia; Dionysos Kathegemon; second cent. CE); *ITralles* 74, 86 (Isis and Sarapis; second cent. CE), 168.

6. *ISmyrna* 600–601 (ca. 158 CE/ca. 163 CE), 622 (ca. 130 CE), 639 (late second cent. CE), 652 (first cent. CE), 729 (ca. 247 CE), 731–32 (ca. 80 CE); cf. *ISmyrna* 728 (Dionysiac-Orphic cult regulation).

Figure 4. Relief of Demeter from Kozçesme in northwestern Asia Minor, now in the Istanbul Archaeological Museum (fourth century BCE*)*

before the city" (*polis*) publicized their honours for Emperor "Hadrian, Olympios, saviour and founder" (*ISmyrna* 622). Another synod of initiates at Smyrna devoted to Demeter could make similar claims of preeminence in the city round about the time of Ignatius, and I return to the implied rivalries in chapter 7.[7] We know little about another group of "fellow-initiates," Ignatius's exact term, mentioned on an epitaph for a deceased member (*ISmyrna* 330).

Inscriptions from Ephesos provide glimpses into various such groups of initiates in the first two centuries, some of which would have been relatively well known in that city and likely familiar to the Christians who heard or read Ignatius's letter. Particularly noteworthy were the initiates of Demeter and those of Dionysos. See figure 4 for an image of the goddess Demeter seated on a throne, from northwestern Asia Minor. The worship of Demeter had a long history in Ephesos specifically (Herodotus *Hist.* 6.16). An association devoted to this deity is first attested in inscriptions by the time of Tiberius, when the group honoured several priests and priestesses who were important benefactors of the city and the association (*IEph* 4337; 19–23 CE).

It is from a monument dating to the time of Domitian that we learn more of this group

7. *ISmyrna* 653–55, 726 (all first–second cent. CE).

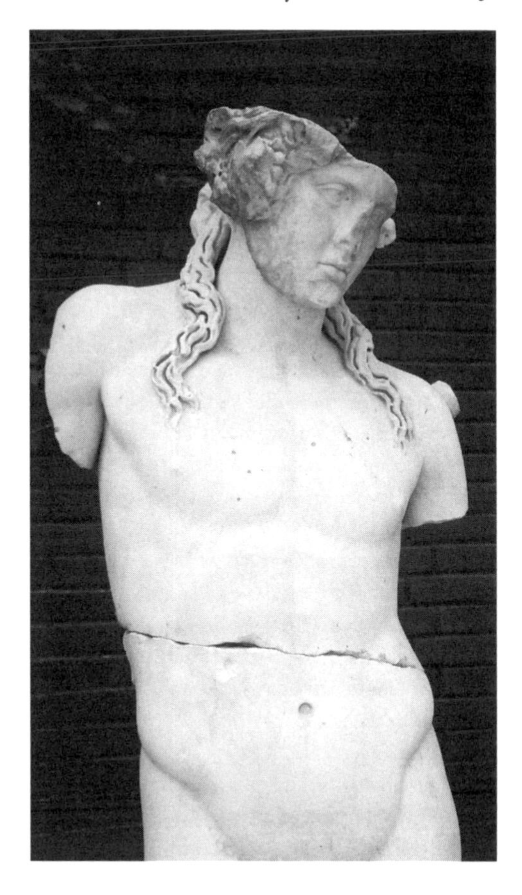

Figure 5. Statue of Dionysos, now in the Selçuk Archaeological Museum

of initiates of Demeter led by priestesses (*IEph* 213; 88–89 CE).[8] Among the regular celebrations of these initiates was a special yearly celebration that included "mysteries and sacrifices" performed "with great purity and lawful customs" in honour of both Fruit-Bearing (Karpophoros) Demeter and the "august" or "revered ones," the emperors as gods. It is worth noting that honours for the emperors, often alongside the gods, were a common feature within the lives of associations in Asia Minor.[9]

The Ephesian initiates of Dionysos are well attested in the epigraphical record as well, with one monument involving honours for the emperor Hadrian (*IEph* 275; cf. *IEph* 293, 434, 1020, 1601). An Ephesian statue of Dionysos, the god of the vine, is pictured in figure 5. Some time in the mid-second century the Dionysiac initiates joined with the initiates of Demeter to become one association, a combination of mysteries attested elsewhere as well (*IEph* 1595).[10] The Christ-bearing fellow-initiates at Ephesos had their holy-object-bearing counterparts in many of these same groups of initiates of Dionysos, Demeter, and others, which brings us to processions and bearers of sacred things.

---

8. Cf. *IEph* 1210, 1270; *NewDocs* IV 22.
9. See Harland 2000 and 2003.
10. Cf. *IG* IX.2 573, from Larisa, Macedonia.

Processions and Bearers of Sacred Things

Ignatius's characterization of the Christian group at Ephesos clearly evokes images from the world of processions when he speaks of them as "fellow-travellers, God-bearers, temple-bearers, Christ-bearers and holy-object-bearers adorned in every respect with the commandments of Jesus Christ" (σύνοδοι πάντες, θεοφόροι καὶ ναοφόροι, χριστοφόροι, ἁγιοφόροι, κατὰ πάντα κεκοσμημένοι ἐν ἐντολαῖς Ἰησοῦ Χριστοῦ; *Eph.* 9.1–2).[11] Also alluding to processions is his brief but perhaps no less significant summary of the Smyrnaeans' identity as, among other things, "the holy-object-bearing" congregation that is "most fitting for its God" (ἐκκλησίᾳ . . . θεοπρεπεστάτῃ καὶ ἁγιοφόρῳ; *Smyrn.* inscr.) [12]

Ignatius was not the first to draw on the analogy of processions to express (metaphorically) devotion to the gods, or to the Judean God specifically. Both Epictetus and Plutarch (Greco-Roman philosophers) speak metaphorically of bearing god, or sacred objects, within the soul as an analogy for fitting worship (Plutarch *Isis and Osiris* 352B). In seeking to correct someone's behavior, Epictetus (in Arrian's presentation) argues:

> You are bearing god about with you, you poor wretch, and know it not! Do you suppose I am speaking of some external god, made of silver or gold? It is within yourself that you bear him, and do not perceive that you are defiling him with impure thoughts and filthy actions. Yet in the presence of even an image of god you would not dare to do anything of the things you are now doing. (Epictetus *Discourses* 2.8.12–14)[13]

Perhaps culturally closer to Ignatius's metaphor is Philo's use of holy-object-bearing imagery. In connection with Gaius's attempt to violate Judean law by putting a statue in Jerusalem, Philo emphasizes the Judeans' eagerness to maintain their customs and laws: "Holding that the laws are oracles vouchsafed by God and having been trained in this doctrine from their earliest years, they bear in their souls the images of the commandments" (*Leg. Gai.* 210).[14] The parallel with Ignatius's idea of bearing the commandments of Christ is notable. Elsewhere, Philo speaks of the way in which humanity is made in the image of God, pointing out that it is in respect to "the mind" that humankind is created in the likeness of God: the mind is "in a fashion a god to him who carries and enshrines it as an object of reverence" (*Op. Mund.* 69). Furthermore, the analogy (including the term "Christ-bearer") was to persist within Christian circles long after Ignatius.[15]

---

11. Ignatius's use of the term "adorned" (κοσμ- root words) here also draws on the terminology of processions in connection with bearing sacred objects or wearing sacred garments and other decorative paraphernalia (esp. "ornament" and "to adorn"; cf. Xenophon of Ephesos *An Ephesian Tale* 1.2).

12. In connection with Ignatius's epistolary inscriptions, it is worth mentioning his repeated emphasis on his own name, Theophoros or "God-bearer." Cf. Lightfoot 1889–1890, 2:20–21.

13. Trans. Oldfather 1926–28 (LCL).

14. Trans. Colson 1929–62 (LCL), with adaptations.

15. The processional metaphor of "Christ-bearing" and "God-bearing" continues in the church fathers (see Clement of Alexandria *Exhortation to the Greeks* 4; Eusebius *HE* 8.10, on "Christ-bearing

Figure 6. Relief depicting a procession of a maenad and two satyrs, from Villa Quintilliana near Rome, now in the British Museum (ca. 100 CE*)*

Turning to the more important local cultural context of Ignatius's imagery, the procession (πομπή) was central to festivals in honour of many gods and goddesses in a variety of settings in the Greco-Roman world, both official (civic and imperial cults) and unofficial (associations).[16] The relief in figure 6 shows a procession involving a maenad (frenzied female follower of Dionysos) and two satyrs (male attendants of the god). Processional rituals in either setting visually communicated the virtues, power, and efficacy of the deity in question, remapping sacred space and ensuring the continued favorable actions of the god or goddess (i.e., benefactions) in relation to the community. These rituals expressed concretely the identity of the god and of the community. Sacred objects, implements, images, and statues of various kinds were essential components in this visual communication for both observers and participants. Those who participated in the procession by proudly carrying the holy objects, even the gods themselves, provided a praiseworthy service to deity and community.

There were appropriate titles for the participants or functionaries who bore objects sacred to particular deities. Several of these correspond directly to Ignatius's list: "god-bearers," "sacred-object-bearers," "basket-bearers," "altar-bearers," "wand-bearers,"

---

martyrs"; Lightfoot 1889–1890, 2:55. The title "Christ-bearer" is attested in papyri (see Bell 1924, 100–102, 108–10, 114–15, on the "Christ-bearing" Paphnutius).

16. There are few studies of processions in the Roman era specifically, but see Nilsson 1961, 1:166–214; Burkert 1985, 99–101; Price 1984, 110–12; Rogers 1991, 80–126.

"symbol-bearers," "sign-bearers," "sacred-stone-bearers," and "phallus-bearers," to name a few attested in inscriptions.[17]

One second-century literary description of such rituals that reflects Ignatius's region of origin, Syria, will serve to illustrate the importance of processions and the carrying of holy objects. In *The Syrian Goddess*, Lucian of Samosata describes the rituals and festivals associated with the sanctuary of Atargatis ("Hera" in Lucian's terms), the mother goddess at Syrian Hierapolis (Bambyke).[18] Here processions and "bearers" of holy things played an important role in honorary activities for Atargatis and two other male deities, likely El and Baal (Zeus and Apollo). Twice yearly, worshippers participated in carrying water from the sea up to the sanctuary in commemoration of a legendary flood which, it is said, ended as a result of a great chasm—a sizable drain—sent by the gods at the site of the sanctuary (*Syr. D.* 12–13). It is on this occasion that a special golden "image" (ξόανον) or "sign" (σημήιον [*sic*]) affixed with symbols associated with Atargatis and the other Syrian gods made its journey, carried by temple functionaries, down to the sea "to fetch the water" (*Syr. D.* 33). Archeological materials (coins from Syrian Hierapolis and Carrhae and a relief from Dura) help to visualize the sign or standard in question, which would consist of a "shaft, the divine symbol or the figure of the deity at the top, symbols or images of deities attached to the shaft" (resembling Roman military standards), as M. Rostovtzeff explains.[19] Groups of "sign-bearers" are attested in connection with associations and mysteries in Asia Minor and elsewhere, as I discuss below.

Lucian points out that the deities of the sanctuary could be quite vocal about when and where the holy things were to be carried. When an oracular response was forthcoming from Baal (Apollo) at Syrian Hierapolis, once again bearers of holy things came to play a role at the god's initiative: "Whenever he wishes to deliver an oracle, he first moves on his throne, and the priests immediately lift him up. If they do not lift him, he begins to sweat and moves still more. When they put him on their shoulders and carry him, he leads them in every direction as he spins around and leaps from one place to another" (*Syr. D.* 36).[20] If the god moves his carriers forward, the answer to the oracle is affirmative, if backward, negative. During festivals called "descents to the lake" (apparently distinguished from the former flood-related festival), both Atargatis and El made the journey in procession, being carried down to the lake, but "Hera [Atargatis] goes first, for the sake of the fish, for fear Zeus [El] sees them first. For if this happens, they say that all the fish perish. He does come to have a look, but she stands in front of him, holds him off, and with many entreaties sends him away" (*Syr. D.* 47).

Ignatius's characterization of Jesus-followers at Ephesos as fellow-processionists bearing sacred objects alludes to aspects of cultural life that would be familiar not only in Syria but also in the cities of western Asia Minor. Processions involving statues and other sacred

17. θεοφόροι, ἱεραφόροι, ἁγιαφόροι, λικναφόροι, καλαθηφόροι, βωμοφόροι, θυρσοφόροι, ναρθηκοφόροι, συμβόλαφόροι, σεμειαφόροι, λιθοφόροι, φαλλοφόροι. See Pleket 1970, 55–88, especially, p. 66, n. 15.

18. On the reliability of this account, see Jones 1986, 41–42. I consult the Greek text of Harmon 1913–67 (LCL).

19. Rostovtzeff 1942, 100 and plates V-VI. Cf. Pleket 1970, 67–72. Rostovzeff (1942) and H. Seyrig (1960, 233–52) show that "Semea" was not a Syrian deity as originally suggested.

20. Trans. Attridge and Oden 1976. Greek text cited from Harmon 1913–67 (LCL).

Figure 7. Statue of Artemis of Ephesos, now in the Selçuk Archaeological Museum

objects were an important component in the civic festivals that honoured Ephesos's official patron deity, Artemis Ephesia, who is pictured in figure 7.[21] There were several boards of functionaries connected with the Artemis sanctuary that were responsible for carrying sacred objects of various kinds in processions, including "ornament-bearers" (κοσμοφόροι) and "gold-bearers" (χρυσοφόροι).[22] In his second-century novel *An Ephesian Tale*, Xenophon of Ephesos begins his story with a description of just such a procession in honour of Artemis, speaking of the "great crowd of Ephesians and visitors alike" who witnessed the procession file past led by well-adorned young girls and youths (ephebes), "first the sacred objects, the torches, the baskets, and the incense" (1.2–3).[23] The procession culminated in a sacrificial ceremony in the sanctuary of the goddess.

Particularly noteworthy in connection with Ignatius's epistle to the Ephesians, however, is that a wealthy Ephesian benefactor, C. Vibius Salutaris, upon his death in 104 CE,

21. Cf. Strabo, *Geography* 14.1.20.
22. See Picard 1922, 240–46. Cf. *IEph* 14, line 23.
23. Trans. Anderson 1989, 125–69. Cf. *The Martyrdom of Saint Timothy* (Keil 1935, 82–92).

pumped a substantial amount of new funds into multiple processions in honour of Artemis, Ephesian mythological and historical figures, and (not surprisingly) Salutaris himself (*IEph* 27).[24] Few inhabitants of Ephesos at the time would have been ignorant of this important foundation, as Salutaris no doubt intended. It established frequent processions, perhaps on average about once every two weeks.[25] Guy MacLean Rogers notes that the throng of 260 participants, "bearing conspicious silver and gold statues through the narrow streets of Ephesos, must have impeded, if not altogether halted, traffic within the city at procession time."[26]

The most prominent participants were the youths (ephebes) who carried gold and silver images or statues of Artemis, of the Ionian and Hellenistic founders, and of the Roman imperial family in the processions through the city. Statues of the emperors, alongside other gods, were an important component in a similar foundation (by C. Julius Demosthenes) for processions at Oenoanda (in Lycia), a function carried out by the "*Sebastoi*-bearers," those who carried images of the emperors as gods.[27]

Also among the beneficiaries and participants of the Ephesian foundation were the hymn-singers of Artemis as well as the elders' organization and boards connected with the Artemis sanctuary, including the "gold-bearers of Artemis."[28] The gold-bearers of Artemis formed a "sanhedrin" which consisted of members drawn from both the priests of the temple and the athletic guild of "sacred victors."[29] Such guilds of "sacred victors from the world" toured Asia Minor, competing in international contests and leaving behind monumental evidence of their victories.[30] Although the appellation "gold-bearer" is attested elsewhere as merely a civic honorary title,[31] it is clear that, in the case of this Ephesian group, literally carrying sacred golden objects in processions was among the key services this group provided. In the time of Hadrian, for instance, they are described as "the priests and sacred victors who carry the golden ornament of the great goddess Artemis" (*IEph* 276).[32] These gold-bearers were, quite literally, god-bearers.

Another informative inscription from the village of Almoura, in the territory of Ephesos (just inland in the Cayster valley), involves the dedication of sacred objects to be carried

24. On this inscription, see Rogers 1991.

25. See Rogers (1991, 83) for the procession schedule.

26. Rogers 1991, 86.

27. Wörrle 1988, 10–11, 216–19 = *SEG* 38 (1988), no. 1462, C (time of Hadrian). Cf. Robert 1969, 2:1275–78. Allen Brent's recent study of "Ignatius of Antioch and the Imperial Cult" (Brent 1998, 30–58) rightly identifies the importance of processions in Ignatius's thought world, but the study is methodologically flawed in its tendency to suggest allusions to imperial cults throughout Ignatius's letters where no explicit identification is possible. See Harland 2003a, 239–51.

28. There was an association at Ephesos called the "gold-bearing icon-bearers" (*IEph* 546). The priests in Magnesia's civic cult may also have been known as "gold-bearing priests of Artemis Leukophryene," as O. Kern suggests (see *IMagnMai* 119).

29. Cf. Rogers 1991, 56–57; *IEph* 27.451–526, 28, 276, 943, 951, 991 (second cent. CE) 3263, 4330 (231–234 CE).

30. Cf. *IAphrodSpect* 66–68, 89–90 (= *IEph* 11), 93; *IDidyma* 107, 201, 272; *TAM* V 977 (Thyatira). On athletic associations see Pleket 1973, 197–227.

31. Cf. *ITralles* 73, 90, 134, 145.

32. See Robert 1975, 324.

in processions for the mysteries of the goddess Demeter and the god Men respectively.[33] In it, P. Aelius Menekrates dedicates income from the shops he owns to purchase a "basket set in silver" for use during the procession as part of Demeter's mysteries. Other inscriptions from Ephesos mention a female functionary called a "basket-bearer" (καλαθηφόρος) whose responsibility it would be to lead in carrying the basket containing the sacred objects in processions like this one at Almoura (see *IEph* 1060, 1070, 1071).[34] In Almoura men were also participants in the procession alongside the priestesses and other women.

The same benefactor, Menekrates, also donated a silver "sign" or "standard" (σημήα [*sic*])—a term we have already encountered in Lucian—to be carried in processions preceding the mysteries and sacred banquet for the god Men, who "presided over the village" as patron. There were corresponding functionaries, called "symbol-bearers," in a cult devoted to Men and Artemis Anaetis in a village near Philadelphia (in Lydia).[35] There was also an association called the "sign-bearers of Apollo Archegetes" at Phrygian Hierapolis which, like many other local associations, was responsible for the upkeep of benefactors' graves. Their name suggests that they carried a standard with symbols of Hierapolis's patron deity in their own rituals and, perhaps, also in a yearly civic celebration (*IHierapJ* 153; second cent. CE).[36] There was also a sign-bearer alongside narthex-bearers, a lamp-bearer and basket-bearers in an association of Dionysiac initiates at Cillae in Thracia (*IGBulg* 1517; third cent. CE).

Other inscriptions from Asia Minor attest to bearers of sacred things, some of them in connection with unofficial associations and groups that celebrated mysteries. These provide an important interpretive framework for Ignatius's description of the unofficial Christian congregation of Christ-bearing fellow-initiates. I turn first to associations devoted to Isis, then to those linked with Dionysos and the Great Mother.

Plutarch's reference (*Moralia* 352B) to the "sacred-object-bearers" (ἱεραφόροι) among initiates in the mysteries of Isis—a favourite literary citation among scholars who deal with Ignatius's analogy[37]—has less-noted counterparts in inscriptions from various locales. Among these are the two "sacred-object-bearers" who set up statues at Pergamon in honour of Sarapis, Isis, Anubis, and other deities in the first century (*IPergamon* 336 = *SIRIS* 313).[38] It is in a similar milieu of Isis worship at Athens that we encounter the synonymous (but less common) "holy-object-bearer" (ἁγιαφόρος), the precise term that Ignatius uses of the Christians (*IG* III 162 = *SIRIS* 16; ca. 120 CE).

Apuleius of Madaura's story of the mysteries of Isis in Cenchreae in Greece describes in detail a sacred procession involving women, musicians, boys, initiates, and priests bearing sacred objects of various kinds (among them a lamp, sacrificial pot, golden palm tree, golden vessel in the shape of a woman's breast, winnowing basket, and wine jar) (*Met.*, book 11).

33. Pleket 1970, 61–74, no. 4 = Lane 1971–76, 1:49–50, no. 75 (mid-second century).

34. Pleket 1970, 63. Cf. Oster 1990, 1671–73.

35. Herrmann 1996, 315–41, no. 27. For discussion see Lane 1971–76, 3:36–37. Cf. *TAM* IV 76 (Nikomedia).

36. See Pleket 1970, 64–72

37. E.g., Schoedel 1985, 67.

38. Cf. *SIRIS* 52 (Thebes), 62 (Chaeronea, third cent. CE), 109 (Thessalonica, second cent. CE), 254 (Samos). There is also an "altar-bearer" attested in connection with Isis at Pergamon (*SIRIS* 315) and a "fire-bearer" at Epidaurus (*SIRIS* 38). Cf. Dunand 1973, 3:63–65.

He also mentions the order of *pastophoroi* (παστοφόροι), which are attested in Greek and Latin inscriptions as well.[39] These were, most likely, "shrine-bearers" who carried miniature temples in processions,[40] which provides a close analogy for Ignatius's "temple-bearers." The bearing of miniature, sacred shrines or temples was not limited to the worship of Isis, as Herodotus's and Didorus Siculus's description of certain Egyptian cults suggests.[41] It seems reasonable to imagine the presence of similar "bearers" of sacred objects among groups of devotees of Isis and Sarapis in Roman Asia, such as the initiates who are attested at Tralles in the early second century (*ITralles* 86 = *SIRIS* 295; time of Hadrian) and, perhaps, the guild of workers in the fishery toll-office at Ephesos which possessed an altar and statue of Isis, probably their patron deity (*IEph* 1503; time of Antoninus Pius). Earlier "cistophoric" coins (second–first cent. BCE) from Tralles, Ephesos, and other locales in Asia Minor depict the basket that was carried in such mystic processions in honour of Isis. [42]

Evidence for such bearers in processions and mysteries is forthcoming from Dionysiac groups, which were widespread in Asia Minor.[43] Several inscriptions from Ephesos mention the title and role of "*thrysus*-bearer," or "wand-bearer" (θυρσοφόρος), in celebrations for Dionysos (*IEph* 1268, 1601–2). The Asian-influenced association of initiates at Torre Nova, Italy (ca. 160 CE), under the direction of their priestess (Pompeia Agrippinilla), included various such functionaries among its members including "winnowing-basket-bearers," "basket-bearers," "fire-bearers," "phallus-bearer," and "god-bearers" (*IGUR* I 160).[44] These were titles and functions of fundamental importance to the mythology and mysteries of the god in question. As M. P. Nilsson notes, the "*liknon* filled with fruit among which a phallus rises, often covered with a cloth, is the characteristic symbol of the Bacchic mysteries of the Roman age."[45] Elsewhere in Asia Minor, near Thyatira, we hear of an association that called itself the "narthex-bearing company." The narthex plant was among the favourite choices for wands in Dionysiac mysteries (*TAM* V 817, 822).

Sacred associations devoted to the Great Mother of Anatolia, Cybele, existed throughout Lydia, Phrygia, and the Roman world generally, including regions such as Moesia and Thracia. In Romanized versions of such groups, "reed-bearers" and "tree-bearers" played a key role, the latter carrying the decorated pine trees in processions that commemorated the death of Attis during the March festival.[46]

Visual depictions on monuments from northwestern Asia Minor help to bring such processions by associations to life. A monument from Kyzikos pictures a procession in

---

39. *SIRIS* 433 (Rome, second or third cent. CE), 709 (Tomi, Moesia Inferior, third cent. CE).

40. Cf. Vidman 1970, 211–12.

41. Cf. Diodorus Siculus 1.97; Herodotus 2.63. If V. Chapot's claim that there was a board of "temple-bearers" at Ephesos is correct, then there is a clear local parallel for Ignatius's use of the term; but Chapot does not cite any specific inscriptions (Chapot 1967 [1904], 516–17; cf. Picard 1922, 242).

42. See Dunand 1973, 78–79; Hölbl 1978, esp. plate XII, no. 1b; Magie 1953, 163–87.

43. See Nilsson 1957.

44. Cf. Vogliano 1933, 215–31; Nilsson 1957, 21–57; *IGBulg* 401, 1517 (Asian-influenced initiates in Thracia).

45. Nilsson 1957, 21.

46. On tree-bearers in the Danubian provinces, see Tacheva-Hitova 1983, 73–74 (no. 4 from Novae), 93–95 (no. 48 from Tomi), 116–18 (no. 101 from Serdica), 148–50.

honour of the Great Mother (*CCCA* I 289; first cent. BCE). The relief depicts Cybele in a quite typical manner, seated on a throne with lions on either side. Below her is shown a procession of eight devotees approaching an altar with upraised hands in adoration of the goddess. The procession would culminate in a sacrificial scene similar to that depicted in another relief from Triglia (near Apamea on the Propontis) set up by the members of the "synagogue of Zeus" in honour of Stratonike, the priestess of Mother Cybele and Apollo (*IApamBith* 35, with photo = *CCCA* I 252; 119 BCE or, more likely, 85 CE). The relief pictures Stratonike, along with a boy guiding the sacrificial victim (a sheep) and a girl playing the Phrygian double flute. They proceed towards the altar with upraised hands in adoration of Cybele and Apollo. Beneath this processional–sacrificial scene are pictured the members of the association reclining for a banquet as they eat souvlaki and listen to flute players.[47] Evidently, processions, along with related functionaries and rituals, were an integral part of activities in many associations, which brings us back to the unofficial congregations addressed by Ignatius.

Conclusion

The case of Ignatius illustrates how certain educated, early Christian authors could draw on familiar concepts and categories from local cultural life, including association life, in order to define and express the identities of congregations. In particular, Ignatius drew on concepts and imagery from the life of local associations devoted to mysteries, characterizing the congregations as groups of fellow-initiates with their own, special mysteries. Alongside this characterization are other analogies drawn from practices in the mysteries and from processions that often involved groups and organizations of various types, including associations.

I would suggest that the effect of such internal self-definitions would be, in part, to provide a sense of place for these Christians within local cultural life despite the other ways in which such minority groups stood apart from others. Ignatius was a relatively educated, literate author, but it seems that his ways of expressing Christian identities nonetheless came to influence others within these congregations. In the next two chapters, I turn to the internal language of belonging that was used among average members within associations, beginning with fictive brother language.

47. See the photo of *GIBM* IV.2 1007 in chapter 1, as well as the discussion of such depictions of association meetings in Harland 2003a, 56–59; Mitropoulou 1990, 472–74.

Part 2

Familial Dimensions of Group Identity

3

"Brothers" in Associations and Congregations

Introduction

Social identity theorists emphasize the role of both internal definitions and external categorizations in dynamics of group identity construction and reformulation. There is a sense in which internal definitions are primary in the construction of identities. In these two chapters I further explore instances of these internal group processes in the ancient context by looking at the use of fictive family language within associations and cultural minority groups, including associations of Christians and of Judeans (Jews).

Identity formation and negotiation take place primarily through social interaction, in this case interaction among members in a particular group. Many social identity theorists stress the importance of language not only in the communication of identities but also in the construction and negotiation of identities, both in terms of internal self-definition and external categorizations.[1] Identities are created or re-created through verbal or nonverbal communication. In surveying the social-scientific literature on how identity is "done," Judith A. Howard stresses how "people actively produce identity through their talk."[2] Discourses of belonging that took place among members within associations, including cultural minority groups, are therefore an excellent place to start in understanding dynamics of group identity.

I argue that Judean and Christian practices of employing family language reflect common modes of formulating and communicating identity or belonging within certain groups in the ancient Mediterranean. These usages suggest ways in which these cultural minority groups mirrored the majority culture in significant ways relating to processes of self-definition and interactions among individual members of a group.

Early Christian congregations, like other associations, could express their identities in a variety of ways, and this included the use of family language to express belonging within the group in certain cases. The language of familial relation, particularly the term "brothers" (ἀδελφοί), is prominent in Paul's letters and subsequently continues with some

1. See Howard 2000, 371–73.

2. Howard 2000, 372.

importance in segments of early Christianity.[3] For example, Paul's first letter to the Christians at Thessalonica, which seeks to comfort Christians faced with "afflictions," is densely packed with references to "the brothers."[4] David G. Horrell notes that "brothers" / "sisters" is used over 112 times in Paul's authentic letters, and Horrell argues that the "prominence of this kinship description would seem to imply that Paul both assumes and promotes the relationship between himself and his addressees, and among the addressees themselves, as one between equal siblings, who share a sense of affection, mutual responsibility, and solidarity."[5] The author of 1 Peter calls on followers of Jesus in Asia Minor to "love the brotherhood" (ἀδελφότης; 1 Pet 2:17; cf. 5:9). Ignatius of Antioch (who knows and uses Paul's letters) reflects continued use of brother language within Christian congregations in Roman Asia and in Syria, yet he also applies the term "brothers" to outsiders as well.[6]

Many scholars pursue the meaning of this figurative sibling language *within* Christianity, especially its Pauline forms, including R. Banks, Wayne A. Meeks, K. Schäfer, K. O. Sandnes, J. H. Hellerman, David G. Horrell, and Trevor J. Burke, in recent years.[7] With the exception of useful studies by Peter Arzt-Grabner and Reidar Aasgaard, very few go beyond this internal Christian usage to focus on other Greco-Roman uses of the sibling metaphor. In particular, we lack studies that sufficiently explore epigraphic and papyrological evidence for fictive kinship within small-group settings or associations in the Greek-speaking, eastern Mediterranean.[8]

One reason for this neglect is that, although many scholars rightly point to the importance of Paul's use of fictive kinship for understanding group identity, this is sometimes explained by scholars in terms of sectarianism in a sociological sense. In particular, Bryan R. Wilson's sociological sect typology has been extremely influential in social-historical studies of early Christianity.[9] So much so that the categorization of early Christian groups as "sects" has become standard practice, as I noted in chapter 1. This chapter further highlights problems in how these groups have been categorized as "sects" and builds on my substantial critique of those approaches in my earlier work.[10]

To provide an influential example of how sibling language is approached, Meeks is among those who correctly emphasize the community-reinforcing impact of the term "brothers" as used in Pauline circles. Yet Meeks goes further to argue that Paul's use of "brothers" is indicative of how "members are taught to conceive of only two classes of humanity: the sect and the outsiders."[11] The use of affective language within Pauline circles

3. E.g., 1 Thess 1:4; 2:1; 3:2; 4:1; 5:1, 4, 12; Matt 5:22–23; 12:49; Acts 2:29; 3:17; 13:15; 1 Pet 2:17; 5:9; Jas 1:2; 2:1; 3:1; 1 John 3:13–16.

4. See 1 Thess 1:4; 2:1; 3:2; 4:1; 5:1, 4, 12.

5. Horrell 2001, 299.

6. Applied to insiders: *Poly.* 5.1; *Smyrn.* 12.1; 13.1; *Eph.* 16.1; *Rom.* 6.2. Applied to outsiders: *Eph.* 10.3. "Brothers" occurs in his letters to Tralles and to Magnesia.

7. Banks 1994 [1980]; Meeks 1983, 85–89; Schäfer 1989; Sandnes 1994; Horrell 2001; Burke 2003. For earlier studies, see especially Schelkle 1954, 631–35.

8. Arzt-Grabner 2002, 185–204; Aasgaard 2004, esp. chs. 4–7.

9. See, for instance, Wilson 1970, 1973, 1982.

10. See Harland 2003a, 177–212.

11. Meeks 1983, 86 (also see pp. 85–88); cf. Lane Fox 1986, 324–25; Sandnes 1994; Elliott 1990, 165–266.

was an important component in "the break with the past and integration into the new community."[12] Most Christian groups strongly set themselves apart from society and the common use of family language is one further indicator of their status as "sects," from this perspective.

An important assumption behind this argument for a sectarian understanding of fictive family language is that such usage is, in some sense, *unique* (or at least peculiar) to early Christians and, to a lesser extent, their close cultural relatives, Judeans.[13] In this view, such modes of address were *not* significant within small-group settings, organizations, or cults in the Greco-Roman world. It is common among some scholars, such as Meeks and Hellerman, both to assert the *rarity* of fictive family language within associations or "clubs" and to discount evidence of such usage that does exist in these settings as lacking any real implications for a sense of belonging or communal identity.[14] Although Meeks admits that fictive sibling terminology was "not unknown in pagan clubs and cult associations," for instance, he does not further explore the evidence and he dismisses some cases he is aware of as insignificant and primarily indicative of "Roman influence."[15]

Meeks, like Robin Lane Fox, Walter Burkert, and others, stresses the differences between associations, on the one hand, and both Christian congregations and Judean gatherings, on the other, and the familial language issue is one component in this contrast.[16] Implied or stated is the idea that, in contrast to Christian groups, most associations (including groups of initiates in the mysteries) lacked a developed sense of communal identity (they were mere "clubs"). In some ways, early Christian groups are taken as ideal or true communities with affective bonds among members.

There is no such consensus concerning fictive kinship terms among scholars of Greco-Roman religions, epigraphy, and associations specifically. Beginning with Erich Ziebarth in the late nineteenth century, several scholars briefly note occurrences of sibling language within associations. Yet these scholars are generally divided on whether *the practice* was relatively common or infrequent in the Greek East.[17] Several, such as Franz Bömer, Franz Poland, and others who depend on them, argue that the practice of using familial terms for fellow-members ("brothers") was relatively unknown in Greek associations.[18] Furthermore, Bömer suggests that the cases where it is attested in Greek inscriptions are results of

---

12. Meeks 1983, 88.

13. Both Franz Bömer and Meeks emphasize the distinctiveness of Christian usage while also suggesting Judean influence (Bömer 1981 [1958–63], 179; Meeks 1983, 87). Cf. Lieu 2004, 166–67.

14. Cf. Meeks 1983, 225 n. 73; Burkert 1987, 45; Lane Fox 1986, 324–35; Schmeller 1995, 16–17; McCready 1996, 59–73; Hellerman 2001, 21–25.

15. Meeks 1983, 87. Cf. Bömer (1981 [1958–63], 172), who considers fictive brother-language "un-Greek."

16. Lane Fox 1986, 85, 324–25; Burkert 1987, 30–53.

17. Ziebarth 1896, 100–101; Waltzing 1895–1900, 1.329–30 n. 3 (on the West primarily); Poland 1909, 54–56; Nock 1924, 105; San Nicolo 1972, 1.33–34 n. 4; Schelkle 1954, 631–634; Bömer 1981 [1958–63], 172–78; Fraser 1977, 74, 78, 164–65 nn. 433–37; Burkert 1987, 45, 149 n. 77; Kloppenborg 1996b, 259; van Nijf 1997, 46–49; Ustinova 1999, 185–88; Harland 2003a, 31–33; Ascough 2003, 76–77.

18. Poland suggests that the only clear case of fictive "brothers" in associations involves the "adopted brothers" at Tanais (Poland 1909, 54–55). Other potential cases are dismissed as Christian or as involving real siblings.

Roman or western influence, and therefore lacking significance for understanding association life in the Greek East.[19]

On the other hand, studies by A. D. Nock, Mariano San Nicolo, K. H. Schelkle, P. M. Fraser, and G. H. R. Horsley suggest that, despite the partial nature of our evidence, familial terminology may have been more common within cults and associations in the Greek East (and elsewhere) than often assumed.[20] Apparently no one has assembled and fully discussed the range of epigraphic evidence, and considerable evidence has come to light recently. Presenting and discussing the Greek inscriptional and papyrological evidence for fictive familial address here may help to clarify this issue in a more satisfactory manner.

Here I use some intriguing first-century archeological evidence from Paul's home-province, Cilicia, as an entry-way into the language of belonging within unofficial associations and guilds, particularly fictive kinship language and the sibling solidarity metaphor. The aim is to draw attention to familial expressions of identity within associations and cults of various kinds with special attention to the Greek-speaking, eastern part of the empire. I argue that there is no reason to minimize the significance of familial expressions of belonging within non-Christian, Greco-Roman contexts in the Greek East while doing the contrary in the case of Christianity. In both cases we are witnessing processes whereby connections among members of a group could be formed, expressed, and solidified, creating or maintaining a sense of communal identity. This way of putting it may show that I am not concerned with oversimplified issues of "borrowing" and genealogical cultural connections, nor with the unanswerable question of whether Paul derived his usage solely from Judean (e.g., synagogues) or from Hellenistic (e.g., associations) contexts, contexts which were less compartmentalized than often assumed, as we are learning. Instead, I am concerned with exploring shared ways of expressing identity and belonging in small group settings.

The nature of archeology and epigraphy limits the degree to which we should expect to be able to witness or evaluate such relational expressions, which are more suited to personal address (e.g., personal letters or face-to-face encounters as sometimes described in narrative or historical sources). Nonetheless, there are clear indications that *some* Greeks and Romans, like *some* Judeans and *some* followers of Jesus in the first centuries, did express a sense of belonging in an association, guild, or organization by identifying their fellows as "brothers" (or, less often attested, "sisters"). The Greek evidence spans the eastern part of the empire, including Asia Minor, Greece, Macedonia, the Danube, the Bosporan kingdom, and Egypt. Furthermore, the evidence dates to the centuries both before and after Paul, further suggesting that we should not so lightly dismiss its continuing significance within certain social settings.

---

19. Bömer 1981 [1958–63], 172–179; cf. Poland 1909, 54–55 (cf. pp. 371–73). Bömer and Poland influence other scholars: e.g., van Nijf 1997, 46 n. 73; Meeks 1983, 225, n. 73 (cf. Kloppenborg 1996b, 259; Ascough 2003, 76 n. 18).

20. Nock goes so far as to argue that the "cult-association is primarily a family" (Nock 1924, 105; cf. Barton and Horsley 1981, 26; Ascough 2003, 76–77). See San Nicolo 1972, 1.33–34 n. 4. In *NewDocs* V 4 (on p. 73), Horsley critiques N. Turner's dismissal of the use of "brother" within associations, citing several instances of its use.

Cautions on the Nature of Sources

Meeks and others who follow him suggest that brother language was *rare* in Greco-Roman associations or cults and relatively common within Christian groups. Yet it seems that these scholars have not taken into account a key difference in the genre of our sources for early Christian groups as opposed to associations. We have personal letters pertaining to early Christian groups (reflecting personal interactions), but rarely have any literary or epistolary evidence for the internal life of other associations. Instead, we have monuments, including honorary inscriptions and epitaphs on graves.

This has important implications regarding the assessment of things such as fictive family language and its relative frequency or importance in Christian, Judean, or other Greco-Roman settings. For in inscriptions (with their formal restrictions) there would be few occasions incidentally to make reference to the day-to-day language of belonging that was used in real-life settings (beyond the title of the group, for instance). The Judean epigraphic evidence is instructive on this point, for although we know that fictive sibling language was used by some Judeans in the Hellenistic and Roman periods (as reflected in the literature), so far we lack inscriptions that attest to the use of "brothers" among members of diaspora synagogues.[21] More importantly, although we find fictive uses of "brothers" / "sisters" in the mouths of educated Christian authors early on, such as Paul, most *epigraphic* attestations of the use of "brothers" considerably postdate our earliest inscriptional evidence for Christianity (which begins about 180 CE). Although "brother" is commonly used in the literature, the earliest Christian epitaphs that have been found do not use fictive sibling language at all, as far as I can see.[22]

So the probability remains that even if particular associations did use such fictive sibling language on a regular basis in real-life settings to indicate a sense of belonging, this

21. E.g., 1 Macc 12:10, 17; 2 Macc 1:1; 4 Macc 13:23, 26; 14:1; Josephus *War* 2.122, and, of course, the Dead Sea Scrolls (cf. Aasgaard 2004, 125–26; Horrell 2001, 296). See the indices of *CIJ* and *IJO* I-III, for instance. Meeks readily dismisses inscriptional evidence for brother language that does exist because of its supposed infrequency, asserting that "[m]ost likely . . . the early Christians took their usage from the Jews" (Meeks 1983, 87). Yet Meeks does not cite any epigraphic cases of the Judean usage (for the first two centuries), and what he does not mention is that we lack such evidence at this point (notwithstanding the few references to "brotherly/sisterly love" [φιλάδελφοι], only some of which are likely figurative). There is an inconsistency in Meeks's approach.

22. So far as I am aware, there are no clear cases of fictive sibling language in Christian inscriptions and epitaphs from the Greek East and Asia Minor before Constantine, including the "Christian for Christians" inscriptions of Phrygia, for instance (Gibson 1978; cf. Snyder 2003 [1985], 210–65). There are a number of instances of "brother(s)/sister(s)" or "beloved brother(s)" as forms of address in papyri that are quite securely Christian, particularly those dating to the third, fourth, and fifth centuries, e.g., *NewDocs* IV 124 and Snyder 2003 [1985], 270–72 (F), 273–77 (I), 278 (L), 282–84 (Z), 284–85 (CC). One of the difficulties here is that the scholarly assumption that "pagans" did *not* tend to use such terms of familial address has been a criterion for identifying letters as Christian based on the presence of brother language. See the discussion of *PRyl* IV 604 further below, for instance, which is now clearly established as "pagan," but still wrongly categorized as Christian by Snyder 2003 [1985], 281–82 (Y) and others.

would *rarely be expressed* on a monument. Relative rarity of expression in inscriptions should not be confused with rarity of practice. What this does mean is that we should pay special attention to the available Greco-Roman materials, rather than ignoring or dismissing them based on issues of presumed infrequency or insignificance.

Asia Minor, Greece, the Danube, and the Bosporan Region

References to "brother(s)" or "sister(s)" (ἀδελφός, -οί / ἀδελφή, -αί) in Greek inscriptions are, of course, not uncommon (especially in epitaphs), but we have the difficulty of assessing when such references are to fictive rather than "real" siblings. Thankfully, there are occasions when we can be confident in recognizing the figurative use of sibling language, including a clear case from first-century Cilicia, likely Paul's home province.

A series of tombs discovered carved into the mountain rock in the vicinity of Lamos in central Rough Cilicia (southwest of Tarsus) pertains to collective burial sites of associations dating to the period before Vespasian.[23] The majority of these common memorials make no mention of a title for the group or of terminology that members would use in referring to one another. In most of these shared tombs there is simply a list of members' names with no further identification (*IKilikiaBM* II 197, 198, 200, 202), or a statement of the leader's name followed by the list of "those with him" (οἱ μετ' αὐτοῦ; *IKilikiaBM* I 34; *IKilikiaBM* II 201). Certainly there are clear signs of belonging in all of these cases in the sense that these individuals consciously "joined together," as one inscription puts it, and they were concerned to ensure that only their members and no one else was to be buried there (*IKilikiaBM* I 34).

So although there are several associations at this locale, only one of them incidentally provides a glimpse into the terminology of belonging which could be used among members, in this case fictive brother language. The inscription in question (*IKilikiaBM* II 201) from Lamos reads as follows:

> *column a = lines 1–20*
>
> Rhodon son of Kydimasas, Selgian, and those with him: Pyramos son of Pyramos, Selgian, Mindyberas son of Arestes, Selgian, Aetomeros Manis, Lylous son of Menos, Selgian, Ketomaneis son of Kibrios, Zezis son of Oubramis, Kendeis son of Zenonis, Aigylis son of Oubramis, Dinneon son of Pigemis, Selgian. This is our common memorial and it is not lawful for anyone to bury another body here. But if anyone buries another here let him pay a pair of oxen and three *mina* (= 100 drachmai) to Zeus, three *mina* and a pair of oxen to Apollo, and three *mina* to the people (δῆμος). But if anyone should go up and wish to sell his common ownership (κοινωνεία), it is not lawful . . .

23. Bean and Mitford 1962, 209–11, nos. 33–35; *IKilikiaBM* I 34; *IKilikiaBM* II 197, 198, 202, 205; cf. *IKilikiaBM* II 189–202 for Lamos generally. The tombs are dated to the time of Vespasian (69–70 CE) or earlier based on the fact that they use "*drachmai*" rather than "*denaria*," which suggests that they date to the period before Vespasian joined Rough Cilicia with the Cilician plain (see notes to *IKilikiaBM* II 196).

column b = lines 21–35

> For it is not lawful to sell from abroad (or, possibly: sell outside the group), but let him take from the common treasury 30 *staters* and let him depart. But if some brother wants to sell, let the other brothers (ἀδελφοὶ) purchase it. But if the brothers so wish, then let them receive the coins mentioned above and let them depart from the association (κονοῦ [*sic*]).
> But whenever someone dies, and has no one to carry out the funeral . . .
> (see the Greek text of column b = lines 21–35 in the note).[24]

The membership in the association consists of ten men under the leadership of Rhodon from Selge, and four other members are likewise immigrants from that city (*polis*) in Pamphylia. We know from several other tombs in the vicinity (near the modern sites of Adanda and Direvli) that Selgian immigrants were particularly prominent in the profession of masonry.[25] The Rhodon in question may be identified with the artisan who carved another tomb in the area (*IKilikiaBM* II 199) and who was responsible for some sculptural work at nearby Selinos (*IKilikiaBM* II 156). It may well be that the members of this association shared this profession, though this is not expressly the case. It may also be that most or all of the members (beyond the Selgians) were immigrants to the area, forming an association along the lines of the sort of immigrant associations I discuss in chapter 5.

What interests us most here is the incidental reference to terminology of belonging used among members of the group. In outlining rules concerning members' share in the tomb and the question of selling this share, the group had decided to emphasize the need to ensure that portions within the tomb remained among members of the group. They consistently refer to such fellow-members as "brothers."[26] In the event that one of the "brothers" wished to "go up," perhaps to his hometown (Selge may be in mind), then he must not sell from abroad, or outside of the current membership. Instead, the departing member should receive his payment back or the other "brothers" may purchase the portion. The final stipulation (before the gap) is unclear but seems to suggest that if a number of the members decide to leave (returning to their hometowns, perhaps), then they too may receive their payments back.

There are other cases from Asia Minor involving fellow-members of an association or cultic organization who likewise employ brother terminology. A number of inscriptions pertaining to functionaries in cults at several locales, many of which also refer to "victory" (νίκη), appear to use the term "brother" as a designation for a priest. At Halicarnassos (on the western coast of Asia Minor, opposite the island of Cos) there are two, perhaps three, monuments on which priests (ἱερεῖς) in a temple are referred to as "brother priests" (ἱερεῖς

---

24. ἔξοθεν πωλῆσαι, ἀλ|λ̣ὰ̣ λ̣α̣μβανέτ̣ω ἐκ τοῦ | κοινοῦ στατῆρες τριά|κοντα καὶ ἀποχωρείτω. | ἐὰν δ̣έ τινος ἀδελφὸς | θελήσει ἀποπωλῆσ|α̣ι̣, ἀγοραζέσθωσαν οἱ | ἕτεροι ἀδελφοί. εἰ δὲ μὴ | θέλωσιν οἱ ἀδελφοί, τό|τε λανβάντωσαν τὸ πρ|ογεγραμμένον κερ[μ]|άτιον καὶ ἐκχωρείτω[σα|ν] ἐκ τοῦ κονοῦ (*sic*) ὅταν δέ | τις ἀποθάνῃ καὶ μὴ συνεξενένκῃ τις (column b = lines 21–35).

25. Cf. *IKilikiaBM* I 34; *IKilikiaBM* II 196, 197, 198, 199, 200.

26. Also see van Nijf 1997, 46–49, who recognizes that this is an example of fictive sibling language despite his view that such practice was rare.

ἀδελφοί).[27] A similar dedication for victory involving subordinate temple functionaries has been found at nearby Mylasa, in which two men are called "good, brother under-priests" (καλῶν ἀ|δελφῶν ὑποιερέ|ων; *IMylasa* 544). Further north and east in the province of Asia, at Synaos in the Aezanatis valley (northeast of Sardis), a recently discovered epitaph of the second century involves an individual functionary consecrated to the god (a ἱερός) who is referred to as "brother *hieros*" (*MAMA* X 437; cf. *SEG* 43 [1993], no. 893). Although we know very little about these functionaries, a pattern of usage is becoming clear which extends beyond just one locale. It would be difficult to explain these cases away as references to real brothers who happened to be fellow-priests, as Poland seems aware.[28] The term brother could be used of fellow-functionaries as a term of belonging in the setting of sanctuaries, as was also the case in Egypt as I discuss below.

Other evidence is forthcoming from Asia Minor, the Aegean, and Greece, this time involving unofficial associations. A monument dedicated to "God Most High" (Theos Hypsistos) at Sinope in Pontus, which need not be considered Judean in any way, refers to the group as "the vowing brothers (οἱ ἀδελφοὶ εὐξάμενοι)."[29] Although less than certain, it is quite possible that the four named men on a grave (ἡρῷον) from the vicinity of Iasos (north of Halicarnassos) who refer to themselves as "the brotherly-loving and unwavering male shippers of Phileros" (τῶν Φιλέρωτος φι|λαδέλφων ἀνδρων ναυκλήρων ἀπλανήτων) may not literally be brothers, but rather members of a guild under the leadership of Phileros.[30] It is worth noting that there are comparable, figurative uses of "brotherly love" or "familial affection" (φιλάδελφοι) in connection with fellow-members of an association at Latium (Italy) devoted to Hygeia (*IG* XIV 902a, p. 694 [addenda]) and among members of Judean groups in Egypt, Rome, and, possibly, Syria.[31] Quite well known are Paul's and 1 Peter's use of "brotherly / sisterly love" (φιλαδελφία) terminology of the relationship

27. *IGLAM* 503 a and b; Newton and Pullan 1862–63, 2.704–5, no. 12c; cf. Bean and Cook 1955, 103, no. 17; *IAsMinLyk* I 1. These and other "victory" inscriptions which have been found at Halikarnassos, Mylasa, Didyma, and Kos are sometimes etched (almost as graffiti) onto preexisting monuments (cf. *IMylasa* 541–564). Unfounded is the suggestion of G. Cousin and Ch. Diehl (followed uncritically by F. H. Marshall in the notes to *GIBM* IV 920 and 934) that all of the victory inscriptions, especially those that mention "brothers," are Christian epitaphs or remembrances referring to victory through martyrdom (Cousin and Diehl 1890, 114–18, no. 18). See *IKos* 65 and 69–72, where E. L. Hicks and W. R. Paton (1891) reject the previous view and more reasonably suggest that these inscriptions refer to victory in competitions (cf. *IKos* 65 and *IMylasa* 554, which involve ephebes). It is worth mentioning the possibility that some of these are dedications by priests within guilds of athletes or performers, where "priest" was a common title for a cultic functionary (see the discussion of athletic guilds further below).

28. Poland prefers to dismiss these apparent cases of pagan "brother priests" by categorizing the inscriptions as Christian, citing no evidence in support (Poland 1909, 55 n. ***); he is likely depending on the problematic suggestion of Cousin and Diehl (see previous note). Secondarily, he suggests that if they are pagan, then these are real brothers.

29. Doublet 1889, 303–4, no. 7; cf. Ustinova 1999, 185–86. It is unsatisfactory to reject this case with a claim that this is Judean syncretism (and therefore not Greek), as does Bömer 1981 [1958–63], 173. Poland mentions this case but suggests that these are probably real brothers (Poland 1909, 55).

30. Cousin and Deschamps 1894, 21, no. 11. On the use of φιλάδελφοι, -αι among blood relatives see *NewDocs* II 80 and III 74; *MAMA* VIII 132, line 13; *IBithynia* III 2 (= *IKlaudiupolis* 75), 7 and 8.

31. For likely figurative Judean uses, see *IEgJud* 114 (near Heliopolis; first cent. BCE or first cent.

among members of congregations, as when Paul exhorts followers of Jesus at Rome to demonstrate "heart-felt affections toward one another with brotherly love" (τῇ φιλαδελφίᾳ εἰς ἀλλήλους φιλόστοργοι) (Rom 12:10).[32]

In connection with such means of expressing ties with fellow members of a group, it is important to point out another clear case from Asia Minor in which similar terms of familial closeness are used among members of an association, even though brother language happens not to be evident. In an epitaph from Tlos in Lycia, the members of a "society" (θίασος) honour a deceased member, setting up the grave stone "on account of" their "heart-felt affection" (φιλοστοργία) for the deceased society-member.[33] With regard to the root for love or affection (φιλ-), in chapter 1 I discussed the fact that the term "dear ones" or "friends" (οἱ φίλοι) was a common means of expressing positive connections with others within associations, particularly in Asia Minor. And we will soon encounter instances where "brothers" and "friends" are used almost interchangeably as terms of belonging within associations in Egypt.

There are other incidental references from around the Aegean that attest to the use of fictive sibling language within associations. In discussing the associations of late Hellenistic Rhodes, P. M. Fraser draws attention to two cases where sibling language is likely used of fellow-members of immigrant or ethnic associations.[34] The clearer of the two involves a funerary dedication for a man and a woman who are also termed "heroized siblings" (ἀδελφῶν ἡρώων). As Fraser points out, this is a clear case where the basic meaning of "blood siblings" is not possible. He argues that although the meaning of "spouse" as in Egyptian papyri remains a possibility, it seems "more plausible to regard both parties, male and female, who are foreigners, as 'brothers' in the sense of fellow members of a koinon [association]."[35]

In a similar vein, Onno van Nijf, who in other respects downplays the frequency of brother-language, nonetheless discusses a third-century inscription from Thessalonica in Macedonia. This involves a collective tomb of an association with individually allotted niches: "For Tyche. I have made this niche in commemoration of my own partner out of joint efforts. If one of my brothers dares to open this niche, he shall pay . . ." (*IG* X.2.1 824). Interestingly enough, as van Nijf argues, here one sees fictive sibling language of belonging alongside a concern to preserve this particular niche from further use by the very same fellow-members of the association. "Brotherhood apparently failed to prevent some brethren from reopening niches to add the remains of another deceased person, or even to remove the remains of the lawful occupant."[36]

There are also some surviving instances from Greece and elsewhere in which those of

---

CE), *IEurJud* II 528 (Rome), and *IJO* III Syr70 (with David Noy's notes; cf. 2 Macc 15:14). Cf. *IEgJud* 86, *IEurJud* II 171 (Rome; third-fourth cent. CE) (either literal or fictive). Also see 1 Pet 3:8.

32. Cf. 1 Thess 4:9; 1 Pet 1:22 and 3:8; Heb 13:1; 2 Pet 1:7.

33. ὁ θίασος ἐπὶ Μάσᾳ τῷ θ[ια]σείτᾳ | φιλοστοργίας ἕνεκε[ν] (*TAM* II 640). On the meaning of φιλοστοργία ("affection" or "heartfelt love," as Horsley puts it in one case), see Robert 1965, 38–42, and, more extensively, Horsley in *NewDocs* II 80, III 11, and IV 33 (cf. Rom 12:10). Horsley had not yet encountered this case, it seems.

34. Fraser 1977, 74, 78, 164–65 nn. 430–37. Cf. *NewDocs* II 14.

35. Fraser 1977, 74.

36. Van Nijf 1997, 46 (with trans).

a common occupation or common civic position, sometimes members of an ongoing guild or organization, address one another as "brother" in a figurative sense. A third-century decree from Chalcis in Euboia (Greece) involves an important civic board (συνέδριον) and the people (δῆμος). In response to a temple-warden's (Aurelius Hermodoros's) generous benefactions to the sanctuary, Amyntas and Ulpius Pamphilos propose that Hermodoros's descendants be honoured with continuous possession of this temple-wardenship (likely of Tyche). The inscription happens to preserve the statement of the clerk of the board who seeks a vote on whether the members of the board agree to grant these honours "according to all of your intentions and the proposal of the brother Pamphilos" (*SIG*³ 898 = *IG* XII.9 906, lines 18–20).[37] Here a fellow-member of the organization is clearly addressed as "brother" in an incidental manner, which suggests that this was normal practice in this setting. There are several other instances of persons of a common occupation (sometimes, though not always, involving membership in a guild) referring to one another (in Greek) as "brother," including a rhetor at Baeterrae in Gaul who called another "the brother rhetor" (*IG* XIV 2516), athletes at Rome (*IGUR* 246), and several different professionals in Egypt, which I discuss below, including undertakers and athletes.[38] Arzt-Grabner also deals with a number of cases in papyri involving officials or business partners who address one another as "brother."[39]

Turning north of Greece and Asia Minor, fictive sibling language occurs in the associations of the Bosporus region on the northern coast of the Black Sea, in what is now southern Ukraine and southern Russia.[40] Greek inscriptions from Tanais attest to numerous associations devoted to "God Most High" (Theos Hypsistos) in the first three centuries (*CIRB* 1260–88). Membership consisted of men only who were drawn from the mixed Greek and Iranian (Sarmatian) populations of this community. The groups used several self-designations, some calling themselves "the synod which is gathered around Theos Hypsistos," or "the synod which is gathered around the priest."[41] These particular inscriptions happen not to make any reference to any informal, fraternal language of belonging that was used among members. But several inscriptions do indicate that an important leader within many of these groups held the title of "father of the synod" (*CIRB* 1263, 1277, 1282, 1288).

Particularly significant here are four inscriptions from Tanais (dating to the first decades of the third century) which pertain to an association that took on fictive sibling language as an *official title* for the group over several decades, calling themselves "the adopted brothers worshiping Theos Hypsistos' (ἰσοποιητοὶ ἀδελφοὶ σεβόμενοι θεὸν ὕψιστον; *CIRB* 1281, 1283, 1285, 1286; ca. 212–240 CE). In a fifth inscription, the editors have restored the title of another association as the "society of brothers" (θίησ[ος τῶν ἀ]δελ[φῶν] [*sic*]; *CIRB* 1284). The idea that we are here witnessing the development of fraternal language from

37. Bömer attributes this case to "Roman influence" without explanation (Bömer 1981 [1958–63], 172). Cf. *PTebtunis* I 12 (118 BCE), 19 (114 BCE), and 55 (late second cent. BCE); cf. Moulton and Milligan 1952, 9; Arzt-Grabner 2002, 188 n. 13.

38. Cf. Fraser 1977, 164 n. 433.

39. Arzt-Grabner 2002, 189–92, 195–99.

40. See Ustinova 1999, 183–96.

41. *CIRB* 1278, 1279, 1280, 1282, for the former; *CIRB* 1260, 1262, 1263, 1264, 1277, 1287, 1288, for the latter.

informal usage among members of associations into a title, and that brother language was likely common in these and other groups from the region at earlier points, is further suggested by epitaphs from Iluraton (mid-second century) and Panticipaion (early third century). Members in these two associations, at least, had been using the informal address of "brother" but had not come to take on this fraternal language as a group title. In each case, the membership of a "synod" honours a deceased fellow with a memorial and happens to express in stone its positive feelings for the lost member by calling him "its own brother" (τὸν ἴδιον ἀδελφόν; *CIRB* 104, 967).[42] In the latter group at Panticipaion, familial language was also used of a leader, who was known as "father of the synod."

Since Emil Schürer's study of the Bosporan Hypsistos inscriptions in 1897, it has been common for certain scholars to suggest Judean influence here (especially at Tanais), but this is highly problematic.[43] Many follow Schürer in holding the view that these were associations of gentiles or "god-fearers" honouring the Judean god as Theos Hypsistos, partly because of the coincidence of Acts-like language for gentile sympathizers here and because of evidence from elsewhere for the description of the Judean God as "god most high," following language in the Septuagint (a Greek translation of the Hebrew Bible from the third century BCE). However, Yulia Ustinova's exhaustive study of the Bosporan evidence for associations and for the worship of gods with the epithet Hypsistos convincingly demonstrates the weaknesses of Schürer's proposal and shows that these groups at Tanais, in particular, are best understood as associations devoted to a Hellenized, Iranian deity, with no Judean connection involved.[44]

The case of associations in the Bosporus region draws attention to another facet of familial expressions of identity in the Greek East which should be noticed before going on to brother language within associations in Egypt and in the mysteries. There are numerous examples of "father of the synod" in associations of this region, for instance, and we have seen that, in at least one case from Panticipaion, "father" is used within a group that also (informally) employs the term "brothers" for members (*CIRB* 104).[45] Similarly, as I discuss below, a group of initiates in the mysteries in Egypt referred to its leader as "father" and fellow-initiates also called one another "brothers," and a guild of athletes at Rome likewise used both "father" for a leader and "brother" among members.

As I discuss at length in the next chapter, there are many other times when, although we do not necessarily witness sibling terminology specifically, we do clearly encounter other familial or parental language to express connections or belonging in associations. There is, in fact, strong evidence pointing to the importance of such metaphorical parental and parent–child language in Greek cities generally and within local associations in these

42. Cf. Ustinova 1999, 188, 200.

43. Schürer 1897, 200–25; cf. Goodenough 1956–57. For the revival of Schürer's theory, see Levinskaya 1996, 111, 244–45; Mitchell 1999, 116–17.

44. See Ustinova 1999, 203–39. Cf. Noy, Panayotov, and Bloedhorn 2004, 323, who exclude this Tanais evidence from their collection of Judean inscriptions. While there were small Judean communities at Panticapaion, Gorgippia, and Phanagoria in the Bosporus region, there is no evidence for Judeans several hundred kilometers away at Tanais.

45. Out of thirty attested associations at Panticipaion (*CIRB* 75–108), eight use the title: *CIRB* 77 (second-third cent. CE), 96 (second cent. CE), 98 (214 CE), 99 (221 CE), 100, 103 (third cent. CE), 104 (third cent. CE), 105 (third cent. CE).

cities of Asia Minor, Greece, Thracia, and other regions in the first three centuries. Such evidence highlights the significance of familial terms of identification in many groups and contexts beyond Christianity. In some cases when members of an association regularly referred to their leader as "mother," "father," or even "papa," I would suggest, they were alluding to the same sort of connections and identifications within the group that the term "brothers" or "sisters" would evoke.

Egypt and Initiates in the Mysteries

Evidence from Hellenistic and Roman Egypt also strongly suggests that it would be problematic to argue that fictive familial language was insignificant within associations or that it was merely a late development (from Roman, western influence) within association life in the East. As with epigraphic evidence from other parts of the eastern Mediterranean, inscriptions from Egypt provide only momentary glimpses of the use of sibling language within associations and other cultic settings. For this region, however, the shortcomings of epigraphic evidence are somewhat counterbalanced by the survival of letters and other documents on papyri, the ancient equivalent of paper (as a result of the dry Egyptian climate). Not surprisingly, as with our evidence for Pauline and other Christian groups, it is within the context of personal address in letters that the use of fictive kinship language becomes more visible.

Papyri reveal that kinship terminology was used in a variety of ways within letters in the Hellenistic and Roman periods, including the use of the terms "brother" or "sister" as titles among royalty, as a designation of a spouse, and as a term of affection among close friends.[46] Arzt-Grabner's study collects together a number of clear cases from papyri (dating from the second century BCE to the third century CE) in which those who are not literally related address officials, friends, or business partners as "brothers."[47] Yet there are also other cases of this practice involving co-workers or co-devotees of a deity or deities who were active within the same sanctuaries or who belonged to associations or other organizations.[48]

As early as the second century of the Hellenistic era, we have instances in which persons belonging to a common profession, organization, and/or circle of devotees express connections with their fellows by using fictive kinship terminology. Though it is possible that two papyri regarding associations of embalmers (χοαχύται) at Thebes (late second century) involve actual family members addressed as "siblings," several scholars following

46. Cf. *NewDocs* I 17; *NewDocs* IV 15; *BGU* IV 1209.

47. Arzt-Grabner 2002. Officials: *BGU* VIII 1755, 1770, 1788 (60s BCE); *SB* XVI 12835 (10 CE). Friends: *BGU* VIII 1874 (first cent. BCE); *POxy* XVII 2148; *SB* V 7661; *POxy* XLII 3057 (first-second cent. CE); *SB* XIV 11644 (first-second cent. CE). Business partners: *BGU* I 248–49, II 531, 594–95, 597 (70s CE); *BGU* XVI 2607 (15 BCE); *POxy* LV 3808 (first-second cent. CE); *OClaud* I 158 (110 CE) and II 226 (mid-second cent. CE).

48. For Christian papyri using "beloved brother" as an address see the list in *NewDocs* IV 124. Plutarch shows an awareness of the common fictive use of sibling language within the context of friendships when he speaks against a man "who addresses his companion (ἑταῖρος) as brother in salutations and letters, but does not care even to walk with his own brother" (*De frat. amor.* 479D).

Amedeo Peyron have argued that in some of these cases "brothers" is more likely used of members in a guild that included nonfamily members.[49] More certain is the case in which the head of a military association, the high-priest, is addressed as "brother" in a first century BCE letter (*BGU* VIII 1770; 64/3 BCE).[50]

The so-called Sarapeum correspondence from Memphis in Egypt provides snap-shots of relations among those active within the sanctuaries of the gods Sarapis and Anubis in the second century BCE (see *UPZ* volume 1 for the papyri). Memphis was located on the west bank of the Nile, about 245 km south of Alexandria, or 20 km south of Cairo. Many letters on papyri have survived concerning these closely associated sanctuaries which were on the edge of town, letters that shed light on functionaries and administration, as well as the importance of the "detainees" (κάτοχοι), who were (voluntarily) being "held fast" or "detained" (κατέχω; cf. παρακατέχω) in the service of Sarapis.[51] Most of the correspondence came into the possession of one Ptolemaios, from Macedonia, who was a "detainee" in the Sarapeum for at least twenty years (from 172–152 BCE or beyond). Several of the letters pertain to Ptolemaios's friends, fellow-devotees, and family, including his actual brothers, Sarapion, Hippalos, and Apollonios (the younger).

Long ago, both Brunet de Presle and Walter Otto pointed to the frequency of "brother" as a title of address in the Sarapeum papyri and suggested that brother terminology was used among those who were "detainees" of Sarapis, who formed an association within the Sarapeum at Memphis.[52] Several others have likewise suggested that "detainees," in particular, formed a closely connected "brotherhood," and some of these scholars suggest a parallelism with Christian notions of a brotherhood.[53] However, Ulrich Wilcken challenges the suggestion of widespread sibling language among the "detainees."[54] Wilcken points out that many of the fictive instances of "brother" in the Sarapeum papyri do not certainly involve members of the "detainees" addressing one another as "brother," and he goes as far as to state that the titles "brother" and "father" have "no religious meaning" in this papyri collection.[55]

49. See *UPZ* II 162 = *PTor* 1, column 1, lines 11 and 19–20, and column 6, lines 33–34 (116 BCE); *UPZ* II 180a = *PParis* 5 column 2, line 5 (114 BCE). Early on, Peyron (1827, 68–69), who was aware of the family trees of embalmers, argued that the reference (in *PTor* 1, line 19–20) to "these brothers who offer services in the cemeteries," as well as the "brothers" mentioned in column 1, line 11, and column 6, lines 33–34, involve men that were not all related as brothers, and that the term is here used of fellow-members of a guild (on the family trees, see Pestman 1993, 14–27). Ziebarth (1896, 100–101), Walter Otto (1975 [1905–8], 1.104 n. 2), and San Nicolo (1972, 33–34 n. 4) agree with Peyron's evaluation (cf. Moulton and Milligan 1952, 9).

50. Cf. Arzt-Grabner 2002, 190; San Nicolo 1972, 1.198–200.

51. *UPZ* I 8 = *PLond* I 44, lines 18–19, speaks of a κάτοχος as "one of the therapeutists who are held fast by Sarapis." Also see *IPriene* 195 (line 28) and *ISmyrna* 725 (= *CIG* 3163) for a similar use of being "held fast" by Sarapis. For groups of "therapeutists" devoted to Serapis and/or Isis see *IDelos* 2077, 2080–81 (second-first cent. BCE); *SIRIS* 318–19 (Kyzikos; first cent. CE); *IMagnSip* 15 (= *SIRIS* 307; second cent. BCE and second cent. CE); *IPergamon* 338 (= *SIRIS* 314).

52. See Brunet de Presle's notes to *PParis* 42 (= *UPZ* I 64), in Letronne, de Presle, and Egger 1865, 308; Otto 1975 [1905–8], 1.124 n. 3 (cf. p. 1.119 n. 1).

53. Cf. Deissmann 1901, 87–88; Milligan 1969 [1910], 22; Moulton and Milligan 1952, 9; Liddell and Scott 1940, 20.

54. Wilcken in the notes to *UPZ* I 64, p. 319.

55. Apollonios on several occasions addresses his brother, Ptolemaios, as "father" in a show

Although Wilcken is right that the term "brother" in the Sarapeum papyri is not limited to members of an association, he goes too far in dismissing the potential cultic and social meanings of this term as an expression of attachment among those who were active or served within the sanctuaries of Anubis and Sarapis: that is, fellow-devotees or fellow-functionaries, though not necessarily members of an association. Clearly, there is a relatively high occurrence of "brother" as a fictive form of address in the Serapeum papyri as compared to papyri generally. In several cases, there are indications that the terminology is used among those who feel a sense of solidarity within a circle of friends or in an organization that served the gods within the sanctuaries (*UPZ* I 61, 62, 64, 69, 71, 72, 109). Thus, for instance, Barkaios, an overseer of the guards at the Anubis sanctuary, addresses the younger Apollonios, a guard, as "brother" (*UPZ* I 64 = *PParis* 42; 156 BCE).[56] Barkaios writes to his subordinate, though fellow, functionary in the service of Anubis in order to thank him for his service in reporting prison escapes. Similarly, in another letter the younger Apollonios addresses as "brother" the elder Apollonios, who was then "leader and superintendent of the Anubieum" (*UPZ* I 69 = *PParis* 45; 152 BCE). The younger Apollonios's close ties with this leader in the sanctuary of Anubis are further confirmed by the younger Apollonios's letter to Ptolemaios, at about this time, in which the younger Apollonios expresses concern about the well-being of both his actual brother and this elder Apollonios (*UPZ* I 68; 152 BCE). Finally, in the same year, the elder Apollonios addresses as "brother" Ptolemaios, writing to this "detainee" of Sarapis concerning the younger Apollonios (*UPZ* I 71 = *PParis* 46; 152 BCE).

It is worth mentioning the possibility that some of these correspondents of the younger Apollonios and Ptolemaios were themselves *previously* among the "detainees" in the Sarapeum, as was Apollonios in the summer of 158 BCE alongside his actual brother Ptolemaios, who was held fast for over twenty years. Yet even without this scenario, these letters clearly suggest that we should not so quickly disregard the possible social and cultic meaning of "brother" to express close ties among these men who were consistently involved in the sanctuaries in a functional role and, likely, as devotees of the gods (Sarapis, Anubis, and others) whom they served together.

Other evidence suggests that fictive sibling terminology was also used among initiates in mysteries who sometimes formed associations in Egypt and elsewhere. This despite the fact that initiations and the shared experiences among initiates were highly secretive, and our sources tend to respect this secrecy. As I discuss in the next chapter, parental language ("mother" or "father") was used of leaders within associations devoted to the mysteries of Dionysos, the Great Mother, Sarapis, and others, and the term "papa" was used of functionaries within a group of initiates of Dionysos. Furthermore, a partially damaged third-century CE papyrus from Oxyrhynchos (about 160 km south-southwest of Cairo) contains an oath pertaining to initiation into mysteries. The man pronouncing the oath happens to mention both the leader of the group, "father Sarapion," and his fellow-initiates,

---

of respect (cf. *UPZ* I 65, 68, 70, 93). Apollonios was not a "detainee" at the time, however, as was Ptolemaios.

56. For a translation of this letter see White 1986, 72–73, no. 39.

the "brothers," perhaps "mystical brothers" (μυστικο]ὺς ἀδελφούς).[57] Similarly, in the second and third centuries, those who were initiated into associations in Italy and the West devoted to Jupiter Dolichenus (Syrian Ba'al), Mithras, and others used both fraternal and paternal language (*fratres*, *pater* in Latin) within the group, but in these particular cases we are witnessing primarily Roman phenomena.[58]

Other incidental references to fictive sibling language used among initiates in the Greek mysteries can be cited, some from an earlier era. Although Walter Burkert downplays the notion of community feelings among initiates, he nonetheless acknowledges the use of "brother" among those initiated into the mysteries of Demeter and Kore at Eleusis, near Athens.[59] Thus, for instance, Plato speaks of two men as "brothers" because of their strong friendship arising from their shared participation in both stages ("initiation" and "viewing") of initiation at Eleusis (ξενίξειν τε καὶ μυεῖν καὶ ἐποπτεύειν πραγματεύονται).[60] Several centuries later, Sopatros (Sopater) the rhetor reflects continued use of the term "brother" among those being initiated at Eleusis specifically.[61]

Analogous expressions drawing on the model of the mysteries further confirm this picture. In his second-century treatise on astrology, Vetius Valens addresses the "initiate" in the secrets of astrology as follows: "I entreat you, most honorable brother of mine, along with the others who are initiated . . ." (ὁρκίζω σε, ἀδελφή μου τιμιώτατε, καί τοῦς μυσταγωγουμένους; *Anthology* 4.11.11; ca. 170 CE). The magical papyri also happen to reflect this practice when, in a prayer, the speaker is directed to refer to fellow-devotees in the following manner: "Hail to those to whom the greeting is given with blessing, to brothers and sisters, to holy men and holy women."[62]

Turning from initiates to other associations in Roman Egypt, Robert W. Daniel devotes some attention to the practice of familial address within occupational associations, discussing several papyri from the second and third centuries CE.[63] Several involve associations of athletes (see the bronze statue of an athlete in figure 8). In one third-century letter from Antinoopolis (about 280 km south of Cairo), the leader (ξυστάρχης) of an athletic association writes to one Andronikos, who is addressed as "brother" both in the external address

57. *PSI* X 1162 as read by Wilcken 1932, 257–59.

58. Devotees of Dolichenus at Rome called their priest "father of the candidates" (*pater candidatorum*) and fellow-initiates "brothers" (*fratres*; cf. Hörig und Schwertheim 1987, nos. 274, 373, 375, 376, 381 [second-third cent. CE]; Ebel 2004, 205–7). On the use of "father" (*pater*) or "father of the mysteries" (*pater sacrorum*) in the mysteries of Mithras, see *CIL* III 3384, 3415, 3959, 4041; *CIMRM* 623–24; Tertullian *Apol.* 8. On the "Arval brothers" (*fratres arvales*) in Rome, see Beard, North, and Price 1998, 1:194–96. Cf. Bömer 1981 [1958–63], 176–78; *CIL* VI 467; *CIL* VI 2233; Schelkle 1954, 633; Waltzing 1895–1900, 1.329–30 n. 3.

59. Burkert 1987, 45, 149, n. 77.

60. Plato *Epistles* 333d-e; cf. Plutarch *Dion.* 54.1; Andocides 1.132.

61. *Division of Questions* 339 in Walz 1843, 123 (fourth cent. CE).

62. Trans. by Grese in Betz 1992, 60 (*PGM* IV 1135; ca. 300 CE). Similarly, a member of a pagan circle worshiping Hermes Trismegistus in the fourth century CE (named Theophanes) uses the term "beloved brother" of his fellows (see S. R. Llewelyn's comments in *NewDocs* VI 25, on p. 175; cf. *Corpus Hermetica* 1.32).

63. Daniel 1979, 37–46.

Figure 8. Bronze statue of an athlete scraping oil from his body in connection with a competition, now in the Ephesos Museum, Vienna (Roman copy of a Greek original from ca. 320 BCE)

(verso) and in the text of the letter (*PRyl* IV 604, lines 32–33, as reedited by Daniel).[64] More importantly, all of the names mentioned, no less than four other men (some of whom are also termed "friend" [φίλος]), are likewise designated "brother" in the body of the letter: brother Eutolmios (line 13), brother Heraiskos (15), brother Apynchis (28), and brother Theodosios (34). Daniel convincingly shows that these are fellow-members of an athletic association, not real siblings, being addressed as brothers.[65] Further strengthening this interpretation is another parallel case from Oxyrhynchos. This letter was written from one leader of an athletic guild to another, who is addressed as a "brother." Two others are likewise called "brother" in the body of the letter, which concerns the affairs of a guild of athletes (*PSI* III 236; third century CE).

There is another important, though late, example of such use of familial language

64. The term ἡγεμών is attested in associations and organizations elsewhere: e.g., *IG* II.2 1993–1995 (Athens; ca. 80 CE); *IGR* I 787 (Baccheion of Asians in Thracia).

65. Cf. *OGIS* 189 (89 or 57 BCE, involving a gymnastic organization at Philai); San Nicolo 1972, 1.33–34 n. 4.

Figure 9. Bronze lamp depicting Herakles (patron deity of athletes) fighting a centaur, now in the Ephesos Museum, Vienna (ca. 150–100 BCE)

within a well-established professional guild of athletes at Rome, which is not discussed by Daniel but is worth mentioning here. The "sacred, athletic, wandering, world-wide association," which was devoted to the god Herakles (see a photo of this god in figure 9), had a significantly long history. Originally based in Asia Minor (probably at Ephesos), the headquarters of this guild (which also had local branches at various locations in the East) was moved to Rome some time in the second century, probably around 143 CE.[66] A Greek inscription from the time of Constantine reveals that, at least by this time and likely earlier as well, the members of this "world-wide" organization expressed positive connections with fellow-members using familial metaphors. Well-respected members are repeatedly called "our brother" (τοῦ ἀδελφοῦ ἡμῶν) in the inscription and the high priest of the guild is called "our father" (τοῦ πατρός ἡμῶν) (*IGUR* 246 = *IG* XIV 956B, lines 11, 12, 14). Such evidence from both Egypt and Rome suggests that the practice of using fictive kinship language within groups of athletes and other guilds may have been more widespread than our limited sources would initially suggest.

Finally, Daniel discusses a second-century papyrus from Ptolemais Hermou in the

66. See Pleket 1973, 197–227, on *IGUR* 235–48. Cf. *IEph* 1084, 1089, 1098.

Fayum region of Egypt (about 120 km south of Cairo) that almost certainly involves undertakers (νεκροτάφοι), the successors of our embalmers of the Ptolemaic period, so to speak.[67] These undertakers of the Roman period were formed into guilds, and it is worth mentioning that this occupation, which involved the transportation, embalming, and burial of the dead, was taken on by both men and women.[68] The letter in question is written from Papsaus to Asklas, who is addressed as both "friend" on the outside address and as "brother" in the letter opening (*PPetaus* 28). In light of the evidence discussed thus far, Daniel seems right in arguing that these are not merely "conventional, meaningless terms of address," but rather reflections of the everyday terminology used among members of these (and other) guilds.[69] According to the body of the letter, Papsaus was in trouble and seeking the help of his fellow-undertaker. Papsaus had sent to Asklas the body of a Roman legionary to be sent on to its final destination, but for some reason the body had not reached its final destination. As a result Papsaus was faced with possible disciplinary action by a leader (ἡγεμών) which, as Daniel shows, was most likely the guild president (not a Roman military officer or the provincial prefect in this case). Although partly to blame, here a fellow guild member, as "brother" and "friend," was sought for help.

Conclusion

Owing to the nature of our sources, we cannot be sure that fictive sibling language was widespread within associations or that it had the same meaning that "brothers" developed within certain groups of Jesus-followers, such as those associated with Paul. Yet what is clear is that many scholars have underestimated the evidence and the significance of fictive kinship language as a means of expressing belonging within associations and organizations of various kinds (ethnic, occupational, gymnastic, civic, cultic, and other groups). Inscriptions from Greece, Asia Minor, and Greek cities of the Danube and Bosporus, as well as papyri from Egypt, suggest that familial language was used within small-group settings in reference to fellow-members as "brothers" or (less often) "sisters."

The happenstance nature of evidence from epigraphy would suggest that these are momentary snap-shots of what was likely common usage within some other associations about which we happen to know less. In paying more attention to surviving materials, we begin to see common ground among some associations, synagogues, and congregations in the expression of belonging and group identity. This notwithstanding the fact that it is extremely difficult to measure the relative importance or depth of meaning attached to such familial language in specific instances.

What sorts of social relations and obligations accompanied the metaphorical use of sibling language within associations? It is important to remember that ancient values and social relations would not be the same as our modern notions of family or sibling relations. Although there is little direct information about the meanings which members of

---

67. Cf. Otto 1975 [1905–8], 1.108–10, 2.180 n. 1. On various kinds of occupations and guilds relating to burial, see Youtie 1940, 650–57.

68. See San Nicolo 1972, 97–100.

69. Daniel 1979, 41.

associations attached to calling a fellow-member brother, we can nonetheless make some inferences from literary discussions of familial relations. These discussions help to clarify the real-life experiences and expectations that would give meaning to the metaphor or analogy.

Although presenting ideals of family relations from a philosophical perspective, for instance, Plutarch's discussion *On Brotherly Love* (early second cent. CE) nonetheless reflects commonly held views that would inform fictive uses of these terms of relation in the Greek world, one would expect.[70] For Plutarch and others the ideal sibling relation is marked by "goodwill" (εὔνοια; Plutarch *De frat. amor.* 481C), and brothers are "united in their emotions and actions" (*De frat. amor.* 480C).[71] Foremost is the ideal of solidarity and identification. "Friendship" (φιλία) is one of the strongest analogies that Plutarch can evoke in explaining (in a Platonic manner) the nature of relations among brothers and between parents and children: "For most friendships are in reality shadows, imitations, and images of that first friendship which nature implanted in children toward parents and in brothers toward brothers" (*De frat. amor.* 479C-D). Conversely, the term "brothers" was a natural way of expressing close social relations among friends in an association.

For Plutarch and others in antiquity there is a hierarchy of honour (τιμή, δόξα) that should be the basis of familial and other relations. Brothers come before friends: "even if we feel an equal affection for a friend, we should always be careful to reserve for a brother the first place . . . whenever we deal with occasions which in the eyes of the public give distinction and tend to confer honour" (δόξαν) (*De frat. amor.* 491B). Beyond this, nature and law "have assigned to parents, after gods, first and greatest honour" (τιμὴν) (*De frat. amor.* 479F).

These Greco-Roman family ideals of solidarity, goodwill, affection, friendship, protection, glory, and honour would be the sorts of values that would come to the minds of those who drew on the analogy of family relationships to express connections with other members of the group, I would suggest. When a member of a guild called a fellow "brother" that member was (at times) expressing in down-to-earth terms relations of solidarity, affection, or friendship, such that the association may have been a second home. In the next chapter, I deal with further evidence regarding such familial forms of relation in associations, including those that involve "mothers" and "fathers."

70. Cf. Aasgaard 2004, chapter 6.

71. Trans. Hembold 1927–69 (LCL)

4

"Mothers" and "Fathers" in Associations and Synagogues

Introduction

As I demonstrated in the previous chapter, familial language of belonging could play an important role in internal definitions of identity among members of certain groups. In some cases, an association could to a certain extent be considered a fictive family. This was true not only within Pauline or other Christian congregations, but also within associations where fictive sibling language was used among fellow-members.

That chapter also showed that there are clear problems with interpreting the Christian use of family language as unique, or as a sign of the sectarian or socially distinguished status of these groups. In fact, you could argue that those Jesus-followers who did engage in this practice were adopting and adapting common modes of identity expression from society more broadly. These cultural minority groups were, in certain respects, mirroring society and mirroring associations within that society that looked to the family as a model of community. Familial language, with its accompanying values of honour, solidarity, and affection, served to strengthen bonds within the group and could at times become part of a group's public presentation of itself.

In this chapter, I turn to further evidence for the use of familial terminology in associations, including Judean (Jewish) synagogues. Moreover, the use of parental language within synagogues further demonstrates the ways in which these ethnic associations or cultural minority groups could assimilate widespread means of expressing group identity from the majority culture.

The use of parental metaphors in associations has drawn limited attention within two scholarly circles. On the one hand, those who study Judean synagogues in the diaspora have engaged in some debate regarding the titles "mother of the synagogue" and "father of the synagogue." The focus here has often been on whether or not the title also entailed some functional leadership role within these gatherings.[1] On the other hand, classicists and ancient historians (especially around the turn of the twentieth century) have touched

1. For earlier discussions see, for instance, Schürer 1897, 29–32; Leon 1995 [1960], 186–88; Hengel 1966, 145–83. For a summary of the scholarly debate up to 1982, see Brooten 1982, 57–72. Most recently, see Levine 2000, 404–6.

upon the use of "father" or "mother" as an honorary designation in connection with guilds and associations. Franz Poland (1909), for instance, attempted to deal with the question of whether or not the practice was significant in the Greek East, and came to a negative conclusion.[2] Yet these two scholarly interests have not met in a substantial comparative study of fictive parental language in connection with synagogues and associations. Such a comparison is especially fitting in light of recent scholarship's emphasis on the ways in which Judean synagogues were, in important respects, considered associations.[3]

Furthermore, rarely have scholars in either of the two fields fully explored the social and cultural framework of this usage in the Greek-speaking, eastern Mediterranean and in immigrant Greek-speaking settings in the West. Focusing on this material, I argue that parental metaphors were more widespread in the cities of the eastern, Greek-speaking provinces of the Roman Empire than often acknowledged. This includes substantial evidence regarding associations specifically, which suggests that such terminology was an important way of expressing honour, social hierarchy, and/or belonging within the group.

Although questions of cultural influence are difficult to assess, a careful look at the evidence suggests that we cannot explain many cases in Greek inscriptions with a claim of western influence. In fact, it seems likely that the initial cultural influence was the other way around, from Greek to Roman. Moreover, the practice among synagogues can be better understood in light of the practice within the Greek cities and associations. Attention to this evidence for associations provides a new vantage point on the mothers and fathers of the synagogues, including honorific and functional dimensions associated with parental designations.

Parental Terminology in Judean Synagogues

It is somewhat surprising that scholars who focus on Judean uses of the titles "mother of the synagogue" and "father of the synagogue" do not give sufficient attention to non-Judean instances within associations or within the Greek cities generally.[4] This may be due, in part, to the notion that, as Lee I. Levine puts it, "the term "father" as a title of honour and respect has deep roots in ancient Judaism," which is indeed true in certain respects.[5] For instance, there are hints that some groups in Judea, such as the Dead Sea community, may have used parental titles for those in positions of authority.[6] Yet instead of also exploring Greco-Roman contexts, the focus of debate with regard to synagogues often pertains

---

2. Poland 1909, 371–72; cf. Foucart 1873, 242; Liebenam 1890, 218 n. 2; Waltzing 1895–1900, 3.446–49. For recent studies that deal with these titles in the Roman *collegia* of the West, see, for instance, Perry 1999, 178–92; Liu 2004, 320–21.

3. See Richardson 1996, 90–109; Richardson 2004, 111–34, 187–224; Baumgarten 1998, 93–111; Runesson 2001. Cf. Harland 2003a, 177–264.

4. E.g., Leon 1995 [1960], 186–88; Hengel 1966, 176–81; Brooten 1982, 57–72; Lassen 1992, 257–61; Levine 2000, 404. Do, however, see G. H. R. Horsley's comments in *NewDocs* IV 127, p. 260. Cf. Noy 1993–95, 77–78.

5. Levine 2000, 404; cf. Noy 1993–95, 77.

6. See the *Damascus Document*'s references to "mothers" and "fathers" (4Q270 7 I 13–15, as interpreted by Crawford 2003, 177–91 and Bernstein 2004).

to the internal question of whether the titles were honorific or functional in terms of real-life leadership, particularly with respect to women's leadership. Bernadette J. Brooten's and Levine's arguments for the probable *functional* nature of at least some of these positions is a corrective to the standard claim of mere honorifics.[7] Still, these same scholars do not fully explore the evidence for associations in their brief discussion of non-Judean parallels, evidence that may help to resolve issues in the debate.[8]

I argue that we can make better sense of this Judean practice within the broader framework of parental metaphors in the Greco-Roman world, particularly in connection with cities, cults, and associations of the Greek East.[9] Furthermore, in some ways the scholarly debate concerning the Judean cases, which sometimes involves opposing options of honorific title or functional leadership, is problematic. I argue that addressing leaders or benefactors as "mother," "father," or "papa," as well as "daughter" or "son," were somewhat usual ways of expressing honour, gratitude, belonging, or even affection within a variety of contexts. In some cases, it seems that such titles could be used of external benefactors who were not, in fact, members of the group in question. Yet in many others involving associations, parental metaphors were used to refer to members or leaders who apparently served some functional or active role within the group.

Furthermore, epigraphic evidence for fictive parental language has a broader significance concerning the relation or assimilation of Judean gatherings to Greco-Roman civic life—culturally, institutionally, and socially. Although dealing primarily with the position of "leader of the synagogue" (ἀρχισυνάγωγος), Tessa Rajak and David Noy's comments regarding the ways in which certain Judean groups reflect and interact with surrounding society, I would suggest, also ring true in connection with the assimilation of parental designations in the synagogue:

> The echoing of the city's status system within the Jewish group represents at the very least an external acceptance within the group of civic political values. These echoes would necessarily be both the result and the facilitator of interaction. The result of redefining the archisynagogate in terms of a sound understanding of Greek civic titles, is thus to conclude that it belonged in an outward-looking type of community, which did not see fit to run its affairs in isolation, even if it might parade its cultural distinctiveness in chosen ways.[10]

A brief outline of our epigraphic evidence for parental metaphors among Judean synagogues is in order before turning to the Greek civic context and associations. Judean uses of the titles "mother of the synagogue" or "father of the synagogue" are found at several locales, and many of these cases occur in Greek inscriptions. What is likely among the earliest attested instances of such parental terminology in a Judean context comes from

---

7. Brooten 1982, 57–72; Levine 2000, 404–6.

8. Brooten 1982, 71. Levine (2000, 404) devotes one passing sentence to the Greco-Roman material despite several pages of discussing the Judean cases.

9. Noy (1993–95, 77–78) makes a similar point, though in brief.

10. Rajak and Noy 1993, 89.

Stobi in Macedonia, dating to the late second or early third century.[11] There a Judean man named Claudius Tiberius Polycharmos donated portions of the lower level of his home to the "holy place" in fulfillment of a vow, including banqueting facilities (a *triclinium*). In the process, he refers to himself as "father of the synagogue at Stobi who lived my whole life according to Judean customs" (*IJO* I Mac 1 = *CIJ* 694, lines 4–9). The simplified designation "Polycharmos, the father" is repeated in the fresco floors of the building, which were also donated in fulfillment of a vow.[12] Levine rightly questions the assumption that all cases are merely honorific, suggesting that the Stobi inscription in particular "conveys the impression that this individual played a crucial and pivotal role in synagogue affairs generally."[13]

Most known references to fathers and mothers of the synagogue involve Greek epitaphs from catacombs in the city of Rome.[14] These inscriptions have not been precisely dated, and recent suggestions range from the late second to the fourth century. At Rome the title "father of the synagogue" occurs in at least eight inscriptions, all of them Greek, which suggests that these were Judeans originally from the eastern diaspora.[15] Eastern origins seem even clearer in at least one of these cases, involving the "father of the synagogue of Elaia" (*IEurJud* II 576; cf. II 406). It seems likely that this synagogue was founded by Judean settlers originally from a city called Elaia in Asia Minor (either west of Nikomedia or south of Pergamon).[16]

There are at least two (possibly three) cases of the corresponding "mother of the synagogue" at Rome, one (possibly two) in Greek and one in Latin.[17] The less fragmentary one reads as follows: "Here lies . . . ia Marcella, mother of the synagogue of the Augustesians. May (she?) be remembered (?). In peace her sleep" (*IEurJud* II 542).[18]

In light of the Greek evidence discussed further below, it would be problematic to argue, as does Eva Maria Lassen,[19] that Judean practice at Rome necessarily reflects specifically Roman (rather than Greek or Greco-Roman) influence, since our earliest examples are in Greek and the majority continue to be so. Added to this is the fact that the titles "mother" and "father" are attested in many other Greek inscriptions involving civic bodies and unofficial associations in the Greek part of the empire at an early period, about which Lassen seems unaware. Conversely, parental titles are not well attested in Latin-speaking

---

11. For the second-century dating, see W. Poehlman 1981, 235–47 (refuting Hengel 1966, 145–83). Cf. White 1997, 355; Noy, Panayotov, and Bloedhorn 2004, 56–71.

12. *IJO* I Mac 3–4. Wiseman and Mano-Zissi 1971, 408; cf. White 1997, 355 n. 123.

13. Levine 2000, 405.

14. Cf. Leon 1995 [1960], 186–88; Levine 2000, 405–6.

15. "Father of the synagogue': *IEurJud* II 209 (= *CIJ* 93), 288 (= 88), 540 (= 494), 544 (= 508), 560 (= 319), 576 (= 509), 578 (= 510), 584 (= 537). Also to be noted are two third-century cases of "father of the synagogue" (one in Latin and the other in Greek) from Numidia and Mauretania in Africa. See le Bohec 1981, 192 (no. 74), 194 (no. 79).

16. Cf. *IEurJud* I 18 = *CIJ* 533 (near Ostia). L. Michael White 1998b (chapter about Ostia) conjectures a reconstruction of this inscription which refers to the "father [and patron of the *collegium*]."

17. 'Mother of the synagogue': *IEurJud* II 251 (= *CIJ* 166), 542 (= 496). For the Latin *mater synagogorum*, see *IEurJud* II 577 (= 523). It is worth noting a Latin inscription from Brescia which mentions a "mother of the synagogue" (*matri synagogae*; *IEurJud* I 5; fourth century or earlier).

18. Trans. Noy (*IEurJud* II 542)1995, 425.

19. Lassen 1992, 257–61.

cities, and they only begin to appear in connection with *collegia* by the mid-second century, as I discuss below.

Other clear cases from the Greek East demonstrate continued use of this terminology within Judean circles. There is a papyrus from Egypt (dating 291 CE) that refers to a city councillor from Ono in Roman Palestine, who is also identified as a "father of the synagogue" (*CPJ* III 473).[20] Two other examples, in this case from Greek cities, happen to date to the fourth century. At Mantineia in Greece there was a "father of the people (λαοῦ) for life" who provided a forecourt for the synagogue building (*IJO* I Ach54 = *CIJ* 720). There was an "elder" (πρεσβυτέρος) and "father of the association" (τοῦ στέμμα|τος) in Smyrna, who made a donation for the interior decoration of the Judean meeting place (*IJO* II 41 = *ISmyrna* 844a = *CIJ* 739).[21]

In later centuries, the titles "father" and "mother" (with no further clarification or reference to "the synagogue") became somewhat standard in relation to important figures within Judean circles, at least at Venosa in Apulia (Italy) in the fifth and sixth centuries.[22] However, in some instances, it is uncertain as to whether the title (attested in both Latin and Greek) pertains to the person's relation to the synagogue specifically or to the civic community more broadly, as in the case of "Auxaneios, father and patron of the city" (*IEurJud* I 115 = *CIJ* 619c; cf. *IEurJud* I 116). It is to the broader civic context and to associations within that framework that I now turn.

Parental Metaphors in Greek Cities and Associations

Mothers, Fathers, Daughters, and Sons

The existence of "mothers" or "fathers" of the Roman *collegia* (beginning in the mid-second century) and the practice among some associations in the West of calling leaders "father" (*pater*), especially among initiates in Mithraic mysteries, has gained some attention.[23] Most recently, Emily Hemelrijk (2008) has collected together and discussed all (twenty-six) known cases of "mothers" of the *collegia* in Italy and the Latin provinces (beginning in the mid-second century), but she does not deal with the Greek East. Poland and others point to such Roman instances and too readily dismiss examples in Greek as "late," as under western influence, and as relatively insignificant for understanding association life in the eastern part of the empire.[24] As a result, they fail to further explore the evidence for such familial terminology, including its relation to the Greek cities generally. Despite the vagaries of

---

20. Cf. Levine 2000, 404.

21. On the use of στέμμα for a group or association, see the inscriptions from Philippi published by Chapouthier 1924, 287–303, esp. 287–92. Cf. *CIG* 3995b (Iconium); *MAMA* X 152 (Appia).

22. Cf. *IEurJud* I 56 (= *CIJ* 612), 61 (= 599), 62 (= 590), 86 (= 611), 87 (= 613), 90 (= 614), 114 (= 619b), 115 (= 619c), 116 (= 619d).

23. On the titles "father" and "mother" in *collegia* in the West (and in Latin inscriptions of the East) see Waltzing 1895–1900, 1.446–49, 4.369–70, 372–73 and, more recently, Perry 1999, 178–192, Liu 2004, 320–21, and Hemelrijk 2008 (who lists all cases).

24. Poland 1909, 371–72; cf. Wilcken 1932, 257–59.

archeological finds and the obvious difficulties in precisely dating many inscriptions, it is important to note that the earliest datable case of parental titles in *collegia* (in Latin) dates to 153 CE, with the majority dating considerably later.

On the other hand, there are cases in Greek from at least the second century BCE for Greek cities and from the early first century CE for associations specifically. There is, in fact, strong evidence pointing to the importance of such parental metaphors in the Greek cities and in local associations within these cities. In contrast, Latin parental titles used in civic (as opposed to imperial)[25] contexts in the West and East, such as *pater civitatis*, were a relatively late development (fifth century), in this case a later designation for the office of *curator civitatis*.[26] Moreover, this evidence suggests the likelihood that (if the practice did not develop independently in West and East) the initial direction of influence in the use of parental titles was from the Greek world to the Roman.

Within the realm of honours in the Greek East and Asia Minor in particular, it was not unusual for civic bodies and other organizations to express honour for, or positive relations with, a benefactor or functionary by referring to him or her as "father" (πατήρ) "mother" (μήτηρ), "son" (υἱός), "daughter" (θυγάτηρ), "foster-father" (τροφεύς), or "foster-child" (τρόφιμος). Evidence for this usage begins as early as the second century BCE (as at Teos involving "fathers") and continues with numerous instances in the first, second, and third centuries of our era (see the partial list in the accompanying table).[27] Thus, at Selge in Pisidia (just west of the Cilicia label on the map) there was a "son of the city" (*polis*) among the dedicators of a statue of Athena in the late first or second century (*ISelge* 2); a "mother of the city" who is an important benefactor and also priestess of Tyche in the second or third century (*ISelge* 17); and a "daughter of the city" who is also a priestess of Tyche and Ares in the late third (*ISelge* 20).

As Louis Robert, Riet van Bremen, and others note, these familial analogies evoke images of prominent persons raising the citizens as though they were their own children, or envision civic bodies and groups adopting as sons and daughters those who demonstrate strong feelings of goodwill (εὔνοια) or affection (φιλία) towards the "fatherland" (φιλόπατρις).[28] Van Bremen, who collects together and discusses the cases of "mothers" and "daughters" specifically, notes that the male equivalents of these titles considerably outnumber the female.[29] Nonetheless, she considers these titles in relation to other evidence for limited participation by women within civic life in the Greek East beginning in the first century: "elite women were integrated into civic life not only through office-holding and as liturgists, but on an ideological level too, as members of their families, and

---

25. "Father of the fatherland" (*pater patriae*) was a standardized term for the Roman emperors (cf. Lassen 1997, 112–13), but there is little to suggest that the father metaphor was widespread in reference to patrons or leaders in Roman *cities* of the West in the first century.

26. The *pater civitatis* was in charge of building and renovation projects in some cities. See Roueché 1979, 173–85; Dagron and Feissel 1987, 215–20.

27. The inscription from Teos involves the citizens of Abdera honouring the citizens of Teos, "who are fathers of our *polis*" (*SEG* 49 [1999], no. 1536; 170–166 BCE).

28. Robert 1949, 74–81; Robert 1969, 316–22 (in some cases, an actual adoption may have taken place); Nollé and Schindler 1991, 71; van Bremen 1996, 167–69; Jones 1989.

29. Van Bremen 1996, 68, and her appendix 3, pp. 348–57.

Table: Evidence for "daughters," "sons," "mothers," and "fathers" of civic and official organizations (including the πόλις, δῆμος, γερουσία, and νέοι)

(Organized alphabetically by city or region under each title)	
Daughter	*SEG* 37 (1987), no. 1099bis (Amorion; second-third cent. CE); *IGR* III 90 (Ankyra; second cent. CE), 191 (Ankyra; mid-second cent. CE); *MAMA* VIII 455, 514–17a-b (Aphrodisias; second-third cent. CE); *IEph* 234, 235, 239, 424, 424a, 1601e (late first-early second cent. CE); *SEG* 36 (1986), no. 1241 (Epiphaneia; third cent. CE); Robert 1969, 319–20 (Herakleia Lynkestis; first-second cent. CE); *ICarie* 63–64 (Herakleia Salbake; 60 CE); *IGR* IV 908 (Kibyra; second cent. CE); *IPerge* 117–18, 120–21, 122–25 (time of Trajan and Hadrian); *ISelge* 20 (third cent. CE); *SEG* 43 (1993), no. 955 (Sagalassos; ca. 120 CE); *IG* V.1 116, 593 (Sparta; late second and third cent. CE); *IStratonikeia* 171, 183, 185–87 (late first cent. CE), 214 (first cent. CE), 227 (second cent. CE), 235 (time of Hadrian), 237 (time of Hadrian), 327 (imperial), 707 (time of Hadrian); *TAM* V 976 (Thyatira; first cent. CE).
Son	*SEG* 45 (1995), no. 738 (Beroia, Macedonia; first-second cent. CE); *SIG*[3] 813 A and B (Delphi; first cent. CE); *IGLAM* 53 (Erythrai); *SEG* 45 (1995), no. 765 (Herakleia Lynkestis, Macedonia; imperial period); *BE* (1951) 204, no. 236 (Kition); *SIG*[3] 804 (Kos; 54 CE); *SEG* 44 (1994), no. 695 (Kos; first cent. CE); Robert 1969, 309–11 (Lesbos); *SIG*[3] 854 (Macedonia); Hepding 1907, 327–29, nos. 59–60 (Pergamon); *OGIS* 470.10 (Sardians); *TAM* III 14, 16, 21, 87, 98, 105, 122, 123 (Termessos; second -third cent. CE); *SEG* 44 (1994), no. 1110 (Panemoteichos; ca. 240–270 CE); *IPerge* 56 (81–84 CE); *SEG* 43 (1993), nos. 950 and 952 (Sagalassos; 120 CE); Pouilloux and Dunant 1954–58, no. 238 (first-second cent. CE); *IG* XII.8 525 (Thasos).
Mother	*IGR* III 191 (Ankyra; mid-second cent. CE); *MAMA* VIII 492b (Aphrodisias; first cent. CE); *IG* V.1 499, 587, 589, 597, 608 (Sparta; early third cent. CE); *IKilikiaBM* I 27 (early third cent. CE); Naour 1977, 265–71, no.1 (Tlos; mid-second cent. CE); *SEG* 43 (1993), no. 954 (Sagalassos; ca. 120 CE); *ISelge* 15–17 (early third cent. CE); *TAM* III 57, 58 (Termessos; early third cent. CE); *IG* XII.8 388, 389 (Thasos; early third cent. CE).
Father	Hagel and Tomaschitz 1998, 42 (Antiocheia epi Krago 21) and 130–31 (Iotape 23a); *SEG* 39 (1989), no. 1055, line 18 (Neapolis; 194 CE); *SEG* 49 (1999), no. 1536 (Teos; 170–166 BCE); *TAM* III 83 (Termessos; first cent. CE); Pouilloux and Dunant 1954–58, no. 192 (first cent. BCE–first cent. CE); *IG* XII.8 458, 533 (Thasos).
Foster-father	See Robert 1949, 74–81 (examples from Amastris, Athens, Chersonesos, Histria, Metropolis, Pericharaxis, Selge, Synnada); cf. Dio of Prusa *Or.* 48.
Foster-child or nursling	*IErythrai* 63 (ca. 240 CE; cf. *SEG* 39 [1989], no. 1240; Jones 1989, 194–97).

as such placed in familial and "affectionate" relationships with the city and its constituent political bodies."[30]

Although the titles were conferred as a way of honouring an influential person, in almost all cases the person so honoured also clearly served some functioning role in the cults or institutions of the cities that honoured them. In fact, sometimes it is clear that it is *because* they made some contributions or provided services as a functionary or leader that they were honoured by being called "mother," "father," "daughter," or "son." So the distinction between honorary title and functional role can be blurry.

On many occasions it is the most important civic bodies, the council (βουλή) and/or the people (δῆμος), who honour a benefactor and mention such titles. Yet this way of expressing positive relations with benefactors and leaders was quite common among other groups and organizations in the Greek East,[31] including gymnastic organizations and unofficial associations. Thus organizations of elders (γεραιοί or γερουσία) at Perge, at Erythrai, and on Thasos in the first to third centuries each honoured benefactors as either "son," "daughter," or "mother" of the group (*IPerge* 121; *IGLAM* 53; *IG* XII.8 388–89, 525). On several occasions, a gymnastic organization of youths (νέοι) at Pergamon honoured Gaius Julius Maximus—a military official, civic president (πρύτανις), and priest of Apollo—as "their own son" (τὸν ἑαυτῶν υἱόν)."[32] Along similar lines, H. W. Pleket reconstructs an inscription from Magnesia on the Maeander River which may refer to a young benefactor as the "son of the friends of the revered ones" (ὑὸς [*sic*] τῶν φι[λοσ]ε[βάστω]ν), involving an association devoted to the members of the imperial family as gods.[33]

In light of this widespread practice in Greek cities and despite scholarly neglect of the subject, then, it is not surprising that similar uses of parental metaphors are found within less official associations of various kinds in eastern parts of the empire. The evidence spans Greek-speaking communities across the Mediterranean, especially in the East, and clearly begins as early as the first century CE. Here I approach the materials on a geographical, rather than chronological, basis, clearly indicating dates (when known) along the way.

There are several examples of such paternal or maternal terminology from Greece, sometimes in reference to important religious functionaries. In the Piraeus (port city to Athens) there was an organization in honour of Syrian deities and the Great Mother whose leadership included a priest, a priestess, a "horse," and a "father of the orgeonic synod" (*SIG*³ 1111 = *IG* III 1280a, esp. line 15; ca. 200–211 CE). The "father" is listed alongside these other functional roles without any suggestion that this is merely an honorific title. In connection with Syria, it is worth mentioning the "father of the association" (κοίνου) that set up a monument near Berytos (*IGR* III 1080). The membership list of a "company" devoted to Dionysos at Thessalonica in Macedonia (second or third century) includes several functionaries (both men and women), including a chief initiate (ἀρχιμύστης), alongside the "mother of the company" (σπεῖρας), which may also be a functional position (rather than simply honorific) in this case (*SEG* 49 [1999], no. 814).

30. Van Bremen 1996, 169.

31. See, for instance, Cormack 1943, 39–44 (involving a "son" of the provincial assembly of Macedonia) and *TAM* III 57 (involving a civic tribe).

32. Hepding 1907, 327–29, nos. 59–60.

33. Pleket 1958, 7–8, regarding *IMagnMai* 119 (late second or third century CE).

Most extant Greek evidence of "fathers" and "mothers" in associations happens to come from Greek cities in the provinces just north of Greece and Asia Minor around the Black Sea. One of the earliest examples of this use of "father" for a benefactor of an association, not known to Poland, dates to about 12–15 CE and reflects "Asian" and Greek (not western) influence in important respects. This inscription from Callatis (in Thracia) involves the "society members" (θιασεῖται) passing a decree in honour of Ariston, who is called "father," as well as "benefactor" of the society and founder of the city (πατρὸς ἐὼν εὐεργέτα καὶ κτίστα τᾶς πό| λιος καὶ φιλοτείμου τοῦ θιάσου).[34] The members of this association devoted to Dionysos crown Ariston for his benefactions and virtues in his relations with the citizens of the city and for his goodwill and love of honour toward the "society" during the time of "the foreign Dionysia" (τῶν ξενικῶν Διονυσίων; line 40). This is very likely among the instances of Dionysiac associations founded by Greek-speaking immigrants from Asia Minor who settled in the cities of Thracia and the Danube (sometimes explicitly calling themselves an association "of Asians"), as M. P. Nilsson also observes.[35] So we should beware of attributing instances of "father" language within associations to western influence and of assuming that such usage was a late development.

Another later instance from this region involves a "company" (σπεῖρα) of Dionysos worshipers in nearby Histria. Here the group is also designated as "those gathered around" (οἱ περὶ) their "father," Achilleus son of Achillas, their priest, and their hierophant in a way that suggests that all three were also members with functional roles within the group (*IGLSkythia* I 99; 218–222 CE).[36] The same man was also the "father" of what seems to be a different group called the "hymn-singing elders (ὑμνῳδοὶ πρεσβύτε|ροι) gathered around the great god Dionysos" (*IGLSkythia* I 100, lines 4–5, 10–11). If this was not enough, he was also the "father" of a third association, this one devoted to the Great Mother at Tomis. There he is listed between a priest and a chief tree-bearer (ἀρχιδενδροφόρος), both figures with functional roles in cultic activities of the group (*IGLSkythia* II 83). I return to further instances of such plural affiliations and identities in chapter 7.

The use of parental language for benefactors and leaders is not limited to Dionysiac groups, then. A board of temple-wardens (νεωκόροι) devoted to Saviour Asklepios in Pautalia, Thracia (southwest of Serdica), refers to the leader of the group simply as "the father."[37] At Serdica in Thracia, an all-female "sacred association" (δοῦμος) of initiates of the Great Mother (Cybele) calls one of its prominent members, likely a leader, "mother of the tree-bearers" (*CCCA* VI 342; ca. 200 CE).[38] Similarly, a mixed association of tree-bearers associated with this goddess at Tomis includes among its leaders both a "mother" and a "father"

---

34. *IGLSkythia* III 44 = Sauciuc-Sâveanu 1924, 139–144, no. 2, lines 5–6 (also see Avram 2002, 69–80).

35. See Edson 1948, 154–58; Nilsson 1957, 50–55; Harland 2003a, 36. Another inscription from Callatis likewise involves a group of "society members" and mentions that one member, at least, was from Ephesos (*IGLSkythia* III 35 = Sauciuc-Sâveanu 1924, 126–39, no. 1, line 22). For other associations of "Asians," see *BE* (1952) 160–61, no. 100 (Dionysopolis); *IGBulg* 480 (Montana); *IPerinthos* 56 = *IGR* I 787 (196–198 CE); *IGLSkythia* I 99, 199 (Histria, Moesia); *IGBulg* 1517 (Cillae, Thracia; 241–244 CE); *IG* X.2 309, 480 and Edson 1948, 154–58, no. 1.

36. Cf. *IKilikiaBM* I 34; *TAM* III 910; *IPontEux* IV 207–212.

37. Kalinka 1906, 157–58, no. 177.

38. Also published, with discussion, in Tacheva-Hitova 1983, 116–19, no. 101.

(namely, the Achilleus mentioned above).[39] Both western and "Asian" (Phrygian-Greek) elements can be seen in these groups devoted to the Great Mother as, on the one hand, they are clearly based on the Romanized version of the cult of the Magna Mater focused on the March festival. On the other hand, some of these same groups use distinctively Phrygian–Greek terminology for associations, especially "sacred δοῦμος."[40] It is worth mentioning that instances of the titles *mater* and *pater* (in Latin) in the worship of Cybele from the city of Rome itself are all significantly later (primarily from the late fourth century and on).[41]

As I mentioned in the previous chapter, there are numerous examples of "father of the synod" in associations of the Bosporus region in the first centuries. The case of Panticapaion, among the oldest of the Greek settlements of the region, provides us with at least thirty-three extant Greek inscriptions that involve associations of society members or synod members (θιασῖται, συνοδεῖται; all but two are epitaphs).[42] In at least eight of these inscriptions, an association happens to mention that one of its leaders was known as the "father of the synod" or simply "father," alongside other standard functionaries such as the priest (ἱερεύς), the "gathering leader" (συναγωγός), the "lover-of-what-is-good" (φιλάγαθος), and others.[43] The consistency of the appearance of the "father" position in various groups and the inclusion of the "fathers" alongside others who are clearly functionaries who perform duties are suggestive of an active leadership role for the fathers here, rather than mere honorifics. Other fictive family language, including the use of "brothers" for members, sometimes accompanies the use of father for leaders in these groups of the Bosporus, as I discussed in the previous chapter.

The use of parental language is also attested for associations in Egypt or in groups of Greek-speaking immigrants from Egypt elsewhere in the empire. Some of these involve devotees of gods with mysteries. One inscription from Rome involves a group founded by Greek-speaking immigrants from Alexandria devoted to Sarapis (*IGUR* 77 = *SIRIS* 384; 146 CE). This "sacred company (τάξις) of the Paianistai" devoted to "Zeus Helios, the great Sarapis, and the revered (σέβαστοι) gods" honours Embe, who is called both "prophet" and "father of the company." The use of the term prophet here strongly suggests an active role for this "father" within the group.

Turning to Egypt proper, in a partially damaged third-century CE papyrus from Oxyrhynchos, a man pronounces an oath pertaining to initiation into mysteries, making mention of both the leader of the group, "father Sarapion," and his fellow-initiates, the "brothers," perhaps "mystical brothers" as I discussed in the previous chapter. In connection with mysteries, it is worth mentioning Apuleius's novel, in which the character Lucius, upon initiation in the mysteries of Isis (set at Cenchreae in Greece), refers to the priest as his "parent"

39. *IGLSkythia* II 83 = *IGR* I 614 = Tacheva-Hitova 1983, 93–95, no. 48, lines 14 and 16 (200–201 CE). Cf. Tacheva-Hitova 1983, 77–78, no. 13 (late second cent. CE); *CCCA* VI 454; (late second cent. or early third cent. CE).

40. For δοῦμος as a group self-designation, see *TAM* V 179, 449, 470a, 483a, 536 (Saittai and vicinity); Buresch 1898, 58–62; *SEG* 42 (1992), no. 625 (Thessalonica); Neumann 1999, 345–53; Neumann 2002.

41. See *CCCA* III 233–36, 241b–43, 246, 263, 283–84, 334.

42. See *CIRB* 75–108; cf. Ustinova 1999, 196–97.

43. *CIRB* 77 (second-third cent. CE), 96 (second cent. CE), 98 (214 CE), 99 (221 CE), 100, 103 (third cent. CE), 104 (third cent. CE), 105 (third cent. CE).

(*parens*).[44] Similarly, worshipers of the Syrian Ba'al as Jupiter Dolichenus at Rome (on the Aventine) reflect such terminology, with priests titled "father of the candidates" (*pater candidatorum*) and fellow initiates calling one another "brothers" (*fratres*) in the second and third centuries.[45] Also quite well known are the associations of soldiers devoted to Mithras in the second and following centuries, in which the seventh stage of initiation was "father" (*pater*) or "father of the mysteries" (*pater sacrorum*).[46] It is important to note, however, that with Jupiter Dolichenus and Mithras we are indeed witnessing largely Roman phenomena, and almost all instances of fictive familial terminology are in Latin for these two gods.

"Papa" as a Functionary

Another metaphorical use of parental or nurturing language in associations is a more intimate form of address that eventually also found a place within Christianity ("papa" = pope). The more colloquial and affectionate term "papa" or "daddy" (πάππας/ἄππας in Greek and variants) was used of religious functionaries within some associations, particularly in Asia Minor, as Karl Buresch noted long ago.[47] In the early second century, a group of initiates devoted to Dionysos met in a "sacred house" in the vicinity of Magnesia on the Maeander River. This group included in its membership two men called "papa" (ἄππας) or foster-father of Dionysos (the role often taken on by Silenos in mythology), alongside a chief initiate, priestess, nurse (ὑπότροφος), and hierophant, a revealer of the sacred objects (*IMagnMai* 117). The photo in figure 10 pictures Dionysos as a baby being cared for by the fatherly Silenos. Other members of the group may well have addressed these men using this affective term.

A second-century inscription from a village north of Hierapolis in Phrygia involves the villagers of Thiounta honouring a "brotherhood," φράτρα. This was a common, indigenous term for a cultic association in Phrygia, Lydia, and Mysia (not to be confused with civic organizations called φρατρία).[48] Within this group at Thiounta, one of the functionaries apparently held the title of "papa."[49] Similarly, a grave from the vicinity of Gölde, near Saittai, mentions "Apollonios the friend and Julianos the papa" (line 29) among those who honour the young deceased priest, Lucius. These two persons appear towards the end of a

44. *Met.* 11.25; cf. 11.21. Also see the commentary by Griffiths 1975, 278, 292.

45. Cf. Hörig und Schwertheim 1987, nos. 274, 373, 375, 376, 381 (second-third cent. CE). Cf. Bömer, 1981 [1958–1963], 176–78; Ebel 2004, 205–7.

46. Cf. *CIL* III 3384, 3415, 3959, 4041; *CIMRM* 623–24; Tertullian *Apol.* 8.

47. Buresch 1898, 130–31.

48. For examples of this type of association (devoted to gods such as Men, the Great Mother, and Asklepios), see *IPhrygR* 506 (Akmoneia); Pleket 1970, 61–74, no. 4 (Almoura village near Teira); *IPhrygR* 64 (town near Hierapolis); Pleket 1958, no. 4 (Ilion; first cent. CE); *TAM* V 762, 806, and 1148 (towns near Thyatira); *IGLAM* 1724d (town near Kyme); *TAM* V 451 and 470a (Maionia near Saittai; 28–29 CE and 96 CE); *IGR* IV 548 (Orkistos); *MAMA* IV 230 (Tymandos); Artemidoros, *Oneirokritika* 4.44; 5.82. Cf. *PLond* 2710 = Roberts, Skeat, and Nock 1936, lines 14–15 (Egypt; first cent. BCE). Cf. Seyfarth 1955.

49. Buresch (1898, 130–131) convincingly challenges Ramsay's view that this is a proper name (Appas) and argues that this is far more likely the title of a cultic functionary in this case. Both Robert (1978, 494) and Josef Keil (in *TAM* V) agree with Buresch.

Figure 10. Statue of Silenos caring for the baby Dionysos, now in the Louvre

list and not along with *actual* family members and close relations that appear in the opening lines. This suggests the possibility of the deceased's membership in an association of "friends" (φίλοι) headed by a "papa," as Buresch also points out (*TAM* V 432; 214/215 CE).

Other instances of "papa" do not necessarily involve unofficial associations, yet further confirm the use of the term for functionaries in cultic contexts. A second or third century inscription from Tarsus in Cilicia (*IGR* III 883) involves a professional association (devoted to Demeter) that honours a Roman consul, describing him as director of public works, Ciliciarch, gymnasium-leader, and also "papa" (παπειν). Louis Robert shows that the latter term refers to an "indigenous priestly title."[50] In light of such evidence, D. Feissel seems right in arguing that a first-century inscription from Dorla in southern Lykaonia (north of Lamos) that mentions "Philtatos, the most blessed papa," likely refers to a Greco-Roman cultic functionary, not a Christian priest, as Gertrud Laminger-Pascher too readily assumes.[51]

50. Robert 1978, 492–94, no. 510; cf. Robert 1949, 197–205; Robert 1987, 50–51.

51. Laminger-Pascher 1992, no. 408. If this is a Christian inscription, it would be among the earliest examples of such. For Feissel's view, which corrects Laminger-Pascher, see *BE* (1993) 771 or, briefly, *SEG* 42 (1992), no. 1247.

What is indeed a clear Christian case of the use of "papa" for the leader of a congregation comes from a letter that likely dates to sometime between 264 and 282 CE (*PAmherst* I 3a, with photo in vol. II, plate 25).[52] In it, a certain Christian merchant, then at Rome, writes to his fellow-workers at Arsinoe in the Fayum region of Egypt, who are termed "brothers." He writes to these fellow-workers and fellow-Christians concerning their need to make payment for the shipment of goods either to Primitinos (the shipper) or by way of Maximos, the "papa" (πάπας) of the congregation at Alexandria.[53] We are witnessing similar uses of fictive kinship to express relationships or hierarchies within associations.

The Meanings of Parental Metaphors

In order to understand the potential meanings of parental metaphors, it is important to note the common juxtaposition of parental (primarily paternal) responsibilities and leadership in the civic setting within literature of the classical, Hellenistic, and Roman periods.[54] When authors from Aristotle on discuss the building blocks of society, they stress the household as the basic unit of society, suggesting that good management of the household would mean good management of the city (*polis*). And when they discuss household management, the father's rule over the household is often taken as an analogy for leadership in society more broadly. The household is, in many ways, a microcosm of society or, as expressed by Philo of Alexandria, "a house is a city compressed into small dimensions, and household management may be called a kind of state management" (*Jos.* 38). So comparisons worked both ways. Actual parental leadership was a model for leadership and beneficence in the civic setting and, conversely, leadership or benefaction in civic contexts and associations could be expressed in terms of parental activity.

Often, inscriptions give us only momentary glimpses of social life, so it is difficult to assess the meanings that would be attached to the metaphorical use of parental language in associations and synagogues, as we also saw in the previous chapter regarding sibling language.[55] Mere passing mention of a "mother" or "father" of a group on an inscription tells us little about how these figures were viewed within the group (in cases where they were members and leaders), or about what social relations and obligations accompanied the use of such fictive familial terminology. Still, something can be said about the potential meanings of parental metaphors within associations and synagogues in light of what we know about "family values" from first- and second-century literary sources, such as Plutarch, Hierocles, and Philo of Alexandria.

First of all, the use of fictive parental terms is consistently related to issues of honour and hierarchy. We have seen that for Greek philosophers such as Plutarch there is a hierarchy of honour that characterizes familial relations. Brothers come before friends, but nature and law "have assigned to parents, after gods, first and greatest honor," and "there is

52. For text, translation, and discussion, see Deissmann 1995 [1927], 205–13.

53. On the Christian use of "papa," see Deissmann 1995 [1927], 216–21, esp. p. 219 note 2.

54. On household management see, for instance, Balch 1981.

55. For a discussion of family metaphors generally in the Roman West, see Lassen 1997, 103–20.

nothing which men do that is more acceptable to gods than with goodwill and zeal to repay favours to those who bore them up" (*De frat. amor.* 479F).[56] Hierocles also speaks of parents as "our greatest benefactors, supplying us with the most important things" (Hierocles *On Duties* 4.25.53).[57] Similarly, the Hellenistic-Judean philosopher Philo outlines the nature of the parent–child relation, grouping the role of parent with other socially superior positions, including the benefactor: "Now parents are assigned a place in the higher of these two orders, for they are seniors and instructors and benefactors and rulers and masters; sons and daughters are placed in the lower order, for they are juniors and learners and recipients of benefits and subjects and servants" (*Spec. leg.* 2.226–27).[58] In choosing to call a benefactor or leader of the group a mother or father, then, members of an association, as metaphorical sons or daughters, were putting that figure on a par with the most honoured persons in society, second only to the gods (or God) from this sort of perspective. Association members were also to some extent reaffirming their own lower position in social hierarchies, along with their piety and gratitude to those higher in the social system.[59]

Second, the use of parental metaphors could also be associated with affection, goodwill, and protection. This would have implications for a sense of belonging within the group in cases where a "mother" or "father" was a member or leader. In his treatise *On Affection for Offspring*, for instance, Plutarch stresses how parents, by nature, show great affection (φιλοστοργία) for children, protecting and caring for the well-being of their offspring as a hen cares for its brood.[60] Conversely, the expectation was that children would reciprocate or "repay beneficence" by providing or caring for their parents, at least in older age (cf. Hierocles *On Duties* 4.25.53). This would have metaphorical significance for those who were "adopted" as "son" or "daughter" with a city or group acting as parent. On a larger scale, the vocabulary of goodwill and affection which Plutarch and others associate with family relations was also very common within the system of benefaction and honours that characterized social relations in the cities of the Greco-Roman world, and parental metaphors are part of this picture.

Conclusion

Greek inscriptions point to the relative importance of fictive parental and familial language in cities of the Greek East at the beginning of the common era. This is also the case with associations specifically. If there was cultural influence at work between East and West, it seems that, initially, the early Greek practice impacted later Roman developments, not the other way around. In many respects, this is an important framework for understanding the adoption, continued use, and contemporary interpretation of the titles "mother of the

56. Cf. Hierocles *On Duties* 4.25.53.

57. Trans. Malherbe 1986, 91–93.

58. Cf. Philo *Dec.* 165–67; Balch 1981, 52–56.

59. Cf. Hierocles *On Duties* 4.25.53.

60. On the epigraphic use of φιλοστοργία ("affection" or "heartfelt love," as G. H. R. Horsley puts it) among family members and in relation to benefactors see Robert 1965, 38–42 and Horsley in *NewDocs* II 80, III 11, and IV 33.

synagogue" and "father of the synagogue" within Greek-speaking Judean diaspora contexts. Because of the happenstance nature of archeological materials, such titles begin to appear in the surviving Judean epigraphic record only in the second century in Macedonia.

In cases where we do possess enough information, it seems that the titles "father" and "mother" could be used in reference to those who actually belonged to the association in question and who served some leadership role there. It is noteworthy that Hemelrijk argues a similar point regarding the active membership and functional roles of "mothers" of the *collegia* in Italy and Latin-speaking provinces.[61] So although in the Judean cases we often lack the sort of information necessary to show that such figures served functional roles, the analogy of the associations suggests that this would be highly likely in at least some instances. Furthermore, the fact that parental titles in associations could be used of both function and honour or, perhaps better stated, as a way of honouring those who provided their services or performed duties, suggests that the functionary versus honorary debate concerning the fathers and mothers of the synagogues may be somewhat misguided.[62] In many cases, the line between the benefactor or patron and the functionary could be blurry, even non-existent. In recent years, it has also been amply noted that leadership in many unofficial settings, including associations, synagogues, and congregations, for instance, naturally emerged out of benefaction. Benefactors that could afford to make material contributions (such as a meeting place) could naturally take on functional leadership roles within a given group or association.[63] These observations notwithstanding the fact that in a few cases parental titles may have been used of more remote benefactors who were not ever members or leaders of the group in question. Nonetheless, we should not assume that this was the norm.

The use of parental metaphors or titles as means of identification among both associations and Judean synagogues places these groups solidly within the social, cultural, and civic landscape of the Greek-speaking Mediterranean. Both share this means of expressing honour, hierarchy, positive relation, and belonging within small-group settings. This practice can be understood as one among the ways in which certain Judean groups reflected their social milieu and signaled, whether intentionally or not, their belonging within a broader cultural context. In the next chapter, we will examine other ways in which such ethnic associations such as the Judeans could both find a home within a society of settlement and continue to identify themselves with the cultural practices of the homeland.

---

61. Hemelrijk 2008, 140–41.

62. Similar debates take place in connection with parental titles in *collegia* of the West (see, most recently, Perry 1999, 178–92, and Liu 2004, 320–21). Perry convincingly argues that, in many cases, the use of familial terminology is internal to the group and "indicates something more than a formal patron-client relationship" (Perry 1999, 189). Also see Hemelrijk 2008, who emphasizes the internal participation of "mothers" of the *collegia*.

63. Cf. White 1997; Rajak and Noy 1993, 75–93; Harland 2003a, 31–33.

Part 3

Identity and Acculturation among Judeans and Other Ethnic Associations

5

Other Diasporas

Immigrants, Ethnic Identities, and Acculturation

Introduction

Judeans (Jews) are by far the most studied of immigrants or resettled ethnic groups in the ancient Mediterranean world. Yet there is growing recognition among scholars that gatherings of Judeans abroad should be placed within the framework of other, less-studied immigrant or cultural minority groups—groups that are also worthy of study in their own rights. Thus Martin Goodman opens a recent anthology by posing the question: How different were Judeans from other peoples in the Greco-Roman world? He briefly posits that "the oddities of the Jews . . . were no greater than that of the many other distinctive ethnic groups, such as Idumaeans, Celts, or Numidians."[1] Jack Lightstone's overview of diaspora Judaism assumes that we should approach Judeans as just one among many ethnic groups.[2] The title of Shaye J. D. Cohen and Ernest Frerichs's edited volume, *Diasporas in Antiquity* (1993), is promising but does not fully deliver in terms of the study of migrant diasporas beyond that of the Judeans.

Moreover, Goodman and others correctly point to the importance of comparative studies for our understanding of the identities of individual Judeans and Judean groups abroad. Yet research into other ethnically based associations remains to be done before the comparative enterprise can proceed with success. Our inscriptional evidence for Judeans abroad, most recently gathered in collections such as *Jewish Inscriptions of Western Europe* (3 volumes), *Jewish Inscriptions of Graeco-Roman Egypt*, and *Inscriptiones Judaicae Orientis* (3 volumes), needs to be placed, in the long run, alongside our materials for other immigrants and associations.[3]

Moreover, few scholars analyze evidence for other associations of persons from a

---

1. Goodman 1998, 4.

2. Lightstone 2007, ch. 25.

3. Horbury and Noy 1992; Noy 1993–95; Noy, Panayotov, and Bloedhorn 2004; Noy and Bloedhorn 2004.

common geographical origin, associations whose existence depended on a shared sense of ethnic identity. Some exceptions to this include George La Piana's rather early work of 1927 on "foreigners" in the city of Rome itself, which touches on both Judeans and associations.[4] Some decades later, L. Ruggini's study (1959) of immigrants from the East in Italy placed Judeans within a comparative perspective, but the article was not concerned with social or cultural questions.[5] More recently, David Noy's excellent study (2000) delves more fully into the world of immigrants in the city of Rome specifically, and he usefully employs insights from the social sciences to analyze the evidence, particularly regarding individual immigrants.

While these studies provide insights into life among immigrants, especially individuals, in Italy, there still remains much work to do on ethnic *associations* in other parts of the ancient Mediterranean with special attention to issues of acculturation and ethnic identities. Despite the vagaries of epigraphic evidence and the scattered nature of our materials both geographically and chronologically, the social historian can nonetheless begin to observe certain recurring aspects of life among immigrant associations and draw some tentative conclusions regarding processes of acculturation in the world of Judeans and Christians.

Alongside the need for group-focussed studies beyond Italy is a particular problem regarding how some scholars employ issues of migration and the formation of associations within broader theories about the Hellenistic and Roman ages. Until recently, it was quite common for certain scholars to speak of these eras as periods of social, political, and cultural decline, along with the decline of the *polis*, or Greek city-state. Such theories of decline among influential scholars, such as M. P. Nilsson and E. R. Dodds, were sometimes accompanied by portraits of a general atmosphere of widespread rootlessness among populations. This picture of rootless populations was illustrated by, among other things, increases in migration and the supposed negative experiences of immigrants specifically.[6]

To provide a recent example, Robert Turcan speaks of a "troubled and drifting world" in which "uprooted people," particularly immigrants, lived "on the fringes of a disintegrating world" in both the Hellenistic and Roman eras.[7] Within this framework, Turcan and others oversimplify the picture of associations, including but not limited to ethnically based associations. Such scholars speak of associations primarily as compensatory phenomena which aimed to ameliorate this supposed situation of widespread detachment.[8]

This theory has rightly been criticized.[9] Peter Brown aptly observes that "many modern accounts of religious evolution of the Roman world place great emphasis on the malaise of life in great cities in Hellenistic and Roman times. Yet the loneliness of the great city and the rapid deculturation of immigrants from traditionalist areas are modern ills: they should not be overworked as explanatory devices for the society we are studying. We can be far from certain that [as Dodds asserts] "such loneliness must have been felt by millions. . . ."'[10]

4. La Piana 1927, 183–403.

5. Ruggini 1959, 186–308.

6. See the more extensive discussion of scholarship in Harland 2006, 21–35.

7. Turcan 1996 [1989], 16–17.

8. Although not expressing this overall theory, P. M. Fraser (1977, 60) seems to think of associations as functioning to compensate for negative immigrant experiences.

9. See Harland 2006, 21–35.

10. Brown 1978, 2–3, citing Dodds 1965, 137.

As the material discussed in this chapter shows, an image of widespread rootlessness among immigrant and other populations does not fit well with evidence concerning real-life associations, at least in the case of many Syrian and Judean associations.

Despite the meagre nature of the evidence, a number of cases point to the probability that associations based on shared ethnic identity were a further means by which immigrants were in some significant ways firmly planted not only in traditions of the homeland but also, to various degrees, in their societies of settlement. Yet we should not begin by presupposing widespread rootlessness or relative deprivation and then reduce associations to merely compensatory phenomena within some overall theory.

This case study draws attention to evidence regarding both acculturation and continued attachments to the homeland. This chapter serves to counter notions of widespread rootlessness among immigrants while also laying the groundwork for the comparative study of ethnically based associations, including Judean gatherings. This dual purpose can be accomplished by delving into the evidence for associations of immigrants from the eastern coast of the Mediterranean sea—known as the Levant—especially associations consisting of members formerly from Syria, Phoenicia, and Samaria, regions neighbouring Judea or Galilee. Samaritans (who designate themselves "Israelites" on Delos) are included here not because they necessarily share some particular cultic affinity with Phoenicians, but because they too neighboured Judea and because contemporaries sometimes included Samaritan towns either within the Phoenician sphere or within the Judean sphere.

Several useful studies address evidence regarding immigrants from Syria or Phoenicia, especially individual immigrants or families at places such as Delos and Rhodes, as we shall see. Yet none focuses attention on dynamics of acculturation and the maintenance of ethnic identities in *associations* of Syrians or Phoenicians specifically. Rather than merely theorizing about the general experience of immigrant groups, this case study begins to fill a gap in our knowledge by looking at the concrete ways in which particular Syrian associations adapted to their place of settlement while simultaneously maintaining contacts with their place of origin. This provides a fitting framework for comparison with acculturation and identity among Judean groups in the cities of the Mediterranean world.

Insights from the Social Sciences

Some terminological clarifications that build on my discussion in the introduction are in order before proceeding with the discussion of both immigrant associations in this chapter and Judeans at Hierapolis in the next chapter. As I explained in the introduction, "ethnic identity" is used to refer to a group's shared sense of who they are based on certain experiences and notions of connection deriving from *group members' perceptions* of common geographical, cultural, and ancestral origins. From the (Tajfelian) social identity theorists' perspective, ethnic identity is that aspect of the self-concept that derives from belonging to an ethnic or cultural minority group.[11] These two ways of understanding the term—pertaining to the collective and to the individual—are not mutually exclusive, and both will inform the discussion at certain points.

---

11. Cf. Phinney 1990.

Closely related to studies of identity, particularly ethnic identity, are social-scientific studies of migration and acculturation. There are three main concepts from this area of study that may assist in the analysis of immigrants' processes of negotiation in the place of settlement and in our discussion of Judean families at Hierapolis in the next chapter. The approach I take here is informed primarily by the sociological work of Milton Yinger and by the social-psychological work of John W. Berry, among others.[12] Recent studies of Christians and Judeans successfully employ similar theories of assimilation or acculturation, including David Balch's (1986) study of 1 Peter's household code and John M. G. Barclay's study (1996) of Judeans in the diaspora.

The first important concept is *cultural assimilation*, or *acculturation*, which refers to cultural interchanges and processes of boundary negotiation associated with encounters between two different groups (or individual members of two groups) with distinctive cultural traits.[13] Acculturation can involve the selection, adoption, and adaptation of a variety of cultural elements including language, values, and other cultural conventions that compose the lifestyle and worldview of a particular cultural group. This process is selective and transformative, with some cultural elements being adopted and adapted and other elements being rejected.[14]

It is important to emphasize that in my theoretical framework here acculturation can progress significantly without the disintegration of a group's boundaries in relation to a larger cultural entity. Cultural adaptation is often a twofold process entailing the "maintenance of cultural integrity as well as the movement to become an integral part of a larger societal framework," as Berry puts it.[15] Another related concept is "biculturalism," which is used by Berry and others to refer to a dynamic process involving the individual's participation in both the minority culture and the majority culture.[16] A fully "biculture" individual would be a person who is both highly *en*culturated into the minority group culture and highly acculturated to the majority culture. In the study of modern diasporas (a subfield of migration studies), a similar term is "hybridity," which implies the combination of ethnic or other identities in a particular individual or group. As Stuart Hall puts it, the "diaspora experience . . . is defined, not by essence or purity, but by the recognition of a necessary heterogeneity and diversity; by a conception of 'identity' which lives with and through, not despite, difference; by *hybridity*."[17]

A second main concept is *structural assimilation*, which in Yinger's use refers to degrees of social integration or participation within informal social networks (e.g., neighbourhoods, associations) or formal structures (e.g., political, legal, social, or economic institutions) of a given host society.[18] It is important to note the importance of evaluating different types of social interactions and their implications regarding levels of assimilation. Thus, for instance, a case of intermarriage between individuals of two different cultural groups

12. Berry 1980; Berry 1997, 5–34; Yinger 1981, 249–64; Phinney 1990; Marger 1991, 117–20; Yinger 1994.

13. Cf. Yinger 1981, 249.

14. Cf. Barnett 1954, 973–1002.

15. Berry 1980, 13.

16. Birman 1994.

17. Hall, as cited and discussed in Brubaker 2005, 6.

18. Yinger 1981, 254; cf. Marger 1991, 118; Elise 1995, 275.

would correspond to higher degrees of assimilation than would occasional contacts with someone of a different cultural group within social networks. The difficulty is that there is rarely sufficient evidence from antiquity to assess things such as intermarriage among two different cultural groups or the consistency of contacts between certain people or groups. We do, however, gain occasional glimpses into social interactions, such as contacts between benefactors and beneficiaries, which we need to consider carefully in order to assess what cultural weight we can attach to a particular case of networking.

Third, concepts such as *dissimilation* and *cultural maintenance* provide balance to assessments of social and cultural interchanges between cultural groups, emphasizing variety in outcomes.[19] Milton Gordon (1964) and other assimilationist scholars of previous generations have been rightly criticized for assuming that "all groups are willing to drop their own cultures and take on that of the core," as Sharon Elise points out.[20] I would suggest that such problematic approaches were more in line with societies that, politically, maintained a "melting-pot" view (e.g., the United States) rather than a "mosaic" view (e.g., Canada) of migration and cultural diversity. In a study of recent trends in immigration and history writing, Ewa Morawska states the following:

> The assimilation paradigm in its classical version has been abandoned on account of its excessive simplicity, and the "ethnicity-forever" approach that replaced it [in the 1970s] is also passing away. The sociology and historiography of immigration may now be on their way toward formulating a more encompassing conceptual framework for the interpretation of adaptation . . . that would integrate both the assimilation and ethnicization processes.[21]

Regarding ancient cases, Jane Webster's study (2001) of problems with previous approaches to "Romanization" (a specific form of acculturation to Roman ways) makes similar observations concerning the need for a balanced approach that pays attention to the *blending* of cultural values and practices.[22] This is a balance I attempt to accomplish in my analysis of ancient ethnic associations and cultural minority groups in this chapter and following chapters.

Recent theories of assimilation and acculturation carefully avoid the tendency to assume complete assimilation or the disappearance of group boundaries as the inevitable outcome. Instead, there is an emphasis on varieties in levels of assimilation, as well as attention to certain processes that work to counter assimilation in particular ways and at various points in a certain group's (or individual's) history.[23] Individual members of a cultural minority group (such as Syrians, Judeans, and Christians) are, in an ongoing way, being *en*culturated into the particular ways of that group while also interacting with the majority culture outside of that group.

Yinger, in particular, uses the term "dissimilation" to refer to the way in which

19. Brettell and Hollifield (eds.) 2000.
20. Elise 1995, 277.
21. Morawska 1990, 218.
22. She adapts the concept of "Creolization" as a replacement for "Romanization."
23. Cf. Brettel and Hollifield 2000.

particular minority or ethnic groups make conscious efforts to reassert and strengthen specific group-society differences: "powerful assimilative forces are matched by renewed attention to socio-cultural differences."[24] Moreover, he states:

> In spite of identity shifts and high rates of intermarriage in some settings and extensive acculturation and integration in almost all settings, some subcultural group lines will remain sharp and some individuals will think first of their ethnic group when they appraise their own identities.[25]

As Jean S. Phinney's survey of literature (from 1972–1990) also notes, Berry and others view this as a two-dimensional process involving both the culture of the minority group and the culture of the majority, with four main combinations in outcome: (1) strong identification with both groups, which entails integration or biculturalism; (2) an exclusive identification with the majority culture, which entails assimilation; (3) identification with only the minority group, which entails separation; and, (4) identification with neither group, which entails marginality.[26] Berry explains the first option, "integration," which entails the "maintenance of cultural integrity as well as the movement to become an integral part of a larger societal framework."[27]

Associations of Immigrants from the Levant

Because of the partial and circumstantial nature of archeological evidence for Syrian and other groups in antiquity, we do not have full access to the same sorts of data as the modern social scientist. Nonetheless, the following discussion of Syrian associations assesses particular historical cases by forming and addressing questions regarding the following indicators of acculturation, structural assimilation, and cultural maintenance: expressions of ethnic identities and ties to the homeland; linguistic practices; rituals, including the gods honoured; other social or cultural conventions or practices (indicative of some level of acculturation and/or cultural maintenance); and, social interactions or network connections with individuals, groups, or institutions (indicative of some level of structural assimilation in the society of settlement or continued attachments to the homeland).

The approach here is to look at specific historical cases on a geographical and chronological basis while also asking broader questions regarding the extent and nature of connections between particular Syrian groups, on the one hand, and individuals, groups, institutions, and cultural traditions, on the other. This will allow observations regarding the historical specifics of particular cases while also drawing attention to common factors and patterns that are observable from one Syrian group to another at different locales and in different periods.

Gathering together in an ongoing association to honour the god(s) and to socialize

24. Yinger 1981, 257; see pp. 257–61.

25. Yinger 1981, 261.

26. See Phinney 1990, 501–2.

27. Berry 1980, 13; cf. Berry 1997.

Figure 11. Monument from Delos dedicated "to Apollo and the Italian gods" by the Italian Hermaists, Apolloniasts, and Poseidoniasts, now in the British Museum (GIBM *IV 963 =* IDelosChoix *157; 74 BCE)*

with friends was a tendency shared by migrants from various parts of the Mediterranean. Some should be mentioned before turning to Syrians specifically. On the island of Delos alone, for instance, there were communities of Italians, Samaritans, Judeans, Egyptians, and both Tyrians and Berytians from Syria, amidst others in the Hellenistic era.[28] The monument in figure 11, for instance, involves three different associations of Italian merchants—Hermes-, Apollo-, and Poseidon-devotees—who list their twelve leaders and dedicate the monument "to Apollo and the Italian gods" in the so-called Italian marketplace (*GIBM* IV 963 = *IDelosChoix* 157; 74 BCE). On the island of Rhodes there were associations of immigrants from Herakleia in Pontus, from Perge in Pamphylia, and from nearby Crete.[29] Particularly visible in Asia Minor were the many associations or "settlements" (κατοικοῦντες) of Roman and Italian businessmen at places like Ephesos, Kibyra, Assos, and Apameia.[30]

Those who emigrated from Asia Minor also gathered together in associations based on common geographic origins. There are inscriptions attesting to Milesians settled on Amorgos island and inhabitants from Pontic Herakleia in Scythia.[31] Among the many groups of settlers from Asia Minor at Rome were the *collegium* of Nysaians, the guild of Ephesian

28. Cf. Bruneau 1970, 457–96, 585–630.

29. *IG* XII.1 158 (cf. *IG* XII.1 963; *IGLSkythia* III 72); *ILindos* 391 and 392 (time of Augustus); *IGR* IV 1128 (time of Augustus).

30. See, for instance, Hatzfeld 1919; Müller and Hasenohr 2002.

31. Milesians: *IG* XII.7 395–410 (second-third cent. CE). Herakleians: *IGLSkythia* III 72 = *SEG* 24 (1974), no. 1037 (second cent. CE).

shippers and merchants, and a group of Sardians, to name just a few.[32] Other associations proudly identified cultural attachments to Asia Minor by labeling themselves a "society" or "company" (*thiasos* or *speira*) of "Asians," as with a number of groups in Macedonia, Thracia, Moesia, and Dacia.[33]

Turning to settlers in Syria itself, at Sidon there were associations of soldiers formed based on common geographic origins, including the "corporate bodies" of Kaunians, Termessians, and Pinarians.[34] The formation of such associations based on common geographic origins is itself an important sign of identification with one's homeland and its cultural ways, as well as an indicator of cultural maintenance and the expression of ethnic identities in the society of settlement.

Evidence for Phoenician or Syrian associations abroad in particular is quite considerable in comparison with other settlers that formed associations based on geographic origins or ethnic identity.[35] Although the inscriptions and buildings associated with these Syrian associations provide only momentary glimpses into issues of identity and acculturation, there are common threads running through the surviving materials. There are indications of both identification with the cultural life of the homeland and notable contacts within local social and cultural life in the place of settlement in a number of cases. These contacts can be interpreted in terms of some degree of integration, even though the chronological and geographical distribution of the evidence makes it difficult to determine what degree. We simply do not have sufficient evidence of Syrian immigrants from one time and place to permit a thick description of a particular group's levels of cultural and structural assimilation. What we do have is evidence from various locales over time which can nonetheless provide indications regarding recurring trends among Syrian immigrants.

Attica and the Piraeus in the Hellenistic Era

Some of the earliest evidence for associations of Syrians or Phoenicians comes from the Piraeus, port city to Athens. There we find worship of numerous foreign deities, as well as the establishment of associations based on common geographical origins and a shared sense of ethnic identity, including Egyptians, Carians, Phrygians, and Thracians.[36] Figure 12 depicts a group of athletic youths approaching the goddess Bendis, the patron deity of Thracians settled in the Piraeus. Evidence for Athenian control over the entrance of foreign cults is particularly strong for the fifth and fourth centuries, when "foreigners" were

---

32. Clerc 1885, 124–31, side B, lines 35–45 (the other side of this monument contains *IEph* 22), on which also see Lüderitz 1994, 194–95, with trans. in note 36; *IGUR* 26 and 86. Also see La Piana 1927, 183–403 and Noy 2000.

33. *IG* X.2 309, 480 (second-third cent. CE); *IPerinthos* 56 = *IGR* I 787 (196–198 CE); *BE* 65 (1952), 160, no. 100 (Dionysopolis); *IGBulg* 480 (Montana; second cent. CE). See Edson 1948, 154–58, who discusses numerous cases.

34. Macridy 1904 = Mendel 1912–14, vol. 1 nos. 102–8.

35. On associations or brotherhoods (esp. *hbr* and *mrzh*) in Phoenicia or Syria itself, see Teixidor 1964, 77–82; Eissfeldt 1968, 285–95, 264–70; Milik 1972, 141–281; Teixidor 1977, 6. Walter Ameling (1990, 189–99) lists a number of cases involving diaspora Syrian associations.

36. Garland 1987, 107–9, and pp. 101–38 generally. On associations and foreigners at Athens in the Hellenistic period, see Parker 1996, 333–42; Vestergaard 2000, 81–109.

Figure 12. Marble relief of Bendis, goddess of the Thracians, along with several athletic youths; relief now in the British Museum (ca. 400–375 BCE)

required to submit a formal request for permission to establish a sanctuary for their patron deities. As Robert Garland points out, however, it seems that by the late fourth century this control had lessened, as none of the cults established in the following era makes mention of such a special privilege.[37]

Alongside these groups in the Piraeus are Phoenicians, who are attested as early as the third century BCE in two bilingual inscriptions.[38] One is an epitaph erected for a deceased daughter by a chief-priest of the god Nergal, an Assyrian deity that had been imported into Sidon at an early stage.[39] The more important inscription here includes, in Greek, honours and crowns granted by an "association (κοινόν) of Sidonians" for a fellow Sidonian (*IG* II^2 2946).[40] Above this is a more extensive Phoenician inscription that dates to the third century BCE. In it, Greek-style honours are granted to one Shama'baal, president of the group in charge of the temple. The inscription happens to mention the funds belonging to "god Baal of Sidon," likely the patron deity of the association. The title Baal, "Lord," could of course apply to a number of Canaanite or Phoenician deities. Yet here it most likely refers

37. Garland 1987, 107–109.

38. For Phoenician inscriptions from Cyprus and Greece generally, see *CIS* I 10–96, 114–21. Two later inscriptions attest to the existence of a "priestess of the Syrian deity" at the Piraeus (*IG* II^2 1337, 2361; 95/94 BCE and third cent. CE). The former involves honours offered by an association.

39. See Garland 1987, 237, no. 100; Eiselen 1907, 130.

40. Most recently republished and discussed by Ameling 1990.

to the god Eshmun, who was particularly prominent at Sidon and associated with Astarte, who possessed primary place as patron deity of that city.[41] Regarding Sidonians in Attica, there is an earlier honorary inscription from Athens itself in which the Athenian people honour Apollonides, a Sidonian, on the request of a group of merchants and shippers (*IG* II² 343; ca. 332/331 BCE).[42]

These early cases involving those identified as Sidonian in Attica demonstrate dynamics of identity and acculturation at play. On the one hand, there is the continued use of Phoenician language and the worship of Sidon's native deity. On the other, there are indications of adaptation to local, Greek cultural practices, most notably the use of Greek and the engagement in Greek-style honorary activities (either of which may also have begun before migration with the Hellenization of Syria under the Seleucids beginning in the third century BCE). The fact that a presumably wealthy Sidonian at nearby Athens was honoured not only by a group of merchants but also by the civic institution of the people of Athens shows that such wealthy Syrian immigrants could maintain important links with civic institutions in at least an occasional manner. Shortly, I discuss other cases in which Syrian associations maintained relations either with institutions in the society of settlement, pointing towards some degree of structural assimilation, or with the institutions of the homeland, suggesting areas of cultural maintenance.

Islands of the Aegean, Including Delos, in the Hellenistic Era

Individual immigrants from Syria gathered together in associations on numerous Greek islands of the Aegean, particularly on islands with an importance for shipping and trade networks. Many Phoenicians are attested on the island of Cos, for instance. A fourth century BCE inscription in both Greek and Phoenician involves the identification of the Phoenician goddess Astarte (Ashtoreth) with Aphrodite.[43] And there was at least one "society" (θίασος) in the first century BCE with a Syrian connection worshipping Astarte and Zeus Soter, likely identified with a Lord such as Baal Shamem ("Lord of Heaven").[44] Although worshipped throughout Syria and beyond, Astarte was particularly prominent at Sidon and Tyre.[45]

---

41. Cf. Lucian *Syr. D.*, 4. The suggestion that Astarte held prominent position in relation to Eshmun is based on the practice of Sidonian kings, who called themselves priests of Astarte rather than of Eshmun (see Eiselen 1907, 127–128).

42. Individual Syrians (both men and women) in Athens and Attica:

Berytians: *IG* II² 1008, 1011, 1960, 8407, 8408, 9484

Sidonians: *IG* II² 960, 1043, 2314, 2316, 8358, 8388, 10265–86; *CIS* 115, 116, 119.

Tyrians: *IG* II² 342, 3147, 4540, 4698, 10468–73, 11415.

Sidonian settlements or communities are also attested elsewhere in the Hellenistic era, including Judea and Idumea in the second century BCE. See Isaac 1991, 132–44; Josephus *Ant.* 12.258–264a; *OGIS* 593.

43. See Bonnet 1996, 87–88.

44. *IKos* 165a (Tyrian), 194 (Sidonian) 341 (Tyrian); *IKosSegre* ED 54 (Tyrian), EV 150 (Phoenician). *IRhodM* 496; see Bonnet 1988, 378.

45. Bonnet 1996, 30–44.

An association of Syrians is also attested on Syme island (east of Cos and north of Rhodes). This honorary inscription of the late first century BCE involves honours for an Idumean "resident foreigner" (μετοίκος), who had been a benefactor of several associations and neighbourhoods. Among these groups was an association of Syrians devoted to Adonis, Aphrodite, and Asklepios (*IG* XII.3 6).[46] Here again there is involvement by an expatriot from the Levant (from Idumea) within local networks. Yet in this case there are even clearer signs of multiple connections in the place of settlement, involving links with other immigrants (Syrians) and with native populations (the districts).

There are higher concentrations of evidence regarding immigrant groups at locales with the highest strategic importance for trade routes, including the island of Delos. The majority of our evidence here comes from the second century BCE, especially the period when Delos was under direct rule by Athens (166–88 BCE) and came to be considered a free port by the ascendant Roman power.[47]

There has been a notable amount of research on immigrants settled on Delos in the Hellenistic period, particularly individual immigrants, Italians, merchants, and bankers.[48] Philippe Bruneau's extensive study examines the cults of Delos generally, including those devoted to "foreign" deities.[49] Marie-Françoise Baslez's article begins to scratch the surface of our present concern by arguing that ethnically based associations were mechanisms by which eastern immigrants maintained attachments to their own traditions while also integrating into a new society. Yet Baslez's study is quite general and is primarily focused on issues of organization and on distinguishing associations of "oriental" foreigners from the more typical Greek associations.[50] Here I begin with associations of Phoenicians or Syrians of the second century before turning to Samaritans.

Beyond the numerous individual expatriots from Syria attested on Delos, there is significant evidence for Syrian or Phoenician cults and associations.[51] One monument involves a dedication by three men to "Heracles and Hauronas, the gods who dwell in Jamnia," on behalf of their brothers, relatives, and "the citizens with them."[52] These are Phoenician Jamnians who had ongoing contact with one another (perhaps in an association) in

46. Literary evidence points to the prominence of the cult of Adonis just outside of Berytos at Aphaca. Lucian mentions the rites of Adonis in connection with "Aphrodite" at Byblos, for instance, so it is possible that these Syrians on Syme island have some connection to either Berytos or Byblos. Teixidor 1977, 35; Lucian *Syr. D.*, 6.

47. Cf. Binder 1999, 297.

48. E.g., Bruneau 1970, 585–620; Rauh 1993; Le Dinahet 1997a, 617–66; Le Dinahet 1997b, 325–36; Le Dinahet 2001, 103–23; Müller and Hasenohr 2002. The evidence for Italian or Roman immigrant associations includes *IDelos* 1730–71; *IDelosChoix* 86, 95–98, 105, 107, 116, 131, 138, 144–45, 157, 164.

49. Bruneau 1970, 457–96.

50. Baslez 1988, 147.

51. Individual Syrians on Delos:

Berytians: *IDelos* 2034, 2182, 2593, 2598, 2599, 2633

Sidonians: *IDelos* 1925, 2091a-b, 2100, 2101, 2314, 2396, 2549, 2598, 2612, 2879

Tyrians: *IDelos* 1925, 1937, 2005, 2130, 2366, 2598, 2599, 2612, 2616; *IG* XI.4 777.

52. *IDelos* 2308; cf. 2309. See Isaac 1991, 139; Bruneau 1970, 475.

connection with the sanctuary of these deities on Delos.[53] The gods in question can be identified with the Canaanite or Phoenician deities Melqart (here Herakles) and Hauron (also transliterated Horon).[54] A similar Phoenician connection is evident in dedications by a banker from Ascalon for the "Ascalonian Poseidon" and for the "Palestinian Heavenly Astarte" (around 100 BCE).[55]

A number of inscriptions from the final decades of the second century BCE attest to a cult of Syrian deities on Delos centered around the worship of a goddess called variously the "Pure Goddess" (Ἁγνὴ θεά), "Pure Aphrodite," "Pure Aphrodite, the Syrian Goddess," or "Atargatis, Pure Goddess."[56] This is the same Atargatis that I discussed in connection with processions in chapter 2. Several of these monuments indicate there was a board of functionaries or "therapeutists" (θ̣εραπ̣ε̣υταί) connected with this cult of Syrian deities, and that the cult was led by a priest and priestess.

Some of these priests and priestesses were from Syrian Hierapolis (Bambyke) itself, home of the famous temple of Atargatis as described by Lucian of Samosata.[57] Some though not all of the inscriptions dedicated to this goddess involve expatriots from Syrian towns, including Laodicea, Antioch, and Hierapolis.[58] Among these dedications are those to the deities Atargatis and Hadad, who also seem to have been coupled at the sanctuary of Hierapolis in the homeland. A number of these same inscriptions add a third honoree, "Asklepios," who is likely to be identified with Eshmun, according to H. Seyrig.[59]

More importantly with respect to associations, in one inscription there is mention of the "society members" (θιασῖται) of the "Pure Goddess" under the direction of a "synagogue leader" (συναγωγεύς). A subsequent discovery of another inscription, which likely relates to the same group, now clarifies that this was an ethnic group called "the association of Syrian society members (τὸ κοινὸν τῶν θιασιτῶ[ν] | τῶν Σύρων)."[60] It is worth noting that a similar society of the "ancestral gods" (τῶι κοινῶι τοῦ θιάσου τῶν πατρίω[ν]) devoted to Phoenician deities, including Atargatis, existed on the island of Astypalaia in the third or second century BCE (*IG* XII.3 178). Syrians abroad continued to carefully honour the deities of their native land, and they did so, in part, by forming associations.

Further materials from Delos pertain to Tyrians and, more extensively, Berytians from

---

53. Because of the mixed population of Jamnia, the site is sometimes described as a Phoenician city (Philo of Byblos) and sometimes as a Judean or Palestinian city (see Isaac 1991, 138).

54. Bruneau 1970, 475; Isaac 1991, 139–40. On the god Hauron, see Albright 1936, 1–12; Albright 1941, 7–12.

55. *IDelos* 1719–21; cf. *IDelos* 2305; Bruneau 1970, 474.

56. On this cult, see *IDelos* 2220–2304; Siebert 1968, 359–74; Bruneau 1970, 466–73. For dedicators who label her the "Syrian goddess" or identify the Pure Goddess as Atargatis see, for instance, *IDelos* 2245, 2251, 2252, 2275 (all ca. 100 BCE), 2294, 2299, 2300.

57. E.g., *IDelos* 2257, 2258, 2283.

58. Syrian expatriots are from Antioch (*IDelos* 2224, 2263, 2285), Hierapolis (nos. 2226, 2261), and Laodicea (nos. 2259, 2262, 2264, 2270). Among the other dedicants are an Alexandrian (no. 2225), an Athenian (nos. 2251–52), a man from Marathon (no. 2245), and several Romans (nos. 2255, 2266, 2269).

59. *IDelos* 2224, 2248, 2261, 2264; Lucian *Syr. D.* See Seyrig 1960, 246–47; Bruneau 1970, 470–71.

60. For the inscription with commentary, see Siebert 1968.

Phoenicia. In both cases, it is the economic importance of Delos that brought these immigrants. The "synod of Tyrian merchants and shippers" at Delos is known from just one inscription, dating to 153/152 BCE (*IDelos* 1519 = *IDelosChoix* 85).[61] The inscription recounts the outcome of a particular assembly (ἐκκλησία) of the members of the association, who are also called "society members" (θιασῖται). This group honoured a fellow member, named Patron, who had shown his goodwill by leading an embassy to Athens, which at this point controlled Delos. The embassy had been successful in gaining permission for the group to build its own sanctuary for "Herakles."

What is particularly significant with respect to the expression of ethnic identity here is the patron deity of this association, which suggests important connections with the homeland of Tyre. The merchants' identification of their god Herakles as "founder of the homeland" (ἀρχηγοῦ δὲ τῆς πατρίδος) in line 15 has particular importance here. Corinne Bonnet's study shows the consistency with which Tyrian nationals abroad identified their native deity, Melqart, with Herakles specifically.[62] Primary in this characterization was the notion that the god Melqart was the founder of cities, so the epithet "the founder" (ἀρχηγέτης) often accompanies the identification of Melqart with Herakles. For instance, about the same time these Tyrians on Delos inscribed their honours, two brothers from Tyre who had settled on the Sicilian island of Malta erected a bilingual dedication for "Melqart, Lord of Tyre" (in Phoenician), who is translated as "Herakles the Founder" (in Greek).[63] As Aaron Jed Brody's study shows, both Melqart and a Semitic god identified with "Poseidon" were among the favourite patron deities of Phoenician and Punic sailors and merchants for centuries.[64] The Tyrians on Delos who founded this sanctuary also make mention of a festival in honour of a "Poseidon" (line 40), which brings us to settlers originally from Berytos (Beirut) who were devoted to a "Poseidon."

Evidence for immigrants from Berytos settled on Delos is more substantial than the evidence for Tyrians, including numerous inscriptions. Most of these were found in excavations of the meeting place of the association (*IDelos* 1520, 1772–96, 2325). This group called itself the association (κοινόν) of "Poseidon-worshipping merchants, shippers, and receivers from Berytos." Like the Tyrian guild, this group was active around the middle of the second century BCE. A number of honorary and dedicatory monuments show the continuing importance of the gods of Berytos for these compatriots, as the inscriptions refer to the "ancestral gods" (πατρίοι; *IDelos* 1783, 1785, 1789). The most prevalent native deities on coins from the city of Berytos itself are the deities Poseidon (a Hellenized expression for a Phoenician sea god) and both Eshmun and Astarte (also prevalent at Sidon), so these are among the possibilities for this guild's patron deities.[65] Among the monuments erected by the Berytians on Delos for such gods is the dedication of a meeting place (οἶκος) with "oracles for the ancestral gods" (*IDelos* 1774).

Alongside this sense of cultic attachment to the homeland are indications of adaptation

---

61. A fourth century dedication from Delos involves "sacred shippers" from Tyre, however (*IDelos* 50).

62. Bonnet 1988; cf. Millar 1993, 264–65; Freyne 2001, 185–88.

63. *IG* XIV 600. See Freyne 2001, 185–86; cf. Herodotus *Histories* 2.44.

64. Brody 1998, 22–26, 33–37.

65. On the Phoenician cult of Poseidon see Teixidor 1977, 42–46.

to the cultural landscape of the new home, at least in terms of relations with the powers-that-be and involvements within social networks. On the one hand, there are two inscriptions that concern relations with Athens and its institutions. In one, the association erects a monument "for the people of the Athenians on account of the virtue and goodwill which the people continues to show towards the association" (*IDelos* 1777). Another involves the association's honours for a benefactor named Demokles, likely an Athenian citizen. The monument includes a series of crowns captioned by either "the association" or "the Athenian people" (*IDelos* 1780).

On the other hand, there are signs of interaction with the Italian or Roman mercantile and cultural presence on Delos. Thus, the most extensive inscription pertaining to this Berytian association involves honours for a Roman banker named Marcus Minatius, son of Sextus, around 153 BCE (*IDelos* 1520). Minatius is praised by the association for his contributions in connection with both his financing of the completion of the headquarters and his offering of a special sacrifice and banquets for members. In return, members of the association offer several forms of honour, including the erection of a statue of Minatius in the meeting place and the establishment of special honorary occasions on which to renew their crowning of this benefactor, including a procession with a sacrificial ox. Furthermore, this Roman Minatius himself attends meetings and festivals of the Berytians, along with his own guests. This suggests close connections between these Syrian immigrants and an important Roman merchant on Delos. Some decades later, in about 90 BCE, the same association honoured a Roman benefactor, Gnaius Octavius son of Gnaius, a praetorian provincial governor (*IDelos* 1782).

Perhaps even more important for present purposes is the integration of the goddess Roma (personified Rome) alongside the ancestral gods of Berytos within the cultural life of this group (*IDelos* 1778, 1779). Quite striking is the statue base on which Roma is praised for her positive relations not only with the guild but also with Berytos, the homeland (*IDelos* 1778, lines 1–4). Archeologists excavating the remains of the meeting place have identified three or four shrines in the northwestern section, and there is agreement among scholars that, alongside shrines for Phoenician deities such as Poseidon and Astarte, Roma was assigned a shrine and became integrated within the ritual life of this group, at least by the first half of the first century BCE.[66]

Materials from other parts of the Mediterranean in other periods suggest that, as an immigrant group, the Berytians are not completely unusual in terms of maintaining connections with civic institutions and Roman figures or traditions. In this sense, these indications of assimilation may be indicative of what was going on in other Syrian groups in connection with whom we happen to lack this number of inscriptions.

It is the number and consistency of contacts that stands out in the Berytian case and there are difficulties in assessing to what degree this level of interaction is peculiar or representative. Certain aspects of the Berytians' interactions are characteristic of Delos in the mid-second century, when various individuals and groups vied with one another in seeking some level of recognition in relation to both Athenian and Roman institutions or authori-

66. On the building history see Picard 1920, 263–311; Bruneau 1970, 622–30; Bruneau 1978, 160–90; Meyer 1988, 203–20; Bruneau 1991, 377–88; McLean 1996, 196–205 (who summarizes earlier discussions); Trümper 2002, 265–330.

ties. It should also be noted that the evidence from Delos involves Syrian *merchants* in an economically important centre of the Aegean. These higher levels of involvement in the society of settlement may or may not be consonant with what went on in certain other Syrian associations in this or other locales or periods.

Delos also provides roughly contemporary evidence for another group of expatriots from the Levant, namely "Israelites" or Samaritans, who may or may not have been involved in trade. These inscriptions are particularly important since, to this point, they represent our only evidence for associations of Samaritans in the Hellenistic or early Roman eras. Individual Samaritans are attested in inscriptions from elsewhere, of course, including a Samaritan man who was buried on Rhodes (*IJO* II 11) and several others at Athens or the Piraeus (*IJO* I Ach 35, 36, 37). And there is an interesting case involving a "Samaritan" listed as a member of an ethnically mixed group in the Piraeus, probably a "society" ([οἱ θιασῶ]τα[ι]; *IJO* I Ach 41; fourth or third cent. BCE).

As to the ethnic identities of those labeled "Samaritans," Josephus claims that some Samaritans might identify themselves using the ethnic descriptor of "Sidonians," suggesting a Phoenician connection for some of the population settled in Samaria. However, Josephus also goes on to claim that Samaritans associated with the sanctuary on Mount Gerizim would go so far as to actively identify their god with a Hellenistic deity (Zeus Hellenios; Josephus *Ant.* 12.258–64). Yet a comparable passage in *2 Maccabees* points towards Samaritan hesitancy on precisely such matters, referring to the Samaritans' *refusal* to dedicate their temple on Gerizim to Zeus Xenios ("Protector of Strangers"), along with the Judean refusal to dedicate the Jerusalem temple to Olympian Zeus.[67] So it is difficult to assess what these "Israelites" on Delos would think of themselves in relation to Phoenicians and the cultural landscape of contemporary Hellenistic Syria. What is clear is the continuing attachment to the rites practiced at Gerizim.

Samaritans on Delos are attested in only two inscriptions of the late third or second century BCE. These monuments were found about one hundred meters away from the structure identified as the meeting place of a group of Judeans or Samaritans (GD 80).[68] As in the case of the Tyrians and Berytians on Delos, the Samaritan inscriptions indicate attachments to the cultic life of the homeland. In fact, the group of Samaritans here had incorporated this sense of ethnic and cultic identification within the title of the group itself. The self-designation of the group appears roughly the same in both inscriptions despite the time separation (of between twenty-five and one hundred years) between them, namely, "the Israelites of Delos who contribute to sacred Mount Gerizim" (οἱ ἐν Δήλῳ Ισραελεῖται οἱ ἀ|παρχόμενοι εἰς ἱερὸν Ἀργα|ριζείν). Here attachments to the religious life of Samaria are expressed not only through mention of the holy site. Connections to the homeland are also indicated in the fact that, at least at some point, the group seems to have financially

67. *2 Macc* 6:2. See Isaac 1991, 136–38, 143 n. 45 and Binder 1999, 471. On problems with the anti-Samaritan bias of our sources (including the crucial 2 Kings 17), see Grabbe 1992, 502–7. Grabbe concludes that the Samaritans continued a "conservative Yahwistic cult" and "there is no more evidence of a pagan origin to Samaritan worship than there is to Jewish worship" (Grabbe 1992, 506).

68. Bruneau 1982, 465–504 = *SEG* 37 (1987), no. 809–10 = *NewDocs* VIII 12a-b. See Trümper 2004, 513–98, who likewise leaves open the possibility of Judean or Samaritan identification (cf. Runesson 2001, 185–87). The early presence of Judeans on Delos is suggested by literary evidence: *1 Macc* 15:15–23; Josephus *Ant.* 14.231–32.

supported the ritual activities at Mount Gerizim in a manner comparable to diaspora Judeans' support of the temple in Jerusalem.[69]

The earlier of the two inscriptions (which dates about 250–175 BCE) involves the Israelites honouring one Menippos from Herakleia—along with his descendants—for his contributions to the group (*NewDocs* VIII 12b = *IJO* I Ach 66). The fact that Menippos had arranged to build and dedicate a "prayer house" (προσευχῇ) "in fulfillment of a vow to God" suggests that he too was a devotee of the God worshipped at Gerizim. This draws attention to the complicated and multiple nature of identities. Either Menippos was a gentile who had come to worship the Israelites' God or he was a Samaritan who migrated first to Herakleia before coming to Delos (either to settle or to visit), likely for business purposes. If the latter, then depending on circumstances Menippos might be identified by others—or identify himself—as a Herakleian,[70] a Delian, a Samaritan, or some combination of these identities, as here. I return to the importance of such multiple identities in chapters 6 and 7.

The later honorary inscription (which dates about 150–128 BCE, or possibly as late as 50 BCE) involves the Israelites' crowning Sarapion, son of Jason, from Knossos (*NewDocs* VIII 12a = *IJO* I Ach 67). This man had made some unspecified benefactions to the group. Here there is no indication that this immigrant from the island of Crete is himself a devotee of the God of the Israelites.

Syrian Immigrants in the Roman Empire

In certain ways, the cultural patterns I have been outlining with regard to some Syrian associations in the Hellenistic era continue into Roman times, although we lack substantial evidence for any one locale comparable to Hellenistic Delos. Syrian settlers from Spain in the West to Greek islands in the East still continued to form associations in their place of settlement as a way of expressing their shared sense of ethnic identity.

In some cases we primarily know of the existence of Syrian associations of the Roman era without having any further significant information regarding how they understood their identities. A fragmentary Greek inscription from Malaca (Malaga) in Spain, for instance, mentions merely a "patron and president of the association of Syrians" (*IG* XIV 2540 = *IGR* I 26).[71] So we need to remain aware of the partial and circumstantial nature of epigraphic evidence and to take care in recognizing the tentative nature of any generalizations that can be made regarding levels of assimilation among Syrian immigrant groups.

Still, other monuments of the Roman era do provide further glimpses of involvements within local networks of benefaction. On the Aegean island of Nisyros (located between the islands of Cos and Rhodes), an association of Syrians devoted to "Aphrodite" is among several associations that honoured a prominent citizen of Nisyros (*IG* XII.3 104 = *IGR* IV

69. Cf. Binder 1999, 473–74. The Samaritan temple was destroyed in 128 BCE (Josephus *Ant.* 13.254–56), but rites likely continued afterwards nonetheless.

70. Among the candidates is the island of Herakleia, south of Delos.

71. Hübner's reconstruction suggests the possibility that this is an "association of Syrians an[d Asians]" (see Ameling 1990, 196).

1110). Gnomagoras was not only a soldier in the Roman army but also a civic magistrate, priest of the civic cult of the emperors, and benefactor of the gymnasium. The inscription specifically points out that he supplied oil not only for citizens but also for settlers (τοῖς κατοικοῦσι) and resident foreigners (τοῖς παρεπιδαμεῦσ|ιν). He is praised for how pleasant he has been "towards all of the associations (τοῖς κοινείοις) which are in Nisyros," including the Syrians.

Such evidence of prominent native citizens engaging in at least occasional positive relations with Syrian immigrant associations, which is also attested at various locales in the Hellenistic era, suggests the real-life reception of "foreigners" could go beyond the sort of ethnic stereotypes and derogatory attitudes found in some contemporary literary sources. Benjamin Isaac's survey of xenophobia in Greek and Roman literature shows that "Phoenicians" were often stereotyped as intelligent (in connection with success in trade) but cruel. Those designated "Syrians," along with others of the East, were sometimes viewed as degenerate, servile, or effeminate.[72] We do need to be careful about assuming that negative stereotypes in the literature were somehow normative or consistent in day-to-day life at particular locales.[73] Furthermore, ethnic labeling of oneself or others does "not automatically entail tension between the ethnic groups," as Koen Goudriaan's study of ethnic groups in Greco-Roman Egypt points out.[74] Despite the need for caution in assessing the social implications of such stereotypes in the literature, I return in the next section to the relevance of such stereotypes for the maintenance and development of ethnic identities.

Turning to Syrians settled in Italy in the Roman imperial era, there are two significant pieces of information pertaining to a group of Tyrians at Puteoli, port city of Rome. First, a fragmentary inscription dating to 79 CE reveals that some Tyrians transferred to Puteoli a statue of their native Phoenician deity, here called "Sareptan Helios" (Sarepta was a town between Sidon and Tyre; *OGIS* 594 = *IGR* I 420).

A second, better-preserved monument from about a century later provides a rare glance at some concrete attachments between these immigrant Phoenicians and their homeland of Tyre, "metropolis of Phoenicia" (*OGIS* 595 = *IGR* I 421; 174 CE).[75] The inscription consists of a letter carried by an emissary from the "settlement" of Tyrians at Puteoli (οἱ ἐν Ποτιόλοις κατοικοῦντες) to civic institutions of Tyre concerning the maintenance of the group's "station" or headquarters. The association of traders characterizes the situation thus:

> This station has long been cared for by the Tyrian settlement in Puteoli, who were many and wealthy, but now our number has dwindled to a few, and in paying for sacrifices and the rites of our ancestral gods (τῶν πατρίων ἡμῶν θεῶν) that are established for worship here in temples, we do not have the means to furnish the rent on the station, 250 denarii per year, especially since the payments for the bull

72. Isaac 2004, 324–51.

73. Isaac focuses almost solely on discriminatory ideas rather than the actual treatment of foreigners, but he does acknowledge this limitation of the work (Isaac 2004, 2, 6–7).

74. Goudriaan 1992, 76.

75. See Sosin 1999, 275–85. For earlier discussions, see La Piana 1927, 254–58; D'Arms 1974, 105; Teixidor 1979.

> sacrifice at the games at Puteoli are charged to us in addition. We entreat, therefore, that you provide for the lasting permanence of the station.[76]

As with many of the Syrian associations of the Hellenistic era, concerns to honour the gods of the homeland stand out here at Puteoli, albeit in regard to the expenses involved in maintaining these cults.

The Tyrian settlement had recently fallen on hard times and, as a result of various other expenses, were apparently unable to pay the yearly fee they owed to maintain possession of their headquarters. Integral to the argument of the emissary as presented in the letter were claims of close connections with the homeland and shared social, economic, and cultural interests among compatriots. The request of this group of immigrants was not uncontested, however.

Joshua D. Sosin's analysis of the partially preserved minutes of the civic assembly at Tyre shows how one Philokles may have been attempting a hostile takeover or simply dissolution of the Puteolian station in favour of the station of Tyrians at Rome itself, which is also mentioned in the minutes.[77] Nevertheless, the Tyrian settlers' erection of this monument shows that the council and people of Tyre sided not with Philokles but with the Tyrians of Puteoli. Tyre itself, it seems, took on the cost of maintaining the station at Puteoli, as Sosin argues.[78] Despite debate at home, then, and despite the potential for competition among associations of immigrants from the same homeland, Tyre itself supported the well-being of its citizens abroad, whose attachments to the homeland could be expressed in various ways. The Tyrians' varied identifications with their homeland and its cultural ways suggests that ethnic identity continued to play a key role in internal identifications and in how this group related to others within the society of settlement.

Ethnic Stereotypes and Identity among Cultural Minority Groups

Earlier I noted that evidence for positive social relations between Syrian immigrants and others within the cities—indicative of some level of integration—should caution us against overestimating the impact of negative stereotypes about such cultural minorities, stereotypes that are reflected in literary sources produced by the elites. As usual, the relationship between literary images or rhetoric and social realities as reflected in archeological evidence is a complicated one which is difficult to evaluate, and we should not assume the priority of literary perspectives.

Although we need to avoid exaggerating such negative perceptions, it is nonetheless important here to discuss the significance of such stereotypes when they were expressed and their functions in relation to issues of identity. This is particularly important in relation to issues of dissimilation and cultural maintenance as I explained those concepts earlier. This discussion would apply not only to stereotyping in relation to Syrian ethnic

76. Trans. Sosin 1999, 278, with adaptations.

77. Sosin 1999, 283.

78. Sosin 1999, 281–84.

groups, of course, but also in relation to other cultural minority groups, including Judeans and followers of Jesus. I return to social categorization and stereotypes in chapter 8, which provides a more extensive discussion of accusations of human sacrifice, cannibalism, and sexual impropriety against Judeans and Christians. As many social-identity theorists note, the perceptions of outsiders and processes of labeling do play at least some role in how cultural minority groups or their members define and redefine themselves in relation to other groups.[79]

Here I discuss two important articles on stereotypes and identity, both of which are informed by Henri Tajfel's (1978, 1981, 1982) social identity theory. One, by Louk Hagendoorn (1993), focusses on the functions of stereotypes for the groups doing the evaluation. The other, by Richard Jenkins (1994), draws attention to the role of external categorization (such as that reflected in stereotypes) in processes of identity reformulation for the groups being negatively evaluated by stereotypes.

Hagendoorn explains the function of ethnic stereotypes in terms of their importance for the social identity of the group that is doing the evaluation. Stereotypes are oversimplified sets or configurations of characteristics attributed to members of a particular out-group (outside group) by an in-group (insiders). They involve "generalized knowledge about social categories and thereby implicitly evaluate these categories."[80] Overall, Hagendoorn argues that "[stereotypes] not only evolve from, but also preserve the values of, the in-group by differentiating the in-group from negatively evaluated out-groups."[81]

Hagendoorn's perspective helpfully integrates anthropological, sociological, and social psychological approaches to social or ethnic categorization and negative stereotypes (such as those associated with prejudice, ethnocentrism, and racism). He explains that in anthropology stereotypes are often explained in terms of *cultural misunderstanding*.[82] Members of an in-group evaluate an outside group's customs and activities using insider values and ways of interpreting cultural meaning. When there are differences in practices and in the modes of cultural interpretation between the groups, misunderstandings in the form of stereotypes result. As Hagendoorn points out, although this accurately explains some elements of ethnic categorization and stereotypes, it needs to be supplemented by other theoretical perspectives.

In sociology, negative stereotypes associated with racism are often viewed as *justifications* for "existing differences in influence, power and wealth between the ethnic majority and the minorities."[83] In other words, a Syrian living in Athens may be characterized negatively by certain Athenian citizens in part because this helps to ensure the superior position of those Athenians in maintaining positions of influence.

A third perspective is offered by social psychology. Hagendoorn draws on social-identity theory as developed by Tajfel to explain that stereotypes are a result of the "search for a favourable self-categorization."[84] Stereotypes serve the "cognitive function" of storing

79. Cf. Nazroo and Karlsen 2003, 903–4.
80. Hagendoorn 1993, 33.
81. Hagendoorn 1993, 34.
82. Hagendoorn 1993, 27–28.
83. Hagendoorn 1993, 31.
84. Hagendoorn 1993, 36.

knowledge and experience in a particular configuration in order to facilitate further social categorization. As such stereotypes are developed and called upon, they serve a "value preservation" function for the in-group (e.g., a Roman author's social group) by implicitly evaluating the characteristics of out-groups (e.g., Syrians, Judeans, Christians, "barbarians") using the values and identity of the in-group as the measuring stick. The entire process takes place in such a way that the superiority of the in-group's (e.g., Romans') cultural values and customs are evaluated as superior, those of the out-group (e.g., Syrians or others) as in some way inferior. In other words, the process of categorizing or labelling others (outsiders or the out-group) is, in fact, a process of internal self-definition.

Furthermore, categorizations of various out-groups take place in a hierarchical manner with different out-groups being ranked, so to speak, in relation to the in-group, which maintains the superior position. Hagendoorn emphasizes the importance of these "ethnic hierarchies" that are indicated by social categorizations of ethnic out-groups.

Jenkins's study furthers our understanding of the impact of such stereotypes on the social identity of the negatively evaluated group, in our case the Syrians or Phoenicians. Building on the insights of Fredrik Barth (1969), Jenkins emphasizes the "transactional nature of ethnicity" and points to two main kinds of transactions. First of all, there are processes of internal self-definition whereby members of a group communicate to one another and to outsiders their own sense of who they are.[85] Second, there are external definitions which involve outsiders' social categorizations of the cultural minority group or its members. These external definitions are often pejorative and can entail negative stereotypes, for the reasons already outlined by Hagendoorn. It is worth noting that there are affinities between this twofold, transactional way of explaining identity and Gregory Stone's (1962) concepts of "identity announcements" (a person's communication of who they are) and "identity placements" (categorizations by others) as more recently employed in studying situational identities among immigrants.[86] Jenkins explains this twofold dynamic in this way:

> whereas social groups define themselves, their name(s), their nature(s) and their boundary(s), social categories are identified, defined and delineated by others. Most social collectivities can be characterized as, to some extent, defined in both ways. Each side of the dichotomy is implicated in the other and social identity is the outcome of the conjunction of processes of internal *and* external definition.[87]

Cultural minorities or ethnic groups, or their individual members, such as the Syrians, Samaritans, Judeans, and Christians discussed in this study, may handle external categorizations in a variety of ways. Yet in virtually all cases the external stereotypes play some role in internal self-definition, according to Jenkins and others.

Jenkins explains this process with the concept of "internalization," as "the categorized group is exposed to the terms in which another group defines it and assimilates that cat-

---

85. Jenkins 1994, 198–99.
86. See, for instance, Ajrouch and Kusow 2007.
87. Jenkins 1994, 201.

egorization, in whole or in part, into its own identity."[88] This process of internalization may range from the acceptance of outsiders' categorizations insofar as those categories happen to fit the internal self-definition of the group, to open rejection or resistance to the external definitions. However, even in cases of resistance, Jenkins emphasizes, "the very act of defying categorization, of striving for an autonomy of self-identification, is . . . an effect of being categorized in the first place. The rejected external definition *is* internalized, but paradoxically, as the focus of denial."[89]

I would suggest that similar processes of group identity were at work among immigrant associations in antiquity. These insights regarding social and ethnic identity provide a framework for understanding the potential role of stereotypes regarding Syrians, Phoenicians, Judeans, Jesus-followers, and others. Although Isaac's study of "racism" in antiquity does not fully engage the sort of social-scientific theories outlined here, his discussion of Lucian of Samosata's reactions to stereotypes concerning Syrians is useful for our purposes, particularly since the inscriptions do not supply us with clear evidence of how the stereotypes shaped certain aspects of group self-definition in Syrian associations.[90]

In particular, Isaac points to several passages where Lucian is responding in some way to the stereotypes of outsiders in an ambivalent manner. Here there are clear signs of what Jenkins calls internalization, a process that I discussed in connection with Philo and Josephus in chapter 1 and to which I return in connection with Judeans and Christians in chapter 8. On several occasions, Lucian makes reference to his own identity as a Syrian—a Greek-speaking Syrian, in this case, but a "Syrian" from Samosata nonetheless. Often he adopts the perspective of the (Greek or Roman) outsider who would categorize such a person as a "barbarian" based on perceptions of ethnic identity.

In one particularly noteworthy passage Lucian not only shows an adoption of the external stereotypes (though perhaps tongue in cheek), he also evinces what Hagendoorn calls "ethnic hierarchies" or rankings of ethnic groups. Lucian does this when he compares his own identity as a Syrian "barbarian" to the royal philosopher Anarchasis as a Scythian "barbarian": "Well, my own situation is like that of Anacharsis—and please do not resent my likening myself to a man of regal stature, for he too was a barbarian, and no one could say that we Syrians are inferior to Scythians. It isn't on grounds of royalty that I compare my situation with his, but rather because we are both barbarians" (*Scythian* 9; cf. *Fisherman* 19).[91] The phrase "no one could say that we Syrians are inferior to Scythians" indicates Lucian's perception of widely held notions of ethnic hierarchies within the social categorizations of his Greek and Roman elite readers. Comments by ancient ethnographers such as Herodotus confirm a strongly negative portrayal of Scythian and adjacent peoples.[92] Syrians and Scythians are both barbarians, from Lucian's perspective, but there are inferior and less inferior barbarians. Once again it is the in-group (in this case the Greek or Roman perspective internalized by Lucian) that categorizes various ethnic groups using internal

88. Jenkins 1994, 216.

89. Jenkins 1994, 217.

90. Isaac 2004, 341–45.

91. Trans. Harmon 1913–67 (LCL).

92. See, for instance, the discussion of Scythians in Hartog 1988 [1980] and in Dudko 2001–2002.

values and perceptions as the measuring stick of what is inferior or superior. To some extent, a higher ranking on the ethnic hierarchy for a particular ethnic group is a result of a perception of greater similarities between the in-group's (e.g., Greek-speaking elite Greeks' and Romans') values and those of that other ethnic group (e.g., Syrians) in comparison with still other ethnic groups (e.g., Scythians).

Elsewhere Lucian reflects knowledge of the more specific stereotypes of Phoenicians or Syrians as successful in trade, yet through underhanded means (*Ignorant Book-Collector* 19–20). Here again it seems that Lucian has internalized stereotypes about Syrians as lacking in morals. He does not openly oppose or resist the stereotypes. Still, the overall satirical context here and elsewhere may, as Isaac notes, suggest a more subtle attempt to "parody normal attitudes" rather than accepting them fully as a self-identification.[93] Whether assimilating or resisting, as Jenkins clarifies, some internalization of external categories is often at work in the process of self-identification. Similar dynamics may have been at work among associations of Syrians settled elsewhere in the ancient Mediterranean. This would play a role in the maintenance and development of ethnic identities alongside other areas involving acculturation.

Conclusion

This preliminary investigation into processes of identity construction and assimilation among ethnic associations from just one region of the eastern Mediterranean begins to reveal certain recurring patterns. This is the case despite diversity among specific groups from the Levant and the difficulties associated with assessing materials from such a wide geographical and chronological span. Recurring evidence for involvements in the society of settlement and continued attachments to the homeland speak against notions of a general atmosphere of detachment and rootlessness among immigrant populations in the Hellenistic and Roman eras, at least in a number of cases involving Syrian or Phoenician ethnic groups.

Despite status as "foreigners" and the potential for ethnic stereotypes to influence outsiders' perceptions, it seems that members of these Syrian groups would in certain circumstances identify themselves first and foremost as Syrians, Phoenicians, Sidonians, Tyrians, or Berytians. The multiple, flexible, and circumstantial nature of identities means that this expression of ethnic distinctiveness was by no means incompatible with the creation or maintenance of social ties in the society of settlement. These Syrians could also belong within or interact with other subgroups of that society, such as neighbourhoods, districts, and other guilds or associations.

Although worship of the gods of the homeland within these associations is evident virtually across the board, this could also be accompanied by identifications with, and acculturation to, indigenous, Greek, or Roman deities and customs. Conversely, non-Syrians could come to honour Phoenician deities alongside settlers. This situation was illustrated by non-Syrians attending the sanctuary of the Pure Syrian Goddess on Delos

93. Isaac 2004, 343.

and by the presence of the Roman Minatius and his guests at gatherings of the Berytian association.

Alongside cultural maintenance and acculturation, involvements in social networks in the society of settlement indicate areas of structural assimilation, both informal and formal. Syrian associations' links with local non-Syrian benefactors and, in some cases, with civic institutions or authorities could position a particular group closer to the heart of certain webs of power in the Greek city. Often the meagre state of the evidence does not allow evaluation of differing degrees of engagement from one Syrian group to another. This is further complicated by the fact that a number of cases surveyed here involve Syrian mercantile groups in important economic centres at particular points in time. These cases may or may not be indicative of what was going on in other Syrian associations.

Associations of Syrians and other ethnic groups are worthy of study in their own right. Yet these groups also offer models for comparison with other ethnic groups, including gatherings of Judeans as evidenced by inscriptions. The past few decades have witnessed a considerable shift in approaches to the study of the Judean diaspora. This is particularly the case with respect to questions of how Judeans related to the cultural contexts in which they found themselves. Moreover, this has been a scholarly shift away from characterizing life in the diaspora as a choice between strongly maintaining ethnic identity through separation, on the one hand, and accommodating completely to the surrounding culture, on the other. Instead, recent work by Paul R. Trebilco (1991), John M. G. Barclay (1996), Erich Gruen (1998), Shaye J. D. Cohen (1999), Tessa Rajak (2002), and others stresses variety among Judean gatherings. These scholars also draw attention to the complexities involved in Judeans both maintaining a sense of being Judean (or Jewish) and finding a home for themselves in specific locales throughout the Mediterranean world.

The Syrian associations offer analogies for comparison with Judean gatherings, particularly regarding patterns of cultural maintenance and assimilation. Thus, in both cases there is a consistent concern with honouring the god(s) of the homeland alongside involvements within both formal and informal social networks and structures in the place of settlement, as I discuss at some length in connection with Judeans in the next chapter.[94] Flowing from this, there is also considerable evidence that many Syrian and Judean groups adopted local cultural conventions associated with honours and benefaction.[95]

Judeans and, it seems, Samaritans do stand out from other immigrants from the Levant insofar as cultural maintenance often entailed attention to just one God and this usually excluded identifications of that God with deities honoured by others.[96] Yet this should not be exaggerated to the point of neglecting comparison, for there are also variations among particular Syrian associations and particular Judean groups in the specifics of how a given group engaged in honouring its benefactors, both divine and human.

---

94. Trebilco 1991; Rajak 2002; Harland 2003a, 213–38.

95. See Harland 2003a, 213–38.

96. Javier Teixidor's notion of the rise of the "supreme god" and "a trend towards monotheism" in Near Eastern and Syrian religion in the Greco-Roman era remains largely unsubstantiated and is not borne out in the case of Syrian or Phoenician associations abroad, it seems. See Teixidor 1977, esp. pp. 13–17; Teixidor 1979.

This preliminary case study suggests that further investigations into immigrant associations of various sorts may provide a more complete picture of where diverse gatherings of Judeans fit on the landscape of cultural minorities in the ancient Mediterranean world. Such comparative investigations may allow us to assess the ways in which particular ethnic associations were involved in the social and cultural traditions of their homelands and of their societies of settlement. Now I turn to a case study of Judeans at Hierapolis in Asia Minor, which further fleshes out some of these dynamics of identity and acculturation.

6

Interaction and Integration

Judean Families and Guilds at Hierapolis

Introduction

Previous chapters on family language and on immigrants show how recent studies of the diaspora are beginning to address regional variations among Judean (Jewish) gatherings and are giving attention to the relationships between these groups and the societies in which they found themselves.[1] Social-scientific approaches to migration and ethnicity can assist us in evaluating issues of identity and the relationships between minority groups, such as Judeans and Christians, and majority cultural groups.

The graves of those who had passed on can also further understanding of such cultural interactions among the living.[2] Leonard Victor Rutgers's study of Judean burials at Rome (second–fourth centuries), for instance, demonstrates this well and finds that instead "of living in splendid isolation or longing to assimilate, the Roman Jews . . . appear as actively and, above all, as self-consciously responding to developments in contemporary non-Jewish society."[3] Careful attention to burial customs in other parts of the empire can offer a new vantage point on questions of acculturation and identity among ethnic groups such as Judean gatherings.

This chapter explores cultural interactions with special attention to Judean epitaphs from Phrygian Hierapolis in Asia Minor in the second and third centuries.[4] After discussing the evidence for Judean associations at this locale, I focus my attention on the recently republished family grave of P. Aelius Glykon and Aurelia Amia (ca. 200 CE).[5] This grave

1. On Asia Minor, see, for example, Trebilco 1991, 167–85; Barclay 1996, 259–81, 320–35; Goodman 1998; Rajak 2002, 335–54, 355–72, 447–62; Harland 2003a.

2. On Judean burial in the diaspora, see, for example, van der Horst 1991; Williams 1994b, 165–82; Strubbe 1994 and 1997; Noy 1998, 75–89.

3. Rutgers 1994, 263.

4. Miranda 1999a, 109–55 (= *IHierapMir*); cf. *SEG* 49 (1999), no. 1814–36.

5. This inscription was recently republished (1992–93) with corrections by Tullia Ritti (formerly *CIJ* 777). I was able to examine the monument (in 2004) thanks to permission from Prof. Francesco D'Andria (director of the Italian Archeological Mission at Hierapolis) and the staff at the Hierapolis museum.

illustrates well the complexity of social and ethnic identities and the potential for interactions between Judeans and their neighbours in the cities of Asia Minor. It involves Glykon's bequest to local guilds of purple-dyers and carpet-weavers in order to regularly perform ceremonies at this family grave on both Judean (Passover and Pentecost) and Roman (Kalends) holidays.

Few scholars fully explore this family grave within the framework of burial practices among Judeans in Hierapolis and in relation to association life in Asia Minor. My approach here has significant implications for issues of ethnic and social identities among Judeans and others in a Greek city (*polis*). In looking at this case, I also work to resolve an ongoing debate regarding the composition of the guilds of purple-dyers and carpet-weavers mentioned in the inscription. While several scholars make known their differing views on the composition or ethnic identity of these groups (Judean, non-Judean, or mixed), few sufficiently investigate this issue in relation to other evidence for the purple-dyers at Hierapolis.

This case also offers opportunity to further examine dynamics of assimilation and cultural maintenance among cultural minority groups in the diaspora, building on the discussion in the previous chapter. Moreover, there are both indications of acculturation to the society of settlement and identifications with the cultural ways of the ancestral land among Judeans at Hierapolis.

Judeans at Hierapolis

Recent discoveries of graves have added to our knowledge of Judeans at Hierapolis. Elena Miranda's publication (1999) includes a total of twenty-three Judean grave inscriptions (out of a total of over 360 epitaphs from Hierapolis published by others). This includes thirteen new Judean inscriptions beyond those previously published by Walther Judeich (in 1898) and by Fabrizio A. Pennacchietti (in 1966–67).[6] Most Judean inscriptions (*IHierapMir* 1–21) were found in the northern necropolis, which was extended from the time of Antoninus Pius (138–161 CE); monuments in that necropolis date mostly from the middle of the second to the third century CE.[7] Two Judean tombs were found elsewhere in the area of the eastern burial grounds (*IHierapMir* 22–23).

The Judean inscriptions range in date from the second half of the second century to the third or fourth centuries based on onomastics, the use of names (especially the presence of Aurelius-related names), and on the forms of the lettering in relation to other dated inscriptions. It is difficult to date them with any more certainty, as none expressly supplies a date, and rarely are named figures known from other sources.

The majority of these Judean inscriptions (eighteen) involves an individual identified as "Judean" (Ἰουδαῖος) making provisions for the burial of him- or herself and family members, without explicit reference to a Judean community or gathering. Almost all of these

6. Those previously published are: *IHierapMir* 5 = *IHierapJ* 69 = *CIJ* 776; no. 6 = *IHierapPenn* 14; no. 8 = *IHierapJ* 72 = *CIJ* 778; no. 9 = *IHierapJ* 97; no. 10 = *IHierapJ* 104; no. 11 = *IHierapPenn* 30; no. 16 = *IHierapJ* 212 = *IGR* IV 834 = *CIJ* 775; no. 20 = *IHierapPenn* 46; no. 22 = *IHierapJ* 295; and no. 23 = *IHierapJ* 342 = *CIJ* 777. *IHierapJ* = Judeich 1898, 67–181. *IHierapPenn* = Pennacchietti 1966–67, 287–328. All twenty-three are also now included, with commentary, in Ameling 2004 (= *IJO* II 187–209).

7. Pennacchietti 1966–67, 293–94; cf. Ritti 1992–93, 42.

Figure 13. Grave "of the Judeans" from Hierapolis, with a menorah and lion (IHierapMir *6* = IJO *II 187)*

identify the owners of the grave and surrounding area and list other family members that were to be buried there. Several go further in following standard forms of burial inscriptions in this part of Asia Minor by warning that no one else should be buried there and by providing for fines in the event that anyone attempted to do so.[8] Fines were most often payable to local civic institutions, including the "most sacred treasury" (ταμῖον) of Hierapolis or, in one case, the civic elders' organization (γερουσίᾳ).[9] Several of those that specify fines also mention that a copy of the inscription was placed in the civic archives (ἀρχεῖον),[10] which was another important formal institution in the Greek cities of Asia Minor. The act of placing a copy of these stipulations in the civic archives is suggestive of the formal legal procedures that would be followed in the event that provisions for care and protection of the grave were violated in some way.[11] These institutional factors point to areas of structural assimilation that I return to below.

Several inscriptions (three, or perhaps four, of the twenty-three) use terminology suggestive of an association of Judeans, providing the only available information about gatherings of Judeans at Hierapolis and the self-designations that these groups used (*IHierapMir* 5, 6, 14b, 16). The epitaph pictured in figure 13, which is inscribed with the plural possessive

8. *IHierapMir* 1, 2, 4, 7, 8, 9, 10, 18, 19, 21.

9. *IHierapMir* 1 (γερουσία), 2, 4, 7, 8, 9, 10a, 18, 19, 21.

10. *IHierapMir* 1, 2, 5, 8, 10, 18, 19, 21.

11. On grave violation (τυμβωρυχία) in Asia Minor, see *IHierapJ* 275, 312 (cf. *IIasos* 376, 392). *IHierapJ* 195, which also involves guilds, more directly indicates this legal context in providing a reward (of 800 denaria) for the "one prosecuting the case" for violation. See also Gerner 1941, 230–75, esp. pp. 250–58, and Strubbe 1991, 48 n. 9. For Judean references to the crime, see *IJO* II 146 (Thyatira), 174 (Akmoneia).

Figure 14. Grave mentioning the "people of the Judeans" at Hierapolis (IHierapMir 5 = IJO *II 206)*

"(Grave) of the Judeans" (Ἰουδέων [*sic*]), alongside the depiction of a menorah and lion, likely refers to a *family* of Judeans, rather than an association (*IHierapMir* 6 = *IJO* II 187; cf. *IHierapMir* 10). Still, there are three other definite references to associations of Judeans.

Interestingly enough, each of the three epitaphs uses different self-designations for the groups in question. In one, a woman and a man explicitly identify themselves as belonging to the "people (τῷ λαῷ) of the Judeans" and make fines for violation of their grave payable to this group (see photo in figure 14):

> The grave and the burial ground beneath it together with the base and the place belong to Aurelia Glykonis, daughter of Ammianos, and her husband Marcus Aurelius Alexander Theophilos, also known as Aphelias, of the Judeans. They will be buried in it, but it is not lawful for anyone else to be buried in it. If this is violated, the guilty one will pay a fine of 1000 denaria to the people of the Judeans (τῷ λαῷ | τῶν Ἰουδαίων).[12] A copy of this inscription was placed in the archives (*IHierapMir* 5 = *IJO* II 206; late second or third cent. CE).[13]

12. The designation λαός for a group is quite well attested in epigraphy for Judeans (cf. *CIJ* 662, 699–702, 704–8, 720; *ISmyrna* 296; *DFSJ* 31 = *IJO* II 26).

13. Trans. mine. Here and in the following inscriptions I follow Miranda's readings of the text. Miranda (1999a) suggests the second half of the second century or early third based on the lettering and the onomastics (presence of Aurelia); Ameling (2004) dates this to the second half of the second century.

The Judean couple of this epitaph is following the standard form of burial inscriptions at Hierapolis, providing for fines to be paid for violation, in this case to a local association to which they presumably belonged.

A second inscription refers to the "settlement" (κατοικίᾳ) of Judeans in Hierapolis:

> This grave and the surrounding place belong to Aurelia Augusta, daughter of Zotikos. In it she, her husband, who is called Glykonianos, also known as Hagnos, and their children will be buried. But if anyone else is buried here, the violator will pay a fine of 300 denaria to the settlement of the Judeans who are settled in Hierapolis (τῇ κατοικίᾳ τῶν ἐν Ἱεραπόλει κατοικούντων Ἰουδαί|ων) and 100 denaria to the one who found out about the violation. A copy of this inscription was placed in the archives of the Judeans (*IHierapMir* 16 = *IJO* II 205; mid- to late second cent. CE).[14]

Here the group is described with terminology that is commonly used by ethnically based associations. This is especially well attested in the case of associations of Romans (οἱ κατοικοῦντες Ρωμαῖοι), such as the "settlement" of Romans that existed at nearby Phrygian Apameia (northeast of Hierapolis) from the first to the third century, at least.[15] This suggests that "Judeans" or "those from Judea"—with intertwined geographic, ethnic, and cultural implications—is the best way to translate the term here, as elsewhere. The seemingly redundant "settlement of Judeans who are settled in Hierapolis" also further suggests this sense of settled immigrants originally from elsewhere, involving migration either in this generation or some previous generation.

This inscription includes the common provision for storage of a copy of the inscription, but in this case this is expressly the archives "of the Judeans" rather than the civic archives. Use of the civic archives was the norm in other Judean (and non-Judean) inscriptions. This particular grave suggests a well-established Judean group (by the mid to late second century), such that it would begin to maintain its own archives for a time in imitation of the civic model.

One face (side b) of a third inscription, now published for the first time by Miranda, refers to a group of Judeans as "the most holy synagogue":

> *(Side a)*
> The grave, the burial ground beneath it, and the area around it belong to Nikotimos Lykidas, son of Artemisios. In it he has buried Apphia, his wife. A copy of this inscription was placed into the archives (τὸ ἀρχεῖον). Judean (Ἰουδαηκή).

> *(Side b)*
> The grave and the place around it belong to Aur. Heortasios Julianus, Tripolitan, Judean, now living in Hierapolis (Τριπολείτου Ἰουδέου, νοῖν οἰκο<ῦ>ντ[ος] | ἐν

14. Trans. mine. This rough date is once again based on the presence of the *gentilicium* Aurelius.

15. *IGR* IV 785–86, 788–91, 793–94; *MAMA* VI 177 (ca. 65–69 CE), 183. Cf. *CIG* 2287 (Athenians on Delos) and *OGIS* 595 = *CIG* 5853 (Tyrian merchants at Puteoli).

> Εἰεραπόλι [*sic*]). In it he and his wife, Glykonis, will be buried, and let their children be buried here as well. It is not lawful for anyone other to be buried in it. If someone does such things, he will pay two silver coins to the most holy synagogue (τῇ ἁγιωτά|τῃ συναγωγῇ) (*IHierapMir* 14 = *IJO* II 191; *side a*, late second century CE; *side b*, third or fourth cent. CE).[16]

The earlier of the two sides of the monument (side a) mentions only that the family members buried there were "Judean," and does not mention a community. The reverse of the original inscription (side b) pertains to a family of Judeans whose relation to those buried earlier is unclear. The family's identification of Aur. Heortasios Julianus as both "Tripolitan" and "Judean," alongside his current status as a settler in Hierapolis, illustrates the potential for multiple social and ethnic identities. I return to this at various points in this study, particularly in connection with Glykon below and in chapter 7. This man was a previous inhabitant, or perhaps citizen, of nearby Tripolis.[17] The family assigns any potential fines to "the most holy synagogue." The descriptive term "most holy" (ἁγιοτατ-) and its synonyms are common self-designations among associations and civic bodies in Asia Minor and in Hierapolis specifically, which suggests other dimensions of acculturation to local custom on the part of this gathering of Judeans.[18]

Overall, then, the evidence from Hierapolis indicates that there was a notable number of Judeans living in this city in the period from the mid-second to the third or fourth century who openly identified themselves as such on their family tombs. Through the accidents of survival and discovery, we happen to encounter about twenty or so families who felt it was important to express Judean aspects of their identities in this way (two of them decorating their graves with a menorah or other related symbols). There was at least one ongoing gathering or association of Judeans, though few families chose to mention such an association on their epitaphs. By the late second century, an association of Judeans was organized enough to have its own archives. Still many of the known Judean epitaphs generally follow local custom in having copies of the inscription placed in, and/or fines for violation payable to, civic institutions of Hierapolis.

The Family Tomb of P. Aelius Glykon and Aurelia Amia

One epitaph at Hierapolis does not explicitly use the term "Judean," nor does it refer to an established Judean association. Instead, it clearly indicates Judean connections by referring

---

16. Miranda's (1999a, 125) dating depends primarily on the forms of the lettering in relation to other dated monuments at Hierapolis. Ameling (2004, 408) proposes that side b may date from the fourth century based on the use of *litra*, which Robert (1946, 106) suggested was characteristic of the fourth or fifth centuries.

17. Although likely the local Tripolis (cf. *IHierapPenn* 22), there are known cities of the same name in Pontus, in Syria, and in North Africa. Cf. Leon 1995 [1960], 153–54, 240 (Tripolitan synagogue at Rome).

18. Cf. *IHierapJ* 40, 41, 342; *IHierapPenn* 25.

Figure 15. Grave of P. Aelius Glykon and Aurelia Amia, involving guilds of carpet-weavers and purple-dyers (IHierapMir 23 = IJO *II 196*)

to holy days, or festivals. The family grave of P. Aelius Glykon and Aurelia Amia dates to the late second or early third century of our era, based on the wife's family name, Aurelia, and the forms of the lettering.[19] As shown in figure 15, this is a limestone sarcophagus (with a partially damaged lid) inscribed on its long side (facing northwest).[20] It is located in the southeastern necropolis of Hierapolis near the remains of the Martyrium of St. Philip, with no other surviving graves in its immediate vicinity. Tullia Ritti's rediscovery and thorough new reading of the inscription, which was first inadequately published in 1868, has significantly filled in previous gaps, including the important reference to the feast of Kalends in lines 9–10 and to the name of Glykon's wife.[21]

The inscription provides important evidence regarding cultural identities and the nature of Judean interactions with others in the Greek city. It reads as follows:

---

19. Cf. Ritti 1992–93, 48; Miranda 1999a, 132; Ameling 2004, 416.

20. Measurements: Bottom: approx. 239 cm long, 93 cm tall, and 135 cm wide. Lid: approx. 74 cm tall at its high point. Lettering: approx. 4 cm. The sarcophagus is located at the beginning point of the main gap between two hills near where the main walkway to the Martyrium of St. Philip (now) ends and the staircase ascending to the martyrium begins.

21. Previously partial or undocumented were line 1, much of line 2, lines 9–10, part of line 11, and line 13. For a list of publications of the *original reading* (= *CIJ* 777), which followed and corrected Wagener 1868, 1 (=Wagener 1873, 379–80.), see Ritti 1992–93, or Miranda 1999a, 131–32, no. 23. *New reading:* Ritti 1992–93; *AE* (1994), no. 1660; *SEG* 46 (1996), no. 1656; Labarre and Le Dinahet 1996, 102–3, no. 62; Miranda 1999b, 58–59, no. 23, and Miranda 1999a, 131–32, no. 23; Dittmann-Schöne 2000, 226–27, no. V.5.10; *IJO* II 196 (Ameling 2004).

> This grave and the burial ground beneath it together with the surrounding place belong to Publius Aelius Glykon Zeuxianos Aelianus[22] and to Aurelia Amia, daughter of Amianos Seleukos. In it he will bury himself, his wife, and his children, but no one else is permitted to be buried here. He left behind 200 denaria for the grave-crowning ceremony to the most holy presidency of the purple-dyers (τῇ σεμνοτάτῃ προεδρίᾳ τῶν πορφυραβάφων στεφα|νωτικο[ῦ]), so that it would produce from the interest enough for each to take a share in the seventh month during the festival of Unleavened Bread (τῇ ἑορτῇ τῶν ἀζύμων). Likewise he also left behind 150 denaria for the grave-crowning ceremony to the sanhedrin of carpet-weavers (τῷ συνε|δρίῳ τῶν ἀκαιροδαπισ<τ>ῶν), so that the revenues from the interest should be distributed, half during the festival of Kalends (τῇ ἑορτῇ τῶν καλανδῶν) on eighth day of the fourth month and half during the festival of Pentecost (τῇ ἑορτῇ τῆς πεντηκοστῆς). A copy of this inscription was placed in the archives (Ritti 1992–93 [published 1996] = *IHierapMir* 23 = *IJO* II 196, revising *CIJ* 777; see note for full Greek text).[23]

Judean Aspects of Identity

The request that customary grave ceremonies be held on two Judean holidays clearly points to this family's identification with Judean cultural ways. Glykon has consciously made a decision that his death (and that of his family members) be commemorated indefinitely on the feasts of Unleavened Bread (in the month of Nisan [March-April]) and on Pentecost (the spring harvest festival), two of the most important Judean festivals.[24] The inscription nowhere identifies the owner (Glykon) as "Judean," as do some other Judean epitaphs at Hierapolis, but this would be unnecessary in light of the explicit mention of Judean holy days.[25]

There is the question, then, of whether Glykon and his family descend from immigrants from Judea (or themselves migrated from Judea) or whether they were gentiles who adopted Judean practices ("Judaizers" as they are sometimes labelled in the literature) and then arranged that others (guild members) also engaged in these practices after their deaths. We cannot know for sure. As Ritti notes, seemingly "non-Judean" elements in the inscription which entail local or Roman practices, including the grave-crowning cere-

---

22. Or, possibly: "P. Aelius Glykon, son of Zeuxis Aelianus" (cf. Ameling 2004, 416).

23. [ἡ] σορὸς καὶ τὸ ὑπὸ αὐτὴν θέμα σὺν τῷ βαθρικῷ καὶ τῷ περικειμένῳ τό|πῳ Ποπλίου Αἰλίου Γλύκωνος Ζευξιανοῦ Αἰλια[νοῦ καὶ Αὐ]ρηλίας Ἀμίας | Ἀμιανοῦ τοῦ Σελεύκου, ἐν ᾗ κηδευθήσεται αὐτὸς καὶ ἡ γυνὴ αὐτοῦ | καὶ τὰ τέκνα αὐτῶν, ἑτέρῳ δὲ οὐδενὶ ἐξέσται κηδευθῆναι. Κατέλι|ψεν δὲ [κα]ὶ τῇ σεμνοτάτῃ προεδρίᾳ τῶν πορφυραβάφων στεφα|νωτικο[ῦ] (δηνάρια) διακόσια πρὸς τὸ δίδοσθαι ἀπὸ τῶν τόκων ἑκάστῳ τὸ | αἱροῦν μη(νὸς) ζʹ ἐν τῇ ἑορτῇ τῶν ἀζύμων. ὁμοίως κατέλιπεν καὶ τῷ συνε|δρίῳ τῶν ἀκαιροδαπισ<τ>ῶν στεφανωτικοῦ (δηνάρια) ἑκατὸν πεντήκοντα, ἅτι| *vac.* να καὶ αὐτοι δώσουσι ἐκ τοῦ τόκου | διαμερίσαντες τὸ ἥμισυ ἐν τῇ ἑορτῇ τῶν καλανδῶν, μη(νὸς) δʹ, ηʹ, καὶ τὸ ἥμισυ ἐν τῇ ἑορτῇ τῆς πεντηκοστῆς. | ταύτης τῆς ἐπιγραφῆς τὸ ἀντίγραφον ἀπε<τέ>θη ἐν τοῖς ἀρχείοις.

24. See Barclay 1996, 415–16, on Judean festivals in the diaspora. Cf. Josephus *Ant.* 14.256–58 and 16.45; Reynolds 1977, 244–45, no. 17 (feast of Tabernacles at Berenike, Cyrenaica, ca. 24 CE).

25. Cf. Ritti 1992–93, 59.

monies and the celebration of the Roman New Year, can readily be understood within the framework of a Judean family well adapted to life in Greco-Roman Hierapolis.[26] In this chapter, I approach the inscription with this Judean immigrant status as the principle working hypothesis.

This is not to discount the possibility that Glykon and his family were gentiles with a significant level of involvement in Judean practices, along the lines of the "god-fearers" in Aphrodisias in the fourth century (*IJO* II 14).[27] Shaye J. D. Cohen (1989) surveys a range of possibilities for gentiles' interactions with Judeans ("Jews" in his terms) or with the Judean God, ranging from admiring some aspect of Judean cultural ways, to participating in certain Judean practices, to full adoption of Judean ways (including circumcision). He helpfully distinguishes between the potential participation of gentiles in certain Judean practices, such as festivals, and gentiles who recognize the God of the Judeans to the exclusion of all other gods, which may be relevant to the discussion further below of membership in the guilds. In the event that Glykon was a gentile adopting Judean practices and then arranging for others to participate in some way in the Judean festivals, then we would be witnessing signs of *en*culturation into the Judean minority group on the part of a non-Judean rather than acculturation of Judeans to local or Greco-Roman ways.[28] The problem is that, unlike the case of the "god-fearers" attested in an inscription from Aphrodisias, nothing in the Glykon inscription itself provides a basis for building a solid case that Glykon or his family was *gentile rather than Judean*.[29]

Although there is no clear evidence that Glykon was a gentile, there is indeed corroborating evidence that some members of the purple-dyers' guild mentioned in this inscription were gentiles. The discussion here explores multiple and intertwined facets of identities in the case of this family and the purple-dyers' guild. In the conclusion, I return to the implications for acculturation depending on whether Glykon was a Judean or a gentile adopting Judean cultural customs.

Roman Facets of Identity and the Feast of Kalends

Alongside this family's clear identification with Judean cultural ways are various signs of intertwined Hierapolitan, Hellenistic, and Roman elements, which I explore now. As previous chapters show, Judean identities were by no means incompatible with a sense of belonging within cities in the Greco-Roman world. Before considering indications of assimilation to local cultural life in Hierapolis, which inevitably also involves intertwined Roman elements, it is important to note Roman aspects of identity specifically.

First, P. Aelius Glykon's name indicates that he is a Roman citizen. If the inscription predates or immediately follows the universal grant of citizenship in 212 CE (*Constitutio*

---

26. Ritti 1992–93, 59–60.

27. On the fourth- or fifth-century dating, now see Chaniotis 2002, 209–42.

28. On possible cases of gentile judaizing in Asia Minor and Syria based on Christian literary evidence, see Murray 2004.

29. On the difficulties in identifying inscriptions as Judean, Christian, or pagan, see Kraemer 1989; Williams 1997; Ameling 2004, 16–20. Miranda (1999a, 144–45) is attracted by the hypothesis that Glykon was a "Jewish sympathizer" but admits the difficulties here.

Antoniniana), as most suggest, then Glykon's choice to include his *tria nomina* (three names = praenomen, nomen, and cognomen) indicates some sense of pride in possessing the status of Roman citizen.[30] It is possible that Glykon or his ancestors were formerly slaves who gained Roman citizenship upon manumission, though there is nothing in the inscription or from other sources relating to Hierapolis that would confirm that. With regard to this man's cognomen or personal name, Glykon, it is worth mentioning that personal names with the root Glyk- ("sweet") are very common in Hierapolis and Phrygia generally, and that this was likewise quite common among Judeans at Hierapolis, including those mentioned on some other Judean graves at Hierapolis.[31] This may well point to Glykon's place of birth as Hierapolis or somewhere else in Phrygia, suggesting that he is not a first generation immigrant. So even this man's name indicates Roman and Hierapolitan or Phrygian dimensions of his identities.

Beyond Roman citizenship, we lack clear indications of Glykon's social-economic status within Hierapolis. Still, it is worth mentioning that most monuments in which a family provides a foundation to a local association or guild to perform grave ceremonies, the deceased (or deceased-to-be) was a Roman citizen with some degree of wealth. Glykon's total amount of 350 denaria (200 plus 150) for the grave-crowning ceremonies (στεφανωτικόν) is greater than, yet comparable to, the case of Aurelius Zotikos Epikratos, who gave 150 denaria to the guild (συντεχνίᾳ) of nail-workers (*IHierapJ* 133). On the other hand, Glykon's foundation is less than Publius Aelius Hermogenes' substantial grant of 1,000 denaria to the guild of dyers (*IHierapJ* 195). Tiberius Claudius Kleon, whose position as high-priest suggests he is among the civic elites,[32] donated the largest attested amount for a grave-crowning ceremony at Hierapolis, granting the sum 2,500 denaria to the civic elders' organization (*IHierapJ* 234). So Glykon is among many other Roman citizens there, some of higher and others of lower social-economic or civic status. We do not know whether he was a citizen of Hierapolis and, if so, whether he was among the civic elites who assumed important offices.

A second, more significant sign of Roman cultural ways has been revealed only with the new edition of the epitaph. Glykon chooses to have his family remembered not only on principal Judean holidays, but also on the feast of Kalends, the Roman New Year celebration (held in January). Glykon leaves funds (150 denaria) to the sanhedrin of carpet-weavers, specifying that half of the proceeds from the foundation be used during the feast of Kalends and half during Pentecost.

It is important to say a few words regarding this Roman New Year festival to assess

---

30. Of the twenty-three Judean epitaphs at Hierapolis, sixteen (including the Glykon inscription) provide a name that suggests Roman citizenship, and five of these are dated to the post–212 CE era by Miranda. Eleven are potentially cases of Judeans with Roman citizenship before the universal grant (mainly in the late second or early third cent. CE).

31. See *IHierapMir* 5, 11, 14, and 16 (cited earlier). See Miranda's discussion of onomastics among Judeans at Hierapolis (Miranda 1999a, 136–40).

32. Compare the high-priest Tiberius Claudius Zotikos Boa, who also held other important civic offices or liturgies including στρατηγός ("general"), ἀγωνοθέτης ("festival organizer") and πρεσβευτής ("elder"). He was honoured by both the "most sacred guild of wool-cleaners" and the "most sacred guild of purple-dyers" on two separate monuments (*IHierapJ* 40, 41; probably third century).

its significance here at Hierapolis. The sparseness of our evidence for the celebration of this particular Roman festival in Asia Minor makes the Glykon inscription all the more relevant to issues of provincial cultural exchanges in relation to Roman cultural practices ("Romanization," to use the traditional term).[33] Michel Meslin's study of the festival emphasizes two complementary dimensions: the official ("civic") and the unofficial ("private," in his terms).[34] The official side of the festival was focussed on vows for the well-being of Rome and its empire as one year ended and the new began. Pliny the Younger provides some limited evidence that this aspect of the festival was celebrated in northern Asia Minor (Bithynia and Pontus) by the early second century (Pliny *Ep.* 10.35–36, 100–101; cf. Suetonius *Nero* 46.4). The Glykon inscription now confirms the continuing adoption of this festival in another area of Asia Minor a number of decades later.

There were also unofficial dimensions to the Roman New Year festival, which would likely be of greater relevance to the situation within a local guild at Hierapolis. These informal celebrations were "anchored in the collective psyche of the Romans" and charged with social and cultic significance, as Meslin puts it.[35]

Although the festival originally focussed its attention on the old Italian god Janus (two-faced protector of doors), its significance expanded beyond this focus. Ovid's famous poetic tribute to the Roman festivals (the *Fasti*), written in honour of Augustus, emphasizes the exchanges of "good wishes" and gifts which accompanied the celebration, including "sweet" gifts (e.g., dates, figs, honey), as well as cash, indicating an omen of a sweet year to come (Ovid *Fasti* 1.171–94). Ovid also alludes to the common practice of workers dedicating their occupational activities in connection with the commencement of the new year (*Fasti* 1.169–70), which may be of relevance to workers such as the carpet-weavers at Hierapolis. A statement by Herodian, a third-century Greek historian, confirms the importance of "exchanging friendly greetings and giving each other the pleasure of interchanging gifts" (Herodian *Hist.* 1.16.2). If Tertullian's negative assessment of Christians participating in New Year's gift giving as "idolatry" is any indication, the exchange of gifts (*strenae*) specifically remained prominent as the festival made its way into the provinces, at least in regions such as North Africa around the turn of the third century.[36]

It is likely these social aspects of celebrating the end of the old year and the beginning of the new, exchanging positive wishes and gifts, remained the focus of attention in many settings, including this case at Hierapolis. Not surprisingly, diaspora Judean attitudes and practices in relation to such festivals could extend beyond the views expressed in rabbinic writings (in the *Abodah Zarah* tractates).[37] Rabbinic sources simply assume that Judeans

---

33. Beginning in about 9 BCE and continuing at least into the second century, another new year's celebration was held in the province of Roman Asia on the birthday of Augustus (September 23), and associations were sometimes involved in those celebrations (*IPergamon* 374; and *IEph* 3801). See Price 1984, 54–55; Harland 2003a, 94–95, 102.

34. For the following see Meslin (1970, 23–50) and Nilsson (1916–19, 54–55), who also notes the involvement of *collegia* in the celebrations.

35. Meslin 1970, 23 (trans. from the French is mine).

36. Tertullian *On Idolatry* 10 and 14; cf. *On Military Crowns* 12.3; *Apology* 35.7. On gifts (*strenae*) see Suetonius *Augustus* 57, *Tiberius* 34, *Caligula* 42.

37. Compare Tessa Rajak's (2002 [1985], 358–62) discussion of diaspora Judeans and Greco-Roman festivals, although she did not have this case available to her.

should distance themselves from any relation to major gentile festivals, including Kalends specifically.[38]

Funerary Practices and Associations in Asia Minor

The nature of this family's acculturation to local funerary customs can be better understood in relation to other Judeans in the city and in relation to other (non-Judean) Hierapolitans who involved guilds in funerary provisions. Glykon's choice to include guilds in funerary commemorations on Judean and Roman festivals excluded—whether incidentally or not—the local Judean association from any direct relation to the burial and upkeep of the family grave. Glykon was certainly not alone in failing to even mention the local Judean association on his epitaph, however. Many other known Judean and non-Judean epitaphs make no mention of any local association or synagogue with which the family was affiliated.

A discussion of funerary involvements among associations (including Judean groups) in western Asia Minor will provide important context here, pointing toward common burial customs shared by Judeans (or possibly gentile "Judaizers") such as Glykon and his family.[39] There were three main ways in which guilds and other associations participated in grave-related activities. First, associations could play a role in the burial of their members, sometimes collecting ongoing fees for later use in funerary related expenses (actual burial or funerary banquets, for instance).[40] Local custom varied in the details and in the importance of this role, however. There is limited evidence that associations in some regions of Asia Minor might also have their own *collective* tomb or burial plot for this purpose. This was the case with the guild of flax-workers at Smyrna, who received a vault as a donation, and the guild of bed-builders at Ephesos, who dedicated a common burial plot.[41] As with associations generally, it seems that collective burial by association was not the norm among Judeans in the diaspora. Instead, the shared *family* tomb was common among both Judeans and non-Judeans in Asia Minor (including those who happened to belong to an association).

Still, there is one clear Judean example of collective burial from Tlos in Lycia (in southern Asia Minor) that should be mentioned. There a man named Ptolemais adopted this local, Tlosian practice by preparing a common burial area (ἡρῷον) for his son and for "all the Judeans" (first century CE).[42] This inscription plays a role in a recent debate regarding how common were such collective "Judean cemeteries" in the first two centuries (before the catacombs of Rome). J. H. M. Strubbe draws on the clear Tlos case to argue for the commonality of collective Judean grave plots in Asia Minor (using other less solid evidence

38. Cf. Hadas-Lebel 1979, 426–41; *y. Abod. Zar.* 1.1, II.E; *b. Abod. Zar.* 1.3.

39. On funerary practices, see Strubbe 1991, 1994, and 1997. On the role of associations in the Greek East see, for example, van Nijf 1997, 31–69, and Dittmann-Schöne 2000, 82–93.

40. Cf. Artemidoros *Oneir.* 5.82.

41. *ISmyrna* 218; *IEph* 2213; *IKilikiaBM* II 190–202; *IKos* 155–59; Fraser 1977, 58–70. Also see van Nijf 1997, 43–49.

42. *IJO* II 223 = *CIJ* 757 = *TAM* II 612.

along the way).[43] On the other hand, David Noy argues that "the existence of separate Jewish burial areas before the catacombs seems on the whole fairly unlikely."[44] I would suggest that forms of Judean burial would be dependent on variations in local practice among associations and, in fact, at least two epitaphs from Tlos appear to confirm this point. Like the Judean epitaph, they involve a collective burial area (ἡρῷον). Each lists names (with no mention of familial relation among the names) of those who are to be buried within it, likely members of associations (*TAM* II 604 and 615). Margaret H. Williams makes similar observations regarding local variations in how specific Judean families adopted burial practices from the local ("gentile") populations, which varied from one locale to the next.[45]

Having noted this role of associations in the burial of individual members and a few cases of common burial by association, it is important to point out that there are many epitaphs that simply do not refer to such groups at all. So the Judeans at Hierapolis who failed to mention any affiliation with a Judean association or who did not involve a local guild in funerary arrangements there are not out of the ordinary in this respect.

A second funerary role involves associations being named as recipients of fines for any violation of the grave alongside other civic institutions (e.g., civic treasury, council, people, elders' organization), or alone. Several guilds at Kyzikos are designated as recipients of any fines for violation of the grave, for instance, and a similar picture emerges at Smyrna. There two different families chose an association of porters who worked in the harbour.[46] So in some ways the synagogue leader at Smyrna in the second or third century (a woman named Rufina) was following local custom when she made fines for violation of her household's grave payable to the "most sacred treasury" of Smyrna (1,500 denaria) and to an association (1,000 denaria), in this case the "people" (ἔθνος, *ethnos*) of the Judeans of which she was a leader or benefactor.[47]

A third area of funerary involvement on the part of associations in Asia Minor entails groups being designated recipients of a foundation that made them responsible for visiting and maintaining the grave, including yearly (or more frequent) ceremonies at the site.[48] It was not necessarily the case that the owner of the grave was a member of the association in question, as cases involving multiple guilds also suggest (e.g., *IHierapJ* 133, 227). It seems that the more important factor in decision making (on the part of the deceased-to-be or family members of the deceased) concerned choosing a group that could indeed be trusted to help protect the grave and fulfill other obligations, and sometimes this was a group to which a family member belonged.

Several inscriptions from Ephesos illustrate this function of associations, for instance. In one first-century epitaph, a silversmith and his wife designate the "sanhedrin" of

---

43. Strubbe 1994, 101–2.

44. Noy 1998, 81.

45. Williams 1994b, 173–74.

46. *IKyzikos* 97, 211, 291 (marble-workers, clothing-cleaners, and porters); *ISmyrna* 204, 205; cf. *IAlexTroas* 122 (coppersmiths, second cent. CE), 151–52 (porters).

47. *ISmyrna* 295 = *IJO* II 43 = *CIJ* 741. Cf. *IJO* II 154, 157 (Nikomedia, third cent. CE). It is worth mentioning that the self-designation ἔθνος is also used by other guilds and associations (e.g., *PKöln* 260, line 3; second cent. BCE).

48. On grave visitation, see Garland 2001, 104–20. On Roman burial practices, see Toynbee 1971, 61–64. On crowns, see Goodenough 1953–68, 7.148–71.

silversmiths as recipient for any fines, but they also leave behind specific funds so that the group can "take care of" (κήδεται) the grave site (*IEph* 2212).[49] In another, a physician and his wife leave behind an endowment for the "sanhedrin of physicians in Ephesos who meet in the museum" (μουσεῖον) to take care of the grave (*IEph* 2304). Quite important for present purposes regarding interaction and acculturation is the family epitaph of a chief physician at Ephesos (named Julius), who asked that "the Judeans in Ephesos" (not the sanhedrin of physicians) maintain the tomb.[50] It is unclear as to whether Julius was a Judean or not. Either way, Judeans are participating in local customs in places like Ephesos.

Along similar lines, a devotee of the Judean God (either a Judean or a Christian) in third-century Akmoneia donated several tools to "the neighbourhood of those near the first gateway" (*IJO* II 171).[51] He did so on condition that this neighbourhood association yearly decorated his wife's grave with roses (ῥοδίσαι), most likely performing the Roman ceremony of *rosalia*, which often included a banquet.[52] This offers an interesting parallel to Glykon's request to have grave-crowning ceremonies held on the Roman New Year, led by the carpet-weavers' association.[53] In both cases a traditionally Roman festival is adapted to local custom (involving associations) by families devoted to the Judean God, presumably omitting practices that would evoke honours for other deities (namely, sacrifice).

Guilds at Hierapolis and the Purple-dyers' Identities

Turning to Hierapolis specifically, it is important to give some sense of what role the guilds played in funerary practices there, which will then shed more light on the significance of Glykon's decision to include guilds (and the purple-dyers in particular) in his bequest. Of the sixteen extant inscriptions that refer to occupational associations at Hierapolis, ten

49. Cf. *IEph* 2402 (potters), 2446 (linen-workers).

50. *IEph* 1677 = *IJO* II 32 = *CIJ* 745 (second cent. CE). See *IEurJud* I 76 from Venosa for another Judean chief physician.

51. The inscription uses the so-called Eumeneian formula, which stipulates that violators will have "to reckon with the justice of God." The formula is now known to be used by both Judeans and Christians, contrary to Ramsay's (1895–97, 520) claim of Christian identification. Robert (1960b, 409–12) thought that the owner of the grave was probably Judean, based on the "Semitic" name of the man (Math[i]os) who sold the plot to Aur. Aristeas (assuming that they were "co-religionists") and on the absence of other evidence of Christians in third-century Akmoneia (cf. Trebilco 1991, 78–80; Strubbe 1994, 72–73). For Judeans at Akmoneia, see *IJO* II 168–78. For Christians, see *MAMA* VI 336.

52. On associations and the *rosalia* festival in the Greek East, see *IG* X.2 260; Dimitsas 1896, no. 920; *CIL* III 703, 704, 707 (from Macedonia); *IPergamon* 374B; *CIG* 3874; *IKlaudiupolis* 115; *INikaia* 62, 95, 1283, 1422; *SEG* 49 (1999), no. 1790 and 2508 (from Asia Minor). Cf. Perdrizet 1900, 299–323; Trebilco 1991, 80–81. On *collegia* in the Latin West see Toynbee 1971, 61–64; Lattimore 1962, 137–41 (cf. *CIL* V 2090, 2176, 2315, 4015, 4017, 4448).

53. On the use of crown symbolism in Judean art, architecture, and literature, see Goodenough 1953–68, 7.149–52. For Judean adaptation of granting crowns as a form of honour for living benefactors, see *IJO* II 36 (Phokaia or Kyme; third cent. CE) and Bruneau 1982, 465–504; *NewDocs* VIII 12 (Samaritans on Delos; second-first BCE).

are epitaphs, and six of these expressly involve a guild or guilds in some ongoing grave ceremonies or superintendence of the grave (including the Glykon inscription). Most of these (four) involve the local practice of providing "funds for the grave-crowning" (στεφανωτικόν), which in this form of expression seems peculiar to the Lycos valley, primarily Hierapolis.[54] Another refers to the responsibility of a guild—purple-dyers or, if they fail, the livestock dealers—in "burning the incense (τῶν παπων) on the customary day" (*IHierapJ* 227b; ca. 190–250 CE). Furthermore, five of the ten epitaphs also mention guilds as recipients of any fines for violation of the grave.[55]

Since there are cases involving several guilds on one epitaph, in all there are a total of ten guilds mentioned in connection with funerary arrangements in the extant monuments of Hierapolis: dyers, nail-workers, coppersmiths, purple-dyers, livestock dealers, water-mill engineers, farmers, wool-cleaners, carpet-weavers, and an unknown "guild." The association of purple-dyers, in particular, stands out prominently as a favourite in the funerary monuments that have survived to us, appearing as recipients of fines or bequests for visitation ceremonies on nearly half (four out of ten) of the grave inscriptions involving guilds, including the Glykon family grave itself.[56]

The fact that a family devoted to the Judean God specifically chose to call on the services of the purple-dyers, as well as the carpet-weavers (a guild known only from the Glykon inscription), begs a question regarding the composition of these guilds and the ethnic identities of guild members. This issue is important in evaluating possibilities regarding dynamics of assimilation and interaction here. Scholarly discussions of this inscription, including many based on the earlier reading, which lacked the reference to Kalends, address the question of whether the guilds were (1) solely Judean, (2) solely non-Judean (gentile), or (3) a mixture of both. Seldom do these scholarly discussions make reference to other epigraphical evidence for the purple-dyers at Hierapolis, however. Such evidence shows that for the purple-dyers, at least, the first option is untenable, the second plausible, and the third most likely.

Erich Ziebarth was among the first to suggest that these two guilds were solely Judean in membership, and other scholars have followed suit, including William Ramsay and Shimon Applebaum.[57] Most recently, Miranda suggests that the purple-dyers, at least, were solely Judean, based on the fact that Glykon chose to have the purple-dyers provide their services only on a Judean holiday. The bequest to the carpet-weavers, however, involves both a Roman and a Judean holiday, reflecting Glykon's choice of separate holidays for the gentile and Judean members of that mixed group, in Miranda's view.[58] However, the Glykon inscription does not give any clear indication that either of these guilds were distinctively Judean, nor that they stood out from other such groups in Hierapolis.

More important, a good number of inscriptions (seven in all) concerning purple-dyers at Hierapolis in this period (mid-second to early third centuries) show that, rather

---

54. *IHierapJ* 50, 195; *IHierapPenn* 45; *IHierapMir* 23 = *IHierapJ* 342. On this local ceremony, see Judeich's notes to *IHierapJ* 195, as well as *IHierapJ* 133, 153, 209, 234, 270, 278, 293, 310, 336 (cf. *ILaodikeia* 84, 85).

55. *IHierapJ* 218; *IHierapPenn* 7, 23, 25, 45.

56. *IHierapJ* 133, 227; *IHierapPenn* 23 and *IHierapMir* 23 = *IHierapJ* 342.

57. Ziebarth 1896, 129; Ramsay 1900, 81, and Ramsay 1902, 98–101; Applebaum 1974b, 480–83.

58. Miranda 1999a, 140–45.

than being distinctively Judean, this guild consisted principally of gentiles (at the points we have any evidence for them) and were viewed as a typical guild in the community.[59] Thus, for instance, the purple-dyers (ἡ τέχνη τῶν πορφυραβά[φων]) joined with the city (*polis*) in about 209 CE to dedicate a portion of the theatre (two levels of the architrave) to Apollo Archegetes ("the Founder"), to other gods of the homeland, and to the emperors Septimius Severus and Caracalla.[60] And beyond the Glykon inscription, none of the other four families who included the purple-dyers (or its leadership, "the board of presidents of the purple-dyers") in funerary arrangements expressly indicates any Judean connections regarding either the family who owned the grave or the guild(s) in question, which goes by various titles at different points.[61]

When the "sacred guild of purple-dyers" (ἡ σεμνοτάτη ἐργα|σία τῶν πορφορα|βάφων) set up its own honorary monuments for civic and imperial officials, once again there is no indication that they were distinctively Judean in composition.[62] It is certainly possible, however, that the guild included Judeans in its membership when such honorary activities took place (the membership would no doubt change over generations), especially in light of evidence from elsewhere concerning Judeans' interactions with imperial-connected individuals who were not Judean.[63] So, although we cannot necessarily assume that members in the purple-dyers were solely non-Judeans (gentiles), we do know that they were *not* solely Judeans during the era of the Glykon inscription.

In light of this, there are two main possibilities regarding the composition of these guilds. In either case this is evidence not only for the participation and integration of Judeans in civic life but also for Judean affiliations with, or memberships in, local occupational associations at Hierapolis. On the one hand, if the guild was composed exclusively of gentiles, as Judeich and Conrad Cichorius suggested early on, this is a Judean (or gentile "Judaizer") following burial conventions of non-Judeans in Hierapolis (and Asia generally) by including guilds in funerary provisions.[64] In this case, the reason for Glykon's asking these guilds (instead of a Judean group, for instance) to perform the grave rituals would presumably relate to the fact that he had contacts with purple-dyers and carpet-weavers

---

59. Cf. Judeich 1898, 174; Ritti 1992–93, 66–67. There are slight variations in the terminology used in reference to the purple-dyers (see n. 60). The purple-dyers are to be distinguished from the "dyers" (βαφεῖς), however, who formed a separate guild (*IHierapJ* 50 and 195).

60. Ritti 1985, 108–13.

61. *IHierapJ* 133 (designated simply τῶν πορ[φυραβάφων); *IHierapJ* 227b (referring to τῷ συνεδρίῳ | τῆς προεδρίας τῶν πορφυρα|βάφων, "the board of presidency of the purple-dyers"); *IHierapPenn* 23 (referring to τῇ προεδρίᾳ τῶν πορφυραβάφων, "the presidents of the purple-dyers"). Cf. *IHierapJ* 156; *IHierapPenn* 37 (each involving a purple-*dealer* [πορφυροπώλης] with no Judean connection involved).

62. *IHierapJ* 42; *IHierapJ* 41= *IGR* IV 822 (probably third cent. CE). The use of "most sacred" is typical of associations, organizations, and civic bodies when they express their own identities, namely, when the group in question is the one having the monument inscribed (see n. 20; cf. *IHierapJ* 36, 40).

63. See Harland 2003a, 219–28.

64. Humann, Cichorius, et al. 1898, 46, 51, 174.

within commercial networks, perhaps as a regular customer, vendor, or benefactor of the guilds.[65]

What seems even more likely is that, although consisting principally of non-Judeans, at Glykon's time these two guilds included individual devotees of the Judean God (Judeans, or perhaps gentile "Judaizers" or "Judaizing" Christians),[66] who happened to be purple-dyers or carpet-weavers. Paul R. Trebilco is among those who mention this third possibility, yet he is hesitant to take a stand on which of the three options seems most or least likely.[67] Suggesting the presence of devotees of the Judean God in the guilds would have the advantage of better accounting for Glykon's request that gentile guilds perform the customary grave ceremony on Judean holidays, and we know that Judeans sometimes did engage in clothing and other related occupations.[68]

If this is indeed the case, then we can begin to imagine processes whereby ordinary gentiles might become gentile sympathizers or "god-fearers" (such as those at Aphrodisias in the fourth century). For the Glykon family's choice to corporately involve these guilds in celebrating Judean festivals would involve some gentiles who had little or no previous involvement in Judean practices. Social network connections based on common occupation could become the basis of new adherences, in this case perhaps leading to an increase in the number of gentiles with some level of attachment to the Judean God or to Judeans living in Hierapolis.[69] In fourth-century Aphrodisias, for instance, several Judeans and "god-fearers" came from occupations related to clothing production or sale (rag-dealer, fuller, boot-maker, linen-worker, and purple-dyer) and, in at least one case, the occupation of a named Judean (a bronzesmith) matches that of two "god-fearers," who are also bronzesmiths (*IJO* II 14b, lines 25, 46, 53). In chapter 1 I discussed the role of occupational networks in the foundation and growth of associations of various kinds, including some Judean gatherings.

If there were Judeans (or "god-fearers") as members of these guilds at Hierapolis, as I argue, Glykon's reasons for choosing these two guilds (rather than other known guilds) would involve a combination of factors, including his contacts (for commercial and/or benefaction purposes) with both Judeans and gentiles *and* his ethnic and cultural affiliations with fellow-Judeans (or at least gentile devotees of the Judean God) in Hierapolis. It is this combination of attachments that makes this third option concerning the mixed

---

65. It was common for wealthier individuals to call on the funerary-related services of a guild to which they did *not* belong (see the earlier discussion of Glykon's socio-economic status).

66. On Christians at Hierapolis, see below.

67. Trebilco 1991, 178–79. Kraabel (1968, 134–35) is among the first to mention this option. Ritti (1992–93) further explores this possibility and is less hesitant in suggesting that this may be a mixed guild. Miranda (1999a, 141–44) discusses evidence of Judean occupational organizations (in Palestine and Alexandria) at some length, and suggests that the purple-dyers were likely Judean and that the carpet-weavers may have been mixed. The new edition of Emil Schürer's work (by Vermes, Millar, and Goodman) states that "the members of the guilds must also have been influenced by Judaism" (Schürer 1973–87, 3.27). Cf. *AE* (1994), no. 1660 on the possibility of *theosebeis*.

68. Cf. *CIJ* 787, 873, 929, 931; Acts 16:14–15; 18:2–3.

69. Cf. Reynolds and Tannenbaum 1987, 116–23. Tessa Rajak and David Noy have shown that even those who were designated "synagogue leaders" may have been non-Judean benefactors of Judean groups, for instance. See Rajak and Noy 1993, 75–93; cf. Rajak 2002, 373–91.

composition of the guild most effective in making sense of the evidence. The theory that Judeans at Hierapolis maintained affiliations with or memberships in other groups or associations within the city is also consistent with Judean evidence from other areas.[70] In cases where we know the occupation of Judeans there is a range of activity comparable to the known guilds, and the fact that occupations are mentioned at all on Judean monuments suggests that this was an important component in their identities.[71] So it is not too surprising to find Judeans affiliating with their fellow-workers within occupational networks and guilds. I will return to this important issue of multiple memberships in associations in chapter 7.

Conclusion

Throughout this chapter I have discussed evidence for members of ethnic or cultural minority groups, namely Judeans at Hierapolis, adopting and adapting to local cultural practices and interacting with their Greek or Roman neighbours in the second and third centuries. The case of Hierapolis demonstrates well some dynamics of cultural and structural assimilation, and it is worthwhile placing this evidence within a broader social-scientific framework here.[72]

In the previous chapter I discussed theories of assimilation that help to explain the processes of boundary negotiations that take place when members of two or more cultural groups interact. In particular, it is useful to distinguish between subprocesses of assimilation, the most important here being (1) cultural assimilation, or acculturation, (2) structural assimilation, and (3) dissimilation or cultural maintenance. I have explained each of these in some detail already, but further explanation of the second main subprocess, *structural assimilation*, is important here in connection with Judeans at Hierapolis.

Milton Yinger proposes that structural assimilation entails both informal and formal levels.[73] At the *informal* level, individual members of a given ethnic or cultural group can interact with persons from other cultural groups through personal, social network connections, including memberships in neighbourhoods, clubs, and associations.[74] The *formal* level of structural assimilation involves members of a particular cultural minority group participating in political, legal, social, or economic institutions of society.

These social-scientific insights provide a framework in which to make better sense of the ancient evidence—albeit fragmentary—for Judeans and Judean groups at Hierapolis and elsewhere in the empire. Moreover, both the form and content of the Judean epitaphs at Hierapolis illustrate both cultural and structural assimilation. First of all, we have seen that the form of Judean grave inscriptions indicates acculturation to patterns of other non-

70. See chapter 7 for evidence regarding multiple affiliations among Judeans.

71. See van der Horst 1991, 99–101; Shaye J. D. Cohen 1993, 10; Reynolds and Tannenbaum 1987, 116–23.

72. For others who have drawn on such social-scientific insights in studying groups in the ancient context see Balch 1986, 79–101; Barclay 1996; Noy 2000.

73. Yinger 1981; Yinger 1994. Cf. Marger 1991, 117–120.

74. Cf. Yinger 1981, 254; Marger 1991, 118.

Judean graves from the same locale.[75] Moving beyond the form of epitaphs to the content and its implications, it is important to notice somewhat subtle evidence of *formal structural* assimilation in relation to important institutions of the Greek city (*polis*). The inclusion of formal institutions, usually the civic ("most sacred") treasury, as recipients of fines in many (nine) Judean inscriptions at Hierapolis (and on Judean epitaphs elsewhere) implied some level of civic responsibility for preservation or maintenance of the family tomb.[76] Violators would have to answer not only to the descendants of the family, if any, but also to the city of Hierapolis itself, so to speak. Including local associations, alongside civic institutions or alone, was thought to further bolster this insurance that the family grave would remain intact and undisturbed.

There are other signs of formal structural assimilation among Judeans here. Like their non-Judean counterparts, nearly half (ten) of the Judean epitaphs from Hierapolis (the Glykon grave included) clearly mention that a copy of the epitaph was placed in the civic archives. This, too, has a structural significance beyond its seemingly incidental mention. For placing a copy in the civic archives further ensured that, if anyone should fail to obey the will of the deceased or actually modify (or remove) the original inscription from the tomb, legal action could follow. This expectation of justice from relevant civic institutions is a significant indication of structural integration within local society.

It is within this context of interaction and acculturation that we can better understand the Glykon family grave itself. If, on the one hand, Glykon and his family were gentile sympathizers (or "judaizing" Christians, for instance)[77] who had adopted important Judean practices, which is possible though difficult to establish, then this provides an interesting case of Greek or Phrygian gentiles' acculturation to the ways of local Judeans while also continuing in burial customs characteristic of Hierapolis and Asia Minor. Furthermore, the involvement of a guild (the purple-dyers) which did include non-Judeans (gentiles) in its number is suggestive of at least some level of acculturation to Judean practices on the part of these guild members at Hierapolis. Yet here it is the family, not members of the guilds, who have chosen to have the guilds participate on Judean holy days and on a Roman festival. Unlike the case of the "god-fearers" at Aphrodisias, there is no clear indication that the gentile guild-members were members in the synagogue or in an association devoted solely to the Judean God.

If, on the other hand, Glykon and his family were from Judea as immigrants or

---

75. Among these standard inscriptional patterns (including the common vocabulary used) are: (1) identification of the owner(s) of the tomb and surrounding area; (2) stipulations that no one else, beyond those designated, is to be buried on the site; (3) preventative measures of setting fines should the instructions be violated; (4) arrangements for payment of such fines to civic institutions (treasury or elders' organization) and/or local associations (e.g., Judean synagogues, guilds); and, (5) deposit of a copy of the inscription in the civic archives.

76. Cf. *IJO* II 172 (Akmoneia), 216 (Termessos), 233, 238 (Korykos).

77. Literary evidence shows that followers of Jesus lived at Hierapolis already in the first century (Col 4:13) and continued in subsequent centuries (cf. Eusebius *HE* 3.31.3, 3.36.1–2, 4.26.1). The earliest openly Christian inscriptions from Hierapolis date to Byzantine times, when the martyrium associated with Philip was established (cf. *IHierapJ* 22, 24; fifth century or later). Attempts by those such as Ramsay to identify other inscriptions as Christian based only on the inscription's use of "unusual" language are problematic at best (e.g., *IHierapJ* 227 with notes by Judeich refuting Ramsay's suggestion of Christianity in that inscription; see Ramsay 1895–97, 118–19, no. 28).

descendants of immigrants, this inscription provides further evidence of both cultural and structural assimilation among Judean families at Hierapolis. I have shown that the fabric of this family's identities consisted of intertwined Judean, Roman, and Hierapolitan strands. Most prominently with regard to Judean identity is the concern to have the grave visited on the festivals of Passover and Pentecost. Many Judean families did assert Judean aspects of their identities (in relation to non-Judeans) by using the designation "Judean," and some did so by including symbols such as the menorah on their grave monuments (*IHierapMir* 6, 12). In one case, for instance, it seems that connections with the homeland of Judea or Israel were expressed through a concern to have bones returned to "the ancestral land" (ἐκτὸς τοῦ διακομίσαντος ἡμᾶς εἰς τὴν πατρῴ|αν γῆν; *IHierapMir* 19), a burial practice that is attested in only a limited number of other diaspora cases.[78] Still, the Glykon inscription stands out among the epitaphs of Hierapolis, and even Asia Minor or the empire, in its special concern to carry on Judean *customs* even after death, thereby continuing to express this Judean element of the family's identities within Hierapolis indefinitely.

At the same time, Glykon felt himself to be Roman in some sense, both in proudly indicating his status as Roman citizen and by choosing to include the Roman New Year festival as a time when the family would be remembered by a guild in Hierapolis. In fact, the rarity of epigraphic evidence concerning the celebration of this Roman festival in the provinces draws further attention to its significance here as a sign of the adoption of some Roman practices among Judeans, what has traditionally been labeled Romanization.

Alongside these Judean and Roman identifications, the family clearly experienced a sense of belonging within the community of Hierapolis specifically in many respects. At the formal structural level, this family, like other Judeans, deposited a copy of the inscription in the civic archives, indicating an expectation of some level of justice from local legal procedures and institutions. Furthermore, these Judeans were acculturated to Hierapolitan or Phrygian practice in leaving "grave-crowning funds" and followed regional custom in entrusting their final bequest to occupational associations. Not only that, but the family also chose one of the most popular and, it seems, widely trusted local guilds to fulfill this duty.

Both Glykon and the devotees of the Judean God who belonged to the guilds of purple-dyers and carpet-weavers further illustrate the potential for multiple affiliations with subgroups of local society. Such involvements in local groups are an important factor in processes of informal structural assimilation. Moreover, information concerning the Glykon family, as well as other Judeans at Hierapolis, points toward significant levels of integration on the part of these Judeans within the society of Greco-Roman Hierapolis alongside a continued sense of belonging with others who gave special attention to honouring the God of the Judean homeland. Now that we have looked at some cases of integration and positive intergroup relations, we can turn to instances of ethnic and other rivalries among associations in the civic context.

---

78. On transportation of bones to Jerusalem, see Williams 1998, 75–76; Josephus *Ant.* 10.94–95. However, see Tessa Rajak's discussion of the necropolis at Beth She'arim in the Lower Galilee, which, in her view, was "a glorified local cemetery, whose catchment area happens to be rather large" (including deceased from nearby diaspora locations, including Beirut, Sidon, and Caesarea; Rajak 2002 [1998], 494).

Part 4

Group Interactions and Rivalries

7

Group Rivalries and Multiple Identities

Associations at Sardis and Smyrna

Introduction

Interactions between different groups within society are central to processes of identity formation and reformulation within those groups. In this chapter, monuments and inscriptions from two cities mentioned in John's Revelation, namely, Sardis and Smyrna, offer a window into the complicated world of group interactions and rivalries in the world of the early Christians. In particular, competition among such associations has important implications for issues of belonging and illustrates how group identities could be expressed in relation to, or over against, other groups.

Moreover, the evidence from such locales demonstrates quite clearly that rivalries could encompass various practices, realms of activity (social, cultic, economic, and otherwise), and levels of engagement. While some groups could be more self-consciously competitive than others in specific ways, competition (alongside cooperation) was inherent within civic life in Asia Minor. Virtually all groups took part in this arena in some manner. Associations were contenders for economic support and benefactions and for the honour and prestige that such connections with benefactors entailed. In fact, participation in monumentalizing was one important means by which an association could assert its identity and make claims about its place within society in relation to other groups and institutions. Rivalrous sentiments are also evident in how groups proclaimed their identities in relation to others. Finally, associations were competitors for potential adherents and for the allegiances of members they had. The evidence for certain individuals' affiliations or memberships within various groups draws attention to the multiple nature of identities.

The point of this chapter is not to say that rivalries predominated but rather to examine what significance areas of competition had for issues of identity. Cooperation and positive intergroup relations were also an element in association life generally. In fact, multiple affiliations, for example, may both indicate competition for allegiances and illustrate the somewhat permeable boundaries that could exist between different associations, such that a person might in some cases comfortably belong within more than one group at a time.

Associations at Sardis and Smyrna

A brief overview of the evidence for associations in Sardis and Smyrna (in the first to third centuries CE) will set the stage for a discussion of rivalries and the expression of group identities. Quite well known in scholarship are the Judean (Jewish) gatherings and Christian congregations that are attested in these two cities.[1] The hall within the bath-gymnasium complex at Sardis, which was adapted in the third or fourth century CE and is pictured in figure 16, is among the most studied synagogues in the diaspora, for instance.[2] Josephus refers to a "synod" of Judeans there at least as early as the first century BCE (Josephus *Ant.* 14.259–261; 16.171), and there are numerous inscriptions pertaining to other Judeans as well (see *IJO* II 53–145). At Smyrna, there was a group that called itself the "people of the Judeans" led by a woman, Rufina, who was head of the synagogue in the second or third century (*IJO* II 43), for instance, and I will soon discuss another somewhat controversial inscription involving "former" Judeans at this locale (*ISmyrna* 697).

Christian groups are attested at Smyrna as early as the time of John's Revelation in the late first century. They continue in our line of vision through the likes of Ignatius of Antioch, whose letters address cities in this region, and Polycarp of Smyrna in the second century. Further information for Christian groups at Sardis comes from authors such as Melito, bishop of Sardis in the mid-second century.[3] Alongside these well-studied Judean and Christian minority groups, however, are numerous other associations that have drawn less scholarly attention and which may provide a framework for comparison on issues such as the expression of identities. The range of associations attested at Sardis and Smyrna is, in fact, quite typical of cities in Asia Minor generally.

Beginning with Sardis, the surviving evidence for occupationally based associations here is somewhat limited. Inscriptions do attest to guilds of Italian businessmen in the republican era, slave-merchants in the late first century, and performers devoted to Dionysos in the second century.[4]

More prevalent in the record are other groups that explicitly identify themselves with particular patron deities. There were associations in connection with Attis, Zeus, Apollo, and the emperors as "revered gods."[5] Some inscriptions refer to "initiates" in mysteries (μύσται and ἀρχενβάται) without designating the deity in question, one of which is also a group of athletes (*ISardH* 1, 5). Other monuments from the vicinity of Sardis vaguely refer to other associations using common terminology, such as "association" (κοινόν) and "companions" (συμβίωσις; *ILydiaKP* III 14–15).

Turning to Smyrna, the surviving evidence for associations that epigraphers have managed to document is even more varied. Regarding guilds, here there is more than

---

1. On Sardis and Smyrna, see the volume edited by Ascough 2005. Also see the recent piece on Judeans, Christians, and others at Sardis by Tessa Rajak (2002, 447–62).

2. On the synagogue see, for instance, Seager and Kraabel 1983; Bonz 1990, 1993; Kroll 2001.

3. See Kraabel 1971; Wilken 1976.

4. *SEG* 46 (1996), no. 1521 (ca. 88 BCE), 1524 (90s CE); *ISardBR* 13–14 (time of Hadrian).

5. *ISardBR* 17 (Attis); *ISardBR* 22; *ISardH* 3, 4 (Zeus; first-second cent. CE); *SEG* 46 (1996), no. 1520 (Apollo Pleurenos; first cent. BCE); *ISardH* 2 (Apollo; first cent. CE); *ISardBR* 62 (emperors; second cent. CE).

Figure 16. Synagogue hall within the bath–gymnasium complex at Sardis

one "family" (φαμιλία) of gladiators, a "synod" of athletes, a group of porters (devoted to Asklepios at one point), and guilds of basket-fishermen, tanners, silversmiths, and goldsmiths.[6] As in many cities in the region, there was a group of merchants with Italian connections, this one emphasizing its province-wide character in calling itself the "Romans and Hellenes engaged in business in Asia" (*ISmyrna* 642; mid to late second cent. CE).

Several associations at Smyrna make reference to a favourite god or goddess. Among our earliest evidence is the membership list of a group devoted to the worship of Anubis, an Egyptian deity (*ISmyrna* 765; early third cent. BCE). Particularly prominent in the Roman period was a group of "initiates" devoted to Dionysos Breseus.[7] Other Dionysiac inscriptions, which may or may not be related to the "Breiseans," refer to a sanctuary of Dionysos (with Orphic-influenced purity rules for entrance) and to a "Baccheion," a common term for a meeting place among Dionysiac associations.[8]

The goddesses Demeter and Kore find their place here, too. One inscription refers to those that had "stepped into" (hence ἐνβαταί) Kore's mysteries, and several others refer to a "synod" of initiates of the "great goddess" Demeter.[9] It is likely that the group that calls itself "the former Judeans" on a list of donors was dedicated to the deity of its homeland, as I explain further below (*ISmyrna* 697; about 124 CE). Rulers and emperors once again find their place here, as at Sardis: one group called itself the "friends-of-Agrippa companions"

---

6. Robert 1971 [1940], nos. 225, 240–41; *ISmyrna* 217, 709 (athletes; first cent. CE); *ISmyrna* 204, 205, 713 (porters; ca. 150–180 CE and 225 CE); *ISmyrna* 715 (fishermen; third cent. CE); Petzl 1977, 87, no. 18 (tanners); *ISmyrna* 721 (goldsmiths/silversmiths; ca. 14–37 CE); cf. *ISmyrna* 718.

7. *ISmyrna* 598–99, 600–601, 622, 639, 652, 729–30, 731–32.

8. *ISmyrna* 728, 733 (second-third cent. CE); cf. Nilsson 1957:133–43. On "Baccheion" see *IEph* 434, *IDidyma* 502, *IGBulg* 1864 (Bizye, Thracia), *IGR* I 787 (Heraklea-Perinthos), *IG* II.2 1368 (Athens).

9. *ISmyrna* 726 (Kore; cf. *ISardH* 5), 653–55 (first-second cent. CE).

and another in the nearby village of Mostenae was an association of "Caesarists," regularly engaging in sacrifices for their patron deities, the emperors (*ISmyrna* 331; *IGR* IV 1348).[10] Less certain are the specific identities of other associations that simply call themselves "companions," "fellow-initiates," "society members," "synods," "sanhedrins," or "friends."[11]

Rivalries among Associations and Issues of Identity

As the above survey suggests, we have considerable evidence for associations at Sardis and Smyrna with which to work. At times, however, it will be beneficial to draw on sources from other cities in the same region and from elsewhere in the Mediterranean to shed more light on issues of identity. Here I discuss a range of possibilities in contentious encounters among associations that also reveal important aspects of how members of these groups expressed their identities within broader society. After dealing with the competitive nature of benefaction, I go on to certain associations' proclamations of preeminence for their group or deity. Finally, I consider competition for membership and for the allegiances or loyalties of members, which provides an opportunity to evaluate the significance of multiple affiliations and identities.

Rivalries Related to Benefaction

An important aspect of social exchanges in the Greco-Roman world were what we can call systems of benefaction (more appropriate for the Greek East) or patronage (more appropriate for the Latin West). The social structures and hierarchies of society were maintained, in part, by exchanges of "good deeds" (literal meaning of "benefaction," εὐεργασία), benefits, or favours in return for honours (τιμαί). Those higher in the social strata were expected to make such donations of goodwill (εὔνοια)—be they offering to build a temple, host a festival, support a local association's meetings, or act as a leader of a group. Those who received such benefits were expected to acknowledge them in the form of honours in return. Such honours could entail proclaiming honours during meetings of the group in question or erecting a statue or monument in honour of the donor or donors. Sometimes benefactors might also be invited as a special guest at meetings of the association, for instance. Failure to fittingly honour one's benefactors could result in shame or insult, honour's antithesis. Considerable scholarly work has been done on the nature of honour–shame societies of the Mediterranean world, both ancient and modern.[12] J. E. Lendon's recent work, *Empire of Honour* (1997), provides a particularly vivid portrait of how this system of honour functioned in Greek and Roman societies.

In the mindset of participants in antiquity, this overall system of hierarchy and exchange

---

10. For the former, compare *IG* VI 374 (an association of Agrippiasts at Sparta) and *CIJ* 365, 425, 503 (a synagogue of Agrippesians at Rome). On the synagogues, see Leon 1995 [1960], 140–42 and Richardson 1998, 19–23.

11. *ISmyrna* 330, 534, 706, 716, 718, 720, 734.

12. Cf. Malina 1981; Elliott 1993.

extended to include the cosmos as a whole, as gods and emperors were considered among the most important benefactors deserving of appropriate honours. The most fitting form of honours for the gods was sacrifice (and accompanying meals), alongside practices such as prayer, singing of hymns, and mysteries. Fittingly honouring gods and emperors was a means by which families, associations, cities, and larger regions helped to ensure the safety and security of their communities. Failure to honour the gods was sure to bring famine, earthquake, fire, and other disasters; so this was taken seriously. So what we as moderns might call "worship" or "religion" was for the ancients part of a more encompassing system of social and cultural exchanges and values that involved the gods.

Turning to associations in Sardis and Smyrna, the conventions of benefaction and honours evince several important dimensions of rivalries within the civic context. First, associations were competitors for the benefaction or support of the elites, and such connections with civic, provincial, or imperial notables could also enhance the perceived status and image of the association within local society.[13] Prominent women and men of the city were potentially the benefactors of several groups and institutions (including the city itself). Yet their resources were not limitless, and groups of various kinds were contestants as potential beneficiaries.

Rivalries for connections with a particular benefactor are illustrated by the case of T. Julius Lepidus at Sardis and the Lepidus family elsewhere in Asia Minor. Both the official, gymnastic group of young men (ephebes) and an association of merchants honoured him, probably with expectations of continued support (*ISardBR* 46 with revisions in *SEG* 46 [1996] 1523). The latter group joined with the civic assembly in honouring this prominent benefactor in the first century:

> According to the decree passed by the assembly, the people of the Sardians honoured T. Julius Lepidus, the emperor-loving high priest of both Asia and the city and foremost man of the city, because of his love of glory and unmatched goodwill towards the homeland. Those engaged in business in the slave market ([τῶν ἐν τῷ] | σταταρίῳ πρα[γματευο]|μένων) set up this honour from their own resources.[14]

The guild of merchants was, evidently, quick to join in honouring such a prominent benefactor.

Lepidus's kin at Thyatira, C. Julius Lepidus, was also the benefactor of a gymnastic group (*TAM* V 968). The Thyatiran Lepidus's cousin (or second cousin), Claudia Ammion, included among her beneficiaries the guild of dyers:

> The dyers honoured and set up this monument from their own resources for Claudia Ammion—daughter of Metrodoros Lepidas and wife of Tiberius Claudius Antyllos who was gymnasium director three times—who was priestess of the revered ones (emperors) and high priestess of the city for life, having been

13. Cf. van Nijf 1997, 73–128; Harland 2003a, 137–60.

14. *SEG* 46 (1996), no. 1524 (first cent. CE); cf. *TAM* V 932 (guild of slave-market merchants at Thyatira). Translations are mine unless otherwise noted.

> contest director in a brilliant and extravagant manner with purity and modesty, excelling others.[15]

Claudia's husband was also a benefactor of a gymnastic organization there.[16] Associations, organizations, and institutions of various kinds were in competition for contacts with and financial support from elite families like the Lepidus family.

Making initial connections with a benefactor helped to ensure continued, cross-generational support (financial and otherwise) from the same family, and hence continued success in competing with potential rivals. This is what is hinted at in the following inscription from Sardis: "The therapeutists of Zeus—from among those who enter the shrine—crowned Sokrates Pardalas, son of Polemaios, foremost man of the city, *for following in his ancestors' footsteps* in his piety towards the deity" (*ISardBR* 221).[17] It is more explicit in the case of the guild of dyers at Thyatira who honoured T. Claudius Sokrates, civic benefactor and imperial cult high priest, just before 113 CE, as well as his son, Sakerdotianos, about twenty years later, praising him for his "love of honour since he was a boy."[18]

It is important to remember that inscriptions provide only snapshots of a moving picture, and it is hard to measure the level of competition or the number of groups involved. For example, monuments rarely if ever tell us that an association failed to gain support from a particular benefactor. Not surprisingly, we hear of only the "winners" not the "losers." I would suggest, however, that the associations in question were not assured of such support. Rather, they had to struggle with others, including more official groups or institutions, to be noticed in this way. Successfully gaining such benefaction was a way of raising the profile of the association within broader society, where the identity of the association could be expressed more openly.

Before moving on to the more varied nature of benefaction and its significance, it is worth noting that associations were not always competing *for* benefactors but could become competitors *as* benefactors. Associations could be competitors as donors seeking the appropriate honours and prestige in return. The guild of silversmiths and goldsmiths at Smyrna, for instance, became a benefactor when it repaired a statue of the goddess Athena "for the homeland" (*ISmyrna* 721). Such actions could maintain or improve an association's profile or visibility within the civic community.

A list of donors to civic institutions at Smyrna (dating about 124 CE) included several groups who, because of their willing contributions to the homeland, could expect honour and prestige in return. Here the groups are both cooperating in some ways and competing in others, then. Among the groups listed as donors on this monument were "theologians," a group of "hymn singers," and a group of "former Judeans" (οἱ ποτε Ἰουδαῖοι; *ISmyrna* 697).

The identity of this group of people identified in some way as "Judeans" has been the centre of some scholarly debate. It is important to take some time here to discuss the

15. *TAM* V 972 (ca. 50 CE); cf. Buckler 1913, 296–300, nos. 2–3; Harland 2003a, 143–47 (on the dyers at Thyatira).

16. *TAM* V 975 (first cent. CE); see Harland 2003a, 146, figure 25, for the family tree.

17. Cf. Herrmann 1996, 323.

18. *TAM* V 978–980 = Buckler 1913, 300–306, nos. 4–5 (with family tree).

identity of this particular group before returning to our focus on rivalries and benefaction. Traditionally (following Jean-Baptiste Frey in *CIJ* 742), οἱ ποτε Ἰουδαῖοι (literally "the at one time *Ioudaioi*") has been understood as "former Jews" in the "religious" sense of apostates: "Jews who had acquired Greek citizenship at the price of repudiating their Jewish allegiance."[19] Mary Smallwood, Louis Feldman, and others who understand it as such cite no other inscriptional evidence to support this interpretation. Moreover, it seems that broader assumptions concerning whether or not Judeans could actually participate in such ways within the Greek city (*polis*) without losing their "Jewish" identity play a significant role in the decision to interpret the phrase as apostasy. This view also seems to separate "religion" from social and cultural life generally, as though the historical subjects would compartmentalize life in this modern way.

Thomas Kraabel, who is followed by others, rightly challenges this translation and suggests that the term means "people formerly of Judea."[20] He does not cite inscriptional evidence to back up this use of the term ποτε ("at one time," "at some time") in reference to a group of immigrants, however. He bases his interpretation on the fact that this type of monument erected in connection with benefactions from various groups to the city would be an unlikely place to make a public renunciation of faith, which is true. Ross Kraemer (1989) builds on Kraabel's suggestion and pursues further evidence that suggests the term could indeed be used as a geographical indicator.

Recently, Margaret Williams contests Kraabel's suggestion, arguing that conspicuous Jewish apostasy did occur and "foreign residents are *never* described as 'formerly of such and such a region.'"[21] She makes no positive arguments concerning how to translate this phrase in the inscription, apparently resorting to the unfounded apostasy theory. She is, in fact, mistaken regarding the absence of this practice of describing foreigners as formerly of some region (unless she is still focussed solely on the term ποτε specifically).

There is substantial evidence for the geographic and ethnic (not "[ir]religious") understanding of the phrase. First of all, the most recent studies on how to translate the term "*Ioudaioi*" (e.g., by Philip Esler, Steve Mason, and John H. Elliott) show that geographical meanings, with ethnic and cultural implications, would predominate in the ancient setting, and that it is best to use the term "Judeans" (rather than "Jews" with its specifically "religious" connotations to the modern ear) to translate the term.[22] Furthermore, in this specific case at Smyrna, a lengthy inscription recording various benefactions to the city would be, as Kraabel points out, an unlikely place to make a public statement of apostasy, and there are no other attested epigraphical parallels to this. The announcement of one's former religious status not only as an individual but as a group would also be peculiar considering the ways in which what we call "religion" was embedded within social and cultural life in antiquity.

On the other hand, the clear proclamation of one's geographical origins with its implications regarding ethnic identity and cultural practice is common in inscriptions. In fact, geographical origin—with accompanying notions of ethnic identity and a cultural way of

19. Feldman 1993, 83, citing Smallwood 1976, 507.
20. Kraabel 1982, 455; cf. Trebilco 1991, 175; *ISmyrna* 697, notes to line 20.
21. Williams 1997:251–52 (italics mine).
22. See Esler 2003; Mason 2007; Elliott 2007.

life—is among the most attested means of identification in the majority of inscriptions, as we saw in earlier chapters. Although we have no other *exact* parallels to this specific usage of ποτε ("at one time," "at some time") in the known cases of ethnically or geographically based associations specifically, it is important to point out that our evidence is partial at best. There is no consistently employed form of self-designation by such immigrant groups in Asia Minor, such that we cannot speak of deviations. Perhaps more importantly, there is, in fact, a similar phrase used on inscriptions to designate *former geographical origins* for an individual or several individuals, which parallels closely the case at Smyrna in many regards. In particular, we have the comparable use of πρίν ("before," "formerly") as in the phrase "when Aurelius, son of Theophilos, formerly of Pieria, was secretary."[23] Compare also the use of "now" (νῦν) as with the Judean epitaph discussed in chapter 6: "Aur. Heortasios Julianus, Tripolitan, Judean, now living in Hierapolis" (Τριπολείτου Ἰουδέου, νοῖν οἰκο<ῦ>ντ[ος] | ἐν Εἰεραπόλι) (*IHierapMir* 14b).

So the inscription involving Judeans at Smyrna as donors provides another instance of settlers from the East gathering together as a group, perhaps an ongoing association, much like those groups discussed in our chapter on Syrian immigrants. On this occasion, this ethnically based association joined with other local groups in contributing towards activities in the civic community, engaging in both cooperative and competitive dimensions of benefaction.

Returning to the issue of competition and identity, there was far more to benefaction than simple material support. Connections with the elites could be a source of *prestige and honour* for an association. Here, too, associations were potential rivals as they sought to establish or maintain a place for themselves within society. The case of the initiates of Dionysos Breseus at Smyrna serves well in illustrating the feelings of importance that arose from such connections.

This synod of initiates is first attested in the late first century and evidently had a long life, existing well into the third century (*ISmyrna* 731, 729). At a certain point in the second century, the membership apparently encompassed a significant number of performers (τεχνῖται), who were likely responsible for performing the Bacchic theatrical dances (*ISmyrna* 639).[24] The synod maintained connections with important figures within civic, provincial, and imperial networks. And these connections were a source of prestige for this group, presumably over against other associations within the same milieu. The group honoured a member of the local elite who had displayed love of honour in his role as contest director on one occasion (*ISmryna* 652; first century). About a century later, they erected a monument in honour of a functionary in the imperial cult and in the worship of Dionysos:

> The sacred synod of performers and initiates which are gathered around Dionysos Breseus honoured Marcus Aurelius Julianus, son of Charidemos, twice-asiarch,

---

23. *NewDocs* I 5 = Mitchell 1999, 131, no. 51 (Pydna, Macedonia); cf. *IG* IV 783.b.4; *IG* X.2 564 (Thessalonica); *SEG* 27 (1977), no. 293 (Leukopatra); all third-early fourth cent. CE. I am grateful to John S. Kloppenborg for pointing me to these inscriptions.

24. Cf. Lucian *De saltatione* 79; Artemidoros *Oneirokritika* 4.39; *IPergamon* 486 (association of "dancing cowherds")

> crown-bearer, temple-warden of the revered ones (emperors) and "bacchos" of the god, because of his piety towards the god and his goodwill towards the homeland in everything; because of the greatness of the works which he has done for it; and because of his endowments for them. This was done when Menophilos Amerimnos, son of Metrophanes, was treasurer and Aphrodisios Paulus, son of Phoibion, was superintendent of works (*ISmyrna* 639).

Perhaps more important in illustrating the reputation-enhancing nature of connections is this group's activities and diplomacy in relation to emperors (or emperors-to-be). The group set up a monument in honour of Hadrian, "Olympios, saviour, and founder" (*ISmyrna* 622; ca. 129–131 CE), and even maintained correspondence with both Marcus Aurelius and Antoninus Pius (*ISmyrna* 600).[25] The most well-preserved part of the latter inscription involves the future emperor Marcus Aurelius, then consul for the second time (ca. 158 CE), responding to the initiates who had sent a copy of their honorary decree by way of the proconsul, T. Statilius Maximus. Aurelius's response to the decree, which pertained to the association's celebration at the birth of his son, acknowledges the goodwill of the initiates even though his son had since died. That these diplomatic contacts continued with Lucius Verus when Aurelius was emperor is shown in a fragmentary letter from these emperors to the same group around 161–163 CE, perhaps in response to further honours (*ISmyrna* 601). While this correspondence with emperors on the part of a local association is somewhat special (though certainly not unique),[26] this synod of initiates was by no means alone among associations in regard to engagement in monumental honours.

The significance of such connections for understanding rivalries and the expression of identities is better understood once one realizes that groups sometimes (publicly) advertised their connections by monumentalizing these instances of contacts with important persons in civic, provincial, and imperial networks. In the Roman Empire, setting up a plaque or monument was a means by which individuals and groups advertised connections, enhanced their standing, and made a statement regarding their identity in relation to surrounding society. According to Woolf, "the primary function of monuments in the early Empire was as devices with which to assert the place of individuals [or collectivities] within society."[27] Those who set up a monument were, in a very concrete manner, literally set in stone, attempting to symbolically preserve a particular set of relations and connections within society and the cosmos for passers-by to observe: the visual and textual components of epigraphy "provided a device by which individuals could write their public identities into history, by fixing in permanent form their achievements and their relations with gods, with men [*sic*], with the Empire, and with the city."[28] Monumentalizing, then, was one way in which groups, such as associations, could express their identities within society, simultaneously attempting to enhance their standing in relation to other competitors in the same context.

---

25. Cf. Krier 1980; Petzl 1983.
26. On associations and diplomacy, see Millar 1977, 456–64 and Harland 2003a, 155–60, 220–23.
27. Woolf 1996, 29.
28. Woolf 1996, 39.

The Rhetoric of Rivalry and External Posturing

Competitive mentalities among associations are further indicated in language and expressions of identity, or in what I call "the rhetoric of rivalry" here. I would suggest that the rhetoric of rivalry among associations would, at least on occasion, find social expression in realities of life, as when members of different groups came face to face. Let me illustrate what I mean by the rhetoric of rivalry.

Sometimes associations and guilds express pride in group identity by attaching appropriate appellations to their publicized name. Many, like the Dionysiac initiates at Smyrna, felt that their group was "sacred" or "holy." Others claimed to be particularly "emperor-loving" and still others called themselves "great" or "worldwide"/"ecumenical."[29]

Associations of performers and athletes illustrate the conscious rivalry involved in such titles. Two particular groups, which were quite active throughout Asia Minor, piled on the self-designations: "the sacred, worldwide synod of performers, sacred victors and associate competitors gathered around Dionysos and emperor Trajan . . . new Dionysos," on the one hand; and, "the sacred, athletic, traveling, pious, reverent synod . . . gathered around Herakles and emperor . . . Hadrian . . . ," on the other.[30]

Because of the sporadic nature of archeological finds, rarely is there evidence of explicit claims of superiority by a particular association. Nonetheless, a monumental statement by a Dionysiac association (Iobacchoi) at Athens is suggestive.[31] When this group gathered in assembly they did so "for the honour and glory of the Bacchic association (εἰς κόσμον καὶ δόξαν τοῦ Βακχείου)," acclaiming their new high priest, the wealthy C. Herodes Atticus, and calling for the engravement of the associations' statutes (see the sculpture of Herodes in figure 17). The minutes for the meeting record the enthusiastic shout of members: "Bravo for the priest! Revive the statutes! . . . Health and good order to the Bacchic association!" The meeting culminated with the members' acclamation: "Now we are the best of all Bacchic associations!" Presumably Dionysiac associations were superior to those devoted to other deities, but this group was the best of all, from the perspective of its members.

There are similar rhetorical claims to preeminence among associations, sometimes with reference to the superiority of the patron deity or deities. Occasionally there is rhetoric concerning whose god is the best, most protective, or most worthy of honour. Aelius Aristides of Smyrna reflects this sort of rhetoric among participants in associations in his discussion of those devoted to Sarapis:

---

29. "Sacred/most sacred": *IEph* 636 (silversmiths); *IKyzikos* 97 (guild of marble-workers), 291 (sack-bearers/porters); *IHierapJ* 40 (guild of wool-cleaners), 41, 342 (guild of purple-dyers); *SEG* 36 (1986), nos. 1051–53 (associations of linen-workers, sack-bearers/porters devoted to Hermes); *IGLAM* 656 ("tribe" of leather-tanners at Philadelphia); *ISmyrna* 652 (synod of Breiseans devoted to Dionysos). "Emperor loving": *IEph* 293 (initiates of Dionysos); *IMiletos* 940d (goldsmiths in the theatre). "Great": *IEph* 4117 (*collegium* of imperial freedmen [*Kaisarianoi*]). "Worldwide": *SEG* 36 (1986), no. 1051 (guild of linen-workers at Miletos). "World-wide" was a favourite among guilds of performers and athletes.

30. *IAphrodSpect* 88 (127 CE), 90; cf. *IAphrodSpect* 91–92; *ISardBR* 13–14; *IEph* 22.

31. *IG* II.2 1368 = *LSCG* 51 (ca. 178 CE); cf. Tod 1932, 71–96.

Figure 17. Statue head of Herodes Atticus, now in the British Museum

> And *people exceptionally make this god alone a full partner in their sacrifices*, summoning him to the feast and making him both their chief guest and host, so that *while different gods contribute to different banquets, he is the universal contributor to all banquets* and has the rank of mess president for those who assemble at times for his sake . . . he is a participant in the libations and is the one who receives the libations, and he goes as a guest to the revel and issues the invitations to the revellers, who under his guidance perform a dance. . . . (*Or.* 45.27–28)[32]

Evidently, it was in associations devoted to Sarapis, more so than any others, that participants truly experienced communion with their god, according to the sentiment expressed here.

There is further evidence from Smyrna specifically. Seldom does the rhetoric of rivalry in inscriptions clearly identify the competitors. This is why the case of associations devoted to Demeter and to Dionysos at Smyrna in the first and second centuries is so pertinent to issues of identity and competition. For each of these associations, which existed simultaneously, there are the typical claims regarding the "greatness" of its patron deity. What is even more telling is the terminology used by each group, such that it seems that we are witnessing conscious attempts to rival the other with claims of preeminence. On the one hand is "the synod of initiates of the great goddess *before the city* (πρὸ πόλεως), Demeter Thesmophoros." On the other are "the initiates of the great Dionysos Breseus *before the city*."[33] In reference to the Dionysiac group, Cadoux interpreted "before the city" as a

32. Trans. Behr 1981–86 with adaptations and my italics. See Youtie 1948 and *NewDocs* I 1 for several invitations to such banquets in Egypt, in which Sarapis himself is the host who bids his guests to attend.

33. *ISmyrna* 622 (ca. 129–131 CE), 655 (note the lack of an article in the Greek). For other uses of

simple reference to locality: "his [Dionysos's] temple stood just outside the walls."[34] However, as Louis and Jeanne Robert point out, there is likely a double meaning here that relates to issues of rivalry: "It seems that πρὸ πόλεως is employed with two senses: before the city, protecting the city."[35] Members of each association felt that their deity was foremost in protecting the civic community, and their group, not the other, was therefore pre-eminent in the homeland of Smyrna. They proclaimed their rivalrous identities publicly, in this case in the form of inscriptions.

Rivalries over Membership and Allegiances

Associations could also be competitors for members and for the allegiances or loyalties of those who were already members. The evidence for multiple affiliations suggests that many associations were potential competitors in this regard. Yet there are clear signs that some groups, more than others, were self-consciously competitive for allegiances, sometimes tending towards claims of exclusivity of some sort. This was the case with some Judean gatherings and some groups of Jesus-followers in this same region, but they were not entirely alone.

As I explained in the introduction, many social scientists emphasize the situational character of identities, including ethnic identities. Particular people might choose to identify themselves differently, or may be perceived by others differently, depending on the particular social situation or group setting. Communications and understandings of identity—relating to the questions "who am I?" or "who are we?"—could be different when a particular person was attending one group rather than another. There was potential for an individual to hold plural ethnic and social identities as a result of such multiple group affiliations. I would suggest that the possibility of tensions among such identities in a particular individual would be more prevalent in cases where that individual belonged to at least one group in which certain members or leaders made claims of group exclusivity, including some cultural minority groups or ethnic groups (e.g., certain Christian congregations or certain Judean gatherings).

The most general, yet instructive, evidence regarding the potential for multiple affiliations among associations comes from imperial legislation. In the late second century, Marcus Aurelius and Lucius Verus reenacted a law to the effect that it was not lawful to belong to more than one guild (*non licet autem amplius quam unum collegium legitimum habere*; *Digest* 47.22.1.2). Regardless of the rationale behind, or (in)effectiveness of, such imperial legislation,[36] what is clear from such actions is the commonality of one person belonging to more than one association. In other words, membership in a guild or association was often

"before the city" by associations, see *IEph* 275, 1257, 1595, 3808a, 4337 (cf. Merkelbach 1979; *NewDocs* VI 32). The πρὸ πόλεως is used at Ephesos as an additional title for Artemis, pointing to her prominence as patron deity and protector of the city (*IEph* 276, 650).

34. Cadoux 1938, 175.

35. 'Il semble que πρὸ πόλεως unisse là les deux sens: devant la ville, protégeant la ville" (Robert and Robert 1983, 172; trans. mine).

36. Meiggs (1960, 321–23) rightly doubts strict enforcement of such laws in the second century. In the first two centuries, governmental involvement or interference in the life of associations was very limited and sporadic, on which see Harland 2003a, 161–73.

Figure 18. The meeting place of the builders' guild at Ostia

nonexclusive. Belonging to one group did not hinder the possibility of belonging to, or affiliating with, another.[37] In this regard, associations of various kinds could be competitors both for new members and for the allegiances of the members they had.

The happenstance nature of archeological evidence makes it unlikely that we would witness actual examples of such multiple affiliations at the local level. Nonetheless, there are indeed some inscriptional cases from various locales. Russell Meiggs points to at least six cases of dual or multiple memberships in guilds at Ostia in Italy in the second century.[38] Meiggs points out that membership in an association based on a specific trade was not necessarily confined to those of that same trade. This left open the possibility of participation within more than one guild even if one did not engage in the occupation in question.[39] Most of the Ostian cases happen to involve members who took on leadership or administrative positions, such as Marcus Licinius Privatus, who was president of the builders (whose meeting place is shown in figure 18) and later treasurer and president of the bakers (*CIL* XIV 128, 374, 4569); and L. Calpurnius Chius, who was a treasurer of both the corn-measurers and the woodworkers, as well as a member in associations devoted to Silvanus, Cybele, and others (*CIL* XIV 309).[40]

Further examples of multiple affiliations are attested elsewhere involving associations

37. See also Ascough 2003, 87–88.

38. See Meiggs 1960, 321–322. Cf. Royden 1988, 29, on cases involving the shippers' guild.

39. Meiggs (1960, 321) points to imperial privileges that were granted to specific guilds on condition that only members of the common trade (rather than whoever happened to belong to the guild) were to share in the privilege.

40. Meiggs 1960, 321–22. On Privatus and Chius, see Royden 1988, 70–71, 106–8.

that do not seem to be based primarily on occupational connections. At Lindos on the Greek island of Rhodes (about 115 BCE), a man named Timapolis played a role as leader and member of numerous associations (at least six *koina*), including those devoted to Aphrodite and Apollo (*ILindos* 252, lines 250–260). I have already discussed cases in previous chapters, such as Achilleus son of Achillas, who was "father" of three different associations in Moesia (*IGLSkythia* I 99–100, II 83).

Turning to Roman Asia specifically, there are clear indications of multiple affiliations or memberships in associations or other groups. At Pergamon, L. Aninius Flaccus is named as a member of both the Dionysiac "dancing cowherds" and the association of "hymn singers of god Augustus and goddess Roma" in the second or third decade of the second century.[41] Contemporary evidence from Ephesos shows that M. Antonius Artemidoros was apparently a member of both "the gold-bearers" (on which see chapter 2) and a group of Dionysiac initiates in the time of Emperor Hadrian (*IEph* 276 and 1601).

Quite intriguing are cases of multiple affiliations involving Judeans and followers of Jesus in Asia Minor, particularly since scholarship has often assumed and stressed the "exclusivity" of membership in such groups.[42] In light of our earlier discussions of assimilation among immigrants and cultural minorities, these multiple involvements in associations and organizations provide further instances of what some sociologists call *informal* structural assimilation. Suggestive of such multiple affiliations are the Judeans on membership lists of gymnastic organizations of youths (ephebes) at Iasos in Asia Minor, at Coronea in Greece, and at Cyrene in Cyrenaica, as well as those Judeans (or Christians) who are named as members of local elders' organizations at Eumeneia.[43] There are indications that Judeans may have maintained memberships in local guilds without necessarily giving up their connections to the synagogue, as I argued in the previous chapter on Hierapolis.

In another study, I have shown that members of Christian congregations in the cities of Roman Asia, especially at Pergamon and Thyatira, seem to have maintained affiliations with other local associations or guilds.[44] There they would encounter food sacrificed to the Greco-Roman gods ("idol-food" in John's terms). John "the seer" clearly objects to these multiple affiliations and labels these involvements idolatry (eating idol-food) and "fornication" (see esp. Rev 2:6, 14–17, 19–23). Yet his Christian opponents who engaged in the activities clearly thought otherwise. John's call for exclusive membership along the lines of a strong sectarianism was not necessarily the norm, as I have shown. There were clearly debates among other Jesus-followers regarding whether or not one could eat food sacrificed to Greek or Roman gods (in associations or elsewhere) while also maintaining membership in a congregation, as the discussions in Paul's letter to Corinth and in Acts further suggest (1 Corinthians 8–10; Acts 15; cf. *Didache* 6.3). Associations and guilds were among the more prevalent local social settings in which one might encounter such sacrificial foods or meats.

41. Conze and Schuchhardt 1899, 179–80, no. 31 (ca. 106 CE); *IPergamon* 374.

42. E.g., Meeks 1983.

43. *CIJ* 755; *IJO* I Ach 53; Robert 1946, 100–101; Robert 1960a, 436–39 (second-third cent. CE); Lüderitz 1983, 11–21, nos. 6–7 (Jewish names among the ephebes, or youths, at Cyrene in Cyrenaica, late first cent. BCE—early first cent. CE); Rajak 2002 [1985], 368–69. In contrast to these mixed groups, at Hypaipa (near Ephesos) there seems to have been a group of "younger men" consisting solely of Judeans (Ἰουδα|[ι]ων νε|ωτέ|ρων; *IJO* II 47; second or third cent. CE).

44. See Harland 2000; further developed in Harland 2003a, 259–263.

Turning to other groups at Sardis and Smyrna specifically, there are further indications of multiple affiliations and, in this case, indications of attempts to strengthen allegiances to a particular group. Exclusivistic membership tendencies are often attributed to Judean gatherings and Christian congregations by scholars of early Christianity without attention to a few suggestive instances involving other associations. Quite telling are attempts by a certain association to curb tendencies towards multiple affiliations, making apparently exclusive claims to the loyalties of members. Such was the case with the therapeutists of Zeus in Sardis, who in the mid-second century reengraved a Greek translation of an apparently ancient, Aramaic edict by the Lydian governor (404–359 BCE).[45] The ancient edict instructs that the temple-keeping therapeutists of Zeus "who enter the shrine and who crown the god are not to participate in the mysteries of Sabazios—with those who bring the burnt offerings—and the mysteries of Agdistis and Ma." Moreover, "they instruct Dorates, the temple-warden, to abstain from these mysteries." What is most significant for us here is that the leaders or certain members of this group in the Roman era apparently felt a need to reinforce the allegiances of members in the association at a later time, tending towards a view that would limit participation in other groups that engaged in mysteries.

Turning to comparable evidence from Egypt for a moment, an association devoted to Zeus Most High (Hypsistos) at Philadelphia prohibits "leaving the brotherhood of the president for another brotherhood" (τῆς τοῦ ἡγ[ουμένου φράτρας εἰς ἑτέραν φράτραν) (*PLond* VII 2193, line 14). Such exclusivity was not the norm, but there were indeed some associations with tendencies in this direction. In light of such suggestive evidence, Wayne A. Meeks's assertion that "Christian groups were exclusive and totalistic in a way that no club nor even any pagan cultic association was" seems overstated, particularly in light of evidence mentioned earlier that suggests that some Judeans and Christians (including those at Corinth) could engage in multiple group affiliations.[46]

A similar stress on the need for special loyalty to a god's rites, though not necessarily exclusivity, is evident in one of the so-called confession inscriptions of Lydia. This involves a man from Blaundos who set up a monument after he was punished by the god "frequently" and "for a long time" "because he did not wish to come and take part in the mystery when he was called" (*MAMA* IV 281 = Petzl 1994, 126, no. 108; first-second cent. CE).

It is important to note that even without such calls for allegiance (whether of an "exclusive" variety or not), many associations could count on members' attachments and pride in belonging to the group, whether they felt a sense of belonging in other groups simultaneously or not. A grave epigram now in Manisa Museum (= ancient Magnesia on the Sipylos) expresses a deceased member's renowned identification with the association:

> I, who at one point set up a monument of the leader of the society members, lie here, I who first observed zeal and faith towards the society (*thiasos*). My name was Menophilos. For honour's sake these men have set up this grave inscription. My mother also honoured me, as well as my brother, children and wife (*IManisaMus* 354; 180 or 234 CE).[47]

---

45. *ISardH* 4 = Robert 1975 = CCCA I 456 = *NewDocs* I 3.
46. Meeks 1983, 85.
47. Translation by Malay 1994, with adaptations.

Continuing family traditions of allegiance to the Dionysiac initiates at Smyrna, for instance, show through when members proudly state that their father was also an initiate in the group, claiming the title "ancestral initiate" (*patromystai*; *ISmyrna* 731–32; 80–90 CE).[48] We know that similar patterns of membership from one generation to the next were practiced among the Iobacchoi at Athens, where the rules outline half-price fees for sons of members (*IG* II^2 1368, lines 37–41).[49]

Conclusion

Evidently, interaction among associations entailed some degree of competition, and there were opportunities for tensions to arise in particular cases. Associations could be rivals not only for the support of wealthier benefactors, but also for the loyalties of members who belonged to the group. In this context, certain groups could on occasion make claims of preeminence or superiority in relation to other groups. In this way, group identities were developed and communicated, in part, within the broader arena of intergroup relations and rivalries in the cities of the Roman Empire.

At various points, I have noted the place of both Judeans and Christians in rivalries. Here it is important to conclude with some implications for Judean gatherings and Christian congregations, both of which happen to be cultural minority groups. Rather than thinking primarily in terms of Christian groups versus other groups (as is customary in studies that employ sectarian typologies), the discussion of rivalries in this chapter suggests we can understand various associations, including Judean and Christian ones, as participants in a broader arena of association life marked by both competition and cooperation, tensions and positive relations. The level of tensions between a particular association and other groups in the civic setting would vary from one group to the next and from one situation to another. Some ethnic or cultural minority groups would tend towards higher levels of tension at certain points than some other associations.

Evidence for multiple affiliations specifically is part of the picture of both interactions between groups (with members to some degree bridging connections between associations) and competition for allegiances. Here too there are indications that some Judeans and some Christians as cultural minorities were nonetheless engaged in *informal* assimilation, as I explained that concept in chapters 5 and 6. Some individual Judeans and Christians affiliated with other groups or associations within the civic context while also being *en*culturated into the specific ways of a given minority group. Alongside these areas of assimilation or tendencies towards biculturalism, there were areas of cultural maintenance that could contribute towards rivalries and tensions that arose, in part, from cultural minority positions. In the next chapter, I explore certain cases of such tensions involving stereotypes about cultural minority groups.

---

48. Cf. *IEph* 972, 1573 (πατρογέρων, "son of a *gerousia* member").
49. On reduced rates for sons, see Ziebarth 1896, 156.

8

Perceptions of Cultural Minorities

Anti-Associations and Their Banquets

Introduction

"These people are Antropophagos [*sic*] or Men Eaters." This quotation is found on a map of inland Africa in William Snelgrave's travel report of 1734, *A New Account of Some Parts of Guinea and the Slave-Trade.*[1] At this point, inland Africa was, in reality, unknown to Britons. Yet the characterization of peoples living in a "Kingdom of Temian" as cannibals illustrates common processes of "othering," identity formulation, and boundary marking that were also at work in antiquity.

These processes of describing foreign peoples or cultural minority groups as barbarous and threatening outsiders are reflected in Greek novels, histories, and ancient ethnographic materials. Here "ethnography" refers to ancient writings claiming to describe the customs of other ethnic groups or cultural minorities. In this chapter, I examine how cultural minority groups such as Judean (Jewish) gatherings and Christian congregations could, at times, be a target in these processes of identity construction and expression. Judeans and Christians were involved within ethnic rivalries in the ancient context.

Identity theorists are concerned not only with internal group identification, which has been the primary occupation in many chapters here, but also with how those outside a particular group categorize or label that group or its members.[2] Internally, I have shown numerous ways in which members of Judean gatherings and Christian congregations defined themselves and expressed group identity within a broader context. It is important to note that group identities could sometimes be expressed in ways that converged with certain external perceptions of synagogues and congregations, as I demonstrated regarding shared terminology and self-designations.

In this chapter, I turn to some negative aspects of external perceptions and consider how external processes of categorization were at work in the case of cultural minorities such as Judeans and followers of Jesus. I have already touched on the significance of ethnic stereotyping in discussing ethnic groups such as Syrians, Phoenicians, and Judeans. Social

1. See Wheeler 1999, 16–17.
2. On this, see especially Tajfel 1981; Hagendoorn 1993; Jenkins 1994.

and ethnic identity theorists, including Henri Tajfel and Richard Jenkins, stress that how one is perceived by others, regardless of how far this is from any element of truth, plays some role in the construction, negotiation, and expression of identities and in the redefinition of group boundaries.

On the other hand, the act of describing those outside one's own cultural group is, in part, a process of describing one's own communal identity. It is by defining "them" that the sense of "us" is reinforced or reformulated. So once again this pertains to issues of identity. Yet this chapter focusses on identity from the perspective of how some outsiders described peoples outside of their own group, peoples who were sometimes considered barbarous or dangerous.

Social customs of eating and banquets of associations specifically could play an important role in such discourses of "the other," discourses concerning other peoples or groups considered foreign in some way. In fact, accusations of cannibalism, together with accompanying notions of human sacrifice, were a recurring element in how certain people presented the identities of others—some Christians among them—as destructive to the very fabric of civilized society.

Mary Douglas's anthropological work on the ways in which the human, physical body and activities affecting the body (including eating, sexual customs, etc.) are representative of society and representations of society is suggestive here.[3] From this body/society correspondence-theory perspective, the accusation of eating the human body can be interpreted as the equivalent of charging others with destroying human society itself.

The meal practices of small groups or associations often play a role in these discourses of the other. Several ostensibly historical or openly fictional accounts from the Hellenistic and Roman periods present a picture of what one might call wildly transgressive behaviour within associations. In particular, there are a number of accounts of activities within associations that focus on human sacrifice, cannibalism, and extreme sexual activities, among other things. Within Greek and Roman novels, there is a consistency in the use of bandit associations, in particular, to present a picture of improper social, commensal, and ritual behaviour within informal, small group settings. Yet similar categorizations and stereotypes also inform the likes of Livy's supposedly historical account of the "alien" rites of Dionysiac associations in Rome.

Such stories of wild transgression in both fictional and historical narratives draw on ethnographic stereotypes of "the other" in order to present a frightening picture of the dangerous or alien anti-association within society. This inversion depends on common knowledge of the far more tame convivial and ritual aims of real-life associations as attested in epigraphy. Moreover, the picture of the outlaw or foreign anti-association that emerges in the material discussed here provides an essential interpretive framework for allegations against cultural minority groups, such as the Judeans of Cyrene who were accused of eating human flesh and making belts from the entrails of their victims and the early Christian groups who were charged with Oedipean unions (incest) and Thyestean feasts (cannibalism).

---

3. Douglas 1973, 93–112.

Wildly Transgressive Banquets in the Imagination

Several accounts of scurrilous banquets and rituals attributed to criminal and other low-life groups survive in Greek and Latin novels, such that Susan A. Stephens and John J. Winkler can suggest that these themes constitute a "subgenre in the field of ancient fiction."[4] We shall see that there was a complicated interplay between these literary conventions, on the one hand, and both historical narratives and popular imagination about foreign peoples or cultural minority groups, on the other. In some novels ancient fiction writers specifically have associations in mind (whether an occupational guild, a cultic society, a foreign group, or a mixture of these) when they tell tales of such wild meetings and banquets, particularly in connection with brigands or bandits (*latrones* in Latin, λῃσταί in Greek).[5] In essence, the villainous group can be presented as the antitype of what an association should be, as well as an inversion of all that is pious and right. Discussion of some narratives in both novels and historical works will flesh out this inverted picture of the association at banquet (the "anti-association," as I call it), setting the stage for an evaluation of similar charges against real-life cultural minority groups and associations.

"They Ate and Drank in Utter Disorder"

The connection with associations is most explicit in Apuleius's second-century story of a band of brigands (*latrones*) who captured both Lucius, the ass, and Charite, an upper-class "maiden of refined qualities" (*Met.* 3.28–4.25; 6.25–7.12). These brigands are cast as trained professionals (4.9) and military men, and they are repeatedly termed a "guild" (*collegium*), as when a member addresses his fellows concerned that they behave in a manner "in keeping with the principles of our guild" (*Met.* 6.31; also see 4.15; 7.1, 7, 8).[6] We are also told that the patron deity of this guild is Mars, to whom they offer their sacrifices.

In this story, the overall behaviour of the association at meals is summarized thus:

> They ate and drank in utter disorder, swallowing meat by the heap, bread by the stack, and cups by the legion. They played raucously, sang deafeningly, and joked abusively, and in every other respect behaved just like those half-beasts, the Lapiths and Centaurs (*Met.* 4.8).

Here we are witnessing an inversion of common Greek banqueting values. The brigands are characterized as excessive and subhuman in their banqueting manners, as the comparison with the feast of the Lapiths and Centaurs indicates. The wedding celebration of

---

4. Stephens and Winkler 1995, 7.

5. On brigands in fiction see, most recently, Henrichs 1970, 18–35; Winkler 1980, 155–81; Jones 1980, 243–54; Bertrand 1988, 139–49; Hopwood 1998, 195–204; Trinquier 1999, 257–77; Watanabe 2003. On accusations of banditry as a metaphor for the "de-stated" or "barbaric" nonperson, see Shaw 1984, 3–52.

6. Trans. Hanson 1989 (LCL).

Figure 19. Architrave depicting a struggle between a Lapith and Centaur, from the Parthenon at Athens, now in the British Museum (fifth cent. BCE*)*

Peirithous, a Lapith, ended in utter violence between the two peoples as a result of the drunken behaviour of a Centaur. These mythical figures were considered the epitome of terrible and violent banqueting behaviour, as evidenced in the title of Lucian's satirical *Symposium, or The Lapiths,* and in many artistic representations.[7] Pictured in figure 19 is a struggle between a Lapith and a Centaur as portrayed above the architrave of the Parthenon at Athens (fifth cent. BCE).

The main characteristic of the situation in Apuleius's novel is that disorder prevails within the association, or *collegium.* The conversation of the bandits while feasting heightens the sense of impropriety as it centers on the details of their underhanded activities that day, which are far from appropriate topics for the symposium as outlined by the likes of Plutarch in his *Symposium.* What comes to the fore in other accounts of the brigands' meals is only hinted at in Apuleius's story in connection with their new brigand chief from Thrace who was "nursed on human blood" (*Met.* 7.5; cf. Herodotus *Hist.* 4.64).

7. Cf. Homer *Od.* 21.285–304; Pausanias *Descr.* 1.17.2; 1.28.2; 5.10.8.

"They Sacrificed a Human Being and Partook of the Flesh"

Particularly common in portraits of the antibanquets of brigand and other groups is the transgressive practice of human sacrifice accompanied by a cannibalistic meal, the ultimate parody of the sacrificial banquet. Such tales of human sacrifice are found in a variety of contexts in antiquity, particularly in ethnographic descriptions of foreign peoples or cultural minority groups, in narratives of conspiracy (which effectively barbarize certain Greeks or Romans), and in narratives with entertainment purposes, such as novels.

James Rives's study of the social meaning of human sacrifice in antiquity shows how human sacrifice acts as a sign within discourses of barbarity versus civilization and of piety versus "superstition" or "magic" (namely, activities perceived as inappropriate ritual practice).[8] Moreover, in virtually all accounts of such wild transgressions, we are witnessing ethnographic discourses that deal with description of the other, whether that other is a remote "barbarian" people or a more dangerous enemy within. Here I focus primarily on associations specifically, only touching on broader issues of human sacrifice insofar as they clarify notions of supposed counter-cultural behaviour within small-group settings.

Among the more controversial accounts is the description of a human sacrifice (a child or a servant) and the accompanying meal in fragments of a second-century Greek novel by Lollianos, entitled *A Phoenician Story* (*Phoenikika*).[9] The instigators of the sacrifice in this fragment are never expressly called brigands, even though most scholars who have dealt with the passage assume so.[10] Perhaps we are safer in generally referring to them as "low-lifes" or, as Winkler puts it, "desperadoes."

For present purposes it is important to point to an explicit designation in the fragmentary text: in the midst of the narrative, there is a reference to the "ones being initiated" (τοῖς μυουμένοις). We need not agree with those who read the novels allegorically and see hidden mystic connections throughout (as does Reinhold Merkelbach, reflected in Henrichs), nor with those who, in reaction, tend to downplay the author's explicit references to mysteries (e.g., Winkler and C. P. Jones).[11] I would suggest that we can discuss this episode in terms of a low-life association of initiates, an inverted picture of associations of initiates (μύσται) that are widely attested in the epigraphic record, as discussed in previous chapters. As I show in connection with Livy's account of the Bacchanalia, there are cases when ancient authors ascribe ritual murder and related criminal activities to real-life groups that engaged in mysteries, particularly those devoted to foreign deities.[12]

---

8. Rives 1995, 65–85.

9. *POxy* 1368 + *PColon* 3328 (here the focus is on the narrative in B1 recto). For a critical edition of the text see Henrichs 1972 and, most recently, Stephens and Winkler 1995, 314–57 (with Greek text and extensive commentary).

10. Henrichs goes further in identifying them with the brigand "cowherds" (βουκόλοι) attested in Dio Cassius and in other novels (Henrichs 1970, 33, 35). On the problems with that view, see Stephens and Winkler 1995, 319–21.

11. E.g., Merkelbach 1995. See the critique in Winkler 1980; Jones 1980; Beck 1996, 131–50.

12. On ritual murder and Mithras, see Vermaseren 1963, 166–68; Turcan 1981, 350 nn. 6–7. On "jars of human flesh" accidentally discovered in the temple of Bellona (often identified with the Cappadocian goddess Ma), see Dio Cassius 42.26.2–3.

The fragmentary episode in Lollianos—which begins with the sacrifice of the child or servant, a sacrificial oath ritual, and a sacrificial meal—runs as follows:

> Meanwhile another man, who was naked, walked by, wearing a crimson loincloth, and throwing the body of the *pais* (child or servant) on its back, he cut it up, and tore out its heart and placed it upon the fire. Then, he took up [the cooked heart] and sliced it up to the middle. And on the surface [of the slices] he sprinkled [barley groats] and wet it with oil; and when he had sufficiently prepared them, [he gave them to the] initiates, and those who held (a slice?) [he ordered] to swear in the blood of the heart that they would neither give up nor betray [--------], not [even if they are led off to prison], nor yet if they be tortured.[13]

As Henrichs points out, this whole sacrificial scene follows the usual Greek pattern of sacrifice, including the central importance of the internal organs or entrails (σπλάγχνα).[14] Also not unusual is the accompanying oath ceremony, in which portions of the innards were consumed together as a symbolic means of binding participants. What is extremely unusual, and deliberately inverts what would otherwise be considered pious activity in honour of the gods, is the fact that it is a human, rather than an animal, victim in this ritual.

Following the sacrifice, the oath ceremony, and the meal came further drinking and entertainment as "they sang, drank, had intercourse with the women in full view of Androtimos (either the leader of the initiates or a captive of the outlaws; B1 Verso, lines 20–21).[15] Shortly thereafter the participants put on robes, smeared their faces with black or white, and departed, likely to engage in further criminal activity in disguise. The author of this novel is certainly not the first to combine both human sacrifice and oath-taking in an inversion of common ritual, as the tales of the conspiracy (*coniuratio*; lit., "swearing together") of Cataline clearly show.[16]

Cataline was among the main political opponents of Cicero (for the consulship, the highest political position at that time) in the city of Rome during the Republican era (in the 60s BCE). Legends about his conspiratorial activities involving human sacrifice developed over time: Sallust mentions Cataline and his co-conspirator's oath that was sealed by partaking from "bowls of human blood mixed with wine" (*Bell. Cat.* 22.1–2); Plutarch claims that "they sacrificed a human being and partook of the flesh" (*Cic.* 10.4); and Dio Cassius asserts that the conspirators "sacrificed a *pais* [child or servant] and after administering the oath over his vitals, ate these in company with the others" (37.30.3).[17] Such accusations against one's compatriots were a succinct way of placing opponents, or disliked

---

13. *PColon* 3328, B 1 recto, lines 9–16. Trans. Stephens and Winkler 1995, 338–41.

14. Henrichs 1970, 33–34.

15. Both Jones and Stephens and Winkler point out some striking similarities between the story here and that in Apuleius's *Met.* (esp. 4.8–33), including a reference to Lapiths as prototypes of unruly banqueters, such that some literary relation is likely (see Jones 1980; Winkler 1980; Stephens and Winkler 1995, 322–25).

16. Cf. Dölger 1934, 207–10; Rives 1995, 72–73; Diodorus Siculus 22.3.5; Plutarch *Publ.* 4.1; Philostratus *Vit. Apoll.* 7.11, 20, 33.

17. Trans. Rolfe 1921 (LCL); Perrin 1916–20 (LCL); Cary 1960–84 (LCL).

politicians of the past, beyond the pale of humanity and civilization, a way of "barbarizing" a fellow Greek or Roman, as Rives puts it.[18]

Though references to "initiates" are lacking in some other cases, there are similar stories of human sacrifice in other novels that present bands of brigands as the ultimate criminal cultic group or association. Thus in Xenophon's second-century *Ephesian Tale* we find a band of brigands (ληστήριον), led by one Hippothoos, collecting statues, wood, and garlands in preparation for a sacrifice in honour of their patron deity, Ares. It turns out that the "usual manner" for their sacrifices is to "hang the intended victim, human or animal, from a tree and throw javelins at it from a distance" (*Ephesiaka* 2.13). In this case, their intended victim is saved at the last moment by the police chief of the region of Cilicia in Asia Minor, who has most of the brigands killed.

Another instance involves a close call, but in Achilles Tatius's second-century novel (ca. 150–175 CE) the sacrifice apparently takes place.[19] This episode includes the bandit "herdsmen" or "cowherds" (βουκόλοι) of the Egyptian Delta, based at a place called Nikochis (*Leuc. Clit.* 4.12.8). It combines the internal threat of robbers with the common fear of "barbarian" (here non-Greek) peoples which is characteristic of ancient travel literature, or ethnography. The "cowherds," who are recurring characters not only in novels but also historical writings, are here presented as "wild frightening men, all large and black" and they "all shouted in a foreign language" (3.9). The narrator, Clitophon, wishes that he and his travelling companions had been captured by Greek bandits instead (3.10).

Ultimately, Clitophon and Leucippe, the protagonists, are separated, and Clitophon escapes from the brigands when they are attacked by the Egyptian army (*Leuc. Clit.* 3.13–14). Then, from a distance, Clitophon witnesses his beloved Leucippe, still in the hands of the brigands. The first person narrative heightens the horror as we witness the brigands' preparations for a sacrifice under the direction of their "priest" (ἱερεύς), creating an altar and pouring a libation over Leucippe's head. The participants lead her in a sacrificial procession to the accompaniment of flutes as the Egyptian priest chants a hymn:

> Then at a signal they all moved far away from the altar. One of the attendants laid her on her back and tied her to stakes fixed in the ground. . . . He next raised a sword and plunged it into her heart and then sawed all the way down to her abdomen. Her viscera leaped out. The attendants pulled out her entrails and carried them in their hands over to the altar. When it was well done they carved the whole lot up, and all the bandits shared the meal. . . . All this was done according to the rubrics sanctioned by the priest. (*Leuc. Clit.* 3.15)[20]

Clitophon stood there in "sheer shock," a shock that no doubt is meant to be shared by the reader, or hearer, of this story. But we soon learn that Leucippe is alive and well, and the two men (who had only pretended their allegiance to the brigand group after their capture) had successfully fooled the brigands using some stage props and special effects (animals' entrails and a trick sword).

18. Rives 1995, 73. On the "political cannibal" see McGowan 1994, 431–33.
19. Cf. Bertrand 1988.
20. Trans. Winkler in Reardon 1989, 216.

The sacrifice of a virgin was, in part,[21] to be the "initiation" of these two men into the brigand association, as the chief brigand (λῃστάρχος) informed them: "We have a tradition that sacrifices, especially human sacrifices, must be performed by the newly initiated (πρωτομύσται)." "Yes sir! We are ready to live up to the highest standards of banditry" was the reply of the initiates-to-be (*Leuc. Clit.* 3.22; cf. 3.19).

The case of the "cowherds" of Egypt happens to provide an instance where history and fiction are intimately intertwined, and where the accusations of barbaric human sacrifice recur again in historical sources.[22] We know from Strabo that there were indeed people that went by the designation "cowherds" (βουκόλοι) in the Egyptian Delta region before the time of Augustus. Yet these are initially described as herdspeople who were also brigands (λῃσταί) in a matter-of-fact manner with no elaboration on any extreme social or ritual conventions beyond their occupation, which included the positive role (in the view of earlier Egyptian kings, so Strabo claims) of warding off foreigners, namely Greeks (*Geogr.* 17.1.6; 17.1.19).

Now a papyrus scroll from the Egyptian Delta confirms ongoing references to these brigands in 166/167 CE, where they are described by an outsider as "the impious Neikokeitai (τῶν ἀνοσίων Νεικωκειτῶν)," which is in keeping with the base at Nikochis which Tatius mentions in his novel.[23] The same descriptive term, "impious" (ἀνοσίος), is used of the Judeans in connection with the revolt under Trajan, by the way. Furthermore, another second-century papyrus contains an oracle that deals with disturbances and seems to refer to the death of "cowherds," presumably as part of the solution to the disturbance.[24] By the time Dio Cassius writes his history (ca. 211–222 CE), then, there has been opportunity for the development of tales surrounding these threatening figures of the Delta. As Winkler convincingly argues, we are here witnessing a case of "history imitating story," more so than the other way around.[25]

Dio's account of a revolt in 172/173 CE involving the "cowherds" happens to mention that the group was led by an Egyptian priest (ἱερεύς) Isidorus.[26] Dio claims that some of the "cowherds" dressed as women and pretended to offer ransom for the release of prisoners in order to deceive and capture a Roman centurion and other soldiers involved in quelling the revolt. This is where Dio moves on to the sort of stereotypical accusations that are in keeping with tales of the supposed criminal behaviour of political conspirators and "barbarous"

---

21. The sacrifice was also the means by which the brigands hoped to purify their citadel and gain the upper hand in battles with Egyptian troops (3.19).

22. On the "cowherds," also see Heliodorus *An Ethiopian Story* (cf. Xenophon *An Ephesian Tale* 3.12); Winkler 1980, 175–81; Bowersock 1994, 51–53; Frankfurter 1998, 207–8; Rutherford 2000.

23. See Fuks 1953, 157–58.

24. *PThmouis* 1, col. 104, line 13 and col. 116, lines 4–5. See Shelton 1976, 209–13; Frankfurter 1998, 208 n. 46; cf. Bertrand 1988; Bowersock 1994, 53.

25. Winkler 1980, 178. Cf. Herodotus *Hist.* 4.106, describing the so-called Androphagi.

26. This priestly leadership of the group seems to be echoed in Heliodorus's fictional narrative in which the brigand chief Thyamis is the son of a high priest of Memphis (*An Ethiopian Story* 1.19; cf. Frankfurter 1998, 208). The account in Tatius, discussed above, likewise mentions the presence of a priest within the group.

peoples: "They also sacrificed his [the centurion's] companion, and after swearing an oath over his entrails, they devoured them" (Dio Cassius 72.4.1–2).[27]

Furthermore, there seems to be some consistency in Dio's choice of the charge of human sacrifice and cannibalism against supposedly barbarous peoples in connection with revolts specifically. For when he describes the revolt of Judeans in Cyrene, who were "destroying both the Romans and the Greeks," he claims that "they would eat the flesh of their victims, make belts for themselves of their entrails, anoint themselves with their blood and wear their skins for clothing" (68.32.1–2). For Dio and some others, this was not out of the ordinary for such foreign peoples: Dio suggests that the Judean immigrants in Egypt and on Cyprus had "perpetrated many similar outrages" (68.32.2). The blurring of the line between history and reality, fact and fiction, that Dio's account of the "cowherds" illustrates so well extends to other supposed historical accounts and popular reports concerning real-life associations and cultural minorities.

Accusations of Wild Transgression and Cultural Minority Groups

"Away . . . You Who Suck Men's Blood"

Notorious is the case of the suppression of worshippers of Bacchus, namely Dionysos, in Rome and Italy beginning in 186 BCE (Livy *Hist. Rom.* 39.8–19). Many studies have struggled with historical, political, ritual, and other dimensions of Livy's account of the Bacchanalia and with the epigraphic decree concerning actions by the Roman senate, which shows that Livy is not making the whole thing up.[28] Here I am less concerned with the question of Roman suppression of Bacchic groups in the early second century, which has been dealt with extensively in scholarship. Instead, I want to consider how the Roman historian Livy, in about 20 BCE, presents this particular case as a story of a "foreign" (Greek) association threatening the Roman way of life and contributing to moral decline.[29] I am interested in Livy's account as description of the alien "other" within, and in what accusations of wild transgression are made concerning the nature of the meetings, initiations, and banquets of these Dionysiac associations. It is important to consider to what degree the charges of ritual murder and sexual perversion may be a consequence of Livy's ethnographic, artistic, or novelistic license.

It is important to note the position of this whole incident within Livy's history: the Bacchanalia affair takes place almost immediately following Livy's characterization of the 180s BCE as the "seeds" of moral decline at Rome. From Livy's perspective, the moral decline was due, in large part, to the influence of foreign ways and featured, in particular,

27. Trans. Cary 1960–84 (LCL).

28. See, more recently, North 1979, 85–103; Rousselle 1982; Gruen 1990, 34–78; Walsh 1996, 188–203.

29. Cf. Dio Cassius, 52.36.2.

imported styles of convivial entertainment and elaborate banquets from "Asia" (*Hist. Rom.* 39.6).[30] The Bacchanalia incident is presented as one further case of this decline.

As P. G. Walsh convincingly shows, there is no need to doubt the "bare bones" of Livy's account in terms of the overall incident and the action of the senate. But there is an important distinction to be made regarding the relative reliability of two main sections of the narrative, between the first, longer section (Livy *Hist. Rom.* 39.8.1–39.14.3) and the second, shorter section dealing with the meeting with the senate (from 39.14.3). "What goes before is clearly a romantic and dramatic expansion of [Postumius's] report, whereas what follows is based on senatorial records, and is more solidly historical."[31] It is precisely in the former, novelistic section that descriptions of wild activities of the association are elaborated in most lurid detail.

In agreement with Erich Gruen's observation that the account "evokes the atmosphere of a romantic novel—or better, Hellenistic and Roman New Comedy," Walsh then goes on to argue that evidence in Plautus, a contemporary of the Bacchic suppression, suggests that Bacchic themes "may have featured as the plot of a comic or mimic drama" and that this "has left its mark on the historiographical tradition" (on both Livy's sources and on Livy's own history writing).[32] Among the ongoing jokes in Plautus about the dangers of Bacchic orgies (also cited in this section's subtitle) is one character's statement: "Away from me, sisters [bacchants], you who suck men's blood."[33]

Livy's account begins with the alien nature of these Dionysiac groups, speaking of a "Greek of humble origin" whose "method of infecting people's minds with error was not by the open practice of his rites and the public advertisement of his trade and his system; he was the hierophant [revealer of sacred objects] of secret ceremonies performed at night" (Livy *Hist. Rom.* 39.8).[34] The initiations, Livy continues, "soon began to be widespread among men and women. The pleasures of drinking and feasting were added to the rituals to attract a larger number of followers. When wine had inflamed their feelings, and night and the mingling of the sexes and of different ages had extinguished all power of moral judgement, all sorts of corruption began to be practiced" (39.8). We then learn of other illegal activities, including supply of false witnesses, forging of documents, perjury, and, most frighteningly, wholesale murder.

The most lurid accusations in Livy's account, which spells out the aforementioned "corruption," appear in a passage that is considered among the least historical sections of the story: namely, the first-hand descriptions of the secretive practices of a former member, Hispala, that had for some reason remained undetected until her report.[35] First, Livy has Hispala outline the crimes in private to warn the initiate-to-be, her lover, Aebutius (Livy *Hist. Rom.* 39.9–10). But it is in the second, more official report to the consul, Postumius (39.13), that the lurid details of extreme sex and ritual murder come to the fore.

In this second report to the consul, Hispala relates how initiations in the Dionysiac

---

30. Cf. Walsh 1996, 189–90.

31. Walsh 1996, 193.

32. Gruen 1990, 62; Walsh 1996, 192.

33. *Bacchides* 52ff., 368ff., as cited by Walsh 1996.

34. Trans. Bettenson 1976, with minor adaptations (text in Sage 1965).

35. Cf. North 1979, 88–90; Gruen 1990, 61–65.

mysteries originally only took place three times a year in daylight, but that more recently the meetings had increased to five days each month at night. Not only that, but membership had increased greatly by this time, including participants from among the Roman elites. Then come the details of moral degradation inspired by foreign rites:

> From the time when the rites were held promiscuously, with men and women mixed together, and when the license offered by darkness had been added, no sort of crime, no kind of immorality, was left unattempted. There were more obscenities practiced between men than between men and women. Anyone refusing to submit to outrage or reluctant to commit crimes was slaughtered as a sacrificial victim. To regard nothing as forbidden was among these people the summit of religious achievement. (Livy *Hist. Rom.* 39.13)

Here we are seeing the common stereotypes so familiar to us now of wild banquets combined with human sacrifice. Yet added to this is the accusation of sexual "perversions" that accompanied the drinking.

Ethnographic descriptions in which foreign peoples are accused of unusual sexual practices are common, as in Tacitus's account of the Judeans' supposed "unlawful" sexual behaviour (*Hist.* 5.5.2; cf. Martial *Epigr.* 7.30).[36] This combination of inverted banqueting and perverted sexual practices would recur in the list of counter-cultural practices attributed to the early Christians as well. Livy provides another clear case where fiction informed by ethnographic stereotypes of the criminal tendencies of foreign peoples informs the description of real-life associations, in this case an association with mysteries. Inversion of proper banqueting and drinking practices, as well as distorted sacrificial rites, are again at the heart of the allegations.

Inscriptional and papyrological evidence for the actual banqueting and sacrificial activities of associations of various kinds, including many Dionysiac associations, comes across as far less exciting, one might even say bland, in relation to these more extreme, imaginative materials. In particular, although there are indications of abusive conduct, and drinking was most certainly a component in such matters, there were simultaneously widely shared values which set parameters on banqueting behaviour within associations and which, from time to time, could be carved in stone. Moreover, the association regulations or sacred laws of the Greco-Roman era that have survived and been uncovered (such as the rule of the Iobacchoi at Athens sketched in figure 20) are concerned with issues of order and decorum in meetings, rituals, and banquets.[37] For example, the rules of the devotees of Zeus Hypsistos, which are echoed elsewhere, include the following: "It shall not be permissible for any one of [the members]... to make factions or to leave the brotherhood of the president for another, or for men to enter into one another's pedigrees at the

---

36. Cf. Tertullian *Marc.*, 1, where Tertullian speaks of the unusual sexual practices of the people of Pontus in an attempt to critique his Christian opponent, Marcion of Pontus.

37. See, for instance, the regulations of the *collegium* devoted to Diana and Antinoos at Lanuvium in Italy (*CIL* XIV 2112; 136 CE), the devotees of Bacchos at Athens (*IG* II^2 1368; 176 CE), and several associations at Tebtunis in Egypt (*PMich* V 243–245; mid-first century CE). Cf. Boak 1937, 210–19; Dennis E. Smith 2003, 97–131.

symposium or to abuse one another at the symposium or to chatter or to indict or accuse another or to resign the course of the year or again to bring the symposia to nought . . ." (*PLond* 2710; ca. 69–58 BCE).[38] Although rules may often be drawn up to deal with problems that were actually encountered, the regulations suggest that "good order"—as defined by such groups—remained a prevalent value in many banqueting settings. So we should not imagine that stories of wild transgression are descriptive of real activities in immigrant or cultural minority groups, or in other associations.

"Come! Plunge the Knife into the Baby": Judeans and Jesus-followers

Since the classic work on accusations of infanticide against Christians by F. J. Dölger, a number of studies have focused on explaining the Thyestean feasts (cannibalism) and Oedipean unions (incest) mentioned in connection with the martyrs of Lyons, among them the important contributions by Albert Henrichs and Robert M. Grant.[39] More recently, M. J. Edwards and Andrew McGowan have independently focused their attention on the Christian evidence and have come to similar conclusions regarding the origins of these accusations. Both scholars challenge the suggestion of Grant and others that the accusations emerged out of a misunderstanding of the actual practices of Christians (namely, a misunderstanding of the eucharist—eating the body and blood of Christ—and the custom of addressing one another as "brother" or "sister").[40] Edwards convincingly argues that it is what the Christians did *not* do—that they did not sacrifice to or fully acknowledge the gods of the Greeks and Romans—that made them stand out as foreign. Dölger was "correct to surmise that pagan controversialists were filling a lacuna in their knowledge of Christian practices, just as they were wont to attribute every peculiarity to barbarians."[41]

Although the accusations against Christians, as well as their Judean precedents, have drawn the attention of many scholars, few fully address these allegations within the framework of ethnography and descriptions of dangerous or foreign *associations* specifically. Whereas the material concerning the outlaws in Lollianos's episode figure somewhat importantly in recent discussions of the Christian evidence, especially Henrich's study,[42] few sufficiently place the discussion within the framework of the outlaw or foreign anti-associations discussed here. Nor have these ethnographic discourses and accusations been explained within the framework of theories of social identity and external categorization, which I have outlined in connection with stereotypes about Syrians and others in chapter 5.

Returning to these ancient instances of social categorization, it is important to outline some of the Judean precedents before moving on to allegations against others who hon-

38. Trans. Roberts, Skeat, and Nock 1936, 42, with adaptations.

39. Henrichs 1970. Cf. Henrichs 1981, 195–235; Grant 1981, 161–70.

40. Edwards 1992, 71–82; McGowan 1994. See chapter 3 in this volume, which shows the difficulties in assuming that the Christian practice of calling one another "brother" was unique (which is an assumption behind Grant's theory).

41. Edwards 1992, 74; cf. Rives 1995.

42. Henrichs 1970.

Figure 20. Sketch of the rules of the Bacchic association (Iobacchoi) at Athens, from Harrison 1906, figure 25.

oured the Judean God, namely, followers of Jesus.[43] Many ancient ethnographic descriptions of the Judeans by Greek, Egyptian, and other authors have been gathered together in Menahem Stern's *Greek and Latin Authors on Jews and Judaism* (1974–84) and have been recently discussed in works such as Peter Schäfer's *Judeophobia* (1997). These descriptions provide important evidence regarding external categorizations and stereotypes regarding Judeans.

In discussing the customs of the Judeans, both Damocritos and Apion (or Apion's source) give credence to rumours, or simply create stories, that Judeans engaged in human sacrifice. Attributed to the Greek author Damocritos (perhaps late first century CE) is the idea that Judeans worshiped the statue of an ass and that every seven years they "caught a foreigner and sacrificed him," cutting him into pieces.[44] There is a sense in which the accusation of human sacrifice is a short form for notions of Judeans' supposed hostility

43. On such accusations against Judeans, see Bickerman 1980, 225–55; Feldman 1993, 123–76; Peter Schäfer 1997.

44. Trans. by Stern 1974–84, 1.531.

to foreigners (μισόξενος βίος), as in Hecataeus (ca. 300 BCE), and hatred of human kind (μισανθρωπία), as in Apollonios Molon (first century BCE).[45]

More extensive is the tale of the Judeans' sacrifice of foreigners, namely Greeks, as told by Apion (contemporary of Philo in first-century Alexandria, Egypt). This Apion authored works that critiqued the ways of Judeans and others; this spurred a response by Josephus, appropriately called *Against Apion*. Apion also played a more direct role as an ambassador for the Greeks of Alexandria in their rivalries with local Judeans, which I mentioned in chapter 1 in connection with Philo's role as ambassador for the Judeans.

Apion's account of an incident in connection with the time of Antiochus Epiphanes (160s BCE) claims to be based on the report of a fattened escapee.[46] According to the story, the Judeans had captured this Greek in order to fulfill the "unutterable law of the Judeans": annually, "they would kidnap a Greek foreigner, fatten him up for a year, and then convey him to a wood, where they slew him, sacrificed his body with their customary ritual, partook of his flesh, and, while immolating the Greek, swore an oath of hostility to the Greeks" (Josephus *C. Ap.* 2.91–96).[47]

Here there is once again the reference to making an oath on a human victim, which was common in stories of criminal or political conspiracy, such as those associated with Cataline and the bandits in Lollianos's novel. Similar charges continued against Judean associations in the diaspora specifically. We have already seen this in the case of Dio Cassius's account of the supposed cannibalistic commensal behaviour of Judeans during the revolts in Cyrene, Cyprus, and Egypt.

This brings us, finally, to the anti-banquets attributed to another set of cultural minority groups with Judean connections in the diaspora setting: followers of Jesus. This is not the place to engage in full analysis of all cases that have been discussed at length in scholarship.[48] Yet it will be worthwhile briefly to outline some of the Christian evidence in order to place it in the context of the present discussion of cultural minority groups and discourses of the other. These accusations, like the stories of bandit anti-associations, political conspiracy, and alien cults, arise from a common stockpile of stereotypes of the threatening other, and there is no need to look for any basis in the reality of actual practices.

As early as Pliny the Younger (ca. 110 CE), who as we saw in chapter 1 thinks of the Christians as both an "association" and an un-Roman or foreign "superstition," there are indications that rumours were circulating about the Christians in Pontus. At least this seems to be the case, if we can read Pliny's mention of "food of an ordinary and harmless kind" as an allusion to a rumoured "crime" (*flagitium*) of cannibalism (Pliny *Ep.* 10.96.7; cf. Tacitus *Ann.* 15.44.2).[49] In fact, Pliny seems to have in mind the typical portrait of the criminal, conspiratorial, or low-life association (though not necessarily the Bacchanalia specifically) when he states that these Christians "bind themselves by oath, not for any criminal

45. Texts in Stern 1974–84. Cf. Feldman 1993, 125–48; Peter Schäfer 1997, 15–17, 21–22, 170–79.

46. Schäfer convincingly argues against Bickerman's view that Apion's story originated in the time of Epiphanes (Schäfer 1997, 62–65; cf. Rives 1995, 70–71).

47. Trans. Thackeray 1926 (LCL).

48. See, most recently, Henrichs 1970; Benko 1980, 1055–118; Edwards 1992; McGowan 1994.

49. On rumours of "crimes" (*flagitia*), see Tacitus *Ann.* 15.44 and Suetonius *Nero* 16.2.

purpose, but to abstain from theft, robbery, and adultery, to commit no breach of trust and not to deny a deposit when called upon to restore it" (*Ep.* 10.96.7).[50]

Around 150 CE, Justin Martyr mentions the accusations of sexual licence and eating of human flesh (*Apol.* 1.26.7). The charges of "Thyestean feasts" (cannibalism) and "Oedipean unions" (incest) are explicit in the letter from the Greek-speaking Christians of Vienne and Lyons to the Christians in Asia and Phrygia concerning the martyrdoms in 177 CE. There the accused are also charged with "atheism" (ἄθεος) and "impiety" (ἀσεβές; Eusebius *HE* 5.1.3–5.2.8).

More explicit and detailed charges of infant sacrifice within associations of Jesus-followers come to the fore in the writings of Tertullian and in Minucius Felix. In his discussion of Rumour personified, for instance, Tertullian refutes the charges by exaggerating them to show their absurdity: "Come! plunge the knife into the baby, nobody's enemy, guilty of nothing, everybody's child . . . catch the infant blood; steep your bread with it; eat and enjoy it" (*Apol.* 8.2).

In Minucius Felix's dialogue, Caecilius critiques the atheistic, Christian "gang . . . of discredited and proscribed desperadoes" (*deploratae, inlicitae ac desperatae factionis*) (*Octavius* 8.3).[51] They consist of the dregs of society and women, who are also considered "profane conspirators (*profanae coniurationis*) leagued together by meetings at night and ritual fasts" (*Oct.* 8.3–4). This "superstition" (*superstitio*) is a "promiscuous brotherhood and sisterhood" (*fratres et sorores*) that worship an ass and adore the genitals of their high priest (*Oct.* 9.2–4).

According to Caecilius, the initiation of new members takes place in a sacrificial banquet that once again echoes the anti-banquets we have seen in both novels and ethnographic sources:

> An infant, cased in dough to deceive the unsuspecting, is placed beside the person to be initiated. The novice is thereupon induced to inflict what seems to be harmless blows upon the dough, and unintentionally the infant is killed by his unsuspecting blows; the blood—oh, horrible—they lap up greedily; the limbs they tear to pieces eagerly; and over the victim they make league and covenant, and by complicity in guilt pledge themselves to mutual silence. (*Oct.* 9.5–6)

Finally, reminiscent of Livy's tales of the Bacchanalia, Caecilius speaks of the Christians' banquets in more detail, in which people of all ages and both sexes mingle. After feasting, "when the blood is heated and drink has inflamed the passions of incestuous lust" the lamps are overturned and indiscriminate, incestuous sexual escapades take place in the dark (*Oct.* 9.6–7).

In many respects, then, what we are witnessing with these allegations against Christians is the convergence of several factors: ethnographic stereotypes of the "foreign"

---

50. Trans. Radice 1969 (LCL). I am not convinced by Robert M. Grant's suggestion that Pliny may actually have in mind Livy's account of the Bacchanalia (Grant 1948, 273–74; cf. Grant 1970, 12–17).

51. Trans. Glover and Rendall 1931 (LCL). Caecilius's opinions may draw on an earlier source by Marcus Cornelius Fronto (ca. 100–166 CE), on which see *Oct.* 9.6 and Benko 1980, 1081.

association (e.g., Bacchanalia), common allegations against Judean groups specifically, and novelistic or popular stories of the internal threat often associated with criminal or low-life anti-associations. Overall, this is part of the process of Greek or Roman self-definition by means of external categorizations of foreign peoples or cultural minority groups, in this case Christians. In virtually all the cases in this chapter, the inversion or perversion of the shared meal, along with inherent sacrificial connections, stands out as a symbol of the group's relation to surrounding society, as a sign of an anti-societal threat and the epitome of social and religious disorder.

The reactions of certain Judeans and Christians, including Tertullian, to such stereotypes can be placed within the context of social identity theory regarding the relation of external categorizations to internal self-definition. Jenkins outlines a variety of scenarios in how members of a particular cultural minority group react to and internalize external attempts at categorization, categorizations which may be positive, neutral, or pejorative. There are cases when external categorizations overlap significantly with some internal modes of self-identification, as we saw in connection with Judean gatherings and Christian congregations as associations in chapter 1. In such cases of overlap, there may be ready assimilation of external categories to internal identifications and, as Jenkins notes, "some degree of external reinforcement or validation is crucial for the successful maintenance of internal (group) definitions."[52]

At the other end of the continuum are active attempts to resist or reject negative external categorizations. This is what we are seeing in the likes of Justin and Tertullian, who focus on rebutting characterizations of Jesus-followers. Yet even in such cases of resistance, the categorization nonetheless plays a role in internal reconfigurations of self-definition: "the very act of defying categorization, of striving for an autonomy of self-identification, is, of course, an effect of being categorized in the first place. The rejected external definition *is* internalized, but paradoxically, as the focus of denial."[53]

Judean and Christian Critique of the Associations of "Others"

Furthermore, there is something that we could call a backlash in the form of moral critique of the associations of others by some Judean and Christian authors. Like the stereotypes about minority groups, this critique also emphasizes disorderly or dangerous convivial activities of the associations of others. Judeans and Christians themselves engaged in ethnic rivalries. Once again, it is by characterizing outside groups as dangerous and barbarous that particular Judean or Christian authors engage in the expression of their own identities over against the stereotyped image of other cultural or ethnic groups, such as Greeks, Romans, Canaanites, and Egyptians. Categorizing others in negative terms contributes towards internal group self-definition and the negotiation of boundaries between "us" and "them."

Writing some time in the first century BCE or CE, for instance, the author of the Wisdom of Solomon describes the "detestable" activities of those who inhabited the "holy land"

52. Jenkins 1994, 216.
53. Jenkins 1994, 217.

before the arrival of the Israelites (the Canaanites, predecessors of the Phoenicians). It seems that this gives this Judean author opportunity to critique contemporary associations or societies of initiates outside of the Judean sphere in the process, calling on the same sort of stereotypes we have seen in Greek or Roman slander against Judeans (with the help of certain passages in the Hebrew Bible which also accuse Canaanites of similar things). God "hated them for practicing the most detestable things—deeds of sorcery and unholy rites (τελετὰς ἀνοσίους), merciless slaughters of children, sacrificial feasting on human flesh and blood—those initiates from the midst of a society (ἐκ μέσου μύστας θιάσου) and parents who murder helpless lives, you willed to destroy . . ." (Wis 12:4–5; cf. Wis 14:15–23).[54]

At the same time, personified Wisdom herself is an initiate of another, superior kind, an "initiate (μύστις) in the knowledge of God" (Wis 8:4). Elsewhere the author critiques the "idolatry" of Greeks generally, the "impious ones" (ἀσεβοῦς) who do not know such "divine mysteries" (2:22) and who instead establish their own inferior "mysteries and rites" (μυστήρια καὶ τελετάς; 14:15): "For whether performing ritual murders of children or secret mysteries or frenzied revels connected with strange laws, they no longer keep either their lives or their marriages pure, but they either kill one another by treachery or grieve one another by adultery" (Wis 14:23–24). Once again, ritual murder and sexual perversion converge in this characterization of the associations of another ethnic group.

Torrey Seland's (1996) study explores evidence for associations in Philo's writings, where Philo compares Judean and other associations. Philo paints a negative picture of the associations of outsiders. Thus, for instance, Philo's account of the gatherings of the Judean therapeutists in Egypt draws out a comparison of the therapeutists' "synods and symposia" with the "frenzy and madness" of the Greek, Roman, and Egyptian banquets and drinking parties (*Vit. Cont.* 40–41). For Philo, who views Judean gatherings as associations of a superior kind, the associations of others were "founded on no sound principle but on strong liquor, drunkenness, intoxicated violence and their offspring, wantonness" (*Flacc.* 136–37).[55]

In a manner similar to the stories discussed earlier, Philo also accuses non-Judean associations in Egypt of conspiratorial activity: "the associations and synods (ἑταιρείας καὶ συνόδους) [in Alexandria] . . . were constantly holding feasts under pretext of sacrifice in which drunkenness vented itself in political intrigue" (*Flacc.* 4). Philo is also sounding a bit like other upper-class authors such as Pliny the Younger, cited in chapter 1. In fact, in this particular case, Philo is identifying with, and assessing positively, the actions of Flaccus, the Roman imperial prefect (governor) of Egypt. Flaccus had engaged in actions to control some associations that were under the benefactor Isidoros of Alexandria (another ambassador for the Greeks in opposition to the Judeans); these associations had happened to engage in rivalries with Judean groups in Alexandria (cf. *Flacc.* 135–45).[56]

This attempt to compare a minority group with associations while simultaneously claiming the superiority of the minority group and the inferiority of outside groups is also reflected in sections of Tertullian's *Apology*. Tertullian defends the Christian association

---

54. Trans. NETS, with adaptations.

55. Cf. *Spec. leg.* 2.145–48; *Leg. Gai.* 312–13.

56. On Isodoros, who went from a supporter of Flaccus to a key opponent, also see the so-called *Acts of the Pagan Martyrs* (Musurillo 1954, 98, 117–40; cf. Philo *Flacc.* 137–38).

(*factio, corpus*), in part, by portraying other associations negatively. For instance, he claims that financial contributions made by members of Christian associations are "not spent upon banquets nor drinking-parties nor thankless eating-houses," but on helping the poor and facilitating burial of the dead (*Apol.* 39.5–6 and 38–39).[57]

Though there may be truth in the fact that drinking was a part of the celebrations of associations, scholars need to refrain from adopting the moralists' critique as a sign that Greco-Roman or Egyptian associations were all about partying and could not care less about honouring the gods.[58] With both Philo and Tertullian, we are witnessing the expression of Judean or Christian identities in relation to the associations in a way that illustrates the internalization of external categorizations that I outlined in chapter 1. As well, we are seeing resistance to certain aspects of other external categorizations such as the stereotypes discussed here.

Struggles between Different Minority Groups: Intergroup Rivalries among Christians

There are also times when these ethnographic discourses and rivalries play a role in internal struggles and boundary definitions among different cultural minority groups. Early Christian groups, for instance, struggled to establish their own legitimacy and find a place for themselves in contradistinction to other followers of Jesus whose practices they considered unacceptable, dangerous, or "heretical" in some way.[59]

Here there are similar strategies in the social categorization of others as part of the process of group self-definition and differentiation. Epiphanius's fourth-century rhetorical attacks on the supposed devilish rituals of the Christian Phibionites is among the most extreme cases.[60] There Epiphanius describes in gory detail how "they even foul their assembly, if you please, with dirt from promiscuous fornication; and they eat and handle both human flesh and uncleanness" (*Pan.* 26.3.3).[61] The account in *Panarion* (26.3.3–5.7) culminates in Epiphanius's discussion of this group's supposed ritual slaughter and consumption of the unwanted fetuses that resulted from the sexual rites of the group.

Yet the Christian groups that, ultimately, became marginalized and lost the struggle also made use of similar charges against other followers of Jesus. The second-century *Gospel of Judas* is a case in point. This is among the documents often labelled "gnostic," and it shares in common with other writings of this type the notion that the Judean god of the Bible who created this world (the demiurge, named "Saklas" in this writing) is not the same

57. Trans. Glover and Rendall 1931 (LCL).

58. Nilsson 1957 is among those who tend to adopt the moralistic critique of ancient authors. See Harland 2003a, 55–87; Dennis E. Smith 2003.

59. See Dölger 1934, 217–23. On the Montanists' sacrifice of children, see, for instance, Philastrius *Diversarum hereseon* 49.5; Epiphanius *Panarion* 48.14.5–6; Cyril of Jerusalem *Catech.* 16.8. The Manichees were also charged with "sacrificing men in demonic mysteries" (Theodore bar Konai [seventh cent. CE]; Adam 1969).

60. Now see Frankfurter 2006, 104–8.

61. Trans. Williams 1997, 84.

benevolent God who sent Christ. In this document, the author criticizes other Christian groups by way of the image of the eleven disciples of Jesus. These disciples are portrayed as fatally misunderstanding Jesus and the God who sent Jesus, and they are portrayed as devoted instead to the demiurge, the malevolent creator of the world. In this setting, there is an episode where Jesus interprets a dream that Jesus' disciples had about twelve priests making sacrifices in the temple:

> Jesus said, "What are [the priests] like?" They [said, "Some] were... [for] two weeks. [Others] were sacrificing their own children. Others were sacrificing their wives as a gift [and] they were humiliating each other. Some were sleeping with men. Some were [committing murder]. Yet others were committing a number of sins and lawless acts. And the men standing [beside] the altar [were] calling upon your [Name]. (*Gos. Judas* 39.12–23)[62]

Jesus then interprets the dream as referring to these very disciples who claim to follow Jesus but are, in fact, far from him: "Jesus said to them, 'You are those you saw who presented the offerings upon the altar . . .'" (*Gos. Judas* 39.18–20). Here the author is accusing Christians who do not hold his own particular views regarding the distinction between the demiurge (God of the Judeans) and the God who sent Christ. He draws on ethnographic discourses that characterize their activities as the equivalent of ritual murder of women and children and of what the author of the *Gospel of Judas* considers sexual perversity.

Conclusions

This trio of ritual atrocity (human sacrifice, cannibalism, and sexual perversion) has a long history in discourses of the other, in negative social categorizations, and in processes of identity negotiation. The trio raises its head again not only in accusations against Jews, "heretics," and witches in the medieval and early modern periods, for instance, but also in the more recent "Satanic ritual abuse" scare of the 1980s, as recently discussed by David Frankfurter.[63]

Frankfurter notes how even academic scholarship has sometimes bought into the rhetoric of such charges, including the ancient cases we have been discussing. Thus, scholars might (in less blatant terms) join with Franz Cumont in speaking of the "return to savagery" characteristic of mystery cults, or that, with the "adoption of the Oriental mysteries, barbarous, cruel and obscene practices were undoubtedly spread."[64] Essentially, this reflects the rhetoric of the likes of Livy about threatening and abhorrent foreign rites in a new guise.

In a similar vein and also in connection with "mysteries" (in Lollianos), Henrichs expressed a belief that "even slanderous accounts of ritual performances can be used as reliable evidence of actual religious practices in antiquity if interpreted properly, and that

62. Trans. DeConick 2007, 71–72.

63. Frankfurter 2001, 352–81, now discussed more fully in Frankfurter 2006.

64. Cumont 1956, 6; see Frankfurter 2001, 363–65.

the uniform pattern in the various rumors of ritual murder points to *concrete rites* that were celebrated by ethnic or tribal minorities."[65] Henrichs does seem to back away from accepting such descriptions as realistic in a later publication that deals with human sacrifice, however.[66] Stephen Benko gives credence to accounts of wild sexual and commensal activities, even the most extreme ones described in Epiphanius's critique of the Phibionites.[67] In this problematic view, such accounts refer to actual rituals that were practiced in some fringe groups. It should be noted that these scholars did not necessarily have available the important sociological and anthropological work that has been done on processes of external categorization and group definition, which have informed my own approach.

The approach here has been to emphasize the manner in which charges of wild transgression are part of more encompassing discourses that reflect the methods and rhetoric of ancient ethnography in order to describe and distance the foreign "other" from one's own cultural or ethnic group. In the process of defining one's own group, the activities of others are defined as dangerous inversions of good order. The anti-association or anti-banquet idea is part of this overall strategy. These ancient discourses are best understood within the framework of intergroup rivalries, identity construction, and group-boundary negotiation.

In light of this understanding of the charges in terms of identity theory and discourses of the other, it is important to reiterate some meanings of these discourses. Douglas's anthropological work has taught us how views of the body, including issues of the consumption of food, reflect views of society and the boundaries within and around society.[68] Moreover, the boundaries that are violated in the ritual murder and consumption of fellow-humans can symbolize the destruction of society itself. It is the prior understanding of the other as a dangerous threat to society that leads ancient authors, whether in history or fiction, to draw on a common stockpile of typical antisocietal actions, cannibalism as the ultimate offence. Allegations of destroying and consuming humanity itself are another way of reinforcing the notion that these groups should be labeled as criminal or barbaric threats. Within the context of such discourses, small groups of outlaws or associations of foreigners specifically can play a noteworthy role in representing the alien or criminal threat within society.

Banqueting practices played an important role in discourses of identity, in which certain authors, representative in some ways of their ethnic or cultural group, engaged in the process of defining their own groups as civilized by alienating another as barbarous. These authors of both fiction and history played on what was commonly expected or pious behaviour within associations by presenting alien associations or low-life criminal guilds as the inversion of all that was pious and right. Ritual murder and the accompanying cannibalistic meal, symbolic of inverting piety and destroying society itself, stand out as the epitome of the anti-banquet. Tales of this sort, informed by ethnographic discourses, were frightening precisely because they represented a distortion of the goals of most associa-

65. Henrichs 1970, 33.

66. Do see Henrichs's (1978, 121–60) more cautious approach to maenads and the supposed eating of raw flesh, however.

67. Benko 1980, 1087–89.

68. Douglas 1973.

tions and groups, namely, the intimately related goals of appropriately honouring the gods (through sacrifice) and feasting with friends.

Sometimes, both Judean synagogues and Christian congregations were targets of this technique of defining oneself over against the other, primarily because of the foreignness of their nonparticipation in honouring, or sacrificing to, the Greek or Roman gods, because of their attention to just one, foreign god (their monotheism or monolatrism). In part, it was this failure to acknowledge the gods of others or to honour any gods beyond the Judean God that set Judeans and followers of Jesus apart as cultural minority groups.

Sometimes, though not always, these differences in cultural practice drew the attention of specific outsiders more than the similarities that led to the view that Judean gatherings and Christians congregations were associations of the usual type. This study has shown that Judeans and Christians were very much a part of intergroup relations in the ancient Mediterranean context, relations that facilitated the construction and reformulation of identities among various associations and communities.

Conclusion

This book has explored issues of identity in the world of the early Christians using local archeological and epigraphic evidence and literary sources for associations as a window into that world. There are many other ways to approach the question of early Christian identities within Greco-Roman contexts, and this study has pursued only certain, neglected pieces of the larger puzzle.

Answers to the question who are we or who am I in relation to this group varied from one person, group, or situation to the next, and group identities could and did evolve over time. Dynamics of identity, whether ethnic or social, are helpfully explained in terms of both internal self-definition and external categorizations. Both outside observers and members of Judean gatherings and Christian congregations often recognized these groups as associations, even though they were associations with a peculiar twist relating to their focus on honouring the Judean God (alongside Jesus in the case of Christians) to the exclusion of other Greek and Roman deities. This twist is something that allows the social historian to speak of these particular associations as cultural minorities and to draw on other social-scientific tools for studying ethnic and minority groups.

Josephus and Philo demonstrate the ways in which Judean gatherings were understood within the framework of societies (*thiasoi*) and synods in the Greco-Roman context, as well as the tendency of Judeans, like others, to present their own groups as superior to their rivals. Perceptions among authors such as Pliny the Younger, Lucian, and Celsus further demonstrate how outsiders and even imperial authorities could view Christian groups with the association as a principal model. This is the case despite peculiarities that might on occasion lead a particular upper-class Roman to dismiss such associations as "superstitions" or as secretive or dangerous associations.

From the inside, Ignatius of Antioch clarifies similar internal patterns of definition relating to association life as he draws on local cultural life to express the identities of the Christian congregations in Asia Minor in terms of groups of initiates with their own, superior mysteries. Metaphors drawn from local processions, including the image of bearing holy objects, further facilitate Ignatius's expression of Christian identity in ways that place these congregations within the familiar world of associations in western Asia Minor.

Internal processes of self-definition are integral to any understanding of group identities. The Greco-Roman social model of the family played a significant role for internal modes of identification among members of certain associations, including but not limited to some Christian congregations and Judean gatherings. It is, therefore, problematic to interpret family and brother language within Christian groups as a further sign that all Christian groups should be categorized as sects. These areas of common ground in expressing belonging and hierarchies within a group demonstrate ways in which congregations and gatherings were part of a larger cultural framework in the Roman Empire.

Comparative investigations into immigrant groups or ethnic associations provide important insights into ethnic identity and acculturation in the world of Judeans and Christians. The case study of Syrians and Phoenicians abroad clarified associational tendencies among immigrants in cities during the Hellenistic and Roman eras. Examining such groups offered further insight into self-definition as certain groups maintained and communicated specific ethnic identities within a host society.

Continuing connections with the homeland and its cultural ways, including devotion to the "ancestral gods," illustrate some of the ways in which ethnic groups continued to define themselves in relation to their original homeland. Judean gatherings were, therefore, not alone as ethnic groups with their own distinctive customs and identities that set them apart in certain ways from other groups in the same social setting.

Alongside these areas of cultural maintenance and differentiation, however, were signs of acculturation and assimilation within local cultural and social life among certain associations of Syrians, Berytians, Tyrians, and others. Participation in social networks and interaction with people from other ethnic groups, for instance, point to significant areas of assimilation and integration within the host society. Cultural exchanges go both ways. Certain people from outside the ethnic group were involved in honouring ancestral gods of Syrian towns, or even attended meetings of these ethnic associations. Such evidence points to certain degrees of enculturation into the ways of the ethnic group on the part of outsiders. Here, too, the Syrian associations offer a helpful analogy for understanding the evidence for Judean gatherings' varying degrees of interaction with local cultural and social structures and for contextualizing the involvements of certain non-Judeans (gentiles or god-fearers) in Judean cultural practices and social connections.

Evidence for the maintenance of ethnic identities and attachments to the homeland, on the one hand, and areas of integration within local society, on the other, problematize general theories of rootlessness and detachment among immigrant populations in the ancient Mediterranean. Further comparative studies of such ethnic groups and diasporas may help to map out Judean and other immigrant populations.

Looking at Judean families at a particular locale, Hierapolis, provided further insight into both cultural maintenance and certain levels of integration within local society on the part of such cultural minority groups. The case of the family of Glykon illustrates the potential for multiple affiliations and multiple identities not only on the part of this family, but also on the part of the primarily non-Judean guilds who continued to remember Glykon and his family on both Judean and Roman holidays. Here again interactions took place between members of different ethnic or cultural groups with resulting acculturation or enculturation for those involved. The Judean graves from Hierapolis in the second and third centuries demonstrate areas of cultural and structural assimilation as families looked to local civic institutions as authorities and adopted or adapted local customs in burial arrangements. At the same time, many continued to clearly identify themselves as Judeans in various ways, including open identification as "Judeans," celebration of Judean holy days, and the use of Judean symbols such as the menorah on family graves. The formation of associations of Judeans is itself a clear indication of attachments to the homeland and a means by which certain dimensions of ethnic identities could be strengthened and displayed in the diaspora.

Positive interactions among different groups or certain levels of integration within local society did not preclude areas of tension or rivalry, however. In some respects, involvement in rivalries and competition was a structural feature of social life in Greek cities of the eastern Roman Empire. So the participation of Judean gatherings and Christian congregations in rivalrous interchanges with others is in some sense normal and expected, at least to some degree. Associations in Sardis and Smyrna engaged in competition within social networks of benefaction, both as recipients of support and as donors. Claims of superiority or preeminence for the group or its god were not unusual within this context of the struggle for honour, recognition, and position within local society.

Furthermore, associations of various kinds were, to different degrees, competitors for members or for the loyalties of the members they had. The evidence for multiple memberships or affiliations points to a plurality of identities, including ethnic identities. As individuals found themselves within different situations at different times, one or another identity would play a more significant role than other identities. Suggestive evidence points to the involvement of some Judeans and Christians within multiple groups despite calls for exclusivity on the part of certain leaders, such as the author of John's Revelation.

The minority cultural positions or ethnic identities of certain associations led, on occasion, to negative external categorizations that further illustrate rivalries among different groups. The case of stereotypes regarding Syrians and Phoenicians set the stage for a discussion of other more general categorizations and stereotypes. Although they should not be exaggerated, such stereotypes were significant for identity negotiation when they were expressed and when members of the categorized group reacted to such negative stereotypes.

Ethnic and minority groups that were perceived as "foreign" could be understood by certain outsiders in terms of what I have called the "anti-association," the dangerous and alien association within our midst. Accusations of human sacrifice, cannibalism, and sexual perversion were among the most striking stereotypes aimed at "foreign" peoples or minority groups, including Judeans and Christians.

Such negative characterizations of the "other" by certain people would potentially facilitate negative actions against such "dangerous" or "alien" peoples on particular occasions. This is demonstrated in local and sporadic persecutions of Christians, for instance. The Christians had the added factor of their Judean connections involving a general rejection of the gods of others, which also led some outsiders to label them impious "atheists." It is not surprising to find such accusations in accounts of persecution, such as the account of the Christians at Lyons who were charged with Thyestean feasts and Oedipean unions and the Christians at Smyrna (ca. 160 CE) who were charged with atheism. In this respect, Christians, like Judeans and some other foreigners, were involved within the framework of ethnic rivalries. These rivalries were expressed not only within ancient ethnographic materials produced by the elites, but also, on occasion, within everyday social interactions on the ground.

Yet these cultural minority groups were not merely targets in such processes of identity construction. They also engaged in similar techniques of internal self-definition through stereotyping the "other," including other associations. Thus, on occasion, Philo defines Judean associations by caricaturing the associations of others (Egyptians, Greeks) as dangerous, conspiratorial, drunken revels. And the author of the Wisdom of Solomon calls on the usual trio of atrocities in speaking of the mysteries of outsiders (e.g., Greeks, Romans, and Egyptians) in terms of human sacrifice, cannibalism, and sexual perversion.

Similar techniques of self-definition and differentiation are found among certain Christian authors who sought to distinguish themselves from other Christian groups that these authors considered dangerous or impious heretics. Epiphanius's description of the Phibionites, on the one hand, and the *Gospel of Judas*'s description of Christians who claimed attachments to Jesus' "inferior" disciples, on the other, illustrate these processes of identity negotiation that involve discourses of ethnicity.

This study has focussed on what was common among many groups while also paying attention to certain distinctive features of ethnic groups and cultural minorities. The attention to shared modes of identity construction, negotiation, and communication is not meant to suggest that Christians were not unique. However, Christians were unique or distinctive insofar as every association, minority group, or ethnic group was unique or distinctive, each in its own way. Among the distinctive characteristics of Christians and Judeans that stood out to many insiders and outsiders was their attention to one, Judean God to the exclusion of other deities. This also entailed refraining from involvement in certain social settings where those other gods were honoured. This distinction was a potential source of tensions with many other groups and individuals within their contexts, and it could lead to social harassment and persecution on particular occasions.

Still, despite this highlighted characteristic that makes a concept such as cultural minority group applicable to both Judean gatherings and Christian congregations, these groups were recognizable to many outsiders as another instance of the association, synod, or society. Whether viewed as an association or an anti-association by particular outsiders on specific occasions, some of these cultural minority groups were more or less integrated than others within local social and cultural life in the cities of the Roman Empire.

Abbreviations

Epigraphic and Papyrological Collections Cited in the Text

(Based on the abbreviations listed in the following publications)

Horsley, G. H. R., and John A. L. Lee. 1994. "A Preliminary Checklist of Abbreviations of Greek Epigraphic Volumes." *Epigraphica* 56:129–69.

Oates, John F., William H. Willis, et al., eds., *Checklist of Editions of Greek, Latin, Demotic and Coptic Papyri, Ostraca, and Tablets.* <http://scriptorium.lib.duke.edu/papyrus/texts/clist.html>, accessed September 2009.

AE	Cagnat, Merlin, et al. 1888–
BE	Haussoullier, Reinach, et al. 1888–
BGU	Schubart, Kühn, et al. 1895–
CCCA	Vermaseren 1987
CIG	Boeckh 1828–77
CIJ	Frey 1936–52
CIL	Mommsen, Lommatzsch, et al. 1893
CIMRM	Vermaseren 1956–60
CIRB	Struve 1965
CIS	Academie des Inscriptions et Belles-Lettres 1881–
CPJ	Tcherikover and Fuks 1957–64
DFSJ	Lifshitz 1967
GIBM	Hicks, Hirschfeld, et al. 1874–1916
IAlexandria	Kayser 1994
IAlexTroas	Ricl 1997
IApamBith	Corsten 1987
IAphrodSpect	Roueché 1993
IAsMinLyk I	Benndorf and Niemann 1884
ICarie	Robert and Robert 1954
IDelos	Roussel and Launey 1937
IDelosChoix	Dürrbach 1921
IDidyma	Rehm 1958
IEgJud	Horbury and Noy 1992

IEph	Engelmann, Wankel, et al. 1979–84
IErythrai	Engelmann, Merkelbach 1972–74
IEurJud	Noy 1993–95
IFayum	Bernand 1975–1981
IG	Gaertringen, Lewis, et al. 1873–
IGBulg	Mihailov 1958–70
IGLAM	Le Bas and Waddington 1972 [1870]
IGLSkythia	Pippidi and Russu 1983–
IGLSyria	Sartre 1982
IGR	Cagnat, Toutain, et al. 1906–27
IGUR	Moretti 1968–91
IHierapJ	Judeich 1898
IHierapMir	Miranda 1999a
IHierapPenn	Pennacchietti 1966–67
IIasos	Blümel 1985
IJO I	Noy, Panayotov, et al. 2004
IJO II	Noy, Bloedhorn, et al. 2004
IJO III	Ameling 2004
IKilikiaBM	Bean and Mitford 1965, 1970
IKlaudiupolis	Becker-Bertau 1986
IKos	Hicks and Paton 1891
IKosSegre	Segre 1993
IKyzikos	Schwertheim 1980–
ILaodikeia	Robert 1969
ILindos	Blinkenberg 1941
ILydiaKP I	Keil and Premerstein 1910
ILydiaKP III	Keil and Premerstein 1914
IMagnMai	Kern 1900
IMagnSip	Ihnken 1978
IMiletos	Wiegend, Kawerau, et al. 1889–1997
IMylasa	Blümel 1987–88
INikaia	Sahin 1979–87
IPergamon	Fränkel 1890–95
IPerge	Sahin 1999–2004
IPerinthos	Sayar 1998
IPontEux	Latyschev 1965 [1890–1901]
IPriene	Gaertringen 1906
IPrusaOlymp	Corsten 1991
IPrusiasHyp	Ameling 1985
IRhodM	Maiuri 1925
IRomJud	Noy 1993–1995
ISardBR	Buckler and Robinson 1932
ISardH	Herrmann 1996
ISelge	Nollé and Schindler 1991
ISmyrna	Petzl 1982–90

IStratonikeia	Sahin 1982–90
ITralles	Poljakov 1989
LSAM	Sokolowski 1955
LSCG	Sokolowski 1962
MAMA	Keil, Buckler, et al. 1928–
NewDocs	Horsley and Llewelyn 1981–2002
OClaud	Bingen, Bülow-Jacobsen, et al. 1992–2000
OGIS	Dittenberger 1903–1905
PAmherst	Grenfell and Hunt 1900–1901
PLond	Kenyon, Bell, Skeat 1893–1974
PMich	Edgar, Boak, et al. 1931–
POxy	Egypt Exploration Fund 1898–
PParis	Letronne, de Presle, et al. 1865
PPetaus	Hagedorn, Hagedorn, et al. 1969
PRyl	Johnson, Martin, et al. 1911–52
PSI	Vitelli, Norsa, et al. 1912–1979
PTebtunis	Grenfell, Hunt, et al. 1902–76
PThmouis	Kmabitsis 1985
PTor	Peyron 1827
SB	Preisigke, Bilabel, et al. 1915–
SEG	Roussel, Salav, et al. 1923–
SIRIS	Vidman 1969
TAM	Kalinka, Heberdey, et al. 1920–
UPZ	Wilcken 1927–57

Journal and Series Abbreviations in the Bibliography

Abbreviations of journals and series follow the listing in the *SBL Handbook of Style.* Additional abbreviations are listed below.

AncSoc	*Ancient Society*
EA	*Epigraphica Anatolica*
ERS	*Ethnic and Racial Studies*
IGSK	*Inschriften griechischer Städte aus Kleinasien*
MDAI(A)	*Mitteilungen des Deutschen Archäologischen Instituts (Athen. Abt.)*
RGRW	Religion in the Greco-Roman World
RPh	*Revue de philologie, de littérature et d'histoire anciennes*

Bibliography

1. Epigraphic and Papyrological Collections

Academie des Inscriptions et Belles-Lettres. 1881. *Corpus inscriptionum semiticarum*. Paris: Academie des Inscriptions et Belles-Lettres.

Ameling, Walter. 1985. *Die Inschriften von Prusias ad Hypium*. IGSK 27. Bonn: Rudolf Habelt.

———. 2004. *Inscriptiones Judaicae Orientis: Band II Kleinasien*. TSAJ 99. Tübingen: Mohr Siebeck.

Bean, G. E., and J. M. Cook. 1955. "The Halicarnassus Peninsula." *Annual of the British School at Athens* 50:85–174.

Bean, George E., and Terence Bruce Mitford. 1962. "Sites Old and New in Rough Cilicia." *Anatolian Studies* 12:185–217.

———, and Terence Bruce Mitford. 1965. *Journeys in Rough Cilicia 1962 and 1963 [Part I]*. Denkschriften der österreichischen Akademie der Wissenschaften in Wien, philosophisch-historische Klasse 85. Vienna: Hermann Böhlaus.

———, and Terence Bruce Mitford. 1970. *Journeys in Rough Cilicia 1964–1968 [Part II]*. Denkschriften der österreichischen Akademie der Wissenschaften in Wien, philosophisch-historische Klasse 102.3. Vienna: Hermann Böhlaus.

Becker-Bertau, Friedrich. 1986. *Die Inschriften von Klaudiu polis*. IGSK 31. Bonn: Rudolf Habelt.

Benndorf, O., and G. Niemann. 1884. *Reisen in Lykien und Karien*. Reisen im Südwestlichen Kleinasien 1. Vienna: Codex-Verlag.

Bernand, Étienne. 1975–81. *Recueil des inscriptions grecques du Fayoum*. Bibliothèque d'Étude 79–80. Cairo: Institut Français d'Archéologie Orientale du Caire.

Bingen, J., et al. 1992–2000. *Mons Claudianus: Ostraca graeca et latina*. Institut Français d'Archéologie Orientale, Documents de Fouilles 29. Cairo: Institut Français d'Archéologie Orientale.

Blinkenberg, C. 1941. *Lindos: Fouilles de l'acropole 1902–1914: II Inscriptions*. Berlin: Walter de Gruyter.

Blümel, Wolfgang. 1985. *Die Inschriften von Iasos*. IGSK 28. Bonn: Rudolf Habelt.

———. 1987–88. *Die Inschriften von Mylasa*. IGSK 35. Bonn: Rudolf Habelt.

Boeckh, Augustine. 1828–77. *Corpus inscriptionum graecarum*. Berolini: Georg Reimeri Libraria.

Buckler, W. H. 1913. "Monuments de Thyatire." *RPh* 37:289–331.

———, and D. M. Robinson. 1932. *Sardis. Publications of the American Society for the Excavation of Sardis: Vol. 7, Greek and Latin Inscriptions*. Leiden: E. J. Brill.

Buresch, Karl. 1898. *Aus Lydien: Epigraphisch-geographische Reisefrüchte*. Leipzig: B. G. Teubner.

Cagnat, R., et al. 1888. *L'Année Épigraphique*. Paris: Presses Universitaires de France.

———, J. Toutain, P. Jovgvet, and G. Lafaye. 1906–27. *Inscriptiones graecae ad res romanas pertinentes*. Paris: E. Leroux.

Chapouthier, Fernand. 1924. "Némésis et Niké." *BCH* 48:287–303.

Clerc, M. 1885. "Inscription de Nysa." *BCH* 9:124–31.

Conze, A., and C. Schuchhardt. 1899. "Die Arbeiten zu Pergamon." *MDAI(A)* 24:164–240.

Corsten, Thomas. 1987. *Die Inschriften von Apameia (Bithynien) und Pylai*. IGSK 32. Bonn: Rudolf Habelt.

———. 1991 *Inschriften von Prusa ad Olympum*. IGSK 39. Bonn: Rudolf Habelt.

Cousin, G., and C. H. Diehl. 1890. "Inscriptions d'Halicarnasse." *BCH* 14:90–121.

———, and G. Deschamps. 1894. "Voyage de Milet à Marmara." *BCH* 18:18–32.

Dagron, Gilbert, and Dennis Feissel. 1987. *Inscriptions de Cilicie*. Travaux et mémoires du Centre de Recherche d'Histoire et Civilisation de Byzance 4. Paris: de Boccard.

Dittenberger, Wilhelm. 1903–5. *Orientis graeci inscriptiones selectae: Supplementum sylloge inscriptionum graecarum*. Leipzig: S. Hirzel.

Doublet, G. 1889. "Inscriptions de Paphlagonie." *BCH* 13:293–319.

Dürrbach, Felix. 1921. *Choix d'inscriptions de Délos: avec traduction et commentaire*. Paris: E. Leroux.

Edgar, C. C., A. E. R. Boak, J. G. Winter, and H. C. Youtie. 1931. *Michigan Papyri*. University of Michigan Studies. Humanistic Series. Ann Arbor: University of Michigan Press.

Egypt Exploration Fund. 1898. *The Oxyrhynchus Papyri*. London: Egypt Exploration Fund.

Engelmann, Helmut, H. Wankel, and R. Merkelbach. 1979–84. *Die Inschriften von Ephesos*. IGSK 11–17. Bonn: Rudolf Habelt.

———, and Reinhold Merkelbach. 1972–74. *Die Inschriften von Erythrai und Klazomenai*. IGSK 1. Bonn: Rudolf Habelt.

Fränkel, Max. 1890–95. *Die Inschriften von Pergamon*. Altertümer von Pergamon 8.1–2. Berlin: W. Spemann.

Frey, Jean-Baptiste. 1936–52. *Corpus inscriptionum iudaicarum*. Sussidi allo studio delle anichità cristiane 3. Rome: Pontificio Istituto di Archeologia Cristiana.

Gaertringen, F. Hiller von. 1906. *Die Inschriften von Priene*. Königliche Museen zu Berlin. Berlin: Georg Reimer.

———, et al. 1873. *Inscriptiones graecae, consilio et auctoritate Acadamiae Litterarum Borussicae editae*. Berlin: Walter de Gruyter.

Gibson, Elsa. 1978. *The "Christians for Christians" Inscriptions of Phrygia: Greek Texts, Translation and Commentary*. HTS 32. Missoula, Mont.: Scholars Press.

Grenfell, Bernard P., and A. S. Hunt. 1900–1901. *The Amherst Papyri*. London: H. Frowde.

———, et al. 1902–76. *The Tebtunis Papyri*. University of California Publications, Graeco-Roman Archaeology 2. London: Henry Frowde.

Hagedorn, Ursula, Dieter Hagedorn, Louise C. Youtie, and Herbert C. Youtie. 1969. *Das Archiv des Petaus (P.Petaus)*. Papyrologica Coloniensia 4. Cologne: Westdeutscher Verlag.

Haussoullier, B., et al. 1888. "Bulletin Épigraphique." *REG*.

Hepding, H. 1907. "Die Arbeiten zu Pergamon 1904–1905: II. Die Inschriften." *MDAI(A)* 32:241–377.

Herrmann, Peter. 1996. "Mystenvereine in Sardeis." *Chiron* 26:315–41.

Hicks, E. L., C. T. Newton, Gustav Hirschfeld, and F. H. Marshall. 1874–1916. *The Collection of Ancient Greek Inscriptions in the British Museum*. Oxford: Clarendon.

———, and W. R. Paton. 1891. *The Inscriptions of Cos*. Oxford: Clarendon.

Horbury, William, and David Noy. 1992. *Jewish Inscriptions of Graeco-Roman Egypt*. Cambridge: Cambridge University Press.

Horsley, G. H. R., and S. R. Llewelyn. 1981–2002. *New Documents Illustrating Early Christianity*. North Ryde, Australia: Ancient History Documentary Research Centre, Macquarie University.

Hörig, Monika, and Elmar Schwertheim. 1987. *Corpus Cultus Iovis Dolicheni (CCID)*. Leiden: Brill.

Ihnken, Thomas. 1978. *Die Inschriften von Magnesia am Sipylos*. IGSK 8. Bonn: Rudolf Habelt.

Johnson, J. M., V. Martin, et al. 1911–52. *Catalogue of the Greek Papyri in the John Rylands Library, Manchester*. Manchester: Manchester University Press.

Judeich, Walther. 1898. "Inschriften." In *Altertümer von Hierapolis*, ed. Carl Humann, Conrad Cichorius, Walther Judeich, and Franz Winter, 67–180. Jahrbuch des kaiserlich deutschen Archäologischen Instituts, Ergänzungsheft 4. Berlin: Georg Reimer.

Kalinka, Ernst. 1906. *Antike Denkmäler in Bulgarien*. Schriften der Balkankommission Antiquarische Abteilung 4. Vienna: Alfred Hölder.

———, et al. 1920–89. *Tituli Asiae Minoris collecti et editi auspiciis academiae litterarum austriacae*. Vienna: Academiam Scientiarum Austriacam.

Kayser, François. 1994. *Recueil des inscriptions grecques et latines (non funéraires) d'Alexandrie impériale*. Bibliothèque d'Étude 108. Cairo: Institut Français d'Archéologie Orientale du Caire.

Keil, Josef, and Anton von Premerstein. 1910. *Bericht über eine Reise in Lydien und der südlichen Aiolis*. Denkschriften der kaiserlichen Akademie der Wissenschaften in Wien, philosophisch-historische Klasse 53.2. Vienna: Alfred Hölder.

———, and Anton von Premerstein. 1911. *Bericht über zweite Reise in Lydien*. Denkschriften der kaiserlichen Akademie der Wissenschaften in Wien, philosophisch-historische Klasse 54.2. Vienna: Alfred Hölder.

———, and Anton von Premerstein. 1914. *Bericht über dritte Reise in Lydien*. Denkschriften der kaiserlichen Akademie der Wissenschaften in Wien, philosophisch-historische Klasse 57.1. Vienna: Alfred Hölder.

———, C. W. M. Cox, et al. 1928. *Monumenta asiae minoris antiqua*. Publications of the American Society for Archaeological Research in Asia Minor/JRSM. Manchester/London: Manchester University Press/Society for the Promotion of Roman Studies.

Kenyon, F. G., H. I. Bell, and T.C. Skeat. 1893–1974. *Greek Papyri in the British Museum*. Oxford: University Press.

Kern, Otto. 1900. *Die Inschriften von Magnesia am Maeander*. Königliche Museen zu Berlin. Berlin: W. Spemann.

Kmabitsis, S. 1985. *Le Papyrus Thmouis 1, colonnes 68–160*. Paris: Publications de la Sorbonne.

Kroll, John H. 2001. "The Greek Inscriptions of the Sardis Synagogue." *HTR* 94:5–55.

Labarre, Guy, and Marie-Thérèse Le Dinahet. 1996. "Les metiers du textile en Asie Mineure de l'époque hellénistique a l'époque imperiale." In *Aspects de l'artisanat du textile dans le monde Méditerranéen (Egypte, Grèce, monde romain)*, 49–115. Collection de l'Institut d'Archéologie et d'Histoire de l'Antiquité, Université Lumière-Lyon 2. Paris: de Boccard.

Laminger-Pascher, Gertrud. 1992. *Die kaiserzeitlichen Inschriften Lykaoniens. Faszikel I: Der Süden*. Ergänzungsbände zu den Tituli Asiae Minoris 15. Vienna: Verlag der Österreichischen Akademie der Wissenschaften.

Lane, E. N. 1971–76. *Corpus monumentorum religionis dei Menis (CMRDM)*. EPRO 19. Leiden: E. J. Brill.

Latyschev, Basilius. 1965 [1890–1901]. *Inscriptiones antiquae orae septentrionalis Ponti Euxini graecae et latinae*. Hildesheim: Georg Olms.

Le Bas, Philippe, and William Henry Waddington. 1972 [1870]. *Inscriptions grecques et latines recueillies en Asie Mineure*. Hildesheim: Olms.

Letronne, A. J., W. Brunet de Presle, and E. Egger. 1865. *Notices et textes des papyrus du Musée du Louvre et de la Bibliothèque Impériale*. Notices et extraits des manuscrits de la Bibliothèque Impériale et autres bibliothèques 18.2. Paris.

Lifshitz, B. 1967. *Donateurs et fondateurs dans les synagogues juives: Répertoire des dédicaces grecques relatives à la construction et à la réfection des synagogues*. Cahiers de la Revue Biblique 7. Paris: J. Gabalda.

Lüderitz, Gert. 1983. *Corpus jüdischer Zeugnisse aus der Cyrenaika*. Beihefte zum Tübinger Atlas des vorderen Orients. Wiesbaden: Dr. Ludwig Reichert Verlag.

Macridy, T. 1904. "À travers les nécropoles sidoniennes." *RB* 13:547–72.

Maiuri, A. 1925. *Nuova silloge epigrafica di Rodi e Cos*. Florence: Univ. di Firenze.

Malay, Hasan. 1994. *Greek and Latin Inscriptions in the Manisa Museum*. Ergänzungsbände zu den Tituli Asiae Minoris 19. Vienna: Verlag der österreichischen Akademie der Wissenschaften.

McCabe, Donald F. 1986. *Samos Inscriptions. Texts and Lists*. Princeton Project on the Inscriptions of Anatolia. Princeton, NJ: Institute for Advanced Study.

Merkelbach, Reinhold. 1979. "Die ephesischen Dionysosmysten vor der Stadt." *ZPE* 36:151–56.

Mihailov, Georgius. 1958–70. *Inscriptiones graecae in Bulgaria repertae*. Institutum Archaeologicum, Series Epigraphica 6. Sofia: Academia Litterarum Bulgarica.

Miranda, E. 1999a. "La Comunità Giudaica di Hierapolis di Frigia." *EA* 31:109–55.

———. 1999b. *Le iscrizioni giudaiche di Hierapolis di Frigia*. Naples.

Mommsen, Theodor, E. Lommatzsch, A. Degrassi, and A. U. Stylow. 1893. *Corpus inscriptionum latinarum consilio et auctoritate Academiae Litterarum Refiae Borussicae*. Berlin: Georgium Reimerum.

Moretti, L. 1968–91. *Inscriptiones graecae urbis romae*. Studi pubblicati dall'Istituto Italiano per la Storia Antica 17. Rome: Istututo Italiano per la Storia Antica.

Newton, C. T., and R. P. Pullan. 1862–63. *A History of Discoveries at Halicarnassus, Cnidus and Branchidæ*. London: Day & Son.

Nollé, Johannes, and Friedel Schindler. 1991. *Die Inschriften von Selge*. IGSK 37. Bonn: Rudolf Habelt.

Noy, David. 1993–95. *Jewish Inscriptions of Western Europe*. Cambridge: Cambridge University Press.

———, Alexander Panayotov, and Hanswulf Bloedhorn. 2004. *Inscriptiones Judaicae Orientis: Volume I. Eastern Europe*. TSAJ 101. Tübingen: Mohr Siebeck.

———, and Hanswulf Bloedhorn. 2004. *Inscriptiones Judaicae Orientis: Volume III. Syria and Cyprus*. TSAJ 102. Tübingen: Mohr Siebeck.

Oliver, Graham J., ed. 2000. *The Epigraphy of Death: Studies in the History and Society of Greece and Rome*. Liverpool: Liverpool University Press.

Oster, Richard. 1990. "Ephesus as a Religious Center under the Principate, I. Paganism before Constantine." *ANRW* II.18.3:1661–728.

Otto, Walter. 1975 [1905–8]. *Priester und Tempel im hellenistischen Ägypten*. Ancient Religion and Mythology. New York: Arno.

Packard Humanities Institute. 2008. "Searchable Greek Inscriptions: A Scholarly Tool in Progress." Packard Humanities Institute, http://epigraphy.packhum.org/inscriptions/.

Parker, Robert. 1996. *Athenian Religion: A History*. Oxford: Clarendon.

Pennacchietti, Fabrizio A. 1966–67. "Nuove iscrizioni di Hierapolis Frigia." *Atti della Accademia delle Scienze di Torino: II classe di scienze morali, storiche e filologiche* 101:287–328.

Perdrizet, Paul. 1900. "Inscriptions de Philippes." *BCH* 24:299–323.

Pestman, P. W. 1993. *The Archive of the Theban Choachytes (Second Century B.C.): A Survey of the Demotic and Greek Papyri Contained in the Archive*. Studia Demotica 2. Leuven: Peeters.

Petzl, Georg. 1982–90. *Die Inschriften von Smyrna*. IGSK 23. Bonn: Rudolf Habelt.

Peyron, Amedeo. 1827. "Papyri graeci regii musie Aegyptii Taurinensis." *Memorie della reale accademia delle scienze di Torino. Scienze morali, storiche e filologiche* 31:9–188.

Pippidi, D. M., and I. I. Russu. 1983. *Inscriptiones Scythiae Minoris graecae et latinae*. Inscriptiones Daciae et Scythiae Minoris antiquae. Bucharest: Academia Scientarum Socialum et Politicarum Dacoromana.

Pleket, H. W. 1958. *The Greek Inscriptions in the "Rijksmuseum Van Oudheden" at Leyden*. Leiden: E. J. Brill.

———. 1970. "Nine Greek Inscriptions from the Cayster-Valley in Lydia: A Republication." *Talanta* 2:55–88.

Poljakov, Fjodor B. 1989. *Die Inschriften von Tralleis und Nysa*. IGSK 36. Bonn: Rudolf Habelt.

Pouilloux, Jean, and C. Dunant. 1954–58. *Recherches sur l'histoire et les cultes de Thasos*. École Française d'Athènes études thasiennes 3. Paris: E. de Boccard.

Preisigke, Friedrich, Friedrich Bilabel, et al. 1915. *Sammelbuch griechischer Urkunden aus Ägypten*. Strassburg/Berlin/Wiesbaden: Karl J. Trübner/Walter de Gruyter/Otto Harrassowitz.

Ramsay, W. M. 1895–97. *The Cities and Bishoprics of Phrygia*. Oxford: Clarendon.

Rehm, Albert. 1958. *Didyma. Zweiter Teil: Die Inschriften*. Deutsches Archäologisches Institut. Berlin: Verlag Gebr. Mann.

Reynolds, Joyce. 1977. "Inscriptions." In *Excavations at Sidi Khrebish Benghazi (Berenice). Volume I: Buildings, Coins, Inscriptions, Architectural Decoration*, ed. J. A. Lloyd, 233–54. Supplements to Libya Antiqua 5. Libya: Department of Antiquities, Ministry of Teaching and Education, People's Socialist Libyan Arab Jamahiriya.

———, and Robert Tannenbaum. 1987. *Jews and God-Fearers at Aphrodisias: Greek Inscriptions with Commentary*. CambPhSocSup 12. Cambridge: Cambridge Philological Society.

Ricl, Marijana. 1997. *The Inscriptions of Alexandreia Troas*. IGSK, 53. Bonn: Rudolf Habelt.

Ritti, Tullia. 1985. *Fonti letterarie ed epigrafiche*. Hierapolis scavi e ricerche 1. Rome: Giorgio Bretschneider Editore.

———. 1992–93. "Nuovi dati su una nota epigrafe sepolcrale con stefanotico da Hierapolis di Frigia." *Scienze dell'antichità storia archeologia antropologia* 6–7:41–68.

Robert, Louis. 1937. *Étude anatoliennes: Recherches sur les inscriptions grecques de l'Asie Mineure*. Études orientales publiées par l'Institut Français d'Archéologie de Stamboul 5. Paris: E. de Boccard.

———. 1946. "Un corpus des inscriptions juives." *Hellenica* 1:90–108.

———. 1949. "Sur une monnaie de Synnada ΤΡΟΦΕΥΣ." *Hellenica* 13:74–81.

———. 1960a. "Épitaphes d'Eumeneia de Phrygie." *Hellenica* 11–12:414–39.

———. 1960b. "Épitaphes juives d'Éphèse et de Nicomédie." *Hellenica* 11–12:381–413.

———. 1960c. "Inscriptions d'Asie Mineure au Musée de Leyde." *Hellenica* 11–12:214–62.

———. 1965. "Lycaonie, Isaurie et Pisidie." *Hellenica* 13:25–109.

———. 1969. "Les inscriptions." In *Laodicée du Lycos: Le nymphée campagnes 1961–1963*, 247–389. Université Laval recherches archéologiques. Série I: Fouilles. Québec: Presses de L'Université Laval.

———. 1971 [1940]. *Les gladiateurs dans l'orient grec*. Bibliothèque de l'École des Hautes Études IVe section, sciences historique et philologiques. Amsterdam: Adolf M. Hakkert.

———. 1975. "Une nouvelle inscription grecque de Sardes: Règlement de l'autorité perse relatif à un culte de Zeus." *CRAI*:306–30.

———. 1978. "Documents d'Asie Mineure." *BCH* 102:395–543.

———. 1987. *Documents d'Asie Mineure*. Paris: de Boccard.

———, and Jeanne Robert. 1954. *La Carie: Histoire et géographie historique avec le recueil des inscriptions antiques. Tome II: Le plateau de Tabai et ses environs*. Paris: Adrien-Maisonneuve.

———, and Jeanne Robert. 1983. *Fouilles d'Amyzon en Carie. Tome I: Exploration, histoire, monnaies et inscriptions*. Commission des fouilles et missions archéologiques au ministère des relations extérieures. Paris: de Boccard.

Roberts, Colin, Theodore C. Skeat, and Arthur Darby Nock. 1936. "The Gild of Zeus Hypsistos." *HTR* 29:39–89.

Roueché, Charlotte. 1993. *Performers and Partisans at Aphrodisias in the Roman and Late Roman Periods: A Study Based on Inscriptions from the Current Excavations at Aphrodisias in Caria*. JRSM 6. London: Society for the Promotion of Roman Studies.

Roussel, Pierre, and Marcel Launey. 1937. *Inscriptions de Délos: Décrets postérieurs à 166 av. J.-C. (nos. 1497–1524). Dédicaces postérieures à 166 av. J.-C. (nos. 1525–2219)*. Académie des Inscriptions et Belles-lettres. Paris: Librairie Ancienne Honoré Champion.

Sahin, Sencer. 1979–87. *Katalog der antiken Inschriften des Museums von Iznik (Nikaia)*. IGSK 9. Bonn: Rudolf Habelt.

———. 1982–90. *Die Inschriften von Stratonikeia*. IGSK 21. Bonn: R. Habelt.

———. 1999–2004. *Die Inschriften von Perge*. IGSK 54. Bonn: R. Habelt.

Sartre, Maurice. 1982. *Inscriptions grecques et latines de la Syrie*. Institut Français d'Archéologie du Proche-orient. Bibliothèque archéologique et historique 113. Paris: Librairie Orientaliste Paul Geuthner.

Sauciuc-Sâveanu, Théophile. 1924. "Callatis: rapport préliminaire." *Dacia* 1:108–46.

Sayar, Mustafa Hamdi. 1998. *Perinthos-Herakleia (Marmara Ereglisi) und Umgebung: Geschichte, Testimonien, griechische und lateinische Inschriften*. Denkschriften der Österreichische Akademie der Wissenschaften. Philosophisch-Historische Klasse, Veröffentlichungen der Kleinasiatischen Kommission. Vienna: Verlag der Österreichischen Akademie der Wissenschaften.

Schubart, W., et al. 1895. *Ägyptische Urkunden aus den Königlichen (later Staatlichen) Museen Berlin. Griechische Urkunden*. Berlin: Weidmannsche Buchhandlung.

Schwertheim, Elmar. 1980. *Die Inschriften von Kyzikos und Umgebung*. IGSK 18. Bonn: Rudolf Habelt.

Segre, Mario. 1993. *Inscrizioni di Cos*. Rome: L'Erma di Bretschneider.

Sokolowski, Franciszek. 1955. *Lois sacrées de l'Asie Mineure*. École française d'Athènes. Travaux et mémoires des anciens membres étrangers de l'école et de divers savants 9. Paris: E. de Boccard.

———. 1962. *Lois sacrées des cites grecques*. École française d'Athènes. Travaux et mémoires des anciens membres étrangers de l'école et de divers savants 10. Paris: E. de Boccard.

Struve, Vasilii. 1965. *Corpus Inscriptionum Regni Bosporani (CIRB) (Korpus Bosporskikh Nadpisei)*. Moscow: Akademiia nauk SSSR.

Tcherikover, Victor, and Alexander Fuks. 1957–64. *Corpus papyrorum judaicarum*. Cambridge, MA: Harvard University Press.

Vermaseren, M. J. 1956–60. *Corpus Inscriptionum et Monumentorum Religionis Mithriacae*. The Hague: M. Nijhoff.

Vidman, Ladislav. 1969. *Sylloge inscriptionum religionis Isiacae et Sarapiacae*. Religionsgeschichtliche Versuche und Vorarbeiten 28. Berlin: Walter de Gruyter.

———. 1987. *Corpus cultus Cybelae Attidisque (CCCA): I. Asia Minor*. Leiden: E. J. Brill.

Vitelli, G., M. Norsa, and et al. 1912–79. *Papiri greci e latini*. Pubblicazioni della Società Italiana per la Ricerca dei Papiri Greci e Latini in Egitto. Florence: Publicasioni della Società Italiana.

Wagener, A. 1868. "Inscription grecque inédite." *Revue de l'instruction publique en Belgique* 11:1.

———. 1873. "Auszüge aus Schriften und Berichten der gelehrten Gesellschaften so wie aus Zeitschriften ." *Philologus* 32:379–84.

Wiegend, Theodor, Georg Kawerau, Albert Rehm, and Peter Herrmann. 1889–1997. *Milet: Ergebnisse der Ausgrabungen und Untersuchungen seit dem Jahre 1899*. Berlin: Walter de Gruyter.

Wilcken, Ulrich. 1927–57. *Urkunden der Ptolemäerzeit (ältere Funde)*. Berlin: de Gruyter.

2. Other Primary and Secondary Sources

Aasgaard, Reider. 2004. *My Beloved Brothers and Sisters: Christian Siblingship in Paul.* Early Christianity in Context. London: T&T Clark.

Abrams, Dominic, and Michael A. Hogg, eds. 1990. *Social Identity Theory: Constructive and Critical Advances.* New York: Springer.

Adam, Alfred. 1969. *Texte zum Manichaismus.* Second edition. Berlin: Walter de Gruyter.

Ajrouch, Kristine J., and Abdi M. Kusow. 2007. "Racial and Religious Contexts: Situational Identities among Lebanese and Somali Muslim Immigrants." *ERS* 30:72–94.

Albright, W. F. 1936. "The Canaanite God Hauron." *AJSL* 53:1–12.

———. 1941. "The Egypto-Canaanite Deity Hauron." *BASOR* 84:7–12.

Alföldy, Géza. 1985. *The Social History of Rome.* Translated by David Braund and Frank Pollock. London: Croom Helm.

Ameling, Walter. 1990. "Koinon ΤΩΝ ΣΙΔΩΝΙΩΝ." *ZPE* 81:189–99.

———. 2004. *Inscriptiones Judaicae Orientis: Band II. Kleinasien.* TSAJ 99. Tübingen: Mohr Siebeck.

Anderson, Graham, trans. 1989. "Xenophon of Ephesus: An Ephesian Tale." In *Collected Ancient Greek Novels.* Edited by B. P. Reardon, 125–69. Berkeley: University of California Press.

Anderson, Robert T. 1971. "Voluntary Associations in History." *American Anthropologist* 73:209–22.

Aneziri, Sophia. 2003. *Die Vereine der Dionysischen Techniten im Kontext der hellenistischen Gesellschaft.* Historia Einzelschriften 163. Munich: Steiner.

Applebaum, S. 1974. "The Legal Status of the Jewish Communities in the Diaspora." In *The Jewish People in the First Century: Historical Geography, Political History, Social, Cultural and Religious Life and Institutions.* Edited by S. Safrai and M. Stern, 420–63. CRINT 1. Assen: Van Gorcum.

———. 1974. "The Organization of the Jewish Communities in the Diaspora." In *The Jewish People in the First Century: Historical Geography, Political History, Social, Cultural and Religious Life and Institutions.* Edited by S. Safrai and M. Stern, 464–503. CRINT 1. Assen: Van Gorcum.

Arnaoutoglou, Ilias N. 2002. "Roman Law and *Collegia* in Asia Minor." *RIDA* 49:27–44.

Arzt-Grabner, Peter. 2002. "'Brothers' and 'Sisters' in Documentary Papyri and in Early Christianity." *RivB* 50:185–204.

Ascough, Richard S. 1996. "The Completion of a Religious Duty: The Background of 2 Cor 8.1–15." *NTS* 42:584–99.

———. 1997a. "Translocal Relationships among Voluntary Associations and Early Christianity." *JECS* 5:223–41.

———. 1997b. "Voluntary Associations and Community Formation: Paul's Macedonian Christian Communities in Context." Ph.D. diss. Toronto School of Theology.

———. 1998. *What Are They Saying about the Formation of the Pauline Churches?* New York: Paulist.

———. 2000. "The Thessalonian Christian Community as a Professional Voluntary Association." *JBL* 119:311–28.

———. 2003. *Paul's Macedonian Associations: The Social Context of Philippians and 1 Thessalonians.* WUNT 161. Tübingen: Mohr-Siebeck.

———. 2007. "'A Place to Stand, a Place to Grow': Architectural and Epigraphic Evidence for Expansion in Greco-Roman Associations." In *Identity and Interaction in the Ancient Mediterranean: Jews, Christians and Others. Essays in Honour of Stephen G. Wilson.* Edited by Zeba A. Crook and Philip A. Harland, 76–98. Sheffield: Sheffield Phoenix Press.

———, ed. 2005. *Religious Rivalries and the Struggle for Success in Sardis and Smyrna.* SCJ 14. Waterloo: Wilfrid Laurier University Press.

Attridge, Harold W., and Robert A. Oden, trans. 1976. *The Syrian Goddess (De Dea Syria), Attributed to Lucian.* Missoula, Mont.: Scholars Press.

Ausbüttel, Frank M. 1982. *Untersuchungen zu den Vereinen im Westen des römischen Reiches.* Frankfurter Althistorische Studien 11. Kallmünz: Verlag Michael Lassleben.

Avram, A. 2002. "Der dionysische thiasos in Kallatis: Organisation, Repräsentation, Funktion." In *Religiöse Vereine in der römischen Antike: Untersuchungen zu Organisation, Ritual und Raumordnung.* Edited by U. Egelhaaf-Gaiser and A. Schäfer, 69–80. Tübingen: Mohr Siebeck.

Balch, David L. 1981. *Let Wives Be Submissive: The Domestic Code in 1 Peter.* Chico, CA: Scholars Press.

———. 1986. "Hellenization/Acculturation in 1 Peter." In *Perspectives on First Peter*, 79–101. NABPR Special Studies Series 9. Macon, GA: Mercer University Press.

Banks, Robert J. 1994 [1980]. *Paul's Idea of Community.* Peabody, MA: Hendrickson.

Banton, Michael. 1977. *The Idea of Race.* London: Tavistock.

———. 1983. *Racial and Ethnic Competition.* Cambridge: Cambridge University Press.

———. 2001. "Progress in Ethnic and Racial Studies." *ERS* 24:173–94.

Barclay, John M. G. 1996. *Jews in the Mediterranean Diaspora from Alexander to Trajan (323 BCE–117 CE).* Edinburgh: T&T Clark.

———. 2007. "Constructing Judean Identity after 70 CE: A Study of Josephus's *Against Apion.*" In *Identity and Interaction in the Ancient Mediterranean: Jews, Christians and Others. Essays in Honour of Stephen G. Wilson.* Edited by Zeba A. Crook and Philip A. Harland, 99–112. Sheffield: Sheffield Phoenix Press.

Barth, Fredrik. 1969. *Ethnic Groups and Boundaries.* Oslo: Universitetsforlaget.

Barnett, H. G., et al. 1954. "Acculturation: An Exploratory Formulation." *American Anthropology* 56:973–1002.

Barton S. C., and G. H. R. Horsley. 1981. "A Hellenistic Cult Group and the New Testament Churches." *JAC* 24:7–41.

Baslez, Marie-Francoise. 1988. "Les communautes d'orientaux dans la cité grecque: Formes de sociabilité et modèles associatifs." In *l'Etranger dans le monde grec: Actes du colloque organisé par l'Institut d'Etudes Anciennes, Nancy, mai 1987*, 139–158. Nancy: Presses Universitaires de Nancy.

Baumgarten, Albert. 1998. "Greco-Roman Voluntary Associations and Jewish Sects." In *Jews in a Greco-Roman World.* Edited by M. Goodman, 93–111. Oxford: Oxford University Press.

Beard, Mary. 1991. "Writing and Religion: *Ancient Literacy* and the Function of the Written Word in Roman Religion." In *Literacy in the Roman World*. Edited by J. H. Humphrey, 35–58. JRASup 3. Ann Arbor, MI: Journal of Roman Archaeology.

———, John North, and Simon Price, eds. 1998. *Religions of Rome*. Cambridge: Cambridge University Press.

Beck, Roger. 1996. "Mystery Religions, Aretalogy, and the Ancient Novel." In *The Novel in the Ancient World*. Edited by G. Schmeling, 131–50. Brill: Leiden.

Beckford, James A. 1975. *The Trumpet of Prophecy: A Sociological Study of Jehovah's Witnesses*. Oxford: Basil Blackwell.

Behr, Charles A., trans. 1981–86. *P. Aelius Aristides: The Complete Works*. Leiden: E. J. Brill.

Bell, H. Idris. 1924. *Jews and Christians in Egypt: The Jewish Troubles in Alexandria and the Athanasian Controversy*. Westport, CT: Greenwood Press.

Benko, Stephen. 1980. "Pagan Criticism of Christianity during the First Two Centuries A.D." *ANRW* II.23.2:1055–118.

Benmayor, Rina, and Andor Skotnes. 1994. "Some Reflections on Migration and Identity." *International Yearbook of Oral History and Life Stories* 3:1–18.

Bernstein, Moshe J. 2004. "Women and Children in Legal and Liturgical Texts from Qumran." *Dead Sea Discoveries* 11:191–211.

Berquist, Jon L. 1995. "Deprivation Theory of Social Movements." In *International Encyclopedia of Sociology*. Edited by Frank N. Magill, 349–53. London: Fitzroy Dearborn.

Berry, John W. 1980. "Acculturation as Varieties of Adaptation." In *Acculturation: Theory, Models and Some New Findings*. Edited by Amado M. Padilla, 9–25. AAAS Selected Symposium 39. Boulder, CO: Westview Press.

———. 1997. "Immigration, Acculturation, and Adaptation." *Applied Psychology* 46:5–34.

Bertrand, Jean Marie. 1988. "Les Boucôloi, ou le monde a l'envers." *REA* 90:139–49.

Besnier, Maurice. 1932. "Églises chrétiennes et collèges funéraires." In *Mélange Albert Dufourcq: Études d'histoire religieuse*, 9–19. Paris: Librairie Plon.

Bettenson, Henry, trans. 1976. *Livy: Rome and the Mediterranean*. Harmondsworth: Penguin Books.

Betz, Hans Dieter, ed. 1992. *The Greek Magical Papyri in Translation Including the Demotic Spells*. Second edition. Chicago: University of Chicago Press.

Bickerman, Elias. 1980 [1927]. "Ritualmord und Eselskult: Ein Beitrag zur Geschichte antiker Publizistik." In *Studies in Jewish and Christian History*, 225–55. AGJU 9. Leiden: E. J. Brill.

Bilde, Per, Troels Engberg-Pedersen, Lisa Hannestad, and Jan Zahle, eds. 1992. *Ethnicity in Hellenistic Egypt*. Aarhus: Aarhus University Press.

Binder, Donald. 1999. *Into the Temple Courts: The Place of the Synagogues in the Second Temple Period*. SBLDS 169. Atlanta: Society of Biblical Literature.

Birman, Dina. 1994. "Acculturation and Human Diversity in a Multicultural Society." In *Human Diversity: Perspectives on People in Context*. Edited by Edison J. Trickett, Roderick J. Watts and Dina Birman, 261–84. The Jossey-Bass Social and Behavioural Science Series. San Francisco: Jossey-Bass.

Boak, A. E. R. 1937. "An Ordinance of the Salt Merchants." *AJP* 58:210–19.

Bodel, John, ed. 2001. *Epigraphic Evidence: Ancient History from Inscriptions*. London/New York: Routledge.

Boissevain, Jeremy. 1974. *Friends of Friends: Networks, Manipulators and Coalitions.* Oxford: Basil Blackwell.
Bonnet, Corinne. 1988. *Melqart: Cultes et mythes de l'Héraclès tyrien en Méditerranée.* Namur: Presses Universitaires de Namur.
———. 1996. *Astarte: Dossier documentaire et perspectives historiques. Contributi alla storia della religione Fenicio-Punica* 2. Rome: Consiglio Nazionale della Ricerche.
Bonz, Marianne P. 1990. "The Jewish Community of Ancient Sardis: A Reassessment of Its Rise to Prominence." *HSCP* 93:343–59.
Bömer, Franz. 1981 [1958–63]. *Untersuchungen über die Religion der Sklaven in Griechenland und Rom.* Second edition. Abhandlungen der Geistes- und Sozialwissenschaftlichen Klasse 10.4. Wiesbaaden: Verlag der Akademie der Wissenschaften und der Literatur.
Bowersock, G. W. 1994. *Fiction as History: Nero to Julian.* Sather Classical Lectures 58. Berkeley: University of California Press.
Brashear, William M. 1993. *Vereine im griechisch-römischen Ägypten.* Xenia: Konstanzer althistorische Vorträge und Forschungen 34. Konstanz: Universitätsverlag Konstanz.
Braudel, Fernand. 1949. *La Méditerranée et le monde méditerranéen à l'époque de Philippe II.* Paris: Colin.
Bremen, Riet van. 1996. *The Limits of Participation: Women and Civic Life in the Greek East in the Hellenistic and Roman Periods.* Dutch Monographs on Ancient History and Archaeology 15. Amsterdam: J. C. Gieben.
Brent, Allen. 1998. "Ignatius of Antioch and the Imperial Cult." *VC* 52:30–58.
———. 2006. *Ignatius of Antioch and the Second Sophistic.* Studien und Texte zu Antike und Christentum 36. Tübingen: Mohr Siebeck, 2006.
Brettell, Caroline B., and James F. Hollifield, eds. 2000. *Migration Theory: Talking Across the Disciplines.* New York: Routledge.
Brody, Aaron. 1998. *"Each Man Cried Out to His God": The Specialized Religion of Canaanite and Phoenician Seafarers.* Harvard Semitic Monographs 58. Atlanta: Scholars Press.
Brooten, Bernadette J. 1982. *Women Leaders in the Ancient Synagogue: Inscriptional Evidence and Background Issues.* BJS 36. Atlanta: Scholars Press.
Brown, Peter. 1978. *The Making of Late Antiquity.* Cambridge: Harvard University Press.
Brown, Raymond E. 1979. *The Community of the Beloved Disciple.* New York: Paulist.
———. 1982. *The Epistles of John: Translated with Introduction, Notes, and Commentary.* AB 30. New York: Doubleday.
Brubaker, Rogers. 2005. "The 'diaspora' Diaspora." *ERS* 28:1–19.
Bruneau, Philippe. 1970. *Recherches sur les cultes de Délos a l'époque hellénistique et a l'époque impériale.* Bibliothèque des écoles françaises d'Athènes et de Rome 270. Paris: de Boccard.
———. 1978. "Les cultes de l'établissement des Poseidoniastes de Bérytos à Delos." In *Hommages à Maarten J. Vermaseren.* Edited by Margreet B. de Boer and T. A. Edridge, 160–90. EPRO 68. Leiden: E. J. Brill.
———. 1982. "'Les Israélites de Délos' et la juiverie Délienne." *BCH* 106:465–504.
———. 1991. "Deliaca." *BCH* 115:377–88.
Buell, Denise Kimber. 2005. *Why This New Race: Ethnic Reasoning in Early Christianity.* New York: Columbia University Press.

Burke, Peter J. 1992 [1980]. *History and Social Theory*. Second edition. Ithaca, NY: Cornell University Press.

———. 2003. "Relationships among Multiple Identities." In *Advances in Identity and Research*. Edited by Peter J. Burke, Timothy J. Owens, Richard T. Serpe, and Peggy A. Thoits, 195–216. New York: Kluwer Academic/Plenum.

———, Timothy J. Owens, Richard T. Serpe, and Peggy A. Thoits, eds. 2003. *Advances in Identity and Research*. New York: Kluwer Academic/Plenum.

Burke, Trevor J. 2003. *Family Matters: A Socio-Historical Study of Kinship Metaphors in 1 Thessalonians*. JSNTSup 247. London: T&T Clark.

Burkert, Walter. 1985 [1977]. *Greek Religion*. Trans. John Raffan. Cambridge: Harvard University Press.

———. 1987. *Ancient Mystery Cults*. Cambridge, MA: Harvard University Press.

Cadoux, Cecil John. 1938. *Ancient Smyrna, a History of the City from the Earliest Times to 324 A.D.* Oxford: Basil Blackwell.

Cartledge, Paul. 2002 [1993]. *The Greeks: A Portrait of Self and Others*. Oxford: Oxford University Press.

———. 1994. "The Greeks and Anthropology." *Anthropology Today* 10:3–6.

Cary, Earnest, trans. 1960–84. *Dio's Roman History*. LCL. Cambridge, MA: Harvard University Press.

Cavendish, James C., Michael R. Welch, and David C. Leege. 1998. "Social Network Theory and Predictors of Religiosity for Black and White Catholics: Evidence of a 'Black Sacred Cosmos'?' *JSSR* 37:397–410.

Chadwick, Henry, trans. 1953. *Origen:* Contra Celsum. Cambridge: Cambridge University Press.

Chaniotis, Angelos. 2002. "The Jews of Aphrodisias: New Evidence and Old Problems." *Scripta Classica Israelica* 21:209–42.

Chapot, Victor. 1967 [1904]. *La province romaine proconsulaire d'Asie depuis ses origines jusqu'à la fin du haut-empire*. Studia Historica 35. Rome: Bretschneider.

Chapouthier, Fernand. 1924. "Némésis et Niké." *BCH* 48:287–303.

Chow, John K. 1992. *Patronage and Power: A Study of Social Networks in Corinth*. JSNTSup 75. Sheffield: JSOT Press.

Cohen, Getzel M. 1995. *The Hellenistic Settlements in Europe, the Islands, and Asia Minor*. Berkeley: University of California Press.

Cohen, Naomi G. 1976. "Jewish Names as Cultural Indicators in Antiquity." *JSJ* 7:97–128.

Cohen, Shaye J. D. 1989. "Crossing the Boundary and Becoming a Jew." *HTR* 82:13–33.

———. 1993. "'Those Who Say They Are Jews and Are Not': How Do You Know a Jew in Antiquity When You See One?" In *Diasporas in Antiquity*. Edited by Shaye J. D. Cohen and Ernest S. Frerichs, 1–45. BJS 288. Atlanta: Scholars Press.

———. 1999. *The Beginnings of Jewishness: Boundaries, Varieties, Uncertainties*. Hellenistic Culture and Society 31. Berkeley: University of California Press.

———, and Ernest S. Frerichs, eds. 1993. *Diasporas in Antiquity*. BJS 288. Atlanta: Scholars Press.

Colson, F. H., trans. 1929–62. *Philo*. LCL. Cambridge, MA: Harvard University Press.

Cormack, J. M. R. 1943. "High Priests and Macedoniarchs from Beroea." *JRS* 33:39–44.

Costello, D. P. 1938. "Notes on the Athenian GENH." *JHS* 58:171–79.

Cowey, James M., and Klaus Maresch, *Urkunden des Politeuma der Juden von Herakleopolis (144/3–133/2 v.Chr.) (P. Polit. Iud.)*. Abhandlungen der Rheinisch-Westfälischen Akademie der Wissenschaften 29. Paderborn: Schöningh, 2001.

Crawford, Sidnie White. 2003. "Mothers, Sisters, and Elders: Titles for Women in the Second Temple Jewish and Early Christian Communities." In *The Dead Sea Scrolls as Background to Postbiblical Judaism and Early Christianity. Papers from an International Conference at St. Andrews in 2001*. Edited by James R. Davila, 177–91. STDJ 46. Leiden: Brill.

Cumont, Franz. 1956. *Oriental Religions in Roman Paganism*. New York: Dover.

D'Arms, John H. 1974. "Puteoli in the Second Century of the Roman Empire. A Social and Economic Study." *JRS* 64:104–24.

Daniel, Robert W. 1979. "Notes on the Guilds and Army in Roman Egypt." *BASP* 16:37–46.

De Vos, George A. 1995. "The Role of Ethnicity in Social History." In *Ethnic Identity: Creation, Conflict, and Accommodation*. Edited by Lola Romanucci-Ross and George A. De Vos, 15–47. Walnut Creek: Altamira.

DeConick, April D. 2007. *The Thirteenth Apostle: What the Gospel of Judas Really Says*. London: Continuum.

Deissmann, Adolf. 1901. *Bible Studies*. Edinburgh: T&T Clark.

———. 1995 [1927]. *Light from the Ancient East: The New Testament Illustrated by Recently Discovered Texts of the Graeco-Roman World*. Translated by Lionel R. M. Strachan. Peabody, MA: Hendrickson.

Dittmann-Schöne, Imogen. 2000. *Die Berufsvereine in den Städten des kaiserzeitlichen Kleinasiens*. Theorie und Forschung 690. Regensburg: Roderer.

Dodds, E. R. 1965. *Pagan and Christian in an Age of Anxiety: Some Aspects of Religious Experience from Marcus Aurelius to Constantine*. Cambridge: Cambridge University Press.

Dölger, Franz. 1934. "'Sacramentum infanticidii.' Die Schlachtung eines Kindes und der Genuß seines Fleisches und Blutes als vermeintlicher Einweihungsakt im ältesten Christentum." *Antike und Christentum* 4:188–228.

Douglas, Mary. 1973 [1970]. *Natural Symbols: Explorations in Cosmology*. Second edition. London: Barrie & Jenkins.

Dudko, Dmitrii M. 2001–2. "Mythological Ethnography of Eastern Europe: Herodotus, Pseudo-Zacharias, and Nestor." *Anthropology and Archeology of Eurasia* 40:75–92.

Dunand, Françoise. 1973. *Le culte d'Isis dans le bassin oriental de la Méditerraneé*. EPRO 26. Leiden: Brill.

Dunn, James D. G. 2008. Review of *Paul, Judaism, and the Gentiles: Beyond the New Perspective*. *RBL* <http://www.bookreviews.org/pdf/6165_6591.pdf, accessed Aug. 28, 2009>.

Ebel, Eva. 2004. *Die Attraktivität früher christlicher Gemeinden: Die Gemeinde von Korinth im Spiegel griechisch-römischer Vereine*. WUNT 178. Tübingen: Mohr-Siebeck.

Edson, Charles. 1948. "Cults of Thessalonica (Macedonia III)." *HTR* 41:153–204.

Edwards, Mark J. 1992. "Some Early Christian Immoralities." *AncSoc* 23:71–82.

Egelhaaf-Gaiser, U., and A. Schäfer, eds. 2002. *Religiöse Vereine in der Römischen Antike. Untersuchungen zu Organisation, Ritual und Raumordnung*. Studien und Texte zu Antike und Christentum 13. Tübingen: Mohr-Siebeck.

Eiselen, Frederick Carl. 1907. *Sidon: A Study in Oriental History*. Columbia University Oriental Studies 4. New York: Columbia University Press.

Eissfeldt, O. 1968. *Kleine Schriften*. Tübingen: J. C. B. Mohr.

Elise, Sharon. 1995. "Cultural and Structural Assimilation." In *International Encyclopedia of Sociology*, 275–278. London: Fitzroy Dearborn.

Elliott, John H. 1990 [1981]. *A Home for the Homeless: A Social-Scientific Criticism of I Peter, Its Situation and Strategy*. Second edition. Minneapolis: Fortress.

———. 1993. *What is Social-Scientific Criticism?* Minneapolis: Fortress.

———. 2007. "Jesus the Israelite Was Neither a 'Jew' Nor a 'Christian': On Correcting Misleading Nomenclature." *Journal for the Study of the Historical Jesus* 5:119–54.

Esler, Philip F. 1998a. *Galatians*. London: Routledge.

———. 1998b. "Review of D. G. Horrell, *The Social Ethos of the Corinthian Correspondence*." *JTS* 49:253–60.

———. 2003. *Conflict and Identity in Romans: The Social Setting of Paul's Letter*. Minneapolis: Fortress.

Feldman, Louis H. 1993. *Jew and Gentile in the Ancient World*. Princeton, NJ: Princeton University Press.

Feldmeier, Reinhard. 1992. *Die Christen als Fremde: Die Metapher der Fremde in der antiken Welt, im Urchristentum und im 1.Petrusbrief*. WUNT 64. Tübingen: Mohr Paul Siebeck.

Fellmeth, Ulrich. 1987. "Die römischen Vereine und die Politik: Untersuchungen zur sozialen Schichtung und zum politischen Bewußtsein der städtischen Volksmassen in Rom und Italien." Ph.D. diss. Stuttgart: Historisches Institut der Universität Stuttgart.

———. 1990. "Politisches Bewusstsein in den Vereinen der städtischen Massen in Rom und Italien zur Zeit der Republik und der frühen Kaiserzeit." *Eirene* 27:49–71.

Ferguson, W. S., and A. D. Nock. 1944. "The Attic Orgeones and the Cult of Heroes." *HTR* 37:61–174.

Foucart, Paul. 1873. *Des associations religieuses chez les Grecs—thiases, éranes. orgéones, avec le texte des inscriptions rélative à ces associations*. Paris: Klincksieck.

Frankfurter, David. 1998. *Religion in Roman Egypt: Assimilation and Resistance*. Princeton, NJ: Princeton University Press.

———. 2001. "Ritual as Accusation and Atrocity: Satanic Ritual Abuse, Gnostic Libertinism, and Primal Murders." *HR* 40: 352–81.

———. 2006. *Evil Incarnate: Rumors of Demonic Conspiracy and Ritual Abuse in History*. Princeton, NJ: Princeton University Press.

Franklin, James L., Jr. 1980. *Pompeii: The Electoral Programmata, Campaigns and Politics, A.D. 71–79*. Papers and Monographs of the American Academy in Rome 28. Rome: American Academy.

Fraser, P. M. 1977. *Rhodian Funerary Monuments*. Oxford: Clarendon.

Freyne, Sean. 2001. "Galileans, Phoenicians and Itureans: A Study of Regional Contrasts in the Hellenistic Age." In *Hellenism in the Land of Israel*, 184–217. Notre Dame: University of Notre Dame Press.

Fuks, A. 1953. "The Jewish Revolt in Egypt (AD 115–117) in the Light of the Papyri." *Aegyptus* 33:131–58.

Gager, John G. 1975. *Kingdom and Community: The Social World of Early Christianity*. New Jersey: Prentice-Hall.

Garland, Robert. 1987. *The Piraeus from the Fifth to the First Century B.C.* London: Duckworth.

———. 2001. *The Greek Way of Death*. Second edition. Ithaca, NY: Cornell University Press.

Gasparro, Giulia Sfameni. 1985. *Soteriology and Mystic Aspects in the Cult of Cybele and Attis*. EPRO 130. Leiden: E. J. Brill.

Geertz, Clifford. 1962. "The Rotating Credit Association: A Middle Rung in Development." *Economic Development and Cultural Change* 10:241–63.

———. 1973. *The Interpretation of Cultures: Selected Essays by Clifford Geertz*. New York: Basic Books.

Gerlach, Luther P., and Virginia H. Hine. 1970. *People, Power, Change: Movements of Social Transformation*. Indianapolis: Bobbs-Merrill.

Gerner, Erich. 1941. "Tymborychia." *Zeitschrift der Savigny-Stiftung für Rechtsgeschichte, Romanistische Abteilung* 16:230–75.

Gibson, Elsa. 1978. *The "Christians for Christians" Inscriptions of Phrygia: Greek Texts, Translation and Commentary*. HTS 32. Missoula: Scholars Press.

Gilmour, S. MacLean. 1938. "Church Consciousness in the Letters of Paul." *Journal of Religion* 18:289–302.

Gleason, Philip. 1991. "Minorities (Almost) All: The Minority Concept in American Social Thought." *American Quarterly* 43:392–424.

Glover, T. R., and Gerald H. Rendall, trans. 1931. *Tertullian: Apology, de Spectaculis. Minucius Felix*. LCL. Cambridge, MA: Harvard University Press.

Goodenough, E. R. 1957. "The Bosporus Inscriptions to the Most High God." *JQR* 47:221–44.

———. 1953–68. *Jewish Symbols in the Greco-Roman Period*. New York: Pantheon Books.

Goodman, Martin, ed. 1998. *Jews in the Graeco-Roman World*. Oxford: Clarendon.

Gordon, Milton. 1964. *Assimilation in American Life: The Role of Race, Religion, and National Origins*. New York: Oxford University Press.

Goudriaan, Koen. 1988. *Ethnicity in Ptolemaic Egypt*. Amsterdam: J.C. Gieben.

———. 1992. "Ethnical Strategies in Graeco-Roman Egypt." In *Ethnicity in Hellenistic Egypt*. Edited by Per Bilde, Troels Engberg-Pedersen, Lisa Hannestad, and Jan Zahle, 74–99. Aarhus: Aarhus University Press.

Grabbe, Lester L. 1992. *Judaism from Cyrus to Hadrian*. Minneapolis: Fortress.

Grant, Robert M. 1948. "Pliny and the Christians." *HTR* 41:273–74.

———. 1970. "Sacrifices and Oaths as Required of Early Christians." In *Kyriakon: Festschrift Johannes Quasten*. Edited by Patrick Granfield and Josef A. Jungmann, 12–17. Münster: Aschendorff.

———. 1981. "Charges of 'Immorality' against Various Groups in Antiquity." In *Studies in Gnosticism and Hellenistic Religions*. Edited by R. Broeck and M. J. Vermaseren, 161–70. EPRO 91. Leiden: Brill.

Griffiths, J. Gwyn. 1975. *Apuleius of Madauros: The Isis-Book (Metamorphoses, Book XI)*. EPRO 39. Leiden: E. J. Brill.

Gruen, Erich S. 1990. "The Bacchanalian Affair." In *Studies in Greek Culture and Roman Policy*, 34–78. Cincinnati Classical Studies 7. Leiden: E. J. Brill.

———. 1998. *Heritage and Hellenism: The Reinvention of Jewish Tradition*. Berkeley: University of California Press.

Gurney, Joan Neff, and Kathleen J. Tierney. 1982. "Relative Deprivation and Social Movements: A Critical Look at Twenty Years of Theory and Research." *Sociological Quarterly* 23:33–47.

Guterman, Simeon L. 1951. *Religious Toleration and Persecution in Ancient Rome*. London: Aiglon.

Hadas-Lebel, M. 1979. "Le paganisme à travers les sources rabbiniques des IIe et IIIe siècles. Contribution a l'étude du syncrétisme dans l'empire romain." *ANRW* II.19.2:397–485.

Hagel, S., and K. Tomaschitz. 1998. *Repertorium des westkilikischen Inschriften*. Vienna: Österreichischen Akademie der Wissenschaften.

Hagendoorn, Louk. 1993. "Ethnic Categorization and Outgroup Exclusion: Cultural Values and Social Stereotypes in the Construction of Ethnic Hierarchies." *ERS* 16:26–51.

Hall, Jonathan M. 1997. *Ethnic Identity in Greek Antiquity*. Cambridge: Cambridge University Press.

———. 2002. *Hellenicity: Between Ethnicity and Culture*. Chicago: University of Chicago Press.

Hanson, J. Arthur, trans. 1989. *Apuleius Metamorphoses*. LCL. Cambridge, MA: Harvard University Press.

Harland, Philip A. 1996. "Honours and Worship: Emperors, Imperial Cults and Associations at Ephesus (First to Third Centuries C.E.)." *SR* 25:319–34.

———. 2000. "Honouring the Emperor or Assailing the Beast: Participation in Civic Life Among Associations (Jewish, Christian and Other) in Asia Minor and the Apocalypse of John." *JSNT* 77:99–121.

———. 2002. "Connections with Elites in the World of the Early Christians." In *Handbook of Early Christianity: Social Science Approaches*. Edited by Anthony J. Blasi, Paul-André Turcotte, and Jean Duhaime, 385–408. Walnut Creek, CA: Alta Mira.

———. 2003a. *Associations, Synagogues, and Congregations: Claiming a Place in Ancient Mediterranean Society*. Minneapolis: Fortress.

———. 2003b. "Imperial Cults within Local Cultural Life: Associations in Roman Asia." *Ancient History Bulletin/Zeitschrift für alte Geschichte* 17:85–107.

———. 2006. "The Declining Polis? Religious Rivalries in Ancient Civic Context." In *Religious Rivalries and the Struggle for Success: Methodological Papers*. Edited by Leif E. Vaage, 21–49. Waterloo, ON: Wilfrid Laurier University Press.

Harmon, A. M., and M. D. Macleod, trans. 1913–67. *Lucian*. LCL. Cambridge, MA: Harvard University Press.

Harris, William V. 1989. *Ancient Literacy*. Cambridge, MA: Harvard University Press.

Harrison, Jane Ellen. 1906. *Primitive Athens as Described by Thucydides*. Cambridge: Cambridge University Press.

Hartog, François. 1988 [1980]. *The Mirror of Herodotus: The Representation of the Other in the Writing of History*. Translated by Janet Lloyd. The New Historicism: Studies in Cultural Poetics. Berkeley: University of California Press.

Hatch, Edwin. 1909 [1880]. *The Organization of the Early Christian Churches: Eight Lectures Delivered before the University of Oxford, in the Year 1880*. London: Longmans, Green.

Hatzfeld, Jean. 1919. *Les trafiquants italiens dans l'orient hellénique*. Bibliothéque des écoles françaises d'Athènes et de Rome 115. Paris: E. de Boccard.

Heinrici, Georg. 1876. "Die christengemeinden Korinths und die religiösen Genossenschaften der Griechen." *ZWT* 19:465–526.

———. 1877. "Zur Geschichte der Anfänge paulinischer Gemeinden." *ZWT* 20:89–130.

———. 1881. "Zum genossenschaftlichen Charakter der paulinischen Christengemeinden." *TSK* 54:505–24.

Hellerman, Joseph H. 2001. *The Ancient Church as Family*. Minneapolis: Fortress.

Hembold, W. C., and F. H. Sandbach, trans. 1927–69. *Plutarch: Moralia*. LCL. Cambridge, MA: Harvard University Press.

Hemelrijk, Emily. 2008. "Patronesses and 'Mothers' of Roman Collegia." *Classical Antiquity* 27:115–62.

Hengel, Martin. 1966. "Die Synagogeninschrift von Stobi." *ZNW* 57:145–83.

Henrichs, Albert. 1970. "Pagan Ritual and the Alleged Crimes of the Early Christians." In *Kyriakon: Festschrift Johannes Quasten*. Edited by Patrick Granfield and Josef A. Jungmann, 18–35. Münster: Aschendorff.

———. 1972. *Die Phoinikika des Lollianos: Fragmente eines neuen griechischen Romans*. Papyrologische Texte und Abhandlungen 14. Bonn: Rudolf Habelt.

———. 1978. "Greek Maenadism from Olympias to Messalina." *HSCP* 82:121–60.

———. 1981. "Human Sacrifice in Greek Religion: Three Case Studies." In *Le sacrifice dans l'antiquité*. Edited by Jean Rudhardt and Olivier Reverdin, 195–235. Geneva: Vandoeuvres.

Hermansen, Gustav. 1981. *Ostia: Aspects of Roman City Life*. Edmonton: University of Alberta Press.

Hill, Christopher. 1971. *Antichrist in Seventeenth-Century England*. London: New York, Oxford University Press.

———. 1972. *The World Turned Upside Down; Radical Ideas during the English Revolution*. London: Temple Smith.

Hobsbawm, E. J. 1959. *Primitive Rebels: Studies in Archaic Forms of Social Movements in the 19th and 20th Centuries*. Manchester: Manchester University Press.

———. 1969. *Bandits*. London: Trinity Press.

Hock, Ronald. 1980. *The Social Context of Paul's Ministry: Tentmaking and Apostleship*. Philadelphia: Fortress.

Hölbl, Günther. 1978. *Zeugnisse ägyptischer Religionsvorstellungen für Ephesus*. EPRO 73. Leiden: E. J. Brill.

Hopwood, Keith. 1998. "'All That May Become a Man': The Bandit in the Ancient Novel." In *When Men Were Men: Masculinity, Power and Identity in Classical Antiquity*. Edited by Lin Foxhall and John Salmon, 195–204. London: Routledge.

Horrell, David G. 1996. *The Social Ethos of the Corinthian Correspondence: Interests and Ideology*. Edinburgh: T&T Clark.

———. 2000. "Models and Methods in Social-Scientific Interpretation: A Response to Philip Esler." *JSNT* 78:83–105.

———. 2001. "From *Adelphoi* to *Oikos Theou*: Social Transformation in Pauline Christianity." *JBL* 120:293–311.

———. 2002. "Social Sciences Studying Formative Christian Phenomena: A Creative Movement." In *Handbook of Early Christianity: Social Science Approaches*. Edited by Anthony J. Blasi, Paul-André Turcotte, and Jean Duhaime, 3–28. Walnut Creek, CA: Alta Mira.

———. 2007. "The Label *Christianos:* 1 Peter 4:16 and the Formation of Christian Identity." *JBL* 126:361–81.

Horsley, G. H. R., and John A. L. Lee. 1994. "A Preliminary Checklist of Abbreviations of Greek Epigraphic Volumes." *Epigraphica* 56:129–69.

Horsley, Richard A. 1985. *Bandits, Prophets, and Messiahs: Popular Movements in the Time of Jesus*. Harrisburg: Trinity Press International.

Horst, P. W. van der. 1991. *Ancient Jewish Epitaphs: An Introductory Survey of a Millennium of Jewish Funerary Epigraphy (300 BCE- 700 CE)*. Contributions to Biblical Exegesis and Theology 2. Kampen: Kok Pharos.

Howard, Judith A. 2000. "Social Psychology of Identities." *Annual Review of Sociology* 26:367–93.

Humann, Carl, Conrad Cichorius, Walther Judeich, and Franz Winter, eds. 1898. *Altertümer von Hierapolis*. Jahrbuch des kaiserlich deutschen Archäologischen Instituts, Ergänzungsheft 4. Berlin: Georg Reimer.

Humphries, Mark. 1998. "Trading Gods in Northern Italy." In *Trade, Traders and the Ancient City*. Edited by Helen Parkins and Christopher Smith, 203–24. London: Routledge.

Isaac, Benjamin. 1991. "A Seleucid Inscription from Jamnia-on-the-Sea: Antiochus V Eupator and the Sidonians." *IEJ* 41:132–44.

———. 2004. *The Invention of Racism in Classical Antiquity*. Princeton, NJ: Princeton University Press.

Jenkins, Richard. 1994. "Rethinking Ethnicity: Identity, Categorization and Power." *ERS* 17:197–223.

Johnson, Aaron P. 2006. *Ethnicity and Argument in Eusebius? Praeparatio Evangelica*. Oxford: Oxford University Press.

Jones, C. P. 1980. "Apuleius' Metamorphoses and Lollianus' Phoinikika." *Phoenix* 34:243–54.

———. 1986. *Culture and Society in Lucian*. Cambridge, MA: Harvard University Press.

———. 1989. "TROPHIMOS in an Inscription of Erythrai." *Glotta* 67:194–97.

Judge, E. A. 1960. *The Social Pattern of the Christian Groups in the First Century*. London: Tyndale.

Kasher, Aryeh. 1985. *The Jews in Hellenistic and Roman Egypt*. Tübingen: Mohr Paul Siebeck.

Kaufert, Joseph M. 1977. "Situational Identity and Ethnicity among Ghanaian University Students." *Journal of Modern African Studies* 15:126–35.

Kee, Howard Clark. 1995. "Defining the First-Century CE Synagogue: Problems and Progress." *NTS* 41:481–500.

Keil, J. 1935. "Zum Martyrium des Heiligen Timotheus in Ephesus." *JÖAI* 29:82–92.

Kerri, James Nwannukwu. 1976. "Studying Voluntary Associations as Adaptive Mechanisms: A Review of Anthropological Perspectives." *Current Anthropology* 17:23–47.

Klauck, Hans-Josef. 1981. *Hausgemeinde und Hauskirche im frühen Christentum*. SBS 103. Stuttgart: Verlag Katholisches Bibelwerk.

———. 1982. *Herrenmahl und hellenistischer Kult: Eine religionsgeschichtliche Untersuchung zum ersten Korintherbrief*. NTAbh 15. Münster: Aschendorff.

Kloppenborg, John S. 1993. "Edwin Hatch, Churches and Collegia." In *Origins and Method: Towards a New Understanding of Judaism and Christianity*. Edited by B. H. Maclean, 212–38. Sheffield: JSOT Press.

———. 1996a. "Collegia and *Thiasoi*: Issues in Function, Taxonomy and Membership." In *Voluntary Associations in the Graeco-Roman World*. Edited by John S. Kloppenborg and Stephen G. Wilson, 16–30. London/New York: Routledge.

———. 1996b. "Egalitarianism in the Myth and Rhetoric of Pauline Churches." In *Reimagining Christian Origins: A Colloquium Honoring Burton L. Mack*. Edited by Elizabeth A. Castelli and Hal Taussig, 247–63. Valley Forge, PA: Trinity Press International.

———. 2000. "Dating Theodotus (CIJ II 1404)." *JJS* 51:243–80.

———, and Stephen G. Wilson, eds. 1996. *Voluntary Associations in the Graeco-Roman World*. London/New York: Routledge.

Kraabel, A. T. 1968. "Judaism in Western Asia Minor under the Roman Empire, with a Preliminary Study of the Jewish Community at Sardis, Lydia." Ph.D. diss. Cambridge, MA: Harvard University.

———. 1971. "Melito the Bishop and the Synagogue at Sardis: Text and Context." In *Studies Presented to George M. A. Hanfmann*. Edited by David Gordon Mitten, John Griffiths Pedley, and Jane Ayer Scott, 77–85. Mainz: Philipp von Zabern.

———. 1982. "The Roman Diaspora: Six Questionable Assumptions." *JJS* 33:445–64.

Kraemer, Ross S. 1989. "On the Meaning of the Term 'Jew' in Greco-Roman Inscriptions." *HTR* 82:35–53.

Krier, Jean. 1980. "Zum Brief des Marcus Aurelius Caesar an den dionysischen Kultverein von Smyrna." *Chiron* 10:449–56.

Krysan, Maria, and William d'Antonio. 1992. "Voluntary Associations." In *Encyclopedia of Sociology*. Edited by Edgar F. Borgatta and Marie L. Borgatta, 4.2231–34. New York: Macmillan.

La Piana, George. 1927. "Foreign Groups in Rome during the First Centuries of the Empire." *HTR* 20:183–403.

Lane Fox, Robin. 1986. *Pagans and Christians*. New York: HarperSanFrancisco.

Lassen, Eva Maria. 1992. "Family as Metaphor: Family Images at the Time of the Old Testament and Early Judaism." *SJOT* 6:247–62.

———. 1997. "The Roman Family: Ideal and Metaphor." In *Constructing Early Christian Families*. Edited by Halvor Moxnes, 103–20. New York: Routledge.

Lattimore, Richard Alexander. 1962. *Themes in Greek and Latin Epitaphs*. Urbana: University of Illinois Press.

Layton-Henry, Z. 2001. "Minorities." In *International Encyclopedia of the Social and Behavioral Sciences*. Edited by Neil J. Smelser and Paul B. Baltes, 9894–98. Oxford: Pergamon.

le Bohec, Y. 1981. "Inscriptions juives et judaïsantes de l'Afrique romaine." *Antiquités Africaines* 17:165–207.

Le Dinahet, Marie-Thérèse. 1997a. "Étrangers et commerçants a Delos: quelques enseignements des epitaphes." *REA* 99:325–36.

———. 1997b. "Une famille de notables tyriens a Delos." *BCH* 121:617–66.

———. 2001. "Italiens de Delos: compléments onomastiques et prosopographiques." *REA* 103:103–23.

Le Guen, Brigitte. 2001. *Les Associations de technites dionysiaques à l'époque hellénistique.* Études d'Archéologie Classique 11–12. Nancy: Association pour la Diffusion de la Recherche sur l'Antiquité (de Boccard).

Lendon, J. E. 1997. *Empire of Honour: The Art of Government in the Roman World.* Oxford: Oxford University Press.

Leon, Harry J. 1995 [1960]. *The Jews of Ancient Rome.* Second edition. Introduction by Carolyn A. Osiek. Peabody, MA: Hendrickson.

Levine, Lee I. 2000. *The Ancient Synagogue: The First Thousand Years.* New Haven: Yale University Press.

Levinskaya, Irina. 1996. *The Book of Acts in Its Diaspora Setting.* The Book of Acts in Its First Century Setting 5. Grand Rapids/Carlisle: Eerdmans/Paternoster.

Liddell, Henry George, and Robert Scott. 1940. *A Greek-English Lexicon.* Ninth edition. Oxford: Oxford University Press.

Liebenam, Wilhelm. 1890. *Zur Geschichte und Organisation des römischen Vereinswesens.* Leipzig: B. G. Teubner.

Lieu, Judith. 1996. *Image and Reality: The Jews in the World of the Christians in the Second Century.* Edinburgh: T&T Clark.

———. 2002. *Neither Jew Nor Greek?: Constructing Early Christianity.* London: T&T Clark.

———. 2004. *Christian Identity in the Jewish and Graeco-Roman World.* Oxford: Oxford University Press.

———, John A. North, and Tessa Rajak. 1992. *The Jews among Pagans and Christians in the Roman Empire.* London: Routledge.

Lightfoot, J. B. 1889–90. *The Apostolic Fathers: Clement, Ignatius, and Polycarp.* London: MacMillan.

Lightstone, Jack. 2007. "Roman Diaspora Judaism." In *A Companion to Roman Religion.* Edited by Jörg Rüpke. Malden, MA: Blackwell.

Little, Kenneth. 1957. "The Role of Voluntary Associations in West African Urbanization." *American Anthropologist* 59:579–96.

Liu, Jinyu. 2004. "Occupation, Social Organization, and Public Service in the Collegia Centonariorum in the Roman Empire (First Century BC–Fourth Century AD)." Ph.D. diss. Columbia University.

Lofland, John, and Rodney Stark. 1965. "Becoming a World-Saver: A Theory of Conversion to a Deviant Perspective." *American Sociological Review* 30:862–75.

Lüderitz, Gert. 1994. "What Is a Politeuma?' In *Studies in Early Jewish Epigraphy.* Edited by Jan Willem van Henten and Pieter Willem van der Horst, 183–225. AGJU 21. Leiden: E. J. Brill.

MacDonald, Margaret Y. 1988. *The Pauline Churches: A Socio-Historical Study of Institutionalization in the Pauline and Deutero-Pauline Writings.* Cambridge: Cambridge University Press.

MacMullen, Ramsay. 1974. *Roman Social Relations 50 B.C. to A.D. 284.* New Haven: Yale University Press.

———. 1993. "The Unromanized in Rome." In *Diasporas in Antiquity*. Edited by Shaye J. D. Cohen and Ernest S. Frerichs, 47–64. Atlanta: Scholars Press.

Macridy, T. 1904. "À travers les nécropoles sidoniennes." *RB* 13:547–72.

Magie, David. 1950. *Roman Rule in Asia Minor to the End of the Third Century after Christ*. Princeton, NJ: Princeton University Press.

———. 1953. "Egyptian Deities in Asia Minor in Inscriptions and on Coins." *AJA* 57:163–87.

Malherbe, Abraham J. 1983 [1977]. *Social Aspects of Early Christianity*. Second edition. Philadelphia: Fortress.

———. 1986. *Moral Exhortation: A Greco-Roman Source Book*. LEC. Philadelphia: Westminster.

Malina, Bruce J. 1981. *The New Testament World: Insights from Cultural Anthropology*. Atlanta: John Knox.

Marcus, Ralph, trans. 1933–63. *Josephus: Jewish Antiquities*. LCL. Cambridge, MA: Harvard University Press.

Marger, Martin N. 1991. *Race and Ethnic Relations: American and Global Perspectives*. Second edition. Belmont, CA: Wadsworth.

Martin, Dale B. 1993. "Social-Scientific Criticism." In *To Each Its Own Meaning*. Edited by Stephen R. Haynes and Steven L. McKenzie, 103–19. Louisville: Westminster John Knox.

Mason, Steve. 2007. "Jews, Judaeans, Judaizing, Judaism: Problems of Categorization in Ancient History." *JSJ* 38:457–512.

———. 2008. *Josephus, Judea, and Christian Origins: Methods and Categories*. Peabody, MA: Hendrickson.

McCready, Wayne O. 1996. "*Ekklesia* and Voluntary Associations." In *Voluntary Associations in the Graeco-Roman World*. Edited by John S. Kloppenborg and Stephen G. Wilson, 59–73. London; New York: Routledge.

McGowan, Andrew. 1994. "Eating People: Accusations of Cannibalism against Christians in the Second Century." *JECS* 2:413–42.

McLean, B. Hudson. 1996. "The Place of Cult in Voluntary Associations and Christian Churches on Delos." In *Voluntary Associations in the Graeco-Roman World*. Edited by John S. Kloppenborg and Stephen G. Wilson, 186–225. London; New York: Routledge.

Meeks, Wayne A. 1983. *The First Urban Christians: The Social World of the Apostle Paul*. London/New Haven: Yale University Press.

Meiggs, Russell. 1960. *Roman Ostia*. Oxford: Clarendon.

Mendel, Gustave. 1912–14. *Catalogue des sculptures grecques, romaines et byzantines*. 3 vols. Constantinople: Musée imperial.

Merkelbach, Reinhold. 1979. "Die ephesischen Dionysosmysten vor der Stadt." *ZPE* 36:151–56.

———. 1995. *Isis regina—Zeus Sarapis. Die griechisch-aegyptische Religion nach den Quellen dargestellt*. Stuttgart/Leipzig: B. G. Teubner.

Meslin, Michel. 1970. *La fête des kalendes de janvier dans l'empire romain*. Collection Latomus 115. Brussels: Latomus Revue d'Études Latines.

Meyer, Hugo. 1988. "Zur Chronologie des Poseidoniastenhauses in Delos." *MDAI(A)* 103:203–20.

Meyers, Barton. 1984. "Minority Group: An Ideological Formulation." *Social Problems* 32:1–15.

Milik, J. T. 1972. *Dédicaces faites par des dieux (Palmyre, Hatra, Tyr) et des thiases sémitiques à l'époque romaine*. Paris: Geuthner.

Millar, Fergus. 1966. "The Emperor, the Senate and the Provinces." *JRS* 56:156–66.

———. 1973. "The Imperial Cult and the Persecutions." In *Le culte des souverains dans l'empire Romain*. Entreteins sur l'antiquité classique 19. Geneva: Olivier Reverdin.

———. 1977. *The Emperor in the Roman World (31 BC - AD 337)*. Ithaca, NY: Cornell University Press.

———. 1983. "Empire and City, Augustus to Julian: Obligations, Excuses and Status." *JRS* 73:76–96.

———. 1993. *The Roman Near East, 31 B.C. – A.D. 337*. Cambridge, MA: Harvard University Press.

Milligan, George. 1969 [1910]. *Selections from the Greek Papyri*. Freeport, NY: Books for Libraries.

Mishnun, Florence. 1950. "Voluntary Associations." *Encyclopaedia of the Social Sciences* 15:283–87. New York: MacMillan.

Mitchell, J. Clyde. 1969. "The Concept and Use of Social Networks." In *Social Networks in Urban Situations: Analyses of Personal Relationships in Central African Towns*. Edited by J. Clyde Mitchell, 1–50 Manchester: Manchester University Press.

Mitchell, J. Clyde. 1974. "Social Networks." *Annual Review of Anthropology* 3:279–99.

Mitchell, Stephen. 1993. *Anatolia: Land, Men, and Gods in Asia Minor*. Oxford: Clarendon.

———. 1999. "The Cult of Theos Hypsistos between Pagans, Jews, and Christians." In *Pagan Monotheism in Late Antiquity*. Edited by Polynmnia Athanassiadi and Michael Frede, 81–148. Oxford: Clarendon.

Mitropoulou, Elpis. 1990. "Feasting at Festivals." In *Akten des XIII. internationalen Kongresses für klassische Archäologie, Berlin 1988*, 472–74. Mainz am Rhein: Philipp von Zabern.

———. 1996. "The Goddess Cybele in Funerary Banquets and with an Equestrian Hero." In *Cybele, Attis and Related Cults: Essays in Memory of M. J. Vermaseren*. Edited by Eugene Lane, 135–65 RGRW 131. Leiden: E. J. Brill.

Mitteis, Ludwig. 1963 [1900]. *Reichsrecht und Volksrecht in den östlichen Provinzen des römischen Kaiserreichs*. Hildesheim: George Olms.

Morawska, Ewa. 2005. "The Sociology and History of Immigration: Reflections of a Practitioner." In *International Migration Research: Constructions, Omissions, and the Promises of Interdisciplinarity*. Edited by Michael Bommes and Ewa Morawska, 203–41. Aldershot, Hants, England: Ashgate.

Moulton, James Hope, and George Milligan. 1952. *The Vocabulary of the Greek Testament Illustrated from the Papyri and Other Non-Literary Sources*. London: Hodder & Stoughton.

Moya, Jose C. 2005. "Immigrants and Associations: A Global and Historical Perspective." *Journal of Ethnic and Migration Studies* 31:833–64.

Müller, Christel, and Claire Hasenohr, eds. 2002. *Les Italiens dans le monde grec. IIe siècle av. J.-C.–Ier siècle ap. J.-C. circulation, activités, intégration. Actes de la table ronde. Ecole Normale Supérieure, Paris 14–16 mai 1998*. BCHSup 41. Paris.

Murray, Michele. 2004. *Playing a Jewish Game: Gentile Judaizing in the First and Second Centuries* CE. Studies in Christianity and Judaism. Waterloo, ON: Wilfrid Laurier University Press.

Musurillo, Herbert A., trans. 1954. *The Acts of the Pagan Martyrs: Acta Alexandrinorum*. Greek Texts and Commentaries. New York: Arno.

Nazroo, James Y., and Saffron Karlsen. 2003. "Patterns of Identity among Ethnic Minority People: Diversity and Commonality." *ERS* 26:902–30.

Neumann, Gunter. 1999. "*Doumos*: Belege, Bedeutung, Herkunft, Etymologie." In *Linguisticum. Festschrift für Wolfgang P. Schmid zum 70. Geburtstag*. Edited by E. Eggers, 345–53. Frankfurt am Main: Peter Lang.

———. 2002. "Ein neuer Beleg für *doumos*." *Historische Sprachforschung (KZ)* 115:57–58.

Nijf, Onno van. 1997. *The Civic World of Professional Associations in the Roman East*. Dutch Monographs on Ancient History and Archaeology 17. Amsterdam: J. C. Gieben.

Nilsson, Martin P. 1916–19. "Studien zur Vorgeschichte des Weihnachtsfestes." *Archiv für Religionswissenschaft* 19:50–150.

———. 1957. *The Dionysiac Mysteries of the Hellenistic and Roman Age*. Lund: C. W. K. Gleerup.

———. 1961. *Geschichte der griechischen Religion*. Second edition. Munich: C. H. Beck.

Nock, Arthur Darby. 1924. "The Historical Importance of Cult-Associations." *Classical Review* 38:105–9.

North, J. A. 1979. "Religious Toleration in Republican Rome." *Proceedings of the Cambridge Philological Society* 25:85–103.

Noy, David. 1998. "'Letters Out of Judaea': Echoes of Israel in Jewish Inscriptions from Europe." In *Jewish Local Patriotism and Self-Identification in the Graeco-Roman Period*. Edited by S. Pearce and S. Jones, 106–17. Sheffield: Sheffield Academic Press.

———. 2000. *Foreigners at Rome: Citizens and Strangers*. London: Gerald Duckworth.

Oldfather, William Abbott, ed. 1926–28. *Epictetus. The Discourses as reported by Arrian, the Manual and Fragments, and an English Translation*. LCL. London: Heinemann.

Oliver, Graham J., ed. 2000. *The Epigraphy of Death: Studies in the History and Society of Greece and Rome*. Liverpool: Liverpool University Press.

Oster, Richard. 1990. "Ephesus as a Religious Center under the Principate, I. Paganism before Constantine." *ANRW* II.18.3:1661–728.

Otto, Walter. 1975 [1905–8]. *Priester und Tempel im hellenistischen Ägypten*. Ancient Religion and Mythology. New York: Arno.

Parker, Robert. 1996. *Athenian Religion: A History*. Oxford: Clarendon.

Paulsen, Henning. 1985. *Die Briefe des Ignatius von Antiochia und der Brief des Polykarp von Smyrna*. Tübingen: Mohr.

Perrin, Bernadotte, trans. 1916–20. *Plutarch's Lives*. LCL. Cambridge, MA: Harvard University Press.

Perry, Jonathan Scott. 1999. "A Death in the Familia: The Funerary Colleges of the Roman Empire." Ph.D. diss. University of North Carolina at Chapel Hill.

———. 2006. *The Roman Collegia: The Modern Evolution of an Ancient Concept*. Leiden: Brill.

Petzl, Georg. 1977. "Aus alten Inschriftenkopien." *Talanta* 8–9:80–99.

———. 1994. "Die Beichtinschriften Westkleinasiens." *EA* 22:1–175.

———. 1983. "T. Statilius Maximus—Prokonsul von Asia." *Chiron* 13:33–36.

Phinney, Jean S. 1990. "Ethnic Identity in Adolescents and Adults: Review of Research." *Psychological Bulletin* 108:499–514.

Picard, C. 1920. "Fouilles de Délos (1910): Observations sur la société des Poseidoniastes de Bérytos et sur son histoire." *BCH* 44:263–311.

———. 1922. *Éphèse et Claros: Recherches sur les sanctuaires et les cultes de l'Ionie du nord.* Bibliothèque des Écoles Françaises d'Athènes et de Rome 123. Paris: E. de Boccard.

Pleket, H. W. 1973. "Some Aspects of the History of Athletic Guilds." *ZPE* 10:197–227.

Poehlman, William. 1981. "The Polycharmos Inscription and Synagogue I at Stobi." In *Studies in the Antiquities of Stobi.* Edited by Blaga Aleksova and James Wiseman, 235–47. Titov Veles: Macedonian Review Editions.

Poland, Franz. 1909. *Geschichte des griechischen Vereinswesens.* Leipzig: Teubner.

Price, S. R. F. 1984. *Rituals and Power: The Roman Imperial Cult in Asia Minor.* Cambridge: Cambridge University Press.

Radice, Betty, trans. 1969. *Pliny: Letters and Panegyricus.* LCL. Cambridge, MA: Harvard University Press.

Radt, Wolfgang. 1988. *Pergamon: Geschichte und Bauten, Funde und Erforschung einer antiken Metropole.* Cologne: DuMont.

———. 1989. "Zwei augusteische Dionysos-Altärchen aus Pergamon." In *Festschrift für Jale Inan.* Edited by Nezih Basgelen and Mihin Lugal, 199–209. Istanbul: Arkeoloji ve Sanat Yayinlari.

Rajak, Tessa. 1984. "Was There a Roman Charter for the Jews?" *JRS* 74:107–23.

———. 2002. *The Jewish Dialogue with Greece and Rome: Studies in Cultural and Social Interaction.* Leiden: Brill.

———, and David Noy. 1993. "*Archisynagogoi*: Office, Title and Social Status in the Greco-Jewish Synagogue." *JRS* 83:75–93.

Ramsay, W. M. 1900. "Antiquities of Hierapolis (Humann, Cichorius, Judeich, Winter)." *Classical Review* 14:79–85.

———. 1902. "The Jews in the Graeco-Asiatic Cities." *Expositor* 5:19–33, 92–109.

Rauh, Nicholas K. 1993. *The Sacred Bonds of Commerce: Religion, Economy, and Trade Society at Hellenistic Roman Delos, 166–87* BCE. Amsterdam: J. C. Gieben.

Reardon, B. P., ed. 1989. *Collected Ancient Greek Novels.* Berkeley: University of California Press.

Reicke, Bo. 1951. "Exkurs über die Agitation in den hellenistischen Korporationen." In *Diakonie, Festfreude und Zelos in Verbindung mit der altchristlichen Agapenfeier,* 320–38. Uppsala Universitets Arsskrift 5. Uppsala: Lundequistska Bokhandeln.

Remus, Harold. 1996. "Voluntary Association and Networks: Aelius Aristides at the Asklepieion in Pergamum." In *Voluntary Associations in the Graeco-Roman World.* Edited by John S. Kloppenborg and Stephen G. Wilson. London/New York: Routledge.

Richardson, Peter. 1996. "Early Synagogues as Collegia in the Diaspora and Palestine." In *Voluntary Associations in the Graeco-Roman World.* Edited by John S. Kloppenborg and Stephen G. Wilson, 90–109. London/New York: Routledge.

———. 1998. "Augustan-Era Synagogues in Rome." In *Judaism and Christianity in First-Century Rome.* Edited by Karl P. Donfried and Peter Richardson, 17–29. Grand Rapids: Eerdmans.

———. 2004. *Building Jewish in the Roman East*. Waco, TX: Baylor University Press.

Rives, James B. 1995. *Religion and Authority in Roman Carthage from Augustus to Constantine*. Oxford: Clarendon.

Rogers, Guy MacLean. 1991. *The Sacred Identity of Ephesos: Foundation Myths of a Roman City*. London: Routledge.

Rolfe, J. C., trans. 1921. *Sallust*. LCL. Harvard: Harvard University Press.

Romanucci-Ross, Lola, and George A. De Vos, eds. 1995. *Ethnic Identity: Creation, Conflict, and Accommodation*. Walnut Creek, CA: Altamira.

Rostovtzeff, M. 1942. "*Vexillum* and Victory." *JRS* 32:92–106.

Roueché, Charlotte. 1979. "A New Inscription from Aphrodisias and the Title πατὴρ τῆς πόλεως." *GRBS* 20:173–85.

Rousselle, R. J. 1982. "The Roman Persecution of the Bacchic Cult, 186–180 B.C." Ph.D. diss. State University of New York at Binghamton.

Royden, Halsey L. 1988. *The Magistrates of the Roman Professional Collegia in Italy from the First to the Third Century A.D.* Biblioteca di Studi Antichi 61. Pisa: Giardini Editori e Stampatori.

Ruggini, L. 1959. "Ebrei e orientali nell'Italia settentrionale fra il IV e il VI secolo." *Studia et documenta historiae et iuris* 25:186–308.

Runesson, Anders. 2001. *The Origins of the Synagogue: A Socio-Historical Study*. ConBNT. Stockholm: Almqvist & Wiskell International.

Rutgers, Leonard Victor. 1994. *The Jews in Late Ancient Rome: Evidence of Cultural Interaction in the Roman Diaspora*. Leiden: Brill.

Rutherford, Ian. 2000. "The Genealogy of the Boukoloi: How Greek Literature Appropriated an Egyptian Narrative-Motif." *JHS* 120:106–21.

Sage, Evan T., trans. 1965. *Livy*. LCL. Cambridge, MA: Harvard University Press.

Ste. Croix, G. E. M. de. 1963. "Why Were the Early Christians Persecuted?' *Past and Present* 26:6–38.

———. 1964. "Why Were the Early Christians Persecuted? — A Rejoinder." *Past and Present* 27:28–33.

———. 1981. *The Class Struggle in the Ancient Greek World from the Archaic Age to the Arab Conquests*. Ithaca, NY: Cornell University Press.

San Nicolo, Mariano. 1972 [1912–13]. *Ägyptisches Vereinswesen zur Zeit der Ptolemäer und Römer*. Munich: C. H. Beck.

Sanders, Jimy M. 2002. "Ethnic Boundaries and Identity in Plural Societies." *Annual Review of Sociology* 28:327–57.

Sandnes, K. O. 1994. *A New Family: Conversion and Ecclesiology in the Early Church with Cross-Cultural Comparisons*. New York: Lang.

Schäfer, K. 1989. *Gemeinde als "Bruderschaft": Ein Beitrag zum Kirchenverständnis des Paulus*. Bern: Peter Lang.

Schäfer, Peter. 1997. *Judeophobia: Attitudes toward the Jews in the Ancient World*. Cambridge, MA: Harvard University Press.

Scheid, John. 1986. "Le thiase du Metropolitan Museum (*IGUR I*, 160)." In *L'association dionysiaque dans les sociétés anciennes: Actes de la table ronde organisée par l'École Française de Rome (Rome 24–25 mai 1984)*, 275–90. Collection de l'École Française de Rome 89. Paris: de Boccard.

Schelkle, K. H. 1954. "Bruder." In *Reallexikon für Antike und Christentum*, 631–40. Stuttgart: Hiersemann.

Schmeller, Thomas. 1995. *Hierarchie und Egalität: Eine sozialgeschichtliche Untersuchung paulinischer Gemeinden und griechisch-römischer Vereine*. SBS 162. Stuttgart: Verlag Katholisches Bibelwerk.

Schoedel, William R. 1985. *Ignatius of Antioch: A Commentary on the Letters of Ignatius of Antioch*. Hermeneia. Philadelphia: Fortress.

Schürer, Emil. 1897. "Die Juden im bosporanischen Reiche und die Genossenschaften der σεβόμενοι θεὸν ὕψιστον ebendaselbst." *Sitzungsberichte der königlich preussischen Akademie der Wissenschaften zu Berlin*, 200–225.

———. 1973–87. *The History of the Jewish People in the Age of Jesus Christ (175 B.C.–A.D. 135)*. Edited by Geza Vermes, Millar Fergus, Martin Goodman, and Matthew Black. Edinburgh: T&T Clark.

Schwartz, Daniel R. 1992. *Studies in the Jewish Background of Christianity*. Tübingen: J. C. B. Mohr.

Schwarzer, Holger. 2002. "Vereinslokale im hellenistischen und römischen Pergamon." In *Religiöse Vereine in der römischen Antike: Untersuchungen zu Organisation, Ritual, und Raumordnung*. Edited by Ulrike Egelhaff-Gaiserand and Alfred Schäfer, 221–60. Tübingen: Mohr Siebeck.

Scott, George M. 1990. "A Resynthesis of the Primordial and Circumstantial Approaches to Ethnic Group Solidarity: Towards an Explanatory Model." *ERS* 13:147–71.

Seager, Andrew R., and A. T. Kraabel. 1983. "The Synagogue and the Jewish Community." In *Sardis from Prehistoric to Roman Times*. Edited by George M. A. Hanfmann, 168–90. Cambridge, MA: Harvard University Press.

Seland, Torrey. 1996. "Philo and the Clubs and Associations of Alexandria." In *Voluntary Associations in the Graeco-Roman World*. Edited by John S. Kloppenborg and Stephen G. Wilson, 110–27. London; New York: Routledge.

Sewell, William H. 1999. "The Concept(s) of Culture." In *Beyond the Cultural Turn: New Directions in the Study of Society and Culture*. Edited by Victoria E. Bonnell and Lynn Hunt, 35–61. Berkeley: University of California Press.

Seyfarth, Jutta. 1955. "Φράτρα und φρατρία im nachklassischen Griechentum." *Aegyptus* 35:3–38.

Seyrig, H. 1960. "Les dieux de Hiérapolis." *Syria* 37:233–52.

Sélincourt, Aubrey de, trans. 1972. *Herodotus: The Histories*. Second edition. Penguin Classics. London: Penguin Books.

Shaw, Brent D. 1984. "Bandits in the Roman Empire." *Past and Present* 102:3–52.

Shelton, John C. 1976. "An Astrological Prediction of Disturbances in Egypt." *AncSoc* 7:209–13.

Sherwin-White, A. N. 1966. *The Letters of Pliny: A Historical and Social Commentary*. Oxford: Clarendon.

Siebert, Gérard. 1968. "Sur l'histoire du sanctuaire des dieux syriens a Délos." *BCH* 92:359–74.

Skarsaune, Oskar, and Reidar Hvalvik, eds. 2007. *Jewish Believers in Jesus: The Early Centuries*. Peabody, MA: Hendrickson.

Smallwood, E. Mary. 1976. *The Jews under Roman Rule from Pompey to Diocletian: A Study in Political Relations*. Second edition. SJLA 20. Leiden: E.J. Brill.

Smith, Dennis E. 2003. *From Symposium to Eucharist: The Banquet in the Early Christian World*. Minneapolis: Fortress.

Smith, Jonathan Z. 1990. *Drudgery Divine: On the Comparison of Early Christianities and the Religions of Late Antiquity*. Chicago Studies in the History of Judaism. Chicago: University of Chicago Press.

Snyder, Graydon F. 2003 [1985]. *Ante Pacem: Archaeological Evidence of Church Life before Constantine*. 2nd ed. Macon, GA: Mercer University Press.

Sommer, Stefan. 2006. *Rom und die Vereinigungen im südwestlichen Kleinasien (133 v. Chr.–284 n. Chr.)*. Hennef: M. Clauss.

Sosin, Joshua D. 1999. "Tyrian *stationarii* at Puteoli." *Tyche* 14:275–84.

Spillman, Lyn. 2007. "Culture." In *Blackwell Encyclopedia of Sociology*. Edited by George Ritzer. Oxford: Blackwell. Blackwell Reference Online. Accessed 28 August 2009 <http://www.sociologyencyclopedia.com.ezproxy.library.yorku.ca/subscriber/tocnode?id=g9781405124331_chunk_g97814051243319_ss1-183>.

Stark, Rodney, and William Sims Bainbridge. 1985. *The Future of Religion: Secularization, Revival and Cult Formation*. Berkeley: University of California Press.

Stephens, Susan A., and John J. Winkler. 1995. *Ancient Greek Novels, The Fragments: Introduction, Text, Translation, and Commentary*. Princeton, NJ: Princeton University Press.

Stern, Menahem, ed. and trans. 1974–84. *Greek and Latin Authors on Jews and Judaism*. Jerusalem: Israel Academy of Sciences and Humanities.

Stets, Jan E., and Peter J. Burke. 2003. "A Sociological Approach to Self and Identity." In *Handbook of Self and Identity*. Edited by Mark R. Leary, 128–152. New York: Guilford.

Stone, Gregory. 1962. "Appearance and the Self." In *Human Behavior and Social Processes*. Edited by A. Rose, 86–118. Boston: Houghton Mifflin.

Stowers, Stanley K. 1995. "Greeks Who Sacrifice and Those Who Do Not: Toward an Anthropology of Greek Religion." In *The Social World of the First Christians: Essays in Honor of Wayne A. Meeks*. Edited by L. Michael White and O. Larry Yarbrough, 293–333. Minneapolis: Fortress.

Strubbe, J. H. M. 1991. "'Cursed Be He That Moves My Bones.'" In *Magika Hiera: Ancient Greek Magic and Religion*. Edited by Christopher A. Faraone and Dirk Obbink, 33–59. Oxford: Oxford University Press.

———. 1994. "Curses against Violation of the Grave in Jewish Epitaphs of Asia Minor." In *Studies in Early Jewish Epigraphy*. Edited by Jan Willem van Henten and Pieter Willem van der Horst, 70–128. AGJU 21. Leiden: E. J. Brill.

———. 1997. *ΑΡΑΙ ΕΠΙΤΥΜΒΙΟΙ: Imprecations against Desecrators of the Grave in the Greek Epitaphs of Asia Minor. A Catalogue*. IGSK 52. Bonn: Rudolf Habelt.

Stryker, Sheldon, and Peter J. Burke. 2000. "The Past, Present, and Future of an Identity Theory." *Social Psychology Quarterly* 63:284–97.

Tacheva-Hitova, Margarita. 1983. *Eastern Cults in Moesia Inferior and Thracia*. Leiden: E. J. Brill.

Tajfel, Henri. 1978. *The Social Psychology of Minorities*. London: Minority Rights Group.

———. 1981. *Human Groups and Social Categories: Studies in Social Psychology*. Cambridge: Cambridge University Press.

———, ed. 1982. *Social Identity and Intergroup Relations*. Cambridge: Cambridge University Press.

———, and J. C. Turner. 1986. "The Social Identity Theory of Intergroup Behaviour." In *Psychology of Intergroup Relations*. Edited by S. Worchel and W. G. Austin, 7–24. Chicago: Nelson Hall.

Tanzer, Helen H. 1939. *The Common People of Pompeii: A Study of the Graffiti*. Johns Hopkins University Studies in Archaeology 29. Baltimore: Johns Hopkins Press.

Teixidor, Javier. 1964. "Aramaic Inscriptions of Hatra." *Sumer* 20:77–82.

———. 1977. *The Pagan God*. Princeton, NJ: Princeton University Press.

———. 1979. *The Pantheon of Palmyra*. Leiden: E. J. Brill.

Thackeray, H. S. J. 1926. *Josephus: The Life. Against Apion*. LCL. Cambridge, MA: Harvard University Press.

———, trans. 1927–28. *Josephus: The Jewish War*. LCL. Cambridge, MA: Harvard University Press.

Theissen, Gerd. [1973] 1982. *The Social Setting of Pauline Christianity: Essays on Corinth*. Translated by John H. Schütz. Philadelphia: Fortress.

———. 1978. *Sociology of Early Palestinian Christianity*. Translated by John Bowden. Philadelphia: Fortress.

———. 1999. *The Religion of the Earliest Churches: Creating a Symbolic World*. Translated by John Bowden. Minneapolis: Fortress.

Thompson, E. P. 1964. *The Making of the English Working Class*. New York: Pantheon Books.

Thomson, Randall J., and Michael Armer. 1980. "Respecifying the Effects of Voluntary Association on Individuals in a Traditional Society." *International Journal of Comparative Sociology* 21:288–301.

Tod, Marcus N. 1932. *Sidelights on Greek History*. Oxford: Basic Blackwell.

Toynbee, J. M. C. 1971. *Death and Burial in the Roman World*. London: Thames & Hudson.

Trebilco, Paul R. 1991. *Jewish Communities in Asia Minor*. Cambridge: Cambridge University Press.

———. 1999. "Jews, Christians and the Associations in Ephesos: A Comparative Study of Group Structures." In *100 Jahre Österreichische Forschungen in Ephesos akten des symposions, Wien 1995*. Edited by Barabara Brandt and Karl Krierer, 325–334. Vienna: Verlag der Österreichischen Akademie der Wissenschaften.

Trinquier, J. 1999. "Le motif du repaire des brigands et le topos du locus horridus Apulée, *Métamorphoses*, IV, 6." *RPh* 73:257–77.

Trümper, Monika. 2002. "Das Sanktuarium des 'Établissement des Poseidoniastes de Bérytos' in Delos. Zur Baugeschichte eines griechischen Vereinsheiligtums." *BCH* 126:265–330.

———. 2004. "The Oldest Original Synagogue Building in the Diaspora: The Delos Synagogue Reconsidered." *Hesperia* 73:513–98.

Turcan, Robert. 1981. "Le sacrifice mithraique: innovations de sens et de modalités." In *Le sacrifice dans l'antiquité*. Edited by Jean Rudhardt and Olivier Reverdin, 341–380. Geneva: Vandoeuvres.

———. 1996 [1989]. *The Cults of the Roman Empire*. Translated by Antonia Nevill. The Ancient World. Oxford: Blackwell.

Ustinova, Yulia. 1991–92. "The *Thiasoi* of Theos Hypsistos in Tanais." *HR* 31:150–80.
———. 1999. *The Supreme Gods of the Bosporan Kingdom*. RGRW 135. Leiden: Brill.
Verkuyten, Maykel. 2004. *The Social Psychology of Ethnic Identity*. Hove, UK: Psychology Press.
Vermaseren, M. J. 1963. *Mithras, The Secret God*. London: Chatto & Windus.
Vertovec, Steven. 2007. "Introduction: New Directions in the Anthropology of Migration and Multiculturalism." *ERS* 30:961–78.
Vestergaard, Torben. 2000. "Milesian Immigrants in Late Hellenistic and Roman Athens." In *The Epigraphy of Death: Studies in the History and Society of Greece and Rome*. Edited by Graham J. Oliver, 81–109. Liverpool: Liverpool University Press.
Vidman, Ladislav. 1970. *Isis und Sarapis bei den Griechen und Römern: Epigraphische Studien zur Verbreitung und zu den Trägern des ägyptischen Kultes*. Religionsgeschichtliche Versuch und Vorarbeiten 29. Berlin: Walter de Gruyter.
Vogliano, Achille. 1933. "La grande iscrizione bacchica del Metropolitan Museum." *AJA* 37:215–31.
Wagener, A. 1868. "Inscription grecque inédite." *Revue de l'instruction publique en Belgique* 11:1.
———. 1873. "Auszüge aus Schriften und Berichten der gelehrten Gesellschaften so wie aus Zeitschriften ." *Philologus* 32:379–84.
Wallis, Roy. 1975. "Relative Deprivation and Social Movements: A Cautionary Note." *British Journal of Sociology* 26:360–63.
Walsh, P. G. 1996. "Making a Drama Out of a Crisis: Livy on the Bacchanalia." *G&R* 43:188–203.
Waltzing, Jean-Pierre. 1895–1900. *Étude historique sur les corporations professionnelles chez les Romains depuis les origines jusqu'à la chute de l'empire d'Occident*. Mémoires couronnés et autres mémoires publiée par l'Académie Royale des Sciences, des Lettres et des Beaux-Arts de Belgique 50. Brussels: F. Hayez.
Walz, Christianus. 1843. *Rhetores graeci*. Stuttgart: J. G. Cottae.
Wasserman, Stanley, and Katherine Faust. 1994. *Social Network Analysis: Methods and Applications*. Cambridge: Cambridge University Press.
Watanabe, A. 2003. "Hippothoos the Lover, Bandit, and Friend: A Study on Elite Masculinity in the Novel." Ph.D. diss. Yale University.
Waters, Mary C. 2000. "Multiple Ethnicities and Identity in the United States." In *We Are a People: Narrative and Multiplicity in Constructing Ethnic Identity*. Edited by Paul R. Spickard and W. Jeffrey Burroughs, 23–40. Philadelphia: Temple University Press.
Webster, Jane. 2001. "Creolizing the Roman Provinces." *AJA* 105:209–25.
Weinfeld, Moshe. 1986. *The Organizational Pattern and the Penal Code of the Qumran Sect: A Comparison with Guilds and Religious Associations of the Hellenistic-Roman Period*. Freibourg: Editions Universitaires.
Weinreich, Otto. 1919. *Stiftung und Kultsatzungen eines Privatheiligtums in Philadelphia in Lydien*. Sitzungsberichte der Heidelberger Akademie der Wissenschaften, philosophisch-historische Klasse 16. Heidelberg: Carl Winters.
Welch, Kevin W. 1981. "An Interpersonal Influence Model of Traditional Religious Commitment." *Sociological Quarterly* 22:81–92.

Wellman, Barry. 1983. "Network Analysis: Some Basic Principles." *Sociological Theory* 1:155–200.

Wheeler, Roxann. 1999. "Limited Visions of Africa: Geographies of Savagery and Civility in Early Eighteenth-Century Narratives." In *Writes of Passage: Reading Travel Writing*. Edited by James S. Duncan and Derek Gregory, 14–48. London: Routledge.

White, John L. 1986. *Light from Ancient Letters*. Foundations and Facets. Philadelphia: Fortress.

White, L. Michael, ed. 1992. *Social Networks in the Early Christian Environment: Issues and Methods for Social History*. Semeia 56. Atlanta: Scholars Press.

———. 1988. "Shifting Sectarian Boundaries in Early Christianity." *Bulletin of the John Rylands University Library of Manchester* 70/3:7–24.

———. 1992. "Social Networks: Theoretical Orientation and Historical Application." In *Social Networks in the Early Christian Environment: Issues and Methods for Social History*. Edited by L. Michael White, 23–36. Semeia 56. Atlanta: Scholars Press.

———. 1997. *The Social Origins of Christian Architecture*. HTS 42. Valley Forge, PA: Trinity Press International.

———. 1998. "Counting the Costs of Nobility: The Social Economy of Roman Pergamon." In *Pergamon: Citadel of the Gods. Archaeological Record, Literary Description, and Religious Development*. Edited by Helmut Koester, 331–71. HTS 46. Harrisburg, PA: Trinity Press International.

———. 1998. "Synagogue and Society in Imperial Ostia: Archaeological and Epigraphic Evidence." In *Judaism and Christianity in First-Century Rome*. Edited by Karl P. Donfried and Peter Richardson, 30–68. Grand Rapids: Eerdmans.

Wilcken, Ulrich. 1932. "Urkunden-Referat." *Archiv für Papyrusforschung und verwandte Gebiete* 10:237–79.

Wilken, Robert L. 1972. "Collegia, Philosophical Schools, and Theology." In *Early Church History: The Roman Empire as the Setting of Primitive Christianity*. Edited by Stephen Benko and John J. O'Rourke, 268–91. London: Oliphants.

———. 1976. "Melito, the Jewish Community at Sardis, and the Sacrifice of Isaac." *TS* 37:53–69.

———. 1980. "The Christians as the Romans (and Greeks) Saw Them." In *Jewish and Christian Self-Definition. Volume One: The Shaping of Christianity in the Second and Third Centuries*. Edited by E. P. Sanders, 100–125. Philadelphia: Fortress.

———. 1984. *The Christians as the Romans Saw Them*. London/New Haven: Yale University Press.

Williams, Margaret H. 1992. "The Jews and Godfearers Inscription from Aphrodisias—A Case of Patriarchal Interference in Early 3rd Century Caria?" *Historia* 41:297–310.

———. 1994a. "The Jews of Corycus—A Neglected Diasporan Community from Roman Times." *JSJ* 25:274–86.

———. 1994b. "The Organization of Jewish Burials in Ancient Rome in the Light of Evidence from Palestine and the Diaspora." *ZPE* 101:165–82.

———. 1997. "The Meaning and Function of *Ioudaios* in Graeco-Roman Inscriptions." *ZPE* 116:249–62.

———, ed. 1998. *The Jews among the Greeks and Romans*. Baltimore: Johns Hopkins University Press.

Wilson, Bryan R. 1970. *Religious Sects: A Sociological Study*. London: World University Library.

———. 1973. *Magic and the Millennium*. London: Heinemann Educational Books.

———. 1982. *Religion in Sociological Perspective*. Oxford: Oxford University Press.

———. 1990. *The Social Dimensions of Sectarianism: Sects and New Religious Movements in Contemporary Society*. Oxford: Clarendon.

———, ed. 1967. *Patterns of Sectarianism: Organisation and Ideology in Social and Religious Movements*. London: Heinemann.

Winkler, Jack. 1980. "Lollianos and the Desperadoes." *JHS* 100:155–81.

Wirth, Louis. 1938. "Urbanism as a Way of Life." *American Journal of Sociology* 44:1–24.

Wiseman, J., and D. Mano-Zissi. 1971. "Excavations at Stobi, 1970." *AJA* 75:395–411.

Wood, John Turtle. 1975 [1877]. *Discoveries at Ephesus Including the Site and Remains of the Great Temple of Diana*. Hildesheim: Georg Olms.

Woolf, Greg. 1996. "Monumental Writing and the Expansion of Roman Society in the Early Empire." *JRS* 86:22–39.

Wörrle, M. 1988. *Stadt und Fest in kaiserzeitlichen Kleinasien. Studien zu einer agonistischen Stiftung aus Oenoanda*. Beiträge zur Alte Geschichte 39. Munich: Beck.

Yinger, J. Milton. 1981. "Toward a Theory of Assimilation and Dissimilation." *ERS* 4:249–64.

———. 1994. *Ethnicity: Source of Strength? Source of Conflict?* Albany: State University of New York Press.

Youtie, Herbert C. 1940. "Notes on O. Mich. I." *TAPA* 71:623–59.

———. 1948. "The *Kline* of Sarapis." *HTR* 41:9–29.

———. 1964. "Notes on Papyri." *TAPA* 95:300–32.

Ziebarth, Erich. 1896. *Das griechische Vereinswesen*. Stuttgart: S. Hirzel.

Zimmermann, Carola. 2002. *Handwerkervereine im griechischen Osten des Imperium Romanum*. Monographien/Römisch-Germanisches Zentralmuseum, Forschungsinstitut für Vor- und Frühgeschichte 57. Mainz: Verlag des Römisch-Germanischen Zentralmuseums.

Zuckerman, Constantine. 1985–88. "Hellenistic *Politeuma* and the Jews. A Reconsideration." *Scripta Classica Israelica* 8–9:171–85.

Ancient Sources

Other Greek and Roman Literature

Inscriptions and Papyri

Modern Authors

Names, Places, and Subjects